Gapenski's
Healthcare Finance

Kristin L. Reiter
Paula H. Song

Gapenski's
Healthcare Finance

An Introduction to Accounting and Financial Management

SEVENTH EDITION

AUPHA

Health Administration Press, Chicago, Illinois

Association of University Programs in Health Administration, Washington, DC

Your board, staff, or clients may also benefit from this book's insight. For information on quantity discounts, contact the Health Administration Press Marketing Manager at (312) 424-9450.

25 24 23 22 21   5 4 3 2

Library of Congress Cataloging-in-Publication Data
Names: Reiter, Kristin L. (Kristin Leanne), author. | Song, Paula H., author. | Gapenski, Louis C. Healthcare finance. | Association of University Programs in Health Administration, issuing body.
Title: Gapenski's healthcare finance : an introduction to accounting and financial management / Kristin L. Reiter, Paula H. Song.
Other titles: Healthcare finance
Description: Seventh edition. | Chicago, Illinois : Health Administration Press ; Washington, DC : Association of University Programs in Health Administration, [2021] | Preceded by Healthcare finance / Louis C. Gapenski, Kristin L. Reiter. Sixth edition. 2016. | Includes bibliographical references and index. | Summary: "This best-selling textbook covers the essential concepts of accounting and financial management in healthcare"— Provided by publisher.
Identifiers: LCCN 2020014150 (print) | LCCN 2020014151 (ebook) | ISBN 9781640551862 (hardcover ; alk. paper) | ISBN 9781640551886 (epub) | ISBN 9781640551893 (mobi) | ISBN 9781640551909 (xml)
Subjects: MESH: Financial Management, Hospital | Health Facilities—economics | Accounting | Capital Financing
Classification: LCC RA971.3 (print) | LCC RA971.3 (ebook) | NLM WX 157.1 | DDC 362.11068/1—dc23
LC record available at https://lccn.loc.gov/2020014150
LC ebook record available at https://lccn.loc.gov/2020014151

The paper used in this publication meets the minimum requirements of American National Standard for Information Sciences—Permanence of Paper for Printed Library Materials, ANSI Z39.48-1984. ∞™

Acquisitions editor: Janet Davis; Manuscript editor: Deborah Ring; Project manager: Andrew Baumann; Cover designer: James Slate; Layout: PerfecType

Found an error or a typo? We want to know! Please e-mail it to hapbooks@ache.org, mentioning the book's title and putting "Book Error" in the subject line.

For photocopying and copyright information, please contact Copyright Clearance Center at www.copyright.com or at (978) 750-8400.

Health Administration Press
A division of the Foundation of the American
   College of Healthcare Executives
300 S. Riverside Plaza, Suite 1900
Chicago, IL 60606-6698
(312) 424-2800

Association of University Programs
   in Health Administration
1730 M Street, NW
Suite 407
Washington, DC 20036
(202) 763-7283

To Jack Wheeler and Dean Smith,
for your guidance, mentorship, and support

BRIEF CONTENTS

DETAILED CONTENTS

Part VI   Capital Investment Decisions

PREFACE

The beginnings of *Healthcare Finance: An Introduction to Accounting and Financial Management* trace back more than 20 years. At that time, there was a need to make available material for courses in traditional, nontraditional, and clinician-oriented master of health administration (MHA) programs in which students did not have a formal educational background in finance-related topics. Finance courses in such programs require a book that provides basic information on foundational topics. Furthermore, these courses often are part of programs that contain just one healthcare finance course, so the course must cover both accounting and financial management. Some texts that were published at that time were strong in accounting, and others were strong in financial management. However, none gave equal emphasis to both components of healthcare finance, giving rise to the first edition of this book.

Concept of the Book

The overall concept of this book has not changed since the first edition: to create a textbook that introduces students to the most important principles and applications of healthcare finance, with roughly equal coverage of accounting and financial management. Furthermore, because the book is intended for use primarily in health services administration programs, in which students are trained for professional positions within healthcare provider organizations, its focus is on healthcare finance as it is practiced in such organizations. Thus, the examples in the book are based on such organizations as hospitals, medical practices, clinics, home health agencies, nursing homes, and managed care organizations.

Another consideration in writing the book is that most readers would be seeing the material for the first time, so it is important that the material be explained as clearly and succinctly as possible. We have tried hard to create a book that readers will find user-friendly—one that they will enjoy reading and can learn from on their own. If students don't find a book interesting, understandable, and useful, they won't read it.

The book begins with an introduction to healthcare finance and a description of the current financial environment in which providers operate, with emphasis on health system design, healthcare insurance, and reimbursement methodologies. From there, it takes students through the basics of financial and managerial accounting. Here, our goal is not to turn generalist managers into accountants but to present those accounting concepts that are most critical to managerial decision-making. The book then discusses the foundations of financial management and demonstrates how healthcare managers can apply financial management principles to help make better decisions—where *better* is defined as decisions that promote the financial well-being of the organization.

Relationship to Other Books

Gapenski's Understanding Healthcare Financial Management (UHFM) (by George H. Pink and Paula H. Song)

UHFM is very similar to a traditional corporate finance text, except that it focuses on the financial management of health services organizations. It does not include explicit accounting content that typically is taught in managerial and financial accounting courses, so *UHFM* assumes that students have some familiarity with financial statements and other basic accounting concepts. The book includes a great deal of theory, but the emphasis is on using the theory, as well as the concepts and tools, to make managerial decisions that maximize financial, and hence mission, performance.

The book is designed primarily for use in graduate-level courses for students who have already had exposure to accounting and financial management courses. It can be used for other student clienteles, but the absence of explicit accounting content, the amount of theory, and the nature of the ancillaries make the book most suitable for MHA and MBA (healthcare concentration) students. Also, because *UHFM* is designed to provide students with a higher level of cognition according to Bloom's Taxonomy, the end-of-chapter problems are provided on spreadsheets rather than printed in the textbook. Finally, student comprehension is maximized when *UHFM* is paired with cases—specifically, those contained in *Gapenski's Cases in Healthcare Finance* (see below).

Gapenski's Fundamentals of Healthcare Finance (FHF) (by Kristin L. Reiter and Paula H. Song)

FHF differs from *Healthcare Finance* in that it focuses primarily on financial decisions made at the clinical department level, so it includes only limited content related to decisions made by the financial staff—for example, decisions about organizational financing and capital structure. Because it focuses on the accounting and financial management concepts and decisions that are most relevant to clinical managers, it is shorter than *Healthcare Finance*.

The book is designed primarily for use in undergraduate-level courses for health science or health services management students and for undergraduate or graduate courses in clinical programs such as medicine, nursing, and physical or occupational therapy. It is also useful for professional development programs in healthcare finance.

Gapenski's Cases in Healthcare Finance (CHF) (by George H. Pink and Paula H. Song)

CHF contains 32 accounting and financial management cases. The cases generally focus on a single decision, such as marginal cost pricing or capital allocation. The casebook has spreadsheet models for most of the cases and questions that instructors can provide to students if they require more structure.

The casebook is designed to provide students with a higher level of cognition through the application of healthcare finance theory, concepts, and tools to "real-world" settings. *CHF* typically is used in conjunction with *UHFM* or *Healthcare Finance* in graduate courses for health services management students, but it can be used with other textbooks and in other settings. The cases are especially appreciated by students with work experience, but the availability of questions permits significant leeway in student clienteles. References have been added to most chapters in *Healthcare Finance* to denote the relevant cases from *CHF*.

Intended Market and Use

Healthcare Finance is not targeted for specific types of educational programs. Rather, it is designed to teach health services management students, in one course, the fundamental concepts of healthcare finance, including both accounting and financial management. Thus, the book can be used in a wide variety of settings: undergraduate and graduate programs, traditional and executive programs, on-campus and distance learning programs, and even independently for professional development.

The key to the book's usefulness is not the educational program but the focus of the course. If the course is a stand-alone course for management students designed to cover both healthcare accounting and financial management, the book will fit. In fact, the book easily can be used across a two-course healthcare finance sequence, especially in modular programs where each course is two credit hours. Typically, such a sequence begins with an accounting course and ends with a financial management course. This book, supplemented by cases (and possibly readings), would work well in such a sequence.

The book should also be useful to practicing healthcare professionals who, for one reason or another, must increase their understanding of healthcare finance. Such professionals include clinicians who have some management responsibilities as well as line managers who now require additional finance skills. As an alternative, *Fundamentals of Healthcare Finance* could be used for this purpose, especially when the readers will remain clinicians as opposed to moving into organizational (corporate) management positions.

Finally, many members of financial staffs, especially those who work exclusively in a single area, such as patient accounts, would benefit from having a broader understanding of healthcare finance principles and would find this book useful.

Changes in the Seventh Edition

Since the publication of the sixth edition of this book, we have used it numerous times in many different settings. In addition, we have received many comments from users at other universities. The reactions of students, other professors, and the marketplace in general have been overwhelmingly positive—every comment received indicates that the basic concept of the book is sound. Even so, nothing is perfect, and the healthcare environment is evolving at a dizzying pace. Thus, many changes have been made to the book, the most important of which are listed here:

- First and foremost, this edition was coauthored by Paula H. Song, associate professor at the University of North Carolina at Chapel Hill. Paula has coauthored several leading textbooks in healthcare finance, including *Gapenski's Understanding Healthcare Financial Management* and *Gapenski's Cases in Healthcare Finance*. She has both research and teaching expertise in financial management and payment systems.
- The contents of chapters 1 and 2 have been reorganized and updated to reflect the current status of healthcare reform. For example, the effects of the Tax Cuts and Jobs Act have been included.
- The financial accounting chapters (3–4) have been reorganized to create a more logical progression of concepts. Chapter 3 now begins with an introduction to financial accounting basics before discussing the income statement and the statement of changes in equity. Chapter 4 focuses on developing students' understanding of the balance sheet

and the statement of cash flows. The discussion of the double entry accounting system has been moved out of the chapters into a new supplement to chapter 4. The supplement expands the coverage of the double entry system to include illustrations of journal entries and the general ledger, T-accounts, and the accounting equation. In addition, the financial accounting chapters have been significantly revised to reflect amendments to the financial accounting conceptual framework and the effects of new revenue recognition and not-for-profit reporting standards on the financial statements of not-for-profit healthcare entities.

- Chapter 10 (Financial Risk and Required Return) has been revised extensively to better differentiate risk measures of realized and expected return distributions, to incorporate actual return data for the calculation of beta, and to lay out more explicitly how the capital asset pricing model is used to make investment decisions.
- Two of the chapter supplements have been removed from the textbook. The chapter 1 supplement on health services settings has been moved online. The chapter 2 supplement discussing lesser used Medicare payment methods has been removed altogether in favor of referring readers to the primary source of the information: the Medicare Payment Advisory Commission's Payment Basics series, which is accessible online.
- Financial calculator solutions to valuation problems have been removed from the textbook, in recognition of the fact that most students now use spreadsheets to conduct financial analyses.
- Finally, the following minor changes to the text have occurred: Coverage of the implications of value-based payment for the revenue cycle has been increased; several new exhibits have been added to illustrate concepts such as step-down cost allocation and variance analysis; end-of-chapter problems have been edited for clarity; and references have been updated to include current literature and examples.

All in all, these changes improve the quality and value of the book without affecting its basic concept and approach to learning.

Acknowledgments

This book reflects the efforts of many people. First and foremost, we would like to thank Mark Covaleski of the University of Wisconsin, who made significant contributions to the accounting content when the book was first written. In fact, without his materials, advice, and counsel, the book would not have been born. In addition, Anna McAleer of Arcadia University provided many useful comments for improving both the text and the instructor's manual. Finally, Sara Berney, MHA student at the University of North Carolina at Chapel Hill, provided critical support in clarifying the text and updating the examples in this edition.

Colleagues, students, and staff at the University of North Carolina at Chapel Hill provided inspirational support, as well as more tangible support, during the development and class testing of the text. Also, the Health Administration Press staff was instrumental in ensuring the quality and usefulness of the book.

Errors in the Book

In spite of the significant effort that has been expended by many individuals on this book, it is safe to say that some errors exist. In an attempt to create the most error-free and useful book possible, we strongly encourage both instructors and students to write or email one of us with comments and suggestions for improving the book. We certainly welcome your input. (Please note that many of the healthcare organizations used as examples in this and previous editions are fictitious. Any similarities in organizational name and characteristics are unintentional.)

Conclusion

In the environment faced by healthcare providers today, good financial decision-making is more important than ever to the economic well-being of the enterprise. Managers of all types and at all levels should be thoroughly grounded in finance principles and applications, but this is easier said than done. We hope that *Healthcare Finance: An Introduction to Accounting and Financial Management* will help you understand the finance problems currently faced by healthcare providers and, more important, that it will provide guidance on how best to solve them.

Kristin L. Reiter, PhD
1104H McGavran-Greenberg Hall
135 Dauer Drive, Campus Box 7411
University of North Carolina Gillings School of Global Public Health
Chapel Hill, NC 27599-7411
reiter@email.unc.edu

Paula H. Song, PhD
1105A McGavran-Greenberg Hall
135 Dauer Drive, Campus Box 7411
University of North Carolina Gillings School of Global Public Health
Chapel Hill, NC 27599-7411
psong@unc.edu

Instructor Resources

This book's Instructor Resources include a test bank, presentation PowerPoint slides, solutions to the end-of-chapter questions, and solutions to the end-of-chapter problems.

For the most up-to-date information about this book and its Instructor Resources, go to ache.org/HAP and search for this book's order code (2417I).

This book's Instructor Resources are available to instructors who adopt this book for use in their course. For access information, please e-mail hapbooks@ache.org.

THE HEALTHCARE ENVIRONMENT

Two factors make the provision of health services different from other services. First, many providers are organized as not-for-profit corporations, as opposed to being investor owned. Second, payment for services typically is made by third parties rather than by the patients who receive the services. Thus, it is necessary for students to understand the environment that creates the unique framework for the practice of healthcare finance.

Part I covers many introductory topics that are designed to provide readers with the structural framework in which finance is practiced within healthcare organizations. Such topics include the definition of healthcare finance, the organization and role of the finance staff, health services settings, and key issues facing healthcare managers. In addition, part I contains information on health insurance, the third-party payer system, reimbursement methodologies, and the impact of healthcare reform.

HEALTHCARE FINANCE BASICS

Learning Objectives

After studying this chapter, readers will be able to

- Describe the organization of this book and the learning aids contained in each chapter.
- Define the term *healthcare finance* as it is used in this book.
- Describe the key characteristics of a business.
- Discuss the structure of the finance department, the role of finance in health services organizations, and how this role has changed over time.
- Describe the major players in the health services sector.
- List the key operational issues currently faced by healthcare managers.
- Describe the forms of business organization and corporate ownership and their organizational goals.
- Discuss the key elements of healthcare reform and its expected effect on the provision of health services.

Introduction

In today's healthcare environment, where financial realities play an important role in health services decision-making, it is vital that managers at all levels understand the basic concepts of healthcare finance and how these concepts are used to enhance the financial well-being of the organization. In this chapter, we introduce readers to the book, including its purpose, goals, and organization. Furthermore, we present some basic background information about healthcare finance and the health services system. We sincerely hope that this book will help you in your quest to increase your professional competency in the important area of healthcare finance.

Before You Begin

Before you begin the study of healthcare finance, here are a few tips about the book that will make the process easier.

Purpose of the Book

Many books cover the general topics of accounting and financial management, so why is a book needed that focuses on healthcare finance? The reason is that while all industries have certain individual characteristics, the health services sector is truly unique. For example, the provision of many healthcare services is dominated by *not-for-profit corporations*, both private and governmental; such entities are inherently different from *investor-owned businesses*. Also, the majority of payments made to healthcare providers are not made by the individuals who use the services but by *third-party payers* (e.g., employers, commercial insurance companies, government programs). Throughout this book, the ways in which the unique features of the health services sector influence the application of finance principles and practices are emphasized and supported by examples.

This book is designed to introduce students to healthcare finance. This design has two important implications. First, the book assumes no prior knowledge of the subject matter; thus, the book is totally self-contained, with each topic explained from the beginning in basic terms. Furthermore, because clarity is so important when concepts are introduced, the chapters are written in an easy-to-read style. None of the topics is inherently difficult, but new concepts often take effort to understand. This process is made easier by the writing style used in the book.

Second, because this book is introductory, it contains a broad overview of healthcare finance. The good news is that the book presents virtually all the important healthcare finance principles used by managers in health services organizations. The bad news is that the large number of topics covered prevents us from covering principles in great depth or from including a wide variety of illustrations. Thus, students who use this book are not expected to fully understand every nuance of every finance principle and practice that pertains to every type of health services organization. Nevertheless, this book provides sufficient coverage of healthcare finance concepts so that readers will be better able to function as managers, judge the quality of financial analyses performed by others, and incorporate sound principles and practices into their own personal finance decisions.

Naturally, an introductory finance book cannot contain everything that healthcare financial managers must know to competently perform their jobs. Nevertheless, the book is useful even for those working in finance positions within health services organizations because it presents an overview of the finance function. Often, when working in a specific area of finance, it is easy to lose sight of the context of the work. This book will help provide that context.

Organization of the Book

To ensure that this book meets its goals, the destination has been carefully charted: to provide an introduction to healthcare finance. The book is organized into the following parts to pave the road to this destination.

Part I, The Healthcare Environment, contains fundamental background material that is essential to the practice of healthcare finance. Part I introduces the book, provides insights into the unique nature of the health services field, and provides additional information on how healthcare providers obtain their revenues. Healthcare finance cannot be studied in a vacuum because the practice of finance is profoundly influenced by the economic and social environment of the field, including the different types of ownership and reimbursement methods.

Part II, Financial Accounting, begins the actual discussion of healthcare finance principles and practices. Financial accounting, which involves the creation of statements that summarize a business's financial status, is most useful for outsiders and for long-term planning and management. In this part, we discuss the format and interpretation of the four primary financial statements and provide an overview of the double-entry accounting system used to record financial accounting transactions.

Part III, Managerial Accounting, which consists of four chapters, focuses on the creation of data used in the day-to-day management and control of a business. Here, the emphasis is on the overall organization, before shifting to the subunit (department) level and then to the individual service level. The key topics in part III include costing methods and behavior, profit planning, cost allocation, pricing decisions, and financial planning and budgeting.

In part IV, Basic Financial Management Concepts, the focus moves from accounting to financial management. In the first of two chapters, we cover time value analysis, which provides techniques for valuing future cash flows. In the second chapter, we discuss financial risk and required return. Taken together, these chapters provide readers with knowledge of two of the most important concepts used in financial decision-making.

Part V, Long-Term Financing, turns to the capital acquisition process. Businesses need capital, or funds, to purchase assets, and this part examines the two primary types of financing—long-term debt and equity. In addition, the final chapter of part V provides the framework for analyzing a business's appropriate financing mix and assessing its cost.

Part VI, Capital Investment Decisions, considers the vital topic of how businesses analyze new capital investment opportunities (capital budgeting). Because major capital projects take years to plan and execute, and because these decisions generally are not easily reversed and will affect operations for many years, their impact on the future of an organization is profound. The two chapters in this part first focus on basic capital investment analysis concepts and then turn to project risk assessment and incorporation.

Part VII, Other Topics, covers two diverse topics. The first chapter in this part discusses the revenue cycle and the management of short-term assets, such as cash and inventories, as well as how such assets are financed. The techniques used to analyze a business's financial and operating condition are discussed in the book's final chapter. These topics are presented last because students may benefit from an overview of the other concepts in the book before embarking on these chapters. However, instructors may also choose to combine these chapters with other parts of the book. For example, chapter 16, Revenue Cycle and Current Accounts Management, may be taught near the chapters in part V as this would present students with a picture of the management of short-term versus long-term accounts. Chapter 17, Financial Condition Analysis, may be taught with the financial accounting chapters in part II since much of the chapter involves the analysis of financial accounting data.

Health services managers must be able to assess the current financial condition of their organizations. Even more important, managers must be able to monitor and control current operations and assess ways in which alternative courses of action will affect the organization's future financial condition.

How to Use This Book

As mentioned earlier, this book is designed to introduce students to healthcare finance. It contains several features designed to make the process as easy as possible.

First, pay particular attention to the *Learning Objectives* listed at the beginning of each chapter. These objectives highlight the most important topics in each chapter and identify readers' learning goals for the chapter.

Following each major section in a chapter (except the chapter's introduction), one or more *Self-Test Questions* are included. As you finish reading each major section, try to answer these questions. Your responses do not have to be perfect, but if you are not satisfied with your answer, reread the section before proceeding. Answers are not provided for the self-test questions, so a review of the section is necessary if you are not sure whether your answers are satisfactory.

It is useful for readers to have important equations both embedded in the text to illustrate their use and broken out separately for easy identification and review. The *Key Equation* boxes can be used for both section and chapter review and as an aid to solving the end-of-chapter problems. The book contains several additional types of boxes, such as *For Your Consideration* and *Healthcare in Practice* boxes. Each of these boxes presents an important issue that is relevant to the text discussion and allows readers to pause to think about the issue presented, generate opinions, and draw conclusions. Many instructors use these boxes to stimulate in-class discussions.

Within the book, italics and boldface are used to indicate importance. *Italics* are used whenever a key term is introduced; thus, italics alert readers that a new and important concept is being presented. Italics are also used occasionally for emphasis. **Boldface** indicates terms that are defined in each chapter's running glossary, which complements the glossary at the back of the book. Boldface is also used occasionally for emphasis.

In addition to the in-chapter learning aids, materials designed to help readers learn healthcare finance are included at the end of each chapter. First, each chapter ends with a section titled *Key Concepts*, which summarizes the most important principles and practices covered in that chapter. If the meaning of a key concept is not clear, you may find it useful to review the applicable section. Each chapter also contains a series of *Questions* designed to assess your understanding of the qualitative material in the chapter. In most chapters, the questions are followed by a set of *Problems* designed to assess your understanding of the quantitative material.

Some chapters conclude with a set of *Selected Cases* from *Gapenski's Cases in Healthcare Finance*, sixth edition, that illustrate practical applications of healthcare finance. Additionally, each chapter includes a set of *Resources*. The books and articles cited can provide a more in-depth understanding of the material covered in the chapter. Finally, some chapters contain a *Chapter Supplement*, whose purpose is to present additional information pertaining to topics in the chapter that is useful but not essential.

Taken together, the pedagogic structure of the book is designed to make learning healthcare finance as easy and enjoyable as possible.

SELF-TEST QUESTIONS

1. Why is it necessary to have a book dedicated to healthcare finance?
2. What is the purpose of this book?
3. Briefly describe the organization of this book.
4. What features of this book are designed to make learning easier?

Defining Healthcare Finance

What is healthcare finance? Surprisingly, there is no single answer to that question because the definition of the term depends, for the most part, on the context in which it is used. Thus, in writing this book, the first step was to establish a definition of *healthcare finance*.

We began by examining the *healthcare sector* of the economy, which consists of a diverse collection of subsectors that involve, either directly or indirectly, the healthcare of the population. The major subsectors of healthcare include the following:

provider
An organization that provides healthcare services (treats patients).

- **Health services.** The health services subsector consists of **providers** of health services, including medical practices, hospitals, nursing homes, home health care agencies, and hospice providers.
- **Health insurance.** The health insurance subsector, which makes most of the payments to health services providers, includes government programs, commercial insurers, and self-insurers. Also included here are managed care companies, such as health maintenance organizations (HMOs), which incorporate both insurance and health services (provider) functions.
- **Medical equipment and supplies.** These subsectors include the makers of diagnostic equipment, such as X-ray machines; durable medical equipment, such as wheelchairs; and expendable medical supplies, such as disposable surgical instruments and hypodermic syringes.
- **Pharmaceuticals and biotechnology.** These subsectors develop and market drugs and other therapeutic products.
- **Other.** This broad category includes organizations such as consulting firms that advise hospitals on strategy and operations, educational institutions that train providers and healthcare managers, government agencies that regulate various health services subsectors, and private agencies that provide a wide variety of services.

Most users of this book will become (or already are) managers at health services organizations or at companies such as insurance and consulting firms that deal directly with health services organizations. Thus, to give this book the most value to its primary users, we focus on finance as it applies within the health services subsector.

accounting
The field of finance that involves the measuring and recording of events, in dollar terms, that reflect an organization's operational and financial status.

Now that we have defined the healthcare focus of this book, the term *finance* must be defined. Finance, as the term is used within health services organizations and as it is used in this book, consists of both the accounting and financial management functions. (In many settings, accounting and financial management are separate disciplines.) **Accounting**, as the term implies, is concerned with the recording, in financial terms, of economic events that reflect the operations, resources, and financing of an organization. In general, the purpose of accounting is to create and provide to interested parties, both internal and external, useful information about an organization's operations and financial status.

Whereas accounting provides a rational means by which to measure a business's financial performance and assess operations, **financial management** provides the theory, concepts, and tools necessary to help managers make better financial decisions. Of course, the boundary between accounting and financial management is blurry; certain aspects of accounting involve decision-making, and much of the application of financial management theory and concepts requires accounting data.

financial management
The field of finance that provides the theory, concepts, and tools used by healthcare managers to make financial decisions.

SELF-TEST QUESTIONS

1. What is meant by the term *healthcare finance*?
2. What is the difference between accounting and financial management?

The Concept of a Business

This book focuses on finance as it is practiced within health services businesses, so it is reasonable to ask, What is a *business*?

In this book, we define a business from a financial (economic) perspective. A business can be thought of as an entity (its legal form does not matter) that (1) obtains financing (capital) from the marketplace; (2) uses those funds to buy land, buildings, and equipment; (3) operates those assets to create goods or services; and then (4) sells those goods or services to create revenue. To be financially viable, a business has to have sufficient revenue to pay all of the costs associated with creating and selling its goods or services.

Although this description of a business is surprisingly simple, it tells a great deal about the basic decisions that business managers must make. One of the first decisions is to choose the best legal form for the business. Then, the manager must decide how the business will raise the capital that it needs to get started. Should it borrow the money (use debt financing), raise the money from owners (or from the community if it is a not-for-profit organization), or use some combination of the two sources? Next, once the start-up capital is raised, what physical assets (facilities and equipment) should be acquired to create the services that (in the case of healthcare providers) will be offered to patients?

For Your Consideration

Businesses, Pure Charities, and Government Entities

A healthcare business relies on revenues from sales to create financial sustainability. For example, if a hospital's revenues exceed its costs, cash is being generated that can be used to provide new and improved patient services, and the hospital can continue to meet community needs. On the other hand, pure charities, such as United Way, rely on contributions for their revenues, so the amount of charitable services provided (which typically are free) is limited by the amount of contributions received. Finally, most government units are funded by tax receipts; therefore, as with charities, the amount of services provided is limited, but in this case by the taxing authority's ability to raise revenues. In spite of these differences, all three types of organizations must operate in a financially prudent manner.

What do you think? From a finance perspective, how different are these types of organizations? How does the day-to-day functioning of their respective finance departments vary? Is finance more important in one type of organization than in another?

Note that businesses are profoundly different from *pure charities*. A business, such as a hospital or medical practice, sustains itself financially by selling goods or services. Thus, it is in competition with other businesses for the consumer dollar. A pure charity, such as the American Heart Association, does not sell goods or services. Rather, it obtains funds by soliciting contributions and then uses those funds to supply charitable (free) services. In essence, a pure charity is a budgetary organization in that the amount of contributions fixes its budget for the year.

Businesses are also different from *government agencies* such as local public health departments. In general, government agencies do not receive revenues by selling services or soliciting contributions. Rather, their revenues are derived from taxing the populations that benefit from the government services, so providing additional services typically uses resources without generating additional income. Thus, like a pure charity, a government agency has a budget that is fixed, but by appropriations rather than by contributions.

SELF-TEST QUESTIONS

1. From a financial perspective, briefly describe a business.
2. What is the difference between a business and a pure charity? Between a business and a government agency?

The Role of Finance in Health Services Organizations

The primary role of finance in health services organizations, as in all businesses, is to plan for, acquire, and use resources to maximize the efficiency and value of the organization. As we discuss in the next section, the two broad areas of finance—accounting and financial management—are separate functions in larger organizations, although the accounting function usually is carried out under the direction of the organization's chief financial officer and hence falls under the overall category of finance.

In general, finance activities include the following:

- **Planning and budgeting.** First and foremost, healthcare finance involves evaluating the financial effectiveness of current operations and planning for the future. **Budgets** play an important role in this process.
- **Financial reporting.** For a variety of reasons, it is important for businesses to record and report to outsiders the results of operations and current financial status. This is typically accomplished by a set of **financial statements**.
- **Capital investment decisions.** Although capital investment is typically handled by senior management, managers at all levels must be concerned with the capital investment decision-making process. Decisions that result from this process, which are called **capital budgeting** decisions, focus on the acquisition of land, buildings, and equipment. They are the primary means by which businesses implement strategic plans, and hence they play a key role in an organization's financial future.
- **Financing decisions.** All organizations must raise **capital** to buy the assets necessary to support operations. Such decisions involve the choice between internal and external funds, the use of debt versus equity capital, the use of long-term versus short-term debt, and the use of lease versus conventional financing. Although senior managers typically make financing decisions, these decisions have ramifications for managers at all levels.
- **Revenue cycle and current accounts management.** Revenue cycle management includes the billing and collections function, while current accounts management involves the organization's short-term assets, such as cash and inventories, and short-term liabilities, such as accounts payable and debt. Such functions and accounts must be properly managed both to ensure operational effectiveness and to reduce costs. Generally, managers at all levels are involved to some extent in revenue cycle and current accounts management.
- **Contract management.** In today's healthcare environment, health services organizations must negotiate, sign, and monitor contracts with managed care organizations and third-party payers. The financial staff typically has primary responsibility for these tasks, but managers at all levels are involved in these activities and must be aware of their effects on operating decisions.
- **Financial risk management.** Many financial transactions that take place to support the operations of a business can themselves increase the business's risk. Thus, an important finance activity is to control financial risk.

budget
A detailed plan, in dollar terms, of how a business and its subunits will acquire and use resources during a specified period of time.

financial statements
Statements prepared by accountants that convey the financial status of an organization. The four primary statements are the income statement, balance sheet, statement of changes in equity, and statement of cash flows.

capital budgeting
The process of analyzing and choosing new long-term assets such as land, buildings, and equipment.

capital
The funds raised by a business that will be invested in assets, such as land, buildings, and equipment that support the organizational mission.

four Cs
A mnemonic for the four basic finance activities: costs, cash, capital, and control.

cost
A resource use associated with providing or supporting a specific service.

These specific finance activities can be summarized by the **four Cs**: costs, cash, capital, and control. The measurement and minimization of **costs** is vital to the financial success of any business. *Cash* is the "lubricant" that makes the wheels of a business run smoothly—without it, the business grinds to a halt. *Capital* represents the funds used to acquire land, buildings, and equipment. Without capital, businesses would not have the physical resources needed to provide goods and services. Finally, a business must have adequate *control* mechanisms to ensure that its capital is being wisely employed and its physical resources are protected for future use.

In times of high profitability and abundant financial resources, the finance function tends to decline in importance. Thus, at the time when most healthcare providers were reimbursed on the basis of costs incurred, the role of finance was minimal. The most critical finance function was cost identification because it was more important to account for costs than it was to control them. In response to payer (primarily Medicare) requirements, providers (primarily hospitals) churned out a multitude of reports both to comply with regulations and to maximize revenues. The complexities of cost reimbursement meant that a large amount of time had to be spent on cumbersome accounting, billing, and collection procedures. Thus, instead of focusing on value-adding activities, most finance work focused on bureaucratic functions.

Now, finance functions are typically much more strategic and sophisticated in recognition of the changes that have occurred in the health services sector. Although billing and collections remain important, to be of maximum value to the enterprise today, the finance function must support a much broader array of activities, including strategy development, cost containment efforts, third-party payer contract negotiations, joint venture decisions, risk management, and clinical integration. In essence, finance must help lead organizations into the future rather than merely record what has happened in the past.

In this book, the emphasis is on the finance function, but there are no unimportant functions in healthcare organizations. Senior executives must understand a multitude of other functions, such as operations, marketing, facilities management, quality improvement, and human resource management, in addition to finance. Still, all business decisions have financial implications, so all managers—whether they are in finance or not—must know enough about finance to properly incorporate any financial implications into decisions made within their own specialized areas.

SELF-TEST QUESTIONS

1. What is the role of finance in today's health services organizations?
2. How has this role changed over time?
3. What are the four Cs?

The Structure of the Finance Department

The size and structure of the finance department within health services organizations depend on the type of provider and its size. Still, the finance department within larger provider organizations generally follows the model described here.

The head of the finance department holds the title *chief financial officer (CFO)* or sometimes *vice president of finance*. This individual typically reports directly to the organization's *chief executive officer (CEO)* and is responsible for all finance activities within the organization.

The CFO directs two senior managers who help manage finance activities. First is the *comptroller* (pronounced, and sometimes spelled, "controller"), who is responsible for accounting and reporting activities such as routine budgeting, preparation of financial statements, payables management, and patient accounts management. For the most part, the comptroller is involved in the activities covered in chapters 3–8 of this text. Second is the *treasurer*, who is responsible for the acquisition and management of capital (funds). The treasurer's activities include the acquisition and employment of capital, cash and debt management, lease financing, financial risk management, and endowment fund management (within not-for-profits). In general, the treasurer is involved in the activities discussed in chapters 11–17 of this text.

Of course, in larger organizations, the comptroller and treasurer have managers with responsibility for specific functions, such as the *patient accounts manager*, who reports to the comptroller, and the *cash manager*, who reports to the treasurer.

In very small businesses, many of the finance responsibilities are combined and assigned to just a few individuals. In the smallest health services organizations, the entire finance function is managed by one person, often called the *business (practice) manager*.

SELF-TEST QUESTIONS

1. Briefly describe the typical structure of the finance department within a health services organization.
2. How does the structure of the finance department differ between small and large health services organizations?

Health Services Settings

Health services are provided in a variety of settings, including hospitals, ambulatory care facilities, long-term care facilities, and even at home.

Before the 1980s, most health services organizations were independent and not formally linked with other organizations. Those that were linked tended to be part of horizontally integrated systems that controlled a single type of healthcare facility, such as hospitals or nursing homes. Over time, however, many health services organizations have diversified and become vertically integrated through either direct ownership or contractual arrangements.

Most readers of this text are familiar with health services settings either through previous courses or work in the field. For readers who have not had exposure to health services settings, the chapter 1 supplement, available online at ache.org/books/HCFinance7, provides additional information.

<table>
<tr><td>SELF-TEST
QUESTIONS</td><td>1. Name a few settings in which health services are provided.
2. Briefly describe horizontal and vertical integration.</td></tr>
</table>

Current Managerial Challenges

In recent years, the American College of Healthcare Executives has surveyed CEOs regarding the most critical concerns of healthcare managers. Financial concerns have headed the list of challenges every year since the survey began in 2002. When asked to rank their specific financial concerns, in 2018, CEOs put costs for staff, supplies, and other expenses; Medicaid reimbursement; and operating costs at the forefront.[1] (Reimbursement is discussed in chapter 2.)

In a survey of senior healthcare executives conducted by the Advisory Board in 2019, respondents reported that their most pressing issues were revenue growth, population health, and accountable care organization strategy and cost containment.[2] Finally, a survey conducted by the Healthcare Financial Management Association identified improving the accuracy of clinical documentation as a key revenue cycle (billing and collecting on a timely basis) concern.[3]

Taken together, the results of these surveys confirm that finance is of primary importance to today's healthcare managers. The remainder of this book is dedicated to helping you confront and solve these issues.

<table>
<tr><td>SELF-TEST
QUESTION</td><td>1. What are some important issues facing healthcare managers today?</td></tr>
</table>

Legal Forms of Businesses

Throughout this book, the focus is on business finance—that is, the practice of accounting and financial management within business organizations. There are three primary legal forms of *business organization:* proprietorship, partnership, and corporation. In addition, there are several hybrid forms. Because most health services managers work for corporations, and because not-for-profit businesses are organized as corporations, this form of organization is emphasized. However, some medical practices are organized as proprietorships, and partnerships and hybrid forms are common in group practices and joint ventures, so health services managers must be familiar with all forms of business organization.

Proprietorships

A **proprietorship**, sometimes called a *sole proprietorship*, is a business owned by one individual. Going into business as a proprietor is easy—the owner simply begins business operations. However, most cities require even the smallest businesses to be licensed, and state licensure is required for most healthcare professionals.

proprietorship
A simple form of business owned by a single individual; also called *sole proprietorship*.

Partnerships

A **partnership** is formed when two or more people associate to conduct a business that is not incorporated. Partnerships may operate under different degrees of formality, ranging from informal oral understandings to formal agreements filed with the state in which the partnership does business. Both the proprietorship and partnership forms of organization are easily and inexpensively formed, are subject to few government regulations, and pay no corporate income taxes. All earnings of the business, whether reinvested in the business or withdrawn by the owner(s), are taxed as personal income to the proprietor or partner.

partnership
A nonincorporated business entity that is created by two or more individuals.

Proprietorships and partnerships have several disadvantages, including the following:

- Selling their interest in the business is difficult for the owners.
- The owners have unlimited personal liability for the debts of the business, which can result in losses greater than the amount invested in the business. In a proprietorship, unlimited liability means that the owner is personally responsible for the debts of the business. In a partnership, it means that if any partner is unable to meet his or her obligation in the event of bankruptcy, the remaining partners are responsible for the unsatisfied claims and must draw on their personal assets if necessary.

- The life of the business is limited to the life of the owners.
- It is difficult for proprietorships and partnerships to raise large amounts of capital. This is generally not a problem when the business is very small or when the owners are very wealthy; however, the difficulty of attracting capital becomes a real handicap if the business needs to grow substantially to take advantage of market opportunities.

Corporations

corporation
A legal business entity that is separate and distinct from its owners (or community) and managers.

A **corporation** is a legal entity that is separate and distinct from its owners and managers. The creation of a separate business entity gives these primary advantages:

- A corporation has an unlimited life and can continue in existence after its original owners and managers have died or left the company.
- It is easy to transfer ownership in a corporation because ownership is divided into shares of stock that can be sold.
- The owners of a corporation have limited liability.

To illustrate limited liability, suppose that an individual made an investment of $10,000 in a partnership that subsequently went bankrupt, owing $100,000. Because the partners are liable for the debts of the partnership, that partner could be assessed for a share of the partnership's debt in addition to the loss of his or her initial $10,000 contribution. In fact, if the other partners were unable to pay their shares of the indebtedness, one partner would be held liable for the entire $100,000. However, if the $10,000 had been invested in a corporation that went bankrupt, the potential loss for the investor would be limited to the $10,000 initial investment. (However, in the case of small, financially weak corporations, the limited liability feature of ownership is often fictitious because bankers and other lenders will require personal guarantees from the stockholders.) Because of these three factors—unlimited life, ease of ownership transfer, and limited liability—corporations can more easily raise money in the financial markets than can sole proprietorships or partnerships.

The corporate form of organization has two primary disadvantages. First, corporate earnings of taxable entities are subject to double taxation—once at the corporate level and then again at the personal level. Second, setting up a corporation, and then filing the required periodic state and federal reports, is more costly and time-consuming than what is required to establish a proprietorship or partnership.

Setting up a corporation requires that the founders, or their attorney, prepare a charter and a set of bylaws. Today, attorneys have standard templates for charters and bylaws, so they can set up a "no-frills" corporation with modest effort. In addition, several companies offer online services that help with the incorporation process. Still, setting up a corporation remains relatively difficult compared with a proprietorship or partnership, and it is even more difficult if the corporation has nonstandard features, such as multiple classes of stock.

Hybrid Forms of Organization

Although the three basic forms of organization—proprietorship, partnership, and corporation—historically have dominated the business scene, several hybrid forms of organization have become quite popular in recent years.

In general, the hybrid forms are designed to limit owners' liability without having to fully incorporate. For example, in a **limited liability partnership (LLP)**, the partners have joint liability for all actions of the partnership, including personal injuries and indebtedness. However, all partners enjoy limited liability regarding professional malpractice because partners are only liable for their own individual malpractice actions, not those of the other partners. In spite of limited malpractice liability, the partners are jointly liable for the partnership's debts. Other hybrid forms of organization include limited liability companies (LLCs), professional corporations (PCs), and professional associations (PAs).

limited liability partnership (LLP)
A partnership form of organization that limits the professional (malpractice) liability of its partners.

---

1. What are the three primary forms of business organization, and how do they differ?
2. What is the purpose of hybrid forms of business organization?

SELF-TEST QUESTIONS

Corporate Ownership

In the previous section, we discussed the different legal forms of businesses. Now, we turn our attention to the two ownership forms of corporations: for-profit and not-for-profit. Unlike other sectors in the economy, not-for-profit corporations play a major role in the healthcare sector, especially among providers. For example, about 56 percent of the community hospitals in the United States are private, not-for-profit hospitals. Only 25 percent of all community hospitals are investor owned; the remaining 19 percent are government hospitals.[4] Furthermore, not-for-profit ownership is common in the nursing home, home health care, hospice, and health insurance industries.

Investor-Owned Corporations

investor-owned (for-profit) corporation
A corporation that is owned by shareholders who furnish capital and expect to earn a return on their investment.

When you think of a corporation, an **investor-owned**, or **for-profit, corporation** likely comes to mind. For example, Ford (www.ford.com), IBM (www.ibm.com), and Microsoft (www.microsoft.com) are investor-owned corporations. In health services, corporations such as HCA Healthcare (https://hcahealthcare.com) and Community Health Systems (www.chs.net) are examples of large for-profit hospital systems; Kindred Healthcare (www.kindredhealthcare.com) and Brookdale Senior Living (www.brookdale.com) are examples of long-term care providers; Select Medical (www.selectmedical.com) and Encompass Health (www.encompasshealth.com) offer rehabilitation services; and MEDNAX (www.mednax.com) offers pediatric services. Individuals become owners of for-profit corporations by buying shares of *common stock* in the company. The *stockholders* (also called *shareholders*) are the owners of investor-owned corporations. As owners, they have two basic rights:

- **The right of control.** Common stockholders have the right to vote for the corporation's *board of directors*, which oversees the management of the company. Each year, a company's stockholders receive a *proxy* ballot, which they use to vote for directors and to vote on other issues that are proposed by management or stockholders. In this way, stockholders exercise control over the corporation. In the voting process, stockholders cast one vote for each common share held.
- **A claim on the residual earnings of the firm.** A corporation sells products or services and realizes revenues from the sales. To produce these revenues, the corporation must incur expenses for materials, labor, insurance, debt capital, and so on. Any excess of revenues over expenses—the *residual earnings*—belongs to the shareholders of the business. Often, a portion of these earnings is paid out in the form of *dividends*, which are cash payments to stockholders, or *stock repurchases*, in which the company buys back shares held by stockholders. However, management typically elects to reinvest some (or all) of the residual earnings in the business, which presumably will produce even higher payouts to stockholders in the future.

Compared with not-for-profit corporations (discussed next), three key features make investor-owned corporations different. First, the owners (stockholders) of the corporation are well defined and exercise control of the business by voting for directors. Second, the residual earnings of the business belong to the owners, so management is responsible only to the stockholders for the profitability of the firm. Finally, investor-owned corporations are subject to various forms of taxation at the local, state, and federal levels.

Not-for-Profit Corporations

If an organization meets a set of stringent requirements, it can qualify for incorporation as a **tax-exempt**, or **not-for-profit**, **corporation**. Tax-exempt corporations are sometimes called *nonprofit corporations*. Because nonprofit businesses (as opposed to pure charities such as United Way) need profits to sustain operations, and because it is hard to explain why nonprofit corporations should earn profits, the term *not-for-profit* better describes such health services corporations. Examples of not-for-profit health services corporations include Kaiser Permanente (https://healthy.kaiserpermanente.org), Catholic Health Initiatives (www.catholichealthinitiatives.org), and the Mayo Clinic Health System (www.mayoclinic.org).

> **tax-exempt (not-for-profit) corporation**
> A corporation that has a charitable purpose, is tax exempt, and has no owners; also called *nonprofit corporation*.

Tax-exempt status is granted to corporations that meet the tax definition of a charitable organization as defined by Internal Revenue Service (IRS) tax code section 501(c)(3) or 501(c)(4). Hence, such corporations are also known as *501(c)(3) or 501(c)(4) corporations*. The tax code defines a charitable organization as "any corporation, community chest, fund, or foundation that is organized and operated exclusively for religious, charitable, scientific, public safety, literary, or educational purposes." Because the promotion of health is commonly considered a charitable activity, a corporation that provides healthcare services can qualify for tax-exempt status, provided that it meets other requirements.

In addition to the charitable purpose, a not-for-profit corporation must be organized and run so that it operates exclusively for the public, rather than private, interest. Thus, no profits can be used for private gain, and no direct political activity can be conducted. Also, if the corporation is liquidated or sold to an investor-owned business, the proceeds from the liquidation or sale must be used for charitable purposes. Because individuals cannot benefit from the profits of not-for-profit corporations, such organizations cannot pay dividends. However, the prohibition of private gain from profits does not prevent parties, such as managers and physicians, from benefiting through salaries, perquisites, contracts, and so on.

Not-for-profit corporations differ significantly from investor-owned corporations. Because not-for-profit firms have no shareholders, no single body of individuals has ownership rights to the firm's residual earnings or exercises control of the firm. Rather, control is exercised by a *board of trustees* that is not constrained by outside oversight, as is the board of directors of a for-profit corporation, which must answer to stockholders. Also, not-for-profit corporations are generally exempt from taxation, including both property and income taxes, and have the right to issue tax-exempt debt (municipal bonds). Finally, individual contributions to not-for-profit organizations can be deducted from taxable income by the donor, so not-for-profit firms have access to tax-subsidized contribution capital.

For-profit corporations must file annual income tax returns with the IRS. The equivalent filing for not-for-profit corporations is IRS **Form 990**, titled "Return of Organization Exempt from Income Tax." Its purpose is to provide both the IRS and the public with financial information about not-for-profit organizations, and it is often the only source of such information. It is also used by government agencies to prevent organizations from abusing their tax-exempt status. Form 990 requires significant disclosures related to governance and boards of trustees. In addition, hospitals are required to file **Schedule H** to Form 990, which includes financial information on the amount and type of community benefit (primarily charity care) provided, bad debt losses, Medicaid patients, and collection practices. IRS regulations require not-for-profit organizations to provide copies of their three most recent Form 990s to anyone who requests them, whether in person or by mail, fax, or email. Form 990s are also available to the public through several online services.

The financial problems facing most federal, state, and local governments have prompted politicians to take a closer look at the tax subsidies provided to not-for-profit hospitals. The Patient Protection and Affordable Care Act (ACA) of 2010 added four requirements that must be met for hospitals to maintain their tax-exempt status: (1) conducting a community health needs assessment every three years and developing plans for implementation; (2) establishing a written financial assistance policy; (3) charging patients who qualify for financial assistance amounts similar to what insured patients are charged; and (4) not engaging in aggressive collection efforts before making an effort to determine whether a patient is eligible for financial assistance.[5]

Likewise, officials in several states have proposed or enacted legislation mandating the minimum amount of charity care to be provided by not-for-profit hospitals and the types of billing and collections procedures that can be applied to the uninsured.[6] For example, Texas has established minimum requirements for charity care that hold not-for-profit hospitals accountable to the public for the tax exemptions they receive. The Texas law specifies four tests, and each hospital must meet at least one of them. The test that most hospitals use to comply with the law requires that at

Form 990
A form filed by not-for-profit organizations with the Internal Revenue Service that reports on governance and charitable activities.

Schedule H
An attachment to Form 990 filed by not-for-profit hospitals that gives additional information on charitable activities.

For Your Consideration
Making Not-for-Profit Hospitals Do Good

Many people have criticized not-for-profit hospitals for not "earning" their charitable exemptions. In a 2010 court ruling, the Illinois Supreme Court concluded that Provena Covenant hospital, located in Urbana, Illinois, was not a charitable institution for property tax purposes. The court's opinion reasoned that the primary use of the hospital property was to provide medical services for a fee, whereas *charity* means providing a gift to the community. The opinion further pointed out that (1) the charity care being provided was subsidized by payments from other patients; (2) many patients granted partial charity care still paid enough to cover costs; and (3) the hospital's community benefit activities, such as a residency program and an education program for emergency responders, also benefited the hospital and thus were not truly gifts to the community. Thus, the hospital property was not in charitable use.

(continued)

least 4 percent of net patient service revenue be spent on charity care.

Finally, municipalities in several states have attacked the property tax exemptions of not-for-profit hospitals that have "neglected" their charitable missions. For example, in 2015, a tax court in New Jersey canceled a not-for-profit hospital's property tax exemption because it was found to have substantial "for-profit" elements and characteristics that made it ineligible for the exemption.[7] According to one estimate, if all not-for-profit hospitals had to pay taxes comparable to their investor-owned counterparts, local, state, and federal governments would receive an additional $17.9 billion in tax revenues.[8] This estimate explains why tax authorities in many jurisdictions are pursuing not-for-profit hospitals as a source of revenue.

(continued from previous page)

Most not-for-profit hospitals today are primarily supported by payments for services rather than by charitable contributions. Under the opinion's reasoning, the property tax exemption may well be hard to maintain. However, a partial dissent by two justices suggests that this case is not the end of the story. The dissent argues that the plurality opinion impinges on the legislative function of setting specific standards for tax exemption, and the issue should be settled by legislative action rather than by courts.

What do you think? Should not-for-profit hospitals lose their property tax or income tax exemptions? Should legislatures set standards that hospitals must meet to maintain their tax-exempt status? If so, how might such standards be specified?

The inherent differences between investor-owned and not-for-profit organizations have profound implications for many elements of healthcare financial management, including organizational goals, financing decisions (i.e., the choice between debt and equity financing and the types of securities issued), and capital investment decisions. Ownership's effect on the application of healthcare financial management theory and concepts is addressed throughout the text.

SELF-TEST QUESTIONS

1. What are the major differences between investor-owned and not-for-profit corporations?
2. What types of requirements have been placed on not-for-profit hospitals to ensure that they meet their charitable mission?
3. What are the purpose and content of IRS Form 990?

Organizational Goals

Healthcare finance is not practiced in a vacuum; it is practiced with some objective in mind. Finance goals within an organization clearly must be consistent with, as well as supportive of, the overall goals of the business. Thus, by discussing organizational goals, a framework for financial decision-making within health services organizations can be established.

Small Businesses

In a small business, regardless of its legal form, the owners generally are also its managers. In theory, the business can be operated for the exclusive benefit of the owners. If the owners want to work very hard to get rich, they can. On the other hand, if every Wednesday is devoted to golf, no outside owner is hurt by such actions. (Of course, the business still has to satisfy its customers or it will not survive.) It is in large, publicly held corporations, in which owners and managers are separate parties, that organizational goals become important to the practice of finance.

Publicly Held Corporations

From a finance perspective, the primary goal of large investor-owned corporations is generally assumed to be *shareholder wealth maximization*, which translates to stock price maximization. Investor-owned corporations do, of course, have other goals. Managers, who make the actual decisions, are interested in their own personal welfare, in their employees' welfare, and in the good of the community and society at large. Still, the goal of stock price maximization is a reasonable operating objective on which to build financial decision-making rules.

Not-for-Profit Corporations

Corporations consist of a number of classes of *stakeholders*, which include all parties that have an interest, usually of a financial nature, in the organization. For example, a not-for-profit hospital's stakeholders include the board of trustees, managers, employees, physician staff, creditors, suppliers, patients, and even potential patients, which may include the entire community. An investor-owned hospital has the same set of stakeholders, plus stockholders, who dictate the goal of shareholder wealth maximization. While managers of investor-owned companies have to please primarily one class of stakeholders—the shareholders—to keep their jobs, managers of not-for-profit firms face a different situation. They have to try to please all of the organization's stakeholders because no single well-defined group exercises control.

Many people argue that managers of not-for-profit corporations do not have to please anyone at all because they tend to lead the boards of trustees that are supposed to exercise oversight. Others argue that managers of not-for-profit corporations have to please all of the business's stakeholders to a greater or lesser extent because all are necessary to the successful performance of the business. Of course, even managers of investor-owned corporations should not attempt to enhance shareholder wealth by treating other stakeholders unfairly, because such actions ultimately will be detrimental to shareholders.

Typically, not-for-profit corporations state their goals in terms of a mission statement. For example, here is the current mission statement of Riverside Hospital, a 450-bed, not-for-profit acute care hospital:

> To care for others as we would care for those we love—to enhance their well-being and improve their health.

Although this mission statement provides Riverside's managers and employees with a framework for developing specific goals and objectives, it does not provide much insight into the goal of the hospital's finance function. For Riverside to accomplish its mission, its managers have identified the following five financial goals:

1. The hospital must maintain its financial viability.

2. The hospital must generate sufficient profits to continue to provide the current range of healthcare services to the community. This means that current buildings and equipment must be replaced as they become obsolete.

3. The hospital must generate sufficient profits to invest in new medical technologies and services as they are developed and needed.

4. Although the hospital has an aggressive philanthropy program in place, it does not want to rely on this program or government grants to fund its operations.

5. The hospital will strive to provide high-quality services to the community as inexpensively as possible, given the financial requirements.

In effect, Riverside's managers are saying that to achieve the hospital's commitment to excellence as stated in its mission, it must remain financially

---

For Your Consideration

Does the Finance Function Differ Among Providers?

Readers of this book understand the difference between for-profit and not-for-profit providers. Not-for-profit providers have a charitable mission, whereas for-profits are in business to make money for owners. Furthermore, all not-for-profit earnings must be reinvested in the enterprise, while some (or all) profits of for-profit health services businesses may be returned to owners in the form of dividends or stock repurchases. Although many studies have tried to assess which type of ownership is better for patients, no consensus has been reached.

But what about the finance function? That is, what about the day-to-day activities of operational managers and the finance staff? Are these appreciably different at not-for-profit providers than at for-profit providers? What about different types of providers—say, medical group practices versus hospitals?

What do you think? Is the finance function at not-for-profit providers appreciably different from that at for-profit providers, or is there an appreciable difference between types of providers? If there are differences, what are they?

strong and profitable. Financially weak organizations cannot continue to accomplish their stated missions over the long run.

Riverside's five financial goals are probably not much different from the financial goals of Jeffersonville Health System (JHS), a for-profit competitor. Of course, JHS has to worry about providing a return to its shareholders, and it receives only a very small amount of contributions and grants. However, to maximize shareholder wealth, JHS also must maintain its financial viability and have the financial resources necessary to offer new services and technologies. Furthermore, competition in the market for hospital services does not permit JHS to charge appreciably more for services than its not-for-profit competitors.

SELF-TEST
QUESTIONS

> 1. What is the difference in goals between investor-owned and not-for-profit businesses?
> 2. Briefly describe the differences in key stakeholders between investor-owned and not-for-profit businesses.

Healthcare Reform and Finance

The Affordable Care Act has been called the most significant healthcare legislation since Medicare and Medicaid were enacted in 1965. The ACA, which became law on March 23, 2010, was designed to provide all US citizens and legal residents with access to affordable health insurance, reduce healthcare costs, and improve care and quality. The legislation put in place comprehensive health insurance exchanges to expand coverage, enacted provisions to hold insurance companies accountable for product cost and quality, required that everyone buy insurance through an individual mandate (this provision was repealed in 2017 as part of the Tax Cuts and Jobs Act), and offered subsidies to low-income individuals. All of these components of the ACA were intended to transform the US healthcare system and make it more affordable and sustainable.

The ACA had numerous aims. However, the central goal was to expand healthcare coverage through shared responsibility among government, individuals, and employers.

Since the ACA's passage, several congressional efforts have been made to repeal and replace the law; however, none has been passed. While the future of healthcare reform is uncertain, major provisions of the ACA remained in effect in 2020. The major implications of healthcare reform for health insurance and provider payments are addressed in chapters 2 and 3, respectively. The major implications of healthcare reform for the institutional setting and the delivery of healthcare services are discussed in the next section of this chapter.

Key Trends Following the Affordable Care Act

Sector Consolidation

Since its passage, the ACA has driven the consolidation of healthcare organizations. It has accelerated health systems' acquisition of hospitals and hospitals' acquisition of physician practices—a trend that is likely to continue for many years. As a result of their greater focus on clinical integration, quality of care, and changing reimbursement methodologies, healthcare organizations are now seeking to restructure healthcare delivery to operate more efficiently and to improve coordination between patients and providers. Healthcare organizations are also looking to gain a competitive advantage by combining assets, staff, and resources.

Consolidation not only provides organizations with access to capital, economies of scale, negotiating power with payers, and market share, but also it may lead to improvements in patient care by making it easier to share patient information, adhere to clinical practice guidelines (thus reducing variations in care), and access high-quality specialist physicians. There is, however, a notable downside to consolidation: increases in prices as healthcare organizations gain greater market share and negotiating power.

Population Health

The ACA is moving providers toward the **population health management** approach to care provision. The goal of population health management is to shift the focus of healthcare from treating illness to maintaining or improving health. The idea is to prevent costly illnesses when possible and hence avoid unnecessary care. This approach is supported by reimbursement models such as capitation, payment bundling, and shared savings (discussed in chapter 2). Instead of providing only preventive and chronic care when patients seek out healthcare for acute problems, healthcare practices that adopt the population health management approach track and monitor the health status of their entire patient population. Doing so requires greater use of health information technology (IT). Key to the success of population health management are greater awareness of the health status of the population and proactive intervention to reduce the use of provider resources and achieve the best population outcomes.

population health management
The concept that the health of all individuals is improved when the health of the entire population is improved.

Social Determinants of Health

In response to increasing incentives to manage healthcare utilization and costs, health systems, government payers, and insurers are taking steps to address the **social determinants of health**. Scholars and healthcare providers increasingly are recognizing that social, economic, and environmental factors such as housing, education, income, and food security have a powerful influence on health outside the healthcare system. Examples of initiatives to address the social determinants of health include screening patients or populations for social needs (e.g., healthy food, housing) and then connecting individuals with resources (e.g., food pantries, information and referral services) in sectors outside healthcare. This goal is consistent with the population health management approach, which focuses on preventing costly illnesses, improving health, and reducing health inequities.

social determinants of health
Social, economic, and environmental conditions in the places where people are born, live, grow, learn, work, and play that affect health.

Clinical Integration

A fundamental component of achieving the goals of healthcare reform is clinical integration. Clinical integration aims to coordinate patient care across conditions, providers, settings, and time to achieve care that is safe, timely, effective, efficient, and patient focused. New payment models and advances in health IT systems are used to facilitate the transition to the clinical integration model and to manage the continuum of care for patients. Provider payments are tied to results for quality, access, and efficiency with the objective of better coordination between hospitals and physicians.

Health IT supports clinical integration by capturing patient information and making it accessible to authorized providers at the point of care. Complete patient information facilitates optimal treatment strategies and reduces the chance of medication errors and conflicting treatment plans. However, the sharing of patient data requires that policies and procedures be in place to protect patient privacy and to guarantee the security of data transferred among patients, caregivers, and organizations.

Technology

Technology has a major impact on the delivery and financial management of healthcare, as shown by the adoption of electronic health record systems starting in the 2000s; however, healthcare as a sector has been slow to adopt new technology because of privacy and safety concerns. A new technology, *blockchain*, has the potential to drastically change the way healthcare providers protect their data and communicate with each other. Blockchain is a system of securing data by linking pieces of data together in chains; thus, a change to one piece of data will update the rest of the chain. While this technology has the potential to revolutionize the sharing of electronic health data, there are still some concerns about ensuring patient privacy.

Electronic health data are still hard to share among providers. However, the increasing emphases on collaboration among clinicians and on quality patient care are spurring healthcare organizations to invest in integrated health IT systems to collect large quantities of patient and provider data (so-called *big data*). Data analytic systems are capable of analyzing large amounts of patient data to better understand clinical processes and to identify problems and opportunities for improvement in the provision of healthcare services. New, complex IT systems and applications of artificial intelligence will facilitate the analysis of care coordination, patient safety, and healthcare utilization.

Staffing Shortages

Healthcare reform has increased the number of patients who can access the healthcare system. As a result, healthcare organizations are seeing an influx of formerly uninsured patients who are now seeking care because they have insurance or better coverage. As a result, the demand for healthcare professionals—especially primary care physicians, nurse practitioners, and physician assistants—has increased.

Healthcare reform is also driving changes in hospital staffing by emphasizing prevention and value-based care, creating demand for primary care providers, emergency physicians, clinical pharmacists, social workers and care coordinators, and health IT and data specialists. Several strategies may increase the supply and distribution of health professionals (including primary care physicians): scholarships, flexible loan repayment programs, and debt forgiveness have been identified as ways to increase the number of providers and attract them to underserved areas. However, many healthcare organizations likely will face great competition for some healthcare staff.

Key Programs of the Affordable Care Act

Accountable Care Organizations

Accountable care organizations (ACOs), a cornerstone of healthcare reform, integrate local physicians with other members of the healthcare community and reward them for controlling costs and improving quality. While ACOs are not radically different from other attempts to improve the delivery of healthcare services, they are unique in the flexibility of their structures and payment methodologies and in their ability to assume risk while meeting quality targets. Similar to some managed care organizations and integrated healthcare systems such as the Mayo Clinic, ACOs are responsible for the health outcomes of a specific population and tasked with collaboratively improving care to reach cost and quality targets set by Medicare. To help

accountable care organization (ACO)
A network of healthcare providers joined together for the purpose of increasing patient service quality and reducing costs.

achieve cost control and quality goals, ACOs can distribute bonuses when targets are met and impose penalties when targets are missed.

One feature of healthcare reform is a shared savings program in which Medicare pays a fixed (global) payment to ACOs that covers the full cost of care for an entire population. This program establishes cost and quality targets. Any cost savings (i.e., costs that are below the target) are shared between Medicare and the ACO, as long as the ACO also meets its quality targets. If an ACO is unable to save money, it could be liable for the costs of the investments made to improve care; it also may have to pay a penalty if it does not meet performance and savings benchmarks.

To be effective, an ACO should include, at a minimum, primary care physicians, specialists, and a hospital, although some ACOs are being established solely by physician groups.

An ACO can take many forms, such as the following:

- An integrated delivery system that has common ownership of hospitals and physician practices and has electronic health records, team-based care, and resources to support cost-effective care
- A multispecialty group practice that has strong affiliations with hospitals and contracts with multiple health plans
- A physician–hospital organization that is a subset of a hospital's medical staff and functions, such as a multispecialty group practice
- An independent practice association comprising individual physician practices that come together to contract with health plans
- A virtual physician organization that sometimes includes physicians in rural areas

medical home
A team-based model of care led by a personal physician who provides continuous and coordinated care throughout a patient's lifetime with a goal of maximizing health outcomes; also called *patient-centered medical home.*

ACOs should have managerial systems in place to administer payments, set benchmarks, measure performance, and distribute shared savings. A variety of federal, regional, state, and academic hospital initiatives are investigating how best to implement ACOs. Although the concept shows potential, many legal and managerial hurdles must be overcome for ACOs to live up to their promise.

Medical Homes

A **medical home** (or *patient-centered medical home*) is a team-based model of care that is led by a personal physician who provides continuous and coordinated care throughout a patient's lifetime with the goal of maximizing health outcomes. The medical home is responsible for meeting all of a patient's healthcare needs or appropriately arranging care with other qualified professionals. This includes the provision of preventive services, treatment of acute and chronic illnesses, and assistance with end-of-life care. It is a model of practice in which a team of healthcare professionals, coordinated by a personal physician, works collaboratively to ensure coordinated and integrated care, patient access and communication, quality, and safety. The medical home model is independent of the ACO concept, but most ACOs provide an organizational setting that facilitates implementation of the model.

Supporters of the medical home model argue that it allows better access to healthcare, increases patient satisfaction, and improves health. The Agency for Healthcare Research and Quality defines a medical home as a model of primary care that encompasses the following functions and attributes:[9]

- **Comprehensive care.** The medical home includes a team of providers that are responsible for meeting a majority of the patients' physical and mental healthcare needs.
- **Patient-centered.** The medical home partners with patients and families to help patients actively engage in care decisions and manage their care.
- **Coordinated care.** The medical home coordinates care across specialists, hospitals, home health agencies, nursing homes, hospices, and community services.
- **Accessible services.** Medical care and information are available at all times through open scheduling, expanded hours of service, and new and innovative communications technologies.
- **Quality and safety.** Quality and patient safety are ensured by a care planning process, evidence-based medicine, clinical decision support tools, performance measurement, active participation of patients in decision-making, use of IT, and quality improvement activities.
- **Payment-for-value methodologies.** Payment methodologies must recognize the added value provided to patients. Payments should reflect the value of work that falls outside of face-to-face visits, support the adoption and use of health IT for quality improvement, and recognize differences among the patient populations treated within the practice.

SELF-TEST QUESTIONS

1. What is the primary purpose of healthcare reform?
2. What is an accountable care organization (ACO), and what is it designed to accomplish?
3. What is the medical home model, and what is its purpose?

Key Concepts

This chapter provides an introduction to healthcare finance. The key concepts of this chapter are as follows:

- The term *healthcare finance*, as it is used in this book, refers to the accounting and financial management principles and practices used within health services organizations to ensure the financial well-being of the enterprise.
- A *business* maintains its financial viability by selling goods or services, whereas a *pure charity* relies solely on contributions.
- The *primary role of finance* in health services organizations, as in all businesses, is to plan for, acquire, and use resources to maximize the efficiency and value of the organization.
- Finance activities generally include (1) *planning* and *budgeting*, (2) *financial reporting*, (3) *capital investment decisions*, (4) *financing decisions*, (5) *revenue cycle* and *current accounts management*, (6) *contract management*, and (7) *financial risk management*. These activities can be summarized by the *four Cs: costs, cash, capital*, and *control*.
- The size and structure of the finance department within a health services organization depend on the type of provider and its size. The finance department within a larger provider organization generally consists of a *chief financial officer (CFO)*, who typically reports directly to the *chief executive officer (CEO)* and is responsible for all finance activities within the organization. Reporting to the CFO are the *comptroller*, who is responsible for accounting and reporting activities, and the *treasurer*, who is responsible for the acquisition and management of capital (funds).
- In larger organizations, the comptroller and treasurer direct managers who have responsibility for specific functions, such as the *patient accounts manager*, who reports to the comptroller, and the *cash manager*, who reports to the treasurer.
- In small health services organizations, the finance responsibilities are combined and assigned to one individual, often called the *business (practice) manager*.
- All business decisions have *financial implications*, so all managers—whether they are in finance or not—must know enough about finance to incorporate those implications into their own specialized decision-making processes.

(continued)

(continued from previous page)

- Recent surveys of health services executives confirm that healthcare managers regard financial concerns as the most important issue they face.
- The three main forms of business organization are *proprietorship*, *partnership*, and *corporation*. Although each form of organization has its own unique advantages and disadvantages, most large organizations, and all not-for-profit entities, are organized as *corporations*.
- *Investor-owned corporations* have *stockholders* who are the owners of the corporation. As owners, stockholders have claim on the *residual earnings* of the corporation. Investor-owned corporations are fully taxable.
- Charitable organizations that meet certain criteria can be organized as *not-for-profit corporations*. Rather than having a well-defined set of owners, such organizations have a large number of *stakeholders* who have an interest in the organization. Not-for-profit corporations do not pay taxes, they can accept tax-deductible contributions, and they can issue tax-exempt debt.
- In lieu of tax filings, not-for-profit corporations must file IRS *Form 990*, which reports on an organization's governance structure and community benefit services, with the Internal Revenue Service.
- From a financial management perspective, the primary goal of investor-owned corporations is *shareholder wealth maximization*, which translates into stock price maximization. For not-for-profit corporations, a reasonable goal for financial management is to ensure that the organization can fulfill its mission, which translates to *maintaining financial viability*.
- *Healthcare reform*—such as the *Affordable Care Act (ACA)*, federal legislation that was signed into law in 2010—is having a significant impact on health insurers and providers.
- *Accountable care organizations (ACOs)* integrate local physicians with other members of the healthcare community and reward them for controlling costs and improving quality.
- A *medical home* (or *patient-centered medical home*) is a team-based model of care led by a personal physician who provides continuous and coordinated care throughout a patient's lifetime to maximize health outcomes.

In chapter 2, we continue the discussion of the healthcare environment, with an emphasis on health insurance and reimbursement methodologies.

Questions

1.1. Briefly describe the purpose and organization of this book and the learning tools embedded in each chapter.

1.2. a. What are some of the subsectors that make up the healthcare sector?

b. What is meant by the term *healthcare finance* as it is used in this book?

c. What are the two broad areas of healthcare finance?

d. Why is it necessary to have a book on healthcare finance as opposed to a generic finance book?

1.3. What is the difference between a business and a pure charity?

1.4. a. Briefly discuss the role of finance in the health services sector.

b. Has this role increased or decreased in importance in recent years?

1.5. What is the structure of the finance department within health services organizations?

1.6. a. (Hint: The material reviewed in this question is covered in the chapter 1 supplement online.) Briefly describe the following health services settings:

- Hospitals
- Ambulatory care
- Home health care
- Long-term care
- Integrated delivery systems

b. What are the benefits attributed to integrated delivery systems?

1.7. What are the major current concerns of healthcare managers?

1.8. What are the three primary forms of business organization? Describe their advantages and disadvantages.

1.9. What are the primary differences between investor-owned and not-for-profit corporations?

1.10. a. What is the primary goal of investor-owned corporations?

b. What is the primary goal of most not-for-profit healthcare corporations?

c. Are there substantial differences between the finance goals of investor-owned and not-for-profit corporations? Explain.

1.11. Briefly describe the main provisions of the Affordable Care Act and its implications for the practice of healthcare finance.

1.12. Describe the primary features of accountable care organizations and medical homes. What benefits are attributed to them?

Notes

1. American College of Healthcare Executives. 2019. "Survey: Healthcare Finance, Governmental Mandates, Personnel Shortages Cited by CEOs as Top Issues Confronting Hospitals in 2018." Published January 25. www.ache.org/about-ache/news-and-awards/news-releases/top -issues-confronting-hospitals-in-2018.

2. Advisory Board. 2019. "We Asked 90 C-Suite Executives About Their Biggest Concerns. Here's What They Told Us." Published June 13. www.advisory.com/research/health-care-advisory-board/blogs/at -the-helm/2019/06/c-suite.

3. Healthcare Finance Management Association. 2013. "HRMA's Executive Survey: Clinical Documentation Meets Financial Performance." Published November. www.hfma.org/content/dam /hfma/document/research_reports/PDF/20158.pdf.

4. American Hospital Association. 2020. "Fast Facts on U.S. Hospitals, 2020." Accessed January 13. www.aha.org/statistics/fast-facts-us -hospitals.

5. James, J. 2016. "Nonprofit Hospitals' Community Benefit Requirements." Health Policy Brief, *Health Affairs*. Published February 25. www.healthaffairs.org/do/10.1377/hpb20160225 .954803/full/healthpolicybrief_153.pdf.

6. Hilltop Institute. 2015. "Community Benefit State Law Profiles." Published January. www.hilltopinstitute.org/wp-content/uploads /publications/CommunityBenefitStateLawProfiles-January2015.pdf.

7. Chiesa Shahinain & Giantomasi. 2015. "Tax Court Ruling Cancels Property Tax Exemption for Non-Profit Hospital." Published July. www.csglaw.com/hospital-tax-exemption.

8. Rosenbaum, S., D. A. Kindig, J. Bao, M. K. Byrnes, and C. O'Laughlin. 2015. "The Value of the Nonprofit Hospital Tax Exemption Was $24.6 Billion in 2011." *Health Affairs* 34 (7): 1225–33.

9. Agency for Healthcare Research and Quality, Patient-Centered Medical Home Resource Center. 2020. "Defining the PCMH." Accessed January 13. https://pcmh.ahrq.gov/page/defining-pcmh.

Resources

For a general introduction to the healthcare system in the United States, see
Barton, P. L. 2010. *Understanding the U.S. Health Services System.* Chicago: Health Administration Press.
Shi, L., and D. A. Singh. 2013. *Essentials of the U.S. Health Care System.* Burlington, MA: Jones & Bartlett Learning.

For the latest information on events that affect health services organizations, see Modern Healthcare, *published weekly by Crain Communications Inc.:* www .crain.com/brands/modern-healthcare/.

For current information about the Affordable Care Act, see the Kaiser Family Foundation: www.kff.org/.

For information about the patient-centered medical home model of care, see the Agency for Healthcare Research and Quality's Patient-Centered Medical Home Resource Center: https://pcmh.ahrq.gov/page/defining-pcmh.

For discussion of the future of healthcare in the United States and other information pertinent to this chapter, see
Bisognano, M. 2011. "Finance Is Key to Achieving Quality and Cost Goals." *Healthcare Financial Management* 65 (4): 68–71.
French, M. T., J. Homer, G. Gumus, and L. Hickling. 2016. "Key Provisions of the Patient Protection and Affordable Care Act (ACA): A Systematic Review and Presentation of Early Research Findings." *Health Services Research* 51 (5): 1735–71.
Hegwer, L. R., and N. Hut. 2019. "The Healthcare CFO of the Future: How Finance Leaders Are Adapting to Relentless Change." *Healthcare Financial Management.* Published September 1. www.hfma.org/topics/hfm/2019 /september/the-healthcare-cfo-of-the-future.html.
Kim, C., D. Majka, and J. H. Sussman. 2011. "Modeling the Impact of Healthcare Reform." *Healthcare Financial Management* 65(1): 51–60.
Korenstein, D., K. Duan, M. J. Diaz, R. Ahn, and S. Keyhani. 2016. "Do Health Care Delivery System Reforms Improve Value? The Jury Is Still Out." *Medical Care* 54 (1): 55–66.
Lee, J. G., G. Dayal, and D. Fontaine. 2011. "Starting a Medical Home: Better Health at Lower Cost." *Healthcare Financial Management* 65 (6): 71–80.
Mulvany, C. 2011. "Medicare ACOs No Longer Mythical Creatures." *Healthcare Financial Management* 65 (6): 96–104.
Nguyen, J., and B. Choi. 2011. "Accountable Care: Are You Ready?" *Healthcare Financial Management* 65 (8): 92–100.

Rauh, S. S., E. B. Wadsworth, W. B. Weeks, and J. N. Weinstein. 2013. "The Savings Illusion—Why Clinical Quality Improvement Fails to Deliver Bottom-Line Results." *New England Journal of Medicine* 365 (26): e48.

Smith, P. C., and K. Noe. 2012. "New Requirements for Hospitals to Maintain Tax-Exempt Status." *Journal of Health Care Finance* 38 (3): 16–21.

Song, P. H., S. D. Lee, J. A. Alexander, and E. E. Seiber. 2013. "Hospital Ownership and Community Benefit: Looking Beyond Uncompensated Care." *Journal of Healthcare Management* 58 (2): 126–42.

For current information on how the internet affects health and the provision of health services, see the Journal of Medical Internet Research: www.jmir.org.

2

HEALTHCARE INSURANCE AND REIMBURSEMENT METHODOLOGIES

Learning Objectives

After studying this chapter, readers will be able to

- Explain the overall concept of insurance, including adverse selection and moral hazard.
- Briefly describe the third-party payer system.
- Explain the different types of general payment methods.
- Describe the incentives created by the different payment methods and their impact on provider risk.
- Describe the purpose and organization of managed care plans.
- Explain the impact of healthcare reform on insurance and reimbursement methodologies.
- Explain the importance and types of medical coding.

Introduction

Compared with other services, the provision of healthcare services is unique. First, often only a few providers of a particular service exist in a given area. Next, it is often difficult to judge the quality and cost of competing services, although new tools aim to facilitate service comparison.[1] Then, the decision about which services to purchase is usually not made by the consumer but by a physician or some other clinician. Also, full payment to the provider is not normally made by the user of the services but by a healthcare insurer. Finally, for most individuals, health insurance from third-party payers is paid for or subsidized by employers or government agencies, so many patients are partially insulated from the costs of healthcare.

This highly unusual marketplace for healthcare services has a profound effect on the supply of, and demand for, such services. In this chapter, we discuss the concept of insurance, the major providers of healthcare insurance, and the methods used by insurers to pay for health services.

Insurance Concepts

Healthcare services are supported by an insurance system composed of a wide variety of organizations and payers. Because insurance is the cornerstone of the healthcare system, a general understanding of insurance will help you better comprehend the marketplace for healthcare services.

A Simple Illustration

To better understand insurance concepts, consider a simple example. Assume that no health insurance exists and you face only two possible medical outcomes in the coming year:

Outcome	Probability	Cost
Stay healthy	0.99	$ 0
Get sick	0.01	20,000

Furthermore, assume that everyone else faces the same medical outcomes at the same odds and with the same associated costs. What is your expected healthcare cost—$E(Cost)$—for the coming year? To find the answer, we multiply the cost of each outcome by its probability of occurrence and then sum the products:

$$
\begin{aligned}
E(Cost) &= (\text{Probability of outcome } 1 \times \text{Cost of outcome } 1) \\
&\quad + (\text{Probability of outcome } 2 \times \text{Cost of outcome } 2) \\
&= (0.99 \times \$0) + (0.01 \times \$20{,}000) \\
&= \$0 + \$200 = \$200.
\end{aligned}
$$

Now, assume that you, and everyone else, make $20,000 a year. With this salary, you can easily afford the $200 "expected" healthcare cost. The problem is, however, that no one's actual bill will be $200. If you stay healthy, your bill will be zero, but if you are unlucky and get sick, your bill will be $20,000. This cost may force you, as well as other people who get sick, into personal bankruptcy.

Next, suppose that an insurance policy that pays all of your healthcare costs for the coming year is available for $250. Would you purchase the policy, even though it costs $50 more than your expected healthcare costs? Most people would. In general, individuals are risk averse, so they would be willing to pay a $50 premium over their expected costs to eliminate the risk of financial ruin. In effect, policyholders are passing to the insurer the costs associated with the risk of getting sick.

Would an insurer be willing to offer the policy for $250? If an insurance company sold a million policies, its expected total policy payout would be 1 million times the expected payout for each policy, or 1 million × $200 = $200 million. If there were no uncertainty about the $20,000 estimated medical cost per claim, the insurer could forecast its total claims precisely. It would collect 1 million × $250 = $250 million in health insurance premiums; pay out roughly $200 million in claims; and hence have about $50 million to cover administrative costs, create a reserve in case realized claims are greater than predicted by its actuaries, and make a profit.

Basic Characteristics of Insurance

This simple example of health insurance illustrates why individuals would seek health insurance and why insurance companies would be formed to provide such insurance. Needless to say, the concept of insurance is much more complicated in the real world. Insurance is typically defined as having four distinct characteristics:

1. **Pooling of losses.** The pooling, or sharing, of losses is the basis of insurance. Pooling means that losses are spread over a large group of individuals, so that each individual realizes the average loss of the pool (plus administrative expenses) rather than the actual loss incurred. In addition, pooling involves the grouping of a large number of homogeneous exposure units—people or things having the same risk characteristics—so that the *law of large numbers* applies. (In statistics, the law of large numbers states that as the size of the sample increases, the sample mean gets closer and closer to the population mean.) Thus, pooling implies (1) the sharing of losses by the entire group and (2) the prediction of future losses with some accuracy.

2. **Payment only for random losses.** A random loss is one that is unforeseen and unexpected and occurs as a result of chance. Insurance is based on the premise that payments are made only for losses that are random. We discuss the moral hazard problem, which concerns losses that are not random, in a later section of this chapter.

3. **Risk transfer.** An insurance plan almost always involves risk transfer. The sole exception to the element of risk transfer is self-insurance, which is the assumption of a risk by a business (or an individual) itself rather than by an insurance company. (Self-insurance is discussed in a later section.) Risk transfer is the transfer of a risk from an insured to an insurer, which typically is in a better financial position to bear the risk than the insured because of the law of large numbers.

4. **Indemnification.** The final characteristic of insurance is *indemnification* for losses—that is, reimbursement to the insured if a loss occurs. In the context of health insurance, indemnification takes place when the insurer pays the insured, or the provider, in whole or in part for the expenses related to the insured's illness or injury.

Adverse Selection

adverse selection
The problem faced by insurance companies because individuals who are more likely to have claims are also more likely to purchase insurance.

One of the major problems facing healthcare insurers is **adverse selection**. Adverse selection occurs because individuals and businesses that are more likely to have claims are more inclined to purchase insurance than those that are less likely to have claims. For example, an individual without insurance who needs a costly surgical procedure will likely seek health insurance if it is affordable to do so, whereas an individual who does not need surgery is much less likely to purchase insurance. Similarly, consider the likelihood of a 20-year-old to seek health insurance versus the likelihood of a 60-year-old to do so. The older individual, with much greater health risk due to age, is more likely to seek insurance.

If this tendency toward adverse selection goes unchecked, a disproportionate number of sick people, or those who are most likely to become sick, will seek health insurance, and the insurer will experience higher than expected claims. This increase in claims will trigger a premium increase, which will only worsen the problem, because the healthier members of the plan will seek insurance from other firms at a lower cost or may totally forgo insurance. The adverse selection problem exists because of asymmetric information, which occurs when individual buyers of health insurance know more about their health status than do insurers.

The best strategy for healthcare insurers to combat adverse selection is to create a large, well-diversified pool of subscribers. If the pool is sufficiently large and diversified, the costs of adverse selection can be absorbed by the large number of enrollees. Many current health policies, such as health insurance exchanges, attempt to limit adverse selection by creating or requiring these large, diversified risk pools.

moral hazard
The problem faced by insurance companies because individuals are more likely to use unneeded health services when they are not paying the full cost of those services.

Moral Hazard

Insurance is based on the premise that payments are made only for random losses, and from this premise stems the problem of **moral hazard**. An example of moral hazard in a casualty insurance setting is the owner who deliberately sets a failing business on fire to collect the insurance. Moral hazard is also present in health insurance, but it typically takes a less dramatic form; few people are willing to voluntarily sustain injury or illness for the purpose of collecting health insurance proceeds. However, undoubtedly there are people who purposely use healthcare services that are not medically required. For example, some people might visit a physician or a walk-in clinic for the social value of human companionship rather than to address a medical necessity. Also, some hospital discharges might be delayed for the convenience of the patient rather than for medical purposes.

Finally, when insurance covers the full cost or most of the cost of healthcare services, individuals often are quick to agree to an expensive magnetic resonance imaging (MRI) scan or other high-cost procedure that may not be necessary. If the same test required total out-of-pocket payment, individuals would think twice before agreeing to such an expensive procedure unless they clearly understood the medical necessity involved. All in all, when somebody else is paying the costs, patients consume more healthcare services.

Even more insidious is the potential impact of insurance on individual behavior. Individuals may be more likely to forgo preventive actions and embrace unhealthy behaviors when the costs of not taking those actions will be borne by insurers. For example, individuals may be less motivated to stop smoking if the monetary costs associated with smoking-related illnesses are carried by the insurer.

The primary tool that insurers have to combat the moral hazard problem is *coinsurance*, which requires insured individuals to pay a certain percentage of eligible medical expenses—say, 20 percent—in excess of the deductible (the amount that individuals pay before their insurance plan starts to pay). Insurers also use *copayments*, which are similar to coinsurance but are expressed as a dollar amount: $20 per primary care visit, for example. To illustrate coinsurance, assume that Juan Pérez, who has employer-provided medical insurance that pays 80 percent of eligible expenses after the $100 deductible is satisfied, incurs $10,000 in medical expenses during

For Your Consideration

Who Should Pay for Health Services— Users or Insurers?

One of the most confounding questions that arises when discussing healthcare services is who should bear the responsibility for payment. Should the patient be responsible, or should some third party, such as the government or an insurance company, foot the bill?

Many people argue that when individuals bear the cost of their own healthcare, they will be responsible consumers and only pay for necessary services. In addition, they will choose providers on the basis of cost and quality and hence create incentives for providers to offer better yet less expensive services. It is estimated that this action alone would reduce total healthcare costs in the United States by 20 to 30 percent, or even more.

Other people argue that individuals cannot make rational decisions regarding their own healthcare because they do not sufficiently understand the nature of illness and injury. Furthermore, there is insufficient information about provider quality and costs available to guide individuals to good decisions. Finally, individuals would skimp on routine preventive healthcare services to save money, which would create healthcare problems down the road and ultimately lead to higher future costs.

What do you think? Should individuals be held more responsible for their own costs of healthcare services? What about the arguments stated here? Is there some way of balancing the need for more consumerism in healthcare service purchases with the need to protect individuals against the very high costs of many services? Can you think of a current example?

the year. The insurer will pay $0.80 \times (\$10,000 - \$100) = 0.80 \times \$9,900 = \$7,920$, so Juan's responsibility is $\$10,000 - \$7,920 = \$2,080$. The purposes of coinsurance and copayments are to reduce premiums (monthly fees for purchasing the insurance plan) to employers and to prevent overutilization of healthcare services. Because insured individuals pay part of the cost, premiums can be reduced. Additionally, by being forced to pay some of the costs, insured individuals will presumably seek fewer and more cost-effective treatments and embrace a healthier lifestyle.

SELF-TEST QUESTIONS

1. Briefly explain the following characteristics of insurance:
   a. Pooling of losses
   b. Payment only for random losses
   c. Risk transfer
   d. Indemnification
2. What is adverse selection, and how do insurers deal with the problem?
3. What is the moral hazard problem, and how do insurers mitigate it?

Third-Party Payers

Up to this point in the chapter, we have focused on basic insurance concepts. A large proportion of the health services sector receives its revenues not directly from the users of their services—the patients—but from insurers, which are known collectively as **third-party payers**. Because an organization's revenues are critical to its financial viability, this section briefly examines the sources of most revenues in the health services sector. In the next section, the reimbursement methodologies employed by third-party payers are reviewed in more detail.

third-party payer
A generic term for any outside party, typically an insurance company or a government program, that pays for part or all of a patient's healthcare services.

Health insurance originated in Europe in the early 1800s, when mutual benefit societies formed to reduce the financial burden associated with illness or injury. Since then, the concept of health insurance has changed dramatically. Today, health insurers fall into two broad categories: private insurers and public programs.

Private Insurers

In the United States, the concept of public, or government-provided, health insurance is relatively new, while private health insurance has been in existence since the early 1900s. In this section, the major private insurers are discussed: Blue Cross Blue Shield (www.bcbs.com), commercial insurers, and self-insurers.

Blue Cross Blue Shield

Blue Cross Blue Shield organizations trace their roots to the Great Depression, when both hospitals and physicians were concerned about their patients' ability to pay healthcare bills. One example is Florida Blue (www.floridablue.com) (formerly Blue Cross and Blue Shield of Florida), which offers healthcare insurance to individuals and families, Medicare beneficiaries, and business groups that reside in Florida.

Blue Cross originated as a number of separate insurance programs offered by individual hospitals. At that time, many patients were unable to pay their hospital bills, but most people, except the poorest, could afford to purchase some type of hospitalization insurance. Thus, the programs were initially designed to benefit hospitals as well as patients. The programs were all similar in structure: Hospitals agreed to provide a certain amount of services to program members who made periodic payments of fixed amounts to the hospitals, whether services were used or not. In a short time, these programs expanded from single-hospital programs to community-wide, multi-hospital plans called *hospital service plans.* The Blue Cross name was officially adopted by most of these plans in 1939.

Blue Shield plans developed in a manner similar to Blue Cross plans, except that the providers were physicians instead of hospitals. Today, there are 36 Blue Cross Blue Shield organizations (referred to as "the Blues"). Some offer only one of the two plans, but most offer both plans. The Blues are organized as independent corporations, including some for-profit entities, but all belong to a single national association that sets standards that must be met to use the Blue Cross Blue Shield name. Collectively, the Blues provide healthcare coverage for more than 106 million individuals in all 50 states, the District of Columbia, and Puerto Rico.[2]

Commercial Insurers

Commercial health insurance is issued by life insurance companies, casualty insurance companies, and companies that were formed exclusively to offer healthcare insurance. Examples of commercial insurers include Aetna, Humana, and UnitedHealth Group. All commercial insurance companies are taxable (for-profit) entities. Commercial insurers entered the health insurance market following World War II. At that time, the United Auto Workers negotiated the first contract with employers in which fringe benefits were a major part of the contract. Also following the war, the Internal Revenue Service ruled that employer-provided health insurance was not taxable, giving employers an incentive to offer this tax-free benefit. Like those covered under Blue Cross Blue Shield, the majority of individuals with commercial health insurance are covered under *group policies* negotiated by employee groups, professional and other associations, and labor unions.

Self-Insurers

The third major form of private insurance is *self-insurance*. Although it might seem as if all individuals who do not have some form of health insurance are self-insurers, this is not the case. Self-insurers make a conscious decision to bear the risks associated with healthcare costs and then set aside (or have available) funds to pay future costs as they occur. Individuals, except the very wealthy, are not good candidates for self-insurance because they face too much uncertainty concerning healthcare expenses. On the other hand, large groups, especially employers, are good candidates for self-insurance. Today, most large groups are self-insured. For example, employees of the State of Florida are covered by health insurance whose costs are paid directly by the state. Florida Blue is paid a fee to administer the plan, but the state bears all the risks associated with cost and utilization uncertainty.

Public Insurers

Government is a major insurer as well as a direct provider of healthcare services. For example, the US federal government provides healthcare services directly to qualifying individuals through the medical facilities of the US Department of Veterans Affairs; the US Department of Defense and its TRICARE program (health insurance for uniformed service members and their families); and the Public Health Service, part of the *US Department of Health and Human Services (HHS)*. In addition, government either provides or mandates a variety of insurance programs, such as workers' compensation. In this section, however, the focus is on the two major government insurance programs: Medicare and Medicaid.

Medicare

Medicare
A federal government health insurance program that primarily provides benefits to individuals aged 65 or older.

Medicare was established by Congress in 1965 primarily to provide medical benefits to individuals aged 65 or older. About 44 million people have Medicare coverage, which pays for about 21 percent of all US healthcare services.

Over the decades, Medicare has evolved to include four major coverages: Part A, which provides hospital and some skilled nursing facility coverage; (2) Part B, which covers physician services, ambulatory surgical services, outpatient services, and other miscellaneous services; (3) Part C, which is managed care coverage offered by private insurance companies and can be selected in lieu of Parts A and B; and (4) Part D, which covers prescription drugs. In addition, Medicare covers healthcare costs associated with selected disabilities and illnesses, such as kidney failure, regardless of age.

Part A coverage is free to all individuals who are eligible for Social Security benefits. Individuals who are not eligible for Social Security benefits can obtain Part A medical benefits by paying monthly premiums. Part

B is optional for all individuals who have Part A coverage, and it requires a monthly premium from enrollees that varies with income level. About one-third of Medicare enrollees elect to participate in Part C, also called *Medicare Advantage Plans*, rather than Parts A and B. Part D offers prescription drug coverage through plans offered by private companies. Each Part D plan offers somewhat different coverage, so the cost of Part D coverage varies widely.

Administration of the Medicare program falls under the HHS, which creates the specific rules of the program on the basis of enabling legislation. Medicare is administered by an agency within the HHS called the *Centers for Medicare & Medicaid Services (CMS)*. CMS has ten regional offices that oversee the Medicare program and ensure that regulations are followed.[3] Medicare payments to providers are not made directly by CMS but by contractors for 12 Medicare Administrative Contractor (MAC) jurisdictions.

Many private insurers also offer coverage called *Medicare supplement insurance*, or *Medigap*. Such insurance is designed to help pay some of the healthcare costs that traditional Medicare does not cover, such as copayments, coinsurance, and deductibles. In addition, some Medigap policies offer coverage for services that Medicare does not include, for example, medical care when traveling outside the United States. When an individual buys Medigap coverage, Medicare will first pay its share of the Medicare-approved amount for covered costs, and then the Medigap policy pays its share.

Medicaid

Medicaid began in 1966 as a modest program to be jointly funded and operated by the states and the federal government. The goal was to provide a medical safety net for low-income mothers and children and for elderly, blind, and disabled individuals who receive benefits from the Supplemental Security Income (SSI) program. Congress mandated that Medicaid cover hospital and physician care, but states were encouraged to expand the basic package of benefits, either by increasing the range of benefits or by extending the program to cover more people. A mandatory nursing home benefit was added in 1972.

Over the years, Medicaid has provided access to healthcare services for many low-income individuals who otherwise would have no insurance coverage. Furthermore, Medicaid has become an important source of revenue for healthcare providers, especially for nursing homes and other providers that treat large numbers of indigent patients.

It is important to note that both Medicare and Medicaid expenditures have been growing at an alarming rate, which has forced both federal and state policymakers to search for more effective ways to improve the programs' access, quality, and cost.

Medicaid
A federal and state government health insurance program that provides benefits to low-income individuals.

1. What are the different types of private insurers?
2. Briefly, what are the origins and purpose of Medicare?
3. What is Medicaid, and how is it administered?

Managed Care Plans

managed care plan
A combined effort by an insurer and a group of providers that aims both to increase quality of care and to decrease costs.

Managed care plans combine the provision of healthcare services and the insurance function into a single entity. Traditional plans are created by insurers that either directly own a provider network or create one through contractual arrangements with independent providers.

One type of managed care plan is the *health maintenance organization (HMO)*. HMOs are based on the premise that the traditional insurer–provider relationship creates incentives that reward providers for treating patients' illnesses while offering little incentive for providing prevention and rehabilitation services. This is often referred to as *volume over value*. By combining the financing and delivery of comprehensive healthcare services into a single system, HMOs theoretically have as strong an incentive to prevent illnesses as to treat them. However, from a patient perspective, HMOs have several drawbacks, including a limited network of providers and the assignment of a primary care physician (often called a gatekeeper) who acts as the initial contact and authorizes all services received from the HMO.

Another type of managed care plan, the *preferred provider organization (PPO)*, evolved during the early 1980s. PPOs are a hybrid of HMOs and traditional health insurance plans that use many of the cost-saving strategies developed by HMOs. PPOs do not mandate that beneficiaries use specific providers, although financial incentives (i.e., patients pay less for going to more efficient providers) encourage members to use providers that are part of the *provider panel*—those providers that have contracts (usually at discounted prices) with the PPO. Furthermore, PPOs do not require beneficiaries to use preselected gatekeeper physicians.

In an effort to achieve the potential cost savings of managed care plans, most insurance companies now apply managed care strategies to their conventional plans. Such plans, which are called *managed fee-for-service plans*, use preadmission certification (review of patient need before a hospital admission), utilization review (examination of services provided to a patient), and second surgical opinions (another physician validates recommended treatment) to control inappropriate utilization.

Although the distinctions between managed care and conventional plans were once quite apparent, considerable overlap now exists in the strategies and incentives employed. Thus, the term *managed care* now describes a continuum of plans, which can vary significantly in their approaches to providing combined insurance and healthcare services. The common feature in managed care plans is that the insurer has a mechanism by which it controls, or at least influences, patients' utilization of healthcare services.

SELF-TEST QUESTIONS

1. What is meant by the term *managed care*?
2. What are the different types of managed care plans?

Healthcare Reform and Insurance

The Affordable Care Act (ACA) introduced a number of provisions to expand insurance coverage and improve insurance affordability and access. Here we outline some of the act's provisions that focus on healthcare insurance.

Insurance Standards

A number of new insurance standards were specified in the ACA. In terms of coverage, these include the following:

- Children and dependents are permitted to remain on their parents' insurance plans until their twenty-sixth birthday.
- Insurance companies are prohibited from dropping policyholders if they become sick and from denying coverage to individuals due to preexisting conditions.
- Individuals have a right to appeal and request that the insurer review denial of payment.

In terms of costs, the standards include the following:

- Insurers are required to charge the same premium rate to all applicants of the same age and geographic location, regardless of preexisting conditions or sex (this is called *community rating*).
- Insurers are required to spend at least 80 percent of premium dollars on health costs and claims instead of on administrative costs and profits. If the insurer violates this standard, it must issue rebates to policyholders (this is called the *medical loss ratio*).
- Lifetime limits on most benefits are prohibited for all new health insurance plans.

In terms of care, the standards include the following:

- All plans must now include essential benefits, such as ambulatory patient services, emergency services, hospitalization, maternity and newborn care, mental health and substance use disorder services, prescription drugs, laboratory services, preventive and wellness services, chronic disease management, and pediatric services, including oral and vision care.
- Preventive services, such as childhood immunizations, adult vaccinations, and basic medical screenings, must be available to patients free of charge.
- Individuals are permitted to choose a primary care doctor outside the plan's network.
- Individuals can seek emergency care at a hospital outside the health plan's network.

It is important to note that individuals who seek primary or hospital care out-of-network will likely pay more.

Individual Mandate

The individual mandate of the ACA went into effect in January 2014. This mandate required that all eligible individuals (i.e., US citizens and legal residents) who were not covered by an employer-sponsored health plan, Medicaid, or Medicare have a health insurance policy or face a tax penalty. In 2017, passage of the Tax Cuts and Jobs Act repealed the individual mandate (effective January 1, 2019). The Congressional Budget Office estimated that repeal of the individual health insurance mandate would increase the number of uninsured people by 4 million in 2019 and 13 million in 2027.[4]

Medicaid Expansion

One of the key provisions of the ACA was the expansion of Medicaid to all citizens and legal residents between the ages of 19 and 64 who have household incomes below 138 percent of the federal poverty level. Medicaid expansion primarily benefits childless adults who previously did not qualify for Medicaid regardless of their income level as well as low-income parents who previously did not qualify even if their children did qualify. As a result, if every state expanded Medicaid, it is estimated that an additional 16 million people would receive coverage.

Originally, under the ACA, Medicaid expansion was mandatory for all states; states that did not comply were to be penalized by the federal government. However, in 2012, the US Supreme Court ruled that states could opt out of the Medicaid expansion, leaving the decision to participate in the hands of the state's leaders. The court further ruled that the federal government could not penalize states through denial of federal funding if they did not expand Medicaid. Despite these rulings, 37 states and the District of Columbia had expanded Medicaid eligibility as of 2019.[5]

Health Insurance Exchanges

Health insurance exchanges (HIEs) are online marketplaces where people can research and review their options and purchase health insurance. People who are unable to receive health insurance through their employer, the unemployed, or the self-employed can purchase coverage through an exchange. Therefore, HIEs are an important part of ensuring that healthcare access is available to all Americans and legal immigrants. As of 2018, roughly 12 million people used HIEs to buy healthcare insurance coverage.[6] To ensure price transparency, all participating insurance companies are required to post on HIEs the rates for their health insurance plans. This mandate permits individuals and businesses shopping for insurance to compare all plans and rates side by side and select plans that are affordable and meet their needs.

health insurance exchange (HIE) An online marketplace created primarily by the states or the federal government that insurers use to post plan details and consumers use to purchase health insurance.

There are different types of HIEs. Public exchanges are created by state or federal governments and are open to both individuals seeking personal insurance and small-group employers seeking insurance for their workers. All plans listed on an HIE are required to offer core benefits—called *essential health benefits*—such as preventive and wellness services, prescription drugs, and hospital stays. Private exchanges, on the other hand, are created by private-sector firms, such as health insurance companies.

In addition to establishing HIEs, the ACA aimed to make insurance more affordable by offering subsidies to individuals below 400 percent of the federal poverty level that purchase insurance on the HIEs. There are two types of subsidies: (1) premium tax credits that offset the amount of monthly premiums that an individual pays, and (2) cost-sharing subsidies that minimize the amount of out-of-pocket costs an individual pays. There are several challenges associated with HIEs. First, the federal exchange, along with many state exchanges, had a difficult launch as a result of technological challenges. This led to distrust of the system and initially lower enrollment than projected. Second, while coverage on the HIEs is largely affordable for individuals that receive subsidies, it is unaffordable for many individuals with incomes above 400 percent of the federal poverty level who do not receive subsidies.

High-Deductible Health Plans

Many consumers who choose coverage are opting for *high-deductible health plans (HDHPs)*. HDHPs are growing in popularity because they are among the least expensive options on the insurance exchanges. In fact, the rate of enrollment in HDHPs has more than doubled since 2009. These plans have low premiums and high deductibles. Some are linked with health savings accounts or health reimbursement arrangements, under which enrollees can use tax-advantaged accounts to pay for medical expenses. HDHPs aim to provide individuals with control over their healthcare expenditures. Individuals enrolled in an HDHP are required to meet minimum deductibles before the plan starts to cover healthcare expenses.

SELF-TEST QUESTIONS

1. Briefly describe the impact of the ACA on health insurance.
2. What is a health insurance exchange (HIE)?
3. What is a high-deductible health plan (HDHP)?

General Reimbursement Methodologies

Regardless of the payer for a particular healthcare service, a limited number of payment methodologies are used to reimburse providers. Payment methodologies fall into two broad classifications: fee-for-service and capitation. Under **fee-for-service** payment, of which many variations exist, the greater the amount of services provided, the higher the amount of reimbursement. Under **capitation**, a fixed payment is made to providers for each *covered life*, or *enrollee*, independent of the amount of services provided. In this section, we discuss the mechanics, incentives created, and risk implications of alternative reimbursement methodologies.

fee-for-service
A reimbursement methodology that provides payment each time a service is provided.

capitation
A reimbursement methodology that is based on the number of covered lives (or enrollees) as opposed to the amount of services provided.

cost-based reimbursement
A fee-for-service reimbursement method based on the costs incurred in providing services.

Fee-for-Service Methods

The three primary fee-for-service methods of reimbursement are cost based, charge based, and prospective payment.

Cost-Based Reimbursement

Under **cost-based reimbursement**, the payer agrees to reimburse the provider for the costs incurred in providing services to the insured population. Reimbursement is limited to *allowable costs*, usually defined as those costs directly related to the provision of healthcare services. Nevertheless, for all practical purposes, cost-based reimbursement guarantees that a provider's costs will be covered by payments from the payer. Typically, the payer makes *periodic interim payments* to the provider, and a final reconciliation is made after the contract period expires and all costs have been processed through the provider's managerial (cost) accounting system.

During its early years (1966–1982), Medicare reimbursed hospitals on the basis of costs incurred. Now, most hospitals are reimbursed by Medicare, and by other payers, using a per diagnosis prospective payment system (this topic is addressed in more detail later in this chapter). However, *critical access hospitals*, which are small rural hospitals that provide services to remote populations that do not have easy access to other hospitals, are still reimbursed on a cost basis by Medicare.

Charge-Based Reimbursement

When payers pay *billed charges*, or simply *charges*, they pay according to a rate schedule, called a **chargemaster**, established by the provider. To a certain extent, this reimbursement system places payers at the mercy of providers in regard to the cost of healthcare services, especially in markets where competition is limited. In the early days of health insurance, all payers reimbursed providers on the basis of billed charges. Few insurers still reimburse providers according to billed charges; the trend for payers is toward other, less generous reimbursement methods (e.g., discounted charges).

> **chargemaster**
> A list of all items and services provided by a health services organization containing their gross (list) prices.

Most payers that historically reimbursed providers on the basis of billed charges now pay by *negotiated*, or *discounted*, *charges*. This is especially true for insurers that have established managed care plans. Additionally, many conventional insurers have bargaining power because of the large number of patients that they bring to a provider, so they can negotiate discounts from billed charges. Such discounts generally range from 20 to 50 percent, or even more, of billed charges. The effect of these discounts is to create a system similar to hotel or airline pricing, where there are listed rates (e.g., chargemaster prices for providers, and rack rates or full fares for hotels and airlines) that few people pay.

Prospective Payment

Under a **prospective payment** system, the rates paid by payers are established by the payer before the services are provided. Furthermore, payments are not directly related to either costs or chargemaster rates. Here are some common units of payment used in prospective payment systems:

> **prospective payment**
> A fee-for-service reimbursement method in which the payment amount is established beforehand by the third-party payer and, in theory, is not directly related to costs or charges.

- **Per procedure.** Under *per procedure* reimbursement, a separate payment is made for each procedure performed on a patient. Because of the high administrative costs associated with this method when it is applied to complex diagnoses, per procedure reimbursement is more commonly used in outpatient than in inpatient settings.
- **Per diagnosis.** Under the *per diagnosis* reimbursement method, the provider is paid a rate that depends on the patient's diagnosis. Diagnoses that require higher resource utilization, and hence are more costly to treat, have higher reimbursement rates. Medicare pioneered this basis of payment in its *diagnosis-related group (DRG)* system, which it first used for hospital inpatient reimbursement in 1983.

per diem payment
A fee-for-service reimbursement method that pays a set amount for each inpatient day.

- **Per day (per diem).** If reimbursement is based on a **per diem payment**, the provider is paid a fixed amount for each day that service is provided, regardless of the nature of the service. Note that per diem rates, which are applicable only to inpatient settings, can be *stratified*. For example, a hospital may be paid one rate for a medical/surgical day, a higher rate for a critical care unit day, and yet a different rate for an obstetrics day. Stratified per diems recognize that providers incur widely different daily costs for providing different types of care. Per diem rates may also vary by the day of a patient's stay, recognizing that early days of care may be more expensive than those later in a patient's stay.

bundled (global) payment
The fee-for-service payment of a single amount for the complete set of services required to treat a single episode.

- **Bundled.** Under **bundled payment**, payers make a single prospective payment that covers all services delivered in a single episode, whether the services are rendered by a single provider or by multiple providers. For example, a bundled payment may be made for all obstetric services associated with a pregnancy provided by a single physician, including all prenatal and postnatal visits as well as the delivery. For another example, a bundled payment may be made for all physician and hospital services associated with a joint replacement operation. Bundled payments incent hospitals and providers to provide the most efficient and effective care at the lowest cost. Finally, note that, at the extreme, a bundled payment may cover an entire population. In this situation, the payment becomes a *global payment*, which, in effect, is a capitation payment (described in the next section of this chapter).

Capitation

Up to this point, the prospective payment methods presented have been fee-for-service methods—that is, providers are reimbursed on the basis of the amount of services provided. The service may be defined as a visit, a diagnosis, a hospital day, an episode, or in some other manner, but the key feature is that the more services that are performed, the greater the reimbursement amount. *Capitation*, although it is a form of prospective payment, is an entirely different approach to reimbursement and hence deserves to be

---

For Your Consideration

Creating the Proper Provider Incentives

An article in the *Wall Street Journal* on February 18, 2015, described the case of a patient who was discharged from a Kindred Healthcare long-term care hospital after 23 days of treatment for complications from a previous knee surgery. According to family members, the timing of his release did not appear to be related to any improvement in his medical condition. However, it did result in the hospital receiving a higher reimbursement for his stay.

According to billing documents, Kindred collected $35,887.79 from Medicare for his treatment—the maximum amount it could earn for treating patients with his condition. Under Medicare's reimbursement rules, if the patient had left the hospital one day earlier, Kindred would have received a per diem rate that would have resulted in a total payment of roughly $20,000. If

(continued)

treated separately. Under capitated reimbursement, the provider is paid a fixed amount per covered life per period (usually a month) regardless of the amount of services provided. For example, a primary care physician might be paid $15 per member per month for handling 100 members of an HMO plan.

Capitation payment, which is used primarily by managed care plans, dramatically changes the financial environment of healthcare providers. It has implications for financial accounting, managerial accounting, and financial management. Discussion of how capitation, as opposed to fee-for-service reimbursement, affects healthcare finance is provided throughout this book.

(continued from previous page)

he had stayed longer than 23 days, the hospital likely would not have received any additional reimbursement other than the $35,887.79 single payment for an "extended" stay.

What do you think? What incentives are created for providers under the reimbursement method used by Medicare for long-term (as opposed to acute care) hospitals? Can you think of a payment system that would encourage long-term care hospitals to discharge patients at the appropriate time?

SELF-TEST QUESTIONS

1. Briefly explain the following payment methods:
   a. Cost based
   b. Charge based and discounted charges
   c. Per procedure
   d. Per diagnosis
   e. Per diem
   f. Bundled
   g. Capitation
2. What is the major difference between fee-for-service reimbursement and capitation?

Provider Incentives Under Alternative Reimbursement Methodologies

Providers, like individuals and businesses, react to the incentives created by the financial environment. It is interesting to examine the incentives that alternative reimbursement methods have on provider behavior. Under cost-based reimbursement, providers are given a "blank check" to acquire facilities and equipment and incur operating costs. If payers reimburse providers for all costs, the incentive is to incur costs. Facilities will be lavish and conveniently located, and staff will be available to ensure that patients are given "deluxe" treatment. Furthermore, services that may not be medically required will be provided because more services lead to higher costs and hence lead to higher revenues.

Under charge-based reimbursement, providers have incentives to set high charge rates, which lead to high revenues. However, in competitive markets, there will be a constraint on how high providers can go. But, to the extent that insurers, rather than patients, are footing the bill, there is often considerable leeway in setting charges. Because charge-based payment is a fee-for-service type of reimbursement in which more services result in higher revenue, a strong incentive exists to provide the highest possible amount of services. In essence, providers can increase utilization, and hence revenues, by *churning*—that is, by creating more visits, ordering more tests, extending inpatient stays, and so on. Charge-based reimbursement creates incentives for providers to contain costs because (1) the spread between charges and costs represents profits, and the more the better, and (2) lower costs can lead to lower charges, which can increase volume. Still, the incentive to contain costs is weak because charges can be increased more easily than costs can be reduced. Note, however, that discounted charge reimbursement places additional pressure on profitability and hence increases the incentive for providers to lower costs.

Under prospective payment reimbursement, provider incentives are altered. First, under per procedure reimbursement, the profitability of individual procedures varies depending on the relationship between the actual costs incurred and the payment for that procedure. Providers, usually physicians, have an incentive to perform procedures that have the highest profit potential. Furthermore, the more procedures, the better, because each procedure typically generates additional profit.

For Your Consideration
Value-Based Purchasing

Value-based purchasing is based on the concept that buyers of healthcare services should hold providers accountable for quality of care as well as costs. In April 2011, the HHS launched the Hospital Value-Based Purchasing Program, which marked the beginning of a historic change in how Medicare pays healthcare providers. The shift from volume to value is widespread. Currently, 2,800 hospitals across the country are being paid for inpatient acute care services based on care cost and quality, not just the quantity of the services provided.[7]

"Changing the way we pay hospitals will improve the quality of care for seniors and save money for all of us," said former HHS Secretary Kathleen Sebelius. "Under this initiative, Medicare will reward hospitals that provide high-quality care and keep their patients healthy. It's an important part of our work to improve the health of our nation and drive down costs. As hospitals work to improve quality, all patients—not just Medicare patients—will benefit." The measures to determine quality focus on how closely hospitals follow best clinical practices and how well hospitals enhance patients' care experiences. The better a hospital does on its quality measures, the greater the reward it receives from Medicare.

What do you think? Should providers be reimbursed based on quality of care? How should "quality" be measured? Should the additional reimbursement to high-quality providers be obtained by reductions in reimbursement to low-quality providers?

The incentives under per diagnosis reimbursement are similar. Providers, usually hospitals, will seek patients with diagnoses that have the greatest profit potential and discourage (or even discontinue) those services that have the least potential. Furthermore, to the extent that providers have some flexibility in selecting procedures (or assigning diagnoses) to patients, an incentive exists to *upcode* procedures (or diagnoses) to ones that provide the greatest reimbursement.

In all prospective payment methods, providers have an incentive to reduce costs because the amount of reimbursement is fixed and independent of the costs actually incurred. For example, when hospitals are paid under per diagnosis reimbursement, they have an incentive to reduce length of stay and hence costs. Note, however, that when per diem reimbursement is used, hospitals have an incentive to increase length of stay. Because the early days of a hospitalization typically are more costly than the later days, the later days are more profitable. However, as mentioned previously, hospitals have an incentive to reduce costs during each day of a patient stay.

Under bundled pricing, providers do not have the opportunity to be reimbursed for a series of separate services, which is called *unbundling*. For example, a physician's treatment of a fracture could be bundled, and hence billed as one episode, or it could be unbundled, with separate bills submitted for making the diagnosis, taking X-rays, setting the fracture, removing the cast, and so on. The rationale for unbundling is usually to provide more detailed records of treatments rendered, but often the result is higher total charges for the parts than would be charged for the entire package of services. Also, bundled pricing, when applied to multiple providers for a single episode of care, forces involved providers (e.g., physicians and a hospital) to jointly offer the most cost-effective treatment. Such a joint view of cost containment may be more effective than each provider separately attempting to minimize its treatment costs because lowering costs in one phase of treatment could increase costs in another.

Finally, capitation reimbursement changes the playing field by completely reversing the actions that providers must take to ensure financial success. Under all fee-for-service methods, the key to provider success is to work harder, increase utilization, and hence increase profits; under capitation, the key to profitability is to work smarter and decrease utilization. As with prospective payment, capitated providers have an incentive to reduce costs, but now they also have an incentive to reduce utilization. Thus, only those procedures that are truly medically necessary should be performed, and treatment should take place in the lowest-cost setting that can provide the appropriate quality of care. Furthermore, providers have an incentive to promote health, rather than just treat illness and injury, because a healthier population consumes fewer healthcare services.

1. What provider incentives are created under fee-for-service reimbursement? Under capitation?

Medical Coding: The Foundation of Fee-for-Service Reimbursement

medical coding
The process of transforming medical diagnoses and procedures into universally recognized numerical codes.

Medical coding, or medical classification, is the process of transforming descriptions of medical diagnoses and procedures into code numbers that can be universally recognized and interpreted. The diagnoses and procedures are usually taken from a variety of sources within the medical record, such as doctor's notes, laboratory results, and radiological tests. In practice, the basis for most fee-for-service reimbursement is the patient's diagnosis (in the case of inpatient settings) or the procedures performed on the patient (in the case of outpatient settings). Thus, a brief background on clinical coding will enhance your understanding of the reimbursement process.

Diagnosis Codes

International Classification of Diseases (ICD) codes
Numerical codes for designating diseases plus a variety of signs, symptoms, and external causes of injury.

The **International Classification of Diseases** (most commonly known by the abbreviation ICD) is the standard for designating diseases plus a wide variety of signs, symptoms, and external causes of injury. Published by the World Health Organization (WHO), **ICD codes** are used internationally to record many types of health events, including hospital inpatient stays and causes of death. (ICD codes were first used in 1893 to report death statistics.) The WHO periodically revises the diagnostic codes in ICD, which is now in its eleventh version (ICD-11).[8]

The United States has used ICD-10-CM since October 1, 2015. This national variant of ICD-10 was provided by CMS and the National Center for Health Statistics, and the use of ICD-10-CM codes is now mandated for all inpatient medical reporting. There are over 70,000 ICD-10-CM procedure codes and over 69,000 diagnosis codes, compared with about 3,800 procedure codes and roughly 14,000 diagnosis codes found in the ICD-9-CM.

The ICD-10 codes are three to seven characters long. The first three characters refer to the category; the next three characters refer to etiology, anatomic site, severity, or other clinical detail; and the seventh character refers to extension. For example, code S52 describes a fracture of the forearm, while S52.521A describes a torus fracture of the lower end of the right radius, initial encounter for closed fracture.

In practice, the application of ICD codes to diagnoses is complicated and technical. Hospital coders have to understand the coding system and the medical terminology and abbreviations used by clinicians. Because of this complexity, and because proper coding can mean higher reimbursement from third-party payers, ICD coders require a great deal of training and experience to be most effective.

Procedure Codes

While ICD codes are used to specify diseases and conditions, **Current Procedural Terminology (CPT) codes** are used to specify medical procedures (treatments). CPT codes were developed and are copyrighted by the American Medical Association. The purpose of CPT is to create a uniform language (set of descriptive terms and codes) that accurately describes medical, surgical, and diagnostic procedures. CPT and its corresponding codes are revised periodically to reflect current trends in clinical treatments. To increase standardization and the use of electronic health records, federal law requires that physicians and other clinical providers, including laboratory and diagnostic services, use CPT for the coding and transfer of healthcare information. (The same law also requires that ICD codes be used for hospital inpatient services.)

> **Current Procedural Terminology (CPT) codes**
> Codes applied to medical, surgical, and diagnostic procedures.

To illustrate CPT codes, there are ten codes for physician office visits. Five of the codes apply to new patients, while the other five apply to established patients (repeat visits). The differences among the five codes in each category are based on the complexity of the visit, as indicated by three components: (1) extent of patient history review, (2) extent of examination, and (3) difficulty of medical decision-making. For repeat patients, the least complex (typically shortest) office visit is coded 99211, while the most complex (typically longest) is coded 99215.

Because Medicare, Medicaid, and other insurers require additional information from providers beyond that contained in CPT codes, CMS developed an enhanced code set, the **Healthcare Common Procedure Coding System (HCPCS)** (commonly pronounced "hick picks"). The system expands the set of CPT codes to include nonphysician services (e.g., ambulance transportation) and durable medical equipment (e.g., prosthetic devices).

> **Healthcare Common Procedure Coding System (HCPCS)**
> A medical coding system that expands the CPT codes to include nonphysician services and durable medical equipment.

Although CPT and HCPCS codes are not as complex as the ICD codes, coders still must have a high level of training and experience to use them correctly. As in ICD coding, correct CPT coding ensures correct reimbursement. Coding is so important that many businesses offer services, such as books, software, education, and consulting, to hospitals and medical practices to improve coding efficiency.

> **SELF-TEST QUESTIONS**

1. Briefly describe the coding system used in hospitals (ICD codes) and medical practices (CPT codes).
2. What is the link between coding and reimbursement?

Traditionally, there have been a number of ways of estimating physician productivity when tying compensation to performance. For many years, productivity was measured by volume-based metrics such as number of patients seen or amount of revenue billed. Today, however, physician productivity measures and compensation models are rapidly moving toward models based on relative value units (RVUs).

Work RVUs, which are one of three components of RVUs, measure the relative level of time, skill, training, and intensity required of a physician to provide a given service. They are a good proxy for the training required and volume of work expended by a physician in treating patients. A routine well-patient visit, for example, would be assigned a lower RVU than an invasive surgical procedure. Given this relative scale, a physician seeing two or three complex or high-acuity patients per day could accumulate more RVUs than a physician seeing ten or more low-acuity patients per day. Thus, the nature of the work, rather than number of patients or billings, is being measured and hence used for compensation levels.

According to the Medical Group Management Association, well over half of all physicians are compensated, at least in part, on the basis of productivity as measured by work RVUs. Usually, work RVUs are combined with other productivity and quality measures in determining productivity and compensation, but there is little doubt that work RVUs have the dominant role.

Specific Reimbursement Methods

There are many specific reimbursement methods in use today. Typically, the methods differ from one insurer to another. In addition, insurers use different methods for different types of providers and services, such as hospitals versus physicians or even hospital inpatients versus outpatients. In this section, we discuss the specific methods used by Medicare to reimburse hospitals for inpatient services and physicians for all services. Medicare reimbursement methods for other types of providers and other services are described in the Payment Basics series developed and maintained by the Medicare Payment Advisory Commission (MedPAC), available at http://medpac.gov/-documents-/payment-basics.

Hospital Inpatient Services

Medicare's **inpatient prospective payment system (IPPS)** is a prospective payment methodology based on an inpatient's diagnosis at discharge. It starts with two national base payment rates (operating and capital expenses), which are then adjusted to account for two factors that affect the costs of providing care: (1) the patient's condition and treatment and (2) market conditions in the facility's geographic location (see exhibit 2.1).

Discharges are assigned to one of 754 *Medicare severity diagnosis-related groups (MS–DRGs)*, which designate the diagnoses of patients with similar clinical problems, who therefore are expected to consume similar amounts of hospital resources. Each MS–DRG has a relative weight that reflects the expected cost of inpatients in that group. The payment rates for MS–DRGs in each local market are determined by adjusting the base payment rates to reflect the local input price level and then multiplying them by the relative weight for each MS–DRG. The operating and capital payment rates are increased for facilities that operate an approved resident training

inpatient prospective payment system (IPPS)
The method, based on diagnosis, that Medicare uses to reimburse providers for inpatient services.

EXHIBIT 2.1

Medicare
Hospital Acute
Inpatient
Services
Payment
System

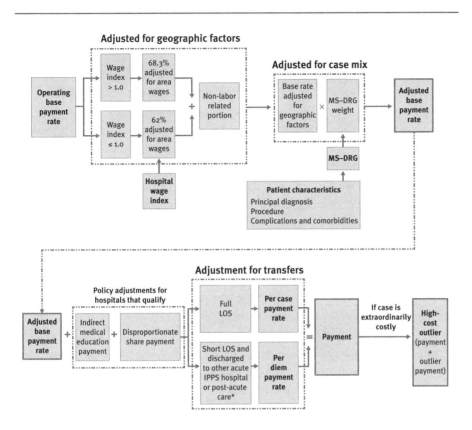

Note: MS–DRG (Medicare severity diagnosis-related group), LOS (length of stay), IPPS (inpatient prospective payment system). Capital payments are determined by a similar system. In addition to the inpatient operating and inpatient capital payments per discharge, hospitals may receive additional payments, such as those related to direct graduate medical education, uncompensated care, and bad debts. Additional payments are also made for certain rural hospitals. Hospitals may receive penalties or additional payments based on their performance on quality standards.

* Transfer policy for cases discharged to post–acute care settings applies for cases in 278 selected MS–DRGs.

Source: Reprinted from MedPAC, "Hospital Acute Inpatient Services Payment System," revised October 2019, http://medpac.gov/docs/default-source/payment-basics/medpac_payment_basics_19_hospital_final_v2_sec.pdf.

program or that treat a disproportionate share of low-income patients. Rates are reduced for transfer cases, and *outlier payments* are added for cases that are extraordinarily costly to protect providers from large financial losses due to unusually expensive cases. Both operating and capital payment rates are updated annually.

The IPPS rates are intended to cover the costs that reasonably efficient providers would incur in providing high-quality care. If the hospital is able to provide the services for less than the fixed reimbursement amount, it can keep the difference. Conversely, if a Medicare patient's treatment costs are more than the reimbursement amount but do not meet the definition of an outlier, the hospital must bear the loss.

Physician Services

Medicare pays for physician services using a *resource-based relative value scale (RBRVS)*. Under the RBRVS system, payments for services are determined by the resource costs needed to provide them as measured by weights called **relative value units (RVUs)**. RVUs consist of three components: (1) a work RVU, which includes the skill level and training required along with the intensity and time required for the service; (2) a practice expense RVU, which includes equipment and supplies costs as well as office support costs, including labor; and (3) a malpractice expense RVU, which accounts for the relative risk and cost of potential malpractice claims. To illustrate, the (total) RVU is 0.52 for a minimal office visit, 1.32 for an average office visit, and 3.06 for a comprehensive office visit. Furthermore, the average office visit RVU is composed of a work RVU of 0.67, a practice expense RVU of 0.62, and a malpractice expense RVU of 0.03.

The RVU values then are adjusted to reflect variations in local input prices, and the total is multiplied by a standard dollar value—called the conversion factor—to arrive at the payment amount. Medicare's payment rates may also be adjusted to reflect provider characteristics, geographic designations, and other factors. The provider is paid the final amount, less any beneficiary coinsurance (see exhibit 2.2).

relative value unit (RVU)
A measure of the amount of resources consumed to provide a particular service. When applied to physicians, a measure of the amount of work, practice expenses, and liability costs associated with a particular service.

1. Briefly describe the method used by Medicare to reimburse providers for inpatient services.
2. Explain the method used by Medicare to reimburse providers for physician services.

Healthcare Reform and Reimbursement Methods

In addition to improving healthcare delivery through focusing on access and quality, the ACA has significantly changed the way providers are reimbursed. The key reforms include an increased focus on quality and efficiency and a move from a fee-for-service model to a prospective payment model, which may include bundled payments or capitation. These new payment methods aim to shift from reimbursement based on the amount of services provided (volume) to reimbursement based on value and better outcomes. Despite efforts to repeal and replace the ACA, most experts predict that the shift toward value-based payment will continue.

The new payment methods are specifically designed to accomplish the following:

- Encourage providers to deliver care in a high-quality, cost-efficient manner
- Support coordination of care among multiple providers
- Adopt evidence-based care standards and protocols that result in the best outcomes for patients
- Provide accountability and transparency
- Discourage overtreatment and medically unnecessary procedures
- Eliminate or reduce the occurrence of adverse events
- Discourage cost shifting

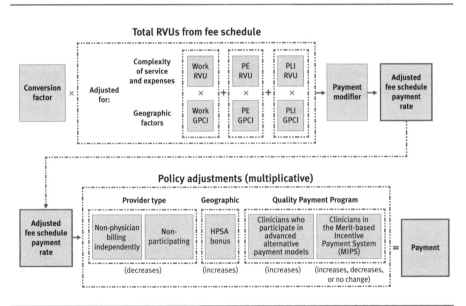

EXHIBIT 2.2
Medicare
Physician
Services
Payment
System

Note: RVU (relative value unit), GPCI (geographic practice cost index), PE (practice expense), PLI (professional liability insurance), HPSA (health professional shortage area). This figure depicts Medicare program payments only. The fee schedule lists separate PE RVUs for facility and nonfacility settings. Fee schedule payments are often reduced when specified nonphysician practitioners bill Medicare independently, but not when services are provided "incident to" a physician's services and billed under a physician's billing number. Clinicians who participate in advanced alternative payment models receive an incentive payment of 5 percent of their professional services payments. Clinicians in MIPS (the Merit-based Incentive Payment System) receive a positive or negative payment adjustment (or no change) based on their performance in four areas: quality, resource use, advancing care information, and clinical practice improvement.

Source: Reprinted from MedPAC, "Physician and Other Health Professional Payment System," revised October 2019, http://medpac.gov/docs/default-source/payment-basics/medpac _payment_basics_19_physician_final_sec.pdf.

The sections that follow describe a few of the important implications for provider payments.

Value-Based Purchasing

value-based
purchasing (VBP)
An approach
to provider
reimbursement
that rewards
quality and
efficiency of
care rather than
quantity of care.

Value-based purchasing (VBP) is a Medicare initiative that rewards acute care hospitals with incentive payments for efficiently providing high-quality care to Medicare beneficiaries. This should lead to lower costs and better clinical outcomes for all hospitalized patients. The amounts of these payments are based on outcome measures such as mortality, healthcare-associated infections, patient safety and experience, process of care, and efficiency and cost reduction. Hospitals may be rewarded for their performance compared with all other hospitals, or for how well they improved their own performance compared with performance during a baseline period. Medicare also uses value-based payment programs for end-stage renal disease, skilled nursing facilities, and home health.

Quality-Based Clinician Compensation

In addition to VBP for hospitals, Medicare factors quality into payments for physicians and most other clinicians. Quality-based compensation is part of Medicare's effort to shift medicine away from the volume-based focus, where clinicians are paid for each service regardless of quality. Clinicians can earn additional compensation based on the quality of care they provide to their patients. Bonuses and penalties are calculated on the basis of performance on quality measures, which vary by specialty. As with VBP programs for hospitals, quality-based clinician reimbursement programs can be paired with shared savings programs, discussed next.

Shared Savings Programs

Shared savings is an approach to reducing healthcare costs and a mechanism for encouraging the creation of accountable care organizations (ACOs). Under shared savings, if a provider reduces total healthcare spending for its patients below the level that the payer expected, the provider is then rewarded with a portion of the savings. The benefits are twofold: (1) The payer spends less than it would otherwise, and (2) the provider gets more revenue than it expected. The savings can arise from the more efficient, cost-effective use of hospital or outpatient services that enhance quality, reduce costs over time, and improve outcomes. It can be applied to hospital episodes of care, including physician services, or to physician office care.

Bundled Payment Models

Bundled payment models are a form of fee-for-service reimbursement in which a single sum covers all healthcare services related to a specific procedure. The objective of bundled payments is to promote more efficient use of resources and reward providers for improving the coordination, quality, and efficiency of care. If the cost of services is less than the bundled payment, the physicians and other providers retain the difference. But if the costs exceed the bundled payment, physicians and other providers are not compensated for the difference.

In some circumstances, an ACO may receive the bundled payment and subsequently divide the payment among participating physicians and providers. In other situations, the payer may pay participating physicians and providers independently, but it may adjust each payment according to negotiated predefined rules to ensure that the total payments to all the providers do not exceed the total bundled payment amount. This type of reimbursement is called *virtual bundling*. For providers, the challenges of bundled payments include determining who owns the episode of care and apportioning the payment among the providers.

Readmissions Reduction Program
The Hospital Readmissions Reduction Program is a Medicare initiative that financially penalizes hospitals if they experience excessive readmission rates compared with expected levels of readmission. The penalties are based on a 30-day readmission measure for conditions such as heart attack, heart failure, and pneumonia.

Hospital-Acquired Conditions Reduction Program
The Hospital-Acquired Conditions Reduction Program is a Medicare initiative to encourage hospitals to improve patient safety. Under the program, hospitals in the worst-performing quartile for hospital-acquired conditions such as bed sores, infections, complications from extended use of catheters, and injuries caused by falls are penalized 1 percent of inpatient payments for all discharges.

SELF-TEST QUESTION

1. Briefly describe the impact of healthcare reform on payments to providers.

Key Concepts

This chapter covers important background material related to health-care insurance and provider reimbursement. The key concepts of this chapter are as follows:

- Health insurance is widely used in the United States because individuals are risk averse and insurance firms can take advantage of the *law of large numbers.*
- Insurance is based on four key characteristics: (1) *pooling of losses*, (2) *payment for random losses*, (3) *risk transfer*, and (4) *indemnification*.
- *Adverse selection* occurs when individuals most likely to have claims purchase insurance while those least likely to have claims do not.
- *Moral hazard* occurs when an insured individual purposely sustains a loss, as opposed to a random loss. In a health insurance setting, moral hazard is more subtle, producing such behaviors as seeking more services than needed and engaging in unhealthy behavior because the costs of the potential consequences are borne by the insurer.
- Most provider revenue is not obtained directly from patients but from healthcare insurers, known collectively as *third-party payers.*
- Third-party payers are classified as *private insurers* (Blue Cross Blue Shield, commercial, and self-insurers) and *public insurers* (Medicare and Medicaid).
- *Managed care plans*, such as health maintenance organizations (HMOs), strive to combine the insurance function and the provision of healthcare services.
- Third-party payers use many different payment methods that fall into two broad classifications: *fee-for-service* and *capitation*. Each payment method creates a unique set of incentives and risk for providers.
- When payers pay *billed charges*, they pay according to a schedule of rates established by the provider called a *chargemaster.*
- *Negotiated charges*, which are discounted from billed charges, are used by insurers with sufficient market power to demand price reductions.
- Under a *cost-based reimbursement system*, payers agree to pay providers certain allowable costs incurred when providing services to the payers' enrollees.

(continued)

(continued from previous page)

- In a *prospective payment system*, the rates paid by payers are determined in advance and are not tied directly to reimbursable costs or billed charges. Typically, prospective payments are made on the basis of the following service definitions: (1) *per procedure*, (2) *per diagnosis*, (3) *per diem* (per day), or (4) *bundled pricing*.

- *Capitation* is a flat periodic payment to a physician or another healthcare provider; it is the sole reimbursement for providing services to a defined population. Capitation payments are generally expressed as some dollar amount per member per month, where the word *member* typically refers to an enrollee in some managed care plan.

- *Medical coding* is the foundation of fee-for-service reimbursement systems. In inpatient settings, *International Classification of Diseases (ICD)* codes are used to designate diagnoses, while in outpatient settings, *Current Procedural Terminology (CPT)* codes are used to specify procedures.

- Medicare uses the *inpatient prospective payment system (IPPS)* for hospital inpatient reimbursement. Under IPPS, the amount of the payment is determined by the patient's *Medicare severity diagnosis-related group (MS–DRG)*.

- To provide some cushion for the high costs associated with severely ill patients within each diagnosis, IPPS includes a provision for *outlier payments*.

- Physicians are reimbursed by Medicare using the *resource-based relative value scale (RBRVS)*. Under RBRVS, reimbursement is based on *relative value units (RVUs)*, which consist of three resource components: (1) *physician work*, (2) *practice expenses*, and (3) *malpractice insurance expenses*. The RVU for each service is multiplied by a dollar conversion factor to determine the payment amount.

- Healthcare reform is having a significant impact on health insurance and on the way providers are reimbursed. More people now have access to insurance coverage, and new provider payment methods emphasize value, efficiency, and patient outcomes over volume.

Because the managers of health services organizations must make financial decisions within the constraints imposed by the economic environment, the insurance and reimbursement concepts discussed in this chapter will be used throughout the remainder of the book.

Questions

2.1. Briefly explain the following characteristics of insurance:
   a. Pooling of losses
   b. Payment only for random losses
   c. Risk transfer
   d. Indemnification

2.2. What is adverse selection, and how do insurers deal with the problem?

2.3. What is the moral hazard problem?

2.4. Briefly describe the major third-party payers.

2.5. a. What are the primary characteristics of managed care plans?
   b. Describe different types of managed care plans.

2.6. What is the difference between fee-for-service reimbursement and capitation?

2.7. Describe the provider incentives under each of the following reimbursement methods:
   a. Cost based
   b. Charge based (including discounted charges)
   c. Per procedure
   d. Per diagnosis
   e. Per diem
   f. Bundled payment
   g. Capitation

2.8. What medical coding systems are used to support fee-for-service payment methodologies?

2.9. Briefly describe how Medicare pays for the following:
   a. Inpatient services
   b. Physician services

2.10. What are some features of healthcare reform that affect healthcare insurance and reimbursement?

Selected Cases

Three cases in *Gapenski's Cases in Healthcare Finance*, sixth edition, are applicable to this chapter: Case 1: New England Healthcare; Case 2: Orlando Family Physicians; and Case 3: Santa Fe Healthcare.

Notes

1. See, for example, the Hospital Compare tool of the Centers for Medicare & Medicaid Services (www.medicare.gov/hospitalcompare /search.html) and Medicare.gov's Procedure Price Lookup (www .medicare.gov/procedure-price-lookup).

2. Blue Cross Blue Shield Association. 2018. "Blue Facts: Healthcare Coverage Designed for Your Community, Accessible Across the Country." Published May. www.bcbs.com/sites/default/files/file -attachments/page/BCBS.Facts__0.pdf.

3. Centers for Medicare & Medicaid Services. 2018. "CMS Regional Offices." Modified April 18. www.cms.gov/Medicare/Coding /ICD10/CMS-Regional-Offices.html.

4. Congressional Budget Office. 2017. "Repealing the Individual Health Insurance Mandate: An Updated Estimate." Published November 8. www.cbo.gov/publication/53300.

5. Medicaid.gov. 2020. "October 2019 Medicaid & CHIP Enrollment Data Highlights." Accessed January 29. www.medicaid.gov/medicaid /program-information/medicaid-and-chip-enrollment-data/report -highlights/index.html.

6. Kaiser Family Foundation. 2020. "Marketplace Enrollment, 2014– 2019." Accessed January 29. www.kff.org/health-reform/state -indicator/marketplace-enrollment/?currentTimeframe=0&sortModel =%7B%22colId%22:%22Location%22,%22sort%22:%22asc%22%7D.

7. Centers for Medicare & Medicaid Services. 2020. "The Hospital Value-Based Purchasing (VCP) Program." Modified January 6. www.cms.gov/Medicare/Quality-Initiatives-Patient-Assessment -Instruments/Value-Based-Programs/HVBP/Hospital-Value-Based -Purchasing.html.

8. World Health Organization. 2020. "International Classification of Diseases, 11th Revision." Accessed January 13. https://icd.who.int /en/.

Resources

For the latest information on events that affect the healthcare sector, see Modern Healthcare, *published weekly by Crain Communications Inc.:* www.crain.com/ brands/modern-healthcare/.

Other resources pertaining to this chapter include

Beagle, J. T. 2010. "Episode-Based Payment: Bundling for Better Results." *Healthcare Financial Management* 64 (2): 36–39.

D'Cruz, M. J., and T. L. Welter. 2010. "Is Your Organization Ready for Value-Based Payments?" *Healthcare Financial Management* 64 (1): 64–70, 72.

———. 2008. "Major Trends Affecting Hospital Payment." *Healthcare Financial Management* 62 (1): 52–58, 60.

Harris, J., I. Elizondo, and A. Isdaner. 2014. "Medicare Bundled Payment: What Is It Worth to You?" *Healthcare Financial Management* 68 (1): 76–82.

Kaplan, R. S., and M. E. Porter. 2011. "The Big Idea: How to Solve the Cost Crisis in Health Care." *Harvard Business Review* 89 (9): 46–52, 54, 56–61.

Kentros, C., and C. Barbato. 2013. "Using Normalized RVU Reporting to Evaluate Physician Productivity." *Healthcare Financial Management* 67 (8): 98–105.

Kim, C., D. Majka, and J. H. Sussman. 2011. "Modeling the Impact of Healthcare Reform." *Healthcare Financial Management* 65 (1): 51–60.

Mulvany, C. 2013. "Insurance Market Reform: The Grand Experiment." *Healthcare Financial Management* 67 (4): 82–86, 88.

———. 2010. "Healthcare Reform: The Good, the Bad, and the Transformational." *Healthcare Financial Management* 64 (6): 52–59.

Patton, T. L. 2009. "The IRS's Version of Community Benefit: A Look at the Redesigned Form 990 and New Schedule H." *Healthcare Financial Management* 63 (2): 50–54.

Pearce, J. W., and J. M. Harris. 2010. "The Medicare Bundled Payment Pilot Program: Participation Considerations." *Healthcare Financial Management* 64 (9): 52–56, 58, 60.

Ronning, P. L. 2011. "ICD-10: Obligations and Opportunities." *Healthcare Financial Management* 65 (8): 48–51.

Saqr, H., O. Mikhail, and J. Langabeer. 2008. "The Financial Impact of the Medicare Prospective Payment System on Long-Term Acute Care Hospitals." *Journal of Health Care Finance* 35 (1): 58–69.

Shoemaker, P. 2011. "What Value-Based Purchasing Means to Your Hospital." *Healthcare Financial Management* 65 (8): 60–68.

Tyson, P. 2010. "Preparing for the New Landscape of Payment Reform." *Healthcare Financial Management* 64 (12): 42–48.

Wilensky, G. R. 2011. "Continuing Uncertainty Dominates the Healthcare Landscape." *Healthcare Financial Management* 65 (3): 34, 36.

Williams, J. 2013. "A New Model for Care: Population Management." *Healthcare Financial Management* 67 (3): 68–76.

Woodson, W., and S. Jenkins. 2010. "Payment Reform: How Should Your Organization Prepare?" *Healthcare Financial Management* 64 (1): 74–79.

FINANCIAL ACCOUNTING

Part I discussed the unique environment that creates the framework for the practice of healthcare finance. In part II, we begin the actual coverage of healthcare finance by discussing financial accounting, which involves the measurement and recording of economic events and the preparation of a business's financial statements. These statements are designed to provide pertinent financial information about an organization to its investors, lenders, and other creditors. Other stakeholders, such as regulators and managers, may find the information useful as well.

The coverage of financial accounting extends over several chapters. Chapter 3 begins with an introduction to basic financial accounting concepts and an explanation of how organizations report financial performance, specifically revenues, expenses, and profits. Then, in chapter 4, the discussion is extended to the reporting of financial status, which includes an organization's assets, liabilities, and equity. In addition, chapter 4 covers the way in which organizations report cash flows. The chapter 4 supplement discusses the recording of transactions, which is the first step in the creation of a business's financial statements.

Finally, chapter 17 discusses how interested parties use financial statement data to assess the financial condition of an organization. Chapter 17 is placed at the end of the book because the nuances of financial statement analysis may be better understood after learning more about the financial workings of a business. Part II and chapter 17, taken together, will provide readers with a basic understanding of how financial statements are created and used to make judgments regarding the operational status and financial condition of health services organizations.

FINANCIAL ACCOUNTING BASICS, THE INCOME STATEMENT, AND THE STATEMENT OF CHANGES IN EQUITY

Learning Objectives

After studying this chapter, readers will be able to

- Name the primary financial statements that make up financial reporting.
- Define the five account types used in financial accounting.
- Explain why financial statements are so important both to managers and to outside parties.
- Describe the standard-setting process (operating procedures) under which financial accounting information is created and reported, as well as the underlying principles applied.
- Describe the components of the income statement—revenues, expenses, and profitability—and the relationships within and among these components.
- Explain the differences between operating income and net income and between net income and cash flow.
- Describe the format and use of the statement of changes in equity.

Introduction

Financial accounting involves identifying, measuring, recording, and communicating in dollar terms the economic events and status of an organization. This information is summarized and presented in a set of *financial statements*, or just *financials*. Because these statements communicate important information about an organization, financial accounting is often called "the language of business." Managers of health services organizations must understand the basics of financial accounting because financial statements are the best way to summarize a business's financial status and performance.

> **financial accounting**
> The field of accounting that focuses on the measurement and communication of the economic events and status of an entire organization.

Financial Statements

A full set of financial statements communicates information about an organization's financial position, changes in its financial position, transactions with owners, cash flows, and any additional information needed to interpret or understand the information provided in the statements. A complete set of financial statements includes five components: (1) balance sheet, (2) income statement, (3) statement of changes in equity, (4) statement of cash flows, and (5) notes. Each of these components provides a different kind of information; certain individual statements may be of more interest to particular users than others.

annual report
A report issued annually by an organization to its stakeholders that contains descriptive information and financial statements for the prior year.

Often, the primary means of disseminating this information to outsiders is the business's **annual report**. It typically begins with a descriptive section that discusses, in general terms, the organization's operating results over the past year as well as developments that are expected to affect future operations. The descriptive section is followed by the business's financial statements.

Because the actual financial statements cannot possibly contain all relevant information, additional information is provided in the *notes* section. For health services organizations, these notes contain information on such topics as accounting practices, the composition of long-term debt, pension plan status, the amount of charity care provided, and the cost of malpractice insurance.

In addition to the body of the financial statements and the notes section, organizations are often required to provide certain *supplementary information*. Other supplementary information may be provided voluntarily by the reporting organization. For example, a healthcare system may report the revenues of its primary subsidiaries as supplementary data even though its financial statements focus on the aggregate revenues of the entire system. Because the notes and supplementary information sections contain a great deal of information that is essential to a good understanding of the financial statements, a thorough examination always considers the information contained in these two sections.

The income statement and statement of changes in equity are discussed in more detail later in this chapter. The balance sheet and statement of cash flows are covered in chapter 4. For now, it is enough to understand that financial reporting entails a variety of components that together meet the objective of communicating important information about an organization to users.

The Building Blocks of Financial Accounting

asset
An item that either possesses or creates economic value for an organization.

The financial accounting model is built on five types of accounts that are summarized in the financial statements: assets, liabilities, equity, revenues, and expenses. **Assets** are the resources, or things of value, that are owned or controlled by the business. Assets either possess (e.g., cash) or create (e.g., equipment) economic value for the organization.

Liabilities are the fixed financial obligations of the organization (e.g., debt). Liabilities represent claims on the assets of the organization by creditors.

Equity is the "book value" of the ownership position in an organization. It is the value of the assets as reported on an organization's financial statements that remains after subtracting the liabilities.

Revenues are inflows of assets, such as cash, that result from the exchange of goods or services with customers. Because revenues increase the assets of an organization without increasing liabilities, revenues add to the organization's equity.

Expenses are the costs incurred by an organization to produce revenues. Because expenses represent the consumption of assets (e.g., cash) to provide goods and services, expenses decrease the organization's equity.

The relationships among the five account types, their presentation in the financial statements of an organization, and their use in recording economic activity are discussed throughout this chapter, as well as in chapter 4 and the chapter 4 supplement. Before we begin, however, we provide some background to help readers better understand financial accounting and reporting.

> **liability**
> A fixed financial obligation of an organization.
>
> **equity**
> Assets minus liabilities; in other words, the "book value" of the ownership position of a business.
>
> **revenues**
> Inflows of assets resulting from the exchange of goods or services with customers.
>
> **expenses**
> The costs of doing business; the dollar value of resources used to provide goods or services.

SELF-TEST QUESTIONS

1. What are the five components of a full set of financial statements?
2. Why are the notes and supplementary information sections important parts of the financial statements?
3. What are the five account types used in financial accounting?

Historical Foundations of Financial Accounting

It is easy to think of financial statements merely as pieces of paper with numbers written on them, rather than in terms of the economic events and *physical assets*—such as land, buildings, and equipment—that the numbers represent. If readers of financial statements understand how and why financial accounting began and how financial statements are used, they can better understand what is happening within a business and why financial accounting information is so important.

Thousands of years ago, individuals and families were self-contained. They gathered their own food, made their own clothes, and built their own shelters. Eventually, people began to specialize: Some individuals or families became good at hunting, others at making spearheads, others at making clothing, and so on. With specialization came trade, initially by bartering one type of goods for another. At first, each producer worked alone, and trade was strictly local. Over time, some people set up production shops that employed workers, simple forms of money were used, and trade expanded beyond the local area. As these simple economies expanded, more formal forms of money developed and a primitive form of banking emerged, as wealthy merchants lent profits from their past dealings to enterprising shop owners and traders who needed money to expand their operations.

When the first loans were made, lenders could physically inspect borrowers' assets and judge the likelihood of repayment. Eventually, lending became much more complex. Industrial borrowers were developing large factories, merchants were acquiring fleets of ships and wagons, and loans were being made to finance business activities at distant locations. At that point, lenders could no longer easily inspect the assets that backed their loans, and they needed a practical way of summarizing the value of those assets. Also, some loans were made on the basis of a share of the profits of the business, so a uniform, widely accepted method for documenting income was required. In addition, owners required reports to see how effectively their own enterprises were being operated, and governments needed information to assess taxes. For all these reasons, a need arose for financial statements, for accountants to prepare the statements, and for auditors to verify the accuracy of the accountants' work.

The economic systems of industrialized countries have grown enormously since the early days of trade, and financial accounting has become much more complex. However, the original reasons for creating financial statements still apply: Bankers and other investors need accounting information to make intelligent investment decisions; managers need it to operate their organizations efficiently; and taxing authorities need it to assess taxes equitably.

Although financial reporting may seem straightforward, translating physical assets and economic events into accounting numbers involves many decisions, assumptions, and estimates. Nevertheless, that is what accountants must do when they construct financial statements. To ensure the usefulness of financial reports, regulators determine the form and disclosure of financial information to users. This creates structure that facilitates comparisons and raises the confidence in the information being reported.

SELF-TEST QUESTION

1. What are the historical foundations of financial accounting statements?

The Users of Financial Accounting Information

The predominant users of financial accounting information are those parties that have a *financial interest* in the organization and hence are concerned with its economic status. All organizations, whether not-for-profit or investor owned, have **stakeholders** that have an interest in the business. In a not-for-profit organization, such as a community hospital, the stakeholders include managers, staff physicians, employees, suppliers, creditors, patients, and even the community. Investor-owned hospitals have essentially the same set of stakeholders, plus owners. Because all stakeholders, by definition, have an interest in the organization, all stakeholders have an interest in its financial condition.

Among the outside stakeholders, *investors*, who supply the *capital* (funds) needed by businesses, typically have the greatest financial interest in health services organizations. Investors fall into two categories: (1) owners who supply equity capital to investor-owned businesses and (2) *creditors* (or *lenders*) who supply debt capital to both investor-owned and not-for-profit businesses. (In a sense, communities supply equity capital to not-for-profit organizations, so they, too, are investors.) In general, there is only one category of owners. However, creditors constitute a diverse group of investors that includes banks, suppliers granting trade credit, and bondholders. Because of their direct financial interest in healthcare businesses, investors are the primary outside users of financial accounting information. They use the information to form judgments about whether to make a particular investment as well as to set the return required on the investment. (Investor-supplied capital is covered in greater detail in chapters 11, 12, and 13.)

Although the field of financial accounting developed primarily to meet the information needs of outside parties, the managers of an organization, including its board of directors (trustees), also are important users of the information. After all, managers are charged with ensuring that the organization has the financial capability to accomplish its mission, whether that mission is to maximize the wealth of its owners or to provide healthcare services to the community. Thus, an organization's managers not only are involved with creating financial statements but also are important users of those statements, both to assess the current financial condition of the organization and to formulate plans to ensure that the future financial condition of the organization will support its goals.

In summary, investors and managers are the predominant users of financial accounting information as a result of their direct financial interest in the organization. Furthermore, investors are not merely passive users of financial accounting information; they do more than just read and interpret the statements. Often, they create financial targets based on the numbers reported in the financial statements that managers must attain or suffer some undesirable consequence. For example, many debt agreements require borrowers to maintain stated financial standards, such as a minimum earnings level, to keep the debt in force. If the standards are not met, the lender can demand that the business immediately repay the full amount of the loan. If the business fails to do so, it may be forced into bankruptcy.

stakeholder
A party that has an interest, often financial, in a business. Stakeholders can be affected by the business's actions, objectives, or policies.

SELF-TEST QUESTIONS

1. What is a stakeholder?
2. Who are the primary users of financial accounting information?
3. How do investors use this information?

Regulation and Standards in Financial Accounting

Securities and Exchange Commission (SEC)
The federal government agency that regulates the sale of securities and the operations of securities exchanges. This agency also has overall responsibility for the format and content of financial statements.

As a consequence of the Great Depression of the 1930s, which caused many businesses to fail and almost brought down the entire securities industry, the federal government began regulating the form and disclosure of information related to publicly traded securities. The regulation is based on the theory that financial information constructed and presented according to standardized rules allows investors to make the best-informed decisions. The **Securities and Exchange Commission (SEC)**, an independent regulatory agency of the US government formed in 1934, was given the authority to establish and enforce the form and content of financial statements. Nonconforming companies—that is, those whose financial statements do not conform to SEC standards—are prohibited from selling securities to the public, so many businesses comply to gain access to capital. Not-for-profit corporations that do not sell securities still must file financial statements with state authorities that conform to SEC standards. Finally, most for-profit businesses that do not sell securities to the public are willing to follow the SEC-established guidelines to ensure uniformity of presentation of financial data. The result is that all businesses, except for the smallest, create SEC-conforming financial statements.

Financial Accounting Standards Board (FASB)
A private organization whose mission is to establish and improve the standards of financial accounting and reporting for private businesses.

Rather than directly manage the process, the SEC designates other organizations to create and implement the standards system. For the most part, the SEC has delegated the responsibility for establishing reporting standards to the **Financial Accounting Standards Board (FASB)**—a private organization whose mission is to establish and improve standards of financial accounting and reporting for private businesses. (The *Governmental Accounting Standards Board* has the identical responsibility for businesses that are partially or totally funded by a government entity.) Typically, the guidance issued by the FASB, which is promulgated by numbered *statements*, applies across a wide range of industries and, by design, is general in nature. More specific implementation guidance, especially when industry-unique circumstances must be addressed, is provided by *industry committees* established by the **American Institute of Certified Public Accountants (AICPA)**—the professional association of public (financial) accountants. For example, financial statements in the health services sector are based on the

American Institute of Certified Public Accountants (AICPA)
The professional association of public (financial) accountants.

AICPA Audit and Accounting Guide titled *Health Care Entities*, which was published most recently on September 1, 2018.

Because of the large number of statements and pronouncements that have been issued by the FASB and other standard-setting organizations, the FASB combined all of the previously issued standards into a single set called the *FASB Accounting Standards Codification*, which became effective on September 15, 2009. The purpose of the codification is to simplify access to accounting standards by placing them in a single source and creating a system that allows users to more easily research and reference accounting standards data.

When more specific guidance is required than the standards provide, other professional organizations may participate in the process, although such work does not have the same degree of influence as codification has. For example, the Healthcare Financial Management Association has established the *Principles and Practices Board*, which develops position statements and analyses on issues that require further guidance.

When taken together, all the guidance contained in the codification and the amplifying information constitute a set of guidelines called **generally accepted accounting principles (GAAP)**. GAAP can be thought of as a set of objectives, conventions, and principles that have evolved through the years to guide the preparation and presentation of financial statements. In essence, GAAP sets the rules for financial statement preparation. Note, however, that GAAP applies only to the area of financial accounting (financial statements), as distinct from other areas of accounting, such as managerial accounting (discussed in later chapters) and tax accounting.

generally accepted accounting principles (GAAP) The set of guidelines that has evolved to foster the consistent preparation and presentation of financial statements.

It should be no surprise that the field of financial accounting is typically classified as a social science rather than a physical science. However, financial accounting is as much an art as a science, and the end result represents negotiation, compromise, and interpretation. The organizations involved in setting standards are continuously reviewing and revising GAAP to ensure the best possible development and presentation of financial data. This task, which is essential to economic prosperity, is motivated by the fact that the US economy is constantly evolving, with new types of business arrangements and securities being created almost daily.

For large organizations, the final step in the financial statement quality assurance process is the *external audit*, which is performed by an independent (outside) *auditor*—usually one of the major accounting firms. The results of the external audit are reported in the *auditor's opinion*, which is a letter that is attached to the financial statements stating whether the statements are a fair presentation of the business's operations, cash flows, and financial position as specified by GAAP.

There are several categories of opinions given by auditors. The most favorable, which is essentially a "clean bill of health," is called an *unqualified opinion.* Such an opinion means that, in the auditor's view, the financial statements conform to GAAP, are presented fairly and consistently, and contain all necessary disclosures. A *qualified opinion* means that the auditor has some reservations about the statements, while an *adverse opinion* means that the auditor believes that the statements do not present a fair picture of the financial status of the business. The entire audit process, which is performed by the organization's internal auditors and the external auditor, is a means of verifying and validating the organization's financial statements. Of course, an unqualified opinion gives users, especially those external to the organization, more confidence that the statements truly represent the business's current financial condition.

Although the guidance given under GAAP, along with auditing rules, would seem to be sufficient to prevent fraudulent financial statements, in the first decade of the twenty-first century, several large companies, including HealthSouth (now called Encompass Health), which operates the nation's largest network of rehabilitation services, were found to be manipulating financial information.[2] Because the US financial system is so dependent on the reliability of financial statements, in 2002, Congress passed the *Sarbanes-Oxley Act*, generally known as *SOX*, as a measure to improve transparency in financial accounting and to prevent fraud. (According to the SEC, *transparency* means the timely, meaningful, and reliable disclosure of a business's financial information.) Here are just a few of the more important provisions of SOX:

- An independent body, the Public Accounting Oversight Board, was created to oversee the entire audit process.
- Auditors can no longer provide non-auditing (consulting) services to the companies that they audit.
- The lead partners of the audit team for any company must rotate off the team every five years (or more often).

- Senior managers involved in the audits of their companies cannot have been employed by the auditing firm during the one-year period preceding the audit.
- Each member of the audit committee shall be a member of the company's board of directors and shall otherwise be independent of the audit function.
- The chief executive officer and chief financial officer shall personally certify that the business's financial statements are complete and accurate. Penalties for certifying reports that are known to be false range up to a $5 million fine, 20 years in prison, or both. In addition, if the financial statements must be restated because they are false, certain bonuses and equity-based compensation that certifying executives earned must be returned to the company.[3]

These provisions, along with others in SOX, are intended to deter future fraudulent behavior by managers and auditors.

SELF-TEST QUESTIONS

1. Why are widely accepted principles important for the measurement and recording of economic events?
2. What entities are involved in regulating the development and presentation of financial statements?
3. What does GAAP stand for, and what is its primary purpose?
4. What is the purpose of the auditor's opinion?
5. What is the purpose of the Sarbanes-Oxley Act (SOX), and what are some of its provisions?

Conceptual Framework of Financial Reporting

Because the actual preparation of financial statements is done by accountants, a detailed presentation of accounting theory is not required in this book. However, to better understand the content of financial statements, it is useful to discuss some aspects of the conceptual framework that accountants apply when they develop financial accounting data and prepare an organization's financial statements. By understanding this framework, readers will be better prepared to understand and interpret the financial statements of healthcare organizations.

In Statement of Financial Accounting Concepts No. 8, which was amended in August 2018, the FASB states, "The objective of general purpose financial reporting is to provide financial information about the reporting entity that is useful to existing and potential investors, lenders, and other creditors in making decisions about providing resources to the entity."[4] To achieve this objective, the FASB specifies the fundamental concepts, assumptions, and principles that underlie the development of financial accounting and reporting guidance (i.e., GAAP).

Qualitative Characteristics of Financial Accounting Data
Relevance
Financial accounting data are relevant if the information has the potential to make a difference in the decisions of users. Relevant data help users make predictions about an organization's future performance or confirm their prior or current understanding of the organization's performance.

Faithful Representation
Financial accounting data faithfully represent economic activity if they are complete, neutral (free of bias, either positive or negative), and free from error. It is important to note that faithful representation does not necessarily mean that information is accurate; since many assumptions and estimates are required in measuring and reporting economic activity, accuracy cannot always be determined with certainty.

      The usefulness of financial accounting data is additionally enhanced if those data possess four characteristics:

1. **Comparability.** Comparability means that similar items are measured and reported in a similar way to allow comparisons across different organizations as well as within organizations over time.
2. **Verifiability.** Financial accounting information is verifiable if independent observers, such as auditors, would concede that the data faithfully represent economic activity.
3. **Timeliness.** Timeliness means that decision makers have data in time to influence their decisions.
4. **Understandability.** Understandability means that data are classified, characterized, and presented in a way that users can understand the information that is being conveyed.

Assumptions
Accounting Entity

accounting entity
The entity (business) for which a set of financial statements applies.

The first assumption is the ability to define the **accounting entity**, which is important for two reasons. First, for investor-owned businesses, financial accounting data must be pertinent to the business activity as opposed to the personal affairs of the owners. Second, within any business, the accounting entity defines the specific areas of the business to be included in the statements. For example, a healthcare system may create one set of financial statements for the system as a whole and separate sets of statements for its subsidiary hospitals. In effect, the accounting entity specification establishes boundaries that tell readers what business (or businesses) is being reported on.

Going Concern

It is assumed that the accounting entity will operate as a *going concern* and hence will have an indefinite life. Going concern means that assets, in general, should be valued on the basis of their contribution to an ongoing business as opposed to their current fair market value. For example, the land, buildings, and equipment of a hospital may have a value of $50 million when they are used to provide patient services, but if they were sold to an outside party for other purposes, the value of these assets might only be $20 million. The going concern assumption, coupled with the fact that financial statements must be prepared for relatively short periods (as explained next), means that financial accounting data are not exact, but rather represent logical and systematic approaches applied to complex measurement problems.

Periodicity

Because accounting entities are assumed to have an indefinite life, but users of financial statements require timely information, it is common to report financial results on a relatively short periodic basis. The period covered, called an **accounting period**, can be any length of time over which an organization's managers, or outside parties, want to evaluate operational and financial results. Most health services organizations use calendar periods— months, quarters, and years—as their accounting periods. However, occasionally an organization will use a **fiscal year** (financial year) that does not coincide with the calendar year. For example, the federal government's fiscal year runs from October 1 to September 30. Although annual accounting periods are typically used for illustrations in this book, financial statements commonly are prepared for periods shorter than one year. For example, many organizations prepare semiannual and quarterly financial statements in addition to annual statements.

accounting period
The period (amount of time) covered by a set of financial statements— often a year, but sometimes a quarter or another time period.

Monetary Unit

The *monetary unit* provides the common basis by which economic events are measured. In the United States, this unit is the dollar, unadjusted for inflation or deflation. Thus, all transactions and events must be expressed in dollar terms.

fiscal year
The year covered by an organization's financial statements; it usually, but not necessarily, coincides with the calendar year.

Principles

Historical Cost

The **historical cost** principle requires organizations to report the values of many assets based on acquisition costs rather than fair market value, which implies that the dollar has constant purchasing power over time. In other

historical cost
In accounting, the purchase price of an asset.

words, land that cost $1 million 20 years ago might be worth $2 million today, but it is still reported at its initial cost of $1 million. The accounting profession has grappled with the inflation impact problem for years but has not yet developed a feasible solution. The historical cost principle removes subjectivity in the measurement of an asset's value, but it does not provide the most current information. We should note, however, that some items (primarily financial security holdings) are reported at fair market value.

Revenue Recognition

revenue recognition principle
The concept that revenues must be recognized in the accounting period in which they are realizable and earned.

The **revenue recognition principle** requires that revenues be recognized in the period in which they are realizable and earned. Generally, this is the period in which the service is rendered, because at that point, the price is known (realizable) and the service has been provided (earned). However, in some instances, difficulties in revenue recognition arise, primarily when the revenue amount or the completion of the service is uncertain.

Expense Matching

The *expense-matching principle* requires that an organization's expenses be matched, to the extent possible, with the revenues to which they relate. In other words, after the revenues have been allocated to a particular accounting period, all expenses associated with producing those revenues should be matched to the same period. Although this concept is straightforward, implementation of the matching principle creates some challenges. For example, consider long-lived assets such as buildings and equipment. Because such assets—for example, a magnetic resonance imaging (MRI) machine—provide revenues for several years, the expense-matching principle dictates that its acquisition cost should be spread over the same number of years. Thus, methods are required for estimating the amount of assets to be moved to expenses in a given year.

Full Disclosure

Financial statements must contain a complete picture of the economic events of the business. Anything less would be misleading by omission. Furthermore, because financial statements must be relevant to a diversity of users, the *full-disclosure principle* pushes preparers to include even more information in financial statements. However, the complexity of the information presented can be mitigated to some extent by placing some information in the notes or supplementary information sections as opposed to the body of the financial statements.

Thresholds and Constraints
Materiality Threshold

If the financial statements contained all possible information, they would be so long and detailed that making inferences about the organization would be difficult without a great deal of analysis. Thus, to keep the statements manageable, only entries that are important to the operational and financial status of the organization need to be separately identified. For example, medical equipment manufacturers carry large inventories of materials that are both substantial in dollar value relative to other assets and instrumental to their core business, so such businesses report inventories as a separate asset item on the balance sheet. Hospitals, on the other hand, carry relatively small inventories. Thus, many hospitals and other healthcare providers do not report inventories separately but combine them with other assets. In general, the *materiality threshold* affects the presentation of the financial statements rather than their aggregate financial content (i.e., the final numbers).

Cost–Benefit Constraint
There are costs associated with financial statement information for both the preparers of the statements and the users. Preparers must collect, record, verify, and report financial information, while users must analyze and interpret the information. As a result, financial statements cannot report all possible information that every potential user might find relevant. When deciding what information should be reported, and how that information should be reported, standards setters and accountants must determine whether the benefits of the information outweigh the associated costs.

SELF-TEST QUESTIONS

1. Why is it important to understand the basic concepts that underlie the preparation of financial statements?
2. What is the goal of financial reporting?
3. Briefly explain the following concepts as they apply to the preparation of financial statements:
   a. Relevance
   b. Faithful representation
   c. Accounting entity
   d. Going concern
   e. Accounting period
   f. Monetary unit
   g. Historical cost
   h. Revenue recognition
   i. Expense matching
   j. Full disclosure
   k. Materiality
   l. Cost–benefit

Accounting Methods: Cash Versus Accrual

In the implementation of the conceptual framework discussed in the previous section, two methods can be applied: cash accounting and accrual accounting. Although, as we discuss later, each method has its own set of advantages and disadvantages, GAAP specifies that only the accrual method can receive an unqualified auditor's opinion, so accrual accounting dominates the preparation of financial statements. Still, many small businesses that do not require audited financial statements use the cash method, and knowledge of the cash method aids our understanding of the accrual method, so we discuss both methods here.

Cash Accounting

cash accounting
The recording of economic events when a cash exchange takes place.

Under **cash accounting**, often called *cash basis accounting*, economic events are recognized—that is, put into the financial statements—when the cash transaction occurs. For example, suppose Sunnyvale Clinic, a large, multispecialty group practice, provided services to a patient in December 2020. At that time, the clinic billed Florida Blue (formerly Blue Cross and Blue Shield of Florida) $700, the full amount that the insurer was obligated to pay. However, Sunnyvale did not receive payment from the insurer until February 2021. If it used cash accounting, the $700 obligation on the part of Florida Blue would not appear in Sunnyvale's 2020 financial statements. Rather, the revenue would be recognized when the cash was actually received in February 2021.

The core argument in favor of cash accounting is that the most important event to record on the financial statements is the receipt of cash, not the provision of the service (i.e., the obligation to pay). Similarly, Sunnyvale's costs of providing services would be recognized as the cash is physically paid out: Inventory costs would be recognized as supplies are purchased, labor costs would be recognized when employees are paid, new equipment purchases would be recognized when the invoices are paid, and so on. To put it simply, cash accounting records the actual flow of money into and out of a business.

Cash accounting has two advantages. First, it is simple and easy to understand. No complex accounting rules are required for the preparation of financial statements. Second, cash accounting is closely aligned with accounting for tax purposes, and hence it is easy to translate cash accounting statements into income tax filing data. Because of these advantages, about 80 percent of all medical practices, typically smaller ones, use cash accounting. However, cash accounting also has disadvantages—primarily, that in its pure form, it does not present information on revenues owed to a business by payers or the business's existing payment obligations.

Before closing our discussion of cash accounting, we should note that most businesses that use cash accounting do not use the "pure" method described here but rather a hybrid method called *modified cash basis accounting*. The modified statements combine some features of cash accounting, usually to report revenues and expenses, and some features of accrual accounting, usually to report assets and liabilities. Still, the cash method presents an incomplete picture of the financial status of a business and hence the preference for accrual accounting by GAAP.

Accrual Accounting

Under **accrual accounting**, often called *accrual basis accounting*, the economic event that creates the financial transaction (e.g., patient surgery is performed), rather than the financial transaction itself (e.g., insurer pays the hospital for the surgery), provides the basis for the accounting entry. When applied to revenues, the accrual concept implies that revenue earned and reported does not necessarily correspond to the actual receipt of cash at the time the revenue is reported. Why? Earned revenue is recognized in financial statements when a service is provided *that creates a payment obligation* on the part of the payer, rather than when the payment is actually received. For healthcare providers, the payment obligation typically falls on the patient, a third-party payer, or both. If the obligation is satisfied immediately—for example, when a patient makes full payment at the time the service is rendered—the revenue is in the form of cash. In such cases, the revenue is recorded at the time of service regardless of whether cash or accrual accounting is used.

However, in most cases, the bulk of the payment for a service comes from a third-party payer and is not received until later, perhaps several months after the service is provided. In this situation, the revenue created by the service does not create an immediate cash payment. If the payment is received within an accounting period—one year, for our purposes—the conversion of revenues to cash will be completed, and as far as the financial statements are concerned, the reported revenue is cash. However, when the revenue is recorded (i.e., the service is provided) in one accounting period and payment does not occur until the next period, the revenue reported has not yet been collected.

Consider the Sunnyvale Clinic example presented in our discussion of cash accounting. Although the services were provided in December 2020, the clinic did not receive its $700 payment until February 2021. Because Sunnyvale's accounting year ended on December 31 and the clinic uses accrual accounting, the clinic's books were closed after the revenue had been recorded but before the cash was received. Thus, Sunnyvale reported this $700 of revenue on its 2020 financial statements, even though no cash

accrual accounting
The recording of economic events in the periods in which the events occur, even if the associated cash receipts or payments happen in a different period.

was collected. When accrual accounting is used, the amount of revenues not collected is listed as a receivable (the amount due to Sunnyvale) in the financial statements, so users will know that not all reported revenues represent cash receipts.

The accrual accounting concept also applies to expenses. To illustrate, assume that Sunnyvale had payroll obligations of $20,000 for employees' work during the last week of 2020 that would not be paid until the first payday in 2021. Because the employees actually performed the work, the obligation to pay the salaries was created in 2020. An expense would be recorded in 2020 even though no cash payment would be made until 2021. Under cash basis accounting, Sunnyvale would not recognize the labor expense until it was paid—in this case, in 2021. But under accrual accounting, the $20,000 would be shown as an expense on the financial statements in 2020, and, at the same time, the statements would indicate a $20,000 liability (or obligation to pay employees). ·

SELF-TEST QUESTIONS

1. Briefly explain the differences between cash and accrual accounting and give an example of each.
2. What is modified cash basis accounting?
3. Why does GAAP favor accrual over cash accounting?

Income Statement Basics

In this section, we begin our coverage of the four primary financial statements by discussing the income statement. Then, in a later section, we discuss the statement of changes in equity. In chapter 4, the remaining two statements—the balance sheet and the statement of cash flows—are discussed. The supplement to chapter 4 discusses the method of recording and compiling the financial accounting data contained in the financial statements. Unfortunately, the names of the statements are not consistent across types of organizations. We will introduce the alternative names of each statement as it is discussed.

The purpose of our financial accounting discussion is to provide readers with a *basic understanding* of the preparation, content, and interpretation of a business's financial statements. The financial statements of large organizations can be long and complex, and there is significant leeway regarding the format used, even within health services organizations. Thus, in our discussion of the statements, we use *simplified illustrations* that focus on key issues. In a sense, the financial statements presented here are summaries of actual financial statements, but this is the best way to learn the basics; the nuances must be left to other books that focus exclusively on accounting matters.

Perhaps the most frequently asked, and the most important, question about a business is this: Is it making money? The **income statement** summarizes the operations (activities) of an organization with a focus on its revenues, expenses, and profitability. The income statement is also called the *statement of operations, statement of activities,* or *statement of revenues and expenses.*

The income statements of Sunnyvale Clinic are presented in exhibit 3.1. Because Sunnyvale is a not-for-profit organization, its income statement is called the statement of operations. The statement also includes changes in net assets, which is the not-for-profit equivalent of the statement of changes in equity. For now, we will focus on the statement of operations. The statement of changes in net assets is discussed later in this chapter.

Most financial statements contain two or three years of data, with the most recent year presented first. The *title section* tells us that these are annual income statements, ending on December 31, for the years 2020 and 2019. Whereas the balance sheet, which is covered in chapter 4, reports a business's financial position at a single point in time, the income statement contains operational results *over a specified period of time*. Because these income statements are part of Sunnyvale's annual report, the time (accounting) period is one year. Also, the dollar amounts reported are listed in *thousands of dollars*, so the $148,118 listed as net patient service revenue for 2020 is actually $148,118,000.

The core components of the income statement are straightforward: revenues, expenses, and profitability (net operating income and net income). *Revenues*, as discussed in the section on cash versus accrual accounting, represent both the cash received and the unpaid obligations of payers for services provided during each year presented. For healthcare providers, revenues result mostly from the provision of patient and patient-related services.

To produce revenues, organizations must incur *expenses*, which are classified as *operating* or *capital*. Although they are not separately broken out on Sunnyvale's income statement, *operating expenses* consist of salaries, supplies, insurance, and other costs directly related to providing services. *Capital costs* are the costs associated with the buildings and equipment used by the organization, such as depreciation and interest expenses. Expenses decrease the profitability of a business, so expenses are subtracted from revenues to determine an organization's profitability. Sunnyvale's income statement reports two different measures of profitability: operating income and net income (called *excess of revenues over expenses*).

The income statement, then, summarizes the organization's ability to generate profits. Basically, it lists the organization's revenues (and income),

income statement A financial statement, prepared in accordance with generally accepted accounting principles (GAAP), that summarizes a business's revenues, expenses, and profitability.

EXHIBIT 3.1
Sunnyvale
Clinic:
Statements
of Operations
and Changes
in Net Assets,
Years Ended
December 31,
2020 and 2019
(in thousands)

	2020	2019
Operations		
Operating Revenues:		
Net patient service revenue	$ 148,118	$ 121,765
Premium revenue	17,316	16,455
Other revenue	3,079	2,704
Net operating revenues	$168,513	$140,924
Expenses:		
Salaries and benefits	$126,223	$102,334
Supplies	20,568	18,673
Insurance	4,518	3,710
Purchased services	3,189	2,603
Depreciation	6,405	5,798
Interest	5,329	3,476
Total expenses	$166,232	$136,594
Operating income	$ 2,281	$ 4,330
Nonoperating income:		
Contributions	$ 243	$ 198
Investment income	3,870	3,678
Total nonoperating income	$ 4,113	$ 3,876
Excess of revenues over expenses (net income)	$ 6,394	$ 8,206
Changes in Net Assets		
Changes in net assets without donor restrictions:		
Excess of revenues over expenses	$ 6,394	$ 8,206
Increase in net assets without donor restrictions	$ 6,394	$ 8,206
Changes in net assets with donor restrictions:		
Gifts and bequests	$ 1,466	$ 0
Increase in net assets with donor restrictions	$ 1,466	$ 0
Increase in net assets	$ 7,860	$ 8,206
Net assets at beginning of year	$ 46,208	$ 38,002
Net assets at end of year	$ 54,068	$ 46,208

the expenses that must be incurred to produce the revenues, and the differences between the two. In the following sections, the major components of the income statement are discussed in detail.

SELF-TEST
QUESTIONS

1. What is the primary purpose of the income statement?
2. In regard to time, how do the income statement and balance sheet differ?
3. What are the major components of the income statement?

Revenues

Revenues can be shown on the income statement in several different formats. In fact, there is more latitude in the construction of the income statement than there is in that of the balance sheet, so the income statements for different types of healthcare providers tend to differ more in presentation than their balance sheets. (See problems 3.2 and 3.3, as well as exhibit 17.1, for examples of income statements from other types of providers.)

Sunnyvale's operating revenues section (see exhibit 3.1) focuses on revenues that stem from the provision of patient and patient-related services; in other words, they derive from operations. As we discuss in a later section, Sunnyvale also has revenues from contributions and securities investments (nonoperating income), but because such income is not related to core business activities, it is reported separately on the income statement.

The first line of the operating revenues section reports net **patient service revenue** of $148,118,000 for 2020. The key term here is *net patient service. Patient service* means that this line contains revenues that stem solely from patient services, as opposed to revenues that stem from related sources, such as parking fees or food services, which are reported on a separate line (other revenue) in the operating revenues section. Also, as discussed later, patient service revenue that stems from capitated patients may be reported separately (e.g., premium revenue). If this is the case, the $148,118,000 reported by Sunnyvale as patient service revenue includes only revenue from fee-for-service patients.

Net patient service revenue means that the patient service revenue reported is the amount that Sunnyvale expects to receive for providing patient care after accounting for certain deductions. Sunnyvale, like all healthcare providers, has a charge description master file, or chargemaster, that contains the charge code and *gross price* for each item and service that it provides. However, the chargemaster price rarely represents the amount

patient service revenue
Revenue that stems solely from the provision of patient services; in some situations, it may only reflect revenue from fee-for-service patients.

the clinic expects to be paid for a particular service. For example, the price for a particular service might be $800, but the contract with a particular payer might specify a 40 percent *discount* from charges, which would result in a reimbursement of only $480. In addition to negotiated discounts, government payers such as Medicare and Medicaid reimburse providers a set amount that often is well below the chargemaster (gross) price.

Because recorded revenue must reflect only amounts that are realizable (collectible), differences between chargemaster prices and actual reimbursement amounts are incorporated before the revenue is recorded on the net patient service revenue line. Thus, the net patient service revenue shown on the income statement is reported after *contractual allowances* have been considered and hence represents the actual reimbursement amount expected.

To add to the complexity of revenue reporting, some services have been provided as *financial assistance* (charity care) to indigent patients. (*Indigent patients* are those who presumably are willing to pay for services provided but do not have the ability to do so.) Sunnyvale has no expectation of ever collecting for these services, so, like contractual allowances, charges for charity care services are not reflected in the $148,118,000 net patient service revenue reported for 2020.

Finally, some payments for patient services that are owed will never be collected. Prior to 2018 (for public entities) and 2019 (for nonpublic entities), estimates of these amounts were reported separately on the income statement as a deduction from patient service revenue titled *provision for bad debts* or *provision for uncollectible accounts* (see exhibit 3.2, column labeled "Before"). However, in 2014, the FASB issued a new accounting pronouncement that changed the reporting of patient service revenue beginning in 2018 or 2019 depending on the type of organization.[5] After its adoption, the majority (or all) of what previously would have been classified as provision for uncollectible accounts and presented as a

Healthcare in Practice
Revenue Reporting in the "Good Old Days"

About 20 years ago, hospital revenues were reported differently than they are today. Then, the revenues section would begin with gross patient services revenue based on chargemaster prices. In other words, every service provided would be recorded at its chargemaster price, and those prices would be aggregated to calculate reported revenues.

Then, the total amount of discounts and allowances would be listed, followed by the total amount of charity care provided, and those values would be subtracted from gross patient service revenue to obtain net patient service revenue. In this format, discounts and allowances and charity care were prominently displayed at the top of the income statement. At the time, estimates of bad debt losses were reported as an expense. Later, bad debt losses were treated as a revenue deduction, and now they are treated mostly as an implicit price concession and not reported separately. Today, if these amounts (discounts and allowances, charity care, and bad debt losses) are listed at all, they typically are listed in the notes to the financial statements rather than in the income statement itself.

What do you think? Is the "old" way or the current system best? Why do you think GAAP was changed to report only the net amount expected to be collected, as opposed to the gross amount billed less all of the deductions?

Statement of Operations and Changes in Net Assets (in thousands)

	After	Before
Patient service revenue net of contractual discounts and allowances		$8,308,889
Provision for uncollectible accounts		(254,569)
Net patient service revenue	$8,054,320	$8,054,320

EXHIBIT 3.2
Presentation of Patient Service Revenue Before and After Implementation of the FASB's New Revenue Recognition Standard

reduction to patient service revenue on the income statement must now be treated as a price concession that reduces the transaction price reported as net patient service revenue.

The FASB defines two types of price concessions: explicit and implicit. Explicit price concessions are based on contractual agreements, established discount policies, and historical experience (e.g., contractual allowances and financial assistance, as discussed previously). Implicit price concessions represent differences between amounts billed and estimated amounts expected to be received from patients based on historical collection experience and current market factors. Thus, what was previously classified as bad debt is now considered an implicit price concession and treated like contractual allowances and financial assistance in the presentation of net patient service revenue. As shown in exhibit 3.2 (column labeled "After"), all that is now reported is a single line titled *net patient service revenue*, which is net of discounts and allowances, charity care and financial assistance, and implicit price concessions. Any true (unpredictable) bad debt losses are reported as an expense under the new accounting standard. While the change affects the presentation of patient service revenue on the income statement, it is not expected to materially affect net income.

A description of policies regarding discounts and charity care often appears in the notes to the financial statements. Sunnyvale's financial statements include the following two notes:

Revenues. Sunnyvale has entered into agreements with third-party payers, including government programs, under which it is paid for services on the basis of established charges, the cost of providing services, predetermined rates, or discounts from established charges. Revenues are recorded at estimated amounts due from patients and third-party payers for the services provided. Settlements under reimbursement agreements with third-party payers are estimated and recorded in the period the related services are rendered and are adjusted in future periods, as final settlements are determined. The adjustments to estimated settlements for prior years are not considered material and thus are not shown in the financial statements or notes.

Charity care. Sunnyvale has a policy of providing charity care to indigent patients in emergency situations. These services, which are not reported as revenues, amounted to $67,541 in 2020 and $51,344 in 2019.

Even though Sunnyvale ultimately expects to collect all of its reported net patient service revenue, the clinic did not actually receive $148,118,000 in cash payments from fee-for-service patients and insurers in 2020. Rather, some of the revenue has not yet been collected. As readers will learn in chapter 4, the yet-to-be-collected portion of the net patient service revenue—$28,509,000—appears on the balance sheet (see exhibit 4.1) as net patient accounts receivable.

If a provider has a significant amount of revenue stemming from capitation contracts, it is often reported separately in the operating revenues section as **premium revenue**. Sunnyvale reported premium revenue of $17,316,000 for 2020. The key difference is that patient service revenue is reported when services are provided, but premium revenue is reported at the start of each contract payment period—typically the beginning of each month. Thus, premium revenue implies an obligation on the part of the reporting organization to provide future services, while patient service revenue represents an obligation on the part of payers to pay the reporting organization for services already provided. Also, different types of providers may use different terminology for revenues; for example, some nursing homes report *resident service revenue.*

Most health services organizations have revenue related to, but not arising directly from, patient services, and Sunnyvale is no exception. In 2020, Sunnyvale reported *other revenue* of $3,079,000. Examples of other revenue include parking fees; nonpatient food service charges; office and concession rentals; and sales of pharmaceuticals to employees, staff, and visitors.

When all the revenue associated with patient services is totaled, the amount reported as *net operating revenues* for 2020 is $168,513,000. This amount represents the net amount of revenue that stems from a provider's core operations—the provision of patient services. Income that results from noncore activities—primarily contributions and securities investments—is reported at the bottom of the income statement.

premium revenue
Patient service revenue that stems from capitated patients as opposed to fee-for-service patients.

SELF-TEST QUESTIONS

1. What categories of revenue are reported on the income statement?
2. Briefly, what is the difference between gross patient service revenue and net patient service revenue?

3. Describe how the following adjustments to revenue are reported on the income statement:
   a. Contractual discounts and allowances
   b. Charity care
   c. Implicit price concessions (formerly bad debt losses)
4. Is income from securities investments included in the operating revenue section? If not, why not?

Expenses

Expenses are the costs of doing business. As shown in exhibit 3.1, Sunnyvale reports its expenses in categories such as salaries and benefits, supplies, insurance, and so on. According to GAAP, expenses may be reported using either a *natural classification*, which classifies expenses by the nature of the expense, as Sunnyvale does, or a *functional classification*, which classifies expenses by purpose, such as inpatient services, outpatient services, and administrative.

The number and nature of expense items reported on the income statement can vary widely depending on the nature and complexity of the organization. For example, some businesses, typically smaller ones, may report only two categories of expenses: health services and administrative. Others may report many categories. Sunnyvale takes a middle-of-the-road approach to the number of expense categories. Most users of financial statements would prefer more expense categories, as well as a mixing of classifications, because more insights can be gleaned if an organization reports revenues and expenses both by service breakdown (e.g., inpatient versus outpatient) and by type (e.g., salaries versus supplies). To assist readers, some organizations present additional detail on expenses in the notes to the financial statements.

Sunnyvale is typical of most healthcare providers in that its cost structure is primarily related to labor. The clinic reported *salaries and benefits* of $126,223,000 for 2020, which amounts to 75 percent of Sunnyvale's total expenses. The way in which these expenses are broken down—by department or by contract—and the relationship of these expenses to the volume or type of services provided is not part of the financial accounting information system. However, such information, which is very important to managers, is available in Sunnyvale's managerial accounting system. Chapters 5–8 focus on managerial accounting.

The expense item titled *supplies* represents the cost of supplies (primarily medical) used in providing patient services. Sunnyvale does not order and pay for supplies when a particular patient service requires them. Rather, the clinic's manager estimates the use of individual supply items, orders them beforehand, and then maintains a supplies inventory. As readers will see in chapter 4, the amount of supplies on hand is reported on the balance sheet. The income statement expense reported by Sunnyvale represents the cost—$20,568,000—of the supplies **actually consumed** in providing patient services for 2020 (recall the expense-matching principle). Thus, the expense reported for supplies does **not** reflect the actual cash spent by Sunnyvale on supplies purchased during the year. In theory, Sunnyvale could have several years' worth of supplies in its inventories at the beginning of 2020; it could have used some of those supplies without replenishing inventories, and hence it might not have actually spent any cash on supplies during 2020.

Sunnyvale uses commercial insurance to protect against many risks, including property risks, such as fire and damaging weather, and liability risks, such as managerial malfeasance and professional (medical) liability. The cost of this protection is reported on the income statement as *insurance* expense, which amounted to $4,518,000 in 2020.

Sunnyvale uses a third-party provider for its reference laboratory. This $3,189,000 expense for 2020 is reported as *purchased services* on the income statement.

depreciation
A noncash charge against earnings on the income statement that reflects the "wear and tear" on a business's fixed assets (property and equipment).

The next expense category, **depreciation**, requires closer examination. Businesses require *property and equipment (fixed assets)* to provide goods and services. Sunnyvale owns most of the fixed assets necessary to support its mission. When fixed assets are initially purchased, Sunnyvale does not report their cost as an expense on the income statement. The reason is that the expense-matching principle dictates that such costs be matched to the accounting periods during which the asset produces revenues. A more pragmatic reason for not reporting the costs of fixed assets when they are acquired is that reported earnings can fluctuate widely from year to year depending on the amount of fixed assets acquired.

To match the cost of fixed assets to the revenues produced by such long-lived assets, accountants use the concept of depreciation expense, which spreads the cost of a fixed asset over many years. Note that most people use the terms *cost* and *expense* interchangeably. To accountants, however, the terms can have different meanings. Depreciation expense is a good example. Here, the term *cost* is applied to the actual cash outlay (total expenditure) for a fixed asset, whereas the term *expense* is used to describe the allocation of that cost over time.

The calculation of depreciation expense is somewhat arbitrary, so the amount of depreciation expense applied to a fixed asset in any year generally is not closely related to the actual use of the asset or its loss in fair market value. To illustrate, Sunnyvale owns a piece of diagnostic equipment that it uses infrequently. In 2019, it was used 23 times, but in 2020, it was used only nine times. Still, the depreciation expense associated with this equipment was the same in both years. Also, the clinic owns another piece of equipment that could be sold today for about the same price that Sunnyvale paid for it four years ago, yet each year the clinic reports a depreciation expense for that equipment, which implies a loss of value.

Depreciation expense, like all other financial statement entries, is calculated in accordance with GAAP. The calculation typically uses the *straight-line method*—that is, the depreciation expense is obtained by dividing the historical cost of the asset, less its estimated salvage value, by the number of years of its estimated useful life (the period of time over which the asset is in service and generates revenues). *Salvage value* is the amount, if any, expected to be received when final disposition occurs at the end of an asset's useful life. The result is the asset's annual depreciation expense, which is the charge reflected in each year's income statement over the estimated life of the asset. In 2020, Sunnyvale reported depreciation expense of $6,405,000, which represents the total amount of deprecation taken on all of the clinic's fixed assets during the year. (The term *straight line* stems from the fact that the depreciation expense is constant in each year, and hence the implied value of the asset declines evenly—like a straight line—over time.) As readers will discover in chapter 4, depreciation is accumulated over time on the organization's balance sheet.

In addition to depreciation calculated for financial statement purposes, which is called *book depreciation*, for-profit businesses must calculate depreciation for tax purposes. *Tax depreciation* is calculated in accordance with Internal Revenue Service regulations, as opposed to GAAP. Also, note that land is not depreciated for either financial reporting or tax purposes.

In closing our discussion of depreciation expense, note that depreciation is a *noncash expense*, meaning there is no actual payment associated with the expense. The cash payment may have been made many years before the expense appears on the income statement. The impact of noncash expenses on a business's cash flows is covered in a later section of this chapter.

Key Equation: Straight-Line Depreciation Calculation

Suppose Sunnyvale Clinic purchases an X-ray machine for $150,000. Its useful life, according to accounting guidelines, is ten years, and the machine's expected salvage value at that time is $25,000. The annual depreciation expense, calculated as follows, is $12,500:

$$\text{Annual depreciation expense} = (\text{Initial cost} - \text{Salvage value}) \div \text{Useful life}$$
$$= (\$150,000 - \$25,000) \div 10 \text{ years}$$
$$= \$125,000 \div 10$$
$$= \$12,500.$$

The final expense line reports *interest expense*. Sunnyvale owes or paid its lenders $5,329,000 in interest expense for debt capital supplied during 2020. Not all of the interest expense reported has been paid, because Sunnyvale typically pays interest monthly or semiannually, and hence interest has accrued on some loans that will not be paid until 2021. The amount of interest expense reported by an organization is influenced primarily by its *capital structure*, which reflects the amount of debt that it uses. Also, interest expense is affected by the borrower's creditworthiness, its mix of long-term versus short-term debt, and the general level of interest rates. (These factors are discussed in detail in later chapters.)

In closing our discussion of expenses, note that many income statements contain a catchall category labeled "other." Listed here are general and administrative expenses that individually are too small to list separately, including items such as marketing expenses and external auditor fees. Although organizations cannot possibly report every expense item separately, it is frustrating for users of financial statement information to come across a large, unexplained expense item. Thus, income statements that include the "other" category often add a note that provides additional detail regarding these expenses.

1. What is an expense?
2. Briefly, what are some of the commonly reported expense categories?
3. What is the logic behind depreciation expense?

Operating Income

Although the reporting of revenues and expenses is clearly important, the most important information on the income statement is profitability. As shown in exhibit 3.1, two different profit measures can be reported on the income statement. (Not all healthcare organizations report both measures. Some report only the final measure—net income.)

operating income
The earnings of a business directly related to core activities; for a healthcare provider, earnings are related to patient services.

The first profitability measure reported by Sunnyvale Clinic is **operating income**, which is calculated in exhibit 3.1 as net operating revenues minus total expenses. The precise calculation is tied to the format of the income statement, but the general idea of operating income is to focus on revenues and expenses that are related to operations (the provision of patient services).

Because net operating revenues in exhibit 3.1 are all related to patient services, operating income measures the profitability of core operations (patient services and related endeavors). Many healthcare providers, especially large ones, have significant revenues that stem from non-patient-service-related activities, so it is useful to report the inherent profitability of the core business separately from the overall profitability of the enterprise.

Sunnyvale reported $2,281,000 of operating income in 2020, which means that the provision of healthcare services and directly related activities generated a profit of that amount. Operating income is an important measure of a healthcare business's profitability because it focuses on the core activities of the business. Some healthcare businesses report a positive net income (net income is discussed later) but a negative operating income (an operating loss). This situation is worrisome, because a business is on shaky financial ground if its core operations are losing money, especially if they do so year after year.

The operating income reported on the income statement is defined by GAAP and represents an estimate of the long-run operating profitability of the business. It has some shortcomings—for one, it does not represent cash flow—that are similar to the shortcomings related to net income, which are discussed in a later section of this chapter. Still, measuring the core profitability of a business is critical to understanding its financial status.

For Your Consideration

Will the Real Operating Income Please Stand Up?

Who would think it would be hard to measure operating income? After all, the basic definition is straightforward: operating revenues minus operating expenses. Still, different analysts can look at the same set of revenue and expense data and calculate different values for operating income.

The problem in calculating operating income lies primarily in the definition of what constitutes a provider's operations (core activities). There are at least three approaches: Operations include (1) only patient care activities; (2) patient care and directly related activities, such as cafeteria and parking garage operations; and (3) patient care, directly related activities, and government appropriations. Each definition results in a different value for operating income. In general, as the definition of core operations expands, the value calculated for operating income increases.

What do you think? Consider the hospital sector. What activities should be considered part of core operations? Should hospitals be required by GAAP to report multiple measures of operating income, each using a different definition of core activities?

SELF-TEST QUESTIONS

1. What is operating income?
2. Why is operating income such an important measure of profitability?

Nonoperating Income

nonoperating income
The earnings of a business that are unrelated to core activities; for a healthcare provider, the most common sources are contributions and investment income.

The next section of the income statement lists **nonoperating income**. As mentioned earlier, reporting the income of operating and nonoperating activities separately is useful. The nonoperating income section of Sunnyvale's income statement shown in exhibit 3.1 reports the income generated from activities unrelated to the provision of healthcare services.

The first category of nonoperating income listed is *contributions*. Many not-for-profit organizations, especially those with large, well-endowed foundations, rely heavily on charitable contributions as an income source. Those charitable contributions that can be used immediately for any purpose (spent now) are reported as nonoperating income. However, contributions that create a permanent endowment fund or are otherwise limited to a specific future use by the donor, and hence are not available for immediate use, are not reported on the income statement. Rather, these contributions appear on the statement of changes in net assets as changes in net assets with donor restrictions.

The second category of nonoperating income is *investment income*, another type of income on which not-for-profit organizations rely heavily. It stems from two primary sources:

1. Healthcare businesses usually have funds available that exceed the minimum necessary to meet current cash expenses. Because cash earns no interest, these "excess" funds usually are invested in short-term, interest-earning securities, such as Treasury bills (a short-term debt obligation) or money market mutual funds. Sometimes these invested funds can be quite large—say, when a business is building up cash to make a tax payment or to start a large construction project. Also, prudent businesses keep a reserve of funds on hand to meet unexpected emergencies. The interest earned on such funds is listed as investment income.

2. Not-for-profit businesses may have a large amount of endowment fund contributions. When these contributions are received, they are not reported as income because the funds are not available to be spent. However, the income from securities purchased with endowment funds is available to the healthcare organization, and hence this income is reported as nonoperating (investment) income.

In total, Sunnyvale reported $4,113,000 of nonoperating income for 2020, consisting of $243,000 in spendable contributions and $3,870,000 earned on the investment of excess cash and endowments. Nonoperating income is not central to the core business, which is providing healthcare services. Overreliance on nonoperating income could mask operational inefficiencies such as overspending on supplies that, if not corrected, could lead to future financial problems. Note that the costs associated with creating nonoperating income are not reported separately by Sunnyvale. Thus, the expenses associated with soliciting contributions or investing excess cash and endowments must be deducted before the income is reported on the income statement. Other organizations may choose to report nonoperating income and expenses separately.

Finally, note that the income statements of some providers do not contain a separate section titled *nonoperating income*. Rather, nonoperating income is included in the revenue section that heads the income statement. In this situation, total revenues include both operating and nonoperating revenues.

SELF-TEST
QUESTIONS

1. What is nonoperating income?
2. Why is nonoperating income reported separately from revenues? Is this always the case?

Net Income

The second profitability measure reported by Sunnyvale Clinic is **net income**, which in exhibit 3.1 is labeled *excess of revenues over expenses*. Sunnyvale's net income is equal to Operating income + Total nonoperating income. Sunnyvale reported net income of $6,394,000 for 2020: $2,281,000 + $4,113,000 = $6,394,000. (Not-for-profit organizations use the term *excess of revenues over expenses*, but we call this measure *net income* because that is the more universally recognized term. Also, one could argue that there are three profitability measures on Sunnyvale's income statement: operating income, nonoperating income, and net income. We do not object to that position, but accountants generally view nonoperating income as an entry on the statement rather than a calculated profitability measure.)

net income
The total earnings of a business, including both operating and nonoperating income.

Because of its location on the income statement and its importance, net income is often referred to as the *bottom line*. Even though Sunnyvale is a not-for-profit organization, **it still must make a profit**. If the business is to offer new services in the future, it must earn a profit today to produce the funds needed for new assets. Furthermore, because of inflation, Sunnyvale could not replace its existing assets as they wear out or become obsolete without the funds generated by positive profitability. Thus, turning a profit is essential for all businesses, including not-for-profits.

What happens to a business's net income? For the most part, it is reinvested in the business. Not-for-profit corporations **must** reinvest all earnings in the business. This reinvestment of earnings increases the equity of the organization. The relationship between net income and equity can be seen in Sunnyvale Clinic's statement of changes in net assets. The increase in net assets without donor restrictions from 2019 to 2020 is equal to Sunnyvale's net income (excess of revenues over expenses) of $6,394,000.

An investor-owned corporation, on the other hand, may return a portion or all of its net income to owners in the form of dividend payments. The amount of profits reinvested in an investor-owned business, therefore, is net income minus the amount paid out as dividends. (Some for-profit businesses distribute profits to owners in the form of bonuses, which often occurs in medical practices. However, when this is done, the distribution becomes an expense item that reduces net income rather than a distribution of net income. The end result is the same—monies are distributed to owners—but the reporting mechanism is much different.)

Note that both operating income and net income measure profitability **as defined by GAAP**. In establishing GAAP, accountants have created guidelines that attempt to measure the *economic income* of a business, which is a difficult task because economic gains and losses often are not tied to easily identifiable events.

Furthermore, some of the income statement items involve estimates (e.g., implicit price concessions) and others (e.g., depreciation expense) do not represent actual cash costs. Because of accrual accounting and other factors, the fact that Sunnyvale reported net income of $6,394,000 for 2020 does not mean that the business actually experienced a net cash inflow of that amount. This point is discussed in greater detail in the next section.

SELF-TEST QUESTIONS

1. Why is net income called the "bottom line"?
2. What is the difference between net income and operating income?
3. What happens to net income?

Net Income Versus Cash Flow

As stated previously, the income statement reports total profitability (net income), which is determined in accordance with GAAP. Although net income is an important measure of profitability, an organization's financial condition, at least in the short run, depends more on the actual cash flow into and out of the business than it does on reported net income. Thus, occasionally a business will go bankrupt even though its net income has historically been positive. More commonly, many businesses that have reported negative net incomes (i.e., net losses) have survived with little or no financial damage. How can this happen?

Consider exhibit 3.1. Sunnyvale reported net operating revenues of $168,513,000 for 2020. Yet this is not the amount of cash that was actually collected during the year, because some of these revenues will not be collected until 2021. Furthermore, some revenues reported for 2019 were actually collected in 2020, but these do not appear on the 2020 income statement. This is because of accrual accounting; reported revenue is not the same as cash revenue. The same logic applies to expenses; few of the values reported as expenses on the income statement are the same as the actual cash outflows. To make matters even more confusing, not one cent of depreciation expense was paid out as cash. Depreciation expense is an accounting reflection of the cost of fixed assets "used up" during the year, but Sunnyvale did not actually pay out $6,405,000 in cash to anyone (e.g., a collector of depreciation). According to the balance sheet (see exhibit 4.1), Sunnyvale actually paid out $88,549,000 at some point in the past to purchase the clinic's total fixed assets. Of Sunnyvale's total fixed assets, $6,405,000 was recognized in 2020 as a cost of doing business, just as salaries and fringe benefits are a cost of doing business.

Can net income be converted to *cash flow*—the actual amount of cash generated during the year? As a rough estimate, cash flow can be thought of as net income plus noncash expenses. Thus, the estimated cash flow generated by Sunnyvale in 2020 is not only the $6,394,000 reported net income, but this amount plus the $6,405,000 shown for depreciation, for a total of $12,799,000. Depreciation expense must be added back to net income to get cash flow because it initially was subtracted from revenues to obtain net income even though there was no associated cash outlay.[6]

Key Equation: Net Income to Cash Flow Conversion

Because of accrual accounting, net income does not represent an estimate of the organization's cash flow for the reporting period. The following equation is used to convert net income to a rough estimate of cash flow: Cash flow = Net income + Noncash expenses. Because depreciation often is the only noncash expense, the equation can be rewritten as Cash flow = Net income + Depreciation. To illustrate, Sunnyvale reported net income of $8,206,000 and depreciation of $5,798,000 in 2019. Thus, a rough measure of its 2019 cash flow is $14,004,000:

$$\text{Cash flow} = \text{Net income} + \text{Depreciation}$$
$$= \$8,206,000 + \$5,798,000$$
$$= \$14,004,000.$$

Here is another way of looking at cash flow versus net income: If Sunnyvale showed no net income for 2020, it would still be generating cash of $6,405,000 (depreciation amount) because that amount was deducted from revenues but not actually paid out in cash. The rationale for the income statement treatment is that Sunnyvale would be able to set aside the depreciation amount, which is above and beyond its cash expenses, this year and in future years. Eventually, Sunnyvale would use the accumulated total of *depreciation cash flow* to replace its fixed assets as they wear out or become obsolete.

Thus, the incorporation of depreciation expense into the cost and, ultimately, the price structure of services provided is designed to ensure the ability of an organization to replace its fixed assets as needed, assuming that the assets could be purchased at their historical cost. To be more realistic, businesses must plan to generate net income, in addition to the accumulated depreciation funds, sufficient to replace existing fixed assets in the future at inflated costs or even to expand the asset base. It appears that Sunnyvale does have such capabilities, as reflected in its $6,394,000 net income and $12,799,000 cash flow for 2020.

It is important to understand that the $12,799,000 cash flow calculated here is only an *estimate* of actual cash flow for 2020, because almost every item of revenues and expenses listed on the income statement does not equal its cash flow counterpart. The greater the difference between the reported values and cash values, the less reliable is the rough estimate of cash flow defined here. The value of knowing the precise amount of cash generated or lost has not gone unnoticed by accountants. In chapter 4, readers will learn about the statement of cash flows, which can be thought of as an income statement that is recast to focus on cash flow.

SELF-TEST QUESTIONS

1. What is the difference between net income and cash flow?
2. How can income statement data be used to estimate cash flow?
3. What is depreciation cash flow, and what is its expected use?
4. Why do not-for-profit businesses need to make a profit?

Income Statements of Investor-Owned Businesses

Our income statement discussion focused on a not-for-profit organization: Sunnyvale Clinic. What do the income statements for investor-owned businesses, such as Community Health Systems (www.chs.net) and Brookdale Senior Living (www.brookdale.com), look like? The financial statements of investor-owned and not-for-profit businesses are generally similar except for entries that are applicable only to one form of ownership, such as tax payments. Because the transactions of all health services organizations are similar in nature, ownership plays only a minor role in the presentation of financial statement data. In reality, more differences in financial statements are attributable to differences in lines of business (e.g., hospitals versus nursing homes versus managed care plans) than to ownership.

The impact of taxes and depreciation on net income and cash flow for for-profit businesses deserves discussion. Exhibit 3.3 presents four income statements that are based on Sunnyvale's 2020 income statement, shown in exhibit 3.1. First, note that the statements in exhibit 3.3 are condensed to show only total revenues (including nonoperating income); all expenses except depreciation; depreciation; and net income. Lines for taxable income, taxes, and cash flow have also been added. The column labeled "Not-for-Profit" presents Sunnyvale's income statement assuming not-for-profit status (zero taxes), so the reported net income and cash flow are the same as those discussed previously.

Now consider the column labeled "For-Profit A," which assumes that Sunnyvale is a for-profit business with a 20 percent tax rate. Here, the clinic must pay taxes of $0.20 \times \$6,394,000 = \$1,279,000$, which reduces net income by a like amount: $\$6,394,000 - \$1,279,000 = \$5,115,000$. In the next column, labeled "For-Profit B," the tax rate is assumed to be 30 percent, which results in higher taxes of $\$1,918,000$ and a lower net income of $\$4,476,000$. The impact of taxes on net income is clear: The addition of taxes reduces net income, and the greater the tax rate, the greater the reduction.

Finally, let's examine the impact of depreciation and taxes on cash flow (net income plus depreciation). The rightmost column, labeled "For-Profit C," is the same as the "For-Profit B" column, except the depreciation expense is assumed to be zero rather than $\$6,405,000$. What is the impact of depreciation expense? Depreciation expense lowers taxable income by a like amount and hence lowers taxes by $T \times$ Depreciation expense, where T is the tax rate. The amount of taxes saved—$0.30 \times \$6,405,000 = \$1,921,500$—is called the **depreciation shield**. It is the dollar amount of taxes that will not have to be paid because of the business's depreciation expense.

Let's check our work. According to exhibit 3.3, the taxes due without depreciation expense are $\$3,839,700$, but with depreciation, they

depreciation shield
The dollar amount of taxes that will not have to be paid because of the business's depreciation expense.

EXHIBIT 3.3

Sunnyvale Clinic: Condensed Income Statements Under Alternative Tax Assumptions,
Year Ended December 31, 2020 (in thousands)

	Not-for-Profit (Tax rate = 0%)	For-Profit A (Tax rate = 20%)	For-Profit B (Tax rate = 30%)	For-Profit C (Tax rate = 30%)
Total revenues	$172,626	$172,626	$172,626	$172,626
Expenses:				
All except depreciation	$159,827	$159,827	$159,827	$159,827
Depreciation	6,405	6,405	6,405	0
Total expenses	$166,232	$166,232	$166,232	$159,827
Taxable income	$ 6,394	$ 6,394	$ 6,394	$ 12,799
Taxes	0	1,279	1,918	3,840
Net income	$ 6,394	$ 5,115	$ 4,476	$ 8,959
Estimated cash flow (NI + depreciation)	$ 12,799	$ 11,520	$ 10,881	$ 8,959

Note: Total revenues = Net operating revenues + Total nonoperating income. NI = net income.

are $1,918,200. Thus, the depreciation expense has saved the business $3,839,700 − $1,918,200 = $1,921,500, which is the amount of the depreciation shield calculated above. Also, note that the cash flow is higher by the same amount, so the depreciation expense, which reduces taxes but does not impact cash flow, has increased cash flow by the amount of the tax reduction (the depreciation shield).

Key Equation: Depreciation Shield

Because depreciation expense reduces taxes, it is said to shield a for-profit business from taxes; therefore, the amount of taxes saved is called the depreciation shield. If a business has $500,000 in depreciation expense and pays taxes at a 30 percent rate, its depreciation shield is $150,000:

$$\text{Depreciation shield} = T \times \text{Depreciation expense} = 0.30 \times \$500,000$$
$$= \$150,000.$$

1. Are there appreciable differences in the income statements of not-for-profit businesses and investor-owned businesses?
2. What are the impacts of taxes and depreciation on net income and cash flow?
3. What is the depreciation shield?

Statement of Changes in Equity

As discussed in a previous section, all or some portion of a business's net income will be retained in the business. The **statement of changes in equity**, also called the *statement of changes in net assets*, is a financial statement that indicates how much of an organization's net income will be retained in the business and hence increase the amount of equity shown on the balance sheet. As Sunnyvale Clinic did in exhibit 3.1, not-for-profit organizations often will combine the income statement and the statement of changes in equity into a single statement called the *statement of operations and changes in net assets*.

> **statement of changes in equity**
> A financial statement that reports how much of a business's income statement earnings flows to the balance sheet equity account.

Exhibit 3.4 contains Sunnyvale's statements of changes in equity. Because we have simplified the financial statements presented in this book to facilitate understanding, the statements shown here are very basic. In most situations, the statements shown in exhibit 3.4 would contain many more lines reflecting transactions that affect equity (net assets) on the balance sheet.

Exhibit 3.4 tells us that in 2020, the entire amount of Sunnyvale's net income of $6,394,000 was retained in the business. Therefore, the equity (net assets) without donor restrictions of the clinic increased from $39,368,000 at the beginning of the year to $45,762,000 at the end of the year. Exhibit 3.4 also tells us that in 2020, Sunnyvale Clinic received donor-restricted contributions in the amount of $1,466,000. Thus, the equity (net assets) with donor restrictions increased from $6,840,000 at the beginning of the year to $8,306,000 at the end of the year. Total net assets increased from $46,208,000 at the beginning of the year to $54,068,000 at the end of the year. This can be confirmed by the amount of equity shown for 2020 in exhibit 4.1 and exhibit 4.5 (see chapter 4).

To illustrate statements of changes in equity in a for-profit organization, consider exhibit 3.5, which presents information for North River Healthcare. Now, some portion of the earnings (net income) of the business is paid out as dividends to owners. In 2020, the business had a net income

EXHIBIT 3.4
Sunnyvale
Clinic:
Statements
of Changes
in Equity
(Net Assets),
Years Ended
December 31,
2020 and 2019
(in thousands)

	2020	2019
Changes in net assets without donor restrictions:		
Excess of revenues over expenses	$ 6,394	$ 8,206
Increase in net assets without donor restrictions	$ 6,394	$ 8,206
Changes in net assets with donor restrictions:		
Gifts and bequests	$ 1,466	$ 0
Increase in net assets with donor restrictions	$ 1,466	$ 0
Increase in net assets	$ 7,860	$ 8,206
Net assets at beginning of year	$46,208	$38,002
Net assets at end of year	$54,068	$46,208

of $7,860,000, but $2,000,000 of this amount was paid to owners. Thus, only $7,860,000 – $2,000,000 = $5,860,000 is available to increase the balance sheet equity account. Note that, in total, the 2020 ending equity was $54,068,000 – $50,168,000 = $3,900,000 greater in exhibit 3.4 than in exhibit 3.5. The difference is caused by the fact that North River paid out $3,900,000 total in dividends over 2019 and 2020; hence, the amount retained in the business was reduced by a like amount. (For simplicity, we did not reduce the net income in exhibit 3.5 by the amount of taxes that would be paid if North River were a for-profit corporation.)

SELF-TEST
QUESTIONS

1. What is the purpose of the statement of changes in equity (net assets)?
2. How does the statement differ between not-for-profit and for-profit entities?

A Look Ahead: Using Income Statement Data in Financial Statement Analysis

Chapter 17 discusses in detail the techniques used to analyze financial statements to gain insights into a business's financial condition. One of the most

	2020	2019
Net income	$ 7,860	$ 8,206
Less: Dividends paid	2,000	1,900
Increase in equity	$ 5,860	$ 6,306
Equity, beginning of year	44,308	38,002
Equity, end of year	$50,168	$44,308

EXHIBIT 3.5
North River Healthcare: Statements of Changes in Equity, Years Ended December 31, 2020 and 2019 (in thousands)

important techniques used in financial condition analysis is *financial ratio analysis*. In financial ratio analysis, values found on the financial statements are combined to form ratios that have economic meaning and help managers and investors interpret the numbers.

To illustrate financial ratio analysis, **total profit margin**, a ratio that is often called *total margin*, is defined as net income divided by total revenues, which includes nonoperating income. For Sunnyvale Clinic, the total margin for 2020 was $6,394,000 ÷ ($168,513,000 + $4,113,000) = $6,394,000 ÷ $172,626,000 = 0.037 = 3.7%. The ratio tells us that each dollar of revenues (including nonoperating income) generated by the clinic produced 3.7 cents of profit (i.e., net income). Thus, each dollar of revenues and income required 96.3 cents of expenses. The total margin is a measure of expense control; for a given amount of revenues and income, the higher the net income, and hence total margin, the lower the expenses. If the total margin for other similar clinics were known, judgments about how well Sunnyvale is doing in the area of expense control, relative to its peers, could be made.

Sunnyvale's total margin for 2019 was $8,206,000 ÷ $144,800,000 = 0.057 = 5.7%, meaning that the clinic's total margin slipped from 2019 to 2020. This finding should alert managers to carefully examine the increase in expenses in 2020. In effect, Sunnyvale's expenses increased faster than its revenues plus investment income, which resulted in falling profitability as measured by total margin. If this trend continues, it will not take long for the clinic to be operating in the red (i.e., losing money).

Finally, let's take a quick look at another financial ratio, **operating margin**, which is defined as operating income divided by net operating revenues. For 2020, Sunnyvale's operating margin was $2,281,000 ÷ $168,513,000 = 0.014 = 1.4%. Thus, each dollar of operating revenues generated by the clinic produced 1.4 cents of profit (operating income). Because operating margin does not include noncore revenues (contributions

total (profit) margin
Net income divided by total revenues; it measures the amount of total profit per dollar of total revenues.

operating margin
Operating income divided by net operating revenues; it measures the amount of operating profit per dollar of operating revenues and focuses on the core activities of a business.

and investment income), it is lower than Sunnyvale's total margin, which does include such income.

A complete discussion of financial ratio analysis can be found in chapter 17. The discussion here, along with a brief discussion in chapter 4, is intended to give readers a preview of how financial statement data can be used to make judgments about a business's financial condition.

SELF-TEST QUESTIONS

1. Explain how ratio analysis can be used to help interpret income statement data.
2. What is the total profit margin, and what does it measure?

Key Concepts

Financial accounting information is the result of a process of identifying, measuring, recording, and communicating the economic events and status of an organization to interested parties. This information is summarized and presented in four primary financial statements: the income statement, the statement of changes in equity, the balance sheet, and the statement of cash flows. The key concepts of this chapter are as follows:

- The five types of accounts used in financial accounting are assets, liabilities, equity, revenues, and expenses.
- The predominant *users of financial accounting information* are parties who have a direct financial interest in the economic status of a business—primarily its managers and investors.
- *Generally accepted accounting principles (GAAP)* establish the standards for financial accounting measurement and reporting. These principles have been sanctioned by the *Securities and Exchange Commission (SEC)*, developed by the *Financial Accounting Standards Board (FASB)*, and refined by the *American Institute of Certified Public Accountants (AICPA)* and other organizations.
- The *goal* of financial accounting is to provide information about organizations that is useful to present and future investors

(continued)

(continued from previous page)

and other users in making rational financial and investment decisions.

- The preparation and presentation of financial accounting data are based on the following concepts: (1) *relevance*, (2) *faithful representation*, (3) *accounting entity*, (4) *going concern*, (5) *accounting period*, (6) *monetary unit*, (7) *historical cost*, (8) *revenue recognition*, (9) *expense matching*, (10) *full disclosure*, (11) *materiality*, and (12) *cost–benefit*.

- Under *cash accounting*, economic events are recognized when the cash transaction occurs. Under *accrual accounting*, economic events are recognized when the obligation to make payment occurs. GAAP requires that businesses use accrual accounting because it provides a better picture of a business's true financial status.

- The *income statement* reports on an organization's operations over a period of time. Its basic structure consists of *revenues*, *expenses*, and one or more *profit* measures.

- *Operating revenues* are monies collected or expected to be collected that are related to the core business, namely, patient services. Operating revenues are broken down into categories such as *net patient service revenue*, *premium revenue*, and *other revenue*.

- *Expenses* are the economic costs associated with the provision of services.

- *Nonoperating income* reports earnings that are unrelated to patient services, typically unrestricted contributions and investment income.

- *Operating income* focuses on the profitability of a provider's core operations (patient services), while *net income* represents the total economic profitability of a business as defined by GAAP.

- Because the income statement is constructed using accrual accounting, net income does not represent the actual amount of cash that has been earned or lost during the reporting period. To estimate *cash flow*, noncash expenses (primarily depreciation) must be added back to net income.

(continued)

(continued from previous page)

- The income statements of investor-owned and not-for-profit businesses tend to look very much alike. However, the income statements of health services organizations in different lines of business can vary. The good news is that all income statements have essentially the same financial content.
- For-profit (taxable) entities must include taxes as an income statement expense item. Because depreciation expense reduces operating (taxable) income, and hence a business's tax liability, it creates a *depreciation shield* equal to the tax rate times the depreciation expense. However, as a noncash expense, depreciation itself does not reduce cash flow, so the greater the amount of depreciation (and therefore, the depreciation shield), the greater the cash flow.
- The *statement of changes in equity* indicates how much of the total profitability (net income) is retained for use by the reporting organization.
- *Financial ratio analysis*, which combines values that are found in the financial statements, helps managers and investors interpret the data with the goal of making judgments about the financial condition of the business.

In this chapter, we focused on financial accounting basics, the income statement, and the statement of changes in equity. In chapter 4, the discussion of financial accounting continues with the remaining two statements: the balance sheet and statement of cash flows. The chapter 4 supplement discusses the methods used in recording financial accounting information.

Questions

3.1. a. What is a stakeholder?
   b. Which stakeholders are most interested in the financial condition of a healthcare provider?
   c. What is the goal of financial accounting?

3.2. a. What are generally accepted accounting principles (GAAP)?

    b. What is the purpose of GAAP?

    c. What organizations are involved in establishing GAAP?

3.3. Briefly describe the following concepts as they apply to the preparation of financial statements:

    a. Relevance

    b. Faithful representation

    c. Accounting entity

    d. Going concern

    e. Accounting period

    f. Monetary unit

    g. Historical cost

    h. Revenue recognition

    i. Expense matching

    j. Full disclosure

    k. Materiality

    l. Cost–benefit

3.4. Explain the difference between cash accounting and accrual accounting. Be sure to include a discussion of the revenue recognition and matching principles.

3.5. Briefly describe the format of the income statement.

3.6. a. What is the difference between gross revenues and net revenues? (Hint: Think about contractual allowances/discounts, financial assistance/charity care, and bad debt/implicit price concessions.)

    b. What is the difference between patient service revenue and other revenue?

3.7. a. What is meant by the term *expense*?

    b. What is depreciation expense, and what is its purpose?

    c. What are some other categories of expenses?

3.8. a. What is the difference between operating income and net income?

    b. Why is net income called the "bottom line"?

    c. What is the difference between net income and cash flow?

    d. Is financial condition more closely related to net income or to cash flow?

3.9. a. What is the purpose of the statement of changes in equity?

    b. What is its basic format?

Problems

3.1. Entries for the Warren Clinic's 2020 income statement are listed below in alphabetical order. Reorder the data in the proper format.

Depreciation expense	$ 90,000
General/administrative expenses	70,000
Interest expense	20,000
Investment income	40,000
Net income	30,000
Net operating income (loss)	(10,000)
Net operating revenues	410,000
Net patient service revenue	400,000
Other revenue	10,000
Purchased services	90,000
Salaries and benefits	150,000
Total expenses	420,000

3.2. Consider the following income statement:

BestCare HMO Statement of Operations Year Ended June 30, 2020 (in thousands)	
Revenue:	
Healthcare premiums	$26,682
Fees and other revenue	1,689
Net investment income	242
Total revenues	$28,613
Benefits and expenses:	
Healthcare costs	$15,154
Operating expenses:	
General and administrative expenses	7,874
Selling expenses	3,963
Interest expense	385
Total benefits and expenses	$27,376
Net income	$ 1,237

a. How does this income statement differ from the one presented in exhibit 3.1?

b. What is BestCare's total profit margin? How can it be interpreted?

3.3. Consider this income statement:

Green Valley Nursing Home, Inc.	
Statement of Income	
Year Ended December 31, 2020	
Revenue:	
Net resident services revenue	$3,053,258
Other revenue	106,146
Total revenues	$3,159,404
Expenses:	
Salaries and benefits	$1,515,438
Medical supplies and drugs	966,781
Insurance and other	296,357
Depreciation	85,000
Interest	206,780
Total expenses	$3,070,356
Operating income	$ 89,048
Income tax expense	31,167
Net income	$ 57,881

a. How does this income statement differ from the ones presented in exhibit 3.1 and problem 3.2?

b. Why does Green Valley show an income tax expense, while the other two income statements do not?

c. What is Green Valley's total profit margin? How does this value compare with the values for Sunnyvale Clinic and BestCare?

d. The before-tax profit margin for Green Valley is operating income divided by total revenues. Calculate Green Valley's before-tax profit margin. Why might this be a better measure of expense control when comparing an investor-owned business with a not-for-profit business?

3.4. Great Forks Hospital reported net income for 2020 of $2.4 million on total revenues of $30 million. Depreciation expense totaled $1 million.

a. What were total expenses for 2020?

      b. What were total cash expenses for 2020? (Hint: Assume that all expenses, except depreciation, were cash expenses.)

      c. What was the hospital's 2020 cash flow?

3.5. Brandywine Homecare, a not-for-profit business, had revenues of $12 million in 2020. Expenses other than depreciation totaled 75 percent of revenues, and depreciation expense was $1.5 million. All revenues were collected in cash during the year, and all expenses other than depreciation were paid in cash.

      a. Construct Brandywine's 2020 income statement.

      b. What were Brandywine's net income, total profit margin, and cash flow?

      c. Now, suppose the company changed its depreciation calculation procedures (still within GAAP) such that its depreciation expense doubled. How would this change affect Brandywine's net income, total profit margin, and cash flow?

      d. Suppose the change had halved, rather than doubled, the firm's depreciation expense. Now, what would be the impact on net income, total profit margin, and cash flow?

3.6. Assume that Mainline Homecare, a for-profit corporation, had exactly the same situation as reported in problem 3.5. However, Mainline must pay taxes at a rate of 30 percent of pretax (operating) income. Assuming that the same revenues and expenses reported for financial accounting purposes would be reported for tax purposes, redo problem 3.5 for Mainline.

3.7. Consider Southeast Home Care, a for-profit business. In 2020, its net income was $1,500,000 and it distributed $500,000 to owners in the form of dividends. Its beginning-of-year equity balance was $12,000,000. Use this information to construct the business's statement of changes in equity. What is the ending 2020 value of the business's equity account?

3.8. Bright Horizons Skilled Nursing Facility, an investor-owned company, constructed a new building to replace its outdated facility. The new building was completed on January 1, 2020, and Bright Horizons began recording depreciation immediately. The total cost of the new facility was $18,000,000, comprising $10 million in construction costs and $8 million for the land. Bright Horizons estimated that the new facility would have a useful life of 20 years. The salvage value of the building at the end of its useful life was estimated to be $1,500,000.

      a. Using the straight-line method of depreciation, calculate annual depreciation expense on the new facility.

b. Assuming a 30 percent income tax rate, how much did Bright Horizons save in income taxes for the year ended December 31, 2020, as a result of the depreciation recorded on the new facility (i.e., what was the depreciation shield)?

c. Does the depreciation shield result in cash or noncash savings for Bright Horizons? Explain.

3.9. Integrated Physicians & Associates, an investor-owned company, had the following account balances at the end of 2020:

Gross patient service revenue (total charges)	$975,000
Contractual discounts and allowances to third-party payers	250,000
Charges for charity (indigent) care	100,000
Estimated bad debts (implicit price concessions)	50,000

a. Calculate the net patient service revenue amount that would be shown on Integrated Physicians & Associates' income statement for the year ended December 31, 2020.

b. Suppose the 2020 contractual discounts and allowances balance reported above is understated by $50,000. In other words, the correct balance should be $300,000. Assuming a 30 percent income tax rate, what would be the effect of the misstatement on Integrated Physicians & Associates' 2020 reported:

i. Net patient service revenue?

ii. Total expenses, including income tax expense?

iii. Net income?

For each item, indicate whether the balance is overstated, understated, or not affected by the misstatement. If overstated or understated, indicate by how much.

Notes

1. Reinstein, A., and N. T. Churyk. 2012. "FASB's ASU 2011-7 Changes Financial Statement Reporting Requirements." *Healthcare Financial Management* 66 (2): 40–42.

2. Freudenheim, M. 2004. "HealthSouth Audit Finds as Much as $4.6 Billion in Fraud." *New York Times.* Published January 21. www.nytimes.com/2004/01/21/business/healthsouth-audit-finds-as-much-as-4.6-billion-in-fraud.html.

3. Giniat, E., and J. Saporito. 2007. "Sarbanes-Oxley: Impetus for Enterprise Risk Management." *Healthcare Financial Management* 61 (8): 65–70.

4. Financial Accounting Standards Board. 2018. "Statement of Financial Accounting Concepts No. 8 As Amended." Published August. www .fasb.org/jsp/FASB/Document_C/DocumentPage?cid=11761711113 98&acceptedDisclaimer=true.

5. Financial Accounting Standards Board. 2014. "Revenue from Contracts with Customers (Topic 606)." Accounting Standards Update 2014-09. Published May 28. www.fasb.org/jsp/FASB /FASBContent_C/CompletedProjectPage&cid=1175805486538.

6. Holmes, J. R., and D. Felsenthal. 2009. "Depreciating and Stating the Value of Hospital Buildings: What You Need to Know." *Healthcare Financial Management* 63 (10): 88–92.

Resources

American Institute of Certified Public Accountants (AICPA). 2014. *Audit and Accounting Guide for Healthcare Entities.* New York: AICPA.

Duis, T. E. 1994. "Unravelling the Confusion Caused by GASB, FASB Accounting Rules." *Healthcare Financial Management* 48 (11): 66–69.

———. 1993. "The Need for Consistency in Healthcare Reporting." *Healthcare Financial Management* 47 (7): 40–44.

Healthcare Financial Management Association. 2019. "Revenue Recognition, Including Implicit Price Concession and Bad Debt Considerations, for Healthcare Organizations: Accounting Issues and Trends." Principles and Practices Board Issue Analysis. Published January. www.hfma.org/content/dam/hfma/ Documents/PDFs/Revenue%20Recognition%20Including%20Implicit%20 Price%20Concession%20and%20Bad%20Debt%20Considerations.pdf.

Heuer, C., and M. K. Travers. 2010. "FASB Issues New Accounting Standards for Business Combinations." *Healthcare Financial Management* 64 (6): 40–43.

Maco, P. S., and S. J. Weinstein. 2000. "Accounting and Accountability: Observations on the AHERF Settlements." *Healthcare Financial Management* 54 (10): 41–46.

Peregrine, M. W., and J. R. Schwartz. 2002. "What CFOs Should Know—and Do—About Corporate Responsibility." *Healthcare Financial Management* 56 (12): 60–63.

4

THE BALANCE SHEET AND STATEMENT OF CASH FLOWS

Learning Objectives

After studying this chapter, readers will be able to

- Explain the purpose of the balance sheet.
- Describe the contents of the balance sheet and its interrelationships with the income statement and the statement of changes in equity.
- Explain the purpose of the statement of cash flows.
- Describe the contents of the statement of cash flows and how it differs from the income statement.
- Describe how a business's transactions affect its income statement and balance sheet (see the chapter 4 supplement).

Introduction

Although the income statement, which was covered in chapter 3, contains information about an organization's revenues, expenses, and income, it does not provide information about the resources needed to produce the income or how those resources were financed. Another financial statement, the balance sheet, contains information concerning an organization's assets and the financing used to acquire those assets.

In addition to recognizing the need to disclose resources and financing, accountants and managers increasingly are aware that income alone does not give a complete picture of an organization's financial condition. Although operating income and net income—which reflect an organization's long-run economic profitability as defined by generally accepted accounting principles (GAAP)—are important profitability measures, financial condition, especially in the short run, is also related to the actual flow of cash into and out of a business. The second financial statement discussed in this chapter, the statement of cash flows, focuses on this important determinant of financial condition.

Although understanding the composition of the financial statements is essential, it is also important that managers understand the relationships among the financial statements. Thus, emphasis is placed on the inter-relationships among the statements throughout the chapter. Finally, the chapter supplement contains a brief introduction to how actual business transactions work their way into an organization's financial statements. Our purpose here is to give readers a feel for how financial statements are actually created.

Balance Sheet Basics

balance sheet
A financial statement that lists a business's assets, liabilities, and equity (fund capital).

Whereas the income statement reports the results of operations *over a period of time*, the **balance sheet** presents a snapshot of the financial position of an organization *at a given point in time*. For this reason, the balance sheet is also called the *statement of financial position*. The balance sheet changes every day as a business increases or decreases its assets or changes the composition of its financing. The important point is that the balance sheet, unlike the income statement, reflects a business's financial position on a specific date; the data in it typically become invalid by the next day, even when both dates are in the same accounting period. Healthcare providers with seasonal demand, such as a walk-in clinic in Fort Lauderdale, Florida, have especially large changes in their balance sheets during the year. For such businesses, a balance sheet constructed in February can look quite different from one prepared in August. Also, businesses that are growing rapidly will have significant changes in their balance sheets over relatively short periods of time.

The balance sheet lists, as of the end of the reporting period, the resources of an organization and the claims against those resources. In other words, the balance sheet reports the assets of an organization and how those assets were financed. The balance sheet has the following basic structure:

Assets	Liabilities and Equity
Current assets	Current liabilities
Long-term assets	Long-term liabilities
	Equity
Total assets	Total liabilities and equity

The assets side (left side) of the balance sheet lists, in dollar terms, all the resources, or assets, owned by the organization. In general, assets are broken down into categories that distinguish short-lived (current) assets from long-lived assets. The liabilities and equity side (claims side or right side) lists the claims against these resources, again in dollar terms.

In essence, the right side reports the sources of financing (capital) used to acquire the assets listed on the left side. The sources of capital are divided into two broad categories: liabilities, which are claims that are fixed by contract, and equity, which is a residual claim that depends on asset values and the amount of liabilities. Like assets, liabilities are listed by maturity (short term versus long term).

Perhaps the most important characteristic of the balance sheet is simply that it must balance—that is, the left side must equal the right side. This relationship, which is called the *accounting identity* or *basic accounting equation*, is expressed in equation form as follows:

$$\text{Assets} = \text{Liabilities} + \text{Equity}.$$

Because liability claims are paid before equity claims if a healthcare organization is liquidated, liabilities are shown before equity both on the balance sheet and in the basic accounting equation.

Note that the accounting identity can be rearranged as follows:

$$\text{Equity} = \text{Assets} - \text{Liabilities}.$$

This format reinforces the concept that equity represents a residual claim against the total assets of the business and the fact that equity can be negative. If a business writes down (decreases) the value of its assets, perhaps due to obsolescence, its liabilities are unaffected because these amounts are still owed to creditors and others. If total assets are written down so much that their value drops below that of total liabilities, the equity reported on the balance sheet becomes a negative amount.

Exhibit 4.1 contains Sunnyvale's balance sheet, which follows the basic structure as previously explained. As the title of the exhibit indicates, the data are presented for the entire clinic. The balance sheet cannot provide much information, if any, about the subunits of an organization, such as departments or service lines. Rather, the balance sheet provides an overview of the economic position of the organization as a whole. As we discussed in chapter 3, for ease of understanding, the balance sheet presented here is simplified compared with most actual statements, but it contains all of the essential elements.

The time frame for the data in the balance sheet is also apparent in the title. The data are reported for 2020 and 2019 as of December 31. Whereas Sunnyvale's income statements indicate that the data are for the **year ended** on December 31, the balance sheets merely indicate a closing date. This minor difference in terminology reinforces the point that the income

EXHIBIT 4.1
Sunnyvale Clinic:
Balance Sheets,
December 31,
2020 and 2019
(in thousands)

Assets	2020	2019
Current Assets:		
Cash and cash equivalents	$ 12,102	$ 6,486
Short-term investments	10,000	5,000
Net patient accounts receivable	28,509	25,927
Inventories	3,695	2,302
Total current assets	$ 54,306	$ 39,715
Long-term investments	48,059	25,837
Net property and equipment	52,450	49,549
Total assets	$154,815	$115,101

Liabilities and Equity		
Current Liabilities:		
Notes payable	$ 4,334	$ 3,345
Accounts payable	5,022	6,933
Accrued expenses	6,069	5,037
Total current liabilities	$ 15,425	$ 15,315
Long-term debt	85,322	53,578
Total liabilities	$100,747	$68,893
Net assets (Equity)	54,068	46,208
Total liabilities and equity	$154,815	$115,101

statement reports operational results **over a period** of time, while the balance sheet reports financial position **at a single point** in time. Finally, the amounts reported on Sunnyvale's balance sheet, just as on its income statement, are expressed in thousands of dollars.

The format of the balance sheet emphasizes the basic accounting equation. For example, as of December 31, 2020, Sunnyvale had a total of $154,815,000 in assets that were financed by a total of $154,815,000 in liabilities and equity. Besides the obvious confirmation that the balance sheet balances, this statement indicates that Sunnyvale's total assets were valued, according to GAAP, at $154,815,000. Liabilities and equity represent claims against the assets of the business by various classes of creditors, other claim-ants with fixed claims, and "owners." Creditors and other claimants have first priority in claims for $100,747,000, and "owners" follow with a residual claim of $54,068,000. The right side of the balance sheet (liabilities and equity, which are in the bottom section of exhibit 4.1) reflects the manner in which Sunnyvale raised the capital needed to acquire its assets. Because the balance sheet must balance, each dollar on the asset (left) side must be matched by a dollar on the capital (right) side.

1. What is the purpose of the balance sheet?
2. What are the three major sections of the balance sheet?
3. What is the accounting identity, and what information does it provide?
4. What is the relationship between assets and financing (capital)?

Assets

Assets either possess or create economic value for the organization. Exhibit 4.1 contains three major categories of assets: current assets, long-term investments, and net property and equipment. The following sections describe each asset category in detail.

Current Assets

Current assets include cash and other assets that are expected to be converted into cash **within one accounting period**, which in this example is one year. For Sunnyvale, current assets total $54,306,000 at the end of 2020. Suppose the short-term investments on the books at that time were converted into cash as they matured; the receivables were collected; and the inventories were used, billed to patients, and collected, all at the values stated on the balance sheet. With all else the same, Sunnyvale would have $54,306,000 in cash at the end of 2021. Of course, all else will not be the same, so Sunnyvale's 2021 reported cash balance will undoubtedly be different from $54,306,000. Still, this exercise reinforces the concept behind the current asset category: the assumption that these assets will be converted into cash during the next accounting period.

current asset An asset that is expected to be converted into cash within one accounting period (often a year).

The conversion of current assets into cash is expected to provide all or part of the funds that will be needed to pay off the $15,425,000 in current liabilities outstanding at the end of 2020 as they become due in 2021. Thus, current assets are one element that contributes to the liquidity of the organization. (A business is *liquid* if it has the cash available to pay its bills as they become due.)

The difference between total current assets and total current liabilities is called **net working capital**. Thus, at the end of 2020, Sunnyvale had net working capital of $54,306,000 − $15,425,000 = $38,881,000. From a pure liquidity standpoint, the greater the net working capital, the better. However,

net working capital A liquidity measure equal to current assets minus current liabilities.

as we discuss in chapter 16, there are costs to carrying current assets, so health services organizations have to balance the need for liquidity against the associated costs of maintaining liquidity. Also, as we discuss in later chapters, there are other factors, such as expected cash inflows, that contribute to a business's overall liquidity.

Within Sunnyvale's current assets, there is $12,102,000 in *cash and cash equivalents*. Cash represents actual cash in hand plus money held in commercial checking accounts (demand deposits). Cash equivalents are short-term securities investments that are readily convertible into cash. In general, accountants interpret that to mean securities that have a maturity of three months or less. Note that cash and cash equivalents are carried on the same line of the balance sheet, so readers cannot determine the relative sizes of each type of asset, which confirms the fact that these are considered to be identical in nature.

In addition to cash and cash equivalents, there is $10,000,000 of *short-term investments* (sometimes called *marketable securities*), which represent cash that has been temporarily invested in highly liquid, low-risk securities such as money market mutual funds, US Treasury bills, or prime commercial paper having a maturity greater than 90 days but less than one year. (*Money market mutual funds* are mutual funds that invest in safe, short-term securities such as Treasury bills and commercial paper. *Treasury bills* are short-term debt instruments issued by the US government. *Commercial paper* is short-term debt issued by very large and financially strong corporations. All of these securities are relatively safe investments because there is virtually 100 percent assurance that the borrowers will repay the loans when they mature.)

Organizations hold cash equivalents and short-term investments because cash earns no interest and money held in commercial checking accounts earns very little interest. Thus, businesses should hold only enough cash and checking account balances to pay their recurring operating expenses—any funds on hand in excess of immediate needs should be invested in safe, short-term, highly liquid (but interest-bearing) securities. Additionally, short-term investments are built up periodically to meet projected nonoperating cash outlays such as tax payments, investments in property and equipment, and legal judgments. Even though short-term investments pay relatively low interest, any return is better than none, so such investments are preferable to cash holdings.

Short-term investments normally are reported on the balance sheet *at cost*, which is the amount initially paid for the securities. However, because of changing interest rates and other factors, these securities may actually be worth more or less than their purchase price. Still, because short-term investments have maturities of less than one year, it is rare for their market values to be substantially different from their costs.

Net patient accounts receivable, often called simply *receivables*, represents money owed to Sunnyvale for services that the clinic has already provided. As discussed in chapter 2 and reiterated in chapter 3, third-party payers make most payments for healthcare services, and those payments often take weeks or months to be billed, processed, and ultimately paid. Sunnyvale's patient accounts receivable amount of $28,509,000 at the end of 2020 is listed on the balance sheet *net* of explicit price concessions such as contractual allowances and charity care discounts, and implicit price concessions (formerly, primarily the provision for bad debt losses). Thus, the presentation on the balance sheet is consistent with the chapter 3 discussion concerning net patient service revenue.

> **net patient accounts receivable (receivables)**
> The amount of money billed for services provided but not yet collected.

The $28,509,000 net receivable amount's relationship to the income statement's net operating revenues of $168,513,000 for 2020 (see exhibit 3.1 in chapter 3) is as follows: A total of $168,513,000 was billed to patients and payers, and was expected to be collected, during 2020. This is a "net" number, as there is a higher amount of gross charges in Sunnyvale's managerial accounting system that reflects charges before deductions for contractual allowances, charity care, and nonpayment. The fact that $28,509,000 of this revenue remains to be collected suggests that the difference between $168,513,000 and $28,509,000, which totals $140,004,000, was collected during 2020. Where is this collected cash? It could be anywhere. Most of it went right out the door to pay operating expenses. Some of the collected cash may have been used to purchase assets (e.g., new equipment) and hence may be sitting in one of the other asset accounts on the balance sheet. If the clinic were to close its doors on the last day of 2020, its patient accounts receivable balance of $28,509,000 would fall to zero when the entire amount was eventually collected (except for any errors in the implicit price concessions forecast). However, if Sunnyvale continues as an ongoing enterprise, the receivables balance will never fall to zero. Although Sunnyvale's collections are lowering its receivables balance, new services are constantly being provided that create new billings, and hence new receivables, that are added to it.

The final current asset listed in exhibit 4.1 is *inventories*, which primarily reflects Sunnyvale's purchases of medical supplies. The value of supplies on hand at the end of 2020 was $3,695,000. The value of supplies used during 2020 was reflected in supplies expense on the income statement. As with the cash account, it is not in a business's best interest to hold excessive inventories. There is a certain level of supplies necessary to meet medical needs and to maintain a safety stock to guard against unexpected surges in use, but any inventories above this level create unnecessary costs.

Businesses that hold large amounts of inventories, such as medical supply companies, typically include a note to the financial statements that discusses the holdings in some detail. However, most healthcare providers hold relatively small levels of inventories, and hence extensive note information is not often provided. In fact, because of the materiality threshold discussed in chapter 3, some providers do not break out inventories as a separate item on their balance sheets but rather include the value of inventories in a catchall balance sheet account called *other current assets*.

It should be obvious that the primary purposes served by the current asset accounts are to support the operations of the organization and to provide liquidity. However, current assets do not generate high returns. For example, cash earns no or very little return, and cash equivalents and short-term investments generally earn relatively low returns. The receivables account does not earn interest income or generate new patient service revenue, and inventories represent dollar amounts invested in items sitting on shelves, which earn no return until those items are used and patients are billed for their use. Because of the low (or zero) return earned on current assets, businesses try to minimize these account values yet ensure that the levels on hand are sufficient to support operations and maintain liquidity. (Current asset management is covered in much greater detail in chapter 16.)

Note that the current assets section of the balance sheet is listed in order of liquidity, or nearness to cash. Cash and cash equivalents, as the most liquid assets, are listed first, while the least liquid of current assets—inventories—is listed last. Dollars invested in inventories will first move into patient accounts receivable as the patients are billed for the supplies used. Then, accounts receivable will be converted into cash when they are collected and, perhaps, shifted to securities if the cash is not needed to pay current bills.

The importance of converting nonearning current assets into short-term investments as quickly as possible, and hence converting zero-return assets into some-return assets, cannot be overemphasized. Under most reimbursement methods, providers first must build the current assets necessary to provide the services; they then must actually do the work; and finally, at some later time (often 45 days or more), they get paid. Providers that operate under capitation have a significant liquidity advantage compared with those that primarily receive fee-for-service revenue. Because capitated payments are received before the services are provided, organizations that are predominantly capitated will have much smaller accounts receivable balances and much larger cash and short-term investment balances than providers, such as Sunnyvale, that operate in a predominantly fee-for-service environment.

financial asset
A security, such as a stock or bond, that represents a claim on a business's cash flows. Financial assets are purchased with the expectation of receiving future payments.

Long-Term Investments

The second major asset category, after current assets, is *long-term investments*, which reports the amount the organization has invested in long-term (maturities that exceed one year) securities. This account represents investments in **financial assets** such as stocks and bonds, as opposed to investments in **real assets** such as buildings and magnetic resonance imaging machines, which are listed next on the balance sheet as net property and equipment. The $48,059,000 reported by Sunnyvale at the end of 2020 represents the amount the clinic has invested in stocks, bonds, and other securities that have a longer maturity than its short-term investments in the hope that they will provide higher returns.

real asset
A physical asset, such as a medical office building or a piece of diagnostic equipment, that has the potential to generate future cash inflows.

Long-term securities investments are reported on the balance sheet at *fair market value* (or just *fair value*), rather than initial cost. This is so that changes in market conditions over time will cause the value of the account to change, even if the securities held remain the same. Changes in market values of long-term investments result in unrealized gains or losses on the investments, which have additional financial statement implications that are beyond the scope of this book. A note to the financial statements usually will explain the details of the types of security investments held by the organization and the resulting gains and losses. The income earned on both short-term and long-term investments is reported on the income statement under nonoperating income. As discussed in chapter 3, Sunnyvale reported investment income of $3,870,000 for 2020.

The discussion of current assets emphasized that businesses try to minimize the amounts held, maintaining only the amounts necessary to support operations. One of the benefits of prudent current asset management is that more money can be moved into long-term investments, both financial and real, which are expected to generate greater returns than those provided by current assets. The ultimate rewards for minimizing an organization's current assets are the reduction in carrying costs (current assets cost money because each dollar in assets has to be matched by a dollar of financing) and the increased return expected from long-term investments.

Not-for-profit organizations typically carry large amounts of long-term securities investments, some funded from depreciation cash flow and hence often called *funded depreciation*. (As we discussed in chapter 3, depreciation is a noncash expense; hence, it creates cash flow in addition to the amount of net income.) Eventually, these funds will be used to purchase real assets that provide new or improved services to Sunnyvale's patients. In essence, the long-term investments account is a savings account that ultimately will be used to purchase new land, buildings, and equipment that either replaces worn-out or obsolete assets or adds to the asset base to accommodate volume growth or provide new services.

In contrast, investor-owned businesses usually do not build up such reserves. Any cash flow in excess of the amount needed for near-term reinvestment in the business is likely to be returned to the capital suppliers (creditors and stockholders), either by debt repurchases or, more typically, by dividends or stock repurchases. When additional capital is needed for long-term investment in property and equipment, an investor-owned business simply goes to the capital (bond and stock) markets and obtains additional debt or equity financing.

Net Property and Equipment

fixed assets
A business's long-term assets, such as land, buildings, and equipment; usually labeled *net property and equipment* on the balance sheet.

The third major asset category is *net property and equipment*, often called **fixed assets**. Fixed assets, compared with current assets and even compared with long-term securities investments, are highly illiquid and typically are used over long periods of time by the organization. Whereas current assets rise and fall spontaneously with the organization's level of operations, fixed assets, such as land, buildings, and equipment, are normally maintained at a level sufficient to handle peak patient demand.

The property and equipment value listed on the balance sheet represents the value of Sunnyvale's fixed assets net of depreciation, so the effects of "wear and tear" are incorporated. The calculation of net property and equipment is included in the notes to the financial statements. To illustrate, exhibit 4.2 contains Sunnyvale's calculation.

The fixed assets (land, buildings, and equipment) are first listed at *historical cost* (the purchase price). The total of such historical costs is labeled *gross property and equipment. Accumulated depreciation* represents the cumulative total dollars of depreciation that have been expensed on the income statement against the historical cost of the organization's fixed assets. Numerically, the amounts of depreciation expense reported on the income statement each year are totaled (accumulated) over time to create the accumulated depreciation account. The accumulated depreciation account is an example of a *contra-asset* account because it is a negative asset. The greater the value of this account, the smaller an organization's net property and equipment account. Contra accounts reduce the value of "parent" accounts; in this case, the parent account is gross property and equipment.

For Sunnyvale, the net balance of property and equipment is $52,450,000 at the end of 2020. The historical cost of these assets is $88,549,000. Some of the fixed assets were purchased in 2020, some in 2019, some in 2018, and some in prior years, but the total purchase price

EXHIBIT 4.2 Sunnyvale Clinic: Net Property and Equipment		2020	2019
	Property and equipment		
	Land	$ 2,954	$ 2,035
	Buildings and equipment	85,595	77,208
	Gross property and equipment	$88,549	$79,243
	Less: Accumulated depreciation	36,099	29,694
	Net property and equipment	$52,450	$49,549

of all the fixed assets being used by Sunnyvale on December 31, 2020, is $88,549,000. The accumulated depreciation on these assets through December 31, 2020, is $36,099,000, which accounts for that portion of the value of the assets that was "spent" in producing income. The difference, or net, of $52,450,000, which reflects the remaining **book value** of the clinic's property and equipment, is the amount reported on the balance sheet. The connection of the balance sheet net property and equipment account to the income statement is through depreciation expense. The accumulated depreciation of $36,099,000 reported in the notes at the end of 2020 is $6,405,000 greater than the 2019 amount of $29,694,000. The $6,405,000 is the 2020 depreciation expense reported on the income statement.

book value
The value of a business's assets, liabilities, and equity as reported on the balance sheet; in other words, the value in accordance with generally accepted accounting principles (GAAP).

Key Equation: Accumulated Depreciation

Accumulated depreciation at the end of an accounting period is determined by adding the current year's depreciation expense to the accumulated depreciation balance at the end of the previous accounting period. The calculation would be more complicated if property or equipment were sold or written off during the year, but that level of detail is beyond the scope of this book. To illustrate, Sunnyvale reported accumulated depreciation of $29,694,000 as of December 31, 2019. For the year ended December 31, 2020, Sunnyvale reported $6,405,000 of depreciation expense on its income statement. Thus, accumulated depreciation as of December 31, 2020, is $36,099,000 calculated as:

> Accumulated depreciation as of December 31, 2019
> + Depreciation expense for the year ended December 31, 2020
> = Accumulated depreciation as of December 31, 2020

or

> $29,694,000
> +   6,405,000
> = $36,099,000.

Depreciation, even though it typically does not reflect the true change in value of a fixed asset over time, at least ensures an orderly recognition of value loss. Occasionally, assets experience a sudden, unexpected loss of value. One example is when technological advancements make a piece of diagnostic equipment obsolete and hence worthless. When this occurs, the asset that has experienced the decline in value is *written off*, which means that its value on the balance sheet is reduced (perhaps to zero) and the amount of the reduction is taken as an expense on the income statement. Such adjustments, called *impairment of capital* by accountants, are routinely made to the plant and equipment accounts on the balance sheet (and to revenues and expenses on the income statement) when assets are sold or lose value. However, a discussion of these adjustments is beyond the scope of this book.

In closing our discussion of assets, note that many providers report a fourth asset category: *other assets*. This is really a catchall category of miscellaneous long-term assets, which may or may not be significant. Examples include fixed assets not used in the provision of healthcare services and funds that were used to support long-term debt sales that will be expensed over time.

SELF-TEST QUESTIONS

1. What are the three major categories of asset accounts?
2. What is the primary difference between current assets and the remainder of the asset section of the balance sheet?
3. Give some examples of current asset accounts.
4. What is the difference between gross property and equipment and net property and equipment?
5. How does accumulated depreciation relate to the income statement?

Liabilities

Liabilities and equity, which appear on the right side of the balance sheet, are shown in the lower section of exhibit 4.1. Together, they represent the *capital* (the money) that has been raised by an organization to acquire the assets shown on the left side. Again, by definition, total capital (the sum of liabilities and equity) must equal total assets. Another way of looking at this is that every dollar of assets on the left side of the balance sheet must be matched by a dollar of liabilities or equity on the right side.

Liabilities represent claims against the assets of an organization that are fixed by contract. Some of the liability claims are made by workers for unpaid wages and salaries, some are made by tax authorities for unpaid taxes, and some are made by vendors that grant credit when supplies are purchased. Even not-for-profit organizations, which do not pay income taxes, have some tax liabilities—typically, unpaid payroll and withholding taxes on their employees. Usually, the largest liability claims are made by *creditors* (lenders) that have made loans (supplied debt capital) to the business.

Most creditors' claims are *unsecured*, meaning that they are not tied to specific assets pledged as collateral for the loan. In the event of **default** by the borrower—nonpayment of interest or principal—creditors have the right to force the business into *bankruptcy*, with *liquidation* as a possible consequence. If the assets of the business are sold (liquidated), bankruptcy law requires that any proceeds be used first to satisfy liability claims before

default
When a borrower fails to make a promised debt payment; technical default occurs when the borrower fails to meet one of the restrictions in the loan agreement but is still making the required payments.

any funds can be paid to owners or, in the case of not-for-profits, used for charitable purposes. Furthermore, the dollar value of each liability claim is fixed by the amount shown on the balance sheet, while the owners, including the community at large for not-for-profit organizations, have a claim to the residual proceeds of the liquidation rather than to a fixed amount. Finally, secured creditors have first right to the sale proceeds of assets pledged as collateral for the loan.

Like assets, the balance sheet presentation of liabilities follows a logical format. Current liabilities, which are those liabilities that come due (must be paid) within one accounting period (one year in this example), are listed first. Long-term debt, distinguished from short-term debt by having maturities greater than one accounting period, is listed second. As shown in exhibit 4.1, Sunnyvale had total liabilities at the end of 2020 of $100,747,000, which consisted of two parts: total current liabilities of $15,425,000 and long-term debt of $85,322,000. The following sections describe each liability account in detail.

Current Liabilities

Current liabilities include liabilities that must be paid within one accounting period. Many healthcare businesses use short-term debt—obligations that have a maturity of less than one accounting period—to finance seasonal or cyclical working capital (current asset) needs. For

> ## For Your Consideration
> ### Should Governments Report Like Businesses?
>
> Historically, states and cities used cash accounting methods to report infrastructure assets such as roads, bridges, and water and sewer facilities. Thus, the cost of an infrastructure investment was reported as an expense on the income statement when it occurred, but the value of the physical asset did not appear on the balance sheet. In other words, the value of all infrastructure assets was off the books. The rationale for this treatment is that infrastructure assets are, for the most part, immovable and of value only to the government unit (and its residents). Because infrastructure assets cannot be sold, there is no "value" to be reported on the balance sheet.
>
> In actuality, of course, physical infrastructure assets such as roads and bridges generally continue to have value, or usefulness, long after government units have incurred the cost of construction. And, just as business assets depreciate in value, the value of infrastructure assets also declines over time. Thus, in 2001, the Governmental Accounting Standards Board mandated that states and cities treat infrastructure assets just like businesses do—record them on the balance sheet at initial cost and depreciate their value over time. The idea is that the new treatment would improve financial reporting, enhance awareness of fiscal issues facing government units, and emphasize the importance of maintaining infrastructure assets.
>
> What do you think? Should government entities have been required to report financial status in the same way as businesses? Will the change in how infrastructure assets are treated cause states and cities to act differently?

example, in preparation for the busy winter season, the Fort Lauderdale walk-in clinic builds up its inventories of medical supplies, but when the season is over, supplies fall back to a lower off-season level. This temporary increase in current assets is typically funded by a bank loan of some type. When listed on the balance sheet, short-term debt is called *notes payable*. We see that Sunnyvale had $4,334,000 of short-term debt outstanding at the end of 2020.

Accounts payable, as well as accrued expenses, represent payment obligations incurred as of the balance sheet date that have not yet been paid. In particular, accounts payable represent amounts due to vendors for supplies purchases. Often, suppliers offer their customers **credit terms**, which allow payment sometime after the purchase is made. For example, one of Sunnyvale's suppliers offers credit terms of 2/10, net 30, which means that if Sunnyvale pays the invoice in ten days, it will receive a 2 percent discount off the list price; otherwise, the total amount of the invoice is due in 30 days. In effect, by allowing Sunnyvale to pay either 10 or 30 days after the supplies have been received, the supplier is acting as a creditor, and the credit being offered is called **trade credit**. The balance sheet tells us that suppliers, at the end of 2020, had extended Sunnyvale $5,022,000 of such credit.

credit terms
The statement of terms that extends credit to a buyer.

trade credit
The credit offered to businesses by suppliers (vendors) when credit terms are offered.

Wages and benefits due to employees resulting from work performed at the end of the accounting period, interest due on debt financing, utilities expenses not yet paid, taxes due to government authorities, and similar items are included on the balance sheet as **accrued expenses**, or just *accruals*. Such expenses occur because the business has incurred the obligation to pay for services received but has not made payment before the financial accounting period ends (i.e., the books are closed).

accrued expenses
A business liability that stems from the fact that some obligations, such as wages and taxes, are not paid immediately after the obligations are created.

Sunnyvale's employees can help illustrate the logic behind accruals. Sunnyvale's staff earns its wages and benefits on a daily basis as the work is performed. However, the clinic pays its workers every two weeks. Therefore, other than on paydays (assuming no lag in payment), the clinic owes its staff some amount of salaries for work performed. Whenever the obligation to pay wages extends into the next accounting period, an accrual is created on the balance sheet. Sunnyvale reported $6,069,000 in accruals for 2020, which, when added to the other current liabilities, totals $15,425,000.

Healthcare in Practice

Leasing and Financial Statements

Under previous accounting rules (GAAP), leases were reported on a lessee's balance sheets in two ways. For long-term (capital) leases, the leased property was reported as an asset, and the present value of lease payments was reported as a liability. But for short-term (operating) leases, the leased property did not appear on the balance sheet at all. Rather, operating lease obligations were reported in the notes to the financial statements. Because short-term leases were not shown directly on the balance sheet, such leases were

(continued)

Long-Term Debt

The *long-term debt* section of the balance sheet represents debt financing to the organization with maturities of more than one accounting period. In the Sunnyvale example, repayment is not required during the coming year. The long-term debt section lists any debt owed to banks and other creditors (e.g., bondholders) as well as obligations under certain types of lease arrangements. Detailed information relative to the specific characteristics of the long-term debt is disclosed in the notes to the financial statements.

To understand how debt financing is handled on the financial statements, it is useful to briefly discuss the mechanics of a loan. Assume that Sunnyvale takes out a $300,000 bank loan with a maturity (term) of three years. For simplicity, assume that the loan agreement requires payments to the bank as shown in exhibit 4.3.

When the loan is first obtained, $300,000 will be added to the long-term debt account and appear on the balance sheet. At the end of the first year, Sunny-vale will pay the bank a total of $130,000, consisting of $30,000 interest on the loan and $100,000 repayment on the *principal* portion of the loan. The $30,000 interest expense, which is paid to the bank for the use of its money, appears as an expense on the income statement. The $100,000 principal repayment, on the other hand, is not an expense item; rather, it reduces the

(continued from previous page)

called *off-balance-sheet financing*. Note, however, that all lease payments were listed as expenses on the income statement, regardless of length.

These rules, which had been in effect since 1977, were replaced by new standards that took effect on January 1, 2019. Although a complete discussion of the old and new rules is beyond the scope of this text, we note here that the most important change is that leases are no longer classified by accountants as operating or capital. Instead, almost all leases are accounted for in the same way on the balance sheet—there is no difference between short-term and long-term leases. All leased property is listed on the asset side as *right-to-use assets* and on the liability side as *lease liabilities*. The ultimate effect of the proposed rule is to eliminate operating leases as a source of off-balance-sheet financing.

What do you think about the rule change? Do analysts find it easier to perform financial statement analyses? Do you think that the new rules will reduce the amount of leasing that currently takes place?

$300,000 carried in the long-term debt account on the balance sheet. In the second year, the loan will be treated in a similar way: $20,000 in interest will appear as an expense on the income statement, and the loan amount on the balance sheet will be reduced by $100,000. (The features of long-term debt are discussed in detail in chapter 11.)

In this example, as with many sources of long-term debt financing, some portion of the borrowed amount (the principal) must be repaid in each year. In addition, some long-term debt that was issued in the past may mature (come due) in any given year. The portion of long-term debt that

	Year 1	Year 2	Year 3
Loan Repayment Schedule:			
Interest on loan	$ 30,000	$ 20,000	$ 10,000
Principal repayment	100,000	100,000	100,000
Total payment	$130,000	$120,000	$ 110,000

EXHIBIT 4.3
Sunnyvale Clinic: Bank Loan with Three-Year Maturity

must be paid in the coming year (accounting period) is recorded on the balance sheet as a **current** liability titled *current portion of long-term debt*. Sunnyvale had no long-term debt payments due in either 2020 or 2019, but if it did, they would appear on the first line of the current liabilities section as current portion of long-term debt.

Liabilities Summary

Sunnyvale had *total liabilities*, consisting of current liabilities and long-term debt, of $100,747,000 at the end of 2020. As we discuss in the next section, Sunnyvale reported $54,068,000 in net assets (equity), for total capital (which must equal total assets) of $154,815,000. Thus, based on the values recorded on the balance sheet, or *book values*, Sunnyvale uses much more debt financing than equity financing. The choice between debt and equity financing is discussed in chapter 13, while chapter 17 includes coverage of alternative ways to measure the amount of debt financing used and its effect on a business's financial condition.

SELF-TEST QUESTIONS

1. What are liabilities?
2. What are some of the accounts that would be classified as current liabilities?
3. Briefly describe accruals and provide an example.
4. What is the difference between notes payable and long-term debt?
5. What is the difference between long-term debt and current portion of long-term debt?

Net Assets (Equity)

net assets
The dollar value, according to GAAP, of a business's assets after subtracting the business's liabilities; in not-for-profit businesses, the term often is used on the balance sheet in place of *equity*.

On the balance sheet of a not-for-profit organization, the ownership claim on the organization's assets is called **net assets** rather than equity. As the term *net* implies, net assets represent the dollar value of assets remaining after subtracting a business's liabilities. However, as discussed in chapter 1, there are numerous forms of ownership for businesses in the health services sector. This variation in ownership results in differences in classifications and terminology used for the equity portion of the balance sheet. For example, depending on the type of business organization, the equity section of the balance sheet may be called *stockholders' equity, owner's net worth, net worth, proprietor's worth, partners' worth,* or something else.

To keep things manageable in this book, the term *equity* typically is used, but the terms all indicate the same thing: the amount of total assets financed by nonliability capital, or total assets minus total liabilities. To determine what belongs to the owners, whether explicitly recognized in for-profit businesses or implied in not-for-profit organizations, fixed claims (liabilities) are subtracted from the book value of the business's assets. The remainder, the net assets (equity), represents the residual value of the assets of the organization.

The equity section of the balance sheet is extremely important because it, more than anything else in the financial statements, reflects the ownership status of the organization. Because exhibit 4.1 lists the equity as *net assets*, it is obvious that Sunnyvale is a not-for-profit corporation. In addition, the net assets are classified based on whether or not their use has been restricted by donors. Some of Sunnyvale's equity capital reported on the balance sheet came from charitable contributions. Fund accounting is discussed in more detail later in this chapter. The vast majority of Sunnyvale's equity capital was obtained by reinvesting earnings within the business and therefore does not have donor restrictions. As discussed in chapter 3, for a not-for-profit organization such as Sunnyvale, **all earnings must be reinvested in the business**.

Sunnyvale's equity increased by $54,068,000 – $46,208,000 = $7,860,000 from 2019 to 2020. Net assets without donor restrictions increased by $45,762,000 – $39,368,000 = $6,394,000, which is the same amount that Sunnyvale reported as net income for 2020. It is important to recognize that this connection between the bottom line of the income statement and the equity section of the balance sheet is a mathematical necessity. In the case of not-for-profit businesses, there is simply nowhere else for those earnings to go. This highlights another connection between the balance sheet and the income statement: In practice, organizations often record other non-income-statement activities that either increase or decrease the amount that flows to the balance sheet equity account. For example, Sunnyvale Clinic reported $1,466,000 in donor-restricted contributions in 2020, which, in addition to net income of $6,394,000, contributed to the $7,860,000 increase in total net assets from 2019 to 2020. Since donor-restricted contributions are not available for immediate use, they are not recorded as revenue or nonoperating income on the income statement. Rather, the $1,466,000 is shown on the statement of changes in net assets as an increase in net assets with donor restrictions. There are many more adjustments to net assets that are beyond the scope of this book, but would be shown on the statement of changes in equity discussed in chapter 3.

Sunnyvale's balance sheet shows an equal amount of assets and liabilities and equity (it balances) because the increase in equity of $7,860,000 was matched by the same increase in assets, along with asset increases that resulted from other financing. The asset increases might be in cash, receivables, supplies, or some other account. The key point is that the equity balance is **not** a store of cash. As Sunnyvale earned profits over the years that increased the equity account, these funds were invested in supplies, property and equipment, and other assets to provide future services that would likely generate even larger profits in the future. Sunnyvale's total assets grew by $154,815,000 – $115,101,000 = $39,714,000 in 2020, which was supported by an increase in total liabilities of $100,747,000 – $68,893,000 = $31,854,000 and an increase in equity of $54,068,000 – $46,208,000 = $7,860,000.

The net assets type of equity section shown in exhibit 4.1 is typical of not-for-profit organizations such as community or religious hospitals. However, a relatively rare form of not-for-profit organization can sell stock privately, and such organizations may show a limited amount of stock outstanding. This type of stock is not sold in the open market, though, and does not convey ownership rights, as does the stock of investor-owned companies. For example, Ashe Memorial, a not-for-profit hospital in North Carolina, is owned by community members who can purchase shares for $100. While shareholders do not benefit financially, they elect the board of trustees and see their dollars invested back in the facility (see www.ashememorial.org/home/about-us.aspx).

Thus far, the discussion of the balance sheet has focused on Sunnyvale, a not-for-profit corporation. In general, the asset and liability sections of the balance sheet are much the same regardless of ownership status. The equity section tends to differ in presentation for different types of ownership because each type has a different form of equity. That is the bad news. The good news is that the economic substance of the equity section remains the same.

Exhibit 4.4 contains the equity section of the balance sheet assuming that Sunnyvale, now with a new name (North River Healthcare), is an investor-owned (for-profit) corporation. This is the type of presentation that would be seen on the balance sheets of for-profit health services businesses such as Community Health Systems (www.chs.net) and Brookdale Senior Living (www.brookdale.com). The first major difference is the title of the section "Stockholders' Equity." This title, or a similar title, such as "Shareholders' Equity," explicitly recognizes that stockholders (shareholders) own the business. (Chapter 12 provides details on stockholders' rights and privileges.)

North River Healthcare was incorporated in 1980, with the bylaws authorizing issuance of 1.5 million shares of common stock. At that time, 1 million shares were sold at a price of $10 per share, so $10 million was collected. Thus, this amount is shown in exhibit 4.4 on the line labeled "common stock."

The *retained earnings* account represents the accumulation of earnings over time that are reinvested in the business. Each year, the amount of net income shown on the income statement, less the amount paid out to stockholders as dividends along with other adjustments, is transferred

	2020	2019
Stockholders' Equity:		
Common stock	$10,000	$10,000
Retained earnings	44,068	36,208
Total equity	$54,068	$46,208

EXHIBIT 4.4
North River Healthcare: Balance Sheet Equity Section, December 31, 2020 and 2019 (in thousands)

from the income statement to the balance sheet. Suppose that North River Healthcare had actually earned $7,860,000 in 2020. Because the firm's retained earnings account increased by a like amount, no distributions were made to stockholders during the year.

Retained earnings, like all equity accounts, represent a claim against assets and are not necessarily available to buy new equipment, to pay dividends, or for any other purpose. The financing represented by retained earnings has already been used within the business to buy property and equipment; to buy supplies; and to increase the cash and cash equivalents, short-term investments, and long-term investments accounts. Only the portion of retained earnings that is sitting in the cash account is immediately available to the business for use.

Although exhibit 4.4 shows only the equity section, it is likely that the values of other balance sheet accounts would differ between investor-owned and not-for-profit businesses. For example, it is unlikely that a for-profit healthcare business would amass such a large amount of long-term investments (securities) unless the funds were earmarked for a particular use in the next few years. North River's stockholders would question why the company had more than $48 million in long-term securities because they would prefer to have all of the business's capital invested in operating assets, which, as indicated earlier, usually earn a higher return than do securities investments. In addition, stockholders prefer to make their own decisions about how to invest excess funds in securities investments. Thus, there would be stockholder pressure on management to either invest this capital in more financially productive operating assets or return it to owners (as dividends or stock repurchases) for redeployment. Stockholders have invested in North River Healthcare because it is a healthcare provider; if they had wanted to own a bank, they would have bought bank stock. If and when North River requires more capital for asset acquisitions, it can always obtain additional debt financing or sell more common stock. Access to the capital markets is seen as an economic advantage that for-profit businesses—whether they are hospitals, medical practices, or managed care plans—have over not-for-profit businesses. However, accessing capital does not come without a cost.

SELF-TEST
QUESTIONS

1. What are net assets (equity)?
2. What are the differences in the equity sections of not-for-profit and investor-owned providers?
3. What is the relationship between the retained earnings account (net assets without donor restrictions) on the balance sheet and earnings (net income or excess of revenues over expenses) reported on the income statement?
4. What is the purpose of the statement of changes in equity?

Fund Accounting

One unique feature of many not-for-profit balance sheets is that they classify certain asset and net asset (equity) accounts as being *restricted*. When a not-for-profit organization receives contributions that donors have indicated must be used for a specific purpose, the organization must create multiple funds to separately track these assets and equity.

A *fund* is defined as a self-contained pool set up to account for a specific resource, activity, or project. Each fund typically has assets, liabilities, and an equity balance. Because the balance sheet of an organization that receives restricted contributions is separated into restricted and unrestricted funds, this form of accounting is called **fund accounting**. Only contributions to not-for-profit organizations are tax deductible to the donor; hence, few contributions are made to investor-owned healthcare businesses. Thus, fund accounting is applicable only to not-for-profit organizations.

To gain a better appreciation of fund accounting, consider exhibit 4.5, which contains Sunnyvale's net assets listing. The first line in exhibit 4.5 lists net assets *without donor restrictions*. These include funds that are derived from operating activities (operating income), investment earnings, and unrestricted contributions—in other words, funds that are not contractually required to be used for a specific purpose. Such funds, as they are generated, are available to Sunnyvale to pay operating expenses, to acquire new property and equipment, or for any other legitimate purpose. Remember, though, that the $45,762,000 in unrestricted net assets is not a pot of money that is available for use at the end of 2020. Most, or all, of it has already been spent.

The next line contains net assets *with donor restrictions*. These funds are provided by donors who have placed conditions on their use. For example, a donor may specify that a contribution cannot be used until three years have elapsed or until the new children's hospital is built. These types of restrictions are temporary because eventually the organization can

fund accounting
A system for recording financial statement data that categorizes accounts whose use has been limited.

	2020	2019
Net Assets (Equity):		
Net assets without donor restrictions:	$45,762	$39,368
Net assets with donor restrictions	$ 8,306	$ 6,840
Total net assets	$54,068	$46,208

EXHIBIT 4.5
Sunnyvale Clinic: Balance Sheet Net Assets (Equity) Section Under Fund Accounting, December 31, 2020 and 2019

satisfy the requirement. When the temporary restriction is met, assuming there are no additional restrictions, such monies are transferred to the unrestricted fund.

Donors may also provide contributions that must be maintained permanently by the organization; however, all or part of the associated earnings can be spent. The permanently restricted portion of such funds is not available for discretionary use. Temporarily and permanently restricted net assets used to be reported as separate line items in the equity section of not-for-profit organizations' balance sheets. However, in August 2016, the Financial Accounting Standards Board issued new accounting guidance that simplifies the presentation from three classes of net assets to two (effective for fiscal years beginning after December 15, 2017). The new guidance also requires organizations to disclose in the notes how different designations, appropriations, and restrictions on assets affect the use of resources.

Restricted contributions impose legal and fiduciary responsibilities on health services organizations to carry out the written wishes of donors. Numerous rules are associated with fund accounting that go well beyond the scope of this book. The good news is that GAAP encourages organizations that use fund accounting to present outside parties with balance sheets that look roughly like the one presented in exhibit 4.1.

SELF-TEST QUESTIONS

1. What is fund accounting?
2. What type of health services organization is most likely to use fund accounting?
3. Explain the differences between funds with and without donor restrictions.
4. Is there a significant difference in the economic content of balance sheets created using fund accounting and those prepared under conventional accounting guidelines?

Statement of Cash Flows

statement of cash flows
A financial statement that focuses on the cash flows that come into and go out of a business.

The balance sheet and income statement are traditional financial statements that have been required for many years. In contrast, the **statement of cash flows** has only been required since 1989 for for-profit businesses and since 1995 for not-for-profit businesses. This financial statement was created by accountants in response to demands by users for better information about a firm's cash inflows and outflows.

While the balance sheet reports the cash balance on hand at the end of the accounting period, it does not provide details on why the cash account is greater or lesser than the previous year's value, nor does the income statement give detailed information on cash flows. In addition to the problems of accrual accounting and noncash expenses discussed in chapter 3, there may be cash raised by means other than operations that does not even appear on the income statement. For example, Sunnyvale may have raised cash during 2020 by taking on more debt or by selling some fixed assets. Such flows, which are not shown on the income statement, affect a firm's cash balance. Finally, the cash coming into a business does not sit in the cash account forever. Most of it goes to pay operating expenses or to purchase other assets, or, for investor-owned firms, some may be paid out as dividends or used to repurchase stock. Thus, the cash account does not increase by the gross amount of cash generated, and it would be useful to know how the difference was spent. The statement of cash flows details where a business gets its cash and what happens to it.

Two formats can be used for the statement of cash flows: the direct format and the indirect format. Most healthcare providers prefer the indirect format. Sunnyvale's 2020 and 2019 statements are presented in exhibit 4.6 in the indirect format. To simplify the discussion, the data in the statements have been reduced; they are somewhat shorter and easier to comprehend than most real-world statements. Nevertheless, an understanding of the composition and presentation of exhibit 4.6 will give readers an excellent appreciation of the value of the statement of cash flows.

The statement of cash flows is formatted to make it easy to understand why Sunnyvale's cash position increased by $5,616,000 during 2020. In other words, it tells us Sunnyvale's sources of cash and how this cash is used. The statement is divided into three major sections: cash flows from operating activities, cash flows from investing activities, and cash flows from financing activities.

Cash Flows from Operating Activities

The first section, *cash flows from operating activities*, focuses on the sources and uses of cash that are **tied directly to operations**. Of course, the most

	2020	2019
Cash Flows from Operating Activities:		
Operating income	$ 2,281	$ 4,330
Adjustments:		
Depreciation	6,405	5,798
Increase in net patient accounts receivable	(2,582)	(1,423)
Increase in inventories	(1,393)	(673)
Decrease in accounts payable	(1,911)	(966)
Increase in accrued expenses	1,032	865
Net cash from operations	$ 3,832	$ 7,931
Cash Flows from Investing Activities:		
Capital expenditures	($ 9,306)	($ 1,953)
Nonoperating income	4,113	3,876
Purchase of short-term securities	(5,000)	0
Purchase of long-term securities	(22,222)	(20,667)
Net cash from investing	($32,415)	($18,744)
Cash Flows from Financing Activities:		
Restricted gifts and bequests	$ 1,466	$ 0
Proceeds from bank loan (notes payable)	989	0
Proceeds from issuance of long-term debt	31,744	0
Net cash from financing	$34,199	$ 0
Net increase (decrease) in cash	$ 5,616	($ 10,813)
Cash and cash equivalents, beginning of year	6,486	17,299
Cash and cash equivalents, end of year	$ 12,102	$ 6,486

EXHIBIT 4.6
Sunnyvale
Clinic:
Statements of
Cash Flows,
Years Ended
December 31,
2020 and 2019
(in thousands)

important source of operating cash flow is operating income, so its value for 2020 ($2,281,000) is listed first. However, because operating income does not equal cash flow, adjustments must be made. The first, and typically most important, adjustment is to add back the noncash expenses that appear on the income statement. As we explained in chapter 3, as a first approximation, the cash flow of a business can be estimated by adding back depreciation, so Operating cash flow = Operating income + Depreciation = $2,281,000 + $6,405,000 = $8,686,000. Thus, depreciation expense of $6,405,000 is the first adjustment entry.

Note that we have started the section labeled "cash flows from operating activities" with operating income. An alternative format is to begin the section with net income or with the total change in net assets. This format does not separately identify operating and nonoperating income on the statement of cash flows. Because Sunnyvale does report operating income on the income statement, it makes the most sense to use it as the starting point for this section of the statement of cash flows.

Adjustments are then made for changes in those balance sheet current asset and liability accounts that are tied directly to operations. For Sunnyvale, this means the net patient accounts receivable, inventories, accounts payable, and accrued expenses accounts. The rationale for these adjustments is that changes in the values of these accounts stem directly from operations; hence, any cash that is generated by or used for these accounts should be included as part of cash flow from operations. In addition, using balance sheet data to calculate operating cash flow recognizes that, under accrual accounting, not every dollar of revenues or expenses listed on the income statement represents a dollar of cash flow.

Note that short-term investments and notes payable, although they are current accounts, reflect investment and financing decisions of a business rather than operations, and hence these accounts are not included in the first section of the statement of cash flows. Also, the entire statement focuses on the change in cash and equivalents, so that will be the output of the statement rather than one of its entries.

To illustrate the adjustments to operating cash flow, Sunnyvale's net patient accounts receivable increased from $25,927,000 to $28,509,000, or by $2,582,000, during 2020. This amount was included in 2020 revenues and hence reported as operating income; however, it was added to receivables instead of collected. Therefore, it is not available as cash flow to Sunnyvale, and it appears as a deduction (negative adjustment) to operating cash flow. To make this point another way, an increase in an asset account requires that the business use cash, so the $2,582,000 increase in receivables reduces the cash flow available for other purposes. For another illustration, accrued expenses increased by $1,032,000 in 2020. Because an increase in accruals, which is on the right (liabilities and equity) side of the balance sheet, creates financing for the clinic and represents a source of cash (as opposed to a use), this change is shown as an addition to operating cash flow.

When all the adjustments were made, Sunnyvale reported $3,832,000 in net cash from operations for 2020. For a business, whether investor owned or not-for-profit, to be financially sustainable, it must generate a positive cash flow from operations. Thus, at least for 2020 and 2019, Sunnyvale's operations are doing what they should be doing—generating cash. However, the clinic's cash flow from operations decreased from 2019 to 2020, so its managers should identify why this happened and then take appropriate action. Unlike Sunnyvale's situation, a consistent negative net cash flow from operations sends a warning to managers and investors that the business may not be economically sustainable.

Cash Flows from Investing Activities

The second major section on the statement of cash flows is *cash flows from investing activities.* For purposes of the statement of cash flows, investing activities are defined as both property and equipment (fixed assets) investments and securities investments.

Because depreciation is accounted for in the cash flows from operating activities section, the focus in this section is on the gross (total) investment in fixed assets. As detailed in Sunnyvale's notes to the financial statements and as reported earlier in this chapter, the 2019 to 2020 change in gross property and equipment is calculated as 2020 Gross property and equipment – 2019 Gross property and equipment = $88,549,000 – $79,243,000 = $9,306,000. Thus, Sunnyvale spent this amount of cash to acquire additional fixed assets during 2020. This fact should not be alarming, even though the amount was greater than the cash flow from operations, as long as the investments are prudent. (Chapters 14 and 15 contain a great number of insights into what makes a prudent capital investment, at least from a financial perspective.)

In addition to investments in fixed assets, Sunnyvale invests in securities and earns nonoperating income. As reported on the income statement, Sunnyvale earned $4,113,000 in total nonoperating income in 2020, which is reported on the second line of the investing section of the cash flow statement. Finally, the clinic made additional securities investments in 2020. Sunnyvale's short-term investments account on the balance sheet increased by $5,000,000, which means it used this amount of cash to buy short-term securities, hence an outflow was posted in the statement of cash flows. Also from the balance sheet, long-term investments increased by $48,059,000 – $25,837,000 = $22,222,000, so this purchase of long-term securities is shown as an outflow in the cash flows from investing activities section.

When all of the 2020 investing activities are considered, Sunnyvale's resulting net cash flow is an outflow of $32,415,000. Even though it earned $4,113,000 in nonoperating income, it spent $9,306,000 on plant and equipment and further invested a total of $27,222,000 in short- and long-term securities.

Cash Flows from Financing Activities

The final major section of the statement of cash flows is *cash flows from financing activities*, which focuses on Sunnyvale's use of contributions and securities to finance its operations and other business activities. The statement of changes in net assets shows restricted gifts and bequests of $1,466,000 in 2020. The changes in balance sheet accounts from 2019 to 2020 indicate that the clinic took out a new bank loan of $989,000 and hence increased its notes payable by $989,000, which is a source of cash. Additionally, Sunnyvale took on an additional $85,322,000 − $53,578,000 = $31,744,000 in long-term debt, another source of cash. Net, Sunnyvale generated a $34,199,000 cash inflow from financing activities.

The previous (cash flows from investing activities) section of the statement of cash flows shows that Sunnyvale used $27,222,000, the vast majority of the new debt financing, to purchase securities. In general, new debt would be used to acquire real assets rather than financial assets. However, Sunnyvale is planning to acquire a large group practice in 2021, and the financing activities undertaken in 2020 were in preparation for this purchase.

Net Increase (Decrease) in Cash and Equivalents and Reconciliation

The next line of the statement of cash flows is the *net increase (decrease) in cash*. It is merely the sum of the totals from the three major sections. For Sunnyvale, there is a net increase in cash of $3,832,000 − $32,415,000 + $34,199,000 = $5,616,000 in 2020. Unlike the "bottom line" of the income statement, the change in cash line has limited value in assessing an organization's financial condition because it can be manipulated by financing activities. If an organization is losing cash on operations but its managers want to report an increase in the cash and equivalents account, in most cases, they simply can borrow the funds necessary to show a net cash increase on the statement of cash flows. Thus, the net cash from operations line is a more important indicator of financial well-being than the net increase (decrease) in cash line.

The net increase (decrease) in cash line is used to verify the entries on the statement of cash flows. As shown in exhibit 4.6, the $5,616,000 increase in cash reported by Sunnyvale for 2020 is added to the beginning-of-year cash and equivalents balance, $6,486,000, to get an end-of-year total of $12,102,000. A check of the end-of-2020 cash and cash equivalents balance shown in exhibit 4.1 confirms the amount calculated on the statement of cash flows.

In summary, the income statement focuses on accounting profitability, while the statement of cash flows focuses on the movement of cash: Where did the money come from, and how did the organization use it? While the major concern of the income statement is economic profitability as defined by GAAP, the statement of cash flows is concerned with cash viability. Is the organization generating, and will it continue to generate, sufficient cash to meet both short-term and long-term needs?

<table>
<tr><td>

1. How does the statement of cash flows differ from the income statement?

2. Briefly explain the three major categories shown on the cash flow statement.

3. In your view, what is the most important piece of information reported on the cash flow statement?

</td><td>

SELF-TEST QUESTIONS

</td></tr>
</table>

Another Look Ahead: Using Balance Sheet Data in Financial Statement Analysis

Chapter 3 provided an introduction to ratio analysis. In this section, we continue the discussion using balance sheet data. The **debt ratio** (or *debt-to-assets ratio*) is defined as total debt divided by total assets. Total debt can be defined several ways, depending on the use of the ratio, but for our purposes here, assume that total debt includes all liabilities (i.e., all non-equity capital). (An alternative would be to include only interest-bearing debt in our definition.) Using the data from exhibit 4.1, Sunnyvale's debt ratio at the end of 2020 was total debt (liabilities) divided by total assets = $100,747,000 ÷ $154,815,000 = 0.65 = 65%. This ratio reveals that each dollar of assets was financed by 65 cents of debt and, by inference, 35 cents of equity.

debt ratio
A debt utilization ratio that measures the proportion of debt (versus equity) financing; typically defined as total debt (liabilities) divided by total assets.

Sunnyvale's debt ratio at the end of 2019 was $68,893,000 ÷ $115,101,000 = 0.60 = 60%. Thus, the clinic increased its proportional use of debt financing by 5 percentage points in one year. That information is important to Sunnyvale's managers and creditors. (The consequences of increased debt utilization are discussed throughout this book, but primarily in chapter 13.) Also, it should be clear that judgments about Sunnyvale's capital structure could not be made easily without constructing the debt ratio and other ratios; interpreting the dollar values directly is very difficult.

Key Concepts

Chapter 3 contained an introduction to financial accounting along with a discussion of the first two financial statements: the income statement and statement of changes in equity. This chapter extends the discussion to cover the balance sheet and statement of cash flows, with emphasis on the interrelationships among the four statements. A demonstration of how economic events (transactions) work their way onto the balance sheet is presented in the chapter supplement. The key concepts of this chapter are as follows:

- The *balance sheet* may be thought of as a snapshot of the financial position of a business at a given point in time.
- The *accounting identity* specifies that assets must equal liabilities plus equity (total assets must equal total claims). When rearranged, the accounting identity reminds us that a business's equity is a residual amount that represents the difference between assets and liabilities.
- *Assets* identify the resources owned by a health services organization in dollars. Assets are listed *by maturity* (i.e., by order of when the assets are expected to be converted into cash). *Current assets* are expected to be converted into cash during the next accounting period.
- *Liabilities* are fixed claims by employees, suppliers, tax authorities, and lenders against a business's assets. *Current liabilities*—those obligations that fall due within one accounting period—are listed first. *Long-term liabilities* (typically debt with maturities greater than one accounting period) are listed second.
- *Equity* is the ownership claim against total assets. Depending on the form of organization and ownership, this claim may be called *net assets, stockholders' equity, proprietor's net worth*, or something else.
- There are several *important interrelationships* between the balance sheet and the income statement. First, the annual depreciation expense shown on the income statement accumulates on the balance sheet in the accumulated depreciation account. Second, revenues recorded on the

(continued)

(continued from previous page)

income statement that have not yet been collected are recorded on the balance sheet as net patient accounts receivable. Revenues that are collected are recorded as cash. Third, all earnings from the income statement that are reinvested in the business accumulate on the balance sheet in the equity account. (The statement of changes in equity creates the bridge between income statement earnings and balance sheet equity.) Finally, inventory balances on the balance sheet are reduced by the amount of supplies expense reported on the income statement.

- The structure of the liabilities and equity side of the balance sheet (i.e., the proportions of debt and equity financing) defines the organization's *capital structure*.

- *Fund accounting* is used by organizations that have donor-restricted contributions. Under fund accounting, net assets are separated into accounts *with* and *without donor restrictions*. Fund accounting complicates internal accounting procedures and adds detail to the balance sheet. However, fund accounting does not alter the basic format of the balance sheet or its economic interpretation.

- The *statement of cash flows* shows where an organization gets its cash and how it is used. It combines information found on the income statement and the balance sheet.

- The statement of cash flows has three major sections: *cash flows from operating activities*, *cash flows from investing activities*, and *cash flows from financing activities*.

- The "bottom line" of the statement of cash flows is the *net increase (decrease) in cash*. Although this amount is useful in verifying the accuracy of the statement, its economic content is not as meaningful as the statement's component amounts.

Except for the chapter supplement, this temporarily ends the discussion of financial accounting. The next chapter begins our discussion of managerial accounting. However, the concepts presented in chapters 3 and 4 are used repeatedly throughout the remainder of the book. In addition, financial accounting concepts are revisited in chapter 17, which focuses on using the financial statements to assess financial performance.

Questions

4.1. a. What is the difference between the income statement and balance sheet in regard to timing?

  b. What is wrong with the following statement? "The clinic's cash balance for 2020 was $150,000, while its net income on December 31, 2020, was $50,000."

4.2. a. What is the accounting identity?

  b. What is the implication of the accounting identity for the numbers on a balance sheet?

  c. What does the accounting identity tell us about a business's equity?

4.3. a. What are assets?

  b. What are the three major categories of assets?

4.4. a. What makes an asset a current asset?

  b. Provide some examples of current assets.

  c. What is net working capital, and what does it measure?

4.5. a. On the balance sheet, what is the difference between long-term investments and property and equipment?

  b. What is the difference between gross fixed assets and net fixed assets?

  c. How does depreciation expense on the income statement relate to accumulated depreciation on the balance sheet?

4.6. a. What is the difference between liabilities and equity?

  b. What makes a liability a current liability?

  c. Provide some examples of current liabilities.

  d. What is the difference between long-term debt and notes payable?

4.7. a. Explain the difference between the equity section of a not-for-profit business and an investor-owned business.

  b. What is the relationship between net income on the income statement and the equity section on a balance sheet?

4.8. What is fund accounting, and why is it important to some healthcare providers?

4.9. a. What is the statement of cash flows, and how does it differ from the income statement?

  b. What are the three major sections of the statement of cash flows?

  c. What is the bottom line of the statement of cash flows, and how important is it?

Problems

4.1. Middletown Clinic had total assets of $500,000 and an equity balance of $350,000 at the end of 2019. One year later, at the end of 2020, the clinic had $575,000 in assets and $380,000 in equity. What was the clinic's dollar growth in assets during 2020, and how was this growth financed?

4.2. San Mateo Healthcare had an equity balance of $1.38 million at the beginning of the year. At the end of the year, its equity balance was $1.98 million.

   a. Assume that San Mateo is a not-for-profit organization. What was its net income for the period?

   b. Now, assume that San Mateo is an investor-owned business.
   - Assuming zero dividends, what was San Mateo's net income?
   - Assuming $200,000 in dividends, what was its net income?
   - Assuming $200,000 in dividends and $300,000 in additional stock sales, what was San Mateo's net income?

4.3. Here is financial statement information on four not-for-profit clinics:

	Pittman	Rose	Beckman	Jaffe
December 31, 2019:				
Assets	$80,000	$100,000	g	$150,000
Liabilities	50,000	d	$75,000	j
Net assets	a	60,000	45,000	90,000
December 31, 2020:				
Assets	b	130,000	180,000	k
Liabilities	55,000	62,000	h	80,000
Net assets	45,000	e	110,000	145,000
During 2020:				
Total revenues	c	400,000	i	500,000
Total expenses	330,000	f	360,000	l

Fill in the missing values labeled a through l.

4.4. The following are selected account balances for Warrenton Clinic as of December 31, 2020, in alphabetical order. Create Warrenton Clinic's balance sheet.

Accounts payable	$ 20,000
Accounts receivable, net	60,000
Cash	30,000
Equity	230,000
Long-term debt	120,000
Long-term investments	100,000
Net property and equipment	150,000
Other assets	40,000
Other long-term liabilities	10,000

4.5. Consider the following balance sheet:

BestCare HMO
Balance Sheet
June 30, 2020
(in thousands)

Assets
Current Assets:

Cash and cash equivalents	$2,737
Net premiums receivable	821
Other current assets	387
Total current assets	$3,945
Long-term investments	$4,424
Net property and equipment	1,500
Total assets	$9,869

Liabilities and Equity

Healthcare costs payable	$2,145
Accrued expenses	929
Unearned premiums	382
Total current liabilities	$3,456
Long-term debt	4,295
Total liabilities	$7,751
Equity	2,118
Total liabilities and equity	$9,869

a. How does this balance sheet differ from the one presented in exhibit 4.1 for Sunnyvale?

b. What is BestCare's net working capital for 2020?

c. What is BestCare's debt ratio? How does it compare with Sunnyvale's debt ratio?

4.6. Consider this balance sheet:

Blue Sky Nursing Home, Inc.	
Balance Sheet	
December 31, 2020	
Assets	
Current Assets:	
Cash and cash equivalents	$ 105,737
Short-term securities investments	200,000
Net accounts receivable	215,600
Supplies	87,655
Total current assets	$ 608,992
Property and equipment	$ 2,250,000
Less accumulated depreciation	356,000
Net property and equipment	$ 1,894,000
Total assets	$ 2,502,992
Liabilities and Shareholders' Equity	
Current Liabilities:	
Accounts payable	$ 72,250
Accrued expenses	192,900
Notes payable	100,000
Current portion of long-term debt	80,000
Total current liabilities	$ 445,150
Long-term debt	1,700,000
Total liabilities	$ 2,145,150
Shareholders' Equity:	
Common stock, $10 par value	$ 100,000
Retained earnings	257,842
Total shareholders' equity	$ 357,842
Total liabilities and shareholders' equity	$ 2,502,992

a. How does this balance sheet differ from the ones presented in exhibit 4.1 and problem 4.5?

b. What is Blue Sky's net working capital for 2020?

c. What is Blue Sky's debt ratio? How does it compare with the debt ratios for Sunnyvale and BestCare?

4.7. Refer to the transactions pertaining to Bayshore Radiology Center presented in the supplement to this chapter. Restate the impact of the transactions on Bayshore's balance sheet using these data: (Hint: It may be helpful to review the chapter supplement before completing this problem.)

a. Transaction 2: The $200,000 equipment purchase is made with long-term borrowings instead of cash.

b. Transaction 3: The $20,000 in supplies are purchased with cash instead of on trade credit.

c. Transaction 4: The $50,000 in services provided are immediately paid for by patients instead of billed to third-party payers.

4.8. Given below are balance sheets as of December 31, 2020, and December 31, 2019, for James Hospital. Using the balance sheets and the additional information provided, complete the income statement of James Hospital for the year ended December 31, 2020. Hint: It may be helpful to review the chapter supplement before completing this problem.

	James Hospital Balance Sheets December 31	
	2020	2019
Assets		
Cash	$ 75,000	$ 50,000
Accounts receivable	32,000	22,000
Net property, plant, and equipment	90,000	100,000
Total assets	$ 197,000	$ 172,000
Liabilities	$ 37,000	$ 30,000
Equity	160,000	142,000
Total liabilities and equity	$ 197,000	$ 172,000

Additional information:
- James Hospital paid no dividends, and there were no other transactions affecting equity during 2020.
- There were no collections during 2020 on accounts receivable outstanding at December 31, 2019, but all receivables are considered collectible.

- There was no charity care or contractual discounts and allowances during 2020.
- James Hospital purchases all medical supplies on account.
- James Hospital did not purchase or sell any property, plant, and equipment during 2020.

James Hospital Income Statement Year Ended December 31, 2020	
Net patient service revenue	?
Total revenue	?
Supplies expense	?
Depreciation expense	?
Total expenses	?
Net income	?

4.9. Oak Street Clinic, a not-for-profit, began 2020 with the following account balances on January 1:

Cash	$ 70,000
Accounts receivable	227,000
Supplies inventory	24,000
Equipment	1,500,000
Accumulated depreciation	300,000
Accounts payable	21,000
Notes payable	500,000
Net assets	1,000,000

During 2020, the accounting clerk recorded the following transactions:

1. Billed patients for services rendered	$1,700,000
2. Purchased medical supplies on credit	12,000
3. Employee salaries earned	712,000
4. Employee salaries paid	683,000
5. Annual depreciation on equipment	150,000

6. Received a bank loan	250,000
7. Cash collections on patient billings	1,124,000
8. Made payment on bank loan	75,000
9. Used medical supplies in patient care	10,000

Oak Street Clinic's year-end is December 31. Construct the 2020 balance sheet and income statement for the clinic, using the beginning account balances and incorporating the effects of each transaction. Hint: It may be helpful to review the chapter supplement before completing this problem.

Resources

American Institute of Certified Public Accountants (AICPA). 2014. *Audit and Accounting Guide for Healthcare Entities.* New York: AICPA.

Doody, D. 2007. "Fair Valuation of Alternatives: Clearing the Audit Hurdle." *Healthcare Financial Management* 61 (9): 158–62.

———. 2006. "The Balance Sheet: A Snapshot of Your Financial Health." *Healthcare Financial Management* 60 (5): 124–25.

Financial Accounting Standards Board. 2016. "Presentation of Financial Statements for Not-for-Profit Entities." Accounting Standards Update 2016-14. Published August. www.fasb.org/jsp/FASB/Document_C/DocumentPage?cid=1176168381847&acceptedDisclaimer=true.

———. 2014. "Revenue from Contracts with Customers." Accounting Standards Update 2014-09. Published May. www.fasb.org/jsp/FASB/Document_C/DocumentPage?cid=1176164076069&acceptedDisclaimer=true.

Song, P. H., and K. L. Reiter. 2010. "Trends in Asset Structure Between Not-for-Profit and Investor-Owned Hospitals." *Medical Care Research and Review* 67 (6): 694–706.

Waldron, D. J. 2005. "Technology Strategy and the Balance Sheet: 3 Points to Consider." *Healthcare Financial Management* 59 (5): 70–76.

4

RECORDING AND COMPILING FINANCIAL ACCOUNTING DATA

The ultimate goal of a business's financial accounting system is to produce financial statements. However, the road from the recording of basic accounting data to the completion of the financial statements is long and arduous, especially for large, complex organizations. Complete coverage of the art and science of financial accounting is not possible in an introductory textbook. Thus, the goal of this chapter supplement is to introduce the processes and procedures used to record and compile financial accounting data.

The Accounting Cycle

The *accounting cycle* is the process of completing all of the accounting tasks for an accounting period. The accounting cycle is repeated beginning with each new accounting period. The starting point for the identification and recording of financial accounting information is a *transaction*, which is defined as an exchange of goods or services between one individual or enterprise and another. To ensure that the transaction is faithfully represented and verifiable—two qualitative characteristics of useful financial information under the conceptual framework of financial accounting—each transaction must be supported by relevant documentation, which is retained for some required length of time.

Once a transaction is identified, its value must be measured and the transaction recorded with a *journal entry*. A journal entry shows the date of the transaction and the amounts by which specific *accounts* are increased or decreased. Accounts are the means by which financial accounting data are sorted and stored. There is one account, or record of transactions, for each uniquely identified activity. For example, under the general heading of cash, separate accounts might be established for petty cash, payroll checks, vendor checks, other checks, and the like. A large business can easily have hundreds or even thousands of separate *primary accounts*, plus *subsidiary accounts* that support the primary accounts. The subsidiary accounts, which pertain to specific assets or liabilities or to individual patients or vendors, are aggregated to create data for a primary account. For example, individual patient charges,

chart of accounts
A document that assigns a unique numerical identifier to every account of an organization.

general ledger
The master listing of an organization's primary accounts, which record the transactions that are used to create a business's financial statements.

which are carried in subsidiary accounts, are aggregated into one or more primary revenue accounts.

To help manage the large number of accounts, businesses use a document called a **chart of accounts**, which assigns a unique numerical code to each account. For example, the petty cash account might have the code 1-1000-00, while the account for checks written might have the code 1-1100-00. The first 1 indicates that the account is an asset account; the second 1 indicates a cash account; and the next digit, 0 or 1, indicates the specific cash account. Additional numbers can be used if the organization decides to subdivide either the petty cash or the checks-written account into subsidiary accounts. For example, the next digit of the checks-written account might indicate the purpose of the check: 1 for payroll, 2 for vendor payments, and so on. Because everyone who deals with the accounts is familiar with the business's chart of accounts, transactions can be easily sorted by account code to ensure that they are recorded in the correct account.

Once a transaction has been recorded, the next step in the accounting cycle is *posting* the information from a journal entry to the appropriate accounts in the **general ledger**. Whereas journal entries summarize the effects of individual transactions on relevant accounts (e.g., a patient receives and pays for services, and the organization records a journal entry to increase cash and increase patient service revenue), the general ledger summarizes all of the transactions affecting each unique account (e.g., all of the transactions during the year that resulted in increases or decreases to the cash account). Examples are provided in exhibit S4.1.

Because the effects of all transactions on each individual account are summarized, the general ledger is the starting point for creating the organization's financial statements. Ultimately, the amounts that are recorded are verified, consolidated, and reconciled in a *trial balance* (which verifies that debits equal credits in the general ledger); any adjusting entries are made; and the information is transferred to the business's financial statements. At the end of the accounting cycle, the accounting records are *closed*, and the process begins again.

Within the system of primary and subsidiary accounts, accounts are further classified as follows:

- *Permanent accounts* include items that must be carried from one accounting period to another. Thus, permanent accounts remain active until the items in the account are no longer "on the books" of the business. For example, an account might be created, or opened, to contain all transactions related to a five-year bank loan. The account would remain open to record transactions relating to the loan—say, annual principal payments—until the loan is paid off in five years,

Assume that on November 1, a patient receives and pays for $300 worth of services. This exchange results in an increase in cash and an increase in net patient service revenue. The transaction is first recorded with a journal entry, such as the one shown below:

EXHIBIT S4.1
Journal Entries and the General Ledger

Date	Account Title and Explanation	Account	Debit	Credit
11/1	Cash	100	$300	
	Net patient service revenue	400		$300

Note: Provided patient care services to self-pay patient.

The first column shows the date of the transaction; the second column, the account title; the third column, the account number from the chart of accounts; and the fourth and fifth columns, the dollar impacts of the transaction on the accounts. The note at the bottom of the entry briefly explains the transaction. The terms *debit* and *credit* are discussed later in this supplement. For now, the key point is that the journal entry records all of the effects of an individual transaction.

For the preparation of financial statements, information from the journal entries must be summarized for each account. The process of *posting* transfers information from the journal entry to the general ledger. Below, the information from the previous journal entry is posted to the cash account in the general ledger.

Date	Explanation	Debit	Credit
11/1	Cash received for patient services	$300	

The cash account in the general ledger accumulates all increases and decreases in cash over the accounting period. The $300 in patient service revenue is posted to a different general ledger account called net patient service revenue.

at which time the account would be closed. At the start of a new accounting period, permanent accounts typically have a nonzero beginning balance because amounts are carried forward from the previous period. Balance sheet accounts are permanent accounts because they reflect the cumulative activity in the account as of a particular date.

- *Temporary accounts* are for those items that will automatically be *closed* at the end of each accounting period. For example, a business's revenue and expense accounts are closed at the end of the accounting period, and the final balances are transferred to the organization's equity account. The revenue and expense accounts begin with a zero balance at the start of each new accounting period. Income statement accounts are temporary accounts because they reflect all of the activity in the accounts over a certain period of time.

- *Contra accounts* are special accounts that convert the gross value of some other account into a net value. For example, a contra asset account is associated with depreciation expense, called accumulated depreciation, that accounts for the loss of value of buildings and equipment over time.

The Double Entry Accounting System

The system used to make journal entries is called the **double entry system**, because each transaction must be entered in at least two different accounts— once as a *debit* and once as a *credit*. In this system, debit simply means "left" and credit means "right." Whether an entry is a debit or a credit depends both on the nature of the entry (e.g., whether the value of the account is being increased or decreased) and the type of account (e.g., revenue, expense, asset, etc.). For that reason, debit and credit entries may not be intuitive to someone who is not familiar with the double entry system.

double entry system
The system used to make accounting journal entries; called *double entry* because each transaction must be entered in at least two different accounts.

Briefly, debits and credits follow the basic accounting equation (also called the *accounting identity*) that was introduced in chapter 4:

$$\text{Assets} = \text{Liabilities} + \text{Equity}$$

Since asset accounts are on the left side of the accounting equation, these accounts are increased with a debit (left-side) entry and decreased with a credit (right-side) entry. Conversely, since liability and equity accounts are on the right side of the accounting equation, these accounts are increased with a credit (right-side) entry and decreased with a debit (left-side) entry. Because most accounts have both debit and credit entries, they traditionally have been set up in a "T" format, and hence they are called *T-accounts*, with debits entered on the left side of the vertical line and credits entered on the right side.

The accounting equation can be expanded by recognizing that revenue and expense accounts (temporary income statement accounts) accumulate changes in the organization's equity balance over the accounting period. Revenue accounts accumulate increases in equity, while expense accounts accumulate decreases in equity.

Thus, the accounting equation can be rewritten as follows:

Assets = Liabilities + Beginning equity + Revenues − Expenses

Adding a time element, we see that:

$$
\begin{array}{l}
\text{Assets as of} \\
\text{12/31/2020}
\end{array}
=
\begin{array}{l}
\text{Liabilities as of} \\
\text{12/31/2020}
\end{array}
+
\begin{array}{l}
\text{Beginning} \\
\text{equity as of} \\
\text{1/1/2020}
\end{array}
+
\begin{array}{l}
\text{Revenues for} \\
\text{the year ended} \\
\text{12/31/2020}
\end{array}
-
\begin{array}{l}
\text{Expenses for} \\
\text{the year ended} \\
\text{12/31/2020}
\end{array}
$$

Revenues minus expenses equals
net income for the year ended
12/31/2020. Therefore, we have:

$$
\begin{array}{l}
\text{Assets as of} \\
\text{12/31/2020}
\end{array}
=
\begin{array}{l}
\text{Liabilities as of} \\
\text{12/31/2020}
\end{array}
+
\begin{array}{l}
\text{Ending equity as of 12/31/2020, where ending} \\
\text{equity is the beginning equity balance plus net} \\
\text{income for the year}
\end{array}
$$

Using the expanded form of the accounting equation, the equation can be rearranged as follows:

Assets + Expenses = Equity + Revenues

Now it is clear that expenses, like assets, increase on the left side of the equation. Thus, expense accounts are increased with a debit (left-side) entry and decreased with a credit (right-side) entry. In contrast, revenue accounts (which appear on the right side of the equation) increase with a credit (right-side) entry and decrease with a debit (left-side) entry. An example is provided in exhibit S4.2.

EXHIBIT S4.2
Recording
Transactions
Using
T-Accounts

Returning to the example in exhibit S4.1, assume that an organization provides and receives payment for $300 worth of patient services on November 1. The transaction involves two accounts: cash and net patient service revenue. The T-accounts are shown below:

Cash		Net Patient Service Revenue	
Debit (+)	**Credit (−)**	**Debit (−)**	**Credit (+)**
$300			$300

Cash is an asset account; therefore, it is increased with a debit (left-side entry). Net patient service revenue is a temporary revenue account; its balance will be transferred to equity when the account is closed. Increases in revenue increase the organization's equity. Therefore, net patient service revenue is increased with a credit (right-side entry).

SELF-TEST QUESTION

1. Briefly explain the following terms used in the recording and compiling of accounting data:
   a. Transaction
   b. Account
   c. Journal entry
   d. Posting
   e. Chart of accounts
   f. General ledger
   g. T-account
   h. Double entry system

Transactions

As we previously discussed, the recording of transactions by the accounting staff is the first step in the creation of a business's financial statements. Understanding how transactions ultimately affect the financial statements will help managers better understand and interpret their content.

The transactions that flow to the income statement are relatively apparent. For example, net operating revenues stem directly from the provision of patient services, and there is an expectation of receiving payment. Thus, the provision of services that have a reimbursement amount of $1,000 would increase the net patient service revenue account by $1,000. Most expenses are treated in the same way: For example, the obligation to pay wages of $150 to an employee for a day's work would increase the salaries expense line by a like amount. However, the way in which transactions flow to the balance sheet can be less obvious. In this section, ten typical transactions are presented. Understanding these transactions will help readers understand how an organization's economic events are transformed into financial statement data. The primary concept behind all transactions is that the basic accounting equation must be preserved—that is, the balance sheet must balance. Thus, each transaction must have a dual effect, either one on the left side and one on the right side of the accounting equation, or offsetting effects on the same side.

Because this is an introductory textbook, we do not discuss T-accounts, debits, or credits in what follows. Rather, it is easier for the beginner to think about how accounts *increase* or *decrease* as a result of economic events.

1. **Investment by owners.** Suppose five radiologists decide to open a diagnostic center that they incorporate as an investor-owned business called Bayshore Radiology Center. They each invest $200,000 cash in the business in exchange for $200,000 of common stock. The transaction results in an equal increase in both assets and equity. In this case, there is an increase in the cash account of $1,000,000 (asset) and an increase in the common stock account of $1,000,000 (equity). The $1,000,000 is reported directly as equity on the balance sheet and not as revenue on the income statement because it is an investment in the organization in exchange for ownership. It is not money that Bayshore Radiology Center has earned by providing patient services. After the transaction, the balance sheet looks like this:

Assets		Liabilities and Equity	
Cash	$1,000,000	Common stock	$1,000,000
Total assets	$1,000,000	Total equity	$1,000,000

2. **Purchase of equipment for cash.** To support operations, the business needs diagnostic equipment. Assume that the first piece of equipment purchased costs $200,000 and it is paid for in cash. This transaction results in a change in the composition of the business's assets, but the totals are unaffected. Cash (an asset) is decreased by $200,000 and a new asset account, net fixed assets, is increased by $200,000:

Assets		Liabilities and Equity	
Cash	$ 800,000		
Net fixed assets	200,000	Common stock	$1,000,000
Total assets	$1,000,000	Total equity	$1,000,000

Total assets and total equity still amount to $1,000,000 because no new capital (liabilities or equity) was acquired by the business.

3. **Purchase of supplies on credit.** Assume that Bayshore purchases medical supplies for $20,000 but does not use any of the supplies immediately. The supplier's terms give the center 60 days to pay the bill. Assets are increased by this transaction because of the expected benefit of using these supplies in the future to provide services. A new asset account, *supplies inventory*, is added with a balance of $20,000 reflecting the value of the supplies on hand. Also, liabilities (accounts payable) are increased by the amount due the supplier:

Assets		Liabilities and Equity	
Cash	$ 800,000	Accounts payable	$ 20,000
Supplies inventory	20,000		
Net fixed assets	200,000	Common stock	1,000,000
Total assets	$1,020,000	Total liabilities and equity	$1,020,000

4. **Services rendered on credit.** Assume that Bayshore provides patient services that result in $50,000 in billings to third-party payers. Assume that no cash is initially collected. This transaction affects both the balance sheet and the income statement. This transaction will increase assets (accounts receivable) by $50,000 to show that Bayshore is owed this amount by payers. The second half of the "double entry" is slightly more complicated. Because Bayshore has provided services and therefore earned the $50,000, this amount is recorded as net patient service revenue and reported on Bayshore's income statement. Because revenue accounts are temporary, at the end of the accounting period, the revenue account will be closed and the $50,000 will be transferred to the retained earnings portion of equity. Thus, on the balance sheet, the provision of patient services increases assets (accounts receivable) and equity (retained earnings) by $50,000:

Assets		Liabilities and Equity	
Cash	$ 800,000	Accounts payable	$ 20,000
Accounts receivable	50,000		
Supplies inventory	20,000	Common stock	1,000,000
Net fixed assets	200,000	Retained earnings	50,000
Total assets	$1,070,000	Total liabilities and equity	$1,070,000

Note here that retained earnings (equity) is increased when revenues are earned, even though no cash has been generated. When accounts receivable are collected at a later date, cash will be increased and receivables will be decreased (see transaction 10), but there will be no effect on revenue since the revenue has already been recorded.

5. **Purchase of advertising on credit.** Bayshore receives a bill for $10,000 from the *Daily News* for advertising its grand opening, but it does not have to pay the newspaper for 30 days. The transaction results in an increase in liabilities (accounts payable) of $10,000 for the amount owed to the newspaper. The transaction also results in an

increase in advertising expense, shown on the income statement. Since expenses are temporary accounts (like revenues), they are closed at the end of the accounting period and their value is transferred to the retained earnings (equity) account. Whereas revenues increase equity, expenses decrease equity. Thus, retained earnings is decreased by $10,000:

Assets		Liabilities and Equity	
Cash	$ 800,000	Accounts payable	$ 30,000
Accounts receivable	50,000		
Supplies inventory	20,000	Common stock	1,000,000
Net fixed assets	200,000	Retained earnings	40,000
Total assets	$1,070,000	Total liabilities and equity	$1,070,000

Here, equity is reduced when expenses are incurred. When payment is made at a later date, both accounts payable and cash will decrease (see transaction 8), but there will be no effect on the expense itself. The expense has already been recorded and the amount must be retained in the records and reported to reflect the fact that the advertising cost was incurred. Advertising is an expense, as opposed to an asset (such as supplies inventory), because the benefits of the outlay have been immediately realized.

6. **Payment of expenses.** Assume that the center paid $50,000 in cash for rent, salaries, and utilities. These payments result in an equal decrease in cash and equity. The decrease in equity will be matched by expenses, and therefore a reduction in net income, on the income statement:

Assets		Liabilities and Equity	
Cash	$ 750,000	Accounts payable	$ 30,000
Accounts receivable	50,000		
Supplies inventory	20,000	Common stock	1,000,000
Net fixed assets	200,000	Retained earnings	(10,000)
Total assets	$1,020,000	Total liabilities and equity	$1,020,000

Note that Bayshore's retained earnings are driven negative by this transaction. In essence, the equity of the center ($1,020,000 in assets − $30,000 in liabilities = $990,000 in equity) is now worth less than the total capital supplied by the center's physician stockholders.

Chapter 4 Supplement

7. **Recognition of supplies used.** Assume that $2,000 worth of supplies inventory was used in providing healthcare services to Bayshore's patients. Because these supplies are no longer available for future use, the supplies inventory asset must be reduced by $2,000. The same amount, $2,000, is recorded as supplies expense on the income statement to reflect the cost of supplies incurred to produce patient care. This reduces retained earnings (equity) by $2,000:

Assets		Liabilities and Equity	
Cash	$ 750,000	Accounts payable	$ 30,000
Accounts receivable	50,000		
Supplies inventory	18,000	Common stock	1,000,000
Net fixed assets	200,000	Retained earnings	(12,000)
Total assets	$1,018,000	Total liabilities and equity	$1,018,000

Note, however, that supplies typically are expended in providing services, so revenue would likely also be created that would increase assets and equity.

8. **Payment of accounts payable (advertising bill).** Assume that the center paid its $10,000 advertising bill, which was due in 30 days. (The supplies bill is not due for 60 days.) The advertising bill was previously recorded in transaction 5 as a payable. This payment on an account for an expense already recognized decreases both assets (cash) and liabilities (accounts payable):

Assets		Liabilities and Equity	
Cash	$ 740,000	Accounts payable	$ 20,000
Accounts receivable	50,000		
Supplies inventory	18,000	Common stock	1,000,000
Net fixed assets	200,000	Retained earnings	(12,000)
Total assets	$1,008,000	Total liabilities and equity	$1,008,000

Payment of a liability related to an expense that has previously been incurred does not affect the expense account or equity. Rather, the liability is reduced on the balance sheet to show that the amount is no longer owed by the organization.

9. **Payment of accounts payable (supplies bill).** One month later, assume that Bayshore paid its $20,000 supplies bill, which decreases cash and accounts payable. Recall that the supplies bill was previously

recorded in transaction 3 as an increase in both assets (supplies inventory) and liabilities (accounts payable). Furthermore, part of the supplies were used and recorded in transaction 7 as a decrease in assets (supplies inventory) and equity (through the recording of supplies expense on the income statement):

Assets		Liabilities and Equity	
Cash	$720,000	Accounts payable	$ 0
Accounts receivable	50,000		
Supplies inventory	18,000	Common stock	1,000,000
Net fixed assets	200,000	Retained earnings	(12,000)
Total assets	$988,000	Total liabilities and equity	$ 988,000

A payment of a liability related to an asset that has previously been recorded does not affect equity. Equity is not affected until the asset has been consumed.

10. **Receipt of cash from a third-party payer.** Assume that $5,000 is received in payment for patient services rendered from one of Bayshore's third-party payers. This transaction does not change Bayshore's total assets or its liabilities or equity. It does change the total assets composition by reducing receivables and increasing cash:

Assets		Liabilities and Equity	
Cash	$725,000	Accounts payable	$ 0
Accounts receivable	45,000		
Supplies inventory	18,000	Common stock	1,000,000
Net fixed assets	200,000	Retained earnings	(12,000)
Total assets	$988,000	Total liabilities and equity	$ 988,000

A collection for services previously billed and recorded does not affect equity. Revenue was already recorded in transaction 4 and cannot be recorded again.

Of course, an almost limitless number of transactions occur in everyday business activities. The purpose of this section is to give readers a sense of how transactions provide the foundation for a business's financial statements.

Before leaving the topic of financial accounting, it is useful to revisit the financial statements one final time. Note that as the ten transactions were recorded, the balance sheet accounts were adjusted accordingly. The account balances from the previous balance sheet were carried forward and additions or subtractions were made to reflect new activity. At the end of the accounting period (i.e., at the end of transaction 10), the balance sheet reflects Bayshore Radiology's assets, liabilities, and equity at that moment in time.

In contrast, the income statement reflects revenues and expenses (and thus changes in equity) over a period of time. To construct Bayshore's income statement for the accounting period, it is necessary to go through the transactions and "collect" those amounts that were recorded as revenues or expenses. Of course, the accounting system would easily allow for these amounts to be identified. For the period reflected by the ten transactions, Bayshore's income statement would appear as follows:

Revenues

Net patient service revenue (from transaction 4)	$50,000
Total revenues	$50,000
Expenses	
Advertising (from transaction 5)	$10,000
Rent, salaries, and utilities (from transaction 6)	50,000
Supplies (from transaction 7)	2,000
Total expenses	$62,000
Net income (loss)	($12,000)

Note that the $12,000 loss is the same amount reflected in the final retained earnings balance on the balance sheet. This is because Bayshore started the period with no retained earnings. The $12,000 loss reduced Bayshore's total equity from the beginning balance of $1,000,000 to $988,000 at the end of the period.

SELF-TEST QUESTIONS

1. What condition must be met when entering transactions on the balance sheet?
2. What is the effect on a business's equity account of a payment on a bill that has already been recorded as an accounts payable?
3. What is the effect of the collection of a receivable on a business's equity account?

III

MANAGERIAL ACCOUNTING

Thus far, the book has concentrated on the healthcare finance environment and the basics of financial accounting. Part III focuses on managerial accounting, which is concerned with the development and use of information designed to help health services managers perform management and control functions in their organizations. Chapter 5 covers cost behavior, cost estimation at the organizational level, and profit (cost-volume-profit) analysis—topics that many consider the cornerstones of managerial accounting. Chapters 6, 7, and 8 focus on costing at the department and service levels, pricing, and financial planning and budgeting. After studying the four chapters that compose part III, readers will have a good understanding of the mechanics of managerial accounting and its value to health services managers.

COST BEHAVIOR, ORGANIZATIONAL COSTING, AND PROFIT ANALYSIS

Learning Objectives

After studying this chapter, readers will be able to

- Explain the differences between financial and managerial accounting.
- Describe how costs are classified according to their relationship to volume.
- Conduct profit (cost-volume-profit) analyses to analyze the impact of changing assumptions on profitability and breakeven points.
- Explain the primary differences between profit analyses under fee-for-service reimbursement versus capitation.

Introduction

Managers of healthcare businesses have many responsibilities. Some of the more important ones are planning and budgeting, establishing policies that control the operations of the organization, and overseeing the day-to-day activities of subordinates. All of these activities require information—a great deal of information. This information has to be presented in a format that facilitates analysis, interpretation, and decision-making. This is where *managerial accounting* comes in. Without a timely and effective managerial accounting system, healthcare managers would be unable to make decisions on the basis of good information. Of course, accurate information does not ensure good decision-making, but without it, good decision-making is almost impossible.

The Basics of Managerial Accounting

Whereas financial accounting focuses primarily on historical, organization-level data for presentation in a business's financial statements, **managerial accounting** focuses on data at all levels of an organization—the business as

managerial (management) accounting
The field of accounting that focuses on all levels of an organization and is used internally for managerial decision-making.

a whole as well as the departments, individual services, and even individual patients—for purposes of planning, decision-making, and control. Managerial accounting data are used internally for making decisions such as routine budgeting, allocation of managerial bonuses, and pricing. Also, managerial accounting data can be compiled for special projects, such as assessing alternative modes of delivery or projecting the profitability of a proposed third-party payer contract.

In short, the focus of managerial accounting is to develop information to meet the needs of managers at all levels in the organization, rather than interested parties outside the organization (mainly investors). Thus, while financial accounting information is driven by the needs of outsiders, managerial accounting information is driven by the needs of managers. Note that the term *management accounting* is sometimes used in place of *managerial accounting*. Although some accountants differentiate between managerial and management accounting, the differences are minor and beyond the scope of this book. For purposes here, managerial accounting and management accounting are the same.

Managers are more concerned with what will happen in the future than what has happened in the past. Thus, unlike financial accounting, managerial accounting is, for the most part, forward-looking. In managerial accounting, managers embark on budgeting and pricing decisions, which require them to make many assumptions about factors such as utilization (volume), reimbursement rates, and costs. The need to make assumptions about the future, combined with the lack of agreed-upon rules for developing managerial accounting data, makes those data much more flexible, but also more uncertain than financial accounting data.

In general, financial accounting can be thought of as reporting work, while managerial accounting is best described as decision work. We do not mean to imply that there is little value in financial accounting data. Indeed, as you will see in chapter 17, financial statements are essential to understanding a business's overall financial condition. Still, the managerial decisions made on a daily basis that create this condition are influenced much more by managerial accounting data, which focus on individual activities within the business, than by financial accounting data, which focus on the entire organization.

A critical part of managerial accounting is the measurement of costs. In fact, the concept of costs is so important that it has spawned its own field of accounting—cost accounting. *Cost accounting* generally is considered to be a subset of managerial accounting, although cost accounting systems also are used to develop the expense data reported on a business's income statement. Therefore, cost accounting bridges managerial and financial accounting.

There is no single definition of the term *cost*. Rather, there are different costs for different purposes. For healthcare providers, a cost typically involves a resource use associated with providing or supporting a specific service. However, the cost per service identified for pricing purposes can differ from the cost per service used for management control purposes. Also, the cost per service used for long-range planning purposes may differ from the cost per service defined for short-term purposes. Finally, as we discussed in chapters 3 and 4, costs do not necessarily reflect actual cash outflows.

SELF-TEST QUESTIONS

1. What are the primary differences between financial and managerial accounting?
2. What is meant by the term *cost*?

Cost Behavior: Fixed Versus Variable Costs

We can classify costs in many ways, depending on the situation and managerial information needs. Let's begin by identifying two types of costs on the basis of their relationship to the amount of services provided, which is often referred to as *activity*, *utilization*, or *volume*. The way that total costs change in response to a change in volume is referred to as *cost behavior*. In general, costs behave in one of two ways as volume changes—they are either fixed or variable.

   Cost classifications first require the specification of a likely range of volumes. In dealing with the future, volume—measured as the number of patient days, number of visits, number of enrollees, number of laboratory tests, and so on—is always uncertain. However, healthcare managers often have an idea of the potential range of volume over some future time period. For example, the business manager of Northside Clinic, an urgent care clinic that is open seven days a week, might estimate that the number of visits next year will range from 12,000 to 14,000 (34 to 40 per day). If it is unlikely that annual utilization will fall outside these bounds, then the range of 12,000 to 14,000 visits defines the clinic's **relevant range**. The relevant range pertains to a particular time period—in this case, next year. For other time periods, the relevant range might differ from its estimate for the coming year.

Fixed Costs

Some costs, called **fixed costs**, are more or less known with certainty, regardless of the volume within the relevant range. For example, Northside Clinic has a labor force of well-trained, salaried permanent employees who are capable of handling up to 14,000 patient visits. This force would be increased or decreased only under unusual circumstances. As long as volume falls within

relevant range
The range of volume expected over some planning period. Alternatively, the range over which fixed costs remain constant—if volume falls outside the relevant range, the fixed cost estimate may be invalid.

fixed cost
A cost that is not related to the volume of services delivered; for example, facilities costs. Total fixed costs do not change if volume remains within the relevant range.

the relevant range of 12,000 to 14,000 visits, total labor costs at the clinic are fixed for the coming year, regardless of the number of patient visits.

Other examples of fixed costs include expenditures on facilities, diagnostic equipment, and information systems. After an organization has acquired these assets, it typically is locked in to them for some time, regardless of volume. Of course, no costs are fixed over the long run. At some point of increasing volume, healthcare businesses must incur additional fixed costs for new facilities and equipment, additional staffing, and so on. Likewise, if volume decreases by a substantial amount, an organization will likely reduce fixed costs by shedding part of its facilities and equipment and reducing its labor force.

It is important to note that fixed costs are fixed *in total* over the relevant range of volume. Because total fixed costs do not increase as volume goes up, average fixed costs *per unit of volume* decline as volume increases. This will become important when we discuss average cost. For now, it is important simply to distinguish between the behavior of fixed costs in total versus fixed costs per unit of volume.

Variable Costs

variable cost
A cost that is directly related to the volume of services delivered and changes in total with changes in volume; for example, the cost of clinical supplies.

Whereas some costs are fixed regardless of volume (within the relevant range), other resources are consumed as volume dictates. Costs that are directly related to volume are called **variable costs**. For example, the costs of the clinical supplies (e.g., rubber gloves, tongue depressors, hypodermics) used by the clinic would be classified as variable costs. If the number of patient visits increases, more supplies will be needed, so *total* variable costs will increase. Variable costs *per unit of volume* typically are considered to be constant and independent of the relevant range, so the relationship between volume and total variable costs is linear. However, the variable cost per unit can vary over time. For example, the costs of supplies may increase as a result of inflation.

In some cases, it is possible to convert fixed costs to variable costs. For example, some of the diagnostic equipment used in the clinic may be leased on a per procedure basis, which converts the cost of the equipment from a fixed cost to a variable cost. Similarly, some health services organizations pay their employees on the basis of the amount of work performed (e.g., hourly), which converts labor costs from fixed to variable.

The main idea behind cost behavior is that some costs (fixed) are more or less predictable because they are independent of volume, while other costs (variable) are much less predictable because they are related to volume. There are other cost classifications based on volume in addition to fixed costs and variable costs. These include semi-fixed costs, which we discuss in the supplement to this chapter.

> 1. Define the term *relevant range.*
> 2. Explain the features and provide examples of fixed and variable costs.
> 3. How does the time period affect the estimation of fixed and variable costs?

Underlying Cost Structure

Health services managers are particularly interested in how total costs are affected by changes in volume. The relationship between an organization's total costs and volume, called **underlying cost structure**, is used by managers in planning, controlling, and decision-making. The primary reason for defining an organization's underlying cost structure is to provide healthcare managers with a tool for forecasting costs (and, ultimately, profits) at different volumes.

underlying cost structure
The relationship between an organization's fixed costs, variable costs, and total costs; also called *cost structure.*

     To illustrate the concept of underlying cost structure, consider the hypothetical cost data presented in exhibit 5.1 for a hospital's clinical laboratory. The cost structure consists of both fixed and variable costs—that is, some of the costs are expected to be volume sensitive and some are not. This structure of fixed and variable costs is typical in healthcare organizations, as well as in most other businesses. To begin our discussion of cost structure, we assume that the relevant range is zero to 20,000 tests. In effect, we are assuming that the laboratory's cost structure holds (stays constant) for volumes of zero to 20,000 tests. (We are purposely using unrealistic volume and cost assumptions for ease of illustration.)

     According to exhibit 5.1, the laboratory has $150,000 in fixed costs, which consist primarily of labor, facilities, and equipment costs. Assuming the laboratory is kept open, it will incur these costs no matter how many tests it performs. In addition to the fixed costs, each test, on average, requires $10 in laboratory supplies, such as glass slides and reagents. The per unit (per test in this example) variable cost of $10 is defined as the **variable cost rate**. If the laboratory's volume doubles—for example, from 500 to 1,000 tests—*total variable costs* will double, from $5,000 to $10,000. However, the variable cost rate of $10 per test remains the same regardless of whether the test is the first, the hundredth, or the thousandth. Total variable costs, therefore, increase or decrease proportionately as volume changes, but the variable cost *rate* remains constant as long as volume remains within the relevant range.

variable cost rate
The variable cost of one unit of output (volume).

     In contrast to total variable costs, total fixed costs remain unchanged as volume varies. When volume doubles from 500 to 1,000 tests, fixed costs

EXHIBIT 5.1
Cost Structure
Illustration:
Fixed and
Variable Costs

Variable Costs per Test		Fixed Costs per Year	
Laboratory supplies	$10	Labor	$100,000
		Other fixed costs	50,000
			$150,000

Volume	Fixed Costs	Total Variable Costs	Total Costs	Average Cost per Test[a]
0	$150,000	$ 0	$150,000	—
1	150,000	10	150,010	$150,010.00
50	150,000	500	150,500	3,010.00
100	150,000	1,000	151,000	1,510.00
500	150,000	5,000	155,000	310.00
1,000	150,000	10,000	160,000	160.00
5,000	150,000	50,000	200,000	40.00
10,000	150,000	100,000	250,000	25.00
15,000	150,000	150,000	300,000	20.00
20,000	150,000	200,000	350,000	17.50

[a] Average cost per test is calculated as Total costs ÷ Volume.

remain at $150,000. Indeed, fixed costs are $150,000 for all volumes within the relevant range.

Because all costs in this example are either fixed or variable, total costs are simply the sum of the two. For example, at 5,000 tests, total costs are Fixed costs + Total variable costs = $150,000 + (5,000 × $10) = $150,000 + $50,000 = $200,000. Because they are tied to volume, total variable costs—and hence total costs—increase as volume increases, even though fixed costs remain constant.

The rightmost column in exhibit 5.1 contains the *average cost* per unit of volume, which in this example is the average cost per test. Average cost is calculated by dividing total costs by volume. For example, at 5,000 tests, with total costs of $200,000, the average cost per test is $200,000 ÷ 5,000 = $40. Because fixed costs, which are constant, are spread over more tests as volume increases, the average cost per test declines as volume increases. For example, when volume doubles from 5,000 to 10,000 tests, fixed costs remain at $150,000, but the fixed cost per test declines from $150,000 ÷ 5,000 = $30 to $150,000 ÷ 10,000 = $15. As the fixed cost per test declines from $30 to $15, the average cost per test declines from $30 + $10 = $40 to $15 + $10 = $25. Higher volume reduces average fixed costs and the average cost per unit of volume. This fact has important implications for the effect of volume changes on profitability. These implications are discussed further in a later section of this chapter.

The cost structure presented in tabular format in exhibit 5.1 is presented in graphical format in exhibit 5.2. Here, costs are shown on the vertical (y) axis, and volume (number of tests) is shown on the horizontal (x) axis. Because fixed costs are independent of volume, they are shown as a horizontal dashed line at $150,000. Total variable costs appear as an upward-sloping dotted line that starts at the origin (0 tests, $0 costs) and rises at a rate of $10 for each additional test. Thus, the slope of the total variable costs line is the variable cost rate. When fixed costs and total variable costs are combined to obtain total costs, the result is the upward-sloping solid line parallel to the total variable costs line but beginning at the y axis at a value of $150,000 (the fixed costs amount). In effect, the total costs line is nothing more than the total variable costs line shifted upward by the amount of fixed costs.

Note that exhibit 5.2 is not drawn to scale. Furthermore, the relevant range is unrealistically large. The intent here is to emphasize the general shape of a cost structure graph and not its exact position. Also, total variable costs are plotted as a straight line (i.e., they are linear) because the variable cost rate is assumed to be constant over the relevant range. Although a curved total

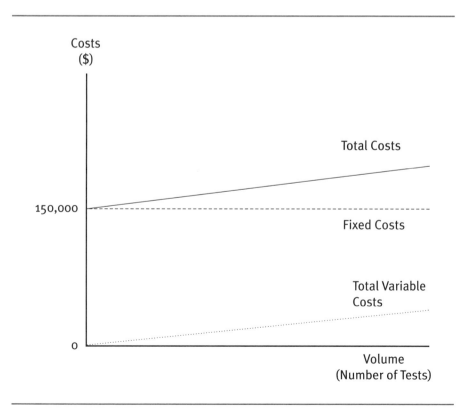

EXHIBIT 5.2
Cost Structure
Graph

variable costs line can occur in some situations, we assume throughout the book that the variable cost rate is constant, and hence total variable costs are linear, at least within the relevant range. This assumption is not unreasonable for most health services organizations in most situations.

1. What is meant by the term *underlying cost structure*?
2. Construct a simple table like the one in exhibit 5.1 for medical supplies with a relevant range of 0 to 500 procedures (unit), $20 in variable costs per procedure, and $500,000 fixed costs. Discuss its elements.
3. Sketch and explain a simple graph similar to the one in exhibit 5.2 to match your table.

Profit Analysis

profit analysis
A technique applied to an organization's cost and revenue structure that analyzes the effect of volume changes on costs and profits; also called *CVP (cost-volume-profit) analysis.*

Profit analysis is an analytical technique used primarily to analyze the effects of volume changes on profit. However, the same procedures can be used to assess the effects of volume changes on costs, so this type of analysis is often called *cost-volume-profit (CVP) analysis.* CVP analysis allows managers to examine the effects of alternative assumptions about costs, volume, and prices. Clearly, such information is useful as managers evaluate future courses of action regarding pricing and the introduction of new services.

Basic Data

Exhibit 5.3 presents the estimated annual costs for Atlanta Clinic, a subsidiary of Atlanta Health Services, for 2021. These costs are based on the clinic's most likely estimate (best guess) of volume—75,000 visits. The most likely estimate often is called the *base case*, so the data in exhibit 5.3 represent the clinic's base case cost forecast. Expected total costs for 2021 are $7,080,962. Because these costs support 75,000 visits, the forecast average cost per visit is $7,080,962 ÷ 75,000 = $94.41.

Focusing solely on total costs, however, does not provide the clinic's managers with much information regarding alternative financial outcomes for 2021. Using this single amount (total costs) suggests that the clinic's costs will remain constant regardless of the number of patient visits. Similarly, the base case average cost per visit amount of $94.41 implicitly treats all costs as variable costs, suggesting that the cost per visit would be $94.41 regardless

	Variable Costs	Fixed Costs	Total Costs
Salaries and Benefits:			
Management and supervision	$ 0	$ 928,687	$ 928,687
Coordinators	442,617	598,063	1,040,680
Specialists	0	38,600	38,600
Technicians	681,383	552,670	1,234,053
Clerical/administrative	71,182	58,240	129,422
Social security taxes	89,622	163,188	252,810
Group health insurance	115,924	211,081	327,005
Professional fees	325,489	383,360	708,849
Supplies	313,283	231,184	544,467
Utilities	74,000	45,040	119,040
Allocated costs	0	1,757,349	1,757,349
Total	$2,113,500	$4,967,462	$7,080,962

EXHIBIT 5.3
Atlanta Clinic: Forecast Cost Data for 2021 (based on 75,000 patient visits)

of volume. Total cost information is necessary and useful, but the detailed breakdown of costs given in exhibit 5.3 gives the clinic's managers more insight into prospective financial outcomes for 2021 than is possible with only total cost information.

Exhibit 5.3 categorizes the clinic's total costs of $7,080,962 into two components: total variable costs of $2,113,500 and total fixed costs of $4,967,462. These cost amounts are fundamentally different, in both quantitative and qualitative terms. The total fixed costs of $4,967,462 are expected to be borne by the clinic regardless of the actual volume in 2021. However, the total variable costs of $2,113,500 apply only to a volume of 75,000 patient visits. If the actual number of visits realized in 2021 is less than or greater than 75,000, total variable costs will be, respectively, less than or greater than $2,113,500. (Of course, this is the primary reason that costs are classified as fixed and variable in the first place.)

The best way to show that total variable costs vary with volume is to express variable costs on a per unit (variable cost rate) basis. For Atlanta Clinic, the implied variable cost rate is $2,113,500 ÷ 75,000 visits = $28.18 per visit. Thus, the clinic's total costs at any volume within the relevant range can be calculated as follows:

Total costs = Fixed costs + Total variable costs
　　　　　= $4,967,462 + ($28.18 × Number of visits).

> ***Key Equation: Underlying Cost Structure***
> The underlying cost structure of a healthcare entity defines the relationship between volume and costs. To illustrate, assume that a clinical laboratory has fixed costs of $500,000 and a variable cost rate of $20. The underlying cost structure of the laboratory can be written as follows:
>
> $$\text{Total costs} = \text{Fixed costs} + \text{Total variable costs}$$
> $$= \$500,000 + (\$20 \times \text{Volume}).$$
>
> Thus, at a volume of 20,000 tests, total costs equal $900,000:
>
> $$\text{Total costs} = \$500,000 + (\$20 \times 20,000)$$
> $$= \$500,000 + \$400,000$$
> $$= \$900,000.$$

This equation, representing Atlanta Clinic's underlying cost structure, explicitly shows that total costs depend on volume. To illustrate the use of the cost structure model, consider three potential volumes for 2021: 70,000, 75,000, and 80,000 patient visits:

Volume = 70,000:
$$\text{Total costs} = \$4,967,462 + (\$28.18 \times 70,000)$$
$$= \$4,967,462 + \$1,972,600 = \$6,940,062$$
Volume = 75,000:
$$\text{Total costs} = \$4,967,462 + (\$28.18 \times 75,000)$$
$$= \$4,967,462 + \$2,113,500 = \$7,080,962$$
Volume = 80,000:
$$\text{Total costs} = \$4,967,462 + (\$28.18 \times 80,000)$$
$$= \$4,967,462 + \$2,254,400 = \$7,221,862$$

When an organization's costs are expressed in this way, it is easy to see that higher volume leads to higher total costs.

Atlanta Clinic's underlying cost structure is plotted in exhibit 5.4. (To simplify the graph, we assume that the relevant range extends to zero visits.) As in exhibit 5.2, fixed costs are shown as a horizontal dashed line, and total costs are shown as an upward-sloping solid line with a slope (rise over run) equal to the variable cost rate—$28.18 per visit. In exhibit 5.4, the graphical presentation has been simplified by not showing total variable costs as a separate line starting at the origin. Rather, total variable costs are represented in exhibit 5.4 by the vertical distance between the total costs line and the fixed costs line.

Note that Atlanta Clinic does not literally write a check for $28.18 for each patient visit, although there may be examples of variable costs in which this is the case. Rather, Atlanta's cost structure indicates that the clinic uses certain resources that its managers have defined as inherently variable, and the best estimate of the value of those resources is $28.18 per visit.

The cost structure data in exhibit 5.3 could be estimated in several ways. One way would be to use a time–motion study (a quantitative study that collects information on duration and movements required to complete specific tasks) and interviews with clinic personnel. For a less intrusive approach, cost accountants could plot the total costs of the clinic at different volume levels for the past several years and then run a regression on those data. In this case, the beta term (slope) of the regression would be the variable cost rate—$28.18— and the alpha term (intercept) would be fixed costs—$4,967,462.

To complete the profit (CVP) model, a revenue component must be added. For 2021, Atlanta Clinic expects fee-for-service revenues, on average, to be $100 per patient visit. Total revenues are plotted in exhibit 5.4 as an upward-sloping solid line starting at the origin with a slope of $100 per visit. If there were no visits, total revenues would be zero; at one visit, total revenues would be $100; at ten visits, total revenues would be $1,000; at 75,000 visits, total revenues would be $7,500,000; and so on. Note that the vertical dashed line is drawn at the point where total revenues equal total

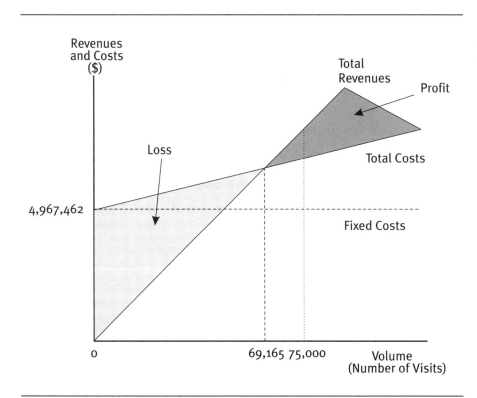

EXHIBIT 5.4
Atlanta Clinic:
CVP Graphical
Model

For Your Consideration
Underlying Cost Structure and Relevant Range

In general, an organization's underlying cost structure is defined for a specified relevant range. For example, Atlanta Clinic's underlying cost structure is given as follows:

Total costs = Fixed costs + Total variable costs
= $4,967,462 + ($28.18 × Number of visits),

and the relevant range for this structure is 65,000 to 85,000 visits.

Now, assume that a new payer makes a proposal to the clinic that would increase next year's volume by 15,000 visits, which would increase the expected number of visits to 90,000. The financial staff presents you, the CEO, with an analysis of the proposal that uses the above cost structure. For example, total costs are calculated as follows:

Total costs = $4,967,462 + ($28.18 × 90,000)
= $4,967,462 + $2,536,200
= $7,503,662.

What is your initial reaction to the analysis? Is it valid, or must it be redone? Which variable in the total costs calculation is most likely to change?

costs, and the vertical dotted line is drawn at the base case volume estimate—75,000 visits. We examine the significance of these lines in later sections of this chapter.

Before we close our discussion of Atlanta's cost structure, it is important to emphasize that this cost structure (primarily the fixed cost estimate) is valid only within the relevant range.

The Projected P&L Statement

One of the first steps that Atlanta Clinic's managers could take in terms of the profit analysis is to construct a statement that shows the forecast profit for 2021, given the most likely assumptions. Such a forecast is called the base case **profit and loss (P&L) statement**. The term *profit and loss* distinguishes this statement from Atlanta Clinic's audited income statement. There are two primary differences between a P&L statement and an income statement. First, P&L statements, as with all managerial accounting data, can be developed to best serve decision-making purposes within the organization, as opposed to following generally accepted accounting principles (GAAP). Second, P&L statements can be created for any subunit within an organization, whereas income statements normally are created only for the overall organization and major subsidiaries.

Atlanta Clinic's 2021 base case projected P&L statement is shown in exhibit 5.5. The bottom line, designated by a double underline, shows Atlanta's 2021 profit forecast using base case values for costs, volume, and prices (reimbursement rates). Note that the format of a P&L statement used for profit analysis purposes distinguishes between variable and fixed costs, whereas a typical income statement (or a P&L statement used for another purpose) does not make this distinction. Also, the projected P&L statement contains a line labeled "total contribution margin." This important concept is discussed in the next section.

The projected P&L statement used in profit analysis contains four variables—three of the variables are assumed, and the fourth is calculated. In exhibit 5.5, the assumed variables are expected volume (75,000 visits),

profit and loss (P&L) statement
A statement that summarizes the revenues, expenses, and profitability of either the entire organization or a subunit of it; can be formatted in different ways for different purposes and does not conform to generally accepted accounting principles (GAAP).

Total revenues ($100 × 75,000)	$7,500,000
Total variable costs ($28.18 × 75,000)	2,113,500
Total contribution margin ($71.82 × 75,000)	$5,386,500
Fixed costs	4,967,462
Profit	$419,038

EXHIBIT 5.5
Atlanta Clinic: 2021 Base Case Forecast P&L Statement (based on 75,000 patient visits)

expected price ($100 per visit reimbursement), and expected costs (delineated in terms of the clinic's underlying cost structure). Profit, the fourth variable, is calculated on the basis of the values assumed for the other three variables.

The base case forecast P&L statement shown in exhibit 5.5 represents only one point on the graphical model in exhibit 5.4. This point is denoted by the dotted vertical line at a volume of 75,000 patient visits. Moving up along this dotted line, the distance from the x axis to the horizontal fixed costs line represents the $4,967,462 in fixed costs. The distance from the fixed costs line to the total costs line represents the $2,113,500 in total variable costs. The distance between the total costs line and the total revenues line represents the $419,038 in profit. As in previous graphs, exhibit 5.4 is not drawn to scale because it will not be used to develop numerical data. Rather, it provides the clinic's managers with a pictorial representation of its projected financial future.

Contribution Margin

The base case forecast P&L statement in exhibit 5.5 introduces the concept of **contribution margin**, which is defined as the difference between per unit revenue and per unit variable cost (the variable cost rate). In this illustration, the contribution margin is Per visit revenue – Variable cost rate = $100.00 – $28.18 = $71.82. What is the meaning of this contribution margin value of $71.82? The contribution margin may seem like profit because it is calculated as revenue minus cost. However, none of the fixed costs of providing service have been included in the cost amount used in the calculation, so it is **not** profit. Because only variable costs have been subtracted from revenues, rather than total costs, the contribution margin is the dollar amount per visit that is available to cover Atlanta Clinic's fixed costs. Only after fixed costs are fully covered does the contribution margin begin to contribute to profit.

With a contribution margin of $71.82 for each of the clinic's 75,000 visits, the projected base case *total contribution margin* for 2021 is $71.82 × 75,000 = $5,386,500, which is sufficient to cover the clinic's fixed costs of $4,967,462 and then provide a $5,386,500 – $4,967,462 = $419,038 profit. After fixed costs have been covered, any additional visits contribute to the clinic's profit at a rate of $71.82 per visit. Contribution margin is a concept that will be used again and again as our discussion of profit analysis continues.

contribution margin
The difference between per unit revenue and per unit cost (variable cost rate); in other words, the dollar amount that each unit of volume contributes to covering fixed costs and, once fixed costs are covered, to profit.

1. Construct a simple P&L statement like the one shown in exhibit 5.5 and discuss its elements.
2. Sketch and explain a simple graph to match your P&L statement.
3. Define and explain the concept of *contribution margin*.

Breakeven Analysis

breakeven analysis
A type of analysis that estimates the amount of some variable—such as volume, price, or variable cost rate—that is needed to break even.

In healthcare finance, **breakeven analysis** is applied in many different situations, so it is necessary to understand the context to fully understand the meaning of the term *breakeven*. Generically, breakeven analysis is used to determine a *breakeven point*, which is the value of a given input variable that produces some minimum desired result. For now, we will use breakeven analysis to determine the volume at which a business becomes financially self-sufficient, called the *breakeven volume*. The breakeven analysis discussed here is actually part of profit (CVP) analysis. Therefore, it can be applied not only to entire businesses but also to subunits within businesses such as departments and individual services.

accounting breakeven
The volume required to produce revenues sufficient to cover all accounting costs; in other words, zero profitability.

Businesses can conduct volume breakeven analysis, which can be defined in two ways. **Accounting breakeven** is defined as the volume needed to produce zero profit. In other words, it is the volume that produces revenues equal to accounting costs. Alternatively, **economic breakeven** is the volume needed to produce a specified profit level—that is, the volume that produces revenues equal to accounting costs plus some desired profit amount.

economic breakeven
The volume required to produce revenues sufficient to cover all accounting costs and to provide a specified profit level.

As mentioned in the previous section, the P&L statement format used here is a four-variable model. When the focus is projected profit, the three assumed variables are costs, volume, and price (reimbursement amount), and profit is calculated. When the focus is volume breakeven, the same four variables are used, but profit is assumed to be known, and volume is the unknown (calculated) value. However, it is also possible to assume a value for profit, volume, and price (or costs) and then calculate the breakeven value for costs (or price). To illustrate volume breakeven, the projected P&L statement presented in exhibit 5.5 can be expressed algebraically as the following equation:

$$\text{Total revenues} - \text{Total variable costs} - \text{Fixed costs} = \text{Profit}$$
$$(\$100 \times \text{Volume}) - (\$28.18 \times \text{Volume}) - \$4{,}967{,}462 = \text{Profit}.$$

Here, we have simply taken the P&L statement, which is presented vertically, and transformed it into an equation, which is presented horizontally and treats volume as an unknown quantity. At accounting breakeven, the clinic's profit equals zero, so the equation can be rewritten with zero in place of the profit amount:

$$(\$100 \times \text{Volume}) - (\$28.18 \times \text{Volume}) - \$4,967,462 = \$0.$$

Rearranging the terms so that only the terms related to volume appear on the left side produces this equation:

$$(\$100 \times \text{Volume}) - (\$28.18 \times \text{Volume}) = \$4,967,462.$$

Using basic algebra, the two terms on the left side can be combined because volume appears in both. The end result is this:

$$(\$100 - \$28.18) \times \text{Volume} = \$4,967,462$$
$$\$71.82 \times \text{Volume} = \$4,967,462.$$

Key Equation: Volume Breakeven

Suppose a clinical laboratory has fixed costs of $500,000, a variable cost rate of $20, and average revenue per test of $50. Volume breakeven is obtained by solving the following equation for volume:

$$\text{Total revenues} - \text{Total variable costs} - \text{Fixed costs} = \text{Profit}$$
$$(\$50 \times \text{Volume}) - (\$20 \times \text{Volume}) - \$500,000 = \text{Profit}.$$

For accounting breakeven, profit is zero, so the equation becomes:

$$(\$50 \times \text{Volume}) - (\$20 \times \text{Volume}) = \$500,000.$$

And solving for volume gives the breakeven amount:

$$(\$30 \times \text{Volume}) = \$500,000$$
$$\text{Volume} = 16,667 \text{ tests.}$$

Note that $30 is the contribution margin, so the equation for breakeven volume can be simplified as follows:

$$(\text{Contribution margin} \times \text{Volume}) = \text{Fixed costs}$$
$$(\$30 \times \text{Volume}) = \$500,000$$
$$\text{Volume} = 16,667 \text{ tests.}$$

For economic breakeven, insert the desired profit amount on the right side of the equation in place of $0.

The left side of the breakeven equation now contains the contribution margin, $71.82, multiplied by volume. Here, the previous conclusion that the clinic will break even when the total contribution margin equals fixed costs is reaffirmed. Solving the equation for volume results in a breakeven point of $4,967,462 ÷ $71.82 = 69,165 visits. Any volume greater than 69,165 visits produces a profit for the clinic, while any volume less than 69,165 results in a loss.

The logic behind the breakeven point is this: Each patient visit brings in $100, of which $28.18 is the variable cost to treat the patient. This leaves a $71.82 contribution margin from each visit. If the clinic sets the contribution margin aside for the first 69,165 visits in 2021, it will have $4,967,430, which is enough (except for a small rounding difference) to cover its fixed costs. Once the clinic exceeds breakeven volume, each visit's contribution margin will flow directly to profit. If the clinic achieves its volume estimate of 75,000 visits, the 5,835 visits above the breakeven point will produce a total profit of 5,835 × $71.82 = $419,070, which matches the profit (again except for a rounding difference) shown on the clinic's base case forecast P&L statement in exhibit 5.5.

We can use the graph in exhibit 5.4 to visualize the breakeven concept. At accounting breakeven, the profit is zero, so total revenues must equal total costs. In exhibit 5.4, this condition holds at the intersection of the total revenues line and the total costs line. This point is indicated by a vertical dashed line drawn at a volume of 69,165 visits. The logic of the breakeven point shown in exhibit 5.4 goes back to the clinic's fixed and variable cost structure. Before even one patient walks in the door, the clinic has already committed to $4,967,462 in fixed costs. Because the total revenues line is steeper than the total variable costs line, and hence the total costs line, as volume increases, total revenues eventually catch up to the clinic's total costs. Any level of utilization to the right of the breakeven point produces a profit, which is shown as a dark shaded area; any level of utilization to the left of the breakeven point results in a loss, which is shown as a light-shaded area.

The relationship between breakeven analysis and the forecast P&L statement is important to understand. Based on the clinic's base case projection of 75,000 visits, it can anticipate a profit of $419,038. However, management may worry that the clinic will not achieve this projected volume and ask the following question: What is the minimum number of visits needed to at least break even? The answer is 69,165 visits.

To verify the breakeven point calculation, exhibit 5.6 presents the forecast P&L statement for 69,165 visits. Except for a small rounding difference, the profit at the accounting breakeven point is $0. (The breakeven point is actually 69,165.4 visits.) As mentioned previously, at accounting breakeven volume, the total contribution margin only covers fixed costs, resulting in zero profit.

This breakeven analysis contains three important assumptions. The first assumption is that the price or set of prices for different types of patients and different payers is independent of volume. In other words, volume increases are not attained by lowering prices, and price increases are not met with volume declines. The second assumption is that costs can be reasonably subdivided into fixed and variable components. The third assumption is that both fixed costs and the variable cost rate are independent of volume over the relevant range, so both the total costs line and the total revenues line are linear.

Breakeven analysis is often performed in an iterative manner. After the breakeven volume is calculated, managers must determine whether the resulting volume can realistically be achieved at the price assumed in the analysis. If the price appears to be unreasonable for the breakeven volume, a new price has to be estimated and the breakeven analysis repeated. Likewise, if the cost structure used for the calculation appears to be unrealistic at the breakeven volume, operational assumptions and hence cost assumptions should be changed and the analysis repeated.

Instead of seeking the number of visits needed for accounting breakeven, Atlanta Clinic's managers may ask for the number of visits needed to achieve a $100,000 profit—or any other profit level. By building a profit target into the breakeven analysis, the focus shifts to *economic breakeven*. The clinic will have a $419,038 profit if it has 75,000 visits, and it will have no profit if it has 69,165 visits. Thus, the number of visits required to achieve a $100,000 profit target (economic breakeven) is somewhere between 69,165 and 75,000. In fact, the number of visits required is 70,558:

$$\text{Total revenues} - \text{Total variable costs} - \text{Fixed costs} = \text{Profit}$$
$$(\$100 \times \text{Volume}) - (\$28.18 \times \text{Volume}) - \$4{,}967{,}462 = \$100{,}000$$
$$(\$71.82 \times \text{Volume}) - \$4{,}967{,}462 = \$100{,}000$$
$$\$71.82 \times \text{Volume} = \$5{,}067{,}462$$
$$\text{Volume} = 70{,}558.$$

Total revenues ($100 × 69,165)	$6,916,500
Total variable costs ($28.18 × 69,165)	1,949,070
Total contribution margin	$4,967,430
Fixed costs	4,967,462
Profit	($ 32)

EXHIBIT 5.6
Atlanta Clinic: 2021 Projected P&L Statement (based on 69,165 patient visits)

We could also calculate the economic breakeven of 70,558 using the contribution margin concept. With a contribution margin of $71.82, it takes $100,000 ÷ $71.82 = 1,392 visits to generate an additional $100,000 in profit contribution after all accounting costs are covered. Thus, economic breakeven occurs at a volume of accounting breakeven + 1,392 = 69,165 + 1,392 = 70,557 visits. This is the same economic breakeven point (except for a rounding difference) that we calculated using the equation above.

1. What is the purpose of breakeven analysis?
2. What is the equation for volume breakeven?
3. Why is breakeven analysis often conducted in an iterative manner?
4. What is the difference between accounting breakeven and economic breakeven?

Profit Analysis in a Discounted Fee-for-Service Environment

As noted in the previous discussion, profit analysis is valuable to healthcare managers because it provides information about expected costs and profitability under alternative estimates of volume (or costs or prices). To learn more about its usefulness, suppose that one-third (25,000) of Atlanta Clinic's expected 75,000 visits come from Peachtree HMO, which has proposed that its new contract with the clinic contain a 40 percent discount from charges. Thus, the net price for its patients would be $60 instead of the undiscounted $100. If the clinic refuses this proposal, Peachtree has threatened to take its members to another provider.

On its face, Peachtree's proposal appears to be unacceptable. Among other reasons, $60 is less than the full average cost of providing service, which was determined to be $94.41 per visit at a volume of 75,000. Thus, on a full-cost basis, Atlanta would lose $94.41 − $60 = $34.41 per visit on Peachtree's patients. With an estimated 25,000 visits, the discounted contract would result in a total profit loss of 25,000 × $34.41 = $860,250. However, before Atlanta's managers reject Peachtree's proposal, it must be examined more closely.

The Impact of Rejecting the Proposal
If Atlanta's managers rejected the proposal, the clinic would lose market share—an estimated 25,000 visits. The forecast P&L statement that would result, which is based on 50,000 undiscounted visits, is shown in exhibit

5.7. At the lower volume, the clinic's total revenues, total variable costs, and total contribution margin decrease proportionately (i.e., by one-third). However, fixed costs are not reduced, so Atlanta would not be able to cover its fixed costs, incurring a loss of $3,591,000 − $4,967,462 = −$1,376,462. To view the situation another way, the expected volume of 50,000 visits is 19,165 short of the breakeven point, so the clinic would be operating to the left of the breakeven point in exhibit 5.4. This shortfall of 19,165 visits, multiplied by the contribution margin of $71.82, produces a loss of $1,376,430, which is the same as shown in exhibit 5.7 (except for a rounding difference).

Clearly, the major factor behind the projected loss is the clinic's fixed cost structure of $4,967,462. With a projected decrease in volume of 33 percent, perhaps the clinic could reduce its fixed costs. The relevant range of 65,000 to 85,000 visits for the existing cost structure provides some evidence that fixed costs could be reduced if volume fell to 50,000 visits.

If Atlanta's managers perceive the volume reduction to be permanent, they may begin to reduce the fixed costs currently in place to meet an anticipated volume of 75,000 visits. However, if the clinic's managers believe that the loss of volume is merely a temporary occurrence, they may choose to maintain the current fixed cost structure and absorb the loss expected for next year. It would not make sense for them to start selling off facilities and equipment and laying off staff, only to reverse these actions one year later. The critical point, though, is that the loss of volume caused by rejecting Peachtree's proposal could have a significant negative impact on the clinic's profitability.

The Impact of Accepting the Proposal

An alternative strategy for the clinic's managers would be to accept Peachtree's proposal. The resulting projected P&L statement is presented in exhibit 5.8. The weighted average revenue per visit of serving the two different payer groups is $(2/3 \times \$100) + (1/3 \times \$60) = \$86.67$. Total revenues based on this average revenue per visit would be $75,000 \times \$86.67 = \$6,500,250$, which equals the value for total revenues shown in exhibit 5.8 (except for a rounding difference). With a lower average revenue per visit, the contribution margin falls to $86.67 − $28.18 = $58.49, which leads to a lower total contribution margin.

The critical point here is that the clinic's total revenues have decreased significantly from the previous situation in which all visits bring in $100 in revenue (see exhibit 5.5). However, the clinic's total costs remain the same because it is handling the same number of visits—75,000. The discount only affects revenues, and the result of accepting Peachtree's proposal is a projected loss of $580,962.

EXHIBIT 5.7
Atlanta Clinic:
2021 Projected
P&L Statement
(based on
50,000
undiscounted
patient visits)

Total revenues ($100 × 50,000)	$5,000,000
Total variable costs ($28.18 × 50,000)	1,409,000
Total contribution margin ($71.82 × 50,000)	$3,591,000
Fixed costs	4,967,462
Profit (Loss)	($1,376,462)

Another way of confirming the expected loss at 75,000 visits is to calculate the clinic's accounting breakeven point at the new average revenue per visit of $86.67. The new breakeven point is 84,928 visits, which confirms that the clinic will lose money at 75,000 visits. Because the clinic is projected to be 84,928 – 75,000 = 9,928 visits below breakeven, and the contribution margin is now $58.49, the projected loss is 9,928 × $58.49 = $580,689, which is the amount shown in exhibit 5.8 (except for a rounding difference).

The change in breakeven point that results from accepting Peachtree's proposal is graphed in exhibit 5.9, along with the original breakeven point. The new total revenues line (the dot-dashed line) is flatter than the original line, so when it is combined with the existing cost structure, the breakeven point is pushed to the right, to 84,928 visits. However, any cost control actions taken by Atlanta's managers would either flatten (if variable costs are lowered) or lower (if fixed costs are reduced) the total costs line and hence push the breakeven point back to the left.

In the new discounted charge environment, the core economic underpinnings have not changed. The clinic is worse off economically, but the clinic's cost structure, managerial incentives, and solutions to financial problems are essentially the same. To increase profit, more services must be provided or costs must be cut. In short, the movement from charges to discounted charges is not radical with regard to its impact on profit analysis and managerial decision-making. The major difference is that the clinic is now under greater financial pressure.

Evaluating the Alternative Strategies

What should Atlanta's managers do? If Peachtree's discount proposal is accepted, the clinic is expected to lose $580,962 rather than make a profit of $419,038. The difference is a swing of $1 million in profit in the wrong direction—hardly an enticing prospect. What happened to the "missing" $1 million? It is now in the hands of Peachtree HMO, which is paying $1 million less to one of its providers (25,000 visits × $40 savings = $1,000,000). This will be reflected as a cost savings on Peachtree's income statement and, if the savings are not passed on to the payers (typically employers), result in a $1 million profit increase for Peachtree HMO.

Undiscounted revenue ($100 × 50,000)	$5,000,000
Discounted revenue ($60 × 25,000)	1,500,000
Total revenues ($86.67 × 75,000)	$6,500,000
Total variable costs ($28.18 × 75,000)	2,113,500
Total contribution margin ($58.49 × 75,000)	$4,386,500
Fixed costs	4,967,462
Profit	($ 580,962)

EXHIBIT 5.8
Atlanta Clinic: 2021 Projected P&L Statement (based on 50,000 visits at $100 and 25,000 visits at $60)

If market forces in Atlanta Clinic's service area suggest that making a counteroffer to Peachtree is not feasible—perhaps because the clinic is competing against another provider—the comparison of a loss of $580,792 to a profit of $419,038 is irrelevant. The only relevant issue in the short term is the comparison of the $580,792 loss if the clinic accepts the proposal to the $1,376,462 loss if the proposal is rejected and Peachtree's patients are lost to the clinic.

Although neither outcome is appealing, accepting the discount appears to be the lesser of two evils. In fact, accepting the discount is better by $1,376,462 − $580,792 = $795,670. Accepting the discount proposal

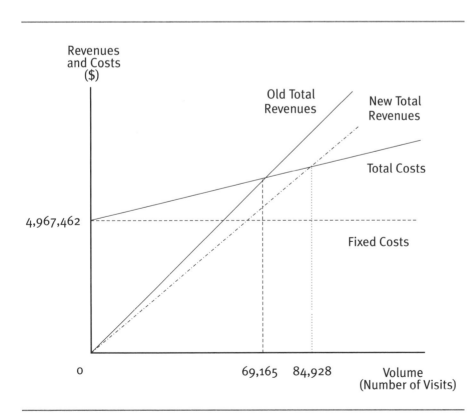

EXHIBIT 5.9
Atlanta Clinic: Breakeven Point with Discounted Revenue

appears to be Atlanta's best **short-term** strategy because Peachtree's patients still produce a positive contribution margin of $60 − $28.18 = $31.82 per visit, which would be forgone if the clinic rebuffed Peachtree's offer. That $31.82 per visit contribution margin, when multiplied by the expected 25,000 visits on the contract, produces $795,500 in total contribution margin that otherwise would be lost. This $795,500 can contribute to covering Atlanta Clinic's fixed costs while it considers whether and how to cut costs.

However, Atlanta's managers cannot ignore the **long-term** implications of accepting the proposal. These implications are not addressed in detail here, but clearly the clinic cannot survive either scenario in the long run because its revenues are not covering the full costs of providing services. In the meantime, taking a $580,962 loss in 2021 may be better than bleeding $1,376,462 until the clinic can adjust to market forces in its service area. This adjustment may be as simple as merely absorbing the losses while the clinic's competitors, perhaps in poorer financial condition, exit the market as they face the same difficult economic choices. Should this happen, a new equilibrium would be established in the marketplace that would allow the clinic to raise its prices. If the long-term solution is not that simple, Atlanta Clinic must reduce its cost structure.

Another problem associated with accepting the discount offer is that the clinic's other payers will undoubtedly learn about the reduced payments and want to renegotiate their contracts with the same, or an even greater, discount. Such a reaction would clearly place the clinic under even more financial pressure, requiring a draconian change in either volume or operating costs to ensure its survival.

Marginal Analysis

The Atlanta/Peachtree illustration points out one way in which the contribution margin can be used in managerial decision-making. To reinforce the concept, the analysis can be viewed from a different perspective. Suppose the clinic forecasts a base case volume of only **50,000 visits** for 2021 and Peachtree HMO offers to provide the clinic 25,000 additional visits at $60 revenue per visit. These 25,000 visits are called *marginal*, or *incremental*, *visits*, because they add to the existing base volume of visits. Should Atlanta's managers accept this offer? (For purposes of this marginal analysis illustration, assume the relevant range begins at 50,000 visits.)

marginal cost
The cost of one additional unit of volume; for example, one more inpatient day or patient visit.

Although each marginal visit from the contract brings in only $60 compared with $100 on the clinic's other contracts, the **marginal cost**, or *incremental cost*—the cost associated with each additional visit—is the variable cost rate of $28.18. If we assume that the relevant range extends to 75,000 patient visits, the clinic's $4,967,462 in fixed costs will be incurred whether the volume is 50,000 or 75,000 visits. Because fixed costs are assumed to be unaffected by the offer, these costs are not relevant to the analysis. In finance terms, the clinic's fixed costs are said to be *nonincremental* to the decision. With each new visit having a contribution margin (the *marginal contribution margin*) of $60.00 – $28.18 = $31.82, each visit contributes positively to Atlanta's recovery of fixed costs and potentially to profits, so the offer must be seriously considered.

Because fixed costs are often difficult to change quickly, in the short term, contribution margin (as opposed to full costs) is the most important consideration in many managerial decisions. As the Atlanta/Peachtree illustration demonstrates, Atlanta Clinic would have been financially worse off had it walked away from the Peachtree contract because the $60 reimbursement rate was not sufficient to cover its full costs (variable and fixed costs). In the long term, however, full costs must be covered (or costs must be cut) for the organization to remain viable.

Finally, note that the analysis would change if 75,000 visits were beyond the relevant range. In that case, new fixed costs would have to be incurred, which would be incremental to the decision. In this situation, the marginal cost would consist of the variable cost rate **plus** the incremental fixed cost per additional visit. If this pushes the marginal cost per visit above $60, the offer loses its financial attractiveness.

SELF-TEST QUESTIONS

1. What is the impact of a discount contract on fixed costs, total variable costs, and the breakeven point?
2. What is meant by *marginal analysis*?
3. What is meant by the statement "Marginal analysis is made more complicated by long-term considerations"?
4. Do marginal costs always consist only of variable costs?

Profit Analysis in a Capitated Environment

The analysis changes when a provider operates in a capitated, rather than a fee-for-service, environment. Although the extent of third-party payer use of capitation has varied over time, capitation is being used more as healthcare reform forces payers to grapple with the problem of increasing quality while constraining costs. For example, one payment strategy for accountable care organizations is to couple capitation payments to providers with meaningful incentives to ensure quality. Our discussion of capitated payment profit analysis both provides an excellent review of the concepts presented in previous sections and highlights the basic differences between capitation and fee-for-service reimbursement methodologies.

To begin, assume that the purchaser of services from Atlanta Clinic is the Alliance, a local business coalition. As in previous illustrations, assume the Alliance is paying the clinic $7,500,000 to provide services for an expected 75,000 visits, but now the amount is capitated. Although projected total revenues remain the same as the previous base case (see exhibit 5.5), the nature of the capitated revenues is different. The $7,500,000 that the Alliance is paying is not explicitly related to the amount of services (number of visits) provided by the clinic, but rather to the size of the covered employee group. In essence, Atlanta Clinic is no longer merely selling healthcare services as it had in the fee-for-service or discounted fee-for-service environment. Now the clinic is taking on the insurance function in the sense that it is responsible for the health status (utilization) of the covered population and must bear the associated risks. If the total costs of services delivered by the clinic exceed the premium revenue (paid monthly on a per member basis), the clinic will suffer the financial consequences. However, if the clinic can efficiently manage the healthcare of the covered population and keep the costs of services delivered by the clinic below the premium revenue, it will benefit financially.

How might Atlanta's managers evaluate whether the $7,500,000 revenue attached to the contract is adequate? To do the analysis, they need two critical pieces of information: cost information and actuarial (utilization) information. The clinic already has the cost accounting information—the full average cost per visit is expected to be $94.41 (at a volume of 75,000 visits), with an underlying cost structure of $28.18 per visit in variable costs and $4,967,462 in fixed costs. For its actuarial information, Atlanta's managers estimate that the Alliance will have a covered population of 18,750 members, with an expected utilization rate of four visits per member per year. Thus, the total number of visits expected is $18,750 \times 4 = 75,000$. Although this appears to be the same 75,000 visits as in the fee-for-service environment, the implications of the Alliance volume differ significantly. Because there is no direct link between the volume of services provided and revenues, utilization above the expected level will bring increased costs with **no corresponding increase** in revenues.

The revenues expected from this contract—$7,500,000—exceed the expected costs of serving this population, which are 75,000 visits multiplied by $94.41 per visit, or $7,080,750. Thus, this contract is expected to generate a profit of $419,250, which, not surprisingly, is the same as the original base case in the fee-for-service environment (except for a rounding difference) (see exhibit 5.5).

A Graphical View in Terms of Utilization
Exhibit 5.10 presents a graphical profit (CVP) analysis for the capitation contract that is constructed similar to the fee-for-service graphs shown previously

for Atlanta Clinic. The horizontal axis shows volume (number of visits), while the vertical axis shows revenues and costs. The graph also shows the same underlying cost structure of $4,967,462 in fixed costs coupled with a variable cost rate of $28.18. One significant difference, however, is that instead of being upward sloping, the total revenues line is horizontal, which means that total revenue is $7,500,000 regardless of volume **as measured by the number of visits**.

Several subtle messages are inherent in this flat revenue line. First, it tells managers that revenue is driven by something other than the volume of services provided. Under capitation, revenue is driven by the insurance contract (i.e., by the premium payment and the number of covered lives, or *enrollees*). This change in revenue source is the core of the logic switch from fee-for-service to capitation: The clinic is being rewarded to manage the healthcare of the population served rather than merely to provide services. However, the clinic's costs are still driven by the amount of services provided (the number of visits).

A second critical point about exhibit 5.10 is the difference between the flat revenue and the flat fixed cost base. Atlanta has a spread of $7,500,000 − $4,967,462 = $2,532,538 to work with in managing the healthcare of this population for the period of the contract. If total variable costs equal $2,532,538, the clinic breaks even; if total variable costs exceed $2,532,538, the clinic loses. Thus, to make a profit, the number of visits must be less than $2,532,538 ÷ $28.18 = 89,870. If everyone in the organization, especially the managers and clinicians, does not understand or effectively manage the utilization risk under capitation, the clinic could find itself in serious financial trouble. On the other hand, if Atlanta's managers and clinicians at all levels understand and manage this utilization risk, they may gain a substantial financial reward. (Note that the breakeven volume of 89,870 visits exceeds the relevant range maximum of 85,000 visits for the cost structure used. Thus, it is likely that costs will be greater than predicted, and hence the breakeven volume is even less than 89,870 visits.)

A key feature of capitation is the reversal of the profit and loss portions of the graph. To see this, compare exhibit 5.10 with exhibit 5.4. The idea that profits occur at lower volumes under capitation is contrary to the fee-for-service environment. It is obvious, however, when one recognizes that the contribution margin, on a per visit basis, is $0 − $28.18 = −$28.18. Thus, each additional visit increases costs by $28.18 without bringing in additional revenue.

The optimal short-term response to capitation from a purely financial perspective is to take the money and provide as few services as legally possible. Of course, the clinic would not have the contract renewed in subsequent years, but it would have maximized short-term profit. Obviously, this course of action is neither appropriate nor feasible. Still, its implications are

EXHIBIT 5.10
Atlanta Clinic:
Breakeven
Point Under
Capitation
Using Number
of Visits as
the Volume
Measure

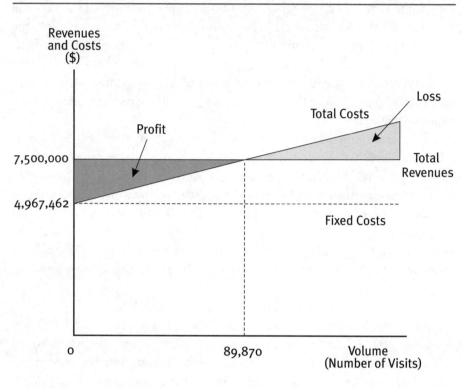

at the heart of concerns expressed by critics of capitation about the incentive created to withhold patient care. The solution to this problem is to monitor and reward (with bonus payments) providers that maintain or improve quality and, at the same time, reduce costs.

A Graphical View in Terms of Membership

Looking at exhibit 5.10, the horizontal axis does not measure the volume to which revenues are related; that is, exhibit 5.10 only includes the number of visits on the horizontal axis, just as if Atlanta Clinic were selling healthcare services. It is not; it is now selling healthcare assurance to a defined population, and it is being paid on the basis of population size, so the appropriate horizontal axis value is the number of members (enrollees).

Exhibit 5.11 recognizes that membership, rather than the amount of services provided, drives revenues. With the **number of members** on the horizontal axis, the total revenues line is no longer flat; revenues only look flat when they are considered relative to the number of visits. The revenue earned by the clinic is actually $7,500,000 ÷ 18,750 = $400 per member, which can be broken down to a monthly premium of $400 ÷ 12 = $33.33. Thus, the expected $7,500,000 revenue shown in exhibit 5.5 results from an expected enrollee population of 18,750 members.

The cost structure can easily be expressed on a membership basis as well. Fixed costs are no problem within the relevant range; they are inherently volume insensitive regardless of whether volume is measured by number of visits or number of members. Thus, exhibit 5.11 shows fixed costs as the same flat, dashed line as before. However, the variable cost rate based on number of members is not the same as the variable cost rate based on number of visits. Per member variable cost must be estimated using two factors: the variable cost rate of $28.18 per visit and the expected utilization rate of four visits per year. The combination of the two is 4 × $28.18 = $112.72, which is the clinic's expected variable cost per member. Expressed on a per member basis, the contribution margin is now $400 − $112.72 = $287.28, as opposed to −$28.18 when volume is based on number of visits.

The analysis based on number of members reveals that two elements are critical to controlling total variable costs under capitation: the underlying variable cost of the service ($28.18 per visit) and the number of visits per member (four). The two-variable nature of the variable cost rate makes cost control more difficult under capitation. In a fee-for-service environment, cost control entails only minimizing per visit expenses; utilization is not an issue. If anything, utilization is good because per visit revenue almost always exceeds the variable cost rate. (In other words, there is a positive contribution margin.)

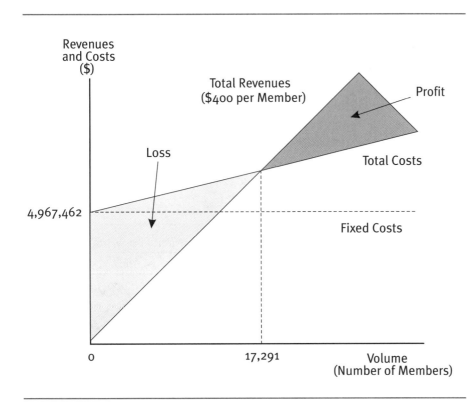

EXHIBIT 5.11
Atlanta Clinic: Breakeven Point Under Capitation Using Number of Members as the Volume Measure

Capitation requires a change in managerial thinking because utilization is now a component of the variable cost rate and hence total variable costs. Of course, control of fixed costs is always financially prudent, regardless of the type of reimbursement.

Conversely, there is one positive feature of the variable cost structure under capitation. With two elements to control, the clinic has more opportunity to lower the variable cost rate under capitation than under fee-for-service reimbursement. The key is the ability of Atlanta's managers to control utilization. If both utilization and per visit costs can be reduced, the clinic can reap greater benefits (profits) than are possible under fee-for-service reimbursement.

Projected P&L Statement Analysis

Exhibit 5.12 shows three projected P&L statements in this capitated environment, each for a different volume level. Let's start with the middle column—the one that contains the expected 75,000 patient visits. The bottom line—$419,038—is the same as in the fee-for-service analysis, which reinforces the point that, at least superficially, the capitated contract is not inherently better or worse than the fee-for-service contract.

What would happen if the clinic experienced more visits than predicted? If the number of visits increases by 10 percent, or by 7,500, to 82,500, the rightmost column in exhibit 5.12 shows that profit would decrease by $419,038 − $207,688 = $211,350. This occurs because total revenues stay constant while costs increase at a rate of $28.18 for each additional visit. With 7,500 additional visits, the clinic's costs increase by 7,500 × $28.18 = $211,350. Obviously, this is quite different from the significant increase in profit at this volume level that would occur in a fee-for-service environment.

Under capitation, a decrease in visits will improve the profitability of the clinic. When the number of visits decreases to 69,165, which is the breakeven point in a fee-for-service environment, profit in a capitated environment increases by $164,430 to $583,468. This increase is explained by the decrease in visits (5,835) multiplied by the per visit contribution margin

EXHIBIT 5.12
Atlanta Clinic:
2021 Projected
P&L Statements
Under Capitation
(based on
69,165, 75,000,
and 82,500
patient visits)

	Number of Visits		
	69,165	75,000	82,500
Total revenues	$7,500,000	$7,500,000	$7,500,000
Total variable costs ($28.18 × Volume)	1,949,070	2,113,500	2,324,850
Total contribution margin	$5,550,930	$5,386,500	$5,175,150
Fixed costs	4,967,462	4,967,462	4,967,462
Profit	$ 583,468	$ 419,038	$ 207,688

under capitation (–$28.18), which results in a $164,430 decrease in costs while revenues remain constant.

The Importance of Utilization

Exhibit 5.12 provides information on the impact of utilization changes on profitability. The center column, the base case, is once again our starting point. With an assumed utilization of four visits for each of the Alliance's 18,750 members, 75,000 visits result in a projected profit of $419,038.

However, if Atlanta's managers are not able to limit utilization to the level forecast (or less), the clinic's profit will fall. Assume that realized utilization is actually 4.4 visits per member, rather than the 4.0 forecast. This higher utilization would result in 4.4 × 18,750 = 82,500 visits, which produces the profit of $207,688 shown in the rightmost column in exhibit 5.12. Because revenues are fixed and total costs are tied to visit volume, higher utilization leads to higher costs and lower profit. With the same 82,500 visits but with total variable costs of $2,324,850 at the higher utilization rate, the variable cost per member increases to $2,324,850 ÷ 18,750 = $123.99, which could also be found by multiplying 4.4 visits per member by the variable cost rate of $28.18.

The left-hand column of exhibit 5.12 shows that the clinic's profitability would increase to $583,468 if utilization were reduced to 3.69 visits per member, producing about 69,165 total visits. With lower utilization, total variable costs are reduced and profit increases. The point is that the ability of a provider to control utilization is the primary key to profitability in a capitated environment. Less utilization means lower total costs, and lower total costs mean greater profit.

The Importance of the Number of Members

Exhibit 5.13 contains the projected P&L statements under capitation, recast to focus on the number of members. Assuming a per member utilization of four visits per year, a 10 percent membership increase to 20,625 members increases the projected profit by about 128 percent. However, if membership declines to 17,291, the clinic just breaks even.

We can use the breakeven equation to verify the breakeven point:

$$\text{Total revenues} - \text{Total variable costs} - \text{Fixed costs} = \text{Profit}$$
$$(\$400 \times \text{Members}) - (\$112.72 \times \text{Members}) - \$4{,}967{,}462 = \$0$$
$$\$287.28 \times \text{Members} = \$4{,}967{,}462$$
$$\text{Members} = 17{,}291.$$

Breakeven analysis reaffirms that the clinic needs 17,291 members in its contract with the Alliance to break even, given the assumed cost structure,

EXHIBIT 5.13
Atlanta Clinic:
2021 Projected
P&L Statements
Under
Capitation
(based on
17,291, 18,750,
and 20,625
members)

	Number of Members		
	17,291	18,750	20,625
Total revenues ($400 × Number of members)	$6,916,400	$7,500,000	$8,250,000
Total variable costs ($112.72 × Members)	1,949,042	2,113,500	2,324,850
Total contribution margin	$4,967,358	$5,386,500	$5,925,150
Fixed costs	4,967,462	4,967,462	4,967,462
Profit	($ 104)	$ 419,038	$ 957,688

which, in turn, assumes utilization of four visits per member and a variable cost rate of $28.18 per visit.

Assuming constant per member utilization, a greater number of members increases profitability because additional members create additional revenues that presumably exceed their incremental (variable) costs. Indeed, the degree of operating leverage (DOL) concept (discussed in the chapter 5 supplement) can be applied here. As shown in exhibit 5.13, a 10 percent increase to 20,625 members from a base case membership of 18,750 results in a (roughly) 128.5 percent increase in profit (from $419,038 to $957,688, or by $538,650). Thus, each 1 percent increase in membership increases profitability by 12.85 percent. Similarly, if membership decreases to the breakeven point of 17,291, a decrease of 7.8 percent, profitability falls by 7.8% × 12.85% = 100%, which leads to a profit of zero.

1. Under capitation, what is the difference between a CVP graph with the number of visits on the x axis and one with the number of members on the x axis?
2. What is unique about the contribution margin under capitation?
3. Why is utilization management so important in a capitated environment?
4. Why is the number of members so important in a capitated environment?

The Impact of Cost Structure on Financial Risk

The financial risk to a healthcare provider, at least in theory, is minimized by having a cost structure that matches its revenue structure. To illustrate, consider a clinic with all payers using fee-for-service reimbursement and hence generating revenues directly related to volume. If the clinic's cost structure consisted of all variable costs (no fixed costs), then each visit would incur costs but at the same time create revenues. Assuming that the per visit revenue exceeds the variable cost rate (i.e., per visit costs), the clinic would realize a profit on each visit. The total profitability of the clinic would be uncertain, as it is tied to volume, but the ability of the clinic to generate a profit would be guaranteed.

At the other extreme, consider a clinic that is totally capitated. In this situation, assuming a fixed number of members, the clinic's revenue stream is fixed regardless of the volume of services provided. Now, to match the revenue and cost structures, the clinic must have all fixed (no variable) costs. Assuming that annual fixed revenue exceeds annual fixed costs, the clinic has a guaranteed profit at the end of the year.

In both illustrations, the key to minimizing risk (ensuring a profit) is to create a cost structure that matches the revenue structure: variable costs for fee-for-service revenues and fixed costs for capitated revenues. Of course, real-world problems occur when a provider tries to implement a cost structure that matches its revenue structure. First, few providers are reimbursed solely on a fee-for-service or a capitated basis. Most providers encounter a mix of reimbursement methods. Still, they are either predominantly fee-for-service or predominantly capitated.

Second, providers do not have complete control over their cost structures. It is impossible for providers to create cost structures with all variable or all fixed costs. Nevertheless, managers can take actions to change their existing cost structure to one that is more compatible with the expected long-term revenue structure (has less risk). For example, assume a medical group practice is reimbursed almost exclusively on a per procedure basis. To minimize financial risk, the practice can take actions such as paying physicians on a per procedure basis and using per procedure leases for diagnostic equipment. The greater the proportion of variable costs in the practice's cost structure, the lower its financial risk.

For Your Consideration
Matching Cost and Revenue Structures

Healthcare providers can lower their financial risk by matching the cost structure to the revenue structure. For example, providers that are primarily reimbursed on a fee-for-service basis can lower risk by converting fixed costs to variable costs. Conversely, providers that are primarily reimbursed on a capitated basis can lower risk by converting variable costs to fixed costs.

Assume that you are the business manager of a large cardiology group practice. Virtually all of the practice's revenues are on a fee-for-service basis. However, the practice's two largest cost categories, labor and diagnostic equipment, are fixed. You are concerned about the potential for volumes to fall in the future and want to take some actions to reduce the financial risk of the practice.

What cost structure is optimal for the practice? What can be done to labor costs to improve the cost structure? To equipment costs? Suppose the change in cost structure will increase overall practice costs at next year's expected volume.

1. Explain this statement: "To minimize financial risk, match the cost structure to the revenue structure."
2. What cost structure would minimize risk if a provider had all fee-for-service reimbursement?
3. What cost structure would minimize risk if a provider were entirely capitated?
4. What are real-world constraints on creating matching cost structures?

Key Concepts

Managers rely on managerial accounting information to plan for and control a business's operations. A critical part of managerial accounting information is the measurement of costs and the use of this information in profit analysis. The key concepts of this chapter are as follows:

- Costs can be classified by their relationship to the *volume of services provided*.
- *Variable costs* are those costs that are expected to increase and decrease in total with changes in volume (patient days, number of visits, and so on), while *fixed costs* are the costs that are expected to remain constant (in total) regardless of volume within some *relevant range*.
- The relationship between cost and activity (volume) is called *underlying cost structure*.
- *Profit analysis*, often called *cost-volume-profit (CVP) analysis*, is an analytical technique that typically is used to analyze the effects of volume changes on revenues, costs, and profit.
- A *projected profit and loss (P&L) statement* is a profit projection that, in a profit analysis context, uses assumed values for volume, price, and costs.
- *Breakeven analysis* is used to estimate the volume needed (or the value of another variable, such as price) for the organization to break even in profitability.

(continued)

(continued from previous page)

- *Accounting breakeven* occurs when revenues equal accounting costs (zero profit), while *economic breakeven* occurs when revenues equal accounting costs plus some profit target.
- *Contribution margin* is the difference between per unit price and the *variable cost rate*. Hence, contribution margin is the per unit dollar amount available to first cover an organization's fixed costs and then to contribute to profits.
- In *marginal analysis*, the focus is the incremental (marginal) profitability associated with increasing or decreasing volume. If fixed costs are not expected to change, this can be measured by contribution margin.
- A *capitated environment* differs dramatically from a fee-for-service environment. In essence, a capitated provider takes on the insurance function.
- The keys to success in a capitated environment are to manage (maintain or reduce) utilization and increase the number of members covered.
- To minimize financial risk, a provider should strive to attain a cost structure that matches its revenue structure.

In chapter 6, the discussion of managerial accounting continues with an examination of costing at the department level.

Questions

5.1. Explain the differences between fixed costs and variable costs.

5.2. What components make up total costs?

5.3. a. What is cost-volume-profit (CVP) analysis?

  b. Why is it so useful to health services managers?

5.4. a. Define contribution margin.

  b. What is its economic meaning?

5.5. a. Write out and explain the equation for volume breakeven.

  b. What role does contribution margin play in this equation?

5.6. What elements of profit analysis change when a provider moves from a fee-for-service to a discounted fee-for-service environment?

5.7. What are the critical differences in profit analysis when it is conducted in a capitated environment versus a fee-for-service environment?

5.8. How do provider incentives differ when the provider moves from a fee-for-service to a capitated environment?

5.9. a. What cost structure is best when a provider is primarily capitated? Explain.

   b. What cost structure is best when a provider is reimbursed primarily by fee-for-service? Explain.

Problems

5.1. Consider the CVP graphs below for two providers operating in a fee-for-service environment:

   a. Assuming the graphs are drawn to the same scale, which provider has the greater fixed costs? The greater variable cost rate? The greater per unit revenue?

   b. Which provider has the greater contribution margin?

   c. Which provider needs the higher volume to break even?

   d. How would the graphs below change if the providers were operating in a discounted fee-for-service environment? In a capitated environment?

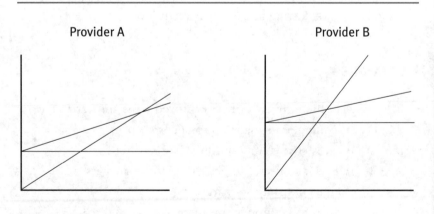

Provider A   Provider B

5.2. Consider the data in the table below for three independent health services organizations:

	Revenues	Total Variable Costs	Fixed Costs	Total Costs	Profit
a.	$2,000	$1,400	?	$2,000	?
b.	?	1,000	?	1,600	$2,400
c.	4,000	?	$600	?	400

Fill in the missing data indicated by question marks.

5.3. Assume that a radiologist group practice has the following cost structure:

Fixed costs	$500,000
Variable cost per procedure	25
Charge (revenue) per procedure	100

Furthermore, assume that the group expects to perform 7,500 procedures in the coming year.

a. Construct the group's base case projected P&L statement.

b. What is the group's contribution margin? What is its accounting breakeven point?

c. What volume is required to produce a pretax profit of $100,000? A pretax profit of $200,000?

d. Sketch out a CVP analysis graph depicting the base case situation.

Now assume that the practice contracts with one HMO, and the plan proposes a 20 percent discount from charges. Answer questions a, b, c, and d under these conditions.

5.4. General Hospital, a not-for-profit acute care facility, has the following cost structure for its inpatient services:

Fixed costs	$10,000,000
Variable cost per inpatient day	200
Charge (revenue) per inpatient day	1,000

The hospital expects to have a patient load of 15,000 inpatient days next year.

a. Construct the hospital's base case projected P&L statement.

b. What is the hospital's accounting breakeven point?

c. What volume is required to produce a profit of $1,000,000? A profit of $500,000?

d. Now assume that 20 percent of the hospital's inpatient days come from a managed care plan that wants a 25 percent discount from charges. If the hospital does not agree, assume it will lose the inpatient days to another provider. Should the hospital agree to the discount proposal?

5.5. You are considering starting a walk-in clinic. Your financial projections for the first year of operations are as follows:

Revenues (10,000 visits)	$400,000
Wages and benefits	220,000
Rent	5,000
Depreciation	30,000
Utilities	2,500
Medical supplies	50,000
Administrative supplies	10,000

Assume that all costs are fixed, except supply costs (medical and administrative), which are variable. Furthermore, assume that the clinic must pay taxes at a 30 percent rate.

a. Construct the clinic's projected P&L statement.

b. What number of visits is required to break even (revenue covers all accounting costs)?

c. What number of visits is required to produce an after-tax profit of $100,000?

5.6. Review the walk-in clinic data presented in problem 5.5. Construct projected P&L statements at volume levels of 8,000, 9,000, 10,000, 11,000, and 12,000 visits. (Hint: The concept of operating leverage, reviewed in this problem, is covered in the chapter 5 supplement.)

a. Assume that the base case forecast is 10,000 visits. What is the clinic's degree of operating leverage (DOL) at this volume level? Confirm the net incomes at the other volume levels using the DOL combined with the percent changes in volume.

b. Now assume that the base case volume is 9,000 visits. What is the DOL at this volume?

5.7. Grandview Clinic has fixed costs of $2 million and an average variable cost rate of $15 per visit. Its sole payer, an HMO, has proposed an annual capitation payment of $150 for each of its 20,000 members. Past experience indicates the population served will average two visits per year.

  a. Construct the base case projected P&L statement on the contract.

  b. Sketch two CVP analysis graphs for the clinic—one with number of visits on the x axis and one with number of members on the x axis. Compare and contrast these graphs with the one in problem 5.3.d.

  c. What is the clinic's contribution margin on the contract per visit? What is the contribution margin per member? How do these values compare with the value in problem 5.3.b?

  d. What profit gain can be realized if the clinic can lower per member utilization to 1.8 visits?

5.8. Triangle Health Center currently provides 1,000 visits per year at a price of $50 per visit. The variable cost per visit (variable cost rate) is $30, and total fixed costs are $15,000. The business manager suggests that Triangle Health Center can increase the number of visits to 1,200 per year by cutting the price per visit by $5 and increasing the fixed advertising budget by $5,000.

  a. Construct the base case projected P&L statement and the projected P&L statement incorporating the proposed changes. Should Triangle Health Center make the suggested changes?

  b. How much would visit volume need to increase for Triangle Health Center to break even (revenues equal to accounting costs) with the proposed changes?

5.9. Charity Hospital, a not-for-profit, has a maximum capacity of 15,000 discharges per year. Variable patient service costs are $495 per discharge. Variable general and administrative costs are $5 per discharge. Fixed hospital overhead costs are $4,000,000 per year. The current reimbursement rate is $1,000 per discharge.

  a. What is Charity's accounting breakeven volume in number of discharges?

  b. Now assume that Charity's total discharges for 2019 totaled 10,000. In late 2019, a specialty cardiac hospital opened near Charity, so discharges in 2020 will reach only 8,500. Management is planning to cut fixed costs so that the total for 2020 will be $1,000,000 less than in 2019. Management is also considering reducing variable staffing costs to earn a target profit that will be the same dollar amount as the profit earned in 2019. Charity has already had 4,000 discharges in 2020 at a reimbursement rate of $1,000 per discharge with variable costs unchanged. What contribution margin per unit is needed on the remaining 4,500 discharges to reach the target profit?

Selected Cases

Two cases in *Gapenski's Cases in Healthcare Finance*, sixth edition, are applicable to this chapter: Case 4: Tulsa Memorial House; and Case 5: Shasta Faculty Practice.

Resources

For a more in-depth treatment of cost measurement in health services organizations, see
Finkler, S. A., D. M. Ward, and T. D. Calabrese. 2019. *Accounting Fundamentals for Health Care Management*, 3rd ed. Sudbury, MA: Jones & Bartlett.
Young, D. W. 2019. *Management Accounting in Health Care Organizations*, 4th ed. Stoneham, MA: Crimson Press.

In addition, see
Al-Hajeri, M., M. Hartmann, S. Jabr, P. C. Smith, and M. Z. Younis. 2011. "Cost-Volume-Profit Analysis and Expected Benefit of Health Services: A Study of Cardiac Catheterization Services." *Journal of Health Care Finance* 37 (3): 87–100.
Angert, S., and H. Seabrook. 2011. "Next-Generation Cost Management." *Healthcare Financial Management* 65 (3): 46–52.
Arredondo, R. 2014. "Why Revisit Your Cost-Accounting Strategy." *Healthcare Financial Management* 68 (7): 68–73.
Boles, K. E., and S. T. Fleming. 1996. "Breakeven Under Capitation: Pure and Simple?" *Health Care Management Review* 21 (1): 38–47.
Cleverley, W. O., and J. O. Cleverley. 2011. "A Better Way to Measure Volume and Benchmark Costs." *Healthcare Financial Management* 65 (3): 78–86.
———. 2010. "Cost Reduction: Identifying the Opportunities." *Healthcare Financial Management* 64 (3): 52–59.
Daly, R. 2014. "Innovations in Cost Management." *Healthcare Financial Management* 68 (3): 50–56.
Farmer, S. A., J. Shalowitz, M. George, F. McStay, K. Patel, J. Perrin, A. Moghtaderi, and M. McClellan. 2016. "Fully Capitated Payment Breakeven Rate for a Mid-size Pediatric Practice." *Pediatrics* 138 (2): e20154367.
Koutsakos, G. 2011. "Measuring Cost When Inpatient Service Acuity Varies." *Healthcare Financial Management* 65 (11): 52–54, 56.
Liu, L. L., D. A. Forgione, and M. Z. Younis. 2012. "A Comparative Analysis of the CVP Structure of Nonprofit Teaching and For-Profit Non-teaching Hospitals." *Journal of Health Care Finance* 39 (1): 12–38.

Rauh, S. S., E. Wadsworth, and W. B. Weeks. 2010. "The Fixed-Cost Dilemma: What Counts When Counting Cost-Reduction Efforts?" *Healthcare Financial Management* 64 (3): 60–63.

Selivanoff, P. 2011. "The Impact of Healthcare Reform on Hospital Costing Systems." *Healthcare Financial Management* 65 (5): 110–14, 116.

Spence, J. 2013. "5 Ways to Make Cost Accounting a Strategic Function in Hospitals." *Healthcare Financial Management* 67 (3): 40.

5

SEMI-FIXED COSTS AND OPERATING LEVERAGE

Semi-fixed Costs

Fixed and variable costs represent two ends of the volume classification spectrum. Within the relevant range, costs are either independent of volume (fixed) or directly related to volume (variable). A third classification, *semi-fixed costs*, falls in between the two extremes. A semi-fixed cost is a cost that is fixed over some range of volume, but this range is smaller than the relevant range used in the analysis. Note that another volume classification is *semi-variable costs*. Such costs have both a fixed and a variable component. An example might be a business's telephone costs, which could include a fixed (base) charge plus additional charges that depend on the number of minutes of usage.

To illustrate semi-fixed costs, assume that the actual relevant range of volume for the clinical laboratory discussed in chapter 5 is 10,000 to 20,000 tests. However, the laboratory's current workforce can only handle up to 15,000 tests per year, so an additional technician, at an annual cost of $35,000, would have to be hired if volume exceeded that level. Now, labor costs are fixed from 10,000 to 15,000 tests, and then again fixed at a higher level from 15,000 to 20,000 tests, but they are not fixed at the same level throughout the entire relevant range of 10,000 to 20,000 tests. Semi-fixed costs are fixed *within* ranges of volume, but there are multiple ranges of semi-fixed costs within the relevant range. Because a graph of semi-fixed costs versus volume looks like stair steps, such costs sometimes are called *step-fixed costs* or *step costs*.

Exhibits S5.1 and S5.2 illustrate the cost structure of the laboratory within the new relevant range and with the addition of semi-fixed costs. As shown in exhibit S5.1, the inclusion of semi-fixed costs prevents average fixed cost and average cost per test from continuously declining throughout the relevant range. At volumes above 15,000 tests, the laboratory must add a technician at a cost of $35,000. This causes a jump in total fixed costs (consisting of fixed and semi-fixed costs), average fixed cost,

EXHIBIT S5.1
Cost Structure
Illustration:
Fixed, Semi-
fixed, and
Variable Costs

Variable Costs per Test	Fixed Costs per Year		Semi-fixed Costs	
Laboratory supplies $10	Labor	$100,000	Increase in labor costs	
	Other fixed costs	50,000	above 15,000 tests	$35,000
		$150,000		

Volume	Fixed Costs	Semi-fixed Costs	Total Fixed Costs	Total Variable Costs	Total Costs	Average Cost per Test
10,000	$150,000	$ 0	$150,000	$100,000	$250,000	$25.00
14,000	150,000	0	150,000	140,000	290,000	20.71
15,000	150,000	0	150,000	150,000	300,000	20.00
16,000	150,000	35,000	185,000	160,000	345,000	21.56
20,000	150,000	35,000	185,000	200,000	385,000	19.25

total costs, and average cost per test. However, once this jump (or step) occurs, average fixed cost and average cost per test begin to decline again as volume increases.

The jump in total costs is easily identified on the total costs line shown in exhibit S5.2. Because of the negative impact of this sudden increase in total costs, the laboratory department head would probably try to avoid hiring an additional technician when volume exceeds 15,000 tests, especially if volume is expected to be only slightly above the jump point or to be temporary. Perhaps new incentives could be put into place to encourage the current technicians to be more productive. Such an action could lower costs in general and create a situation in which the average cost per test would decline continuously throughout the relevant range.

Although semi-fixed costs are common in health services organizations, they add a level of complexity to profit analysis—also called cost-volume-profit (CVP) analysis—without adding a great deal of additional insight. Thus, the examples presented in chapter 5 assume that an organization's cost structure consists only of fixed and variable costs.

SELF-TEST QUESTIONS

1. What is a semi-fixed cost?
2. How does the addition of semi-fixed costs change a cost structure graph?
3. What is the impact of semi-fixed costs on per unit average cost?

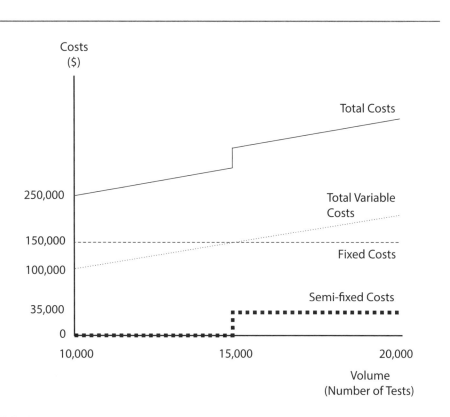

EXHIBIT S5.2
Cost Structure
Graph

Operating Leverage

As we demonstrate in chapter 5, profit analysis is used to examine how changes in volume affect profits and to estimate breakeven points. Assume now that Atlanta Clinic's managers believe that changes in the local market for healthcare services will occur that will increase their volume estimate for 2021 to 82,500 visits—an increase of 7,500 visits over the original 75,000 visit base case estimate. (The relevant range for Atlanta's cost structure is 65,000 to 85,000 visits.) Exhibit S5.3 contains the clinic's projected P&L statements at 69,165 (accounting breakeven), 75,000 (base case), and 82,500 visits. The first two columns were constructed in chapter 5, while the third column, which represents the 82,500 visit estimate, is new.

Now that P&L statements have been created at three different volume levels, the consequences of volume changes can be better understood. As the clinic's forecast volume moves from 75,000 visits to 82,500 visits, its profit increases by $957,688 – $419,038 = $538,650. This increase is equal to the

EXHIBIT S5.3
Atlanta Clinic:
2021 Projected
P&L Statements
(based on
69,165, 75,000,
and 82,500
patient
visits)

	Number of Visits		
	69,165	75,000	82,500
Total revenues ($100 × Volume)	$6,916,500	$7,500,000	$8,250,000
Total variable costs ($28.18 × Volume)	1,949,070	2,113,500	2,324,850
Total contribution margin ($71.82 × Volume)	$4,967,430	$5,386,500	$5,925,150
Fixed costs	4,967,462	4,967,462	4,967,462
Profit	($ 32)	$ 419,038	$ 957,688

additional 7,500 visits multiplied by the $71.82 contribution margin. When the volume is beyond the accounting breakeven point, any additional visits equate to additional profit—that is, the clinic's fixed costs are now covered, so all contribution margin additions flow directly to profit. Similarly, the outcome is known if the clinic's projected volume dropped from 75,000 to 69,165 visits. In this case, the decrease of 5,835 visits × $71.82 contribution margin = $419,070, which is the loss of profit (except for a rounding difference) that results from the volume decrease.

The movement from 75,000 to 82,500 visits resulted in a $(82,500 - 75,000) \div 75,000 = 7,500 \div 75,000 = 0.10 = 10\%$ increase in volume and thus total revenues. While the top line of the P&L statement—total revenues—increased by 10 percent, the bottom line of the statement—profit—increased by 128.5 percent ($538,650 \div $419,038 = 1.285 = 128.5\%$). This incredible increase in profit occurs because the clinic is reaping the benefit of its cost structure, which includes fixed costs that do not increase with volume.

If a high proportion of a business's total costs are fixed, the business is said to have high *operating leverage*. In finance, high operating leverage means that a relatively small change in volume results in a large change in profit.

Operating leverage is measured by the *degree of operating leverage (DOL)*, which in this illustration is calculated at any given volume by dividing the total contribution margin by profit. At a volume of 75,000 visits, Atlanta Clinic's DOL is Total contribution margin ÷ Profit = $5,386,500 ÷ $419,038 = 12.85. The DOL indicates how much profit will change for each 1 percent change in volume. Thus, at a volume of 75,000 visits, each 1 percent change in volume produces a 12.85 percent change in profit, so a 10 percent increase in volume results in a $10\% \times 12.85\% = 128.5\%$ increase in profit. Note, however, that the DOL changes with volume, so the 12.85 DOL calculated here is applicable only to a starting volume of 75,000 visits.

Cost structures differ widely among industries and among organizations within a given sector. The DOL is greatest in health services organizations with a large proportion of fixed costs and, consequently, a low proportion of variable costs. The result is a high contribution margin, which contributes to a high DOL. In economics terminology, high-DOL businesses are said to have *economies of scale* because higher volumes lead to lower per unit total costs. In such businesses, a small increase in revenue produces a relatively large increase in profit. However, high-DOL businesses have relatively high breakeven points, increasing the risk of losses. Also, operating leverage is a double-edged sword: High-DOL businesses suffer large profit declines, and potentially large losses, if volume falls.

To illustrate the negative effect of a high DOL, consider this question: What would happen to Atlanta Clinic's profit if volume fell by 7.8 percent from the base case level of 75,000 visits? To answer this question, recognize that profit would decline by $7.8\% \times 12.85\% = 100\%$, so the clinic's profit would fall to zero. The data in exhibit S5.3 confirm this answer. At a projected volume of 69,165 visits (a decrease of 7.8 percent from 75,000 visits), the clinic's profit is zero (except for a rounding difference). Of course, this volume was previously identified in the chapter as the breakeven point.

To what extent can managers influence a business's operating leverage? In many respects, operating leverage is determined by the inherent nature of the business. In general, hospitals and other institutional providers must make large investments in fixed assets (land, buildings, and equipment), and hence they have a high proportion of fixed costs and high operating leverage. Conversely, home healthcare businesses and other noninstitutional providers need few fixed assets, so they tend to have relatively low operating leverage. Still, managers can somewhat influence operating leverage. For example, organizations can make use of temporary, rather than permanent, employees to handle peak patient loads. Also, assets can be leased on a per use (per procedure) basis, rather than purchased or leased on a fixed rental basis. Actions such as these tend to reduce the proportion of fixed costs in an organization's cost structure and can help reduce operating leverage.

SELF-TEST QUESTIONS

1. What is operating leverage, and how is it measured?
2. Why is the operating leverage concept important to managers?
3. Can managers influence their firms' operating leverage?
4. How does an organization's cost structure affect its exposure to economies of scale?

DEPARTMENTAL COSTING AND COST ALLOCATION

Learning Objectives

After studying this chapter, readers will be able to

- Differentiate between direct and indirect (overhead) costs.
- Explain why proper cost allocation is important to health services organizations.
- Define a cost driver and explain the characteristics of a good driver as opposed to a poor one.
- Describe the three primary methods used to allocate overhead costs among revenue-producing departments.
- Apply cost allocation principles across a wide range of situations in health services organizations.

Introduction

In chapter 5, we discussed organizational costing, which requires the classification of costs according to their relationship to volume. In this chapter, we introduce departmental costing, which requires an additional classification of costs according to their relationship to the unit (e.g., department) being analyzed. In essence, we will see that some costs are unique to the department, while other costs stem from resources that belong to the organization as a whole. Once it is recognized that some costs are organizational in nature rather than department specific, it becomes necessary to create a system for allocating organizational costs to individual departments. For now, we will focus on costing at the department level. In chapter 7, we discuss costing (and pricing) of individual service lines. Although some of the material in this chapter is conceptual, much of it involves the application of allocation techniques. Thus, a considerable portion of this chapter is devoted to examples of cost allocation in different settings.

Direct Versus Indirect (Overhead) Costs

Some costs in an organization are unique to the reporting subunit, and therefore they can be identified with relative certainty. To illustrate, consider a hospital's clinical laboratory department. Certain costs are unique to that department—for example, the salaries and benefits for the managers and technicians who work there and the costs of the equipment and supplies used to conduct the tests. These costs, which would not be incurred if the laboratory were closed, are classified as the **direct costs** of the department.

direct cost
A cost that is tied exclusively to a subunit of an organization, such as the salaries of a department's employees. When a subunit is eliminated, its direct costs disappear.

Direct costs constitute only a portion of the laboratory department's cost structure. The remaining resources used by the laboratory are not unique to the laboratory; the department uses many shared resources of the hospital as a whole. For example, the laboratory shares the organization's physical space (facilities) as well as its infrastructure, which includes information systems, utilities, housekeeping, maintenance, medical records, and general administration. The costs that are not borne exclusively by the laboratory department are called **indirect costs**, or *overhead costs*.

Indirect costs, in contrast to direct costs, are much more difficult to measure at the department level precisely because they arise from shared resources—that is, if the laboratory department were closed, the indirect costs would not disappear. Perhaps some indirect costs could be reduced, but the hospital would still require a basic infrastructure to operate its remaining departments. The direct/indirect classification has relevance only at the subunit level; if the unit of analysis is the entire organization, all costs are direct by definition. Thus, in our discussion of organizational costing in chapter 5, we did not have to introduce the concept of direct versus indirect costs.

indirect (overhead) cost
A cost that is tied to shared resources rather than to an individual subunit of an organization; for example, facilities costs.

Note that the two cost classifications (fixed/variable and direct/indirect) overlay one another. That is, fixed costs typically include both direct costs (e.g., a supervisor's salary in a patient services department) and indirect costs (e.g., the portion of the hospital CEO's salary allocated to a patient services department), while variable costs, in most cases, include only direct costs (e.g., medical supplies in a patient services department), although they can include both direct and indirect costs (e.g., variable housekeeping supplies allocated to a patient services department). Conversely, direct costs usually include fixed and variable costs, while indirect costs typically include primarily fixed costs.

SELF-TEST QUESTIONS

1. What is the difference between direct and indirect costs?
2. Give several examples of indirect and direct costs for a hospital's emergency services department.

Introduction to Cost Allocation

A critical part of cost measurement at the department level is the assignment, or *allocation*, of indirect costs. **Cost allocation** is essentially a pricing process within the organization whereby managers allocate the costs of one department to other departments. Because this pricing process does not occur in a market setting, no objective standard exists that establishes the price for the transferred services. Thus, cost allocation within a business must, to the extent possible, establish prices that approximate those that would be set under market conditions.

cost allocation
The process by which overhead costs are assigned (allocated) to individual departments within an organization.

What costs within a health services organization must be allocated? Typically, the overhead costs of the business, such as those incurred by administrators, facilities management personnel, financial staffs, and housekeeping and maintenance personnel, must be allocated to the departments that generate revenues for the organization (generally patient services departments). The allocation of overhead costs to patient services departments is necessary because there would be no need for such costs in the first place if there were no patient services departments. Long-term decisions regarding the pricing and service offerings of the patient services departments must be based on the *full costs* associated with each service, including both direct and overhead (indirect) costs. Clearly, the proper allocation of overhead costs is essential to good decision-making within health services organizations.

The goal of cost allocation is to assign all of the costs of an organization to the activities that cause them to be incurred. With complete cost data accessible in the organization's managerial accounting system, managers can make better decisions regarding cost control, what services should be offered, and how those services should be priced. Of course, the more complex the managerial accounting system, the higher the costs of developing, implementing, and operating the system will be. As in all situations, the benefits associated with more accurate cost data must be weighed against the costs required to develop and manage such data.

Interestingly, much of the motivation for more accurate cost allocation systems comes from the recipients of overhead services. Managers at all levels within health services organizations are under pressure to optimize financial performance, which translates into reducing costs. Indeed, many department heads are evaluated, and hence compensated and promoted, primarily on the basis of profitability, assuming that performance along other dimensions is satisfactory. For such a performance evaluation system to work, all parties must perceive the cost allocation process to be accurate and fair if managers are held accountable for both the direct and indirect costs of their departments. In other words, department heads may be held accountable for the full costs associated with the services performed by their departments.

1. What is meant by the term *cost allocation*? By the term *full costs*?
2. What is the goal of cost allocation?
3. Why is cost allocation important to health services managers?

Cost Allocation Basics

cost pool
A group of overhead costs to be allocated; for example, facilities costs or marketing costs.

cost driver
The basis on which a cost pool is allocated; for example, square footage for facilities costs.

allocation rate
The numerical value used to allocate overhead costs; for example, $10 of facilities costs per square foot of occupied space.

To assign costs from one activity to another, two important elements must be identified: a cost pool and a cost driver. A **cost pool** is a grouping of similar costs to be allocated, while a **cost driver** is the basis on which the allocation is made. For example, the costs of a hospital's housekeeping department might be allocated to the other departments on the basis of the size of each department's physical space. The logic here is that the amount of housekeeping resources expended in each department is directly related to the physical size of that department. In this situation, total housekeeping costs would be the *cost pool*, and the number of square feet of occupied space would be the *cost driver*.

When the cost pool amount is divided by the total amount of the cost driver, the result is the overhead **allocation rate**. Thus, in the housekeeping illustration, the allocation rate is the total housekeeping costs of the organization divided by the total space (square footage) occupied by the departments *receiving* the allocation. Note that the space (square footage) occupied by the housekeeping department itself is not included in the total amount of the cost driver. This procedure results in an allocation rate measured in dollars cost per square foot of space used. In the patient services departments, full (total) costs would include the direct costs of each department and an allocation for housekeeping services, made on the basis of the amount of occupied space.

Cost Pools

Typically, a cost pool consists of all of the direct costs of one support (overhead) department. However, if a single support department offers several substantially different services, and the patient services departments use those services in different relative amounts, it may be beneficial to separate the costs of that support department into multiple pools.

For example, suppose a hospital's financial services department provides two significantly different services: patient billing/collections and budgeting. Furthermore, assume that the routine care department uses proportionally more patient billing/collections services than does the laboratory department, but the laboratory department uses proportionally more budgeting services than does the routine care department. In this situation, it would be best to create two cost pools for one support department. To do this, the total costs of financial services would be divided into a billing/collections pool and a budgeting pool. Then, cost drivers would be chosen for each pool and the costs allocated to the patient services departments as described in the following sections.

Cost Drivers

Perhaps the most important step in the cost allocation process is the identification of proper cost drivers. Traditionally, overhead costs were aggregated across all support departments and then divided by a rough measure of organizational volume, resulting in an allocation rate of some dollar amount of generic overhead per unit of volume.

For example, the total inpatient overhead costs of a hospital might be divided by total inpatient days, giving an allocation rate of so many dollars per patient day, which is called the *per diem overhead rate*. If a hospital had 72,000 patient days in 2020 and its total inpatient overhead costs were $36 million, the overhead allocation rate would be $36,000,000 ÷ 72,000 = $500 per patient day (per diem). Regardless of the type of patients treated within an inpatient services department (adult versus child, trauma versus illness, acute versus critical care, and so on), the $500 per diem allocation rate would be applied to determine the total indirect cost allocation for that department.

However, not all overhead costs are tied to the number of patient days. For example, overhead costs associated with admission, discharge, and billing typically are not related to the number of patient days but to the number of admissions. Thus, tying all overhead costs to a single cost driver improperly allocates such costs, which distorts reported costs for patient services and hence raises concerns about the effectiveness of decisions based on such costs. In state-of-the-art cost management systems, overhead costs are separated into different cost pools, and the most appropriate cost driver for each pool is identified. These systems require substantial resources and thus are found most often in large health systems.

The theoretical basis for identifying cost drivers is the extent to which costs from a pool actually vary as the value of the driver changes. For example, does a patient services department with 10,000 square feet of space use twice the amount of housekeeping services as a department with only 5,000 square feet of space? The better the relationship (correlation) between actual resource expenditures at each subunit and the cost driver, the better the cost driver and the better the resulting cost allocations will be.

Healthcare in Practice
Hospitals and Housekeeping Cost Drivers

Most hospitals use square footage to allocate housekeeping costs. The rationale, of course, is that a patient services department that is twice as big as another will require twice the expenditure of housekeeping resources. The advantage of this cost driver is that it is easy to measure and does not change very often.

The disadvantage of using square footage as the cost driver is that some patient services departments require more housekeeping support because of the nature of the service, even when similar-sized spaces are occupied. For example, surgery departments require more intense housekeeping services than do rehabilitation units.

Is there a better cost driver available for allocating housekeeping costs? If so, what is it? Describe how the "new and improved" cost driver would improve the measurement of full costs.

Effective cost drivers possess two important characteristics. The first, and perhaps the less important of the two, is *fairness*—that is, does the cost driver chosen result in an allocation that is fair to the patient services departments? The second, and perhaps more important, characteristic is *cost control*—that is, does the cost driver chosen create incentives for departments to use less of that overhead service?

For example, there is little that a patient services department manager can do to influence overhead cost allocations if the cost driver is patient days. In fact, the action needed to reduce patient days might lead to negative financial consequences for the organization if it is reimbursed on a fee-for-service or a per diem basis. An effective cost driver will encourage patient services department managers to take overhead cost reduction actions that do not have negative implications for the organization. A well-chosen cost driver makes patient services department heads accountable for the use of support department resources, which is the starting point for gaining control of overhead costs in any organization. The remainder of this chapter emphasizes the importance of effective

EXHIBIT 6.1
Prairie View Clinic: Allocation of Housekeeping Overhead to the Physical Therapy Department

Step 1: Determine the Cost Pool
The departmental costs to be allocated pertain to the housekeeping department, which has total budgeted costs for 2021 of $100,000.

Step 2: Determine the Cost Driver
The best cost driver was judged to be the number of hours of housekeeping services provided. An expected total of 10,000 hours of such services will be provided in 2021 to those departments that will receive the allocation.

Step 3: Calculate the Allocation Rate
$100,000 ÷ 10,000 hours = $10 per hour of housekeeping services provided.

Step 4: Determine the Allocation Amount
The physical therapy department uses 3,000 of the total 10,000 hours of housekeeping services, so its allocation of housekeeping department overhead is $10 × 3,000 = $30,000.

cost drivers, including several illustrations that distinguish good drivers from poor ones.

The Allocation Process

The steps involved in allocating overhead costs are summarized in exhibit 6.1, which illustrates how Prairie View Clinic allocated its housekeeping costs for 2021. Cost allocation takes place both for historical purposes, in which realized costs over the past year are allocated, and for planning purposes, in which estimated future costs are allocated to aid in pricing and other decisions. The examples in this chapter generally assume that the purpose of the allocation is financial planning and budgeting, so the data presented are estimated for the coming year—2021.

The first step in the allocation process is to establish the cost pool. In this case, the clinic is allocating housekeeping costs, so the cost pool is the projected total costs of the housekeeping department—$100,000. Next, the most effective cost driver must be identified. After considerable investigation, Prairie View's managers concluded that the best cost driver for housekeeping costs is labor hours—that is, the number of hours of housekeeping services required by the clinic's departments is the variable most closely related to the actual cost of providing these services. The intent here, of course, is to pick the cost driver that provides the most accurate cause-and-effect relationship between the use of housekeeping services and the costs of the housekeeping department. For 2021, Prairie View's managers estimate that the housekeeping department will provide 10,000 hours of service to the departments that will receive the allocation.

Now that the cost pool and cost driver have been defined and measured, the allocation rate is established by dividing the expected total overhead cost (the cost pool) by the expected total volume of the cost driver: $100,000 ÷ 10,000 hours = $10 per hour of services provided.

Key Equation: Allocation Rate

The allocation rate is the rate used to calculate each receiving department's allocation of an overhead cost pool. To illustrate, assume the financial services department has $1,000,000 in total costs (the cost pool). In total, the patient services departments generate 500,000 bills (the cost driver). Therefore, the allocation rate is $2 per bill:

$$\text{Allocation rate} = \text{Cost pool amount} \div \text{Cost driver volume}$$
$$= \$1,000,000 \div 500,000 \text{ bills}$$
$$= \$2 \text{ per bill.}$$

The final step in the process is to make the allocation to each department. To illustrate the allocation, consider the physical therapy (PT) department—one of Prairie View's patient services departments. For 2021, PT is expected to use 3,000 hours of housekeeping services, so the dollar amount of housekeeping overhead allocated to PT is $10 \times 3,000 = \$30,000$. Other departments within the clinic also use housekeeping services, and their allocations can be made in a similar manner—the $10 allocation rate per hour of services used is multiplied by the amount of each department's hourly utilization of housekeeping services. When all departments are considered, the 10,000 hours of housekeeping services is fully distributed among the departments using those services. For any one department, the amount allocated depends on both the allocation rate and the amount of housekeeping services used.

SELF-TEST QUESTIONS

1. What are the definitions of a *cost pool*, a *cost driver*, and an *allocation rate*?
2. Under what conditions should a single overhead department be divided into multiple cost pools?
3. On what theoretical basis are cost drivers chosen?
4. What two characteristics make an effective cost driver?
5. What are the four steps in the cost allocation process?

Cost Allocation Methods

Mathematically, cost allocation can be accomplished in a variety of ways, and the method used is somewhat discretionary. No matter which method is chosen, all support department costs eventually must be allocated to the departments (generally patient services departments) that create the need for those costs.

The key difference among the methods is the way support services provided by one department are allocated to **other support departments** (e.g., housekeeping services provided to the financial services department). The direct method of cost allocation totally ignores services provided by one support department to another. Two other allocation methods address intrasupport department allocations. The reciprocal method recognizes all of the intrasupport department services, and the step-down method recognizes some, but not all, of the intrasupport department services. Regardless of the method chosen, all of the support costs within an organization ultimately

EXHIBIT 6.2
Prairie
View Clinic:
Alternative
Cost Allocation
Methods

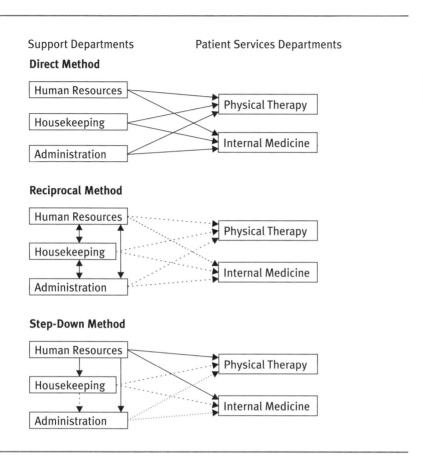

are allocated from support departments to the departments that generate revenues for the organization.

Exhibit 6.2 summarizes the three allocation methods. Prairie View Clinic, which is used in the illustration, has three support departments (human resources, housekeeping, and administration) and two patient services departments (PT and internal medicine).

Under the **direct method** of allocation, shown in the top section of exhibit 6.2, each support department's costs are allocated directly to the patient services departments that use the services. Thus, none of the support services costs are allocated to other support departments. In the illustration, both PT and internal medicine use the services of all three support departments, so the costs of each support department are allocated to both patient services departments. The key feature of the direct method—and the feature that makes it relatively simple to apply—is that no intrasupport department allocations are recognized. Thus, under the direct method, only the direct costs of the support departments are allocated to the patient services

direct method
A cost allocation method in which all overhead costs are allocated directly from the overhead departments to the patient services departments with no recognition that overhead services are provided to other support departments.

departments because no indirect costs have been created by intrasupport department allocations.

reciprocal method
A cost allocation method that recognizes all of the overhead services provided by one support department to another.

As shown in the center section of exhibit 6.2, the **reciprocal method** of allocation recognizes the interdependencies among human resources, housekeeping, and administration; therefore, it is generally considered to be more accurate and objective than the direct method. The reciprocal method derives its name from the fact that it recognizes all of the services that departments provide to and receive from other departments. The good news is that this method captures all of the intrasupport department relationships, so no information is ignored and no biases are introduced into the cost allocation process. The bad news is that the reciprocal method relies on the simultaneous solution of a series of equations representing the utilization of intrasupport department services. Thus, it is relatively complex, which makes it difficult to explain to department heads and typically more costly to implement.

step-down method
A cost allocation method that recognizes some of the overhead services provided by one support department to another.

The **step-down method** of allocation, which is shown in the lower section of exhibit 6.2, represents a compromise between the simplicity of the direct method and the complexity of the reciprocal method. It recognizes some of the intrasupport department effects that the direct method ignores, but it does not recognize the full range of interdependencies that the reciprocal method accounts for. The step-down method derives its name from the sequential, stair-step pattern of the allocation process, which requires that the allocation take place in a specific sequence. As shown in exhibit 6.2, all the direct costs of human resources are first allocated to both the patient services departments and the other two support departments. Human resources is then *closed out* because all of its costs have been allocated. Next, housekeeping costs, which now consist of both direct and indirect costs (the direct costs of housekeeping plus the allocation from human resources), are allocated to the patient services departments and the remaining support department—administration. Finally, the direct and indirect costs of administration are allocated to the patient services departments. The final allocation from administration includes human resources and housekeeping costs because a portion of these support costs has been allocated or "stepped down" to administration.

The critical difference between the step-down and reciprocal cost allocation methods is that after each allocation is made in the step-down method, a support department is removed from the process. Even though housekeeping and administration provide support services back to human resources, these indirect costs are not recognized because human resources is removed from the allocation process after the initial allocation. Such costs are recognized in the reciprocal method.

1. What are the three primary methods of cost allocation?
2. Explain how they differ.
3. Which method do you think is the most accurate? Which is the least accurate?

Direct Method Illustration

The best way to gain a more in-depth understanding of cost allocation is to work through several allocation illustrations. We begin with the direct method. As shown in exhibit 6.3, Kennington Hospital has three revenue-producing patient services departments: routine care, laboratory, and radiology. Accountants often call the patient services departments **profit centers**, because they not only incur costs but also generate revenues. Conversely, overhead departments are called **cost centers** because they incur costs but do not generate revenues.

Hospital costs are divided into those costs attributable to the profit centers (direct costs) and those costs attributable to the support departments (overhead costs). Of course, the overhead costs are direct costs to the support departments, but when they are allocated to the patient services departments, these direct costs become indirect (overhead) costs.

Data for Kennington Hospital show that the revenues for each of the patient services departments are much greater than their direct costs. Furthermore, Kennington's projected total revenues of $27,000,000 exceed the hospital's projected total costs of $25,450,000. However, the aggregate revenue and cost amounts provide no information to Kennington's managers concerning the true profitability of each patient services department. To determine true profitability by profit center, the *full costs* of providing patient services, including both direct and indirect costs, must be measured. Only then can the hospital's managers develop rational pricing and cost control strategies.

As previously discussed, three decisions are required when allocating costs: how to define the cost pools, what the cost drivers are, and which method of allocation to use. We begin by illustrating the direct method of cost allocation. The step-down method is discussed in the chapter 6 supplement.

The cost pools (total costs) for the support departments are given in the lower section of exhibit 6.3. Financial services costs are $1,500,000; facilities costs equal $3,800,000; housekeeping costs are $1,600,000; general administration costs total $4,400,000; and human resources costs equal $2,550,000. Thus, overhead costs at the hospital total $13,850,000, which

profit center
A business unit (in our examples, typically a department) that generates revenues as well as costs, hence its profitability can be measured.

cost center
A business unit that does not generate revenues, hence only its costs can be measured.

EXHIBIT 6.3
Kennington
Hospital: 2021
Revenue and
Cost Projections

Projected Revenues by Patient Services Department

Routine Care	$16,000,000
Laboratory	5,000,000
Radiology	6,000,000
Total revenues	$27,000,000

Projected Costs for All Departments

Patient Services Departments (Direct Costs):

Routine Care	$ 5,500,000
Laboratory	3,300,000
Radiology	2,800,000
Total costs	$11,600,000

Support Services Departments (Overhead Costs):

Financial Services	$ 1,500,000
Facilities	3,800,000
Housekeeping	1,600,000
General Administration	4,400,000
Human Resources	2,550,000
Total overhead costs	$13,850,000
Total costs of both patient and support services	$25,450,000
Projected profit	$ 1,550,000

ultimately must be allocated to the hospital's three patient services departments. Kennington's managers believe that little is to be gained by dividing any of the support departments into multiple cost pools, so each support department constitutes one cost pool.

The next step in the allocation process is to identify the best cost drivers for each cost pool. Exhibit 6.4 provides a summary of the support departments and their assigned cost drivers. Unfortunately, the selection of cost drivers is not an easy process, and to a large extent, the usefulness of the cost allocation process depends on choosing the most effective drivers. As discussed later, Kennington's selection of cost drivers, like many selections made in real-world situations, is somewhat of a compromise between effectiveness and simplicity.

The cost driver chosen for financial services is patient services revenue. The financial services department provides a full range of financial support to the hospital. The bulk of its efforts are devoted to patient billing and

Support Services Department	Cost Driver
Financial Services	Patient services revenue
Facilities	Space utilization (square footage)
Housekeeping	Labor hours
General Administration	Salary dollars
Human Resources	Salary dollars

EXHIBIT 6.4
Kennington
Hospital:
Assigned Cost
Drivers

collections, but it is also involved in financial and managerial accounting, budgeting and report preparation, and many other financial tasks. Tying the allocation of this support department to the amount of patient services revenues assumes a strong positive relationship between the amount of financial services provided to each patient services department and revenues generated by that department. However, this assumption is incorrect, making patient services revenue a relatively inaccurate cost driver. The resulting cost allocation thus has limitations. In the next section, we discuss the benefits of moving from a poor cost driver to a better one.

The amount of space used (square footage) is the basis for allocating the costs of facilities. This cost driver is often used by health services organizations to allocate the initial costs of land, buildings, and equipment, as well as the costs of maintenance and other facilities services. The logic applied here is that the patient services departments with the most space require the most facilities and hence the most facilities support. Of course, this assumption does not always hold. For example, in any year, facilities may be required to support a special large project for one of the patient services departments, resulting in costs that far exceed that department's proportional space utilization. Nevertheless, over the long run at Kennington Hospital, the relative costs of facilities utilization by the patient services departments track closely with the space occupied by those departments.

Two of the remaining support departments, general administration and human resources, also use a relatively poor cost driver, salary dollars. If radiology has payroll costs that are five times larger than those of laboratory, radiology will be charged (allocated) five times as much of the costs incurred by administration and human resources. While this cost driver is often used by health organizations because of its simplicity, in reality, it is not a very good measure. In this case, the allocated costs from general administration and human resources probably do not truly represent the relative amounts of utilization of these overhead services.

Housekeeping has perhaps the best cost driver—namely, the number of labor hours of housekeeping services consumed. In many organizations, housekeeping costs are allocated on the basis of square footage, using the logic that the amount of space occupied by a department accurately reflects housekeeping efforts and hence costs. This assumption may or may not be valid, however. In effect, large-space departments may be subsidizing small-space departments, such as emergency services, where space may be limited but the intensity of work requires a significant amount of housekeeping services. To account for such situations at Kennington Hospital, housekeeping is using a better cost driver—one that more closely aligns to the actual resources expended in providing support to the patient services departments.

The development and use of the best cost driver is a cost–benefit issue. Housekeeping must devote resources to tracking where its workers spend their time, an effort that would not be required if the cost driver were square footage. The benefit, of course, is a cost driver that makes it easier for Kennington's senior managers to hold department heads responsible for both direct and indirect costs. If the head of the radiology department does not like the amount of housekeeping costs that are being charged to the department, she can do something about it: use fewer housekeeping services. With an inferior cost driver, such as square footage, there is little that patient services department heads can do if they do not like the housekeeping allocation. In most cases, reduction of square footage is not a practical way to deal with excessive housekeeping costs.

With labor hours consumed as the cost driver, the cost control solution for patient services department heads is to reduce the amount of housekeeping services used. If the hospital has the right incentive system in place, ultimately, all patient services department heads have an incentive to be as efficient as possible in using housekeeping services. In the long run, the direct costs of the housekeeping department—currently $1,600,000—will fall as these services are used more efficiently. In reality, the secondary benefit of choosing a more effective cost driver is a more equitable allocation. The primary benefit is that a good cost driver creates an incentive for department heads to use less of the support service, which ultimately leads to lower overhead costs for the organization.

Exhibit 6.5 contains the initial data necessary for the allocation. The first column of the exhibit lists the patient services departments. The amounts of the chosen cost drivers consumed by each patient services department are listed after that: patient services revenue used for allocating financial services costs, square footage used for facilities allocations, housekeeping labor hours used for housekeeping allocations, and departmental salary dollars used for both general administration and human resources allocations.

If Kennington were using the step-down or reciprocal allocation methods, the information shown in exhibit 6.5 would have to include the support departments because the data would be needed for intrasupport department allocations. By using the direct method, the hospital ignores intrasupport department dependencies. The totals indicated at the bottom

Department	Patient Services Revenues	Square Feet	Housekeeping Labor Hours	Salary Dollars
Routine Care	$16,000,000	199,800	76,000	$ 5,709,000
Laboratory	5,000,000	39,600	6,000	2,035,000
Radiology	6,000,000	61,200	9,000	2,439,000
Total	$27,000,000	300,600	91,000	$10,183,000

EXHIBIT 6.5
Kennington Hospital: Patient Services Departmental Summary Data

of each column only reflect the use of support services by the patient services departments, to which all of the support costs are allocated.

Exhibit 6.6 divides the dollar amount of each cost pool by the total amount of each cost driver to derive the allocation rates. For example, the cost pool (direct costs) for financial services totals $1,500,000, which will be allocated as indirect (overhead) costs to the patient services departments that have a total of $27,000,000 in patient services revenues. The allocation rate for financial services, therefore, is $1,500,000 ÷ $27,000,000 = $0.05556 per dollar of patient services revenue.

As previously mentioned, the allocation of indirect costs can be viewed as an internal pricing mechanism. Thus, the heads of the revenue-producing departments can look at exhibit 6.6 and see the rate that they are being charged for support services, which amounts to the following:

- $0.05556 for each dollar of patient services revenue generated for financial services support
- $12.64 per square foot of space used for facilities support
- $17.58 per labor hour consumed for housekeeping support
- $0.432 per salary dollar paid to department employees for general administrative overhead
- $0.250 per salary dollar for human resources support

Department	Cost Pool (total costs)	Cost Driver	Total Utilization	Allocation Rate[a]
Financial Services	$1,500,000	Patient revenue	$27,000,000	$0.05556
Facilities	3,800,000	Square feet	300,600	12.64
Housekeeping	1,600,000	Labor hours	91,000	17.58
General Administration	4,400,000	Salary dollars	$10,183,000	0.432
Human Resources	2,550,000	Salary dollars	$10,183,000	0.250

EXHIBIT 6.6
Kennington Hospital: Overhead Allocation Rates

[a] Dollars per unit of the cost driver.

EXHIBIT 6.7
Kennington Hospital: Final Allocations

Support Department (allocation rate)	Routine Care		Patient Services Department — Laboratory		Radiology	
Financial Services ($0.0556)	× $16,000,000 =	$ 888,960	× $5,000,000 =	$ 277,800	× $6,000,000 =	$ 333,360
Facilities ($12.64)	× 199,800 =	2,525,472	× 39,600 =	500,544	× 61,200 =	773,568
Housekeeping ($17.58)	× 76,000 =	1,336,080	× 6,000 =	105,480	× 9,000 =	158,220
Administration ($0.432)	× 5,709,000 =	2,466,288	× 2,035,000 =	879,120	× 2,439,000 =	1,053,648
Human Resources ($0.250)	× 5,709,000 =	1,427,250	× 2,035,000 =	508,750	× 2,439,000 =	609,750
Total indirect costs		$ 8,644,050		$ 2,271,694		$ 2,928,546
Direct costs		$ 5,500,000		$ 3,300,000		$ 2,800,000
Total costs		$ 14,144,050		$ 5,571,694		$ 5,728,546

Total indirect costs = $8,644,050 + $2,271,694 + $2,928,546 = $13,844,290.

Total costs = $14,144,050 + $5,571,694 + $5,728,546 = $25,444,290.

Note: Because of rounding in the allocation process, the totals here differ slightly from the values contained in exhibit 6.3.

If radiology pays a technician $10 an hour in direct labor costs for each hour the technician works, the department will also be charged 0.432 × $10.00 = $4.32 for general administrative overhead and 0.250 × $10.00 = $2.50 for human resources overhead, plus additional allocations for financial services, facilities, and housekeeping support. Having two cost pools—in this case, the general administration and human resources departments—that use the same cost driver (salary dollars) is not unusual. However, the allocation rate is different for the two support departments because they have different cost pool amounts.

The final step in the allocation process is to calculate the actual dollar allocation to each of the patient services departments, which is shown in exhibit 6.7. The support departments are listed in the first column, along with the applicable allocation rate, while the patient services departments are listed across the top. To illustrate the calculations, consider the routine care department. It produces $16,000,000 in patient services revenue, and the overhead allocation rate for financial services is $0.05556 per dollar of patient services revenue, so the allocation for such support is $0.05556 × $16,000,000 = $888,960. Furthermore, routine care has 199,800 square feet of space; with a facilities rate of $12.64 per square foot, its allocation for facilities support is $12.64 × 199,800 = $2,525,472.

The allocations to the routine care department for housekeeping, general administration, and human resources support shown in exhibit 6.7 were calculated similarly. The end result is that $8,644,050 out of a total of $13,850,000 of the indirect (overhead) costs of Kennington Hospital are allocated to routine care. Routine care also has direct costs of $5,500,000, so the full (total) costs of the department, including both direct and indirect, are $8,644,050 + $5,500,000 = $14,144,050. The cost allocations and total cost calculations for the laboratory and radiology departments shown in exhibit 6.7 were done in a similar manner.

For general management purposes, understanding the mechanics of the allocation is less important than recognizing the value of choosing effective cost drivers. The cost driver for housekeeping services (i.e., the number of service hours provided) is good in the sense that it reflects the true level of effort expended by this department in support of the patient services departments. The patient services department heads are being fairly charged for these services, and, more important, patient services department heads can take actions to lower the allocated amounts by reducing the amount of housekeeping services used.

In closing this illustration, note how exhibit 6.7 after the allocation process reconciles with exhibit 6.3 before the allocation process. First, as shown in exhibit 6.3, total support services (overhead) costs are $13,850,000. This is the same amount (except for a rounding difference) shown in exhibit 6.7 as the total overhead allocated to the patient services departments: $8,644,050 (to routine care) + $2,271,694 (to laboratory) + $2,928,546 (to radiology) = $13,844,290. The total after-allocation costs of $25,444,290 shown in exhibit 6.7 also equal the original forecast of total costs in exhibit 6.3 of $25,450,000 (again, except for a rounding difference).

SELF-TEST QUESTIONS

1. Briefly outline the allocation procedures used by Kennington Hospital.
2. What underlying characteristic creates a good cost driver?
3. What are the two properties of an effective cost driver?
4. What is the most important organizational benefit derived from the selection of an effective cost driver?

Cost Allocation and Departmental Profitability

At this point, you might be thinking that Kennington Hospital spent a lot of time and effort in the cost allocation process. Was it all worth it? What did Kennington's managers gain from the effort? Well, the answer is this: They now know the profitability of the patient services departments when all costs, including indirect costs, are considered.

Exhibit 6.8 summarizes the profitability of Kennington's patient services departments when viewed from the perspectives of direct costs and total (full) costs. In effect, exhibit 6.8 contains projected profit-and-loss statements for the patient services departments for 2021. Sections 1 and 2 list projected revenues and projected direct costs, respectively, of the three patient services departments. Then, section 3 lists the profitability of each department when only direct costs are considered. As you see, all three patient services departments are profitable in this situation, which may make everyone happy, at least temporarily.

Note that the values in parentheses in section 3 are *profit margins*, defined as Profit ÷ Revenues. For example, the profit margin listed for the routine care department is $10,500,000 ÷ $16,000,000 = 0.656 = 65.6%, which can be interpreted as each dollar of revenues leading to 65.6 cents in profits when only direct costs are considered. The higher the margin, the more profitable the department. Profit margins make it easier for healthcare managers to compare the relative profitability of departments. Based on the margin values in section 3, we see that the aggregate profit of all patient services departments is 57.0 percent, so routine care is doing better than average, radiology is slightly worse than average, and laboratory is doing much worse than average. Still, all departments are profitable.

EXHIBIT 6.8
Kennington
Hospital: 2021
Patient Services
Department
Revenue, Cost,
and Profitability
Projections
(margins listed
in parentheses)

1. Projected Revenues

Routine Care	$16,000,000	
Laboratory	5,000,000	
Radiology	6,000,000	
Total revenues	$27,000,000	

2. Projected Direct Costs

Routine Care	$ 5,500,000	
Laboratory	3,300,000	
Radiology	2,800,000	
Total direct costs	$11,600,000	

3. Projected Profit on Direct Costs

Routine Care	$10,500,000	(65.6%)
Laboratory	1,700,000	(34.0)
Radiology	3,200,000	(53.3)
Aggregate profit on direct costs	$15,400,000	(57.0%)

4. Projected Indirect Costs

Routine Care	$ 8,644,050	
Laboratory	2,271,694	
Radiology	2,928,546	
Total indirect costs	$13,844,290	

5. Projected Profit on Total Costs

Routine Care	$ 1,855,950	(11.6%)
Laboratory	−571,694	(−11.4)
Radiology	271,454	(4.5)
Aggregate profit on total costs	$ 1,555,710	(5.8%)

Note: Because of rounding in the allocation process, some of the values here differ slightly from the values contained in exhibit 6.3.

Section 4 of exhibit 6.8 lists the indirect costs allocated to each patient services department, which were taken from exhibit 6.7, and section 5 lists patient services department profitability when total (full) costs, including direct and indirect, are considered. Now, based on the data in section 5, we see that one of the three patient services departments, laboratory, is expected to experience an 11.4 percent profit margin loss in 2021. In addition, the true profitability of the patient services departments is not nearly as high as shown in section 3 when only direct costs were considered. Now, the aggregate (average) margin is only 5.8 percent compared with 57.0 percent when only direct costs are considered.

The lesson of this story is that looking at departmental profitability solely on the basis of direct costs, although valuable for some purposes, does not give a complete picture of each department's financial status. To obtain the best measure of departmental profitability, it is necessary to include both direct and indirect costs in the analysis.

Changing to a More Effective Cost Driver

The Kennington Hospital example illustrated the direct method of cost allocation. In this section, we illustrate the benefits of moving from a poor cost driver to a better one.

Kennington historically has allocated the $1,500,000 in financial services costs on the basis of the patient services revenue generated by patient services departments. However, it was widely recognized that this driver was not highly correlated with the actual amount of overhead services provided by the financial services department to each patient services department, and it was not perceived by the patient services department heads as being fair. More important, it did not create an incentive for overhead cost reduction because patient services department heads would not reduce the amount of services provided (and reduce revenues) just to lower their overhead allocations.

A thorough analysis of the work done by the financial services department indicated that its primary task in support of the patient services departments is generating third-party payer billings and collecting the payments on those bills. Thus, Kennington's managers concluded that the cost of providing financial services is more highly correlated with the number of bills generated than with patient services revenues, so number of bills was chosen as the new cost driver.

Exhibit 6.9 shows the new cost allocations for financial services as well as a comparison with the allocations under the old (patient services revenue) driver. Note that the allocations have changed substantially. Because the average amount

For Your Consideration
Profitability and Bonuses

As shown in exhibit 6.8, the profitability of Kennington Hospital's three patient services departments is forecast for 2021 on the basis of direct costs and full (total) costs, which include indirect costs. When only direct costs are considered, departments can be ranked in terms of their profitability (from high to low) as follows: routine care, radiology, and laboratory. Furthermore, all departments are profitable. However, when indirect costs are added to the mix, the order stays the same, but one of the departments (laboratory) becomes unprofitable.

Now assume that Kennington compensates its department heads using a base salary plus bonus system, with the bonus tied to department profitability as measured by profit margin. If the department is unprofitable, there is no bonus, and the higher the profitability, the greater the bonus. Kennington's chief financial officer argues that

(continued)

of a routine care department bill is much higher than the average amounts of laboratory and radiology department bills, the routine care department has significantly fewer bills than the other patient services departments in spite of its significantly higher revenues. Thus, the new financial services allocation is much lower than the amount under the old driver for the routine care department, but it is much higher for the laboratory and radiology departments.

The move to a different cost driver represents more than just change for the sake of change. It represents an attempt by Kennington's managers to base the allocation of financial services costs on the actual amount of support provided by the financial services department to each patient services department. By doing so, the overhead allocation is more likely to be perceived by patient services department heads as being fair. Furthermore, the new cost driver could encourage patient services department heads to reduce their utilization of financial services support (i.e., consolidating bills results in fewer bills), which would lower Kennington's overhead costs.

(continued from previous page)

bonuses should be based on full costs. "After all," she says, "that's what really counts." On the other hand, the laboratory department head had this to say: "We patient services department heads have no control whatsoever of overhead costs, so why should we be held responsible for them?"

What do you think? Should bonuses be based on profitability measured using only direct costs, or should they be based on full costs? Should bonuses be tied to profitability at all, or should they be tied to patient outcomes or some other metric?

EXHIBIT 6.9
Kennington Hospital: New Financial Services Department Allocations

Utilization of Financial Services

Patient Services Department	Number of Bills Required
Routine Care	3,200
Laboratory	60,300
Radiology	36,500
Total	100,000

Allocation Rate

$1,500,000 ÷ 100,000 = $15.00 per bill.

Allocations

	New		Old	Difference
Routine Care	$15.00 × 3,200	= $ 48,000	$ 888,960	−$ 840,960
Laboratory	15.00 × 60,300	= 904,500	277,800	+626,700
Radiology	15.00 × 36,500	= 547,500	333,360	+ 214,140
Total		$1,500,000	≈$1,500,000	$ 0

In spite of the improvement that results from the change, the new cost driver is not perfect. Other changes could be made to improve the allocation even more. For example, the financial services department performs tasks other than billing, such as generating numerous reports for the organization, including financial statements and budget reports. Indeed, the department has one analyst whose full-time job is creating and interpreting budget reports (budgeting is discussed in detail in chapter 8). A better allocation of financial services department costs, therefore, may require that financial services costs be separated into two (or more) pools, each with its own cost driver. If this were done, some proportion of the department's total costs of $1,500,000 would be assigned to report preparation, and a separate cost driver would be identified to allocate these costs to the patient services departments.

While better and more specific cost drivers can usually be developed, the actual cost allocation that has taken place is still meaningful. Cost accounting studies generally have shown that the relationship between overhead cost consumption and volume, measured either by revenues or by units of service, is not very strong. Indeed, use of volume as the cost driver often results in systematic, as opposed to random, errors in cost allocation. Volume-based allocation schemes create a bias against larger revenue-producing departments by overallocating overhead costs to these departments, while the overhead costs of smaller revenue-producing departments are underallocated. This bias occurs primarily because a volume-based cost driver fails to recognize the economies of scale inherent in larger departments in the utilization of overhead services. For example, it probably costs no more to bill a third-party payer for $5,000 than it does to bill for $500, as far as the resources required to produce and transmit the bill and to monitor and collect the payment. Yet a revenue-based allocation scheme

Healthcare in Practice

Overhead Ratio—A Shortcut to Overhead Cost Allocation

In this chapter, we discussed the traditional method of overhead cost allocation. In essence, overhead costs were grouped into cost pools, appropriate cost drivers were chosen, allocation rates were calculated, and user department allocations were estimated based on the amount of the cost driver consumed.

A simpler method of cost allocation involves use of the *overhead ratio*, which is defined generically as Overhead costs ÷ Revenue. The specific definition of this ratio depends on the setting in which it is used: for example, hospital versus medical practice versus long-term care facility. The values of these ratios also vary by type of provider but usually fall in the range of 50 to 70 percent.

Here is how the shortcut works: Assume that an orthopedic practice has total revenues of $10,000,000 and total overhead costs of $5,000,000. Using the generic definition of the overhead ratio, the practice's overhead ratio is $5,000,000 ÷ $10,000,000 = 0.50, or 50%. Now assume that clinical services, one of the divisions of the practice, has revenues of $6,000,000. To estimate the overhead allocation for that division, simply multiply the division's revenues by the overhead ratio: $6,000,000 × 0.50 = $3,000,000. Thus, based on this simpler allocation method, the clinical services division has $6,000,000 – $3,000,000 = $3,000,000 available to cover its direct costs.

What do you think about this shortcut method of cost allocation? What are its advantages and disadvantages relative to the traditional method described in this chapter?

would allocate more financial services costs to a patient services department with relatively high charges than to a department with relatively low charges that had exactly the same patient load and the same number of bills.

Although the cost driver change made in this example appears to be a zero-sum game (i.e., the routine care department benefits while the other two patient services departments lose), the decision to make the change was not really difficult for Kennington's senior managers. With a better cost driver, the hospital has moved to a more equitable allocation of financial services costs, even though it may not seem that way to the department heads who saw their allocated amounts increase. However, those departments with allocation increases for financial services (laboratory and radiology) are now being allocated their fair share of those overhead expenses. They were formerly being subsidized by the routine care department, whose allocation was too high.

In addition, the heads of revenue-producing departments can now reap the benefits of their efforts to make the billing process more efficient. If the laboratory department director does not like the new higher allocation, he can do something about it—generate fewer bills. The task must be done without lowering the total billing amount, which may not be easy. In fact, the effort will probably have to be done jointly with the financial services department and perhaps with the cooperation of third-party payers.

The critical point is that patient services department heads are now motivated to participate in making the billing process more efficient. If the laboratory department can cut the number of bills in half, it can cut its allocation in half. If other patient services departments can do this, Kennington will eventually discover that it can get along with fewer resources devoted to financial services and can thus reduce total overhead costs. A reduction in overhead costs is the ultimate benefit of moving to a better cost driver.

SELF-TEST QUESTIONS

1. What are the advantages of changing from a poor cost driver to a better one?
2. What are the costs involved in the change?
3. Why is good cost allocation critical to good decision-making?

Final Thoughts on Cost Allocation

This chapter has been more mechanical than conceptual, but readers should not lose sight of the basic principles of cost allocation. First, cost allocation is driven by the need to measure costs and profits at the department level. Thus, the primary goal of cost allocation is to allocate all support department costs to those departments that create the need for those costs (profit centers), typically the patient services departments. In general, cost drivers should be chosen that have a high correlation with the amount of overhead services consumed—the greater the consumption of services, the higher the allocation.

In addition, to be effective, cost drivers must meet two tests. First, they must create an allocation system that is perceived as being fair; managers must believe that the overhead allocations to their departments truly reflect the amount of overhead services consumed. Second, the allocation process should foster cost reduction within the organization. To ensure fairness and cost control incentives, cost drivers must reflect those factors that truly influence the amount of overhead services consumed.

In any organization, the better the cost allocation system meets these two tests, the better the managerial decisions will be. After all, costs play a major role in many provider decisions, such as what prices to charge, what services to offer, and how much clinical managers should be paid. If the cost allocation system is faulty, those decisions may be flawed and the financial condition of the business and employee morale will be degraded. Although the allocation process may seem rather mundane, the more confidence that all managers have in its validity, the better the organization will function.

SELF-TEST QUESTIONS

1. What is the goal of cost allocation?
2. What are the two primary tests that good cost allocation processes pass?
3. Why is the cost allocation process important to health services managers?

Key Concepts

This chapter focuses on costing at the department level, which requires cost allocation. The key concepts are as follows:

- *Direct costs* are the unique and exclusive costs of one unit of an organization, such as the labor costs of one department, and therefore are relatively easy to measure.
- *Indirect costs*, in contrast, are inherently difficult to measure because they involve a shared resource of the organization as a whole, such as general administration costs.

(continued)

(continued from previous page)

- The goal of cost allocation is to assign the overhead costs of an organization to the departments that cause them to be incurred (the patient services departments).

- The motivation to improve cost allocation systems comes largely from the increasing pressure to optimize economic performance within health services organizations and the resultant managerial incentive systems that focus on financial performance.

- A *cost pool* is a dollar amount of overhead services to be allocated. In general, a cost pool consists of the total direct costs of one support department. However, under some circumstances, it may be better to divide the direct costs of a support department into multiple cost pools.

- A *cost driver* is the basis for making allocations from a cost pool. The identification of effective cost drivers is essential to a sound cost allocation system.

- Cost drivers are chosen on the basis of their *correlation* with the amount of overhead services used. The greater the overhead service utilization, the greater the cost allocation.

- An effective cost driver will be perceived by department heads as being *fair* and will promote *cost reduction* within the organization.

- There are three primary *methods for cost allocation:* direct, reciprocal, and step-down.

- The *direct method* recognizes no intrasupport department services. Thus, support department costs are allocated exclusively to patient services departments.

- The *reciprocal method* recognizes all intrasupport department services. The reciprocal method is the most complex to implement and explain to department heads.

- The *step-down method* represents a compromise between the direct and reciprocal methods that recognizes some of the intrasupport department services.

- Regardless of the allocation method, all costs eventually are allocated to the patient services departments.

Although this chapter contained a great deal of detail, the most important point to remember is that a sound cost allocation system is required for making good pricing (and service) decisions, which is the topic of discussion in the next chapter.

Questions

6.1. What are the primary differences between direct and indirect costs?

6.2. What is the goal of cost allocation?

6.3. a. What are the three primary methods of cost allocation?

b. What are the differences among them?

6.4. a. What is a cost pool?

b. What is a cost driver?

c. How is the cost allocation rate determined?

6.5. Under what circumstances should an overhead department be divided into multiple cost pools?

6.6. Effective cost drivers, and the resulting allocation system, must have what two important attributes?

6.7. Briefly describe (illustrate) the cost allocation process. (To keep things simple, use the direct method for your illustration.)

6.8. Which is the better cost driver for the costs of a hospital's financial services department: patient services department revenues or number of bills generated? Explain your rationale.

Problems

6.1. The housekeeping services department of Ruger Clinic, a multispecialty practice, had $100,000 in direct costs in 2020. These costs must be allocated to Ruger's three revenue-producing patient services departments using the direct method. Two cost drivers are under consideration: patient services revenue and hours of housekeeping services used. The patient services departments generated $5 million in total revenues during 2020, and to support these clinical activities, they used 5,000 hours of housekeeping services.

a. What is the value of the cost pool?

b. What is the allocation rate if:

• patient services revenue is used as the cost driver?

• hours of housekeeping services is used as the cost driver?

6.2. Refer to problem 6.1. Assume that the three patient services departments are adult services, pediatric services, and other services. The patient services revenue and hours of housekeeping services for each department are as follows:

Department	Revenue	Housekeeping Hours
Adult services	$3,000,000	1,500
Pediatric services	1,500,000	3,000
Other services	500,000	500
Total	$5,000,000	5,000

a. What is the dollar allocation to each patient services department if patient services revenue is used as the cost driver?

b. What is the dollar allocation to each patient services department if hours of housekeeping support is used as the cost driver?

c. What is the difference in the allocation to each department between the two drivers?

d. Which of the two drivers is better? Why?

The following data pertain to problems 6.3 through 6.6:

St. Benedict's Hospital has three support departments and four patient services departments. The direct costs to each of the support departments are as follows:

General administration	$2,000,000
Facilities	5,000,000
Financial services	3,000,000

Selected data for the three support and four patient services departments are shown below:

Department	Patient Services Revenues	Space (square feet)	Housekeeping Labor Hours	Salary Dollars
Support:				
General administration		10,000	2,000	$ 1,500,000
Facilities		20,000	5,000	3,000,000
Financial services		15,000	3,000	2,000,000
Total		45,000	10,000	$ 6,500,000
Patient Services:				
Routine care	$30,000,000	400,000	150,000	$12,000,000
Intensive care	4,000,000	40,000	30,000	5,000,000
Diagnostic services	6,000,000	60,000	15,000	6,000,000
Other services	10,000,000	100,000	25,000	7,000,000
Total	$50,000,000	600,000	220,000	$30,000,000
Grand total	$50,000,000	645,000	230,000	$36,500,000

6.3. Assume that the hospital uses the direct method for cost allocation. Furthermore, the cost driver for general administration and financial services is patient services revenue, while the cost driver for facilities is space utilization.

   a. What are the appropriate allocation rates?

   b. Use an allocation table similar to exhibit 6.7 to allocate the hospital's overhead costs to the patient services departments.

6.4. Assume that the hospital uses salary dollars as the cost driver for general administration, housekeeping labor hours as the cost driver for facilities, and patient services revenue as the cost driver for financial services. (The majority of the costs of the facilities department stem from the provision of housekeeping services.)

   a. What are the appropriate allocation rates?

   b. Use an allocation table similar to the one used for problem 6.3 to allocate the hospital's overhead costs to the patient services departments.

   c. Compare the dollar allocations with those obtained in problem 6.3. Which departments are allocated more overhead costs? Which are allocated less?

   d. Which of the two cost driver schemes is better? Explain your answer.

6.5. Now assume that the hospital uses the step-down method for cost allocation, with salary dollars as the cost driver for general administration, housekeeping labor hours as the cost driver for facilities, and patient services revenue as the cost driver for financial services. Assume also that the general administration department provides the most services to other support departments, followed closely by the facilities department. The financial services department provides the least services to the other support departments. (Hint: The step-down method of cost allocation, reviewed in this problem, is covered in the chapter 6 supplement.)

   a. Use an allocation table to allocate the hospital's overhead costs to the patient services departments.

   b. Compare the dollar allocations with those obtained in problem 6.4. Which departments are allocated more overhead costs? Which are allocated less?

   c. Is the direct method or the step-down method better for cost allocation within St. Benedict's? Explain your answer.

6.6. Return to the direct method of cost allocation and use the same cost drivers as specified in problem 6.4 for the general administration and facilities departments. However, assume that

$2,000,000 of financial services costs is related to billing and managerial reporting and $1,000,000 is related to payroll and personnel management activities.

a. Devise and implement a cost allocation scheme that recognizes that the financial services department has two widely different functions.

b. Is there any additional information that would be useful in completing the first part of this problem?

c. What are the costs and benefits to St. Benedict's of creating two cost pools for the allocation of financial services costs?

The following data pertain to problems 6.7 and 6.8:

St. Luke's Hospital has three support departments and four patient services departments. The direct costs to each of the support departments are as follows:

General administration	$4,000,000
Maintenance	5,000,000
Employee benefits	4,000,000

Selected data for the three support and four patient services departments are shown below:

Department	Patient Services Revenue	Space (square feet)	Number of Full-Time Equivalent Employees	Salary Dollars
Support:				
General administration		8,000	15	$ 2,500,000
Maintenance		10,000	75	3,500,000
Employee benefits		7,000	50	3,000,000
Total		25,000	140	$ 9,000,000
Patient Services:				
Routine care	$40,000,000	500,000	700	$18,000,000
Intensive care	7,000,000	45,000	200	6,000,000
Obstetrics services	4,000,000	35,000	150	4,000,000
Other services	12,000,000	200,000	400	8,000,000
Total	$63,000,000	780,000	1,450	$36,000,000
Grand total	$63,000,000	805,000	1,590	$45,000,000

6.7. Assume the hospital uses the direct method for cost allocation. Furthermore, the cost driver for general administration is patient services revenue, the cost driver for maintenance is space utilization, and the cost driver for employee benefits is the number of full-time equivalent employees.

a. What are the appropriate allocation rates?

b. Use an allocation table similar to exhibit 6.7 to allocate the hospital's overhead costs to the patient services departments.

6.8. Assume that the hospital uses salary dollars as the cost driver for general administration and employee benefits, and space utilization as the cost driver for maintenance.

a. What are the appropriate allocation rates?

b. Use an allocation table similar to exhibit 6.7 to allocate the hospital's overhead costs to the patient services departments.

c. Compare the dollar allocations with those obtained in problem 6.7. Which departments are allocated more overhead costs? Which are allocated less?

Selected Cases

Three cases in *Gapenski's Cases in Healthcare Finance*, sixth edition, are applicable to this chapter: Case 6: Big Bend Medical Center; Case 7: Eagan Family Practice; and Case 8: Dallas Health Network.

Resources

For a more in-depth treatment of cost measurement in health services organizations, see
Finkler, S. A., D. M. Ward, and T. D. Calabrese. 2019. *Accounting Fundamentals for Health Care Management*, 3rd ed. Sudbury, MA: Jones & Bartlett.
Young, D. W. 2019. *Management Accounting in Health Care Organizations*, 4th ed. Stoneham, MA: Crimson Press.

In addition, see
Arredondo, R. 2014. "Why Revisit Your Cost-Accounting Strategy." *Healthcare Financial Management* 68 (7): 68–73.
Carroll, N., and J. C. Lord. 2016. "The Growing Importance of Cost Accounting for Hospitals." *Journal of Health Care Finance* 43 (2): 171–85.

Cooper, R., and T. R. Kramer. 2008. "The Problem with Revenue-Based Cost Assignment." *MGMA Connection*, April, 44–47.

Hilsenrath, P., C. Eakin, and K. Fischer. 2015. "Price-Transparency and Cost Accounting: Challenges for Health Care Organizations in the Consumer-Driven Era." *Inquiry* 52: 1–5.

Meeting, D. T., and R. O. Harvey. 1998. "Strategic Cost Accounting Helps Create a Competitive Edge." *Healthcare Financial Management* 52 (12): 43–51.

Muise, M. L., and B. A. Amoia. 2006. "Step Up to the Step-Down Method." *Healthcare Financial Management* 60 (5): 72–77.

Young, D. W. 2008. "Profit Centers in Clinical Care Departments: An Idea Whose Time Has Gone." *Healthcare Financial Management* 62 (3): 66–71.

6

STEP-DOWN METHOD ILLUSTRATION

In chapter 6, we noted that there are several methods for allocating overhead costs to user departments. We discussed three methods (direct, step-down, and reciprocal) but only illustrated the direct method. (In fact, there is a fourth method, *double apportionment,* which is not covered in this book.) In this supplement, we use Fargo Medical Associates, which has two support departments (financial services and general administration) and two patient services departments (home care and diagnostic services), to illustrate the step-down method. In the illustration of the direct method presented in chapter 6, support department costs were allocated solely to the patient services departments, with no recognition of the provision of intrasupport department services. Here we recognize, at least partially, that support departments provide services to one another. Note that the reciprocal method would fully recognize the provision of intrasupport department services.

Because the step-down method recognizes that support departments provide services to one another, a new decision must be made: Which of Fargo's two support departments is the most primary? That is, which support department provides more services to the other? This decision will determine the order of allocation. Order is important in the step-down method because costs can be allocated in only one direction. Fargo's managers, after some analysis, concluded that the general administration department provides more support to the financial services department than the financial services department does to general administration. Thus, in the step-down process, the first support department to be allocated is general administration.

Fargo's managers determined that the cost driver for general administration costs is payroll costs, and the cost driver for financial services costs is the number of bills. The managers assembled the summary data shown in exhibit S6.1.

Note that the managers did not include payroll costs for general administration in exhibit S6.1. This does not mean that the general administration department has no payroll costs. Rather, it reflects the nature of the step-down cost allocation method. Since general administration costs are being allocated to only three departments—financial services, home care, and diagnostic services—the payroll costs of general administration must be excluded when calculating the allocation rate. If the general administration payroll costs were included in the denominator of the allocation rate, the rate

EXHIBIT S6.1
Fargo Medical
Associates:
Summary Data

Department	Direct Costs	Payroll Costs	Number of Bills
General Administration	$ 312,425		
Financial Services	665,031	$ 505,321	
Home Care	950,000	3,376,845	10,508
Diagnostic Services	875,000	425,115	3,948
Total	$2,802,456	$4,307,281	14,456

would be too small and not all costs would be allocated. The general administration department cannot allocate costs back to itself.

When determining total units of the cost driver for the allocation
rate, it is important to include only those departments that will *receive* an
allocation. This relationship also holds for the allocation of financial services
costs. Since financial services costs will only be allocated to home care and
diagnostic services, the number of bills produced by general administration
and financial services (if any) is not important.

The calculation of allocation rates and the final allocations are shown
in exhibit S6.2. The first table shows the method for calculating the allocation
rates. The second table summarizes the allocation and the resulting full costs
after the allocation is completed. Note that exhibit S6.2 is laid out slightly differently than the exhibits in chapter 6. This layout shows the stair-step pattern

EXHIBIT S6.2
Fargo Medical
Associates:
Step-Down
Allocation of
Administration
and Financial
Services Costs

	Allocation Rates	
Department:	General Administration	Financial Services
Cost driver:	Payroll costs	Number of bills
Cost pool:	$312,425	$665,031 + $36,653 = $701,684
Relevant units of cost driver:	$4,307,281 payroll dollars	14,456 bills
Allocation rate:	$312,425 ÷ $4,307,281 = $0.072534 per dollar of payroll	$701,684 ÷ 14,456 = $48.53929 per bill

| | | Indirect Cost Allocations | | |
Department	Direct Costs	General Administration	Financial Services	Full Costs
General Administration	$ 312,425	($312,425)		$ 0
Financial Services	665,031	36,653	($701,684)	0
Home Care	950,000	244,937	510,051	1,704,988
Diagnostic Services	875,000	30,835	191,633	1,097,468
Total	$2,802,456	$ 0	$ 0	$2,802,456

of the step-down allocation method; however, the process is similar to that illustrated in chapter 6. The key point is that the formatting of the analysis is not what matters; it is understanding the concepts that is important.

In the direct method, the $312,425 in general administration direct costs would be allocated only to the two patient services departments. However, in the step-down method, the $312,425 is allocated not only to the two patient services (revenue-producing) departments but also to financial services, the other support department.

As shown in the first table of exhibit S6.2, the allocation of general administration costs is made using the payroll costs of the *receiving departments* as the cost driver. The total payroll for Fargo, less the general administration department, is $4,307,281, so the $312,425 in general administration costs are allocated at a rate of $312,425 ÷ $4,307,281 = $0.072534 per dollar of payroll. Based on this allocation rate, the allocation of general administration costs to the financial services department is 0.072534 × $505,321 = $36,653, while the allocation to the home care department is 0.072534 × $3,376,845 = $244,937 and the allocation to the diagnostic services department is 0.072534 × $425,115 = $30,835.

This first step of the step-down allocation is shown in the third column of the second table in exhibit S6.2. The general administration direct costs are removed from the general administration department (the number in parentheses denotes a negative number) and allocated down to three remaining departments: the financial services department, the home care department, and the diagnostic services department. Summing the values in column three provides a check of the calculations—all of the general administration costs should be allocated to the remaining three departments, thus the column should sum to zero.

Now that general administration costs have been allocated among both support and patient services departments, the role of the general administration department in the allocation process is completed. The next step is to allocate financial services costs, which now include both direct costs and the indirect costs from the allocation of general administration overhead. Because previous steps in the process influence the cost pools of subsequent steps, it is critical to complete the allocation of costs from one department before moving to the calculation of the allocation rate for any of the remaining departments. The calculation of the allocation rate for financial services department costs is shown in the first table of exhibit S6.2. Although the financial services department has only $665,031 in direct costs, the total amount to be allocated is $701,684 because the total cost pool now includes $36,653 of allocated general administration overhead. Because some of the costs of general administration now flow through the financial services department, the allocation of financial services costs to the patient services departments is somewhat greater than it would be using the direct method. However, the allocation of general administration costs to the patient services departments is less under the step-down method than under the direct method because some costs that had been allocated directly to patient services departments are now allocated to the financial services department, another support department.

Column four in the second table of exhibit S6.2 shows the allocation of the financial services costs to the two patient service departments. The total cost pool of $701,684 is removed from the financial services department and allocated as follows: $48.53929 per bill $\times$ 10,508 bills = $510,051 to home care and $48.53929 $\times$ 3,948 = $191,633 to diagnostic services. The last column in the table shows the full costs in each department after the step-down allocation is complete. After summing the values across each row, no costs remain in the two support departments. All support department costs have been allocated to the patient service departments. Finally, note that the total organizational costs before the allocation are equal to the total organizational costs after the allocation, showing that the step-down allocation process only "moves" costs; it does not increase or decrease the total costs of the organization.

The step-down method of allocation is somewhat more complicated than the direct method. However, a good managerial accounting system can accomplish either allocation method quite easily. The real disadvantage of the step-down method is that it is more difficult for department heads to understand, especially in large, complex organizations. Still, for the reasons discussed in chapter 6 (fairness and cost control), managers want the best possible allocation system. In addition, Medicare requires that providers use the step-down method when reporting Medicare costs. Thus, in practice, the use of the step-down method dominates the others.

SELF-TEST QUESTIONS

1. What is the primary difference between the direct and step-down methods of cost allocation?
2. Why might organizations adopt a more complicated allocation system rather than use the direct method?

7

SERVICE LINE COSTING AND PRICING

Introduction

In our discussion of managerial accounting, we have examined costing at the organizational level (along with cost behavior and profit analysis) and costing at the department level (and its major feature, cost allocation). Although these are important concepts, the ultimate goal of cost estimation is costing at the service or individual patient level. Thus, we begin this chapter with a discussion of some of the techniques used (and proposed) to estimate costs at the *micro level*.

Among the most important uses of managerial accounting data is establishing a price for a particular service or, given a price, estimating whether the service will be profitable. For example, in a charge-based environment, managers of healthcare providers must set prices for the services that their organizations offer. Managers also must determine whether to offer volume discounts to valued payer groups, such as managed care plans or business coalitions, and how large these discounts should be. Such decisions are called *pricing decisions.*

In other environments, insurers, especially government and managed care plans, dictate reimbursement amounts. Therefore, health services managers do not set prices but must decide whether the payment is sufficient to assume the risks associated with providing services to the covered populations. These decisions are called *service decisions.* Because service decision analyses are similar to pricing decision analyses, they are discussed jointly. Service decisions are discussed in more detail in the chapter 7 supplement. One of the key inputs into both pricing and service decisions is the cost of the services under consideration, which is why the chapter begins with costing at the service and patient level.

Pricing and service decisions affect a business's revenues and costs, and hence its financial condition, which ultimately determines the business's long-term viability. The importance of such decisions is easy to understand. In essence, pricing and service decisions determine both the strategic direction of the business and the ability of the organization to survive, prosper, and meet the needs of the populations served.

Service Line Costing

As discussed in chapters 1 and 2, one of the key elements of healthcare reform is cost reduction at the provider level. This focus is paramount for accountable care organizations, in which the goal is to create shared savings and/or capitated contracts that encourage providers to shift attention from optimizing reimbursement to increasing quality while containing costs. To contain costs, as well as to make better decisions when negotiating contracts, it is necessary to know (or at least have a reasonable idea of) costs at the individual service or even the individual patient level.

Several methods are used to estimate costs at the service level. In this section, we discuss three methods: cost-to-charge ratio (CCR), relative value unit (RVU), and activity-based costing (ABC). In addition, we introduce time-driven activity-based costing (TDABC), a relatively new approach that focuses on costing multiple services provided to individual patients.

The Setting
To illustrate costing at the service level, consider Tarheel Family Practice (TFP), a large physician group that is organized into five departments, one of

	Service X	Service Y	Total	
Annual volume (visits)	5,000	5,000	10,000	
RVUs per visit	10	18		
Annual costs:				
Direct	$242,500	$ 485,000	$ 727,500	
Indirect (overhead)			300,000	
Total costs			$1,027,500	
Annual charges	$700,000	$1,400,000	$2,100,000	
Annual revenues (reimbursements)	$400,000	$ 900,000	$1,300,000	

EXHIBIT 7.1
Tarheel Family Practice: Selected Routine Services Department Data

which is the routine services department. For ease of discussion, we assume that the department provides only two services: X and Y. Data relevant to our illustrations are summarized in exhibit 7.1.

The department has 10,000 visits annually, split evenly between the two services. The department's total annual costs come to $1,027,500. These include $300,000 in department overhead (including both TFP overhead allocated to the department and department overhead that supports both services), $242,500 in direct costs of service X, and $485,000 in direct costs of service Y. Finally, the department's charges (based on chargemaster prices) total $2,100,000, while actual revenues (reimbursements) total $1,300,000, split between the two services as shown in exhibit 7.1. Before we discuss the individual costing methods, we want to emphasize that this example is highly simplified. Its purpose is simply to give you a flavor of the alternative methods available for costing individual services.

Cost-to-Charge Ratio Method

The **cost-to-charge ratio (CCR)** method is the most basic of the three methods of costing individual services. The CCR method is based on two assumptions: First, the indirect (overhead) costs allocated to the services constitute a single cost that is proportional across all services provided. In other words, each service consumes indirect costs in the same proportion as the department as a whole. Second, charges (or, alternatively, reimbursement rates) reflect the level of intensity of the service provided and hence the use of overhead resources, including both TFP-allocated and department-specific overhead.

cost-to-charge ratio (CCR)
A ratio used to estimate the overhead costs of individual services; defined as the ratio of indirect (overhead) costs to charges (or, alternatively, to service revenues).

We begin by focusing on charges. With indirect (overhead) costs of $300,000 supporting total charges of $2,100,000, CCR = Indirect costs ÷ Total charges = $300,000 ÷ $2,100,000 = 0.143 = 14.3%.

Key Equation: Cost-to-Charge Ratio

Suppose a nursing home has annual indirect (overhead) costs of $1,500,000 and $4,500,000 in charges. The CCR is calculated as follows:

$$\text{CCR} = \text{Indirect costs} \div \text{Total charges}$$
$$= \$1,500,000 \div \$4,500,000$$
$$= 0.333 = 33.3\%.$$

Note that the cost-to-charge ratio can also be defined using total revenues (reimbursements) in place of charges.

Once the CCR has been calculated for the department, it is used to estimate the overhead costs for each individual service: Service overhead costs = CCR × Service charges. Thus, the overhead cost allocations for services X and Y are:

Service X: 0.143 × $700,000 = $100,100.
Service Y: 0.143 × $1,400,000 = $200,200.

The total amount of overhead allocated to the two services is $100,100 + $200,200 = $300,300, which, except for a rounding difference, equals the $300,000 in total indirect costs for the department.

To obtain the full costs of each service line, simply add the direct costs to the amounts allocated for overhead: Full (total) service costs = Direct cost + Indirect cost. The results are:

Service X: $242,500 + $100,100 = $342,600.
Service Y: $485,000 + $200,200 = $685,200.

As a check, the full costs of both services total $342,600 + $685,200 = $1,027,800, which, again, except for a rounding difference, equals the total costs of the department.

Finally, to obtain the average cost per visit for each service, divide the full costs by the number of visits:

Service X: $342,600 ÷ 5,000 = $68.52.
Service Y: $685,200 ÷ 5,000 = $137.04.

Note that revenues can be used as an alternative to charges in the CCR method. The procedure is the same as described above, but now revenues are used to calculate the CCR. Here is the calculation: With indirect (overhead) costs of $300,000 supporting total revenues (reimbursements) of $1,300,000, the cost-to-charge ratio is CCR = $300,000 ÷ $1,300,000 = 0.231 = 23.1%. Using this new value for the CCR, and revenues in lieu of charges, the overhead cost allocations are:

Service X: 0.231 × $400,000 = $92,400.

Service Y: 0.231 × $900,000 = $207,900.

Finally, to obtain the full costs of each service line, the calculations are:

Service X: $242,500 + $92,400 = $334,900.

Service Y: $485,000 + $207,900 = $692,900.

As a check, the full costs of both services total $334,900 + $692,900 = $1,027,800, which, again, except for a rounding difference, equals the total costs of the department.

Exhibit 7.2 presents a comparison of the results of the two approaches. In this illustration, there is little difference between the allocation results using charges as the basis for the allocation and using revenues (reimbursements) as the basis.

> **For Your Consideration**
>
> Charges Versus Revenues in the CCR Method
>
> The illustration of the CCR method of costing at the service level presented two possible approaches: One uses charges as the basis of the allocation, and one uses revenues (reimbursements). Although the results of the two vary by only small percentages (–2.25 percent and 1.12 percent), in other situations, the variation could be much larger.
>
> Healthcare providers using the CCR method must decide which approach to use. (For some Medicare calculations, the use of charges is required; however, for internal use, providers may use either charges or revenues.) In theory, the choice should reflect the metric (charges or revenues) that best reflects the relationship to the amount of overhead resources consumed. But is that metric charges or revenues? Charges supposedly reflect the underlying costs of the service—the higher the charges, the higher the costs. However, there is much anecdotal evidence (e.g., the $10 aspirin) that charges are not a good reflection of costs. On the other hand, are revenues a better reflection of costs? Private insurers, Medicare, and Medicaid often have large differences in reimbursement amounts for the same service.
>
> What do you think? Should the CCR method use charges or revenues as the metric? What is the justification for your answer?

Relative Value Unit Method

In contrast to the CCR method, which ties overhead resource consumption to charges (or revenues), the **relative value unit (RVU) method** ties the use of overhead resources to the complexity and time required for each service. In other words, this method uses the intensity of the service provided, as measured by relative value units (RVUs), as the basis for allocating overhead. As we discussed in chapter 2, its use in healthcare pricing and reimbursement is influenced primarily by the *resource-based relative value scale* (*RBRVS*), which uses RVUs to set Medicare payments for physician services.

relative value unit (RVU) method
A method for estimating the overhead costs of individual services based on the intensity of the service provided, as measured by RVUs.

EXHIBIT 7.2
CCR Method:
Comparison of
Results Using
Charges and
Revenues

	Service X	Service Y	Total
Allocation Based on Charges:			
Direct	$242,500	$485,000	$ 727,500
Indirect	100,100	200,200	300,300
Total	$342,600	$685,200	$1,027,800
Allocation Based on Revenues:			
Direct	$242,500	$485,000	$ 727,500
Indirect	92,400	207,900	300,300
Total	$334,900	$692,900	$1,027,800
Difference	–$ 7,700	$ 7,700	$ 0
	–2.25%	1.12%	0.00%

Note: Some rounding differences occur between the data in exhibit 7.1 and those in exhibit 7.2.

To begin our illustration of the RVU method, assume that a study conducted by the medical director of TFP identified the number of RVUs required to perform each service. The result was the assignment of 10 RVUs for service X and 18 RVUs for service Y. (RVU estimates for many healthcare services are available from several sources, including Medicare and professional associations.)

The RVU analysis is summarized in exhibit 7.3. First, the RVUs for each service are multiplied by the annual volume, and the products are summed to obtain the total RVUs for the department—140,000. Now with department overhead costs of $300,000 to support 140,000 RVUs, the overhead cost per RVU is $300,000 ÷ 140,000 = $2.143. The final step in the overhead cost allocation is to multiply the cost per RVU by the total number of RVUs for each service to obtain the overhead allocation:

Service X total overhead cost = $2.143 × 50,000 = $107,150.
Service Y total overhead cost = $2.143 × 90,000 = $192,870.

Now, the total costs of each service are the direct costs of the service plus the overhead allocation:

Service X: $242,500 + $107,150 = $349,650.
Service Y: $485,000 + $192,870 = $677,870.

Service	RVUs	Volume	Total RVUs
X	10	5,000	50,000
Y	18	5,000	90,000
			140,000

EXHIBIT 7.3
RVU Analysis
for Services X
and Y

Overhead cost per RVU = $300,000 ÷ 140,000 = $2.143.

Service X total overhead cost = $2.143 × 50,000 = $107,150.

Service Y total overhead cost = $2.143 × 90,000 = $192,870.

Total overhead costs = $107,150 + $192,870 = $300,020.

Note: Some rounding differences occur between the data in exhibit 7.1 and those in exhibit 7.3.

As a final check, note that the total costs of each service sum to $1,027,520, which, except for a small rounding difference, equals the total costs of the department, $1,027,500.

The goal of RVU costing is to reflect the cost of the overhead resources used to provide the service. Of course, the key to the fairness of RVU costing is how well the number of RVUs assigned to each service matches the cost of the overhead resources consumed. Because of the difficulties involved in initially assigning RVU values to services, this method is used most often when RVU values have already been estimated, such as for procedures performed by physicians.

Activity-Based Costing Method

Our discussion thus far has focused on what might be called **traditional costing** methods. In essence, traditional methods begin with aggregate costs. Overhead costs are then allocated downstream, first to the patient services departments and then, using the CCR or RVU method, to individual services. Thus, traditional methods can be thought of as top-down allocation. Although traditional costing works well for estimating costs at the department level, its usefulness for estimating the costs of activities within or across departments, such as individual tests, services, or diagnoses, or the services used by individual patients is limited. The next approach, **activity-based costing (ABC)**, addresses this limitation and is generally acknowledged to be superior to the traditional methods.

ABC uses an upstream approach to cost allocation. Its premise is that all costs within an organization stem from activities. In ABC, because activities rather than departments are the focus of the process, costs can be

traditional costing A top-down approach to costing that first identifies costs at the department level and then (potentially) assigns those costs to individual services.

activity-based costing (ABC) A bottom-up approach to costing that identifies the activities required to provide a particular service, estimates the costs of those activities, and then aggregates those costs.

more easily assigned to individual patients, individual physicians, particular diagnoses, a reimbursement contract, a managed care population, and so on.

The key to cost allocation under ABC is to identify the activities that are performed to provide a particular service and then aggregate the costs of those activities. The steps required to implement ABC are as follows:

- Identify the relevant activities.
- Estimate the costs of each activity, including both direct and indirect.
- Assign cost drivers for each activity.
- Collect activity data for each service.
- Calculate the total cost of the service by aggregating activity costs.

Note that in some cost accounting systems, direct costs are assigned directly to service units and only indirect costs are included in the ABC process. For simplicity, this example combines direct and indirect costs.

To illustrate the ABC concept, suppose that the routine services department of TFP performs seven services: (1) patient check-in, including insurance verification; (2) preliminary assessment; (3) diagnosis; (4) treatment; (5) prescription writing; (6) patient check-out; and (7) third-party payer billing. As in our previous examples, we must reiterate that this illustration is highly simplified with the purpose of providing a sense of how ABC works.

Exhibit 7.4 contains the initial data and allocation rate calculations. To illustrate, the annual costs of the patient check-in activity, consisting of clerical labor and supplies (direct costs) plus space and other overhead (indirect costs), are $50,000 to support 10,000 total visits, so the allocation rate for the patient check-in activity is $50,000 ÷ 10,000 = $5.00 per visit. For another illustration, the total (direct labor by one nurse and overhead) cost required to conduct the initial assessment is $75,000, spread over (5,000 visits × 5 minutes for service X) + (5,000 visits × 10 minutes for service Y) = 25,000 + 50,000 = 75,000 minutes annually, giving an allocation rate of $75,000 ÷ 75,000 = $1 per minute for the initial assessment activity.

As shown in exhibit 7.5, the final step in the ABC process is to aggregate the activity costs for all of the seven services. Note that this is done on a per visit basis. For example, for service X, the cost of check-in is 1 visit × $5.00 = $5.00; the cost of assessment is 5 minutes × $1.00 = $5.00; and the cost of diagnosis is 10 minutes × $2.00 = $20.00. Other activity costs for service X and service Y were calculated in a similar manner.

The result of summing the individual activity costs associated with each service is an average cost of $75.10 per visit for service X and $130.40 per visit for service Y. The ability of the routine services department to estimate the costs of its individual services allows the services to be priced on

			Activity Data			
Activity	Annual Costs	Cost Driver	Service X	Service Y	Total	Allocation Rate
Check-in	$ 50,000	Visits	5,000	5,000	10,000	$ 5.00
Assessment	75,000	Minutes per visit	5	10	75,000	1.00
Diagnosis	250,000	Minutes per visit	10	15	125,000	2.00
Treatment	450,000	Minutes per visit	10	20	150,000	3.00
Prescription	2,500	Number of drugs per visit	0.5	2	12,500	0.20
Check-out	50,000	Visits	5,000	5,000	10,000	5.00
Billing	150,000	Number of bills per visit	1	2	15,000	10.00
Total costs	$1,027,500					

the basis of actual costs. In addition, cost control is made easier because the activities, and corresponding resource expenditures for each service, have been clearly identified.

Note that the total annual costs of providing service X are 5,000 visits × $75.10 = $375,500, while the total costs for service Y are 5,000 visits × $130.40 = $652,000. Because there are only two services in this simple example, the total costs of the routine services department are $375,500 + $652,000 = $1,027,500, which equals the total cost amount identified in exhibit 7.1.

Clearly, ABC holds great promise for healthcare providers. The ability to assess the costs of individual services with more confidence than in traditional costing methods provides managers with better information regarding the true costs of providing services. However, the information and resource requirements to establish an ABC system far exceed those required for traditional cost allocation. For this reason, traditional cost allocation is the prevalent allocation method for many small healthcare entities, with ABC becoming more widespread as the need for better cost data becomes more important and as providers invest in newer and more powerful managerial accounting systems.

Time-Driven Activity-Based Costing (TDABC) Method

The final method of costing that we discuss is a relatively new concept that, for now, is more of a theoretical approach than one that is widely used in practice. Still, it offers the promise of expanding the concept of cost measurement beyond individual service costing in a way that could lead to better (including lower cost) treatment plans.

EXHIBIT 7.5
ABC Illustration: Final Aggregation of Activity Costs per Visit

Activity	Cost Driver	Rate	Service X		Service Y	
			Consumption	Cost	Consumption	Cost
Check-in	Visits	$ 5.00	1	$ 5.00	1	$ 5.00
Assessment	Number of minutes	1.00	5	5.00	10	10.00
Diagnosis	Number of minutes	2.00	10	20.00	15	30.00
Treatment	Number of minutes	3.00	10	30.00	20	60.00
Prescription	Number of drugs	0.20	0.5	0.10	2	0.40
Check-out	Visits	5.00	1	5.00	1	5.00
Billing	Number of bills	10.00	1	10.00	2	20.00
Cost per service				$75.10		$130.40

The idea behind the **time-driven activity-based costing (TDABC)** method is to simplify ABC. TDABC measures all costs required to deliver healthcare outcomes. It is a simpler method compared with ABC because it requires only two types of information: (1) the costs of resources used and (2) the amount of time the patient spends with each resource. (See the Resources section at the end of this chapter for more information on the TDABC method.)

The TDABC method follows these steps:

- **Select the medical condition to be studied.** For each condition, complications and comorbidities must be considered along with the beginning and end of the patient care cycle. For chronic conditions, the patient care cycle is defined by a period of time, often a year.
- **Define the care delivery chain.** The second step is to define the principal activities that comprise the patient's care. This becomes the road map of the activities involved in a complete cycle of care.
- **Develop process maps of each activity.** In this step, the resources required for each activity are identified, including labor, equipment, supplies, facilities, overhead, and other resources. Also, the amount of time required for each activity must be recorded. (Note that time recording may be treated as a separate step.)
- **Estimate the cost of supplying the patient care resources.** Here, both the direct and indirect costs of each activity are estimated. Generally, direct costs include such items as labor, equipment depreciation or lease costs, and supplies. Indirect costs cover such items as facilities space and furnishings along with billing and collections, general administration, and other typical support functions. (Note that this step can be broken down into several substeps.)
- **Estimate the allocation rates for each activity.** In this step, allocation rates are measured as total activity costs divided by total time devoted to that activity.
- **Calculate the total cost of patient care.** In the final step, the costs of each activity are measured by multiplying a patient's time spent in the activity by the allocation rate. Finally, the costs of all the activities are summed to estimate the total cost of a patient's complete cycle of care.

Although we do not present an illustration of TDABC here, it is clear that this costing method offers hope for creating a healthcare delivery system that truly delivers value. The key is better measurement of both the treatment costs across the continuum of services needed to treat patients and the outcomes that result.

time-driven activity-based costing (TDABC) An approach to costing that focuses on the entire cost of a patient's cycle of care rather than the cost of individual services.

1. Briefly describe the following service costing methods:
    a. Cost-to-charge ratio (CCR)
    b. Relative value unit (RVU)
    c. Activity-based costing (ABC)
2. Explain how time-driven activity-based costing (TDABC) differs from the other three methods.

Healthcare Providers and the Power to Set Prices

Now that we have finished our discussion of costing at the service (and patient) level, it is time to move on to pricing. Healthcare providers' power to set prices ranges between two extremes. At one extreme, providers have no power whatsoever and must accept the reimbursement rates set by the marketplace. At the other extreme, providers can set any prices (within reason) they desire, and payers must accept those prices. Clearly, few real-world markets for healthcare services support such extreme positions across all payers. Nevertheless, thinking in such terms can help health services managers better understand the pricing and service decisions they face.

Providers as Price Takers

As discussed throughout the book, healthcare services are provided in an increasingly competitive marketplace. As providers respond to market competition, managers must assess the ability of their organizations to influence the prices paid for the services offered. If the organization is one of a large number of providers in a service area with many commercial fee-for-service purchasers (payers), and if little distinguishes the services offered by the competing providers, economic theory suggests that prices will be set by local supply-and-demand conditions. Thus, the actions of a single participant, whether that participant is a provider or a payer, cannot influence the prices set in the marketplace. In such a *perfectly competitive market*, healthcare providers are said to be **price takers** because they are constrained by (or "must take") the prices set in the marketplace.

price taker
A business that has no power to influence the prices set by the marketplace (or by government payers).

Although few markets for healthcare services are perfectly competitive, some payers—notably, government payers such as Medicare and insurers with significant market power—can set reimbursement levels on a take-it-or-leave-it basis. In this situation, as in competitive markets, providers also are price takers in the sense that they have little influence over reimbursement rates. Because many markets are either somewhat competitive or dominated by large insurers, and because government payers cover a significant proportion of the population, most providers probably qualify as price takers for a large percentage of their revenue.

As a general rule, providers that are price takers must take price as a given and concentrate managerial efforts on controlling costs and reducing utilization to ensure that their services are profitable. From a purely financial perspective, a price-taking provider should offer every service that can be provided at a cost that is less than the given price, even if that price has fallen because of discounting or other market actions.

Although the pure financial approach to service decisions is obviously simplistic, it raises an important managerial accounting issue: What costs are relevant to the decision at hand? To ensure long-term sustainability, prices must cover full costs. However, prices that do not cover full costs may be acceptable for short periods, and it might be in the provider's best interest in the long run to accept such prices. This matter is discussed later in the chapter.

Providers as Price Setters

In contrast to price takers, healthcare providers with market dominance enjoy large market shares and therefore exercise some pricing power. Within limits, such providers can decide what prices to set for the services offered. Furthermore, if a provider's services can be differentiated from the services of others on the basis of quality, convenience, or some other characteristic, that provider also has the ability—again, within limits—to set prices for the differentiated services. Healthcare providers that have such pricing power are called **price setters**.

The situation would be much easier for managers if a provider's status as a price taker or price setter were fixed for all payers for all services for long periods of time. Unfortunately, the market for healthcare services is always changing, and providers can quickly move from price setter to price taker or vice versa. For example, the merger of two healthcare providers may create sufficient market power to change two price takers, as separate entities, into one price setter, as a combined entity. Furthermore, providers can be price takers for some services and price setters for others, or price takers for some payers and price setters for others. To make matters even more complicated, a large provider that serves separate market areas may be a price taker for a particular service in one geographic market yet be a price setter for the same service in another geographic market.

price setter
A business that has the power to set the market prices for its goods or services.

SELF-TEST QUESTIONS

1. What is the difference between a price taker and a price setter?
2. Are healthcare providers generally price takers or price setters exclusively? Explain your answer.

Price-Setting Strategies

When providers are *price setters*, alternative strategies can be used to price healthcare services. Unfortunately, no single strategy is most appropriate in all situations. In this section, we discuss two of the price-setting strategies most frequently used by health services organizations: full and marginal cost pricing.

Full Cost Pricing

full cost pricing
The process of setting prices to cover all costs plus a profit component.

Full cost pricing recognizes that to remain viable in the long run, health services organizations must set prices that recover all costs associated with operating the business. Thus, the full cost of a service—whether a patient day in a hospital, a visit to a clinic, a laboratory test, or the treatment of a particular diagnosis—must include the following: (1) the direct variable costs of providing the service; (2) the direct fixed costs; (3) the appropriate share of the overhead expenses of the organization; and (4) a profit component, to provide funds for reinvestment and ensure future capability.

Because of the difficulties inherent in estimating the costs of individual services with any confidence, such costs must be viewed with some skepticism. Nevertheless, in the aggregate, revenues must cover both direct and overhead costs, and prices in total must lead to revenues that cover all costs of an organization. Furthermore, all businesses need profits to survive in the long run. In not-for-profit businesses, prices must be set high enough to provide the profits needed to support asset replacement and to meet growth targets. In addition, for-profit providers must provide equity investors with an explicit financial return on their investment. The bottom line here is that to recover full costs, including economic costs, prices must be set to cover accounting costs plus a profit target.

Marginal Cost Pricing

In economics, the *marginal cost* of an item is the cost of providing one additional unit of output, whether that output is a product or a service. For example, suppose that a hospital currently provides 40,000 patient days of care. Its marginal cost, based on inpatient days as the unit of output, is the cost of providing the 40,001st day of care. In this situation, it is likely that fixed costs, both direct and overhead, will not have to increase to support this volume increase, so the marginal cost that must be covered consists solely of the variable costs associated with an additional one-day stay.

Fixed costs do not change in most situations because no additional personnel would be hired nor overtime required (no additional labor cost). The marginal cost, therefore, consists of variable costs such as laundry, food and expendable supplies, and any additional utility services consumed during that day. The marginal cost associated with one additional patient day is far less than the full cost, which must include all costs plus a profit component.

> *(continued from previous page)*
>
> care company, beginning with a single HMO-style managed care plan. Once the managed care plan launches, it will send patients to Space Coast hospitals. Thus, the hospital must make a decision about its pricing policy for its "in-house" managed care plan. Should it price high to maintain strong margins, or should it price low to help the new managed care plan attract members?
>
> What do you think? Does marginal cost pricing or full cost pricing make more sense? Is the optimal pricing strategy the same in the short run as in the long run?

Many proponents of government programs such as Medicare and Medicaid argue that payments to providers should be made on the basis of marginal rather than full costs. The argument is that some price above marginal cost is all that is required for the provider to "make money" on government-sponsored patients. By implication, nongovernment payers would cover all other costs. However, what would happen if all payers for a particular provider set reimbursement rates based on marginal costs? If such a situation occurred, the organization would not recover its total costs, and it would ultimately fail.

Should any prices be set on the basis of marginal costs? In theory, the answer is no. For prices to be equitable, all payers should pay their fair share in covering providers' total costs. In the case that **marginal cost pricing** is adopted, which payer(s) should receive its benefits by being charged lower prices? Should it be the government, because it is taxpayer funded, or should it be the last payer to contract with the provider? There are no good answers to these questions. Conceptually, it is easiest to require all payers to pay full costs and equitably share the burden of the organization's total costs.

marginal cost pricing
The process of setting prices to cover only marginal costs.

As a practical matter, it may make sense for healthcare providers to occasionally use marginal cost pricing to attract a new patient clientele or to retain an existing clientele (i.e., to gain or retain market share). To survive in the long run, however, businesses must earn revenues that cover their full costs. Thus, either marginal cost pricing must be a temporary measure or the organization must employ **cross-subsidization (price shifting)**. In such situations, some payers are overcharged for services, compared with the full costs, while others are undercharged.

Historically, providers used price shifting to support services that were not able to support their full costs, such as emergency care, teaching

cross-subsidization (price shifting)
A pricing approach in which some payers are charged more than full costs to make up for other payers that are paying less than full costs.

and research, and indigent care. Without such price-shifting strategies, many providers would not have been able to offer a full range of services. More recently, price shifting has been used to subsidize government payers, primarily Medicaid, which critics contend is setting reimbursement rates that fall far short of full costs.

Payers that pay in excess of costs were traditionally willing to accept price shifting because of their concern for the greater good and the fact that the additional burden was not excessive. Today, however, overall healthcare costs have risen to the point that the major purchasers of healthcare services are less and less willing to support the costs associated with providing services to others. Purchasers are demanding prices that cover only true costs, without cross-subsidies, while payers feel they do not have the moral responsibility to fund healthcare services for those outside their covered populations.

SELF-TEST QUESTIONS

1. Describe two common pricing strategies used by price setters and their implications for financial survivability.
2. What is cross-subsidization (price shifting)?
3. Is cross-subsidization used by providers as frequently today as it was in the past? If not, why?

Price-Taking Strategies

When providers are *price takers*, alternative strategies can be used to ensure an organization's financial health. In this section, we discuss one of the price-taking strategies most frequently used by health services organizations: **target costing**.

target costing
For price takers, the process of reducing costs (if necessary) to the point at which a profit is earned on the market-determined price.

Target costing is a management strategy that helps providers deal with situations in which they are *price takers*. Target costing assumes that the price for a service is given by the marketplace and then subtracts the desired profit on that service to obtain the target cost level. If possible, management then reduces the full cost of the service to the target level. Essentially, target costing backs into the cost at which a healthcare service must be provided to attain a given profitability target.

Perhaps the greatest value of target costing lies in the fact that it forces managers to recognize that the market, rather than the provider, is setting prices. Thus, to ensure a sound financial condition, a provider must attain a cost structure that is compatible with the revenue stream. A provider that cannot lower costs to the level required to make a profit ultimately will fail.

1. What is target costing?
2. What is its greatest value?

Setting Fee-for-Service Prices on Individual Services

The best way to understand the mechanics of pricing decisions is to work through some illustrations. The first example illustrates the conceptual approach to setting fee-for-service prices on individual services.

Assume that the managers of Windsor Clinic, a not-for-profit provider, plan to offer a new service. The clinic's financial manager has estimated the following cost data for the service:

Variable cost per visit	$ 10
Annual direct fixed costs	100,000
Annual overhead allocation	25,000

Furthermore, the clinic's marketing consultant believes that demand for the new service will be 5,000 patient visits during its first year of operation.

To begin, Windsor's managers want to know what price must be set on each visit for the service to break even during the first year. To answer this question, we will apply the profit (cost-volume-profit) analysis method discussed in chapter 5, but now our focus is price breakeven rather than volume breakeven. For *accounting breakeven*, the expected profit of the service must be zero, so revenues less costs must equal zero. One way to calculate the breakeven price is to express the relationship between revenues, costs, and profit in equation form:

$$\text{Total revenues} - \text{Total costs} = \$0$$
$$\text{Total revenues} - \text{Total variable costs} - \text{Direct fixed costs} - \text{Overhead} = \$0$$
$$(5{,}000 \times \text{Price}) - (5{,}000 \times \$10) - \$100{,}000 - \$25{,}000 = \$0$$
$$(5{,}000 \times \text{Price}) - \$175{,}000 = \$0$$
$$5{,}000 \times \text{Price} = \$175{,}000$$
$$\text{Price} = \$175{,}000 \div 5{,}000 = \$35.$$

Thus, under the utilization and cost assumptions developed by the clinic's managers, a price of $35 per visit must be set on the new service to break even in the accounting sense.

Of course, Windsor's managers want the service to earn a profit and achieve economic breakeven. Suppose the goal is to make a profit of $100,000 on the new service. The previous calculations show that costs at 5,000 visits are expected to total $175,000. Thus, to make a profit of $100,000, service revenues must total $175,000 + $100,000 = $275,000. With 5,000 visits, the price must be set at $275,000 ÷ 5,000 = $55 per visit.

Up to this point, the analysis has focused on full cost pricing. Suppose Windsor's managers want to price the service aggressively to quickly build market share. Now the service must only cover the variable (marginal) cost of $10 per visit, so a price of $10 is all that is required. This price, which is well below the accounting breakeven of $35 and the economic breakeven of $55, would result in a loss of $125,000 ($100,000 in direct fixed costs and $25,000 in overhead) during the first year the service is offered, assuming that the aggressive pricing does not affect the 5,000-visit utilization estimate.

Key Equation: Price Breakeven

Suppose a clinical laboratory has fixed costs of $500,000, a variable cost rate of $20, and a volume of 20,000 tests. Price breakeven is obtained by solving the following equation for price:

Total revenues – Total variable costs – Fixed costs = Profit
(20,000 × Price) – ($20 × 20,000) – $500,000 = Profit.

For accounting breakeven, profit is zero, so the equation becomes

(20,000 × Price) – $400,000 – $500,000 = $0.

Thus, the breakeven price is $45 per test:

(20,000 × Price) = $900,000
Price = $900,000 ÷ 20,000 = $45 per test.

For economic breakeven, insert the desired profit amount on the right side of the equation in place of $0.

What price should Windsor's managers actually set on the new service? One important consideration is the relationship between price and volume. By assuming that the service will produce 5,000 visits regardless of price, the analysis ignores this relationship. A more complete analysis would examine the effect of different prices *and* volumes on profits. Another consideration is how easy it would be to increase the price that is initially set. If price increases are expected to be met with a great deal of resistance, pricing low to gain market share might be a poor long-run strategy.

1. Briefly explain the conceptual process for pricing individual services.
2. What do you think the price should be on Windsor's new service? Justify your answer.

Setting Prices Under Capitation

The second illustration focuses on how one hospital priced a new capitated product. Exhibit 7.6 contains relevant 2021 forecast revenue and cost data for Montana Medical Center (MMC), a 350-bed, not-for-profit hospital. According to its managers' best estimates, MMC expects to earn a profit of $1,662,312 in 2021. The data consist first of a worksheet that breaks down the cost data by payer. Here, the assumption is that all payers use fee-for-service reimbursement, including discounted fee-for-service. The cost data in exhibit 7.6 include the hospital's cost structure, broken down by variable costs; fixed costs, including both direct and overhead (the $71,746,561 given in the profit and loss [P&L] statement); and contribution margin.

EXHIBIT 7.6
Montana Medical Center: Projected Payer Worksheet and P&L Statement for 2021 (fee-for-service reimbursement)

Payer	Number of Admissions	Average Revenue per Admission	Revenue by Payer	Variable Cost per Admission	Total Variable Costs	Contribution Margin
Payer Worksheet:						
Medicare	4,268	$7,327	$ 31,271,636	$2,529	$ 10,793,772	$20,477,864
Medicaid	5,895	5,448	32,115,960	1,575	9,284,625	22,831,335
Montana Care	828	4,305	3,564,540	1,907	1,578,996	1,985,544
Managed Care	1,885	3,842	7,242,170	1,638	3,087,630	4,154,540
Blue Cross	332	5,761	1,912,652	2,366	785,512	1,127,140
Commercial	1,408	11,770	16,572,160	2,969	4,180,352	12,391,808
Self-Pay	1,289	2,053	2,646,317	1,489	1,919,321	726,996
Other	1,149	11,539	13,258,311	3,085	3,544,665	9,713,646
Total	17,054		$108,583,746		$35,174,873	$73,408,873
Weighted average		$6,367		$2,063		
P&L Statement:						
Total revenues		$108,583,746				
Variable costs		35,174,873				
Contribution margin		$ 73,408,873				
Fixed costs		71,746,561				
Profit		$ 1,662,312				

To illustrate the nature of the data, consider MMC's Medicare patients. Medicare is expected to provide the hospital with 4,268 admissions at an average revenue of $7,327 per admission, for total revenues of 4,268 × $7,327 = $31,271,636. Expected variable cost per admission for a Medicare patient is $2,529, which results in expected total variable costs of 4,268 × $2,529 = $10,793,772. The difference between expected total revenues and the expected total variable costs produces a forecast total contribution margin of $31,271,636 − $10,793,772 = $20,477,864 for the Medicare patient group. This total contribution margin is combined with the total contribution margins of the other payer groups to produce an expected aggregate total contribution margin for the hospital of $73,408,873. As shown in the P&L statement portion of exhibit 7.6, the total contribution margin both covers MMC's forecast fixed costs of $71,746,561 and produces an expected profit of $1,662,312.

MMC's managers are considering taking a bold strategic action—offering a capitated plan for inpatient services. One of the first tasks that must be performed is to set the price for the new plan. Exhibit 7.7 contains the key assumptions of the pricing decision. The hospital's managers believe that about 13 percent of the current patient base will be converted to the capitated plan. To be conservative, the assumption was made that no additional patients will be generated. Thus, at least initially, patients in the capitated plan will come from MMC's current patient base. In effect, MMC will have to cannibalize its own business (i.e., reduce the market share of one of the

---

EXHIBIT 7.7
Montana
Medical
Center: Initial
Assumptions for
a Capitated Plan

1. The capitated plan will initially enroll the following percentages of the hospital's current patients:
   a. Medicaid: 20 percent
   b. Commercial: 40 percent
   c. Self-pay: 40 percent
2. Assuming that utilization rates are not affected by the change to a capitated plan, admissions from the capitated group are expected to total (0.20 × 5,895) + (0.40 × 1,408) + (0.40 × 1,289) = 2,258.
3. Based on current coverage information, the patient population under capitation (number of enrollees) would be 25,000.
4. Variable costs for capitated patients will remain the same as currently estimated for each payer group.
5. Total fixed costs will remain the same.
6. All other assumptions inherent in the exhibit 7.6 forecast hold for the capitated plan.
7. The goal for the price set for capitated enrollees will be to generate, at a minimum, the profit forecast in exhibit 7.6 under fee-for-service reimbursement.

hospital's existing products as a result of the introduction of a new product) with the expectation of protecting its current market share and using the capitated plan as a marketing tool to expand its market share in the future.

Assumptions also are made regarding where the cannibalization will occur and the number of admissions under the capitated plan. These data are provided in points 2 and 3 of exhibit 7.7. The patient mix assumptions will be important when costs are estimated for the new plan.

MMC's managers believe, at least initially, that hospital utilization will be unaffected by the conversion of some patients from fee-for-service contracts to capitation. Another expectation is that variable costs for the new plan will be the same as experienced in the past with each payer group. These two assumptions are important. MMC's managers are assuming that the utilization and delivery of healthcare services for the capitated population will be exactly the same as for the fee-for-service population. This is probably a reasonable starting assumption given that the capitated population will represent only a small portion of MMC's overall business. However, if changes in payer reimbursement methodologies lead to a greater proportion of capitated patients, both utilization patterns and the underlying cost structure are likely to change as the hospital responds to the incentives created.

Finally, and perhaps most important in terms of pricing strategy, the capitated price that MMC plans to offer to the market must result in the same profit ($1,662,312) expected if the hospital were to remain totally fee-for-service. This is critical to MMC's financial health and survival as a healthcare entity. The underlying logic here is that MMC's managers want to experiment with capitation, but they are unwilling to do so at the expense of the bottom line. This pricing goal, and the expected cost structure of serving the capitated population, therefore, will drive the monthly premium established for the capitated product. If the goal of preserving the bottom line while adding the new product proves to be unattainable, MMC's managers will have to reevaluate their initial pricing strategy.

Exhibit 7.8 contains an analysis similar to the one shown in exhibit 7.6, except that exhibit 7.8 includes the proposed capitated plan. Changes from the exhibit 7.6 values are shown in boldface. For example, the entire first line of the worksheet, labeled "Capitated," is in boldface because this is MMC's new service line, which does not appear in exhibit 7.6. Also in boldface are selected values on the Medicaid, commercial, and self-pay lines; these values will change because of the shift of some of these payer groups' patients to the capitated plan.

Note that the exhibit 7.8 volume levels reflect the expected patient shifts from fee-for-service to capitation. For example, the Medicaid group reflects the 20 percent decrease resulting from patients shifting to the capitated plan: $0.80 \times 5,895 = 4,716$. The commercial and self-pay payer groups

EXHIBIT 7.8
Montana
Medical Center:
Projected
Analysis
Assuming
25,000
Enrollees and
Constant Profit

Payer	Number of Admissions	Average Revenue per Admission	Revenue by Payer	Variable Cost per Admission	Total Variable Costs	Contribution Margin
Payer Worksheet:						
Capitated	**2,258**	$ 6,250	$ 14,110,583	$1,903	$ 4,296,794	$ 9,813,789
Medicare	4,268	7,327	31,271,636	2,529	10,793,772	20,477,864
Medicaid	**4,716**	5,448	**25,692,768**	1,575	**7,427,700**	18,265,068
Montana Care	828	4,305	3,564,540	1,907	1,578,996	1,985,544
Managed Care	1,885	3,842	7,242,170	1,638	3,087,630	4,154,540
Blue Cross	332	5,761	1,912,652	2,366	785,512	1,127,140
Commercial	**845**	11,770	**9,943,296**	2,969	**2,508,211**	7,435,085
Self-Pay	**773**	2,053	**1,587,790**	1,489	**1,151,593**	**436,198**
Other	1,149	11,539	13,258,331	3,085	3,544,665	9,713,646
Total	17,054		$108,583,746		$35,174,873	$73,408,873
Weighted average		$ 6,367		$2,063		

Annual capitated revenue requirements = $14,110,583÷25,000 = $564.42 per member.
Monthly capitated revenue requirements = $564.42÷12 = $47.04 per member per month (PMPM).

P&L Statement:

Total revenues	$ 108,583,746
Variable costs	35,174,873
Contribution margin	$ 73,408,873
Fixed costs	71,746,561
Profit	$ 1,662,312

also reflect their 40 percent losses in admissions to the new plan. In total, the capitated plan is expected to siphon off $0.20 \times 5,895 = 1,179$ Medicaid admissions; $0.40 \times 1,408 = 563$ commercial admissions; and $0.40 \times 1,289 = 516$ self-pay admissions, for a total of 2,258 admissions.

For now, pass by the revenue columns in exhibit 7.8 and focus on the variable cost columns for the capitated patients. Because each capitated patient is expected to have the same variable cost as under the previous plans, variable costs for the capitated plan are expected to total $(1,179 \times \$1,575) + (563 \times \$2,969) + (516 \times \$1,489) = \$4,296,796$. With an expected number of admissions of 2,258, the average variable cost per capitated admission is $\$4,296,794 \div 2,258 = \$1,903$. (Note that the values in exhibits 7.6 and 7.8 were obtained from a spreadsheet analysis, which does not round to the nearest dollar. Thus, there are some minor rounding differences when the calculations are made by hand.)

Now consider the revenue columns. To keep the projected profit the same as in exhibit 7.6, revenues must total $108,583,746. Furthermore, expected total revenues from all payer groups except the new plan amount to $94,473,163. Thus, the capitated plan must bring in revenue of $108,583,746 – $94,473,163 = $14,110,583 to achieve MMC's target profit. This calculation can be thought of as working backward on (or up) the projected P&L statement shown at the bottom of exhibit 7.8.

With expected admissions of 2,258, the average revenue per admission can be calculated as $14,110,583 ÷ 2,258 = $6,250. However, this implied average revenue per admission has no real meaning in a capitated plan because MMC will not be charging these patients on a per admission basis. The calculated per admission revenue value of $6,250 is a *fee-for-service equivalent revenue*; the hospital will not actually receive $6,250 per admission under the new plan. As MMC's patients move from fee-for-service to capitation, revenue will be based on enrollment rather than admissions.

With all this information at hand, MMC's managers now can price the new plan. Total revenues of $14,110,583 are required from 25,000 enrollees, so the annual revenue per enrollee is $14,110,583 ÷ 25,000 = $564.42. Because premiums are normally expressed on a *per member per month (PMPM)* basis, the annual revenue requirement must be divided by 12 to obtain $47.04 PMPM. This PMPM charge is what MMC's managers will set as the initial price when marketing the new plan.

The illustration presented here describes one way that MMC's managers could establish a price for a new capitated plan. However, this illustration is a base case analysis—it uses the most likely estimates for all input variables, such as the number of enrollees, variable costs, and so on. A complete pricing analysis goes well beyond a base case analysis with a **scenario analysis**, whereby MMC's managers assess the impact of changing assumptions in key variable values. The idea here is to create alternative scenarios in addition to the most likely (base case) scenario. Through the scenario analysis, MMC's managers can gain a sense of the uncertainty involved in creating the new capitated product.

To keep the length of this chapter manageable, we do not illustrate scenario analysis here. However, the value and structure of scenario analysis will be discussed in detail in chapter 15 as part of our coverage of capital budgeting (project) risk analysis.

scenario analysis
A project risk analysis technique that examines alternative outcomes, generally three, as opposed to only the most likely outcome.

SELF-TEST QUESTIONS

1. Briefly explain why the base case analysis required the calculation to move up the P&L statement rather than down (the normal direction).
2. How are capitated revenue requirements typically expressed?
3. What is scenario analysis, and why is it so critical to good pricing decisions?
4. What is the most uncertain variable in MMC's capitated plan pricing analysis?

Key Concepts

Managers rely on managerial accounting and actuarial information to make pricing and service decisions. Pricing decisions involve setting prices on services for which the provider is a price setter, while service decisions involve whether or not to offer a service when the price is set by the payer (the provider is a price taker). Service decisions are illustrated in the supplement to this chapter. The key concepts of this chapter are as follows:

- The primary methods of costing individual services are the (1) *cost-to-charge ratio (CCR)*, (2) *relative value unit (RVU)*, and (3) *activity-based costing (ABC)*.

- In addition, *time-driven activity-based costing (TDABC)* is a relatively new method of estimating the costs of treating individual patient diagnoses over time.

- Long-term pricing decisions are based on an organization's need for revenues to (1) cover the full cost of doing business and (2) provide the profits necessary to acquire new technologies and offer new services.

- *Price takers* are healthcare providers that have to accept, more or less, the prices set in the marketplace for their services, including the prices set by government insurers.

- *Price setters* are healthcare providers that have market power or whose services can be differentiated from others, such as by quality or convenience, and therefore have the ability to set the prices on some or all of their services.

- *Full cost pricing* permits businesses to recover all costs, including direct fixed, direct variable, and overhead, while *marginal cost pricing* recovers only marginal (typically direct variable) costs.

- *Purchasers* of healthcare services exercise considerable market power, thereby restricting the ability of providers to *cross-subsidize (price shift)*.

- *Target costing* takes the prices paid for healthcare services as a given and then determines the cost structure necessary for financial survival given the prices set.

- Pricing decisions are supported by a variety of analyses that use both actuarial and managerial accounting data. Typically, such analyses include a *base case*, which uses the most likely estimates for all input values, plus a *scenario analysis*, which considers the effects of alternative assumptions.

In the next chapter, our coverage of managerial accounting continues with a discussion of planning and budgeting.

Questions

7.1. Describe the following methods used to estimate the cost of individual services:
   a. Cost-to-charge ratio (CCR) method
   b. Relative value unit (RVU) method
   c. Activity-based costing (ABC) method

7.2. What is the time-driven activity-based costing method (TDABC), and how does it differ from the methods listed in question 7.1?

7.3. a. Using a medical group practice to illustrate your answer, explain the difference between a price setter and a price taker.
   b. Can most providers be classified strictly as either a price setter or a price taker?

7.4. Explain the essential differences between full cost pricing and marginal cost pricing strategies.

7.5. What would happen financially to a health services organization over time if its prices were set at:
   a. Full costs?
   b. Marginal costs?

7.6. a. What is cross-subsidization (price shifting)?
   b. Is it as prevalent today as it has been in the past?

7.7. a. What is target costing?
   b. Suppose a hospital was offered a capitation rate for a covered population of $40 per member per month (PMPM). Briefly explain how target costing would be applied in this situation.

7.8. What is the role of accounting information in pricing decisions?

7.9. a. What is scenario analysis as applied to pricing decisions?
   b. Why is it such an important part of the process?

Problems

7.1. Assume that the managers of Fort Winston Hospital are setting the price for a new outpatient service. Here are relevant data estimates:

Variable cost per visit	$ 5.00
Annual direct fixed costs	$500,000
Annual overhead allocation	$ 50,000
Expected annual utilization (visits)	10,000

a. What per visit price must be set for the service to break even? To earn an annual profit of $100,000?

b. Repeat part a, but assume that the variable cost per visit is $10.

c. Return to the data given in the problem. Again repeat part a, but assume that direct fixed costs are $1,000,000.

d. Repeat part a assuming both $10 in variable cost and $1,000,000 in direct fixed costs.

7.2. The audiology department at Randall Clinic offers many services to the clinic's patients. The three most common, along with cost and utilization data, are as follows:

Service	Variable Cost per Service	Annual Direct Fixed Costs	Annual Number of Visits
Basic examination	$ 5	$50,000	3,000
Advanced examination	7	30,000	1,500
Therapy session	10	40,000	500

a. What is the fee schedule for these services, assuming that the goal is to cover only variable and direct fixed costs?

b. Assume that the audiology department is allocated $100,000 in total overhead by the clinic, and the department director has allocated $50,000 of this amount to the three services listed above. What is the fee schedule assuming that these overhead costs must be covered? (To answer this question, assume that the allocation of the $50,000 in overhead costs to each service is made on the basis of number of visits.)

c. Assume that these services must make a combined profit of $25,000. Now what is the fee schedule? (To answer this question, assume that the profit requirement is allocated in the same way as overhead costs. Include the overhead costs from part b in developing the fee schedule.)

7.3. Allied Laboratories is combining some of its most common tests into one-price packages. One such package will contain three tests that have the following variable costs:

	Test A	Test B	Test C
Disposable syringe	$3.00	$3.00	$3.00
Blood vial	0.50	0.50	0.50
Forms	0.15	0.15	0.15
Reagents	0.80	0.60	1.20
Sterile bandage	0.10	0.10	0.10
Breakage/losses	0.05	0.05	0.05

When the tests are combined, only one syringe, form, and sterile bandage will be used. Furthermore, only one charge for breakage/losses will apply. Two blood vials are required, and reagent costs will remain the same (reagents from all three tests are required).

a. As a starting point, what is the price of the combined test assuming marginal cost pricing?

b. Assume that Allied wants a contribution margin of $10 per test. What price must be set to achieve this goal?

c. Allied estimates that 2,000 of the combined tests will be conducted during the first year. The annual allocation of direct fixed and overhead costs totals $40,000. What price must be set to cover full costs? What price must be set to produce a profit of $20,000 on the combined test?

7.4. Assume that Valley Forge Hospital has only the following three payer groups:

	Number of Admissions	Average Revenue per Admission	Variable Cost per Admission
Commercial	1,000	$5,000	$3,000
PennCare	4,000	4,500	4,000
Medicare	8,000	7,000	2,500

The hospital's fixed costs are $38 million.

a. What is the hospital's net income?

b. Assume that half of the 100,000 covered lives in the commercial payer group will be moved into a capitated plan. All utilization and cost data remain the same. What PMPM rate will the hospital have to charge to retain its net income calculated in part a?

     c. What overall net income would be produced if the admission rate of the capitated group were reduced from the commercial level by 10 percent?

     d. Assuming that the utilization reduction also occurs, what overall net income would be produced if the variable cost per admission for the capitated group were lowered to $2,200?

7.5. Bay Pines Medical Center estimates that a capitated population of 50,000 would have the following base case utilization and total cost characteristics:

Service Category	Inpatient Days per 1,000 Enrollees	Average Cost per Day
General	150	$1,500
Surgical	125	1,800
Psychiatric	70	700
Alcohol/drug abuse	38	500
Maternity	42	1,500
Total	425	$1,367

In addition to medical costs, Bay Pines allocates 10 percent of the total premium (total capitated revenue) for administration/ reserves.

     a. What is the PMPM rate that Bay Pines must set to cover medical costs plus administrative expenses?

     b. What would be the rate if a utilization management program were to reduce utilization within each patient service category by 10 percent? By 20 percent?

     c. Return to the initial base case utilization assumption. What rate would be set if the average cost on each service were reduced by 10 percent?

     d. Assume that both utilization and cost reductions were made. What would the premium be?

7.6. Assume that a primary care physician practice performs only physical examinations. However, there are three levels of examination—I, II, and III—that vary in depth and complexity. An RVU analysis indicates that a level I examination requires 10 RVUs, a level II exam 20 RVUs, and a level III exam 30 RVUs. The total costs to run the practice, including a diagnostic laboratory, amount to $500,000 annually, and the numbers of examinations administered annually are 2,400 level I, 800 level II, and 400 level III.

   a. Using RVU methodology, what is the estimated cost per type of examination?

   b. If the goal of the practice is to earn a 20 percent profit margin on each examination, how should the examinations be priced?

7.7. Consider the following data for a clinical laboratory:

Activity Data

Activity	Annual Costs	Cost Driver	Test A	Test B	Test C	Test D
Receive specimen	$ 10,000	Number of tests	2,000	1,500	1,000	500
Set up equipment	25,000	Number of minutes per test	5	5	10	10
Run test	100,000	Number of minutes per test	1	5	10	20
Record results	10,000	Number of minutes per test	2	2	2	4
Transmit results	5,000	Number of minutes per test	3	3	3	3
Total costs	$150,000					

   a. Using ABC techniques, determine the cost allocation rate for each activity.

   b. Now, using these allocation rates, estimate the total cost of performing each test.

   c. Verify that the total annual costs aggregated from individual test costs equal the total annual costs of the laboratory given in the table above.

7.8. A hospital pharmacy fills three types of prescriptions. Prescription A requires refrigeration to maintain the drug's activity. Prescription B has potentially fatal interactions with other drugs and therefore requires careful review by a pharmacist. Prescription C is a basic, common drug that presents little risk to the patient. Prescription A is a brand-name drug still on patent, and therefore the charge for the drug is high relative to its cost. Consider the following data for the hospital pharmacy:

Annual Prescription Volume, Total Direct Costs, and Total Charges

	Prescription (Rx) A	Prescription (Rx) B	Prescription (Rx) C
Annual volume	50	200	1,000
Total direct costs	$ 7,668	$48,840	$31,300
Total charges	$35,000	$70,000	$50,000

(continued)

Budgeted Overhead Costs and Activity Data

Activity	Annual Costs	Cost Driver	Cost Driver Consumption per One Rx		
			Rx A	Rx B	Rx C
Refrigeration	$ 8,000	Number of units requiring refrigeration	1	0	0
Materials handling	24,000	Number of feet to drug storage area	50	20	10
Prescription review	90,000	Number of pharmacist minutes	15	60	3
Total costs	$122,000				

a. Using the cost-to-charges ratio (CCR) method, determine the overhead that would be allocated to each type of prescription, A, B, and C.

b. Determine the total cost (Direct cost + Indirect cost) of filling one of each type of prescription if overhead is allocated using CCR.

c. Using ABC techniques, determine the allocation rate for each overhead activity and determine the overhead that would be allocated to each type of prescription, A, B, and C.

d. Determine the total cost (Direct cost + Indirect cost) of filling one of each type of prescription if overhead is allocated using ABC techniques.

e. Explain the reasons for the difference in the full cost of each prescription in parts b and d.

7.9. Consider the following data for a primary care practice that provides two types of services, A and B:

Activity	Annual Costs	Cost Driver	Activity Data	
			Service A	Service B
Check-in	$ 100,000	Visit volume	7,000	15,000
Assessment	250,000	Minutes per service	15	8
Diagnosis	600,000	Minutes per service	20	10
Treatment	1,200,000	Minutes per service	5	5
Check-out	125,000	Visit volume	7,000	15,000
Billing	250,000	Number of bills	3	1
Total	$2,525,000			

a. Using ABC techniques, determine the allocation rate for each overhead activity.

b. Determine the overhead costs per visit for each type of service.

c. Verify that the total annual costs aggregated from individual visit costs equal the total annual costs of the practice given in the table above.

Selected Case

One case in *Gapenski's Cases in Healthcare Finance*, sixth edition, is applicable to this chapter: Case 9: Cambridge Transplant Center.

Resources

For a more in-depth treatment of the TDABC method of costing, see

Kaplan, R. S. 2014. "Improving Value with Time-Driven Activity-Based Costing (TDABC)." *Healthcare Financial Management* 68 (6): 76–83.

Kaplan, R. S., and M. E. Porter. 2011. "The Big Idea: How to Solve the Cost Crisis in Health Care." *Harvard Business Review* 89 (9): 47–64.

Kaplan, R. S., M. Witkowski, M. Abbott, A. B. Guzman, L. D. Higgins, J. G. Meara, E. Padden, A. S. Shah, P. Waters, M. Weidemeier, S. Wertheimer, and T. W. Feeley. 2014. "Using Time-Driven Activity-Based Costing to Identify Value Improvement Opportunities in Healthcare." *Journal of Healthcare Management* 59 (6): 399–413.

In addition, see

Barton, S., D. Lancaster, and M. Bieker. 2008. "Chargemaster Maintenance: Think 'Spring Cleaning' All Year Round." *Healthcare Financial Management* 62 (11): 42–46.

Bilsky, S. D., and J. M. Aber. 2007. "Lining Up Your Service Lines." *Healthcare Financial Management* 61 (7): 68–73.

Buchler, R. 2014. "Achieving Strategic Cost Reduction in the OR." *Healthcare Financial Management* 68 (10): 42–44, 46.

Cleverley, W. O., and J. O. Cleverley. 2008. "10 Myths of Strategic Pricing." *Healthcare Financial Management* 62 (5): 82–87.

———. 2007. "Setting Defensible and Appropriate Prices in Healthcare." *Healthcare Executive* 22 (1): 9–12.

Greenspun, H., and W. Bercik. 2013. "Cost-Outcomes Focus Is Essential for ACO Success." *Healthcare Financial Management* 67 (2): 96–102.

Griebl, O., and C. Skalka. 2007. "The Growing Imperative of Effective Pricing Strategies and Tools for Not-for-Profit Hospitals." *Healthcare Financial Management* 61 (10): 76–80.

Houck, S., and J. O. Cleverley. 2014. "How Hospitals Approach Price Transparency." *Healthcare Financial Management* 68 (9): 56–62.

Mulaik, M. W., P. Kassing, and K. M. Nichols. 2014. "Medicare's New CT and MRI Cost Centers Demand Accurate Cost Reporting." *Healthcare Financial Management* 68 (10): 28–30.

Pandey, S. 2012. "Applying the ABCs in Provider Organizations." *Healthcare Financial Management* 66 (11): 112–20.

Pederson, C. D. 2005. "Cost-Based Pricing and the Underperforming Physician Group." *Healthcare Financial Management* 59 (10): 62–68.

Richmond, R. 2013. "A Better Approach to Cost Estimation." *Healthcare Financial Management* 67 (3): 87–90.

Stodolak, F. 2008. "Hospital Zero-Base Pricing Can Make a Difference." *Healthcare Financial Management* 62 (9): 102–8.

Sturm, A., and F. Tiedemann. 2013. "Developing a Consumer Pricing Strategy." *Healthcare Financial Management* 67 (5): 104–8.

Wichmann, R., and R. Clark. 2006. "Developing a Defensible Pricing Strategy." *Healthcare Financial Management* 60 (10): 72–80.

Winterhalter, S. J. 2011. "Economic Factors Converge: Force Hospitals to Review Pricing Strategies." *Journal of Health Care Finance* 37 (4): 15–35.

MAKING SERVICE DECISIONS

The primary focus of the illustrations in chapter 7 is *price setting*. In this supplement, we present an illustration of a related decision—the service decision. Now, our focus is on evaluating the attractiveness of contract proposals with given prices.

County Health Plan (CHP), an HMO with 40,000 members, has proposed a new contract that would capitate Baptist Hospital for all inpatient services provided to CHP's commercial enrollees whose primary care physicians are affiliated with the hospital. The proposal calls for a capitation payment of $35 per member per month (PMPM) for the first year of the contract. Baptist's managers must decide whether to accept the proposal.

To begin the analysis, Baptist's managed care analysts developed the inpatient actuarial data contained in exhibit S7.1. The data are presented under two levels of utilization management. The data in the top section are based on a loosely managed population in Baptist's service area. These data represent a bare minimum of utilization management effort and hence reflect relatively poor utilization management practices. The bottom section contains data that represent the best-observed utilization management practices based on hospitals located in service areas that have extremely high managed care penetration. The differences between the two data sets illustrate the potential for improved financial performance that comes with more sophisticated utilization management systems. Both sets of data reflect populations with characteristics similar to CHP's commercial enrollees.

To illustrate the calculations, consider the top line in the top section (General). Under loosely managed utilization, the covered population is expected to use 157 days of general medical services for each 1,000 enrollees. Furthermore, the costs associated with one day of such services total $1,500. Thus, the general services costs for each 1,000 enrollees are expected to be $157 \times \$1,500 = \$235,500$, or $19.62 PMPM ($235,500 \div 1,000 = \$235.50$ per member; $\$235.50 \div 12$ months $= \$19.62$ PMPM). Calculations for other inpatient services were performed similarly and added to obtain total medical costs of $50.39 PMPM.

There are two additional categories of costs besides medical costs. Each section of the exhibit has lines for administrative costs and risk (profit) margin. *Administrative costs* include costs incurred in managing the contract,

EXHIBIT S7.1
CHP/Baptist
Hospital:
Contract
Analysis Under
Two Utilization
Management
Scenarios

Loosely Managed (Suboptimal) Utilization:

Service Category	Inpatient Days per 1,000 Enrollees	Average Cost per Day	Average Cost per Member per Month*
General	157	$1,500	$19.62
Surgical	132	1,800	19.80
Psychiatric	71	700	4.14
Alcohol/Drug abuse	38	500	1.58
Maternity	42	1,500	5.25
Total medical costs	440	$1,374	$50.39
Administrative costs			2.80
Risk (profit) margin			2.80
Total PMPM			$55.99

Tightly Managed (Optimal) Utilization:

Service Category	Inpatient Days per 1,000 Enrollees	Average Cost per Day	Average Cost per Member per Month*
General	79	$1,600	$10.53
Surgical	58	1,900	9.18
Psychiatric	13	800	0.87
Alcohol/Drug abuse	4	600	0.20
Maternity	26	1,600	3.47
Total medical costs	180	$1,617	$24.25
Administrative costs			1.35
Risk (profit) margin			1.35
Total PMPM			$26.95

Note: Some rounding differences occur in the table.
* Based on 40,000 members (enrollees).

such as costs associated with patient verification, utilization management, quality assurance, and member services.

The second category of nonmedical costs is the *risk (profit) margin*. Because Baptist would be bearing inpatient utilization risk for the covered population, it builds in a margin both to provide a profit on the contract commensurate with the risk assumed and to create a reserve that could be tapped if utilization, and hence costs, exceeds the amount estimated. It is Baptist's practice to allow 10 percent of the total premium for these two non-medical costs, so medical costs represent 90 percent of the total premium.

For example, in the upper section of exhibit S7.1, $0.9 \times$ Total premium = $50.39, so Total premium = $50.39 ÷ 0.9 = $55.99. Furthermore, it is Baptist's policy to split the $55.99 – $50.39 = $5.60 in nonmedical costs evenly between the two categories, so administrative costs and risk (profit) margin are allocated $2.80 each.

Baptist's managers use the same 10 percent nonmedical cost allocation for both the loosely managed and tightly managed utilization scenarios. One could argue that the greater the utilization management effort, the higher the administrative costs. Thus, it might be better to allocate a greater percentage for administrative costs in the tightly managed scenario than in the loosely managed scenario. In fact, administrative costs could require a higher dollar allocation under tightly managed utilization, even though the overall premium amount is lower. However, laws often dictate what percentage of the premium must be devoted to clinical services and quality improvement versus administrative costs and profits.

Exhibit S7.1 sends a strong message to Baptist's managers regarding the acceptability of CHP's $35 PMPM contract offer. If Baptist were to accept the offer and then loosely manage the enrollee population, it would lose an estimated $55.99 – $35 = $20.99 PMPM on the contract. The costs in exhibit S7.1 represent full costs as opposed to only variable (marginal) costs. Therefore, Baptist may be able to carry the contract in the short run, but it would not be able to sustain the contract over time. On the other hand, if Baptist could manage the enrollee population in accordance with "best-observed practices," it would make an estimated profit of $35 – $26.95 = $8.05 PMPM on the contract.

The contract also can be analyzed in accounting, rather than actuarial, terms. This format, along with required supporting calculations, is shown in exhibit S7.2. Again, focus on the loosely managed section. In exhibit S7.2, instead of showing inpatient days per 1,000 enrollees as in exhibit S7.1, inpatient days are expressed in terms of the total number of enrollees, which is expected to be 40,000 for this contract. Thus, using utilization data from exhibit S7.1, the total number of patient days of general medical services is $157 \times 40 = 6{,}280$. With an estimated cost of $1,500 per day, total costs for general medical services amount to $6{,}280 \times \$1{,}500 = \$9{,}420{,}000$. The costs for all service categories were calculated in the same way and total $24,192,000. Each nonmedical service cost was calculated as $40{,}000 \times \$2.80 \times 12 = \$1{,}344{,}000$, resulting in total costs under loosely managed utilization of $26,880,000.

Regardless of the level of utilization management, revenues from the contract are expected to total $40{,}000 \times \$35 \times 12 = \$16{,}800{,}000$. Thus, the projected P&L statements in simplified form consist of this revenue amount minus total costs under each utilization scenario. The end result is

EXHIBIT S7.2
CHP/Baptist
Hospital:
Projected
Costs and P&L
Statements

PROJECTED COSTS:
Loosely Managed (Suboptimal) Utilization:

Service Category	Inpatient Days per 40,000 Enrollees	Average Cost per Day	Total Annual Costs
General	6,280	$1,500	$ 9,420,000
Surgical	5,280	1,800	9,504,000
Psychiatric	2,840	700	1,988,000
Alcohol/Drug abuse	1,520	500	760,000
Maternity	1,680	1,500	2,520,000
Total medical costs	17,600	$1,374	$ 24,192,000
Administrative costs			1,344,000
Risk (profit) margin			1,344,000
Total annual costs			$ 26,880,000

Tightly Managed (Optimal) Utilization:

Service Category	Inpatient Days per 40,000 Enrollees	Average Cost per Day	Total Annual Costs
General	3,160	$1,600	$ 5,056,000
Surgical	2,320	1,900	4,408,000
Psychiatric	520	800	416,000
Alcohol/Drug abuse	160	600	96,000
Maternity	1,040	1,600	1,664,000
Total medical costs	7,200	$1,617	$ 11,640,000
Administrative costs			648,000
Risk (profit) margin			648,000
Total annual costs			$ 12,936,000

P&L STATEMENTS:
Loosely Managed (Suboptimal) Utilization:

Total revenues	$16,800,000
Total costs	26,880,000
Profit (Loss)	($10,080,000)

Tightly Managed (Optimal) Utilization:

Total revenues	$16,800,000
Total costs	12,936,000
Profit (Loss)	$ 3,864,000

Note: Some rounding differences occur in the table.

an expected net loss of $10,080,000 under loosely managed utilization and a profit of $3,864,000 under tightly managed utilization.

What should Baptist's managers do regarding the contract? For now, the decision appears simple: Accept the contract if the hospital can tightly manage utilization, or reject the contract if it cannot. Unfortunately, the base case contract analysis, like many financial analyses, raises more questions than it answers. This demonstrates that analyses conducted to help with pricing and service decisions more often raise managers' awareness of potential consequences than offer simple solutions.

What else would Baptist's managers want to know prior to making the decision? One key element of information is the cost structure (fixed versus variable) associated with the contract. Even though the analyses indicate that the contract is unprofitable under loosely managed utilization, the analysis is conducted on a full cost basis. If the costs associated with the contract consist of 50 percent fixed costs and 50 percent variable costs, the variable cost PMPM in the worst case (loosely managed utilization) is $0.50 \times \$55.99 = \$28.00$. At a premium of $35, the marginal PMPM contribution margin is $35 − $28 = $7. Thus, even under loose management, the premium would at least cover the contract's variable (marginal) costs. If Baptist cannot afford to lose the market share associated with CHP's members, its managers may deem the contract acceptable in the short run. Assuming that the hospital can improve its utilization management over time, eventually it will be able to cover the total costs associated with the contract.

Cost structure is not the only variable that can change over time. Perhaps Baptist can demonstrate superior quality and negotiate a higher premium over time. On the downside, perhaps CHP will gain additional market power over time and attempt to push the premium even lower. These are just a few of the imponderables that Baptist's managers must consider when making the service decision.

SELF-TEST QUESTIONS

1. Why does utilization management play such an important role in pricing and service decisions under capitation?
2. Why are nonmedical costs included in the analysis?
3. What would you do regarding the contract if you were the CEO of Baptist Hospital?
4. What other factors should Baptist's managers consider when making the capitation contract decision?

FINANCIAL PLANNING AND BUDGETING

Learning Objectives

After studying this chapter, readers will be able to

- Describe the overall financial planning process and the key components of the financial plan.
- Discuss the format and use of several types of budgets.
- Explain the difference between a static budget and a flexible budget.
- Create a simple operating budget.
- Use variance analysis to assess financial performance and identify operational areas of concern.

Introduction

Financial planning and budgeting play a critical role in the finance function of all health services organizations. In fact, one could argue that planning and budgeting are the most important of all finance-related tasks.

Planning encompasses the overall process of preparing for the future. Because of its importance to organizational success, most health services managers, especially in large organizations, spend a great deal of time on activities related to planning. *Budgeting* is an offshoot of the planning process. A set of *budgets* is the basic managerial accounting tool used to tie together planning and control functions (by allowing comparisons of actual results to expected results). In general, organizational plans focus on the long-term big picture, whereas budgets address the details of planning for the immediate future and, through the control mechanism, ensuring that current performance is consistent with organizational plans and goals.

This chapter introduces the planning process and discusses how financial plans and budgets are used within health services organizations. In particular, the chapter focuses on how managers can use flexible budgets and variance analysis to exercise control over current operations. As this is an introductory book, we only scratch the surface of these important topics.

Strategic and Operational Planning

strategic plan
A document
that defines a
business's long-
term direction
along with the
resources needed
to get there.

Financial plans and budgets are developed within the framework of a business's **strategic plan**. Strategic plans focus an organization's vision and priorities in response to a changing environment. Their primary purpose is to ensure that everyone within the organization is working toward the same goals. Simply put, strategic planning is a continuous process that guides organizational action and behavior. The following are some of the components of the strategic plan.

Values Statement

The "guiding light" for the strategic plan is the organization's *values statement*, because values represent the core priorities that define the organization's culture. To illustrate, consider the following values of Bayview Hospital, a not-for-profit acute care hospital:

- To treat everyone with respect and dignity
- To be compassionate in comfort and care
- To achieve excellence and ensure quality

Mission Statement

The *mission statement*, which must conform to the values statement, defines the organization's overall purpose and reason for existence. The mission may be defined either specifically or in more general terms, but at a minimum, it must describe what the organization does and for whom. For example, here is Bayview's mission statement:

- To provide comprehensive, state-of-the-art patient services
- To emphasize caring and other human values in the treatment of patients and in relations among employees, medical staff, and community
- To provide employees and medical staff with maximum opportunities to achieve their personal and professional goals

Vision Statement

The *vision statement* describes the desired position of the organization at a future point in time—say, ten years from now. The intent is to provide a single goal that motivates managers, employees, and the medical staff to work together to achieve it. Bayview's vision statement is "To be the regional leader in providing state-of-the-art, compassionate care in a humanistic environment."

Bayview's values, mission, and vision statements provide managers with a framework for establishing the specific goals and objectives outlined in the operating plan, which we describe in the next section.

Operational Planning

Whereas strategic planning provides general guidance for the long term, operational planning provides a road map for executing an organization's strategic plan. The key document in operational planning is the **operating plan**, which contains near-term operational objectives and the detailed guidance necessary to meet those objectives. In other words, the operating plan provides the "how to" or perhaps "how we expect to" portion of an organization's overall plan for the future.

Exhibit 8.1 outlines the key elements of Bayview Hospital's operating plan, with an expanded section for the financial plan. A full outline would require several pages, but exhibit 8.1 provides some insights into the format and contents of an operating plan. Note that the financial plan must be linked to the organization's strategic plan.

> **operating plan**
> An organizational road map for the future, often spanning five years, but with most detail for the first year. Operating plans must be based on and consistent with the guidance provided in the organization's strategic plan.

1. Briefly describe the nature and use of the following corporate planning tools:
   a. Strategic plan
   b. Values statement
   c. Mission statement
   d. Vision statement
2. Why do financial planners need to be familiar with the business's strategic plan?

Financial Planning

Whereas strategic and operational planning focus on the overall organization, financial planning focuses on the finance function. Section 1 of the **financial plan** (chapter 7.C of the operating plan in exhibit 8.1) focuses on financial condition, capital investments, and financing at the organizational level. Its first component is a review of the business's current financial condition, which provides the basis, or starting point, for the remainder of the financial plan. (Insights into how this is accomplished are presented in chapter 17.)

The second component is the capital budget, which outlines future plans for capital investment (the purchase of land, buildings, and equipment).

> **financial plan**
> The portion of the operating plan that focuses on the finance function.

EXHIBIT 8.1

Bayview Hospital: Operating Plan Outline

Chapter 1	Organizational values, mission, and vision
Chapter 2	Organizational goals and objectives
Chapter 3	Projected business environment
Chapter 4	Organizational strategies
Chapter 5	Summary of projected business results
Chapter 6	Service line plans
Chapter 7	Functional area plans

    A.   Marketing
    B.   Operations
    C.   Finance
        1. Financial condition, capital investments, and financing
            a.   Financial condition analysis
            b.   Capital budget
            c.   Forecast financial statements
            d.   External financing requirements
        2. Current accounts and revenue cycle management
            a.   Overall policy
            b.   Cash budget
            c.   Cash and marketable securities management
            d.   Inventory management
            e.   Revenue cycle management
            f.   Short-term financing
        3. Budgeting and control
            a.   Statistics budget
            b.   Revenue budget
            c.   Expense budget
            d.   Operating budget
            e.   Control procedures
    D.   Administration and human resources
    E.   Facilities

(Capital budgeting procedures are discussed in chapters 14 and 15.) This information feeds into the forecast financial statements, which are projected for the next five years. The final component is a list of the organization's future financing requirements, along with a plan for obtaining these funds. (Financing decisions are covered in chapters 11, 12, and 13.) As can be seen from its content, Section 1 of the financial plan provides an overview of the financial future of the organization.

Section 2 of the financial plan concerns current accounts management, which encompasses the management of current assets and current liabilities, including *revenue cycle management*. Here the plan provides overall guidance regarding day-to-day, short-term financial operations. (Current accounts and revenue cycle management are covered in chapter 16.) In essence, Section 2 of the financial plan provides short-term operating benchmarks for all facets of current accounts management.

Section 3 is the budgeting and control portion of the financial plan. This section identifies the organization's financial goals at the micro level— for example, by division, contract, or diagnosis—and it is used to control operations through frequent comparisons with actual results. In essence, this portion contains the budgets that provide the benchmarks managers should be striving to attain throughout the year.

Exhibit 8.2 contains the hospital's annual financial planning schedule. This schedule illustrates that, as for most organizations, Bayview's financial planning process is essentially continuous. For Bayview, much of the financial planning function takes place at the department level, with technical assistance from the marketing, planning, and financial staffs. Larger organizations, with divisions, focus the planning process at the divisional level. Each division has its own mission and goals, as well as objectives and budgets designed to support its goals; these plans, when consolidated, constitute the overall operating plan.

Months	Action	
April–May	Marketing department analyzes national and local economic factors likely to influence Bayview's patient volume and reimbursement rates. At this time, a preliminary volume forecast is prepared for each service line.	**EXHIBIT 8.2** Bayview Hospital: Annual Financial Planning Schedule
June–July	Operating departments prepare new project (long-term asset) requirements as well as operating cost estimates based on the preliminary volume forecast.	
August–September	Financial analysts evaluate proposed capital expenditures and department operating plans. Preliminary forecast financial statements are prepared with emphasis on Bayview's overall sources and uses of funds and forecast financial condition.	
October–November	All previous input is reviewed and the hospital's operating plan is drafted by the planning, financial, and departmental staffs. At this stage, the operating and cash budgets are finalized. Any changes that have occurred since the beginning of the planning process are incorporated into the plan.	
December	The operating plan, including all budgets for the coming year, is approved by the hospital's executive committee and submitted to the board of directors for final approval.	

1. Briefly describe the contents of a typical financial plan.
2. What are the primary differences between sections 1, 2, and 3 of the financial plan?

Introduction to Budgeting

budgeting
The process of preparing and using a budget, which is a detailed plan (in dollar terms) that specifies how resources will be obtained and used during some future period.

Budgeting involves detailed plans, expressed in dollar terms, that specify how resources will be obtained and used during a specified future period of time. In general, budgets rely heavily on revenue and cost estimates, so the budgeting process applies many of the managerial accounting concepts presented in chapters 5, 6, and 7.

To be of most use, budgets must be thought of not as accounting tools but as managerial tools. In reality, budgets are more important to line managers than to the financial staff because budgets provide the means to plan and communicate operational expectations within an organization. In addition, the budgeting process and the resulting final budget provide the means for senior executives to allocate financial resources among competing demands within an organization.

Although planning, communication, and allocation are important purposes of the budgeting process, perhaps the greatest value of budgeting is that it establishes financial benchmarks for control. Compared with actual results, budgets provide managers with feedback about the relative financial performance of the entity for which they are accountable. Such comparisons help managers evaluate the performance of individuals and identify areas where they may need to intervene.

When actual results differ from those specified in the budget, managers use *variance analysis* to identify the drivers that caused the divergent performance. In this way, managerial resources can be applied to the areas of operations that need improvement. In addition, the information developed by comparing actual results with expected (planned) results (the control process) is useful in improving the overall accuracy of the planning process. By examining budget variances, managers may identify changes in the operating environment that should be considered during the next planning cycle.

1. What is budgeting?
2. What are its primary purposes and benefits?

Initial Budgeting Decisions

Managers must make many decisions regarding the budgeting process. This section covers decisions that focus on budget timing and the general approach to the budgeting process. The next major section discusses the types of budgets used within healthcare organizations.

Budget Timing

Virtually all health services organizations set annual budgets for the coming year. However, it would take too long for managers to detect adverse trends if budget feedback were provided solely on an annual basis, so most organizations also have quarterly budgets, while some have monthly, weekly, or even daily budgets. Not all budget types or subunits within an organization use the same timing pattern—some may use monthly budgets, while others use weekly budgets. Additionally, many organizations prepare budgets for one or more *out years*, or years beyond the next budget year; these budgets are more closely aligned with financial planning than with operational control.

Conventional Versus Zero-Based Budgets

Traditionally, health services organizations used the **conventional budgeting** approach to develop their budgets. In this approach, the previous budget is used as the starting point for creating the new budget. Each line on the old budget is examined, and then adjustments are made to reflect changes in circumstances. In this approach, it is common for many budget changes to be applied more or less equally across departments and programs. For example, labor costs might be assumed to increase at the same inflation rate for all departments and programs within an organization. The main task under the conventional approach is determining what changes (typically minor) must be made to the previous budget to account for changes in operating environment. In other words, the assumption is made that, except for these changes, the current budget accurately reflects the resource needs of the organization.

> **conventional budgeting**
> An approach to budgeting that uses the previous budget as the starting point for creating the new budget.

As its name implies, **zero-based budgeting** starts with a clean slate—that is, departments begin with a budget of zero and department heads fully justify every line item in their budgets. In effect, departments and programs must justify their contribution (positive or negative) to the organization's financial condition each budget period.

Conceptually, zero-based budgeting is superior to conventional budgeting. Indeed, when zero-based budgeting was introduced in the 1970s, it was widely embraced. However, the managerial resources required for zero-based budgeting far exceed those required for conventional budgeting.

> **zero-based budgeting**
> An approach to budgeting that starts with a "clean slate" and requires complete justification of all budget items.

Therefore, many organizations that initially adopted zero-based budgeting soon concluded that its benefits were not as great as its costs. However, many health services organizations are again using zero-based budgeting, primarily because market forces are requiring providers to implement cost control efforts on a more or less continuous basis.

As a compromise, some health services organizations use conventional budgeting annually but then use a zero-based budget on a less frequent basis—say, every five years. An alternative is to use the conventional approach for 80 percent of the budget each year and the zero-based approach for 20 percent. Then, over every five-year period, the entire budget will be subjected to zero-based budgeting. This approach takes advantage of the benefits of zero-based budgeting without creating a budgeting process that is too time-consuming in any single year for managers.

Top-Down Versus Bottom-Up Budgets

The budget affects virtually everyone in the organization, and individuals' reactions to the budgeting process can have considerable influence on an organization's overall effectiveness. Thus, one of the most important decisions regarding budget preparation is whether the budget should be created from the top down or from the bottom up.

In the *bottom-up*, or *participatory*, *approach*, budgets are developed first by department or program managers. Presumably, such individuals are most knowledgeable regarding their departments' or programs' financial needs. The department budgets are submitted to the finance department for review and compilation into the organizational budget, which then must be approved by senior management. Unfortunately, the aggregation of department or program budgets often results in an organizational budget that is not financially feasible. In such cases, the component budgets must be sent back to the original

---

For Your Consideration
Middle-Out Budgeting

As you know, there are two primary approaches to the budgeting process. In the top-down approach, budgets are established by senior management—for example, the executive committee or board of directors (or trustees). In essence, senior management is dictating the financial resources to be allocated to the department level. In the bottom-up approach, department heads are responsible for creating their own budgets, which are then submitted up the chain for approval. Although the bottom-up approach has many virtues, in large organizations, it is often impractical to have that many people involved in the budget process.

Some organizations are now experimenting with a hybrid budgeting approach called *middle-out budgeting*. In this approach, budgets are prepared at the divisional (services) level—for example, a hospital's inpatient, outpatient, clinical support, and administrative support divisions. Then the budgets are sent to both senior and junior (department) managers for review and ultimate approval. In essence, middle managers—who presumably are in the best position to understand both sides and can create a budget that is adequate yet not excessive—act as go-betweens.

What do you think? Is there any merit to middle-out budgeting? Which approach do you think is best for a small organization, such as a three-doctor medical practice? What about a 600-bed hospital?

preparers for revision, which starts a negotiation process aimed at creating a budget that is acceptable to all parties, or at least to as many parties as possible.

A more authoritarian approach to budgeting is the *top-down approach*, in which little negotiation takes place between middle and upper managers. This approach has the advantages of being relatively expeditious and reflecting top management's perspective from the start. However, by limiting involvement and communication, the top-down approach often results in less commitment among middle managers and employees than the bottom-up approach. The idea of participatory budgeting is to involve as many managers, and even employees, as possible in the budgetary process, because people are more likely to perform better and make greater attempts to achieve budgetary goals if they have played a prominent role in setting those goals.

SELF-TEST QUESTIONS

1. What time periods are used in budgeting?
2. What are the primary differences between conventional budgets and zero-based budgets?
3. What are the primary differences between top-down budgets and bottom-up budgets?

Budget Types

Although an organization's immediate financial expectations are expressed in a document called *the budget* (or *master budget*), in most organizations, "the budget" is actually composed of several different budgets. Unlike an organization's financial statements, budget formats are not specified by external parties in the form of generally accepted accounting principles, or GAAP, so the contents and format of the budget are dictated by the organization's mission and structure and by managerial preferences. That said, several types of budgets are used either formally or informally at virtually all health services organizations.

Statistics Budget

The **statistics budget** is the cornerstone of the budgeting process in that it specifies the patient volume and resource assumptions used in other budgets. Because the statistics budget feeds into all other budgets, accuracy is particularly important. The statistics budget does not provide detailed information on required resources such as staffing or short-term operating asset requirements, but it provides general guidance.

Some organizations, especially smaller ones, may not have a separate statistics budget but instead may incorporate its data directly into the revenue

statistics budget
A budget that contains the patient volume and resource need assumptions used in all other budgets.

and expense budgets or perhaps into a single operating budget. The advantage of having a separate statistics budget is that, in large organizations, it forces all other budgets to use the same set of volume and resource assumptions. Unfortunately, patient volume estimates, which are the heart of the statistics budget and which drive all other forecasts, are among the most difficult to make.

To illustrate the complexities of patient volume forecasting, consider the procedures followed by Bayview Hospital when it prepares its statistics budget. To begin, the demand for services is divided into four major groups: inpatient, outpatient, ancillary, and other services. Volume trends in each of these areas over the past five years are plotted, and a first approximation forecast is made, assuming a continuation of past trends. Next, the level of population growth and disease trends are forecast. For example, what will be the growth in the over-65 population in the hospital's service area? These forecasts are used to develop volume by major diagnoses and to differentiate between normal services and critical care services.

Bayview's managers then analyze the competitive environment. Consideration is given to such factors as the hospital's inpatient and outpatient capacities, its competitors' capacities, and new services or service improvements that either Bayview or its competitors might institute. Next, Bayview's managers consider the effect of the hospital's planned pricing actions on volume. For example, does the hospital have plans to raise outpatient charges to boost profit margins or to lower charges to gain market share and utilize excess capacity? If such actions are expected to affect volume forecasts, these forecasts must be revised to reflect the expected impact. Marketing campaigns and changes in third-party payer contracts also affect volume, so probable developments in these areas also must be considered.

If the hospital's volume forecast is off the mark, the consequences can be serious. First, if the market for any particular service expands more than Bayview has expected and planned for, the hospital will not be able to meet its patients' needs. Potential patients will end up going to competitors, and Bayview will lose market share and perhaps miss a major opportunity. However, if its projections are overly optimistic, Bayview could end up with too much capacity, which means higher-than-necessary costs because of excess facilities and staff.

Revenue Budget

revenue budget
A budget that focuses on the revenues of an organization or its subunits.

Detailed information from the statistics budget feeds into the **revenue budget**, which combines patient volume and reimbursement data to develop revenue forecasts. Bayview's planners consider the hospital's pricing strategy for managed care plans, conventional fee-for-service contracts, and private-pay patients as well as trends in inflation and third-party payer reimbursement, all of which affect operating revenues.

The result is a compilation of operating revenue forecasts by service, both in the aggregate—for example, inpatient revenue—and on an individual diagnosis basis. The individual diagnosis forecasts are summed and then compared with the aggregate service group forecasts. Differences are reconciled, and the result is an operating revenue forecast for the hospital as a whole, broken down by service categories and by individual diagnoses.

In addition to operating revenues, other revenues, such as interest income on investments and lease payments on medical office buildings, must be forecast. Note that in all revenue forecasts, both the amount and the timing are important. Thus, the revenue budget must forecast not only the amount of revenue but also when the revenue is expected to occur, typically by month.

Expense Budget

Like the revenue budget, the **expense budget** is derived from data in the statistics budget. The focus here is on the costs of providing services rather than the resulting revenues. The expense budget typically is divided into labor (salaries, wages, and fringe benefits, including travel and education) and nonlabor components. The nonlabor components include expenses associated with such items as depreciation, leases, utilities, medical supplies, and administration. Expenses normally are broken down into fixed and variable components. (As discussed later in this chapter, cost structure information is required if an organization uses flexible budgeting techniques.)

> **expense budget**
> A budget that focuses on the costs of providing goods or services.

Operating Budget

For larger organizations, the **operating budget** flows from the revenue and expense budgets. For smaller businesses, data typically found in the statistics, revenue, and expense budgets are used to create the operating budget in a single step. Because the operating budget (and, by definition, the revenue and expense budgets) is prepared using accrual accounting methods, it can be roughly thought of as a forecast income statement. However, unlike the income statement, which is typically prepared at the organizational level, operating budgets are prepared at the subunit level—say, a department or product line. Because of its overall importance to the budgeting process, the operating budget is the main focus of this chapter.

> **operating budget**
> A single budget that combines both the revenue and expense budgets.

SELF-TEST QUESTIONS

1. What are some of the budget types used within health services organizations?
2. Briefly describe the purpose and use of each.
3. How are the statistics budget, revenue and expense budgets, and operating budget related?

Constructing a Simple Operating Budget

Exhibit 8.3 contains the 2020 operating budget for Carroll Clinic, an inner-city primary care facility. Most operating budgets are more complex than this illustration, which has been simplified for ease of discussion.

Developing the operating budget requires a number of assumptions. As with most financial forecasts, the starting point for the operating budget, which was developed in October 2019, is patient volume. A *volume projection* gives managers a starting point for making revenue and cost estimates. As shown in part I of exhibit 8.3, Carroll Clinic's expected patient volume for 2020 comes from two sources: a fee-for-service (FFS) population expected to total 36,000 visits and a capitated population expected to average 30,000 members. Historically, annual utilization by the capitated population has averaged 0.15 visits per member-month, so in 2020, this population, which is expected to total 30,000 × 12 = 360,000 member-months, will provide 360,000 × 0.15 = 54,000 visits. In total, therefore, Carroll's patient base is expected to produce 36,000 + 54,000 = 90,000 visits. Armed with this volume projection, Carroll's managers can proceed with revenue and cost projections.

Part II of exhibit 8.3 contains revenue data. The clinic's net collection for each FFS visit averages $25. Some visits will generate greater revenues, and some will generate less. On average, though, expected revenue is assumed to be $25 per visit. Thus, 36,000 visits will produce $25 × 36,000 = $900,000 in FFS revenues. In addition, the premium for the capitated population is $3 per member per month (PMPM), which would generate a revenue of $3 × 360,000 member-months = $1,080,000. Considering both patient sources, total revenues for the clinic are forecast to be $900,000 + $1,080,000 = $1,980,000 in 2020.

Because of the uncertainty inherent in the clinic's volume estimates, it is useful to recognize that total revenues will be $1,980,000 only if the volume forecast holds. In reality, Total revenues = ($25 × Number of FFS visits) + ($3 × Number of capitated member-months). If the actual number of FFS visits is more or less than 90,000 in 2020, or the number of capitated lives (and hence member-months) is something other than 30,000, the resulting revenues will be different from the $1,980,000 forecast. Similarly, if actual reimbursement or premium rates differ from $25 and $3, respectively, then the resulting revenues will be different from the forecast.

Part III of exhibit 8.3 focuses on expenses. To support the forecast 90,000 visits, the clinic is expected to use 48,000 hours of medical labor at an average cost of $25 per hour, for a total labor expense of 48,000 × $25 = $1,200,000. Thus, labor costs are expected to average $1,200,000 ÷ 90,000 = $13.33 per visit in 2020. In reality, all labor costs are not variable, but there are a sufficient number of workers who either work part-time or

I. Volume Assumptions:			
A. FFS	36,000	visits	
B. Capitated lives	30,000	members	
Number of member-months	360,000		
Expected utilization per member-month	0.15		
Number of visits	54,000	visits	
C. Total expected visits	90,000	visits	

EXHIBIT 8.3
Carroll Clinic:
2020 Operating
Budget

II. Revenue Assumptions:

A.   FFS $ 25 per visit
× 36,000 expected visits
$ 900,000

B.   Capitated lives $ 3 PMPM
× 360,000 actual member-months
$1,080,000

C.   Total expected revenues $1,980,000

III. Cost Assumptions:

A.   Variable Costs:

Labor	$1,200,000	(48,000 hours at $25/hour)
Supplies	150,000	(100,000 units at $1.50/unit)
Total variable costs	$1,350,000	
Variable cost per visit	$ 15	($1,350,000 ÷ 90,000)

B.   Fixed Costs:

Overhead, plant, and equipment	$ 500,000
C. Total expected costs	$1,850,000

IV. Pro Forma Profit and Loss (P&L) Statement:

Revenues:	
FFS	$ 900,000
Capitated	1,080,000
Total	$1,980,000
Costs:	
Variable:	
FFS	$ 540,000
Capitated	810,000
Total	$1,350,000
Contribution margin	$ 630,000
Fixed costs	500,000
Projected profit	$ 130,000

are paid on the basis of productivity to closely tie labor hours to the number of visits.

Supplies expense, the bulk of which is inherently variable in nature, historically has averaged about $1.50 per bundle (unit) of supplies, with 100,000 units expected to be used to support 90,000 visits. (A unit of supplies is a more or less standard package that contains both administrative and clinical supplies.) Thus, supplies expense is expected to total $150,000, or $150,000 ÷ 90,000 = $1.67 on a per visit basis. Taken together, Carroll's labor and supplies variable costs are forecast to be $13.33 + $1.67 = $15 per visit in 2020. The same amount can be calculated by dividing total variable costs by the number of visits: $1,350,000 ÷ 90,000 = $15.

Finally, the clinic is expected to incur $500,000 in fixed costs, primarily administrative overhead, some labor costs, depreciation, and lease expense. Therefore, to serve the anticipated 90,000 visits, costs are expected to consist of $1,350,000 in variable costs plus $500,000 in fixed costs, for a total of $1,850,000. Again, it is important to recognize that some costs (in Carroll's case, a majority of costs) are tied to volume. Thus, total costs can be expressed as ($15 × Number of visits) + $500,000. If the actual number of visits in 2020 is more or less than 90,000 or the actual variable cost rate is different from $15, total costs will differ from the $1,850,000 budget estimate.

The final section (part IV) of exhibit 8.3 contains Carroll Clinic's budgeted 2020 profit and loss (P&L) statement, the heart of the operating budget. The difference between the projected revenues of $1,980,000 and the projected variable costs of $1,350,000 produces a total contribution margin of $630,000. Deducting the forecast fixed costs of $500,000 results in a budgeted profit of $130,000.

The true purpose of the operating budget is to set financial goals for the clinic. In effect, the operating budget can be thought of as a contract between the organization and its managers. Thus, the $130,000 profit forecast becomes the overall profit benchmark for the clinic in 2020, and individual managers will be held accountable for the revenues and expenses needed to meet the budget.

SELF-TEST QUESTIONS

1. What are some of the key assumptions required to prepare an operating budget?
2. Do the required assumptions depend on the type of organization and the nature of its reimbursement contracts?
3. Why is the budgeted profit and loss (P&L) statement so important?

Variance Analysis

Variance analysis, which focuses on differences (variances) between realized values and forecasts, is an important technique for controlling operations. This section includes a discussion of the basics of variance analysis, including flexible budgeting, and an illustration of the process.

Variance Analysis Basics

In accounting, a **variance** is the difference between an actual (realized) value and the budgeted value, often called a *standard*. Note that the accounting definition of variance is different from the statistical definition, although both meanings connote a difference from some base value. In effect, *variance analysis* is an examination and interpretation of differences between what has actually happened and what was planned. If the budget is based on realistic expectations, variance analysis can provide managers with useful information. Variance analysis does not provide all the answers, but it does help managers ask the right questions.

Variance analysis is essential to the managerial control process. Actions taken in response to variance analysis often have the potential to dramatically improve the operations and financial performance of the organization. For example, many variances are controllable (can be corrected by managerial actions), so managers can take actions to avoid unfavorable variances in the future.

The primary focus of variance analysis should not be to assign blame for unfavorable results. Rather, the goal of variance analysis is to uncover the cause of operational problems so that these problems can be corrected as quickly as possible and avoided, or at least minimized, in the future. Unfortunately, not all variances are controllable by management. Nevertheless, knowledge of such variances is essential to the overall management and well-being of the organization.

Static Versus Flexible Budgets

To be of maximum use to managers, variance analysis must be approached systematically. The starting point for such analyses is the **static budget**, which is the original approved budget unadjusted for differences between planned and actual (realized) patient volumes. However, at the end of a budget period, it is unlikely that realized volume will equal budgeted volume, and it would be useful to know which variances are due to volume forecast errors and which variances are caused by other factors.

To illustrate this concept, consider Carroll Clinic's 2020 operating budget contained in exhibit 8.3. The profit projection, $130,000, is predicated on specific volume assumptions: 36,000 visits for the FFS population

variance analysis
A technique used in budgeting in which realized values are compared with budgeted values to help control operations.

variance
The difference between what actually happened and what was expected to happen.

static budget
A budget that is prepared at the beginning of a planning period.

and 360,000 member-months, resulting in 54,000 visits, for the capitated population. At the end of the year, the clinic's managers will compare actual profits with budgeted profits. The problem, of course, is that it is highly unlikely that actual profits will result from exactly 36,000 fee-for-service visits and 360,000 member-months (with 54,000 visits) for the capitated population. The number of fee-for-service visits might be higher or lower than forecast, and the capitated population might be greater or less than forecast and use services at a different rate than assumed in the static budget. Thus, if Carroll's managers merely compared the realized profit with the $130,000 profit in the static budget, they would not know whether any profit difference is caused by forecast and realized patient volume differences or by underlying operational differences.

flexible budget
A budget based on the static budget assumptions but adjusted to reflect realized volume.

To provide an explanation of what is driving the profit variance, Carroll's managers must create a flexible budget. A **flexible budget** is one in which the static budget has been adjusted to reflect the actual volume achieved in the budget period. Essentially, a flexible budget is an after-the-fact device that tells managers what the results would have been under the volume level actually attained, **assuming all other budgeting assumptions are held constant**. The flexible budget permits a more detailed analysis than is possible using only actual results compared with the static budget. However, a flexible budget only manipulates variable costs, thus requiring the identification of variable and fixed costs and placing a greater burden on the organization's managerial accounting system.

For Your Consideration
Rolling Budgets

A *rolling budget*, also called a *continuous budget*, is constantly being updated. In essence, a rolling budget is kept current by adding a period to the budget each time a period ends. For example, assume an annual budget is created for January–December 2020. When January 2020 ends, the budget is revised for the period February 2020–January 2021. Thus, the budget remains annual, but the year is rolled forward by adding a month as each month passes. Alternatively, the annual budget could be rolled forward by quarter, in which case it would be extended every three months.

A rolling budget allows managers to incorporate new information into the organizational budget in a timely manner and get a feel for how that information affects annual (but not necessarily fiscal year) results. Thus, forecasts can be revised and the results of managerial actions can be incorporated monthly, with results still forecast on an annual basis.

What do you think? Are rolling budgets a valuable addition to the planning process? What information do rolling budgets provide that is not available in traditional quarterly and annual budgets?

Variance Analysis Illustration

To illustrate variance analysis, consider Carroll's static budget for 2020 (exhibit 8.3), which projects a profit of $130,000. Data used for variance analysis are tracked in Carroll's managerial accounting information system throughout the year, and variance analyses are performed monthly. This allows managers to take necessary actions during the year to positively influence annual results. For purposes of this illustration, however, the monthly feedback is not shown. Rather, the focus is on the year-end results, which are contained in exhibit 8.4.

Creating the Flexible Budget

Exhibit 8.5 contains three sets of data for 2020. The static budget, which is taken from exhibit 8.3, is the forecast made at the beginning of 2020; the actual results, taken from exhibit 8.4, reflect what happened. The flexible budget in the center column of exhibit 8.5 reflects projected revenues and costs at the **realized (actual) volume**, as opposed to the projected volume, **but incorporates all other assumptions that were used in the static (original) budget**. By analyzing differences in these three data sets, Carroll's managers can gain insights into why the clinic ended the year with a loss.

The flexible budget maintains the original budget assumptions of Revenues = ($25 × Number of FFS visits) + ($3 × Number of capitated member-months) and Expenses = ($15 × Number of FFS visits) + ($15 × Number of capitated visits) + $500,000. However, the flexible budget flexes (adjusts) revenues and costs to reflect actual volume levels. Thus, in the flexible budget column, Revenues = ($25 × 40,000) + ($3 × 360,000) = $1,000,000 + $1,080,000 = $2,080,000, and Expenses = ($15 × 40,000) + ($15 × 72,000) + $500,000 = $600,000 + $1,080,000 + $500,000 = $1,680,000 + $500,000 = $2,180,000. The flexible budget uses the original estimates for revenue and variable cost rates but couples these rates with realized volumes. In the static budget, these same rates were used in conjunction with forecast volumes.

The flexible budget can be described as follows. The $2,080,000 in total revenues is what the clinic **would have expected** at the start of the year if the volume estimates had been 40,000 FFS visits and a capitated membership of 30,000. In addition, the total variable costs of $1,680,000 in the flexible budget are the costs that Carroll **would have expected** for 40,000 FFS visits and 72,000 capitated visits (based on a membership of 30,000). By definition, the fixed costs should be the same, within a reasonable range, no matter what the volume level is. On net, the $100,000 loss shown on the flexible budget represents the profit expected given the initial assumed revenue, cost, and volume relationships, coupled with a forecast volume that equals the realized volume.

Conducting the Variance Analysis

As explained earlier, variance analysis involves comparing two amounts; the variance is the difference between the values. For example, if at the beginning of the year, a hospital expected to make a profit of $2 million but the actual profit was $3 million, the variance would be $1 million. The expected, or *standard* value—in this case, $2 million in profits—is the profit goal of

EXHIBIT 8.4
Carroll Clinic:
2020 Results

I. Volume:

A. FFS   40,000   visits
B. Capitated lives   30,000   members
    Number of member-months   360,000
    Actual utilization per
        member-month   0.20
    Number of visits   72,000   visits
C. Total actual visits   112,000   visits

II. Revenues:

A. FFS $ 24   per visit
                                      ×   40,000   actual visits
                                      $ 960,000
B. Capitated lives $ 3   PMPM
                                      × 360,000   actual member-months
                                      $1,080,000
C. Total actual revenues $2,040,000

III. Costs:

A. Variable Costs:
    Labor $1,557,400   (59,900 hours at $26/hour)
    Supplies   234,600   (124,800 units at $1.88/unit)
        Total variable costs $1,792,000
    Variable cost per visit $ 16   ($1,792,000 ÷ 112,000)
B. Fixed Costs:
    Overhead, plant,
        and equipment $ 500,000
C. Total actual costs $2,292,000

IV. Profit and Loss Statement:

    Revenues:
        FFS $ 960,000
        Capitated   1,080,000
        Total $2,040,000
    Costs:
        Variable:
            FFS $ 640,000
            Capitated   1,152,000
            Total $1,792,000
        Contribution margin $ 248,000
        Fixed costs   500,000
        Actual profit   ($ 252,000)

	Static Budget	Flexible Budget	Actual Results
Visits (Volume):			
FFS visits	36,000	40,000	40,000
Capitated visits	54,000	72,000	72,000
Total	90,000	112,000	112,000
Revenues:			
FFS	$ 900,000	$1,000,000	$ 960,000
Capitated	1,080,000	1,080,000	1,080,000
Total	$1,980,000	$2,080,000	$2,040,000
Costs:			
Variable:			
FFS	$ 540,000	$ 600,000	$ 640,000
Capitated	810,000	1,080,000	1,152,000
Total	$1,350,000	$1,680,000	$1,792,000
Contribution margin	$ 630,000	$ 400,000	$ 248,000
Fixed costs	500,000	500,000	500,000
Profit	$ 130,000	($ 100,000)	($ 252,000)

EXHIBIT 8.5
Carroll Clinic: Static and Flexible Budgets and Actual Results for 2020

the hospital as expressed in the budget. As you will see from the following paragraphs, most variances are calculated in more or less the same way.

To begin Carroll Clinic's variance analysis, consider the data contained in exhibit 8.5. The *total*, or *profit*, *variance* is the difference between the realized profit and the static profit. Thus, Profit variance = Actual profit – Static profit, or (–$252,000) – $130,000 = –$382,000. That is, Carroll's 2020 profitability was $382,000 below standard, or $382,000 less than expected. This large negative variance should generate considerable concern among Carroll's managers, and lead to a more detailed analysis to determine the underlying causes.

The first question that Carroll's management likely wants answered is this: Is the large loss (compared with expectations) due to a revenue shortfall, cost overruns, or both? Exhibit 8.6 shows the –$382,000 profit variance at the top and breaks it down into its revenue and cost components.

In calculating all variances, we are using definitions (given in the bottom of each variance exhibit) that show "bad" results as a negative number. Variances can be defined so that the resulting value is either a positive or a negative number. For example, when cost variances are calculated, they can be defined so that a negative variance means costs less than standard, which is good, or costs greater than standard, which is bad, depending on which value is subtracted from the other. In this example, all variances have been defined

EXHIBIT 8.6
Profit Variance
and Revenue
and Cost
Components

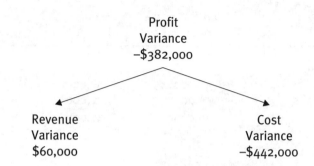

Profit variance = Actual profit – Static profit
Revenue variance = Actual revenues – Static revenues
Cost variance = Static costs – Actual costs

so that a negative number indicates an undesirable variance and not necessarily that the realized value is less than the standard. For example, a higher-than-standard wage rate would be a negative variance, indicating that the variance is harmful to the clinic, even though realized wages were higher than expected.

The *revenue variance* shown in exhibit 8.6 is Actual revenues – Static revenues = $2,040,000 – $1,980,000 = $60,000, which, because it is a positive variance, tells Carroll's managers that realized revenues were actually $60,000 **higher** than expected. However, the *cost variance* of Static costs – Actual costs = $1,350,000 – $1,792,000 = –$442,000 indicates that realized costs were **much greater** than expected. (Remember that our convention is that positive variances are "good" and negative variances are "bad.") The net effect of the revenue and cost variances is the $60,000 + (–$442,000) = –$382,000 profit variance. By breaking down the profit variance into revenue and cost components, it is readily apparent that the major cause of Carroll's poor profit performance in 2020 was that costs were too high. However, the analysis thus far does not discriminate between cost overruns caused by volume forecast errors and those caused by other factors.

Regarding the revenue variance, it would be nice to know whether the greater-than-expected revenues were due to greater-than-expected volume or greater-than-expected prices (reimbursement). Exhibit 8.7 examines the revenue variance in more detail. Here, the $60,000 positive revenue variance is deconstructed into volume and price variances. The *volume variance* is Flexible revenues – Static revenues = $2,080,000 – $1,980,000 = $100,000, and the *price or rate variance* is Actual revenues – Flexible revenues = $2,040,000 – $2,080,000 = –$40,000. These variances tell Carroll's managers that a higher-than-expected volume should have resulted in revenues being $100,000 greater than expected in 2020. However, this potential revenue increase was partially offset by the fact that realized prices (reimbursement rates) were less than expected. The end result of higher volume at lower prices is realized revenue that was $60,000 higher than forecast. To keep this illustration manageable, the number of covered lives (enrollment) was held constant throughout the year. If this had not been the case, two flexible budgets would be required and the volume variance would have two components. (Refer to the note at the bottom of exhibit 8.7.)

Now let's change our focus to the cost side of the variance analysis. Exhibit 8.8 breaks down the –$442,000 cost variance into volume and management components. The *volume variance* of Static costs – Flexible costs = $1,350,000 – $1,680,000 = –$330,000 indicates that a large portion of the $442,000 cost overrun was caused by the incorrect volume forecast: Higher-than-expected volume resulted in higher-than-expected costs. This higher-than-expected volume would not be a financial problem if it were additional fee-for-service patients, in which case higher costs as a result of higher volume would likely be more than offset by higher revenues. However, the fact that a majority of the higher volume (18,000 of 22,000 visits) came from capitated patients means that there was no matching revenue increase.

In addition to the problem of higher-than-expected volume, $112,000 of the $442,000 cost overrun was caused by other factors. This amount is

EXHIBIT 8.7
Revenue
Variance
and Volume
and Price
Components

Revenue variance = Actual revenues – Static revenues
Volume variance = Flexible revenues – Static revenues
Price variance = Actual revenues – Flexible revenues

Note: In our example, there are no enrollment differences. However, if some patients are capitated, and there are enrollment differences between the static budget and realized results, the situation becomes more complex. Then, it is necessary to create two flexible budgets: (1) one flexed for both enrollment and utilization and (2) one flexed only for enrollment. With two flexible budgets, volume variances can be calculated for both changes in the number of covered lives and changes in utilization.

   Volume variance = Flexible (enrollment and utilization) revenues – Static revenues
   Enrollment variance = Flexible (enrollment) revenues – Static revenues
   Utilization variance = Flexible (enrollment and utilization) revenues – Flexible
       (enrollment) revenues

called the *management variance*, which is calculated as Flexible costs − Actual costs = $1,680,000 − $1,792,000 = −$112,000. The management variance gets its name from the assumption that any cost variances not caused by volume forecast inaccuracies are a result of management performance. The theory here is that most clinical managers have limited (if any) control over the volume of services supplied, but they do have control over factors such as the amount of labor used, wage rates, supplies utilization and costs, and so forth. Thus, the $112,000 cost overrun classified as management variance can be influenced by managerial actions. If all standards in the static budget except the volume estimate were met, the cost overrun would have been only $330,000, and not the $442,000 realized.

To attempt to eliminate the management variance in future years, Carroll's managers must determine precisely where the cost overruns lie. The primary resources involved in operating costs are labor and supplies, so it would be valuable to learn which of the two areas contributed most to the management variance. Perhaps a more probing investigation can be made within labor and supplies: Is too much of each resource being used (efficiency/usage), or is too much money being paid for what is being used (rate/price)?

Exhibit 8.9 examines the components of the management variance. We see that $64,067 of the management variance of $112,000 is a result of labor costs, so with no fixed cost variance, the remainder is the result of supplies costs. Furthermore, the $64,067 *labor variance* can be broken down into the portion caused by productivity problems (the *efficiency variance*) and the portion caused by wage rate overages (the *rate variance*). The numbers indicate that a very small portion of the labor cost overrun was caused by productivity problems; the vast majority of the overrun was caused by

EXHIBIT 8.8
Cost Variance and Volume and Management Components

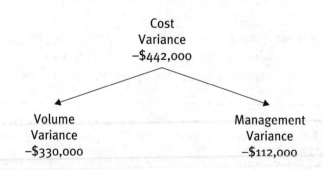

Cost variance = Static costs − Actual costs
Volume variance = Static costs − Flexible costs
Management variance = Flexible costs − Actual costs

higher-than-expected wage rates. This suggests that Carroll's managers have to take a close look to ensure that they are not paying higher wage rates than the local labor market dictates or relying on expensive sources of labor such as contract labor. Of course, Carroll wants to have quality employees, but at the same time, management needs to be concerned about labor costs.

The calculations of the component variances for labor are presented in exhibit 8.10. Calculating the components requires finding per unit input volumes (in this case labor hours) and rates. Labor hours per visit are calculated by dividing total labor hours by visit volume. In the column labeled "Flexible Budget," the static budget assumptions from exhibit 8.3 are combined with actual visit volume. Budgeted labor hours per visit = 48,000 total labor hours ÷ 90,000 total visits = 0.53333 hours per visit, and the budgeted rate per hour is given as $25. The flexible budget total is found by multiplying the values in each of the rows in the flexible budget column: 112,000 × 0.53333 × $25 = $1,493,333. In the column labeled "Adjusted for Input Volume," the actual labor hours per visit is used, while the rate per hour and the visit volume are held constant. Using data from exhibit 8.4, actual labor hours per visit is calculated as 59,900 total hours ÷ 112,000 total visits = 0.534821 hours per visit. The difference between the flexible budget total and the

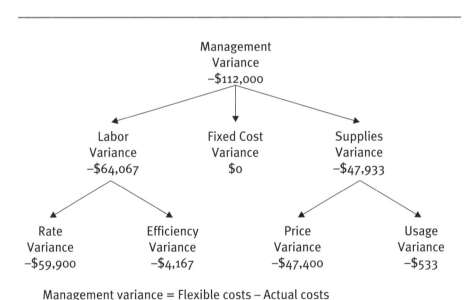

EXHIBIT 8.9
Management Variance and Fixed Costs, Labor, and Supplies Components

Management variance = Flexible costs − Actual costs
Fixed cost variance = Flexible fixed costs − Actual fixed costs
Labor variance = Flexible labor costs − Actual labor costs
Rate variance = (Static rate − Actual rate) × Actual labor hours
Efficiency variance = (Flexible hours − Actual hours) × Static rate
Supplies variance = Flexible supplies costs − Actual supplies costs
Price variance = (Static price − Actual price) × Actual units
Usage variance = (Flexible units − Actual units) × Static price

adjusted for input volume total is the efficiency variance (Efficiency variance = $1,493,333 – $1,497,500 = –$4,167).

Finally, in the column labeled "Actual Results," all of the realized values are used—visit volume, labor hours per visit, and rate per hour—to arrive at actual labor costs. The difference between the adjusted for input volume total and the actual results total is the rate variance (Rate variance = $1,497,500 – $1,557,400 = –$59,900). Moving from left to right, one factor is changed at a time to decompose the labor management variance into its components.

How did Carroll do in 2020 regarding supplies costs? If $64,067 of the management variance of $112,000 is caused by labor costs, the remainder, $47,933, must be caused by supplies costs. Within the $47,933 *supplies variance*, the amount caused by excess usage (the *usage variance*) and the amount caused by price differentials (the *price variance*) can be determined. To begin, $533 of the supplies variance of $47,933 is caused by usage differences; the remainder ($47,400) is caused by price differences. Thus, the supplies cost overrun resulted almost exclusively from price increases—the price paid was higher than that assumed in the static budget. Supplies usage was almost on target when volume differences are accounted for. Thus, it would be prudent for management to investigate the clinic's purchasing policy to see whether prices could be lowered through such actions as changing vendors, making larger purchases at a single time, joining a purchasing alliance, or just negotiating better.

Final Comments on Variance Analysis

Variance analysis helps managers identify the factors that cause realized profits to differ from those expected. If profits are higher than expected, managers can see why and then try to exploit those factors in the future. If profits are lower than expected, managers can identify the causes and then embark

EXHIBIT 8.10 Labor Variance and Efficiency and Rate Components	Flexible Budget	Adjusted for Input Volume	Actual Results
Visits (volume) ×	112,000	112,000	112,000
Labor hours per visit ×	0.533	0.535	0.535
Rate per hour =	$25	$25	$26
Total labor cost	$1,493,333	$1,497,500	$1,557,400

$1,493,333 – $1,497,500 = –$4,167 (efficiency variance)

$1,497,500 – $1,557,400 = –$59,900 (rate variance)

–$4,167 + –$59,900 = –$64,067 (total labor management variance)

Note: The calculations of the component variances may not be exact due to rounding.

on a plan to correct the deficiencies. Larger health services organizations have made significant improvements in their use of variance analysis. The benefit of expanding the level of detail in the variance analysis is that it is easier for managers to isolate and presumably rectify problem areas. Fortunately, the marginal cost of obtaining such detailed information is lower now than ever before because large amounts of managerial accounting information are being generated at many health services organizations to support cost control efforts and to aid in pricing and service decisions.

It is important to recognize that the Carroll Clinic example presented here is meant to illustrate variance analysis techniques rather than illustrate a complete analysis. A complete analysis would encompass many more variances. Furthermore, in most organizations, variance analysis is conducted at the department level as well as at other sublevels, such as service or contract lines, in addition to the organization as a whole. Nevertheless, the Carroll Clinic example gives readers a feel for how variance analysis is conducted and its benefits to the organization.

SELF-TEST QUESTIONS

1. What is variance analysis, and what is its value to healthcare providers?
2. What is the difference between a static budget and a flexible budget?
3. What are the components of profit variance? Of revenue variance? Of cost variance?

Key Concepts

Planning and budgeting are important managerial activities. In particular, budgets allow health services managers to plan for and set expectations for the future, assess financial performance on a timely basis, and ensure that operations are carried out in a manner consistent with expectations. The key concepts of this chapter are as follows:

- *Planning* encompasses the overall process of preparing for the future, while *budgeting* is the accounting process that ties together planning and control functions.
- The *strategic plan*, which provides broad guidance for the long-term future, is the foundation of any organization's planning process.

(continued)

(continued from previous page)

- The *values statement* contains the core beliefs of an organization.
- The *mission statement* defines an organization's overall purpose (its reason for existence).
- The *vision statement* describes the desired position of an organization at some point in the future—say, in ten years.
- The *operating plan*, often called the *five-year plan*, provides more detailed guidance for the short term than is contained in the strategic plan.
- The *financial plan*, which is the financial portion of the operating plan, contains three sections: (1) *financial condition, capital investments, and financing*; (2) *current accounts and revenue cycle*; and (3) *budgeting and control*.
- *Budgeting* provides a means for communication and coordination of organizational expectations as well as allocation of financial resources. In addition, budgeting establishes benchmarks for control.
- The *conventional approach* to budgeting uses the previous budget as the basis for constructing the new budget. *Zero-based budgeting* begins each budget as a clean slate, and all entries have to be justified each budget period.
- *Bottom-up budgeting*, which begins at the unit level, encourages maximum involvement by middle managers. Conversely, *top-down budgeting*, which is less participatory in nature, is a more efficient way to communicate senior management's views.
- There are several types of budgets, including the *statistics budget*, the *revenue budget*, the *expense budget*, and the *operating budget*.
- The *operating budget* is the basic budget of an organization in that it sets the profit target for the budget period.
- When the original budget, or *static budget*, is recast to reflect the actual volume of patients treated, leaving all other assumptions unchanged, the result is called a *flexible budget*.
- A *variance* is the difference between a budgeted (planned) value, or *standard*, and the actual (realized) value. *Variance analysis* examines differences between budgeted and realized amounts with the goal of finding out why things went either badly or well.
- To be most useful, variance analysis examines differences between actual results and the static and flexible budgets.

This chapter concludes the discussion of managerial accounting. Chapter 9 begins the examination of basic financial management concepts.

Questions

8.1. Why are planning and budgeting so important to an organization's success?

8.2. Briefly describe the planning process. Be sure to include summaries of the strategic, operating, and financial plans.

8.3. Describe the components of a financial plan.

8.4. How are the statistics, revenue, expense, and operating budgets related?

8.5. a. What are the advantages and disadvantages of conventional budgeting versus zero-based budgeting?

b. What organizational characteristics create likely candidates for zero-based budgeting?

8.6. If you were the CEO of Bayview Hospital, would you advocate a top-down or a bottom-up approach to budgeting? Explain your rationale.

8.7. What is variance analysis?

8.8. a. Explain the relationships among the static budget, flexible budget, and actual results.

b. Assume that a group practice has both capitated and fee-for-service (FFS) patients. Furthermore, the number of capitated enrollees has changed over the budget period. To calculate the volume variance and break it down into enrollment and utilization components, how many flexible budgets must be constructed?

Problems

8.1. Consider the following 2020 data for Newark General Hospital (in millions of dollars):

	Static Budget	Flexible Budget	Actual Results
Revenues	$4.7	$4.8	$4.5
Costs	4.1	4.1	4.2
Profits	0.6	0.7	0.3

a. Calculate and interpret the profit variance.
b. Calculate and interpret the revenue variance.
c. Calculate and interpret the cost variance.
d. Calculate and interpret the volume and price variances on the revenue side.
e. Calculate and interpret the volume and management variances on the cost side.
f. How are the variances calculated above related?

8.2. Here are the 2020 revenues for the Wendover Group Practice Association for four different budgets (in thousands of dollars):

Static Budget	Flexible (Enrollment/ Utilization) Budget	Flexible (Enrollment) Budget	Actual Results
$425	$200	$180	$300

a. What do the budget data tell you about the nature of Wendover's patients: Are they capitated or fee-for-service? (Hint: See the note to exhibit 8.7.)
b. Calculate and interpret the following variances:
- Revenue variance
- Volume variance
- Price variance
- Enrollment variance
- Utilization variance

8.3. Here are the budgets of Brandon Surgery Center for the most recent historical quarter (in thousands of dollars):

	Static	Flexible	Actual
Number of surgeries	1,200	1,300	1,300
Patient revenue	$2,400	$2,600	$2,535
Salary expense	1,200	1,300	1,365
Nonsalary expense	600	650	585
Profit	$ 600	$ 650	$ 585

The center assumes that all revenues and costs are variable and hence tied directly to patient volume.

a. Explain how each amount in the flexible budget was calculated. (Hint: Examine the static budget to determine the relationship of each budget line to volume.)

b. Determine the variances for each line of the profit and loss statement, both in dollar terms and in percentage terms. (Hint: Each line has a total variance, a volume variance, and a price variance [for revenues] or management variance [for expenses].)

c. What do the results from part b tell Brandon's managers about the surgery center's operations for the quarter?

8.4. Refer to Carroll Clinic's 2020 operating budget contained in exhibit 8.3. Instead of the actual results reported in exhibit 8.4, assume the results reported below:

Carroll Clinic: New 2020 Results		
I. Volume:		
A. FFS	34,000	visits
B. Capitated lives	30,000	members
Number of member-months	360,000	
Actual utilization per member-month	0.12	
Number of visits	43,200	visits
C. Total actual visits	77,200	visits
II. Revenues:		
A. FFS	$ 28	per visit
	× 34,000	actual visits
	$ 952,000	
B. Capitated lives	$ 2.75	PMPM
	× 360,000	actual member-months
	$ 990,000	
C. Total actual revenues	$1,942,000	
III. Costs:		
A. Variable Costs:		
Labor	$1,242,000	(46,000 hours at $27/hour)
Supplies	126,000	(90,000 units at $1.40/unit)
Total variable costs	$1,368,000	
Variable cost per visit	$ 17.72	($1,368,000 ÷ 77,200)
B. Fixed Costs:		
Overhead, plant, and equipment	$ 525,000	
C. Total actual costs	$1,893,000	

(continued)

IV. *Profit and Loss Statement:*

Revenues:

FFS	$ 952,000
Capitated	990,000
Total	$1,975,000

Costs:

Variable:

FFS	$ 602,487
Capitated	765,513
Total	$1,368,000
Contribution margin	$ 574,000
Fixed costs	525,000
Actual profit	$ 49,000

a. Construct Carroll's flexible budget for 2020.

b. What are the profit variance, revenue variance, and cost variance?

c. Consider the revenue variance. What is the component volume variance? The price variance?

d. Break down the cost variance into volume and management components.

e. Break down the management variance into labor, supplies, and fixed costs variances.

f. Break down the labor and supplies variances into rate/price and efficiency/usage components.

g. Interpret your results. In particular, focus on the differences between the variance analysis here and the Carroll Clinic illustration presented in the chapter.

8.5. Instead of the results in problem 8.4, consider the results reported below:

Carroll Clinic: New 2020 Results

I. *Volume:*

A. FFS	34,000	visits
B. Capitated lives	31,000	members
Number of member-months	372,000	
Actual utilization per member-month	0.11613	
Number of visits	43,200	visits
C. Total actual visits	77,200	visits

II. Revenues:

A. FFS $ 28   per visit

                              × 34,000

                          $ 952,000   actual visits

B. Capitated lives $ 2.75   PMPM

                          ×372,000   actual member-months

                          $1,023,000

C. Total actual revenues $1,975,000

III. Costs:

A. Variable Costs:

   Labor $1,242,000   (46,000 hours at $27/hour)

   Supplies   126,000   (90,000 units at $1.40/unit)

      Total variable costs $1,368,000

   Variable cost per visit $ 17.72   ($1,368,000 ÷ 77,200)

B. Fixed Costs:

   Overhead, plant, and
      equipment $ 525,000

C. Total actual costs $1,893,000

IV. Profit and Loss Statement:

   Revenues:

      FFS $ 952,000

      Capitated   1,023,000

         Total $1,975,000

   Costs:

      Variable:

         FFS $ 602,487

         Capitated   765,513

            Total $1,368,000

      Contribution margin $ 607,000

      Fixed costs   525,000

      Actual profit $ 82,000

Assume the results reported in problem 8.4 hold, except that a difference existed among budgeted (static) enrollment and realized enrollment. The corrected results are presented above.

a. Construct Carroll's flexible budgets for 2020. (Hint: Because of a change in enrollment, creating three flexible budgets is necessary. See the note to exhibit 8.7.)

b. What are the profit variance, revenue variance, and cost variance?

c. Focus on the revenue side. What is the volume variance? The price variance? Break the volume variance into enrollment and utilization components. How does your answer here differ from your corresponding answer to problem 8.4?

d. Now consider the cost side. What are the volume and management variances? Break down the management variance into labor, supplies, and fixed costs variances.

e. Interpret your results. In particular, focus on the differences between the variance analysis here and the one in problem 8.4.

8.6. Chelsea Clinic projected the following budget information for 2020:

Total FFS Visit Volume	90,000 visits
Payer Mix:	
Blue Cross	40%
Highmark	60%
Reimbursement Rates:	
Blue Cross	$25 per visit
Highmark	$20 per visit
Variable Costs	
Resource Inputs:	
Labor	48,000 total hours
Supplies	100,000 total units
Resource Input Prices:	
Labor	$25.00 per hour
Supplies	$1.50 per unit
Fixed Costs (overhead, plant, and equipment)	$500,000

a. Construct Chelsea Clinic's operating budget for 2020.

b. Discuss how each key budget assumption might result in a budget variance, and name the variance that would be used to examine results associated with each assumption.

8.7. Refer to problem 8.6. Chelsea Clinic's actual results for 2020 are shown in the table below.

Total FFS Visit Volume	100,000 visits
Payer Mix: Blue Cross	
Blue Cross	40%
Highmark	60%

(continued)

Reimbursement Rates:

Blue Cross	$28 per visit
Highmark	$18 per visit

Variable Costs

Resource Inputs:

Labor	50,000 total hours
Supplies	150,000 total units

Resource Input Prices:

Labor	$28.00 per hour
Supplies	$1.50 per unit
Fixed Costs (overhead, plant, and equipment)	$500,000

a. Construct Chelsea Clinic's flexible budget and actual operating results for 2020.

b. What are the profit variance, revenue variance, and cost variance?

c. Focus on the revenue side. What is the volume variance? The price variance?

d. Now consider the cost side. What are the volume and management variances? Break down the management variance into labor, supplies, and fixed costs variances.

e. Break down the labor and supplies variances into rate/price and efficiency/usage components.

f. Interpret your results.

Selected Case

One case in *Gapenski's Cases in Healthcare Finance*, sixth edition, is applicable to this chapter: Case 10: Cascades Mental Health Clinic.

Resources

Barr, P. 2005. "Flexing Your Budget." *Modern Healthcare*. Published September 12. http://modernhealthcare.com/article/20050912/MAGAZINE/509120317/flexing-your-budget.

Bradley, L. S. 2008. "Budgeting—or Refusing to Budget: How Budget Workshops Can Reduce the Pain." *Healthcare Financial Management* 62 (3): 56–59.

Cardamone, M. A., M. Shaver, and R. Worthman. 2004. "Business Planning: Reasons, Definitions, and Elements." *Healthcare Financial Management* 58 (4): 40–46.

Clark, J. J. 2005. "Improving Hospital Budgeting and Accountability: A Best Practice Approach." *Healthcare Financial Management* 59 (7): 78–83.

Dommert, H. J., and T. E. Getzen. 2005. "On the Money: Making Forecasts What They Should Be." *Healthcare Financial Management* 59 (11): 106–10, 112.

Fuller, J., and M. Anderson. 2009. "Common Ground: Productivity Benchmarking for CFOs and CNOs." *Healthcare Financial Management* 63 (6): 100–108.

Hill, L. E. 2016. "Pioneering a Rolling Forecast." *Healthcare Financial Management* 70 (11): 58–62.

Kolman, C. M. 2017. "Transforming Healthcare Analytics to Manage Costs." *Healthcare Financial Management* 71 (6): 28–33.

Mahler, D. 2016. "Zero-Based Budgeting Is Not a Wonder Diet for Companies." *Harvard Business Review*. Published June 30. https://hbr.org/2016/06/zero-based-budgeting-is-not-a-wonder-diet-for-companies.

May, E. L. 2014. "Financial Planning in a Value-Based World." *Healthcare Executive* 29 (3): 11–18.

Miller, D., M. Allen, S. Schnittger, and T. Hackman. 2013. "How Rolling Forecasting Facilitates Dynamic, Agile Planning." *Healthcare Financial Management* 67 (11): 80–84.

Moore, K. D., and D. Coddington. 2016. "Integrating Health Care's Many Levels of Thinking." *Healthcare Financial Management* 70 (10): 80–81.

Nugent, M. E. 2011. "Budget Planning Under Payment Reform." *Healthcare Financial Management* 65 (7): 38–42.

Person, M. M., III. 1997. *The Zero-Base Hospital*. Chicago: Health Administration Press.

Skinner, J., R. Higbea, D. Buer, and C. Horvath. 2018. "Using Predictive Analytics to Align ED Staffing Resources with Patient Demand." *Healthcare Financial Management* 72 (2): 56–61.

Sorensen, D., and D. Sullivan. 2005. "Managing Trade-Offs Makes Budgeting Processes Pay Off." *Healthcare Financial Management* 59 (11): 54–60.

Swayne, L. M., W. J. Duncan, and P. M. Ginter. 2007. *Strategic Management of Health Care Organizations*. Malden, MA: Blackwell.

IV

BASIC FINANCIAL MANAGEMENT CONCEPTS

Parts II and III were devoted to financial and managerial accounting. Now, we turn our attention to financial management, which provides managers with the tools to make better financial decisions. But before we discuss the application of healthcare financial management theory and concepts to healthcare organizations, it is essential for readers to have a fundamental knowledge of two important foundational topics.

The first topic is time value analysis. Most financial management decisions involve future dollar amounts. For example, when a medical group practice uses debt financing, it is obligated to make a series of future principal and interest payments to the lender. Or when a hospital builds an outpatient surgery center, it expects the investment to provide a series of future cash inflows when the center is up and running. To estimate the financial impact of these transactions, future dollar amounts must be valued. The process of valuing cash flows that occur at different points in time is called time value analysis. Chapter 9 presents the concepts necessary to perform this analysis.

The second foundational topic is financial risk and required return. Virtually all financial decisions involve risk. To illustrate, there is the risk that the medical group practice that obtained debt financing will not be able to make the required loan payments. Or there is the risk that the cash flows expected from the hospital's new outpatient surgery center will be less than those forecast when the center was built. Situations like these involve financial risk. To make good financial decisions, managers must be able to define and measure such risk. Furthermore, risk must be incorporated into the decision-making process by setting a required rate of return that is appropriate for the riskiness of the transaction. Chapter 10 provides the tools required both to understand financial risk and to translate risk into required return.

TIME VALUE ANALYSIS

Learning Objectives

After studying this chapter, readers will be able to

- Explain why time value analysis is so important to healthcare financial management.
- Find the present and future values for lump sums, annuities, and uneven cash flow streams.
- Explain and apply the opportunity cost principle.
- Measure the financial return on an investment in both dollar and percentage terms.
- Describe and apply stated, periodic, and effective annual interest rates.

Introduction

The financial (monetary) value of any asset, whether it is a financial asset, such as a stock or a bond, or a real asset, such as a piece of diagnostic equipment or an ambulatory surgery center, is based on future cash flows. A dollar in hand today is worth more than a dollar to be received in the future because a dollar today can be used for immediate consumption, whereas a dollar expected in the future cannot. If investment opportunities exist, a dollar to be received in the future is worth less than a current dollar because a dollar in hand today can be invested in an interest-bearing account and hence can be worth more than one dollar in the future. Because current dollars are worth more than future dollars, financial management decisions must account for cash flow timing differences.

The process of assigning appropriate values to cash flows that occur at different points in time is called **time value analysis**. It is an important part of healthcare financial management because most financial investment analyses involve the valuation of future cash flows. In fact, of all the financial analysis techniques discussed in this book, none is more important than time value analysis. The concepts presented here are the cornerstones of most financial investment analyses, so a thorough understanding of time value concepts is

time value analysis
The use of time value of money techniques to value future cash flows; sometimes called *discounted cash flow analysis*.

essential to good decision-making. In addition to the material in this chapter, the chapter 9 supplement contains two topics of less importance to healthcare finance: solving for interest rate and time, and amortization.

Time Lines

time line
A graphical representation of time and cash flows; may be an actual line or cells on a spreadsheet.

The creation of a **time line** is the first step in time value analysis, especially when you are first learning time value concepts. Time lines make it easier to visualize when the cash flows in a particular analysis occur. To illustrate the time line concept, consider the following five-period time line:

Time 0 represents the starting point (typically the time of the first cash flow in the analysis); time 1 is one period from the starting point, or the end of period 1; time 2 is two periods from the starting point, or the end of period 2; and so on. Thus, the numbers above the tick marks represent end-of-period values. Often, the periods are years, but other time intervals—such as quarters, months, or days—can be used to fit the timing of the cash flows being evaluated. If the time periods are years, the interval from 0 to 1 will be year 1, and the tick mark labeled 1 will represent both the end of year 1 and the beginning of year 2.

Cash flows are shown on a time line directly below the tick marks that match the point in time when they are expected to occur. The interest rate that is relevant to the analysis is sometimes shown directly above the time line in the first period. Additionally, unknown cash flows—the ones to be determined in the analysis—are sometimes indicated by question marks. To illustrate, consider the following time line:

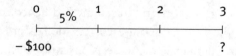

In this situation, the interest rate for each of the three periods is 5 percent, an investment of $100 is made at time 0, and the time 3 value is the unknown. The $100 is an *outflow* because it is shown as a negative cash flow. (Outflows are sometimes designated by parentheses rather than by minus signs.) In more complicated analyses, it is essential to use the proper signs to designate whether a cash flow is an inflow (positive cash flow) or an outflow. Furthermore, some spreadsheet functions require that signs be attached to cash flows in time value analyses, even simple ones, before the calculation can be completed. Thus, to ensure that readers are familiar with the sign convention used in time value analyses, we use them in most illustrations in this book.

Time lines are key to learning and applying time value concepts, and they are extremely helpful for conducting analyses that involve future cash flows. Even experienced financial analysts use time lines when dealing with complex problems. The time line may be an actual line, as illustrated here, or it may be a series of columns (or rows) on a spreadsheet. Time lines are used extensively in the remainder of this book, so get into the habit of creating time lines when conducting analyses that involve future cash flows.

SELF-TEST
QUESTIONS

1. Draw a three-year time line that illustrates the following situation: an investment of $10,000 at time 0; inflows of $5,000 at the end of years 1, 2, and 3; and an interest rate of 10 percent during the entire three years.
2. Why is sign convention important in time value analyses?

Future Value of a Lump Sum: Compounding

The process of going from today's value, or **present value (PV)**, to a future value is called **compounding**. Although compounding is not used extensively in healthcare financial management, it is the best starting point for learning time value analysis. To illustrate *lump sum* compounding, which deals with a single starting amount, suppose that the office manager of Meridian Clinic deposits $100 in a bank account that pays 5 percent annual interest (interest is credited to the account at the end of each year). How much would be in the account at the end of one year? To begin, here are the terms used in this time value analysis:

present value (PV)
The beginning amount (current worth) of an investment of a lump sum, an annuity, or a series of unequal cash flows.

compounding
The process of finding the future value of a lump sum, an annuity, or a series of unequal cash flows.

- $PV = \$100$ = Present value, or beginning amount, of the account.
- $I = 5\%$ = Interest rate the bank pays on the account per year. The interest amount, which is paid at the end of the year, is based on the balance at the beginning of each year. Note that in time value calculations done "by hand," I must be expressed as a decimal, so $I = 0.05$.
- INT = Dollars of interest earned during each year, which equals the beginning amount multiplied by the interest rate. Thus, $INT = PV \times I$.
- FV_N = Future value, or ending amount, of the account at the end of N years. Whereas PV is the value now, or *present value*, FV_N is the value N years in the *future*, after the interest earned has been added to the account.

- N = Number of years involved in the analysis.

In this example, $N = 1$, so FV_N can be calculated as follows:

$$FV_N = FV_1 = PV + INT$$
$$= PV + (PV \times I)$$
$$= PV \times (1 + I).$$

The future value at the end of one year—FV_1—equals the present value multiplied by (1.0 plus the interest rate). This future value relationship can be used to find how much $100 will be worth at the end of one year if it is invested in an account that pays 5 percent interest:

$$FV_1 = PV \times (1 + I) = \$100 \times (1 + 0.05) = \$100 \times 1.05 = \$105.$$

What would be the value of the $100 if Meridian Clinic left the money in the account for five years? Here is a time line that shows the amount at the end of each year:

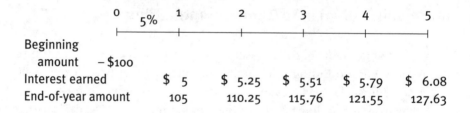

Note the following points:

- The account is opened with a deposit of $100. This is shown as an outflow at year 0.
- Meridian earns $100 × 0.05 = $5 of interest during the first year, so the amount in the account at the end of year 1 is $100 + $5 = $105.
- At the start of the second year, the account balance is $105. Interest of $105 × 0.05 = $5.25 is earned on the now larger amount, so the account balance at the end of the second year is $105 + $5.25 = $110.25. The year 2 interest—$5.25—is higher than the first year's interest—$5—because $5 × 0.05 = $0.25 in interest was earned on the first year's interest.
- This process continues, and because the beginning balance is higher in each succeeding year, the interest earned increases in each year.
- The total interest earned—$27.63—is reflected in the final balance—$127.63—at the end of year 5.

To better understand the mathematics of compounding, note that the year 2 value—$110.25—is equal to

$$
\begin{aligned}
FV_2 &= FV_1 \times (1 + I) \\
&= PV \times (1 + I) \times (1 + I) \\
&= PV \times (1 + I)^2 \\
&= \$100 \times (1.05)^2 = \$110.25.
\end{aligned}
$$

Furthermore, the balance at the end of year 3 is

$$
\begin{aligned}
FV_3 &= FV_2 \times (1 + I) \\
&= PV \times (1 + I)^3 \\
&= \$100 \times (1.05)^3 = \$115.76.
\end{aligned}
$$

Continuing the calculation to the end of year 5 gives

$$
FV_5 = \$100 \times (1.05)^5 = \$127.63.
$$

These calculations show that a pattern clearly exists in future value calculations. In general, the future value of a lump sum at the end of N years can be found by applying this equation:

$$
FV_N = PV \times (1 + I)^N
$$

Future values, and most other time values, can be calculated in three ways: (1) using a regular calculator, (2) using a financial calculator, or (3) using a spreadsheet. This textbook focuses on the regular calculator and spreadsheet solution techniques.

Key Equation: Future Value of a Lump Sum
The future value of a lump sum (single value) can be found using a simple equation. For example, suppose $1,000 was invested for three years in an account paying 10 percent interest. The future value would be $1,331:

$$
\begin{aligned}
FV_N &= PV \times (1 + I)^N \\
FV_3 &= \$1,000 \times (1.10)^3 \\
&= \$1,000 \times 1.10 \times 1.10 \times 1.10 \\
&= \$1,331.00.
\end{aligned}
$$

Here, FV_N is the future value at the end of year N, PV is present value, and I is the interest rate.

Regular Calculator Solution

To use a regular calculator, multiply PV by $(1 + I)$ N times or use the exponential function to raise $(1 + I)$ to the Nth power and then multiply the result by PV. Perhaps the easiest way to find the future value of $100 after five years when it is compounded at 5 percent is to enter $100, then multiply this amount by 1.05 five times. If the calculator is set to display two decimal places, the answer would be $127.63:

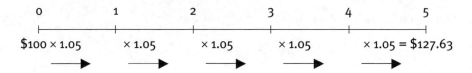

As denoted by the arrows, compounding involves moving to the **right** along the time line. In fact, the term *compounding* is used for finding future values because future values increase, or compound, over time.

Spreadsheet Solution

	A	B	C	D
1				
2	5	Nper	Number of periods	
3	$ 100.00	Pv	Present value	
4	5.0%	Rate	Interest rate	
5				
6	$ 127.63	=100*(1.05)^5 (entered into Cell A6)		
7				
8	$ 127.63	=A3*(1+A4)^A2 (entered into Cell A8)		
9				
10	$ 127.63	=FV(A4,A2,,–A3) (entered into Cell A10)		

Spreadsheet programs, such as Microsoft Excel, are well suited for time value analyses. For simple time value calculations, it is easy to enter the appropriate formula directly into the spreadsheet. For example, you could enter the spreadsheet version of the future value equation into cell A6: = 100*(1.05)^5. Here, = tells the spreadsheet that a formula is being entered into the cell; * is the spreadsheet multiplication sign; and ^ is the spreadsheet exponential, or power, sign. When this formula is entered into cell A6, the value $127.63 appears in the cell (when formatted with a dollar sign to two decimal places). Note that different spreadsheet programs use slightly different syntax in their time value analyses. The examples presented in this text use Excel syntax. Also note that some syntax changes over time as spreadsheet software is updated. If in doubt, use the help feature to ensure that you are using the correct formula.

In most situations, it is more useful to enter a formula that can accommodate changing input values than to embed these values directly in the formula, so it would be better to solve this future value problem with this formula: = A3*(1+A4)^A2, as done in cell A8. Here, the present value ($100) is contained in cell A3, the interest rate (0.05, which is displayed as 5%) in cell A4, and the number of periods (5) in cell A2. With this formula, future values can be easily calculated with different starting amounts, interest rates, or number of years by changing the values in the input cells.

In addition to entering the appropriate time value formulas, most time value solutions are preprogrammed in the spreadsheet software. The preprogrammed time value formulas are called *functions*. Like any formula, a time value function consists of a number of arithmetic calculations combined into one statement. Functions save spreadsheet users the time and tedium of building formulas from scratch.

Each function begins with a unique name that identifies the calculation to be performed, along with one or more *arguments* (the input values for the calculation) enclosed in parentheses. The best way to access the time value functions is to use the spreadsheet's Insert Function feature (also called the Function Wizard), which is designated on the Excel toolbar by *fx*. For this future value problem, first move the cursor to cell A10 (the cell where you want the answer to appear). Then click on the Function Wizard, select "Financial" for the function category and "FV" (future value) for the function name, and click OK. On the next menu, enter A4 for Rate, A2 for Nper (number of periods), and –A3 for Pv. (Note that the Pmt and Type entries

For Your Consideration
The Power of Compounding

"The power of compounding" is a phrase that emphasizes the fact that a relatively small starting value can grow to a large amount when it is invested over a long period, even when the rate of growth (interest rate) is modest. For example, assume that a new parent places $1,000 in a mutual fund to help pay the child's college expenses, which are expected to begin in 18 years. If the mutual fund—say, a common stock fund holding a large number of securities—earns a return of 10 percent per year, after 18 years, the value of the account will be $5,560, which is not an inconsequential sum. (Historically, 10 percent was considered a reasonable estimate for annual returns on a well-diversified portfolio of stocks. However, some market watchers now believe that future returns will be less, say, 8 or 9 percent.)

Now, assume that the money is meant to help fund the child's retirement, which is assumed to occur 65 years in the future. The value of the mutual fund account at that time will be $490,371, or nearly a half million dollars! Imagine that: $1,000 grows to nearly half a million, all because of the power of compounding. The moral of this story is clear: When saving for retirement, or for any other purpose, start early.

are left blank for this problem. Also, note that the cell address entered for Pv has a minus sign. This is necessary for the answer to be displayed as a positive number.) Finally, click OK, and the result—$127.63—appears in cell A10.

Most of the spreadsheet solutions shown in this book follow a similar format. The input values and the output are contained in column A. If a spreadsheet function is used in the solution, the input value (argument) names are shown in column B to the right of the input values. In addition, the formula or function used to calculate the output is shown in column B to the right of the output value. Finally, column C contains the descriptive input names.

The most efficient way to solve most problems that involve time value is to use a spreadsheet. However, the basic mathematics behind the calculations must be understood to set up complex problems before solving them. In addition, the underlying logic must be understood to comprehend stock and bond valuation, lease analysis, capital budgeting analysis, and other important healthcare financial management topics.

SELF-TEST QUESTIONS

1. What is a lump sum?
2. What is compounding? What is interest on interest?
3. What are two solution techniques for solving lump sum compounding problems?
4. How does the future value of a lump sum change as the time is extended and as the interest rate increases?

Present Value of a Lump Sum: Discounting

Suppose that GroupWest Health Plans, which has premium income reserves to invest, has been offered the chance to purchase a low-risk security from a local broker that will pay $127.63 at the end of five years. A local bank is currently offering 5 percent interest on a five-year certificate of deposit (CD), and GroupWest's managers regard the security offered by the broker as having the same risk as the bank CD. The 5 percent interest rate available on the bank CD is GroupWest's *opportunity cost rate*. (Opportunity costs are discussed in detail in the next section of this chapter.) How much would GroupWest be willing to pay for the security that promises to pay $127.63 in five years?

Key Equation: Present Value of a Lump Sum
The present value of a lump sum (single value) can be found using a simple equation. For example, suppose $1,000 was expected to be received in three years and the appropriate interest (discount) rate was 10 percent. The present value would be $751.31:

$$PV_N = FV \div (1 + I)^N$$
$$PV_3 = \$1,000 \div (1.10)^3$$
$$= \$1,000 \div 1.10 \div 1.10 \div 1.10$$
$$= \$751.31.$$

Here, PV_N is the present value of a lump sum to be received N years in the future, FV is future value, and I is the discount rate. This equation can be solved with a regular calculator or a spreadsheet.

The future value example presented in the previous section showed that an initial amount of $100 invested at 5 percent per year would be worth $127.63 at the end of five years. Thus, GroupWest should be indifferent to the choice between $100 today and $127.63 at the end of five years. Today's $100 is defined as the *present value*, or *PV*, of $127.63 due in five years when the opportunity cost rate is 5 percent. If the price of the security being offered is exactly $100, GroupWest could buy it or turn it down because that is the security's "fair value." If the price is less than $100, GroupWest should buy it, while if the price is greater than $100, GroupWest should decline the offer.

Conceptually, the present value of a cash flow due N years in the future is the amount that, if it were on hand today, would grow to equal the future amount when compounded at the opportunity cost rate. Because $100 would grow to $127.63 in five years at a 5 percent interest rate, $100 is the present value of $127.63 due five years in the future when the opportunity cost rate is 5 percent. In effect, the present value tells us what amount would have to be invested to earn the opportunity cost rate. If the investment can be obtained for a lesser amount, a higher rate will be earned. If the investment costs more than the present value, the rate earned will be less than the opportunity cost rate.

Finding present values is called **discounting**, and it is simply the reverse of compounding: If *PV* is known, compound to find *FV*; if *FV* is known, discount to find *PV*. Here are the solution techniques used to solve this discounting problem:

discounting
The process of finding the current (present) value of a lump sum, an annuity, or a series of unequal cash flows.

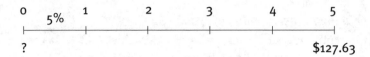

To develop the discounting equation, solve the compounding equation for *PV*:

$$\text{Compounding:} \quad FV_N = PV \times (1+I)^N.$$

$$\text{Discounting:} \quad PV = \frac{FV_N}{(1+I)^N}.$$

The equations show us that compounding problems are solved by multiplication, while discounting problems are solved by division.

Regular Calculator Solution
Enter $127.63 and divide it five times by 1.05:

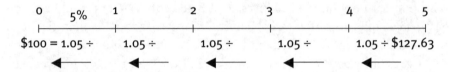

As shown by the arrows, discounting is moving left along a time line. As with compounding, the term *discounting* is descriptive. As we move left along a time line, the values get smaller, or *discount*, over time.

Spreadsheet Solution

	A	B	C	D
1				
2	5	Nper	Number of periods	
3	$ 127.63	Fv	Future value	
4	5.0%	Rate	Interest rate	
5				
6	$ 100.00	=A3/(1+A4)^A2 (entered into Cell A6)		
7				
8	$ 100.00	=PV(A4,A2,,–A3) (entered into Cell A8)		
9				
10				

One solution would be to enter the applicable formula, as shown to the right of cell A6: = A3/(1+A4)^A2. Here, the future value ($127.63) is contained in cell A3, the interest rate (0.05, which is displayed as 5%) in cell A4, and the number of periods (5) in cell A2. With this formula, present values can easily be calculated with different starting future amounts, interest rates, or number of years.

The function approach is illustrated in cell A8. First, move the cursor to that cell (the cell where you want the answer to appear). Then click on the Function Wizard, select "Financial" for the function category and "PV" (present value) for the function name, and click OK. On the next menu, enter A4 for Rate, A2 for Nper (number of periods), and –A3 for Fv. (Note that the Pmt and Type entries are left blank for this problem. Also, note that the cell address entered for Fv has a minus sign. This is necessary for the answer to be displayed as a positive number.) Finally, press OK and the result—$100.00—appears in cell A8.

---

1. What is discounting? How is it related to compounding?
2. What are the two techniques for solving lump sum discounting problems?
3. How does the present value of a lump sum to be received in the future change as the time is extended and as the interest rate increases?

Opportunity Costs

In the last section, the opportunity cost concept was used to set the discount rate on the time value analysis of GroupWest's investment opportunity. The opportunity cost concept plays a critical role in time value analysis. To illustrate, suppose an individual found the winning ticket for the Florida lottery and now has $1 million to invest. At first it might appear that this money has zero cost because its acquisition was purely a matter of luck. However, the winner has to think in terms of the opportunity costs involved. By using the funds to invest in one alternative—for example, in the stock of Quest Diagnostics (www.questdiagnostics.com)—the winner forgoes the opportunity to make some other investment—for example, buying US Treasury bonds. Thus, there is an **opportunity cost** associated with any investment planned for the $1 million, even though the investment capital (the lottery winnings) was "free." The concept of opportunity costs applies to any investment, whether in financial assets or real assets, regardless of the source of the investment funds.

Because one investment decision automatically negates all other possible investments with the same funds, the cash flows expected to be earned from any investment must be discounted at a rate that reflects the return

opportunity cost The cost associated with alternative uses of the same funds. For example, if money is used for one investment, it is no longer available for other uses, creating an opportunity cost.

that could be earned on forgone investment opportunities. The problem is that the number of forgone investment opportunities is virtually infinite, so which one should be chosen to establish the opportunity cost rate? The opportunity cost rate to be applied in time value analysis is the rate that could be earned on alternative investments **of similar risk**. It would not be logical to assign a low opportunity cost rate to a series of risky cash flows, or vice versa. This concept is one of the cornerstones of investment analysis, so it is worth repeating: **The opportunity cost (discount) rate applied to investment cash flows is the rate that could be earned on alternative investments of similar risk.**

It is important to recognize that the discounting process accounts for the opportunity cost of capital (i.e., the loss of use of the funds for other purposes). In effect, discounting a potential investment at, say, 10 percent produces a present value that provides a 10 percent return. Thus, if the investment can be obtained for less than its present value, it will earn more than its opportunity cost rate and hence is a good investment. Alternatively, if the cost of the investment is greater than its present value, it will earn less than the opportunity cost rate and hence, from a financial perspective, is a bad investment.

It is also important to note that the opportunity cost rate does not depend on the source of the funds to be invested. Rather, **the primary determinant of this rate is the riskiness of the cash flows being discounted.** Thus, the same 10 percent opportunity cost rate would be applied to this potential investment regardless of whether the funds to be used for the investment were won in a lottery, taken out of petty cash, or obtained by selling some securities.

Generally, opportunity cost rates are obtained by looking at rates that could be earned—or more precisely, rates that are expected to be earned—on securities such as stocks or bonds. Securities are usually chosen to set opportunity cost rates because their expected returns are more easily estimated than rates of return on real assets such as hospital beds, magnetic resonance imaging (MRI) machines, outpatient surgery centers, and the like. Furthermore, securities traded in efficient markets generally provide the minimum return appropriate for the amount of risk assumed, so securities returns provide a good benchmark for other investments (discussed in chapter 12).

To illustrate the opportunity cost concept, assume that Oakview Community Hospital is considering building a nursing home. The first step in the financial analysis is to forecast the cash flows that the nursing home is expected to produce, including the cost of building and operating the home as well as the expected patient service revenues. These cash flows, then, must be discounted at some opportunity cost rate to determine their present value.

Would the hospital's opportunity cost rate be (1) the expected rate of return on a bank CD; (2) the expected rate of return on the stock of Genesis Health-Care (www.genesishcc.com), which operates a large number of nursing homes and assisted living centers; or (3) the expected rate of return on pork belly futures? (Futures are investments that involve commodity contracts for delivery at some future time.) The answer is the expected rate of return on Genesis HealthCare stock because that is the rate of return available to the hospital on **alternative investments of similar risk**. Bank CDs are low-risk investments, so they would understate the opportunity cost rate in owning a nursing home. Conversely, pork belly futures are high-risk investments, so that rate of return is probably too high to apply to Oakview's nursing home investment.[1]

For Your Consideration

Bastiat's Parable

The parable of the broken window was written by French political economist Frederic Bastiat in 1850. The parable, also known as the glazier's fallacy, goes something like this:

Suppose the careless child of a shopkeeper happens to break a pane of glass in the shop's front window. A bystander to the accident offers the unfortunate shopkeeper this consolation: Everybody must live—what would become of glaziers (window repairers) if panes of glass were never broken? The glazier comes, replaces the pane, receives $100 (as valued today) for his work, and, in his heart, blesses the careless child. This observation prompts the bystander to conclude that it is a good thing to break windows. After all, it causes money to circulate to the benefit of the entire economy.

At this point, Bastiat raises a red flag. "The bystander's observation is flawed," he says, "because the theory is confined to that which is seen; it takes no account of that which is not seen. Because the shopkeeper has spent $100 on the window, it is lost to him forever. If he had not had a window to replace, he might have bought new shoes or added another book to his library. In short, he would have employed his $100 in some other way, which this accident has prevented."

What do you think of Bastiat's logic? Is he correct, or is breaking windows good for society? Should the $100 expenditure be dictated by the child or by the father? How does this parable relate to the opportunity cost concept?

Note that the source of the funds used for the nursing home investment is not relevant to the analysis. Oakview may obtain the needed funds by borrowing, by soliciting contributions, or by using excess cash accumulated from profit retention. (If Oakview were investor owned, the funds could be obtained by selling more stock.) **The discount rate applied to the nursing home cash flows depends only on the riskiness of those cash flows and the returns available on alternative investments of similar risk, not on the source of the investment funds.**

At this point, you may question the ability of real-world analysts to assess the riskiness of a cash flow stream or to choose an opportunity cost rate with any confidence. Fortunately, the process is not as difficult as it may appear here because businesses have benchmarks that can be used as starting points. (Chapter 13 contains a discussion of how benchmark opportunity cost rates are established for capital investments, while chapter 15 presents a detailed discussion of how the riskiness of a cash flow stream can be assessed.)

SELF-TEST QUESTIONS

1. Why does an investment have an opportunity cost rate even when the funds employed have no explicit cost?
2. How are opportunity cost rates established?
3. Does the opportunity cost rate depend on the source of the investment funds?

annuity
A series of payments of a fixed amount for a specified number of equal periods.

payment (PMT)
In time value analysis, the dollar amount of an annuity cash flow.

ordinary (regular) annuity
An annuity with payments occurring at the end of each period.

annuity due
An annuity with payments occurring at the beginning of each period.

Annuities

Whereas a lump sum is a single value, an **annuity** is a series of equal payments made at fixed intervals for a specified number of periods. Annuity **payments**, which are given the symbol PMT or Pmt, can occur at the beginning or end of each period. If the payments occur at the end of each period, as they typically do, the annuity is an **ordinary (regular) annuity**. If payments are made at the beginning of each period, the annuity is an **annuity due**. Because ordinary annuities are far more common in time value problems, when the term *annuity* is used in this book (or in general), payments are assumed to occur at the end of each period. Furthermore, we begin our discussion of annuities by focusing on ordinary annuities.

Ordinary Annuities

If Meridian Clinic were to deposit $100 at the end of each year for three years in an account that paid 5 percent interest per year, how much would Meridian accumulate at the end of three years? The answer to this question is the *future value* of the annuity.

Regular Calculator Solution

One approach to the problem is to compound each individual cash flow through year 3 and then sum the resultant future values.

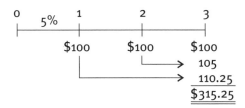

```
0         1        2         3
|---5%----|--------|---------|
         $100    $100     $100
           |        └──────→  105
           └───────────────→  110.25
                             $315.25
```

The future value of any annuity is defined to occur at the end of the final period. Thus, for regular annuities, the future value coincides with the last payment.

Spreadsheet Solution

	A	B	C	D
1				
2	3	Nper	Number of periods	
3	$ (100.00)	Pmt	Payment	
4	5.0%	Rate	Interest rate	
5				
6				
7				
8	$ 315.25	=FV(A4,A2,A3) (entered into Cell A8)		
9				
10				

Here, we again use the future value function, but now we use the payment (Pmt) entry in the Function Wizard to recognize that the problem involves annuities. Place the cursor in cell A8. Then, click on the Function Wizard, select Financial for the function category and FV (future value) for the function name, and press OK. On the next menu, enter A4 for Rate, A2 for Nper (number of periods), and A3 for Pmt. (Note that the Pv and Type entries are left blank for this problem.) Finally, press OK and the result—$315.25—appears in cell A8.

Suppose that Meridian was offered the following alternatives: a three-year annuity with payments of $100 at the end of each year or a lump sum payment today. Meridian has no need for the money during the next three years. If it accepted the annuity, it would deposit the payments in an account that pays 5 percent interest per year. Similarly, the lump sum payment would be deposited into the same account. How large must the lump sum payment be today to make it equivalent to the annuity? The answer to this question is the *present value of the annuity*, which for ordinary annuities occurs one period prior to the first payment.

Regular Calculator Solution

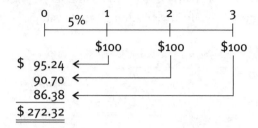

Spreadsheet Solution

	A		B	C	D
1					
2		3	Nper	Number of periods	
3	$	(100.00)	Pmt	Payment	
4		5.0%	Rate	Interest rate	
5					
6					
7					
8	$	272.32	=PV(A4,A2,A3) (entered into Cell A8)		
9					
10					

Here we use the present value function, but again with a payment entry to recognize that the problem involves annuities. Place the cursor in cell A8. Then click on the Function Wizard, select Financial for the function category and PV for the function name, and press OK. On the next menu, enter A4 for Rate, A2 for Nper (number of periods), and A3 for Pmt. (Note that the Fv and Type entries are left blank for this problem.) Finally, press OK and the result—$272.32—appears in cell A8.

An important application of the annuity concept relates to loans with constant payments, such as mortgages, auto loans, and many bank loans to businesses. Such loans are examined in more depth in the chapter 9 supplement.

Annuities Due

If the three $100 payments in the previous example had been made at the beginning

For Your Consideration

If You Win the Lottery, Should You Take the Annuity or the Cash?

Suppose you win the Powerball lottery with a jackpot of $590,500,000. With odds reported at 1 in 175,223,510, you would be very lucky indeed. Winners of Powerball have two choices for how they can receive their winnings. They can receive 30 annual payments (in your case, 30 × $19,683,333) or one lump sum (in your case, $370,896,781). Which option should you choose?

The first step is to determine the discount rate that makes the present value of the annuity due equal to the lump sum; in other words, what is the rate of return that makes the present value

(continued)

of each year, the annuity would have been an *annuity due*. Here are the solution techniques for the **future value of an annuity due**.

Regular Calculator Solution

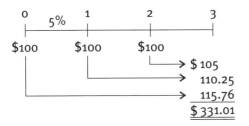

The future value of an annuity due occurs one period after the final payment, whereas the future value of a regular annuity coincides with the final payment. Thus, compared with an ordinary annuity, all the cash flows of an annuity due are compounded for one additional period, and hence the future value of an annuity due is greater than the future value of a similar ordinary annuity by $(1 + I)$. This logic leads to an alternative approach for obtaining the future value of an annuity due:

$$FV(\text{Annuity due}) = FV \text{ of an ordinary annuity} \times (1 + I)$$
$$= \$315.25 \times 1.05 = \$331.01.$$

(continued from previous page)

of 30 annual payments of $19,683,333 equal to the lump sum of $370,896,781? It turns out that a discount rate of 3.59 percent makes the present value of the annuity due equal to the lump sum.

Now what? If you believe that you can achieve an average annual rate of return greater than 3.59 percent through careful investing, you should choose the lump sum and invest it accordingly. However, if you believe that you are unlikely to achieve an average annual rate of return of 3.59 percent, you should choose the annuity. Of course, there are many other financial factors to consider, such as taxes, liquidity, and other assets and liabilities. There are nonfinancial factors as well, such as your family circumstances and age. An 80-year-old Powerball winner likely has a different attitude toward a 30-year annuity than a 20-year-old winner. What do you think? What would you do if you were the winner?

Spreadsheet Solution

	A	B	C	D
1				
2	3	Nper	Number of periods	
3	$ (100.00)	Pmt	Payment	
4	5.0%	Rate	Interest rate	
5				
6	$ 331.01	=FV(A4,A2,A3,,1) (entered into Cell A6)		
7				
8	$ 331.01	=FV(A4,A2,A3)*(1+A4) (entered into Cell A8)		
9				
10				

One approach (shown in cell A6) is to use the spreadsheet future value (FV) function but to enter "1" for Type (as opposed to leaving the cell blank).

Now the spreadsheet treats the entries as an annuity due, and $331.01 is displayed as the answer.

Alternatively, note that the solution is the same as for an ordinary annuity, except the result must be multiplied by (1 + Rate), which is (1 + A4) in this example. This solution is given in cell A8. The result—$331.01—is the future value of the annuity due. Here are the solution techniques for the **present value of an annuity due.**

Regular Calculator Solution

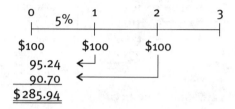

Because the payments are shifted to the left, each payment is discounted for one less year. Thus, the present value of an annuity due is larger than that of a similar regular annuity.

The present value of an annuity due can be thought of as the present value of an ordinary annuity that is compounded for one additional period, so it also can be found as follows:

$$PV(\text{Annuity due}) = PV \text{ of an ordinary annuity} \times (1 + I)$$
$$= \$272.32 \times 1.05 = \$285.94.$$

Spreadsheet Solution

	A	B	C	D
1				
2	3	Nper	Number of periods	
3	$ (100.00)	Pmt	Payment	
4	5.0%	Rate	Interest rate	
5				
6	$ 285.94	=PV(A4,A2,A3,,1) (entered into Cell A6)		
7				
8	$ 285.94	=PV(A4,A2,A3)*(1+A4) (entered into Cell A8)		
9				
10				

As with future value, one approach (shown in cell A6) is to use the spreadsheet present value (PV) function but to enter "1" for Type (as opposed to leaving the cell blank). Now the spreadsheet treats the entries as an annuity due, and $285.94 is displayed as the answer.

The alternative solution is the same as for an ordinary annuity, except the function in cell A8 is multiplied by (1 + A4). The result—$285.94—is the present value of the annuity due.

1. What is an annuity?

2. What is the difference between an ordinary annuity and an annuity due?

3. Which annuity has the greater future value: an ordinary annuity or an annuity due? Why?

4. Which annuity has the greater present value: an ordinary annuity or an annuity due? Why?

Perpetuities

Most annuities call for payments to be made over some finite period of time—for example, $100 per year for three years. However, some annuities go on indefinitely, or perpetually, and hence they are called **perpetuities**. The present value of a perpetuity is found as follows:

perpetuity
An annuity that lasts forever (has no maturity date).

$$PV(\text{Perpetuity}) = \frac{\text{Payment}}{\text{Interest rate}} = \frac{PMT}{I}.$$

Perpetuities can be illustrated by some securities issued by the Canadian Healthcare Board. Each security promises to pay $100 annually in perpetuity (forever). What would each security be worth if the opportunity cost rate, or discount rate, is 10 percent? The answer is $1,000:

$$PV(\text{Perpetuity}) = \frac{\$100}{0.10} = \$1,000.$$

	A	B	C	D
1				
2				
3	$ 100.00	Pmt	Payment	
4	10.0%	Rate	Interest rate	
5				
6				
7				
8	$ 1,000.00	=A3/A4 (entered into Cell A8)		
9				
10				

Using a spreadsheet, simply enter the perpetuity formula into a cell, as shown here in cell A8.

Suppose that interest rates, and hence the opportunity cost rate, rose to 15 percent. What would happen to the security's value? The interest rate increase would decrease the security's value to $666.67:

$$PV(\text{Perpetuity}) = \frac{\$100}{0.15} = \$666.67.$$

Key Equation: Present Value of a Perpetuity

The present value of a perpetuity (never-ending annuity) can be found using a simple equation. For example, suppose a $1,000 annual ordinary annuity had payments that lasted forever and that the appropriate interest (discount) rate was 8 percent. The present value of the perpetuity would be $12,500:

$$
\begin{aligned}
PV &= \text{Payment} \div \text{Interest rate} \\
&= \$1,000 \div 0.08 \\
&= \$12,500.
\end{aligned}
$$

Because the payments last forever, the future value of a perpetuity is undefined.

Assume that interest rates fell to 5 percent. The rate decrease would increase the perpetuity's value to $2,000:

$$PV(\text{Perpetuity}) = \frac{\$100}{0.05} = \$2,000.$$

As illustrated above, the value of a perpetuity changes dramatically when interest rates (opportunity costs) change. All securities' values are affected when such changes occur, but some types, such as perpetuities and long-term government bonds, are more sensitive to interest rate changes than others. Conversely, securities such as short-term government bonds (T-bills) and one-year CDs are affected much less when interest rates change. The risks associated with interest rate changes are discussed in more detail in chapter 11.

SELF-TEST QUESTIONS

1. What is a perpetuity?
2. What happens to the value of a perpetuity when interest rates increase or decrease?

Uneven Cash Flow Streams

The definition of an annuity (or perpetuity) includes the words "constant amount," so annuities involve payments that are the same in every period. Although some financial decisions, such as bond valuation, do involve constant payments, most important healthcare financial analyses involve uneven, or nonconstant, cash flows. For example, the financial evaluation of a proposed outpatient clinic or MRI facility rarely involves constant cash flows.

In general, the term *lump sum* is used with a single dollar amount, the term *payment (PMT)* is reserved for annuities in which there are multiple constant dollar amounts, and the term *cash flow (CF)* is used when there is a series of uneven lump sum amounts.

Present Value

The present value of an uneven cash flow stream is calculated as the sum of the present values of the individual cash flows in the stream. For example, suppose that Wilson Radiology Group is considering the purchase of a new X-ray machine. The group's managers forecast that the operation of the new machine would produce the following stream of cash inflows (in thousands of dollars):

What is the present value of the new X-ray machine investment if the appropriate discount (opportunity cost) rate is 10 percent?

Regular Calculator Solution

The present value of each lump sum cash flow can be found using a regular calculator, and then these values are summed to find the present value of the stream—$580,950:

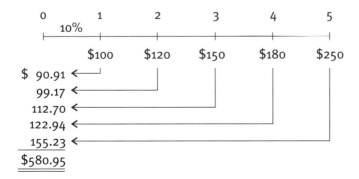

Spreadsheet Solution

	A		B	C	D
1					
2		10.0%	Rate	Interest rate	
3					
4	$	100	Value 1	Year 1 CF	
5	$	120	Value 1	Year 2 CF	
6	$	150	Value 1	Year 3 CF	
7	$	180	Value 1	Year 4 CF	
8	$	250	Value 1	Year 5 CF	
9					
10	$	580.95	=NPV(A2,A4:A8) (entered into Cell A10)		

The NPV (net present value) function calculates the present value of a stream, called a spreadsheet *range*, of cash flows. First, the cash flow values must be entered into consecutive cells in the spreadsheet, as shown above in cells A4–A8. Next, the discount (opportunity cost) rate must be placed into a cell (as in cell A2). Then, place the cursor in cell A10, use the Function Wizard to select "Financial" and "NPV," and press OK. On the next menu, enter A2 as Rate and A4:A8 as Value 1. Press OK, and the value $580.95 is displayed in the cell. (Note that the Value 1 entry is the range of cash flows contained in cells A4–A8.)

The NPV function assumes that cash flows occur at the **end** of each period, so NPV is calculated as of the **beginning** of the period of the first cash flow specified in the range, which is one period before that cash flow occurs. Because the cash flow specified as the first flow in the range is a year 1 value, the calculated NPV occurs at the beginning of year 1, or the end of year 0, which is correct for this illustration. However, if a year 0 cash flow is included in the range, the NPV would be calculated at the beginning of year 0 (the end of year –1), which typically is incorrect. This problem is addressed in the next major section of this chapter.

Future Value

The future value of an uneven cash flow stream is found by compounding each payment to the end of the stream and then summing the future values.

Regular Calculator Solution

The future value of each lump sum cash flow can be found using a regular calculator. Then, these values are summed to find the future value of the stream—$935.63:

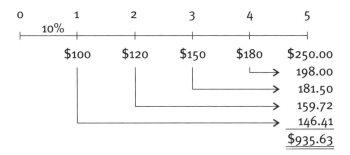

Spreadsheet Solution

Most spreadsheet programs do not have a function that computes the future value of an uneven cash flow stream. However, future values can be found by building a formula in a cell that replicates the regular calculator solution.

1. Give two examples of financial decisions that typically involve uneven cash flows.
2. Describe how present values of uneven cash flow streams are calculated using a regular calculator and using a spreadsheet.
3. What is meant by *net present value?*

Using Time Value Analysis to Measure Return on Investment

In most investments, an individual or a business spends cash today with the expectation of receiving cash in the future. The financial attractiveness of such investments is measured by *return on investment (ROI)*, or just *return*. There are two basic ways of expressing ROI: in dollar terms and in percentage terms.

To illustrate the concept, let's reexamine the cash flows expected to be received if Wilson Radiology Group buys its new X-ray machine (shown on the time line in thousands of dollars). In the last section, we determined that the present value of these flows, when discounted at a 10 percent rate, is $580,950:

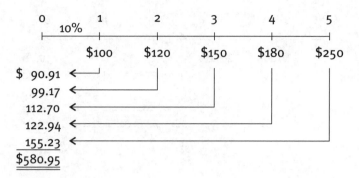

Dollar Return

The $580,950 just calculated represents the present value of the cash flows that the X-ray machine is **expected** to provide to the group, assuming a 10 percent discount (opportunity cost) rate. This result tells us that a 10 percent return on a $580,950 investment would produce a cash flow stream that is identical to one being discounted.

To measure the *dollar return* on the investment, the cost of the X-ray machine must be compared with the present value of the expected benefits (the cash inflows). If the machine will cost $500,000 and the present value of the inflows is $580,950, then the expected dollar return on the machine is $580,950 – $500,000 = $80,950. This measure of dollar return incorporates time value, and hence opportunity costs, through the discounting process. The opportunity cost inherent in the use of the $500,000 is accounted for because the 10 percent discount rate reflects the return that could be earned on alternative investments of similar risk. By virtue of the $80,950 excess return, usually called **net present value**, the X-ray machine has an expected present value that is $80,950 more than would result if it had only a 10 percent return, which is the opportunity cost rate. Thus, the X-ray machine makes sense financially because it creates an excess dollar return for the hospital. The dollar return calculation can be accomplished in one step by adding the cost of the X-ray machine to the time line:

net present value (NPV)
A project return-on-investment (ROI) metric that measures the time value–adjusted expected dollar return.

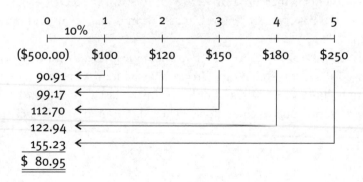

Spreadsheet Solution

The cost of the machine must be added to the cash flow data. Here, it is added to the spreadsheet range.

Note that the situation here is the same as in the previous cash flow stream, except that there is an initial investment outlay of $500 added in cell A3. Because the NPV of the cash inflows in cells A4 through A8 represents the Value 1 period before the first (A4) cash flow, all that must be done is to add the investment outlay to the calculated NPV. This is done in cell A10 above by adding A3 to the NPV function, and the new result—$80.95—appears.

	A	B	C	D
1				
2	10.0%	Rate	Interest rate	
3	$ (500)		Year 0 CF	
4	$ 100	Value 1	Year 1 CF	
5	$ 120	Value 1	Year 2 CF	
6	$ 150	Value 1	Year 3 CF	
7	$ 180	Value 1	Year 4 CF	
8	$ 250	Value 1	Year 5 CF	
9				
10	$ 80.95	=NPV(A2,A4:A8)+A3 (entered into Cell A10)		

Rate of Return

The second way to measure the ROI of an investment is by the *rate of return*, or *percentage return*. This measures the interest rate that must be earned on the investment outlay to generate the expected cash inflows. In other words, this measure provides the expected periodic rate of return on the investment. If the cash flows are annual, as in this example, the rate of return is an annual rate. In effect, we are solving for I—the interest rate that equates the sum of the present values of the cash inflows to the dollar amount of the cash outlay.

Mathematically, if the sum of the present values of the cash inflows equals the investment outlay, the NPV of the investment is forced to $0. This relationship is shown here:

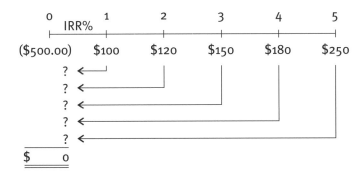

For Your Consideration
What Is the True Rate of Return?

Most investors do not give a lot of thought when expressing investment returns. For example, assume you made an investment of $1,000 that returned $1,100 after one year. Thus, you earned $100 on $1,000, for a rate of return of 10 percent. Sounds good, doesn't it?

But now assume that the inflation rate over the investment period was 4 percent. Because inflation erodes the purchasing power of money, you would have had to earn $40 on your $1,000 investment to just hold your own, so the real (after adjusting for inflation) dollar return was $100 − $40 = $60, giving a real rate of return of 6 percent.

What about taxes? If you were in the 30 percent federal-plus-state tax bracket and the return was fully taxable, 0.30 × $100 = $30 would go into Uncle Sam's pocket, leaving you with a usable (true) dollar return of $100 − $40 (inflation adjustment) − $30 (tax adjustment) = $30, which translates to a true rate of return of just 3 percent.

Disappointing? You bet! Your 10 percent *nominal* rate of return withered away to a mere 3 percent when inflation and taxes were considered. The truth is that nominal returns are more comforting to investors, but they do not give a realistic view of how much usable return is actually earned.

How should investment returns be measured? Do financial services companies have an incentive to provide nominal rather than true rates of return in their advertising? Should they be required to provide nominal, real, and true rates of return?

internal rate of return (IRR)
A return-on-investment (ROI) metric that measures expected rate of (percentage) return.

Note that the rate of return on an investment, particularly an investment in plant or equipment, typically is called the **internal rate of return (IRR)**, a somewhat archaic term that often is used instead of ROI, or just rate of return. Although a trial-and-error procedure could be used on a regular calculator to determine the rate of return, it is better to use a spreadsheet.

Spreadsheet Solution

	A	B	C	D
1				
2	$ (500)	Values	Year 0 CF	
3	$ 100	Values	Year 1 CF	
4	$ 120	Values	Year 2 CF	
5	$ 150	Values	Year 3 CF	
6	$ 180	Values	Year 4 CF	
7	$ 250	Values	Year 5 CF	
8				
9	15.3%	=IRR(A2:A7) (entered into Cell A10)		

The IRR function is used to calculate rate of return. Choose Financial and IRR on the Function Wizard, then enter A2:A7 as Values. The result—15.3%—appears in cell A9, the cell that has the IRR function in it.

The IRR of 15.3 percent tells the group's managers that the expected rate of return on the X-ray machine exceeds the opportunity cost rate by 15.3 – 10.0 = 5.3 percentage points. The expected rate of return is higher than that available on alternative investments of similar risk (the required rate of return), and hence the X-ray machine makes financial sense. Note that both the dollar (NPV) return and the percentage (IRR) return indicate that the X-ray machine should be acquired. In general, the two methods lead to the same conclusion regarding the financial attractiveness of an investment.

Financial returns are discussed in much greater detail in chapters 11, 12, and 14. For now, an understanding of the basic concept is sufficient.

SELF-TEST QUESTIONS

1. What does the term *return on investment* mean?
2. Differentiate between dollar return and rate of return.
3. Is the calculation of financial return an application of time value analysis? Explain your answer.
4. What role does the opportunity cost rate play in calculating financial returns?

Semiannual and Other Compounding Periods

In all the examples thus far, we assumed that interest is earned (compounded) once a year, or annually. This is called *annual compounding*. Suppose, however, that Meridian Clinic puts $100 into a bank account that pays 6 percent annual interest, but it is compounded *semiannually*. How much would the clinic accumulate at the end of one year, two years, or some other period? Semiannual compounding means that interest is paid every six months, so interest is earned more often than under annual compounding.

The Effect of Semiannual Compounding
To illustrate semiannual compounding, assume that the $100 is placed into the account for three years. The following situation occurs under *annual* compounding:

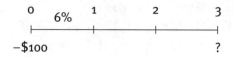

$$FV_N = PV \times (1 + I)^N = \$100 \times (1.06)^3.$$

Regular Calculator Solution

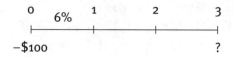

Spreadsheet Solution

	A	B	C	D
1				
2	3	Nper	Number of periods	
3	$ 100.00	Pv	Present value	
4	6.0%	Rate	Interest rate	
5				
6	$ 119.10	=100*(1.06)^3 (entered into Cell A6)		
7				
8	$ 119.10	=A3*(1+A4)^A2 (entered into Cell A8)		
9				
10	$ 119.10	=FV(A4,A2,,-A3) (entered into Cell A10)		

Now, consider what happens under semiannual compounding. Because interest rates usually are stated as annual rates, this situation would be described as 6 percent interest, compounded semiannually. With semiannual compounding, $N = 2 \times 3 = 6$ semiannual periods, and $I = 6 \div 2 = 3\%$ per semiannual period. Here is the solution:

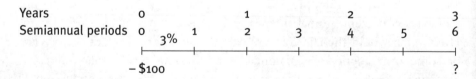

$$FV_N = PV \times (1 + I)^N = \$100 \times (1.03)^6.$$

Regular Calculator Solution

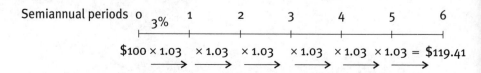

Spreadsheet Solution

	A	B	C	D
1				
2	6	Nper	Number of periods	
3	$ 100.00	Pv	Present value	
4	3.0%	Rate	Interest rate	
5				
6	$ 119.41	=100*(1.03)^6 (entered into Cell A6)		
7				
8	$ 119.41	=A3*(1+A4)^A2 (entered into Cell A8)		
9				
10	$ 119.41	=FV(A4,A2,,-A3) (entered into Cell A10)		

The $100 deposit grows to $119.41 under semiannual compounding, but it grows to only $119.10 under annual compounding. This result occurs because interest on interest is being earned more frequently under semiannual compounding.

Stated Versus Effective Interest Rates

Throughout the economy, different compounding periods are used for different types of investments. For example, bank accounts often compound interest monthly or daily, most bonds pay interest semiannually, and stocks generally pay quarterly dividends.[2] Furthermore, the cash flows that stem from capital investments such as hospital beds or diagnostic equipment can be analyzed in monthly, quarterly, or annual periods or some other interval. To properly compare time value analyses with different compounding periods, they need to be on equivalent periods, which leads to a discussion of stated versus effective interest rates.

The *stated interest rate* in Meridian's semiannual compounding example is 6 percent. That is the rate stated in the contract with the bank. Note that the stated rate is also called the **nominal rate**. The **effective annual rate (EAR)** is the rate that produces the same ending (future) value under annual compounding. In the example, the effective annual rate is the rate that would produce a future value of $119.41 at the end of year 3 under annual compounding. The solution is 6.09 percent, as found here using a spreadsheet:

nominal (stated) interest rate
The interest rate stated in a debt contract; it does not reflect the effect of any compounding that occurs more frequently than annually.

effective annual rate (EAR)
The interest rate that, under annual compounding, produces the same future value as was produced by more frequent compounding.

	A	B	C	D
1				
2				
3	3	Nper	Number of periods	
4	$ (100.00)	Pv	Present value	
5	$ 119.41	Fv	Future value	
6				
7				
8	6.09%	=RATE(A3,A4,A5) (entered into Cell A8)		
9				
10				

Thus, if one bank savings account offered 6 percent stated (nominal) interest with semiannual compounding while another offered 6.09 percent with annual compounding, they both would be paying the identical effective annual rate because their ending values would be the same:

Semiannual periods 0   1   2   3   4   5   6
           3%

$100 × 1.03 × 1.03   × 1.03   × 1.03 × 1.03 × 1.03 = $119.41

Years   0   1   2   3
        6.09%

$100 × 1.0609 × 1.0609 × 1.0609 = $119.41

In general, the EAR can be determined, given the stated rate and number of compounding periods per year, by using this equation:

$$EAR = (1 + I_{Stated}/M)^M - 1.0,$$

where I_{Stated} is the stated (annual) interest rate and M is the number of compounding periods per year. The term I_{Stated}/M is the **periodic interest rate**, so the EAR equation can be recast as follows:

periodic interest rate
In time value of money analysis, the interest rate per period; for example, 2 percent quarterly interest, which equals an 8 percent stated (annual) rate.

$$EAR = (1 + Periodic\ rate)^M - 1.0.$$

To illustrate the use of the EAR equation, the EAR, when the stated rate is 6 percent and semiannual compounding occurs, is 6.09 percent:

$$EAR = (1 + 0.06/2)^2 - 1.0$$
$$= (1.03)^2 - 1.0$$
$$= 1.0609 - 1.0 = 0.0609 = 6.09\%,$$

which confirms the answer that we obtained previously.

As shown in the preceding calculations, semiannual compounding—or for that matter, any compounding that occurs more than once a year—can be handled in two ways. First, the input variables can be expressed as periodic variables rather than annual variables. In the Meridian Clinic example, use N = 6 periods rather than N = 3 years, and I = 3% per period rather than I = 6% per year. Second, find the effective annual rate and then use this rate as an annual rate over the number of years. In the example, use I = 6.09% and N = 3 years.

For another illustration of the EAR concept, consider the interest rate charged on credit cards. Many banks charge 1.0 percent per month and, in their advertising, state that the annual percentage rate (APR) is 12 percent. (*APR* and *annual percentage yield* are terms defined in truth-in-lending and truth-in-savings laws.) APR is defined as Periodic rate × Number of compounding periods per year, so it ignores the consequences of compounding. Although the APR on a credit card with interest charges of 1.0 percent per month is 1.0% × 12 = 12%, the true effective annual rate is 12.7 percent. Consequently, the true cost rate to credit card users is the effective annual rate of 12.7 percent:

$$EAR = (1 + \text{Periodic rate})^M - 1.0$$
$$= (1.01)^{12} - 1.0 = 0.127 = 12.7\%$$

Key Equation: Effective Annual Rate

The effective annual rate (EAR) is used to compare rates of return on investments that have different compounding periods. Suppose that a bank CD pays 8 percent interest compounded quarterly. Its EAR is 8.24 percent:

$$EAR = (1 + I_{Stated}/M)^M - 1.0$$
$$= (1 + 0.08/4)^4 - 1.0 = (1.02)^4 - 1.0$$
$$= 1.0824 - 1.0 = 0.0824$$
$$= 8.24\%.$$

Here, I_{Stated} is the interest rate stated in the contract and M is the number of compounding periods per year.

Time value analysis will be applied in subsequent chapters, so it is important that readers feel comfortable with this material before moving ahead.

SELF-TEST QUESTIONS

1. What changes must be made in the calculations to determine the future value of an amount being compounded at 8 percent semiannually versus one being compounded annually at 8 percent?
2. Why is semiannual compounding better than annual compounding from an investor's standpoint?
3. How does the effective annual rate differ from the stated rate?
4. How does the periodic rate differ from the stated rate?

Key Concepts

Financial decisions often involve situations in which future cash flows must be valued. The process of valuing future cash flows is called time value analysis. The key concepts of this chapter are as follows:

- *Compounding* is the process of determining the *future value (FV)* of a lump sum or a series of payments.
- *Discounting* is the process of finding the *present value (PV)* of a future lump sum or series of payments.
- An *annuity* is a series of equal, periodic *payments (PMT)* for a specified number of periods.
- An annuity that has payments that occur at the end of each period is called an *ordinary* annuity.
- If each annuity payment occurs at the beginning of the period rather than at the end, the annuity is an *annuity due*.
- A *perpetuity* is an annuity that lasts forever.
- If an analysis that involves more than one lump sum does not meet the definition of an annuity, it is called an *uneven cash flow stream*.
- The financial consequence of an investment is measured by *return on investment (ROI)*, or just *return*, which can be expressed either in *dollar terms* or in *percentage (rate of return) terms*.
- The *stated rate* is the annual rate normally quoted in financial contracts.
- The *periodic rate* equals the stated rate divided by the number of compounding periods per year.
- If compounding occurs more frequently than once a year, it is often necessary to calculate the *effective annual rate*, which is the rate that produces the same results under annual compounding as obtained with more frequent compounding.

Questions

9.1. a. What is an opportunity cost rate?
      b. How is this rate used in time value analysis?
      c. Is this rate a single number that is used in all situations?

9.2. What is the difference between a lump sum, an annuity, and an unequal cash flow stream?

9.3. Great Lakes Health Network's net income increased from $3.2 million in 2010 to $6.4 million in 2020. The total growth rate over the ten years is 100 percent, while the annual growth rate is only about 7.2 percent, which is much less than 100 percent divided by ten years.

   a. Why is the annual growth rate less than the total growth rate divided by ten?

   b. Which growth rate has more meaning—the total rate over ten years or the annualized rate?

9.4. Would you rather have a savings account that pays 5 percent compounded semiannually or one that pays 5 percent compounded daily? Explain your answer.

9.5. The present value of a perpetuity is equal to the payment divided by the opportunity cost (interest) rate: $PV = PMT \div I$. What is the future value of a perpetuity?

9.6. When a loan is amortized, what happens over time to the size of the total payment, interest payment, and principal payment? (Hint: This question covers material contained in the chapter supplement.)

9.7. Explain the difference between the stated rate, periodic rate, and effective annual rate.

9.8. What are three techniques for solving time value problems?

9.9. Explain the concept of return on investment (ROI) and the two different approaches to measuring it.

Problems

9.1. Find the following values for a lump sum assuming annual compounding:

   a. The future value of $500 invested at 8 percent for one year

   b. The future value of $500 invested at 8 percent for five years

   c. The present value of $500 to be received in one year when the opportunity cost rate is 8 percent

   d. The present value of $500 to be received in five years when the opportunity cost rate is 8 percent

9.2. Repeat problem 9.1, but assume the following compounding conditions:

   a. Semiannual

   b. Quarterly

9.3. What is the effective annual rate (EAR) if the stated rate is 8 percent and compounding occurs semiannually? Quarterly?

9.4. Find the following values assuming a regular, or ordinary, annuity:

a. The present value of $400 per year for ten years at 10 percent
b. The future value of $400 per year for ten years at 10 percent
c. The present value of $200 per year for five years at 5 percent
d. The future value of $200 per year for five years at 5 percent

9.5. Repeat problem 9.4, but assume the annuities are annuities due.

9.6. Consider the following uneven cash flow stream:

Year	Cash Flow
0	$ 0
1	250
2	400
3	500
4	600
5	600

a. What is the present (year 0) value if the opportunity cost (discount) rate is 10 percent?
b. Add an outflow (or cost) of $1,000 at year 0. What is the present value (or net present value) of the stream?

9.7. Consider another uneven cash flow stream:

Year	Cash Flow
0	$2,000
1	2,000
2	0
3	1,500
4	2,500
5	4,000

a. What is the present (year 0) value of the cash flow stream if the opportunity cost rate is 10 percent?
b. What is the future (year 5) value of the cash flow stream if the cash flows are invested in an account that pays 10 percent annually?
c. What cash flow today (year 0), in lieu of the $2,000 cash flow, would be needed to accumulate $20,000 at the end of year 5?

(Assume that the cash flows for years 1 through 5 remain the same.)

d. Time value analysis involves either discounting or compounding cash flows. Many healthcare financial management decisions—such as bond refunding, capital investment, and lease versus buy—involve discounting projected future cash flows. What factors must executives consider when choosing a discount rate to apply to forecast cash flows?

9.8. What is the present value of a perpetuity of $100 per year if the appropriate discount rate is 7 percent? Suppose that interest rates doubled in the economy and the appropriate discount rate is now 14 percent. What would happen to the present value of the perpetuity?

9.9. Assume that you just won $35 million in the Florida lottery, and hence the state will pay you 20 annual payments of $1.75 million each beginning immediately. If the rate of return on securities of similar risk to the lottery earnings (e.g., the rate on 20-year US Treasury bonds) is 6 percent, what is the present value of your winnings?

9.10. An investment that you are considering promises to pay $2,000 semiannually for the next two years, beginning six months from now. You have determined that the appropriate opportunity cost (discount) rate is 8 percent, compounded quarterly. What is the value of this investment?

9.11. Consider the following investment cash flows:

Year	Cash Flow
0	($1,000)
1	250
2	400
3	500
4	600
5	600

a. What is the return expected on this investment measured in dollar terms if the opportunity cost rate is 10 percent?

b. Provide an explanation, in economic terms, of your answer.

c. What is the return on this investment measured in percentage terms?

d. Should this investment be made? Explain your answer.

9.12. Everly Healthcare has just borrowed $1,000,000 on a five-year, annual payment term loan at a 15 percent rate. The first payment is due one year from now. Construct the amortization schedule for this loan. (Hint: This problem covers material contained in the chapter supplement.)

9.13. Assume that $10,000 was invested in the stock of General Medical Corporation with the intention of selling after one year. The stock pays no dividends, so the entire return will be based on the price of the stock when sold. The opportunity cost of capital on the stock is 10 percent.

a. To begin, assume that the stock sale nets $11,500. What is the dollar return on the stock investment? What is the rate of return?

b. Assume that the stock price falls and the net is only $9,500 when the stock is sold. What are the dollar return and the rate of return?

c. Assume that the sales prices remain the same but the stock is held for two years. Now, what are the dollar return and the rate of return?

9.14. County Hospital is planning to purchase a new piece of medical equipment with a list price of $3,000,000. The medical equipment supplier has been experiencing low sales volume and is currently offering special pricing to boost sales. The medical equipment supplier provides County Hospital with the following two alternative offers:

Offer 1: County Hospital can purchase the medical equipment at a 10 percent discount (sale price) if it pays the full amount at the time of purchase.

Offer 2: County Hospital can purchase the medical equipment at a 5 percent discount (sale price) with two-year, no-cost financing. If County Hospital chooses Offer 2, half of the final purchase price will be due at the end of year 1 and half of the final purchase price will be due at the end of year 2.

Assume that County Hospital has enough cash available to take advantage of either offer and will not need to borrow any money to complete the purchase.

a. Which offer should County Hospital take if its risk-adjusted opportunity cost of capital is 10 percent?

b. Which offer should County Hospital take if its risk-adjusted opportunity cost of capital is 1 percent?

c. Explain why your answers were either the same or different for parts a and b.

9.15. Assume a large healthcare system has just approved a $355,000 annual (per year) bonus to retain its top cardiac surgeon. Assume that $355,000 will be paid to the surgeon as a bonus at the end of each year that he stays, up to ten years. The healthcare system wants to invest a lump sum now to have enough money to cover the bonuses over the ten-year period. Assume the healthcare system can earn a 5 percent stated annual rate of return on its investment, compounded semiannually (twice per year). What amount would the healthcare system need to invest now to have enough money to pay the annual bonus to the surgeon at the end of each of the next ten years?

Selected Case

One case in *Gapenski's Cases in Healthcare Finance*, sixth edition, is applicable to this chapter: Case 11: Gulf Shores Surgery Centers.

Notes

1. Actually, owning a single nursing home is riskier than owning the stock of a firm that has a large number of nursing homes with geographic diversification. Also, an owner of Genesis HealthCare stock can easily sell the stock if things go sour, whereas it would be much more difficult for Oakdale to sell its nursing home. These differences in risk and liquidity suggest that the true opportunity cost rate is probably higher than the return that is expected from owning the stock of a large long-term care company. However, direct ownership of a nursing home implies control, while ownership of the stock of a large firm usually does not. Control rights tend to reduce the opportunity cost rate. The main point here is that, in practice, it may not be possible to obtain a "perfect" opportunity cost rate. Nevertheless, an imprecise one is better than none at all.

2. Some financial institutions pay interest that is compounded *continuously*. Continuous compounding is not relevant to healthcare financial management, so it is not discussed here.

Resources

Brickner, D. R., and L. S. Mahoney. 2018. "Factoring in the Time Value of Money with Excel." *Journal of Accountancy* 225 (3): 42–54.

See also the help menu for your spreadsheet software.

INTEREST RATE AND TIME CALCULATIONS AND AMORTIZATION

9

Solving for Interest Rate and Time

In general, the time value analysis concepts presented in chapter 9 are all that is needed in healthcare financial analysis. However, more can be done with lump sums than merely calculating present and future values. Four time value analysis variables are used when working with lump sums: PV, FV, I, and N. If the values of three of the variables are known, the value of the fourth can be found with the help of a spreadsheet. In chapter 9, the interest rate, I, and the number of years, N, plus either PV or FV are given in the illustrations. In some situations, however, the analysis may require solving for either I or N.

Solving for Interest Rate

Suppose that Family Practice Associates (FPA), a primary care group practice, can buy a bank CD for $78.35 that will return $100 after five years. In this case, PV, FV, and N are known, but I, the interest rate that the bank is paying, is not known.

$$FV_N = PV \times (1 + I)^N$$
$$\$100 = \$78.35 \times (1 + I)^5.$$

Spreadsheet Solution

	A		B	C	D
1					
2		5	Nper	Number of periods	
3	$	(78.35)	Pv	Present value	
4	$	100.00	Fv	Future value	
5					
6					
7					
8		5.00%	=RATE(A2,,A3,A4) (entered into Cell A8)		
9					
10					

Here, the spreadsheet function named RATE is used to solve for I, as illustrated to the right of cell A8. First, click on the Function Wizard, select "Financial" for the function category and "RATE" for the function name, and press OK. On the next menu, enter A2 for Nper (number of periods), A3 for Pv (present value), and A4 for Fv (future value). (Note that the Pmt and Type entries are left blank for this problem. Also note that the Pv was entered as a negative number, as shown on the time line.) Finally, press OK and the result—5%—appears in cell A8. (Note that some spreadsheet programs display the answer in decimal form unless the cell is formatted to display in percent.)

Solving for Time

Suppose that the bank told FPA that a certificate of deposit pays 5 percent interest each year, that it costs $78.35, and that at maturity the practice would receive $100. How many years will it take for the CD to mature? In this case, PV, FV, and I are known, but N, the number of periods, is not known.

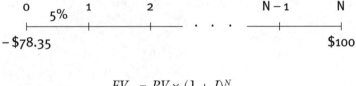

$$FV_N = PV \times (1 + I)^N$$
$$\$100 = \$78.35 \times (1.05)^5.$$

Spreadsheet Solution

	A	B	C	D
1				
2	5.00%	Rate	Interest rate	
3	$ (78.35)	Pv	Present value	
4	$ 100.00	Fv	Future value	
5				
6				
7				
8	5.00	=NPER(A2,,A3,A4)	(entered into Cell A8)	
9				
10				

To solve for time, the spreadsheet function named Nper (number of periods) is used. To begin, place the cursor in cell A8 and click on the Function Wizard. Then select "Financial" for the function category and "Nper" for the function name, and click OK. On the next menu, enter A2 for Rate, A3 for Pv, and A4 for Fv. (Note that the Pmt and Type entries are left blank for this problem. Also, note that the Pv was entered as a negative number, as shown on the time line.) Finally, press OK and the result—5.00—appears in cell A8.

The Rule of 72

The *Rule of 72* gives a simple and quick method for judging the effect of different interest rates on the growth of a lump sum deposit. To find the number of years required to double the value of a lump sum, simply divide the number 72 by the interest rate paid. For example, if the interest rate is 10 percent, it would take $72 \div 10 = 7.2$ years for the money in an account to double in value. The spreadsheet solution is 7.27 years, so the Rule of 72 is relatively accurate, at least when reasonable interest rates are applied.

In a similar manner, the Rule of 72 can be used to determine the interest rate required to double the money in an account in a given number of years. To illustrate, an interest rate of $72 \div 5 = 14.4$ percent is required to double the value of an account in five years. The spreadsheet solution in this case is 14.9 percent, so the Rule of 72 again gives a reasonable approximation of the precise answer.

1. What are a few real-world situations that may require you to solve for interest rate or time?
2. Can spreadsheets easily solve for interest rate or time?
3. Explain the Rule of 72.

Amortized Loans

One important application of time value analysis involves loans that are to be paid off in equal installments over time, including automobile loans, home mortgage loans, and most business debt other than short-term loans and bonds. If a loan is to be repaid in equal periodic amounts—monthly, quarterly, or annually—it is said to be an **amortized loan**. The word *amortize* comes from the Latin *mors*, meaning *death*, so an amortized loan is one that is killed off over time.

To illustrate, suppose that Santa Fe Oncology Group borrows $1 million from the Bank of New Mexico, to be repaid in three equal installments at the end of each of the next three years. The bank is to receive 6 percent interest on the loan balance that is outstanding at the beginning of each year.

amortized (installment) loan A loan that is repaid in equal periodic amounts that include both principal and interest payments.

The first task in analyzing the loan is to determine the amount that Santa Fe must repay each year, or the annual payment. To find this value, recognize that the loan amount represents the present value of an annuity of PMT (payment) dollars per year for three years, discounted at 6 percent.

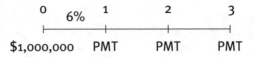

Spreadsheet Solution

	A	B	C	D
1				
2	6.0%	Rate	Interest rate	
3	3	Nper	Number of periods	
4	$ 1,000,000	Pv	Present value	
5				
6				
7				
8	$ 374,110	=PMT(A2,A3,−A4) (entered into Cell A8)		
9				
10				

If Santa Fe pays the bank $374,110 at the end of each of the next three years, the percentage cost to the borrower, and the rate of return to the lender, will be 6 percent.

Each payment made by Santa Fe consists partly of interest and partly of repayment of principal. This breakdown is given in the *amortization schedule* shown in exhibit S9.1. The interest component is largest in the first year,

EXHIBIT S9.1
Loan Amortization Schedule

Year	Beginning Amount (1)	Payment (2)	Interest[a] (3)	Repayment of Principal[b] (4)	Remaining Balance (5)
1	$1,000,000	$ 374,110	$ 60,000	$ 314,110	$685,890
2	685,890	374,110	41,153	332,957	352,933
3	352,933	374,110	21,177	352,933	0
		$1,122,330	$122,330	$1,000,000	

[a] Interest is calculated by multiplying the loan balance at the beginning of each year by the interest rate. Therefore, interest in year 1 is $1,000,000 × 0.06 = $60,000; in year 2, it is $685,890 × 0.06 = $41,153; and in year 3, it is $352,933 × 0.06 = $21,177.

[b] Repayment of principal is equal to the payment of $374,110 minus the interest charge for each year.

and it declines as the outstanding balance of the loan is reduced over time. For tax purposes, a taxable business borrower reports the interest payments in column 3 as a deductible cost each year, while the lender reports these same amounts as taxable income.

1. When constructing an amortization schedule, how is the periodic payment amount calculated?
2. Does the periodic payment remain constant over time?
3. Do the principal and interest components remain constant over time? Explain your answer.

FINANCIAL RISK AND REQUIRED RETURN

> ## Learning Objectives
>
> After studying this chapter, readers will be able to
>
> - Explain in general terms the concept of financial risk.
> - Define and differentiate between stand-alone risk and portfolio risk.
> - Define market risk.
> - Explain the capital asset pricing model (CAPM) relationship between risk and required rate of return.
> - Use the CAPM to determine required returns.

Introduction

Two of the most important concepts in investment analysis are financial risk and required return. What is financial risk, how is it measured, and what effect, if any, does it have on required return (opportunity cost rates) and managerial decisions? Because so much of financial decision-making involves risk and return, it is impossible to understand healthcare finance without having a solid appreciation of risk and return concepts.

If investors—both individuals and organizations—viewed risk as a benign fact of life, it would have little impact on decision-making. However, decision makers for the most part believe that if a risk must be taken, there must be a reward for doing so. Thus, an investment of higher risk, whether it is an individual investor's security investment or a radiology group's investment in diagnostic equipment, must offer a higher return to make it financially attractive.

In this chapter, basic risk concepts are presented from the perspective of both individual investors and businesses. Health services managers must be familiar with both contexts because they must understand how investors make decisions regarding the supply of capital as well as how businesses make decisions regarding their use of that capital. In addition, the chapter discusses the relationship between risk and required rate of return. To be truly useful in financial decision-making, it is necessary to know the impact of risk on investors' views of investment acceptability.

The Many Faces of Financial Risk

A full discussion of financial risk would take many chapters—perhaps even an entire book—because financial risk is a complicated subject. First of all, the nature of financial risk depends on whether the investor is an individual or a business. Then, if the investor is an individual, it depends on the *investment horizon*, or the amount of time until the investment proceeds are needed. To make the situation even more complex, it may be difficult to define, measure, or translate financial risk into something usable for decision-making. For example, the risk that individual investors face when saving for retirement is the risk that the amount of funds accumulated will not be sufficient to fund the lifestyle expected during the full term of retirement. Needless to say, translating such a definition of risk into investment goals is not easy. The good news is that our primary interest in this book is the financial risk inherent in businesses. Thus, our discussion focuses on the fundamental factors that influence the riskiness of real-asset investments (e.g., land, buildings, equipment).

Still, two factors complicate our discussion of financial risk. The first complicating factor is that financial risk is seen both by businesses and by the investors in those businesses. There is some risk inherent in the business that depends on the type of business. For example, biotechnology firms are generally acknowledged to face a great deal of risk, while hospitals typically have less risk. Then, investors, primarily stockholders and debtholders (creditors), bear the riskiness inherent in the business, but as **modified by the nature of the securities they hold**. For example, the stock of Magellan Health (www.magellanhealth.com), a for-profit behavioral health company, is more risky than its debt, although the risk of both securities depends on the inherent risk of a business that operates in the behavioral health sector. The risk differential arises because of contractual differences between equity and debt: Debtholders have a fixed claim against the cash flows and assets of the business, while stockholders have a residual claim to what is left after all other claimants have been paid. Not-for-profit providers have the same partitioning of risk, but the inherent risk of the business is split between the creditors who supply debt capital and the *implied* stockholders (the community at large).

The second complicating factor is that the riskiness of an investment depends on the context in which it is held. For example, a stock held alone (in isolation) is riskier than the same stock held as part of an investor's large portfolio (collection) of stocks. Similarly, a magnetic resonance imaging (MRI) system operated independently is riskier than the same system operated as part of a large, geographically diversified business that owns and operates numerous types of diagnostic equipment.

---

1. What complications arise when dealing with financial risk in a business setting?

SELF-TEST QUESTION

Returns on Investments

The concept of return provides investors with a convenient way to express the financial performance of an investment. To illustrate, suppose you buy ten shares of a stock for $100. The stock pays no dividends, and at the end of one year, you sell the stock for $110. What is the return on your $100 investment?

One way to express an investment's return is in dollar terms:

Dollar return = Amount to be received – Amount invested

= $110 – $100 = $10.

If, at the end of the year, you sell the stock for only $90, your dollar return will be –$10.

Although expressing returns in dollars is easy, two problems arise. First, to make a meaningful judgment about the return, you need to know the scale (size) of the investment; a $100 return on a $100 investment is a great return (assuming the investment is held for one year), but a $100 return on a $10,000 investment is a poor return. Second, you also need to know the timing of the return; a $100 return on a $100 investment is a great return if it occurs after one year, but the same dollar return after 100 years is not very good. The solution to these scale and timing problems is to express investment results as rates of return or percentage returns. For example, when $1,100 is received after one year, the rate of return on the one-year stock investment is 10 percent:

Rate of return = Dollar return ÷ Amount invested

= $100 ÷ $1,000 = 0,10 = 10%.

The rate of return calculation "standardizes" the dollar return by considering the annual return per unit of investment.

Introduction to Financial Risk

Generically, *risk* is defined as a hazard, a peril, or an exposure to loss or injury. Thus, risk refers to the chance that an unfavorable event will occur. If a person engages in skydiving, she risks injury or death. If a person gambles at roulette, he is not risking injury or death but is taking a *financial risk*. Even when a person invests in stocks or bonds, she risks losing money in the hope of earning a positive rate of return. Similarly, when a healthcare business invests in new assets such as diagnostic equipment or a new cancer hospital, it is taking a financial risk.

To illustrate financial risk, consider two potential personal investments. The first investment consists of a one-year, $1,000 face value US Treasury bill (or T-bill) bought for $950. Treasury bills are short-term federal debt that are sold at a *discount* (less than face value) and return *face*, or *par*, *value* at maturity. The investor expects to receive $1,000 at maturity in one year, so the anticipated rate of return on the T-bill investment is ($1,000 − $950) ÷ $950 = $50 ÷ $950 = 0.0526, or 5.26%.

This calculation can be done using a spreadsheet, as follows:

	A	B	C	D
1				
2	1	Nper	Number of periods	
3	$ (950.00)	Pv	Present value	
4	$ 1,000	Fv	Future value	
5				
6				
7				
8	5.26%	=RATE(A2,,A3,A4) (entered into Cell A8)		
9				
10				

The $1,000 payment is fixed by contract (the T-bill promises to pay this amount), and the US government is certain to make the payment, unless a national disaster prevents it, which is unlikely. Thus, there is virtually a 100 percent probability that the investment will actually earn the 5.26 percent rate of return that is expected. In this situation, the investment is defined as being *riskless* or *risk-free*.[1]

Now, assume that the $950 is invested in a biotechnology partnership that will be terminated in one year. If the partnership develops a new, commercially valuable product, its rights will be sold and $2,000 will be received from the partnership, for a rate of return of ($2,000 − $950) ÷ $950 = $1,050 ÷ $950 = 1.1053 = 110.53%:

	A	B	C	D
1				
2	1	Nper	Number of periods	
3	$ (950.00)	Pv	Present value	
4	$ 2,000	Fv	Future value	
5				
6				
7				
8	110.53%	=RATE(A2,,A3,A4) (entered into Cell A8)		
9				
10				

On the other hand, if the partnership does not develop anything worthwhile, it will be worthless, no money will be received, and the rate of return will be ($0 – $950) ÷ $950 = –1.00 = –100%:

	A	B	C	D
1				
2	1	Nper	Number of periods	
3	$ (950.00)	Pv	Present value	
4	$ 0.01	Fv	Future value	
5				
6				
7				
8	–100.00%	=RATE(A2,,A3,A4) (entered into Cell A8)		
9				
10				

financial risk
In an investment context, the risk that the return on an investment will be less than expected. The greater the chance of earning a return far below that expected, the greater the risk. In a capital structure context, it is the risk added to a business (more precisely, to the business's owners) when debt financing is used. The greater the proportion of debt financing, the greater the financial risk.

Note that spreadsheets give no solution when the future value is zero, but if a small number—for example, 0.01—is entered for the future value, the solution for interest rate is –100.00.

Now, assume that there is a 50 percent chance that a valuable product will be developed. In this admittedly unrealistic situation, the expected rate of return (a statistical concept that will be discussed shortly) is the same 5.26 percent as the expected return on the T-bill investment: $(0.50 \times 110.53\%) + [0.50 \times (-100\%)] = 5.26\%$. However, the biotechnology partnership is a far cry from being riskless. If things go poorly, the realized rate of return will be –100 percent, which means that the entire $950 investment will be lost. Because there is a chance of earning a return that is less than expected, the partnership investment is described as risky.

Thus, **financial risk** is related to the probability of earning a return less than expected. The greater the chance of earning a return far below that expected, the greater the amount of financial risk. We should note that defining financial risk as the probability of earning a return far below that expected is somewhat simplistic. As we discussed previously, there are many different ways of viewing financial risk. However, the simple definition presented here is a good starting point for discussing the types of risk that are most relevant to decisions made within health services organizations.

1. What is a generic definition of risk?
2. Give an example of financial risk.

Risk Aversion

Why are defining and measuring financial risk so important? It is because, for the most part, both individual and business investors dislike risk. Suppose you were given the choice between taking a sure $1 million and flipping a coin for either zero or $2 million. You—and just about everyone else—would likely take the sure $1 million. A person who takes the sure thing is said to be *risk averse*; a person who is indifferent between the two alternatives is *risk neutral*; and an individual who prefers the gamble to the sure thing is a *risk seeker*.

Of course, people and businesses do gamble and take other financial risks, so all of us at some time typically exhibit risk-seeking behavior. However, most individuals would never put a sizable portion of their wealth at extreme risk, and most health services managers would never "bet the business." Most people are risk averse when it really matters.

What are the implications of **risk aversion** for financial decision-making? First, given two investments with similar returns but different risk, investors will favor the lower-risk alternative. Second, investors will require higher returns on higher-risk investments. These typical outcomes of risk aversion have a significant impact on many facets of financial decision-making and appear over and over in the remainder of this book.

risk aversion
The tendency of individuals and businesses to dislike risk. The implication of risk aversion is that riskier investments must offer higher expected rates of return to be acceptable.

1. What does the term *risk aversion* mean?
2. What are the implications of risk aversion for financial decision-making?

Probability Distributions

The chance that an event will occur is called *probability of occurrence*, or just *probability*. For example, when rolling a single die, the probability of rolling a two is one out of six, or $1 \div 6 = 0.1667 = 16.67\%$. If all possible outcomes related to a particular event are listed, and a probability is assigned to each outcome, the result is a **probability distribution**. In the example of the roll of a die, the probability distribution looks like this:

Outcome	Probability
1	0.1667 = 16.67%
2	0.1667 = 16.67%
3	0.1667 = 16.67%
4	0.1667 = 16.67%
5	0.1667 = 16.67%
6	0.1667 = 16.67%
	1.0000 = 100%

probability distribution
All possible outcomes of a random event along with their probabilities of occurrence; for example, the probability distribution of rates of return on a proposed investment.

All possible outcomes (i.e., the number of dots showing after the die roll) are listed in the left column, and the probability of each outcome is listed in the right column, in both decimal and percentage format. For a complete probability distribution, which must include all possible outcomes for an event, the probabilities must sum to 1.0, or 100 percent.

Probabilities can also be assigned to possible outcomes—in this case, returns—of personal and business investments. If a person buys stock, the return will usually come in the form of *dividends* and **capital gains** (selling the stock for more than the person paid for it) or **losses** (selling the stock for less than the person paid for it). Because all stock returns are uncertain, there is some chance that the dividends will not be as high as expected and that the stock price will not increase as much as expected or that it will even decrease. The higher the probability of dividends and stock prices having subpar performance, the higher the probability that the return will be significantly less than expected and hence the greater the risk.

capital gain (loss)
The profit (loss) from the sale of certain investments at more (less) than their purchase price.

To illustrate the concept using a business investment, consider a radiology group evaluating the purchase of a new CT scanner. The cost of the scanner is an investment, and the net cash inflows that stem from patient utilization provide the return. The net cash inflows, in turn, depend on the number of procedures performed, the charge per procedure, payer discounts, operating costs, and so on. These values typically are not known with certainty but depend on factors such as patient demographics, physician acceptance of the technology, local market conditions, labor and supplies costs, and so on. The radiology group faces a probability distribution of returns rather than a single return known with certainty. The greater the probability of returns far below the return anticipated, the greater the risk of the scanner investment.

1. What is a probability distribution?
2. How are probability distributions used in financial decision-making?

Expected and Realized Rates of Return

To be most useful, the concept of financial risk must be defined more precisely than "the chances of a return far below that anticipated." Exhibit 10.1 contains the estimated return distributions developed by the financial staff of Suffolk Community Hospital for two proposed projects: an emergency room (ER) expansion and a walk-in clinic. Here, each economic state reflects a combination of factors that dictate each project's profitability. For example, for the ER project, the very poor economic state signifies a competitive market and low general utilization, low reimbursement rates, high usage by uninsured patients, high operating costs, and so on. Conversely, the very good economic state assumes high utilization by insured patients, high reimbursement rates, low operating costs, and so on. The economic states are defined in a similar fashion for the walk-in clinic.

expected rate of return
The return expected, in a statistical sense, on an investment when the purchase is made.

The **expected rate of return**, defined in the statistical sense, is the weighted average of the return distribution, where the weights are the probabilities of occurrence. For example, the expected rate of return on the ER expansion, $E(R_{ER})$, is 10 percent:

$$
\begin{aligned}
E(R_{ER}) = {} & \text{Probability of Return 1} \times \text{Return 1} \\
& + \text{Probability of Return 2} \times \text{Return 2} \\
& + \text{Probability of Return 3} \times \text{Return 3} \\
& + \ldots \\
= {} & [0.10 \times (-10\%)] + (0.20 \times 0\%) + (0.40 \times 10\%) \\
& + (0.20 \times 20\%) + (0.10 \times 30\%) \\
= {} & 10\%.
\end{aligned}
$$

Calculated in a similar manner, the expected rate of return on the walk-in clinic is 15 percent.

The expected rate of return is the average return that would result, given the return distribution, if the investment were randomly repeated many times. In this illustration, if 1,000 clinics were built in different areas, and each faced the return distribution given in exhibit 10.1, the average return on the 1,000 investments would be 15 percent, assuming that the returns in each area are independent of one another (i.e., random). However, only one clinic would actually be built, and the realized rate of return may be less than the expected 15 percent. Therefore, the clinic investment (as well as the ER investment) is risky.

Expected rate of return expresses an expectation for the future. When the managers at Suffolk Community Hospital analyzed the ER investment, they expected it to earn 10 percent. However, assume that economic conditions take a turn for the worse and the very poor economic scenario occurs. In this case, the **realized rate of return**, which is the rate of return that the investment produced as measured at termination, would be –10 percent. It is the potential of realizing a –10 percent return on an investment that has an expected return of +10 percent that produces financial risk.

realized rate of return
The return achieved on an investment when it is terminated.

Note that in many situations, especially those arising in classroom examples, the expected rate of return is not even achievable. For example, an investment that has a 50 percent chance of a 5 percent return and a 50 percent chance of a 15 percent return has an expected rate of return of 10 percent. Yet, assuming that the given distribution truly reflects all of the potential investment outcomes, there is zero probability of actually realizing the 10 percent expected rate of return. Still, the 10 percent expected rate of return is the best measure of the profitability of the investment at the time it is being analyzed.

Key Equation: Expected Value
The expected value of a probability distribution can be found by summing the products of the value in each state multiplied by its probability (Prob.) of occurrence. To illustrate, assume that the returns on an investment have the following probability distribution:

Probability of Occurrence	Rate of Return
0.20	0%
0.60	10
0.20	25

The expected rate of return, $E(R)$, is 11.0 percent:

$$E(R) = (\text{Prob. 1} \times \text{Return 1}) + (\text{Prob. 2} \times \text{Return 2}) + (\text{Prob. 3} \times \text{Return 3})$$
$$= (0.20 \times 0\%) + (0.60 \times 10\%) + (0.20 \times 25\%)$$
$$= 0.0\% + 6.0\% + 5.0\%$$
$$= 11.0\%.$$

Economic State	Probability of Occurrence	Rate of Return if State Occurs	
		ER	Clinic
Very poor	0.10	–10%	–20%
Poor	0.20	0	0
Average	0.40	10	15
Good	0.20	20	30
Very good	0.10	30	50
	1.00		

SELF-TEST
QUESTIONS

1. How is the expected rate of return calculated?
2. What is the economic interpretation of the expected rate of return?
3. What is the difference between the expected rate of return and the realized rate of return?

Stand-Alone Risk

We can look at the two return distributions in exhibit 10.1 and conclude that the clinic is riskier than the ER expansion because the clinic has a chance of a 20 percent loss, while the worst possible loss on the ER is only 10 percent. This intuitive risk assessment is based on the **stand-alone risk** of the two investments—that is, we are focusing on the riskiness of each investment under the assumption that it would be Suffolk's only asset (operated in isolation). In the next section, portfolio effects are introduced, but for now, we can continue our discussion of stand-alone risk.

stand-alone risk
The riskiness of an investment that is held in isolation as opposed to held as part of a portfolio (collection of investments).

Stand-alone risk depends on the "tightness" of an investment's return distribution—that is, the amount of dispersion (size) of the distribution. If an investment has a "tight" return distribution, with returns falling close to the expected return, it has relatively low stand-alone risk. Conversely, an investment with a return distribution that is "loose," and hence has values well below the expected return, is relatively risky in the stand-alone sense.

It is important to recognize that risk and return are *separate* attributes of an investment. An investment may have a tight distribution of returns, and hence low stand-alone risk, but its expected rate of return might be very low, say, 2 percent. In this situation, the investment may not be financially attractive, in spite of its low risk. Similarly, a high-risk investment with a sufficiently high expected rate of return would be attractive.[2]

It is also important to recognize that the size of an investment does not affect its risk. For example, a $1,000 investment in Tenet Healthcare (www.tenethealth.com) bonds has the same risk as a $1,000,000 investment. The amount of capital (money) at risk does not change the riskiness of the investment—the bonds have a certain amount of risk regardless of the amount bought. What may differ, however, is the investor's ability to *bear* that risk. An individual with modest income may be able to bear the risk of the $1,000 investment but not the $1,000,000 investment. On the other hand, a large fixed-income mutual fund would easily be able to bear the risk of the $1,000,000 investment. Remember, though, that the size of an investment does not change its inherent risk.

To be truly useful, any definition of risk must be measurable, so we need some numerical way to specify the "degree of tightness" of an investment's return distribution. One such measure is the **variance**.

Variance is a measure of the dispersion of a distribution around its mean (expected value), but it is less useful than standard deviation because its measurement unit is percent (or dollars) squared, which has no economic meaning. **Standard deviation**, which is often denoted by the symbol σ (lowercase Greek sigma), is a common statistical measure of the dispersion of a distribution around its mean—the smaller the standard deviation, the tighter the distribution and the lower the stand-alone risk of the investment. To illustrate the calculation of standard deviation, consider the estimated returns of the ER investment, as listed in exhibit 10.1. Here are the steps:

standard deviation (σ) A statistical measure of the variability (dispersion) of a probability distribution about the mean (expected value).

1. The expected rate of return on the ER, $E(R_{ER})$, is 10 percent.
2. The *variance* of the return distribution is determined as follows:

$$
\begin{aligned}
\text{Variance} = &\ (\text{Probability of Return 1} \times [\text{Rate of Return 1} - E(R_{ER})]^2) \\
&+ (\text{Probability of Return 2} \times [\text{Rate of Return 2} - E(R_{ER})]^2) \\
&+ \ldots \\
= &\ (0.10 \times [-10\% - 10\%]^2) + (0.20 \times [0\% - 10\%]^2) \\
&+ (0.40 \times [10\% - 10\%]^2) + (0.20 \times [20\% - 10\%]^2) \\
&+ (0.10 \times [30\% - 10\%]^2) \\
= &\ 120.00.
\end{aligned}
$$

3. The standard deviation is defined as the square root of the variance:

$$
\begin{aligned}
\text{Standard deviation}(\sigma) &= \sqrt{\text{Variance}} \\
&= \sqrt{120.00} = 10.95\% \approx 11\%.
\end{aligned}
$$

Most spreadsheet programs have built-in functions that calculate standard deviation. However, these functions assume that the distribution values that are entered have *equal probabilities* of occurrence and are **not** usable with the types of distributions contained in exhibit 10.1. The spreadsheet functions are designed to handle *historical* data, such as annual returns over the past five years, as opposed to *forecast* distributions with unequal probabilities of occurrence.

Using the same procedure, the clinic investment listed in exhibit 10.1 was found to have a standard deviation of returns of about 18 percent. Because the standard deviation of returns of the clinic investment is larger than that of the ER investment, the clinic investment has more stand-alone risk than the ER investment.

SELF-TEST QUESTIONS

1. What is stand-alone risk?
2. Are risk and return separate attributes of an investment? Explain.
3. Does the amount of money at risk affect the riskiness of an investment? Explain.
4. Define and explain the most common measure of stand-alone risk.

Portfolio Risk and Return

The preceding section introduced a risk measure—standard deviation—that applies to investments held in isolation. There is a problem, however, with viewing risk in the stand-alone sense: Most investments are held not in isolation but as part of a collection, or **portfolio**, of investments. Individual investors typically hold portfolios of *securities* (i.e., stocks and bonds), while businesses generally hold portfolios of *projects* (i.e., product or service lines). When investments are held in portfolios, the primary concern of investors is not the realized rate of return on an individual investment but rather the realized rate of return on the entire portfolio. Similarly, the stand-alone risk of each individual investment in the portfolio is not important to the investor; what matters is the *aggregate* risk of the portfolio, or **portfolio risk**. Thus, the nature of risk and how it is defined and measured changes when investments are held not in isolation but as part of a portfolio.

portfolio
A number of individual investments held collectively.

portfolio risk
The riskiness of an individual investment when it is held as part of a diversified portfolio (collection of investments) as opposed to held in isolation.

Portfolio Returns
Consider the realized returns for the seven investment alternatives listed in exhibit 10.2. The individual investment alternatives (investments A, B, C, and D) could be projects under consideration by South West Clinics, Inc., or they could be stocks that are being evaluated as personal investments by Joyce Dunne. The remaining three alternatives in exhibit 10.2 are portfolios.

Portfolio AB consists of 50 percent invested in investment A and 50 percent in investment B (e.g., $10,000 invested in A and $10,000 invested in B); portfolio AC is an equal-weighted portfolio of investments A and C. Portfolio AD is an equal-weighted portfolio of investments A and D. As shown in the bottom of the exhibit, investments A and B have 10 percent expected rates of return, while the expected rates of return for investments C and D are 15 percent and 12 percent, respectively. Investments A and B have identical stand-alone risk as measured by standard deviation (11 percent), while investments C and D have greater stand-alone risk than A and B.

The *rate of return on a portfolio*, R_p, is the weighted average of the expected returns on the assets that make up the portfolio, with the weights reflecting the proportion of the total portfolio invested in each asset:

$$(R_p) = [w_1 \times E(R_1)] + [w_2 \times E(R_2)] + [w_3 \times E(R_3)] + \ldots$$

In this case, w_1 is the proportion of investment 1 in the overall portfolio, $E(R_1)$ is the expected rate of return on investment 1, and so on. Thus, the expected rate of return on portfolio AB is 10 percent:

$$\begin{aligned} R_{AB} &= (w_A \times R_A) + (w_B \times R_B) \\ &= (0.5 \times 10\%) + (0.5 \times 10\%) = 5\% + 5\% = 10\%, \end{aligned}$$

while the expected rate of return on portfolio AC is 12.5 percent and on AD is 13.5 percent.

Alternatively, the expected rate of return on a portfolio can be calculated by looking at the portfolio's return distribution. To illustrate, consider the return distribution for portfolio AC contained in exhibit 10.2. The portfolio return in each economic state is the weighted average of the returns on investments A and C in that state. For example, the return on portfolio AC in the very poor state is $[0.5 \times (-10\%)] + [0.5 \times (-25\%)] = -17.5\%$. Portfolio AC's return in each other state is calculated similarly. Portfolio AC's return distribution now can be used to calculate its expected rate of return:

$$\begin{aligned} R_{AC} &= [0.10 \times (-17.5\%)] + [0.20 \times (-2.5\%)] + (0.40 \times 12.5\%) \\ &\quad + (0.20 \times 27.5\%) + (0.10 \times 42.5\%) \\ &= 12.5\%. \end{aligned}$$

This is the same value as that calculated from the expected rates of return of the two portfolio components:

$$R_{AC} = (0.5 \times 10\%) + (0.5 \times 15\%) = 12.5\%.$$

Portfolio Risk: Two Investments

When an investor holds a portfolio of investments, the portfolio is in effect a stand-alone investment, **so the riskiness of the portfolio is measured by the standard deviation of portfolio returns**, the previously discussed measure of stand-alone risk. How does the riskiness of the individual investments in a portfolio combine to create the overall riskiness of the portfolio? Although the rate of return on a portfolio is the weighted average of the returns on the component investments, a portfolio's standard deviation (i.e., riskiness) is generally **not** the weighted average of the standard deviations of the individual components. The portfolio's riskiness may be smaller than the weighted average of each component's riskiness. Indeed, the riskiness of a portfolio may be less than the least risky portfolio component, and, under certain conditions, a portfolio of risky investments may even be riskless.

A simple example can be used to illustrate this concept. Suppose an individual is given the following opportunity: Flip a coin once; if it comes up heads, he wins $10,000, but if it comes up tails, he loses $8,000. This is a reasonable gamble in that the expected dollar return is $(0.5 \times \$10,000)$ + $[0.5 \times (-\$8,000)]$ = $1,000. However, it is highly risky because the individual has a 50 percent chance of losing $8,000. Thus, risk aversion would cause most people to refuse the gamble, especially if the $8,000 potential loss would result in financial hardship.

Alternatively, suppose an individual is given the opportunity to flip the coin 100 times, and she wins $100 for each heads but loses $80 for each tails. It is possible, although extremely unlikely, that she could flip all heads and win $10,000. It is also possible, and also extremely unlikely, that she could flip all tails and lose $8,000. But the chances are high that she will flip close to 50 heads and 50 tails and net about $1,000. Even if she flipped a few more tails than heads, she would still make money on the gamble.

	Rate of Return if State Occurs						
Year	A	B	C	D	AB	AC	AD
1	−10%	30%	−25%	15%	10%	−17.5%	2.5%
2	0	20	−5	10	10	−2.5	5.0
3	10	10	15	0	10	12.5	5.0
4	20	0	35	25	10	27.5	22.5
5	30	−10	55	35	10	42.5	32.5
Rate of return	10.0%	10.0%	15.0%	17.0%	10.0%	12.5%	13.5%
Standard deviation	15.8%	15.8%	31.6%	13.5%	0.0%	23.7%	13.3%

EXHIBIT 10.2 Realized Returns for Four Individual Investments and Three Portfolios

Although each flip is risky in the stand-alone sense, collectively, the flips are not risky at all. In effect, the multiple flipping creates a portfolio of investments; each flip of the coin can be thought of as one investment, so the individual now has a 100-investment portfolio. Furthermore, the return on each investment is independent of the returns on the other investments: The individual has a 50 percent chance of winning on each flip of the coin regardless of the results of the previous flips. By combining the flips into a single gamble (i.e., into an investment portfolio), the risk associated with each flip of the coin is reduced. In fact, if the gamble consisted of a large enough number of flips, almost all risk would be eliminated: The probability of a near-equal number of heads and tails would be extremely high, and the result would be a sure profit. The key to the risk reduction inherent in the portfolio is that the negative consequences of tossing tails can be offset by the positive consequences of tossing heads.

To examine portfolio effects in more depth, consider portfolio AB in exhibit 10.2. Each investment (A or B) has a standard deviation of returns of 10 percent and is quite risky when held in isolation. However, a portfolio comprising the two investments has a rate of return of 10 percent in every possible state of the economy, so it offers a riskless 10 percent return. This result is verified by the value of zero for portfolio AB's standard deviation of returns. The reason investments A and B can be combined to form a riskless portfolio is that their returns move exactly opposite to one another: In economic states when A's returns are relatively low, those of B are relatively high, and vice versa, so the gains on one investment in the portfolio more than offset losses on the other.

For Your Consideration

The Gambler's Fallacy

On August 18, 1913, at the casino in Monte Carlo, a rare event occurred at the roulette wheel. (A roulette wheel contains black and red spaces, and the ball has roughly a 50/50 chance of landing on either color each time the wheel is spun.) On that day, the ball landed on a black space a record 26 times in a row. As a result, beginning when black had come up a phenomenal 15 times, there was a wild rush to bet on red. As each spin continued to come up black, players doubled and tripled their stakes, and, after 20 spins, many expressed the belief that there was not a chance in a million of another black. By the time the run ended, on the 27th spin, the casino was millions of francs richer.

The players at the roulette wheel that day committed what is known as the "gambler's fallacy," also called the "Monte Carlo fallacy." Simply put, the fallacy rests on the assumption that some result must be "due" simply because what previously happened departed from what was expected to happen. In this example, one spin of the roulette wheel does not affect the next spin. Thus, each time the ball is rolled, there is (ideally) a 50 percent chance of landing on a black and a 50 percent chance of landing on a red. Even after many blacks have occurred in succession, there is still a 50/50 chance of a red because the results of previous spins have no bearing on the outcome of the next spin—the roulette wheel has no memory.

What do you think of the gambler's fallacy? What conditions must hold for the fallacy to apply? Are there situations that might occur that would cause the fallacy to be correct (past results predict future results)? If people are smart enough to recognize the fallacy, why do Las Vegas casino owners make so much money?

correlation
The movement
relationship
between two
variables.

**correlation
coefficient**
A standardized
measure of
correlation that
ranges from –1
(variables move
perfectly opposite
of one another)
to +1 (variables
move in perfect
synchronization);
denoted by *r*.

The movement relationship of two variables (i.e., their tendency to move either together or in opposition) is called **correlation**. The **correlation coefficient**, represented by the variable *r*, measures this relationship. Investments A and B can be combined to form a riskless portfolio because the returns on A and B are *perfectly negatively correlated*, which is designated by $r = -1.0$. For every state in which investment A has a return higher than its expected return, investment B has a return lower than its expected return, and vice versa.

The opposite of perfect negative correlation is *perfect positive correlation*, with $r = +1.0$. Returns on two perfectly positively correlated investments move up and down together as the economic state changes. When the returns on two investments are perfectly positively correlated, combining the investments into a portfolio will **not** lower risk because the standard deviation of the portfolio is simply the weighted average of the standard deviations of the two components.

To illustrate the impact of perfect positive correlation, consider portfolio AC in exhibit 10.2. Its rate of return, R_{AC}, is 12.5 percent, while its standard deviation is 16.4 percent. Because of perfect positive correlation between the returns on A and C, portfolio AC's standard deviation is the weighted average standard deviation of its components:

$$\sigma_{AC} = (0.5 \times 11.0\%) + (0.50 \times 21.95\%) = 16.4\%.$$

There is no risk reduction in this situation. The risk of the portfolio is less than the risk of investment C, but it is more than the risk of investment A. Forming a portfolio does not reduce risk when the returns on the two components are perfectly positively correlated; the portfolio merely *averages* the risk of the two investments.

What happens when a portfolio contains two investments that have positive, but not perfectly positive, correlation? Combining the two investments can eliminate some, but not all, risk. To illustrate, consider portfolio AD in exhibit 10.2. This portfolio has a standard deviation of returns of 10.1 percent, so it is risky. However, portfolio AD's standard deviation is not only less than the weighted average of the component standard deviations, $(0.5 \times 11\%) + (0.5 \times 12.1\%) = 11.6\%$, it also is less than the standard deviation of each component. The correlation coefficient between the return distributions for A and D is 0.53, which indicates that the two investments are positively correlated, but they are not perfectly correlated because the coefficient is less than +1.0. Combining two investments that are positively correlated, but not perfectly so, lowers risk but does not eliminate it.[3]

Because correlation is the factor that drives risk reduction, a logical question arises: What is the correlation among returns on "real-world" investments? Generalizing about the correlations among real-world investment alternatives is difficult. However, it is safe to say that the return distributions of two randomly selected investments—whether they are real assets in a multispecialty group practice's portfolio of service lines or financial assets in an individual's investment portfolio—are virtually never perfectly correlated, so correlation coefficients are never –1.0 or +1.0. In fact, it is almost impossible to find actual investment opportunities with returns that are negatively correlated with one another or even to find investments with returns that are uncorrelated ($r = 0$). Because all investment returns are affected to a greater or lesser degree by general economic conditions, investment returns tend to be positively correlated with one another. However, because investment returns are not affected identically by general economic conditions, returns on most real-world investments are not perfectly positively correlated.

The correlation coefficient between the returns of two randomly chosen investments will usually fall in the range of +0.3 to +0.8. Returns on investments that are similar in nature, such as two inpatient projects in a hospital or two stocks in the same sector, will typically have correlations at the upper end of this range. Conversely, returns on dissimilar projects or securities will tend to have correlations at the lower end of the range.

For real-world correlations, consider exhibit 10.3, which shows the correlation coefficients between several investment classes. The base for all correlations is the Standard & Poor's (S&P) 500 index, which is a diversified portfolio of large-firm stocks. Adding asset classes with negative or low correlation to traditional investments such as the S&P 500 can increase portfolio diversification.

Portfolio Risk: Many Investments

Businesses are not restricted to two projects, and individual investors are not restricted to holding two-security portfolios. Most companies have tens, or even thousands, of individual projects (i.e., product or service lines), and most individual investors hold many different securities or mutual funds that may be composed of a multitude of individual securities. Thus, what is most relevant to investment decision-making is not what happens when two investments are combined into portfolios, but what happens when many investments are combined.

To illustrate the impact on risk of creating large portfolios, consider exhibit 10.4. The graph illustrates the risk inherent in holding *randomly selected* portfolios of one investment, two investments, three investments, four investments, and so on, considering the correlations that occur among real-world investments. The plot is based on *historical* annual returns on common stocks, but the conclusions apply to portfolios made up of any type

EXHIBIT 10.3
Correlations
Among Selected
Asset Classes,
January 2009–
December 2018

Investment 1	Investment 2	Correlation Coefficient
Investment-grade bonds	S&P 500	−0.06
Cash	S&P 500	−0.08
Commodities	S&P 500	0.52
Currencies	S&P 500	−0.52
Global indexes	S&P 500	0.97
Hedge funds	S&P 500	0.74
Real estate investment trusts	S&P 500	0.73
S&P 500	S&P 500	1.00

Source: Guggenheim Investments, "Asset Class Correlation Map," January 2009–December 2018, www.guggenheiminvestments.com/mutual-funds/resources/interactive-tools/asset-class-correlation-map.

of risky investment, including portfolios of real-asset investments held by healthcare providers. The plot shows the average standard deviation of all one-investment (one-stock) portfolios, the average standard deviation of all possible two-investment portfolios, the average standard deviation of all possible three-investment portfolios, and so on.

The risk inherent in holding an average one-investment portfolio is relatively high, as measured by its standard deviation of annual returns. The average two-investment portfolio has a lower standard deviation, so holding an average two-investment portfolio is less risky than holding a single investment of average risk. The average three-investment portfolio has an even lower standard deviation of returns, so an average three-investment portfolio is less risky than an average two-investment portfolio. As more investments are randomly added to create larger and larger portfolios, the riskiness of the portfolio decreases. However, as more and more investments are added, the incremental risk reduction of adding even more investments decreases, and regardless of how many are added, some risk always remains in the portfolio—even with a portfolio of thousands of investments, substantial risk remains.[4]

All risk cannot be eliminated by creating a large portfolio because the returns on the component investments, although not perfectly so, are still positively correlated with one another. In other words, all investments, both real and financial, are affected to a lesser or greater degree by general economic conditions. If the economy is booming, all investments tend to do well, while in a recession, all investments tend to do poorly. It is the positive correlation among real-world investment returns that prevents investors from creating riskless portfolios.

Diversifiable Risk Versus Market Risk

Exhibit 10.4 shows what happens as investors create ever-larger portfolios. As the size of a randomly created portfolio increases, the riskiness of the portfolio decreases, so a large proportion of the stand-alone risk inherent in an individual investment can be eliminated if it is held as part of a large portfolio. For example, if a stock investor wanted to eliminate as much stand-alone risk as possible, he would have to own more than 6,500 stocks. Fortunately, it is not necessary to purchase all the stocks individually because mutual funds that mimic all of the major stock indexes are available.[5] A portfolio that consists of a large number of stocks is called the **market portfolio** because it consists of the entire stock market, or at least one entire segment of the stock market. Studies have found that the market portfolio has only about one-half the standard deviation of an average stock. However, it is not necessary for individual investors to own the market portfolio to take advantage of the risk-reducing benefits of diversification. As illustrated in exhibit 10.4, most of the benefit can be obtained by holding about 50 randomly selected stocks. Such a collection of investments is called a *well-diversified portfolio*.

> **market portfolio**
> A portfolio that contains all publicly traded stocks; often proxied by some market index, such as the S&P 500.

That part of the stand-alone risk of an individual investment that can be eliminated by diversification (i.e., by holding it as part of a well-diversified

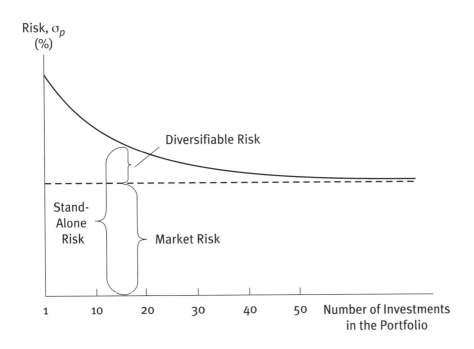

EXHIBIT 10.4
Portfolio Size and Risk

diversifiable risk
The portion of the risk of an investment that can be eliminated by holding the investment as part of a diversified portfolio.

market risk
The risk of an individual investment when it is held as part of a diversified portfolio as opposed to held in isolation.

portfolio) is called **diversifiable risk**. That part of the stand-alone risk of an individual investment that cannot be eliminated by diversification is called **market risk**. Every investment, whether it is the stock of Tenet Healthcare held by an individual investor or a CT scanner operated by a radiology group, has some diversifiable risk that can be eliminated and some portfolio risk that cannot be diversified away. Not all investments benefit to the same degree from portfolio risk-reducing effects, and some portfolios are not truly well diversified. In general, however, any investment will have some of its stand-alone risk eliminated when it is held as part of a portfolio.

Diversifiable risk, as seen by individuals who invest in stocks, is caused by events that are unique to a single business, such as the introduction of a new service, a labor strike, or a lawsuit. Because these events are essentially random, their effects can be eliminated by diversification. When one stock in a large, well-diversified portfolio does worse than expected because of a negative event that is unique to that firm, another stock in the portfolio will do better than expected because of a firm-unique positive event. On average, bad events in some companies will be offset by good events in others, so lower than expected returns on one stock will be offset by higher-than-expected returns on another, leaving the investor with an overall portfolio return closer to that expected than would be the case if only a single stock were held.

> ### Key Equation: Diversifiable Versus Portfolio Risk
> The stand-alone risk of an investment can be broken down into two parts:
>
> $$\text{Stand-alone risk} = \text{Diversifiable risk} + \text{Market risk}.$$
>
> Diversifiable risk is that portion of the stand-alone risk of an investment that can be eliminated by placing it in a well-diversified portfolio, while market risk is the risk that remains (cannot be diversified away).

The same logic can be applied to a business with a portfolio of projects. Perhaps hospital returns generated from inpatient surgery are less than expected because of the trend toward outpatient procedures, but this may be offset by returns that are greater than expected on state-of-the-art diagnostic services. Note that if a hospital offered both inpatient and outpatient surgery, it would be *hedging* against the trend toward more outpatient procedures because reduced demand for inpatient surgery would be offset by increased demand for outpatient surgery.

The point here is that the negative impact of random events that are unique to a particular business, or to a particular service within a business, can be offset by positive events in other businesses or in other products or services. Thus, the risk caused by random, unique events can be eliminated by portfolio diversification. Individual investors can diversify by holding many different securities, and health services businesses can diversify by offering many different services.

All investments do not benefit to the same degree from portfolio risk reduction. Some investments have a large amount of diversifiable risk and hence have a great deal of risk reduction when they are added to a portfolio. Others do not benefit nearly as much from portfolio risk reduction—it depends on the characteristics of both the investment and the portfolio. For example, consider the addition of a hospital management company's stock to two portfolios. The first portfolio consists of the stocks of 50 health-care providers. The second portfolio consists of the stocks of 50 randomly selected companies from many different industries. Much less risk reduction will occur when the hospital stock is added to the healthcare portfolio than when it is added to the randomly selected portfolio. The reason should be obvious: Hospital returns are more highly correlated with healthcare providers than with firms in other industries, and the higher the correlation, the less the risk reduction.

This logic tells us that there is more risk reduction potential inherent in adding a nursing home to a hospital business than there is in adding it to a long-term care business that already owns a large number of such investments. However, recognize that it is probably more difficult for managers of a hospital to manage a nursing home than it is for managers that specialize in such businesses.

Unfortunately, not all risk can be diversified away. Market risk—the risk that remains even in a well-diversified portfolio—stems from factors (e.g., wars, inflation, recessions, high interest rates) that systematically affect all stocks in portfolio or all products and services produced by a system. For example, the increasing market power of managed care organizations or government payers could lower reimbursement levels for all services offered by a hospital. No amount of diversification by the hospital into different health-care service lines could eliminate this risk.

Implications for Investors

The ability to eliminate a portion of the stand-alone risk inherent in individual investments has two significant implications for investors, whether the investor is an individual who holds securities or a healthcare business that offers service lines:

1. **Holding a single investment is not rational.** Holding a large, well-diversified portfolio can eliminate much of the stand-alone risk inherent in individual investments. Investors who are risk averse should

seek to eliminate all diversifiable risk. Individual investors can easily diversify their personal investment portfolios by buying many individual securities or mutual funds that hold diversified portfolios. Businesses cannot diversify their investments as easily as individuals can, but healthcare businesses that offer a diverse line of services are less risky than those that rely on a single service.

2. **Because an investment held in a portfolio has less risk than one held in isolation, the traditional stand-alone risk measure of standard deviation is not appropriate for individual assets when they are held as parts of portfolios.** Thus, it is necessary to rethink the definition and measurement of financial risk for such investments. (Note, though, that standard deviation remains the correct measure for the riskiness of an investor's entire *portfolio* because the portfolio is, in effect, a single investment held in isolation.)

SELF-TEST QUESTIONS

1. What is a portfolio of assets?
2. What is a well-diversified portfolio?
3. What happens to the risk of a single asset when it is held as part of a portfolio of assets?
4. Explain the differences between stand-alone risk, diversifiable risk, and market risk.
5. Why should all investors hold well-diversified portfolios rather than individual assets?
6. Is standard deviation the appropriate risk measure for an individual asset?
7. Is standard deviation the appropriate risk measure for an investor's portfolio of assets?

The Relevant Risk of a Stock

capital asset pricing model (CAPM)
An equilibrium model that specifies the relationship between a stock's value and its market risk, as measured by beta (β).

If investors are risk averse, they will demand a premium for bearing risk—that is, the higher the risk of a security, the higher its expected return must be to induce investors to buy it or to hold it. All risk except that related to broad market movements can easily be eliminated through diversification. This implies that investors are primarily concerned with the risk of their portfolio rather than the risk of the individual securities in the portfolio. How, then, should the risk of an individual stock be measured? The **capital asset pricing model (CAPM)** provides one answer to that question. A stock might be quite risky if it is held by itself, but—because diversification eliminates about half of its risk—the stock's *relevant risk* is its contribution to a well-diversified portfolio's risk, which is much smaller than the stock's stand-alone risk.

A well-diversified portfolio has only market risk. Therefore, the CAPM defines the relevant risk of an individual stock as the amount of risk that the stock contributes to the market portfolio, which is a portfolio containing all stocks. The relevant measure of risk is called the **beta coefficient**, or simply beta (denoted by β). The beta of stock i is calculated as:

> **beta coefficient (β)**
> A measure of the risk of one investment relative to the risk of a collection (portfolio) of investments.

$$\beta_i = (\sigma_i / \sigma_m) \times r_{im},$$

where

σ_i = standard deviation of stock i's returns,

σ_m = standard deviation of the market's returns, and

r_{im} = correlation coefficient between the returns on stock i and the market's returns.

This equation shows that a stock with a high standard deviation, σ_i, will have a high beta, which means that, all else held constant, the stock contributes a lot of risk to a well-diversified portfolio. This makes sense, because a stock with high stand-alone risk will tend to destabilize a portfolio. Note, too, that a stock with a high correlation with the market, r_{im}, will also tend to have a large beta and hence greater risk. This also makes sense, because a high correlation means that diversification is not helping much—the stock will perform well when the portfolio is performing well, and the stock will perform poorly when the portfolio is performing poorly.

The beta of any portfolio of investments is simply the weighted average of the individual investments' betas:

$$\beta_{\text{Portfolio}} = (w_1 \times \beta_1) + (w_2 \times \beta_2) + (w_3 \times \beta_3) + (w_i \times \beta_i), \text{ and so on.}$$

Here, $\beta_{\text{Portfolio}}$ is the beta of the portfolio, which measures the volatility of the entire portfolio; w_i is the fraction of the portfolio invested in each particular asset; and β_i is the beta coefficient of that asset. For ease of illustration, assume that an investor has only the four stocks listed in the following table:

Stock	Beta (β_i)	Weight in Portfolio (w_i)
1	0.6	25%
2	1.0	25%
3	1.4	25%
4	1.8	25%

The weighted average of the stock betas is the portfolio beta:

$$\beta_{Portfolio} = (0.6 \times 0.25) + (1.0 \times 0.25) + (1.4 \times 0.25) + (1.8 \times 0.25)$$
$$= 1.20.$$

Four key points about beta are important to know.

1. Beta determines how much risk a stock contributes to a well-diversified portfolio. If all the stocks' weights in a portfolio are equal, then a stock with a beta that is twice as big as another stock's beta contributes twice as much risk.
2. The average of all stocks' betas is equal to 1; the beta of the market also is equal to 1. Intuitively, this is because the market return is the average of all the stocks' returns.
3. A stock with a beta greater than 1 contributes more risk to a portfolio than does the average stock, and a stock with a beta less than 1 contributes less risk to a portfolio than does the average stock.
4. Most stocks have betas that are between about 0.4 and 1.6.

Estimating Beta

The CAPM is an ex ante model, which means that all of the variables represent before-the-fact, expected values. In particular, the beta coefficient used by investors should reflect the relationship between a stock's expected return and the market's expected return during some future period. However, people generally calculate betas using data from some past period and then assume that the stock's risk will be the same in the future as it was in the past.

Many analysts use four to five years of monthly data, although some use 52 weeks of weekly data. To illustrate, we use the four years (2015–2018) of monthly returns to calculate the betas of Community Health Systems, Tenet Healthcare, and HCA Healthcare using the equation introduced earlier for calculating beta:

	Market (S&P 500)	Community Health Systems	Tenet Healthcare	HCA Healthcare
Symbol	GSPC	CYH	THC	HCA
Standard deviation	3.3%	20.7%	14.4%	7.0%
Correlation with the market		0.37	0.36	0.36
$\beta_i = (\sigma_i/\sigma_m) \times ri_m$		2.32	1.58	0.77

Suppose you plot a stock's returns on the y axis of a graph and the market portfolio's returns on the x axis. The formula for the slope of a regression line is exactly equal to the formula for calculating beta. Therefore, to estimate beta for a security, you can estimate a regression with the stock's returns on the y axis and the market's returns on the x axis using the following equation:

$$r_{it} = a_i + \beta_i \, r_{Mt} + e_{it},$$

where r_{it} and r_{Mt} are the actual returns for the stock and the market for date t; a_i and β_i are the estimated regression coefficients; and e_{it} is the estimated error at date t. Exhibit 10.5 illustrates this approach for Community Health Systems and HCA Healthcare. The blue dots represent each of the 48 data points, with the stock's returns plotted on the y axis and the market's returns on the x axis. We use the Trendline feature in Excel to show the regression equation on the charts (these are colored blue). It is also possible to use Excel's SLOPE function to estimate the slope from a regression: SLOPE (known_y's, known_x's). Exhibit 10.5 shows that Community Health Systems has an estimated beta of 2.32 and HCA Healthcare has an estimated beta of 0.77, the same values that we calculated earlier using the equation for beta. The black line is the plot of market versus market (a 45-degree line with a slope of 1.00).

Notice that the slope of the regression line of Community Health Systems (2.32) is steeper than the slope of the market line (1.00), suggesting that Community Health Systems is riskier than the market. Conversely, the slope of the regression line of HCA (0.77) is flatter than the market, suggesting that HCA is less risky than the market.

It is important to remember that beta cannot be observed; it can only be estimated. Community Health Systems has an estimated beta of 2.32. What does that mean? By definition, the average beta for all stocks is equal to 1, so Community Health Systems contributes 132 percent more risk to a well-diversified portfolio than a typical stock (assuming the two have the same portfolio weight). HCA Healthcare has an estimated beta of 0.77, meaning that it contributes 23 percent less risk to a well-diversified portfolio than a typical stock. When the market is doing well, a high-beta stock such as Community Health Systems tends to do better than an average stock, and when the market does poorly, a high-beta stock also does worse than an average stock. The opposite is true for a low-beta stock: When the market soars, the low-beta stock tends to go up by a smaller amount; when the market falls, the low-beta stock tends to fall less than the market.

The Relationship Between Risk and Return and the Capital Asset Pricing Model

This chapter contains much discussion of the definition and measurement of financial risk. However, the ability to define and measure is of no value in financial decision-making unless risk can be related to return. Planners must consider the question, how much return is required to compensate investors for assuming a given level of risk? In this section, we focus on setting required rates of return on stock investments because the basic theory of risk and return was developed with these in mind. In later chapters, the focus is on setting required rates of return on individual projects within firms.

The relationship between the market risk of a stock, as measured by its market beta, and its required rate of return is given by the CAPM. To begin, some basic definitions are needed:

- $E(R_i)$ = Expected rate of return on stock i (any stock).
- $R(R_i)$ = Required rate of return on stock i.
- RF = Risk-free rate of return. In a CAPM context, RF is generally measured by the return on long-term US Treasury bonds (T-bonds).
- β_i = Market beta coefficient of stock i. The market beta of an average-risk stock is $\beta_A = 1.0$.
- $R(R_M)$ = Required rate of return on a portfolio that consists of all stocks, which is the market portfolio. $R(R_M)$ is also the required rate of return on an average ($\beta_A = 1.0$) stock.
- RP_M = Market risk premium = $R(R_M) - RF$. This is the additional return over the risk-free rate required to compensate investors for assuming average ($\beta_A = 1.0$) risk.
- RP_i = Risk premium on stock i = $[R(R_M) - RF] \times b_i = RP_M \times b_i$. Stock i's risk premium is less than, equal to, or greater than the premium on an average stock, depending on whether its beta is less than, equal to, or greater than 1.0. If $\beta_i = \beta_A = 1.0$, then $RP_i = RP_M$.

EXHIBIT 10.5
Monthly Stock Returns of Community Health Systems, HCA Healthcare, and S&P 500, 2014–2018

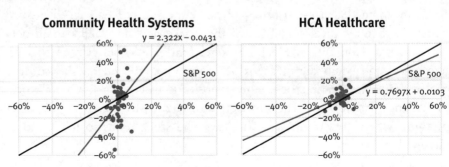

Using these definitions, the CAPM relationship between risk and required rate of return is expressed by the following equation, which specifies a line called the **security market line (SML)**:

Required return on stock i = Risk-free rate + Risk premium for stock i

Required return on stock i = Risk-free rate + (Beta of stock i) × (Market risk premium)

$$R(R_i) = RF + [R(R_M)] - RF) \times \beta_i$$
$$\qquad = RF + (RP_M \times \beta_i).$$

security market line (SML)
The portion of the capital asset pricing model (CAPM) that specifies the relationship between market risk and required rate of return.

The SML equation shows that a stock's required return is determined by the risk-free rate, the market risk premium, and beta.

The Risk-Free Rate

A stock's required return begins with the risk-free rate. To induce investors to take on a risky investment, they will need a return that is at least as big as the risk-free rate. The yield on long-term Treasury bonds is often used to measure the risk-free rate when estimating the required return with the CAPM.

The Market Risk Premium

The market risk premium is the difference between the required rate of return on the market, $R(R_M)$, and the risk-free rate, RF:

Market risk premium = $R(R_M) - RF$

Market risk premium = RP_M.

The market risk premium, RP_M, is the extra rate of return that investors require to invest in the stock market rather than purchase risk-free securities. The size of the market risk premium depends on the degree of risk aversion that investors have on average. When investors are very risk averse, the market risk premium is high; when investors are less concerned about risk, the market risk premium is low. In this example, T-bonds yield an RF of 6 percent, and an average share of stock has a required rate of return, $R(R_M)$, of 10 percent, so RP_M is 4 percentage points. If the degree of risk aversion is increased, $R(R_M)$ might increase to 12 percent, which would cause RPM to increase to 6 percentage points. Thus, the greater the overall degree of risk aversion, the higher the required rate on the market and hence the higher the required rates of return on all stocks.

The Risk Premium for an Individual Stock

The risk premium for an individual stock, RPi, is equal to the product of the stock's beta and the market risk premium:

Risk premium for stock i = (Beta of stock i) × (Market risk premium)

Risk premium for stock i = $[R(R_M)-RF] \times \beta_i$

Risk premium for stock i = $(RP_M \times \beta_i)$.

For an illustration of the use of the SML, assume that RF is 6 percent and $R(R_M)$ is 10 percent. For a low-risk stock with β_{Low} = 0.5, the risk premium for the stock RP_{Low} is:

$$= [R(R_M)-RF] \times \beta_i$$

$$= (RP_M \times \beta_i)$$

$$= (10\% - 6\%) \times 0.5$$

$$= (4\%) \times 0.5$$

$$= 2\%.$$

The Required Rate of Return for an Individual Stock

According to the SML, the required rate of return on the low-risk stock is:

$$R(R_{Low}) = \text{Risk-free rate} + \text{Risk premium for low-risk stock}$$

$$R(R_{Low}) = RF + RP_{Low}$$

$$R(R_{Low}) = 6\% + 2\%$$

$$R(R_{Low}) = 8\%.$$

If a high-risk stock has β_{High} = 2.0, then its required rate of return is 14 percent, as we see here:

$$R(R_{High}) = 6\% + (10\% - 6\%) \times 2.0$$

$$R(R_{High}) = 6\% + (4\%) \times 2.0$$

$$R(R_{High}) = 6\% + 8\%$$

$$R(R_{High}) = 14\%.$$

An average stock with $\beta_{Average}$ = 1.0 has a required return of 10 percent, the same as the market return, which can be seen if we figure it in the following way:

$$R(R_{Average}) = 6\% + (10\% - 6\%) \times 1.0$$

$$R(R_{Average}) = 6\% + (4\%) \times 1.0$$

$$R(R_{Average}) = 6\% + 4\%$$

$$R(R_{Average}) = 10\% = R(R_M).$$

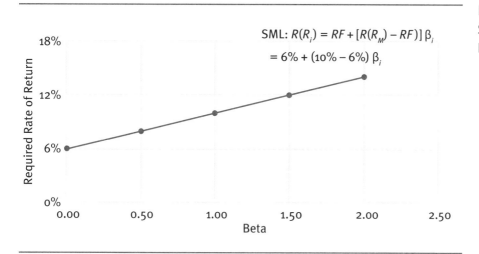

EXHIBIT 10.6
Security Market
Line

The SML is often depicted in graphical form, as in exhibit 10.6, which shows the SML when $RF = 6$ percent and $R(R_M) = 10$ percent.

Here are the relevant points concerning the graph:

- Required rates of return are shown on the vertical axis, while risk as measured by market beta is shown on the horizontal axis.
- Riskless securities have $\beta_i = 0$; therefore, RF is the vertical axis intercept.
- The slope of the SML reflects the degree of risk aversion in the economy. The greater the average investor's aversion to risk, (1) the steeper the slope of the SML, (2) the greater the risk premium for any stock, and (3) the higher the required rate of return on stocks.
- The y axis intercept reflects the level of expected inflation. The higher inflation expectations are, the greater both RF and $R(R_M)$ are, and thus the higher the SML plots on the graph.
- The values previously calculated for the required rates of return on stocks with $\beta_i = 0.5$, $\beta_i = 1.0$, and $\beta_i = 2.0$ agree with the values shown on the graph.

Both the SML and a firm's position on it change over time because of changes in interest rates, investors' risk aversion, and individual firms' betas. Thus, the SML, as well as a firm's risk, must be evaluated on the basis of current information. The SML, its use, and how its input values are estimated are covered in greater detail in chapter 13.

Required Return and Changes in Expected Inflation or Risk Aversion

Change in Expected Inflation
Exhibit 10.7 shows the impact on the SML of a 2 percent increase in expected inflation. The change causes the risk-free interest rate to increase from 6 percent to 8 percent, but there is no change in the market risk premium (10% − 6% = 12% − 8% = 4%). This happens because as the risk-free rate changes, so will the required return on the market, and this will, other things held constant, keep the market risk premium stable. Exhibit 10.7 also shows that the increase in expected inflation leads to an identical increase in the required rate of return on all assets, because the same risk-free rate is built into the required rate of return on all assets. For example, $R(R_M)$ (and the average stock) increases from 10 percent to 12 percent. Other risky securities' returns also rise by 2 percentage points.

Change in Risk Aversion
The slope of the SML reflects the extent to which investors are averse to risk: The steeper the slope of the line, the greater the average investor's aversion to risk. Suppose all investors were indifferent to risk—that is, suppose they were not risk averse. If RF = 6 percent, then risky assets would also provide an expected return of 6 percent. If there were no risk aversion, then there would be no risk premium, and the SML would be a horizontal line. As risk aversion increases, so does the risk premium, and this causes the slope of the SML to become steeper. Exhibit 10.8 illustrates the impact of an increase in risk aversion on the SML. In this case, $R(R_M)$ rises from 10 percent to 12.5 percent. The returns on other risky assets also rise, and the effect of this shift

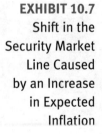

EXHIBIT 10.7
Shift in the Security Market Line Caused by an Increase in Expected Inflation

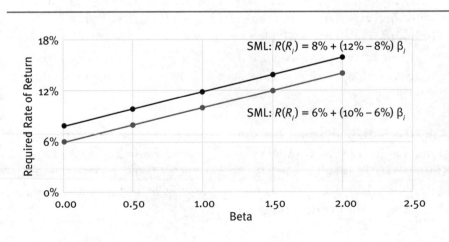

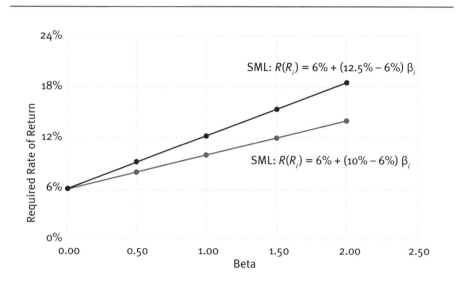

EXHIBIT 10.8
Shift in the
Security Market
Line Caused by
an Increase in
Investor Risk
Aversion

in risk aversion is greater for riskier securities. For example, the required return on a stock with $\beta_i = 0.5$ increases by only 1.25 percentage points, from 8.5 percent to 9.75 percent; the required return on a stock with $\beta_i = 1.0$ increases by 2.5 percentage points, from 10.0 percent to 12.5 percent; and the required return on a stock with $\beta_i = 1.5$ increases by 3.75 percentage points, from 12.0 percent to 15.75 percent.

Comparison of Required Return to Expected Return

The CAPM conceptualizes the required return on stock i, $R(R_i)$, as the risk-free rate plus the extra return (i.e., the risk premium) needed to induce an investor to hold the stock. That is, for a given level of risk as measured by beta, what rate of expected return does an investor require to compensate them for bearing that risk? Here, $R(R_i)$ can be considered the minimum expected return that is required by an average investor.

How do investors use $R(R_i)$? If the expected rate of return, $E(R_i)$, is less than $R(R_i)$, an investor would not purchase stock i or would sell it if it is owned. If $E(R_i)$ is greater than $R(R_i)$, an investor would purchase stock i, and an individual would be indifferent about the purchase if $E(R_i) = R(R_i)$.

Suppose an investor is considering purchase shares of Regis Healthcare, which has a beta of 1.1 and an expected rate of return, $E(R_{\text{Regis}})$, of 15 percent. If RF is 6 percent and $R(R_M)$ is 10 percent, then the required rate of return on Regis Healthcare, $R(R_{\text{Regis}})$, is calculated as follows:

$$R(R_i) = RF + [R(R_M) - RF] \times b_i$$
$$R(R_{Regis}) = 6\% + (10\% - 6\%) \times 1.1$$
$$R(R_{Regis}) = 10.4\%.$$

In this circumstance, the expected rate of return is greater than the required rate of return for Regis Healthcare, so an investor would purchase the stock. In summary,

- If $E(R_i) > R(R_i)$, an investor would purchase stock i.
- If $E(R_i) = R(R_i)$, an investor would be indifferent about purchase of stock i.
- If $E(R_i) < R(R_i)$, an investor would not purchase stock i.

Some Final Thoughts About Beta and the Capital Asset Pricing Model

The CAPM is more than just an abstract theory described in textbooks. It is widely used by analysts, investors, and corporate managers. However, despite its intuitive appeal, at least serious concerns are prompted by the CAPM:

1. It is built on a restrictive set of assumptions that do not conform well to real-world conditions.
2. It is impossible to prove. Studies that do demonstrate the linear relationship between market risk and required return prove nothing because the results stem from the mathematical properties of the model, not because it is theoretically correct.
3. Some studies find no relationship between stocks' returns and market betas.
4. The market betas that are actually used in the CAPM measure the historical relative volatility of a stock, but conditions often change. Thus, its future volatility, which is of real concern to investors, might be quite different from its past volatility.

Despite these concerns, the CAPM is extremely appealing because it is simple and logical. It focuses on the impact that a single investment has on a portfolio, which in most situations is the correct way to think about risk. Furthermore, it tells us that the required rate of return on an investment comprises the risk-free rate, which compensates investors for time value, plus a risk premium that is a function of investors' attitudes toward risk in the aggregate and the specific portfolio risk of the investment being evaluated.

Because of these points, the CAPM is an important conceptual tool. However, its actual use to set required rates of return must be viewed with some caution. We have more to say about CAPM in practice in chapter 13.

1. What is the capital asset pricing model (CAPM)?
2. What is the appropriate measure of risk in the CAPM?
3. Write out the equation for the SML, and graph it.
4. How do changes in risk aversion and inflation expectations affect the SML?
5. What are the pros and cons regarding the CAPM?

Key Concepts

This chapter covers the important topics of financial risk and required return. The key concepts of this chapter are as follows:

- Risk definition and measurement are important in healthcare finance because decision makers, in general, are *risk averse* and require higher returns from investments that have higher risk.
- *Financial risk* is associated with the prospect of returns less than anticipated. The higher the probability of a return being far less than anticipated, the greater the risk.
- The risk of investments held in isolation, called *stand-alone risk*, can be measured by the dispersion of the rate-of-return distribution about its *expected value*. The most commonly used measure of stand-alone risk is the *standard deviation* of the return distribution.
- Most investments are not held in isolation but as part of a *portfolio*. Individual investors hold portfolios of securities, and businesses hold portfolios of projects (i.e., products and services).
- When investments with returns that are less than perfectly positively correlated are combined in a portfolio, risk is reduced. The risk reduction occurs because less than expected returns on some investments are offset by greater than expected returns on other investments. However, among real-world investments, it is

(continued)

(continued from previous page)

impossible to eliminate all risk because the returns on all assets are influenced to a greater or lesser degree by overall economic conditions.

- That portion of the stand-alone risk of an investment that can be eliminated by holding the investment in a portfolio is called *diversifiable risk*, while the risk that remains is called *portfolio risk*.

- *Market risk* is the risk of business projects (or of the stocks of entire businesses) when they are considered as part of an individual investor's well-diversified portfolio of securities.

- Market risk is measured by a project's or stock's *market beta*, which reflects the volatility of a project's (or stock's) returns relative to the volatility of returns on a well-diversified stock portfolio.

- Stand-alone risk is most relevant to investments held in isolation; corporate risk is most relevant to projects held by not-for-profit firms and by small, owner-managed, for-profit businesses; and market risk is most relevant to projects held by large investor-owned corporations.

- The *beta coefficient* (β) *of a portfolio of investments* is the weighted average of the betas of the components of the portfolio, where the weights are the proportion of the overall investment in each component. Therefore, the weighted average of corporate betas of all projects in a business must equal 1.0, while the weighted average of all projects' market betas must equal the market beta of the firm's stock.

- The *capital asset pricing model (CAPM)* is an equilibrium model that describes the relationship between market risk and required rates of return.

- The *security market line (SML)* provides the actual risk–required rate of return relationship. The required rate of return on any stock is equal to the risk-free rate plus the market risk premium times the stock's market beta coefficient: $R(R_i) = RF + [R(R_M) - RF] \times \beta = RF + (RP_M \times \beta)$.

This concludes the discussion of basic financial management concepts. The next chapter begins our coverage of long-term financing.

Questions

10.1. When considering stand-alone risk, the return distribution of a less risky investment is more peaked ("tighter") than that of a riskier investment. What shape would the return distribution have for an investment with (a) completely certain returns and (b) completely uncertain returns?

10.2. Stock A has an expected rate of return of 8 percent, a standard deviation of 20 percent, and a market beta of 0.5. Stock B has an expected rate of return of 12 percent, a standard deviation of 15 percent, and a market beta of 1.5. Which investment is riskier? Why? (Hint: Remember that the risk of an investment depends on its context.)

10.3. a. What is risk aversion?

b. Why is risk aversion so important to financial decision-making?

10.4. Explain why holding investments in portfolios has such a profound impact on the concept of financial risk.

10.5. Assume that two investments are combined in a portfolio.

a. In words, what is the expected rate of return on the portfolio?

b. What condition must be present for the portfolio to have lower risk than the weighted average of the two investments?

c. Is it possible for the portfolio to have lower risk than that of either investment?

d. Is it possible for the portfolio to be riskless? If so, what condition is necessary to create such a portfolio?

10.6. Explain the difference between market risk and diversifiable risk.

10.7. What are the implications of portfolio theory for investors?

10.8. a. What is market risk?

b. How is it defined?

10.9. Under what circumstances is stand-alone and market risk most relevant?

10.10. a. What is the capital asset pricing model (CAPM)? The security market line (SML)?

b. What are the weaknesses of the CAPM?

c. What is the value of the CAPM?

Problems

10.1. Consider the following probability distribution of returns estimated for a proposed project that involves a new ultrasound machine:

State of the Economy	Probability of Occurrence	Rate of Return
Very poor	0.10	−10.0%
Poor	0.20	0.0
Average	0.40	10.0
Good	0.20	20.0
Very good	0.10	30.0

a. What is the expected rate of return on the project?
b. What is the project's standard deviation of returns?
c. In what situation is this risk relevant?

10.2. Suppose that a person won the Florida lottery and was offered a choice of two prizes: (1) $500,000 or (2) a coin-toss gamble in which he would get $1 million for heads and zero for tails.

a. What is the expected dollar return on the gamble?
b. Would the person choose the sure $500,000 or the gamble?
c. If he chooses the sure $500,000, is this person a risk averter or a risk seeker?

10.3. Refer to exhibit 10.2.

a. Construct an equal-weighted (50/50) portfolio of investments B and C. What are the expected rate of return and standard deviation of the portfolio? Explain your results.
b. Construct an equal-weighted (50/50) portfolio of investments B and D. What are the expected rate of return and standard deviation of the portfolio? Explain your results.

10.4. Suppose that the risk-free rate, RF, is 8 percent and the required rate of return on the market, $R(R_M)$, is 14 percent.

a. Write out the security market line (SML) equation, and explain each term.
b. Plot the SML on a sheet of paper.
c. Suppose that inflation expectations increase such that the risk-free rate, RF, increases to 10 percent and the required rate of return on the market, $R(R_M)$, increases to 16 percent. Write out and plot the new SML.

d. Return to the original assumptions in this problem. Now, suppose that investors' risk aversion increases and the required rate of return on the market, $R(R_M)$, increases to 16 percent. (There is no change in the risk-free rate because RF reflects the required rate of return on a riskless investment.) Write out and plot the new SML.

10.5. Several years ago, the Value Line Investment Survey reported the following market betas for the stocks of selected healthcare providers:

Company	Beta
Quorum Health	0.90
Beverly Enterprises	1.20
Health South Corporation	1.45
United Healthcare	1.70

At the time these betas were developed, reasonable estimates for the risk-free rate, RF, and required rate of return on the market, $R(R_M)$, were 6.5 percent and 13.5 percent, respectively.

a. What are the required rates of return on the four stocks?

b. Why do their required rates of return differ?

c. Suppose that a person is planning to invest in only one stock rather than a well-diversified stock portfolio. Are the required rates of return calculated above applicable to the investment? Explain your answer.

10.6. Suppose that Apple Health Services has four different projects. These projects are listed below, along with the amount of capital invested and the market betas:

Project	Amount Invested	Market Beta
Walk-in clinic	$ 500,000	1.1
MRI facility	2,000,000	1.5
Clinical laboratory	1,500,000	0.8
X-ray laboratory	1,000,000	1.0
	$5,000,000	

a. What is the overall market beta of Apple Health Services?

b. How does the riskiness of Apple's stock compare with the riskiness of an average stock?

c. Would stock investors require a rate of return on Apple that is greater than, less than, or the same as the return on an average-risk stock?

10.7. Assume that Community Health Systems is evaluating the feasibility of building a new hospital in an area not currently served by the company. The company's analysts estimate a market beta of 1.1 for the hospital project, which is somewhat higher than the 0.8 market beta of the company's average project. Financial forecasts for the new hospital indicate an expected rate of return on the equity portion of the investment of 20 percent. If the risk-free rate, RF, is 7 percent and the required rate of return on the market, $R(R_M)$, is 12 percent, is the new hospital in the best interest of Community Health Systems' shareholders? Explain your answer.

10.8. Yahoo Finance reported the following market betas for the stocks of selected health insurers:

Company	Beta
UnitedHealth Group	0.70
Humana	1.16
Aetna	0.63
Cigna	0.71

Assume that the risk-free rate, RF, and required rate of return on the market, $R(R_M)$, are 2.0 percent and 8.5 percent, respectively.

a. What are the required rates of return on the four stocks?

b. Which of the stocks is riskiest for investors? Explain your answer.

10.9. Assume that Everly Healthcare, a provider of skilled nursing facility services, is evaluating the feasibility of building a new facility to replace one of its aging facilities in a small, low-volume market. The company's analysts estimate a market beta for the project of 0.8, which is somewhat lower than the 0.91 market beta of the company's average project. The corporate beta for the project is estimated to be 0.5. Financial forecasts for the new facility indicate an expected rate of return on the equity portion of the investment of 7 percent. If the risk-free rate, RF, is 2 percent and the required rate of return on the market, $R(R_M)$, is 10 percent, is the new facility in the best interest of Everly's shareholders? Explain your answer.

Selected Case

One case in *Gapenski's Cases in Healthcare Finance*, sixth edition, is applicable to this chapter: Case 12: Mid-Atlantic Specialty, Inc.

Notes

1. If inflation is considered, the T-bill investment is not truly risk-free. The *real return*, which recognizes inflation effects, is uncertain because it depends on the amount of inflation realized over the year.

2. In markets that are *efficient*, low-risk investments will have low expected returns, while high-risk investments will have high expected returns. However, not all markets are efficient. See chapter 12 for a complete discussion of market efficiency.

3. A portfolio of two investments has lower risk than that of either component only when the correlation coefficient between the returns on the two investments is less than the ratio of the standard deviations, when this ratio is constructed with the lower standard deviation in the numerator. For example, for portfolio AD to have less risk than both A and D, the correlation coefficient between the returns on A and D must be less than σ_A/σ_D = 11.0% ÷ 12.1% = 0.91. The actual correlation coefficient is 0.53, so the condition is met in this example.

4. Although stocks can be combined with complex investments (derivatives) to form riskless portfolios, our emphasis here is on real-asset investments.

5. The Wilshire 5000 Index, also called the Total Stock Market Index, mimics the returns of all publicly traded US stocks.

Resources

Bannow, T. 2018. "ACOs Reluctant to Move to Advanced Risk-Taking Models." *Modern Healthcare*. Published October 8. www.modernhealthcare.com/article /20181006/NEWS/181009954/acos-reluctant-to-move-to-advanced -risk-taking-models.

Beck, W., C. Kelly-Aduli, and B. B. Sanderson. 2018. "Protecting Revenue at Risk." *Healthcare Financial Management* 72 (4): 62–67.

Brigham, E. F., and P. R. Daves. 2017a. "Risk and Return: Part I." In *Intermediate Financial Management*, 13th ed., by E. F. Brigham and P. R. Davies, 56–111. Mason, OH: South-Western Cengage Learning.

————. 2017b. "Risk and Return: Part II." In *Intermediate Financial Management*, 13th ed., by E. F. Brigham and P. R. Davies, 112–48. Mason, OH: South-Western Cengage Learning.

Friesen, C. A. 2018. "Assessing Risk in Healthcare Finance Calls for Stewardship." *Healthcare Financial Management* 72 (4): 1–2.

Kotecki, L. 2018. "Reaping the Benefits of an Actuarial Mindset." *Healthcare Financial Management* 72 (4): 50–54.

Luthi, S. 2018. "Azar Hints at 'Bold' Risk-Based Medicare Payment Models." *Modern Healthcare*. Published September 6. www.modernhealthcare.com/article /20180906/NEWS/180909962/azar-expect-bold-risk-based-medicare -payment-models.

Puchley, T., and C. Toppi. 2018. "ERM: Evolving from Risk Assessment to Strategic Risk Management." *Healthcare Financial Management* 72 (4): 44–49.

LONG-TERM FINANCING

Regardless of size, all health services organizations must have capital (funds) to acquire the facilities, equipment, inventories, and other assets needed to conduct business. Many different types of capital are available to health services organizations. Debt financing is supplied by lenders, while equity financing is obtained from owners in for-profit businesses and from the community at large in not-for-profit businesses. Because the types of financing have different characteristics, managers must understand how the types of capital differ and what effect these differences have on the risk and financial condition of the business. Furthermore, to better understand how capital suppliers decide how much to charge for capital, managers need to know how securities are valued.

Managers of health services organizations have many decisions to make regarding long-term financing. For example, should a hospital use a small or large proportion of debt capital in its financing mix? Such decisions are important because they affect the hospital's risk and the cost of its financing and therefore its potential profitability.

The three chapters in part V introduce readers to the types of capital that are available to health services organizations, how this capital is valued in the marketplace, and how the use of debt financing affects a business's risk and capital costs.

LONG-TERM DEBT FINANCING

11

Learning Objectives

After studying this chapter, readers will be able to

- Describe how interest rates are set in the economy.
- Discuss the types of long-term debt instruments and their features.
- Discuss the components that make up the interest rate on a debt security.
- Explain credit ratings and their importance to both borrowers and lenders.
- Value debt securities.

Introduction

If a business is to operate, it must have assets. To acquire assets, it must raise capital. Capital comes in two basic forms: debt and equity. Historically, capital furnished by the owners of investor-owned businesses (i.e., stockholders of for-profit corporations) was called *equity* capital, while capital obtained by not-for-profit businesses from grants, contributions, and retained earnings was called *fund* capital. Both types of capital serve the same purpose in financing businesses—providing a permanent financing base without a contractually fixed cost—so today the term *equity* is often used to represent nonliability capital regardless of ownership type.

In addition to equity financing, most healthcare businesses use a considerable amount of *debt* financing (loans), which is provided by *creditors*. For example, on average, healthcare providers finance their assets with 5 percent short-term debt (and liabilities), 35 percent long-term debt, and 60 percent equity, as measured by balance sheet amounts.[1] Thus, more than one-third of providers' financing comes from debt.

In this chapter, many facets of debt financing are discussed, including important background material related to how interest rates are set in the economy. The discussion here focuses on long-term debt; short-term debt is discussed in chapter 16. Besides the topics covered within the chapter, the chapter 11 supplement discusses three concepts that are relevant but not essential to understanding debt financing: credit enhancement, the term structure of interest rates, and economic factors that influence interest rate levels.

The Cost of Money

Capital in a free economy is allocated through the price system. The *interest rate* is the price paid to obtain debt capital, whereas for equity capital in for-profit firms, the price (i.e., investors' returns) takes the form of *dividends* and *capital gains* (or *losses*). Four fundamental factors affect the supply of and demand for investment capital—and the cost of money: investment opportunities, time preferences for consumption, risk, and inflation.

To understand how these factors operate, consider the situation facing Lori Gibbs, an entrepreneur who is planning to found a new home health agency. Lori does not have sufficient personal funds to start the business, so she must supplement her equity capital with debt financing.

Investment Opportunities
If Lori estimates that the business will be highly profitable, she will be able to pay creditors a higher interest rate than if the business is barely profitable. Her ability to pay for borrowed capital depends on the business's *investment opportunities*. The higher the profitability of the business, the higher the interest rate that Lori can afford to pay lenders for use of their savings.

Time Preferences for Consumption
The interest rate that lenders charge depends in large part on their *time preferences for consumption*. For example, one potential lender, Jane Wright, may be saving for retirement, so she may be willing to lend funds at a relatively low interest rate because her preference is for future consumption. Another person, John Davis, has a young family to support, so he may be willing to lend funds out of current income, forgoing consumption, but only if the interest rate is high. John is said to have a high time preference for consumption, and Jane has a low time preference. If the entire population of an economy were living right at the subsistence level, time preferences for current consumption would necessarily be high, aggregate savings would be low, interest rates would be high, and the availability of capital would be scarce.

Risk
The *risk* inherent in the prospective home health care business, and thus in Lori's ability to repay the loan, also affects the return that lenders require: the higher the risk, the higher the interest rate. Investors will be unwilling to

lend to high-risk businesses unless the interest rate is higher than the rate on loans to low-risk businesses.

Inflation

Finally, because the value of money in the future is affected by *inflation*, the higher the expected rate of inflation, the higher the interest rate lenders will demand. Debt suppliers must demand higher interest rates when inflation is high to offset the resulting loss of purchasing power.

To simplify matters, the illustration implied that savers lend directly to businesses that need capital, but in most cases, the funds actually pass through a *financial intermediary* such as a bank or a mutual fund. Also, although we used the interest rate on debt capital to illustrate the four factors, the same logic applies to the cost of all investment capital, including equity.

1. What is the "price" of debt capital?
2. What four factors affect the cost of money?

Common Long-Term Debt Instruments

There are many types of long-term debt, which generally is defined as debt that has a maturity greater than one year. Some types of long-term debt, such as home mortgages and auto loans, are used by individuals, while other types are used primarily by businesses. In this section, we discuss the types of long-term debt most commonly used by healthcare organizations.

Long-Term Loans

A **term loan** (short for *long-term loan*) is a contract under which a borrower agrees to make a series of interest and principal payments, on specified dates, to a lender. Term loans usually are negotiated directly between the borrowing business and the lender, which typically is a financial institution such as a commercial bank, a mutual fund, or an insurance company. Thus, term loans are *private placements* as opposed to *public offerings*, which typically are used on bonds (discussed in the next section), the other major type of long-term debt.

term loan
Long-term debt financing obtained directly from a financial institution, often a commercial bank.

Most term loans have maturities of two to ten years. Like home mortgages, term loans are usually amortized (paid) in equal installments over the life of the loan, so part of the principal of the loan is retired with each payment.

Term loans have three major advantages over debt (bonds) sold to the public: speed, flexibility, and low administrative costs. Because term loans are negotiated directly between an institutional lender and the borrower, as opposed to being sold to many lenders, formal documentation is minimized. The key provisions of the loan can be worked out much more quickly, and with more flexibility, than those for a public issue. Furthermore, it is not necessary for a term loan to go through the Securities and Exchange Commission (SEC) (www.sec.gov) registration process. Finally, after a term loan has been negotiated, changes can be made more easily than with bonds if financial circumstances so dictate.

The interest rate on a term loan can be either fixed for the life of the loan or variable. If it is *fixed*, the rate used will be close to the rate on equivalent maturity bonds issued by businesses of comparable risk. If the rate is *variable*, it is usually set at a certain number of percentage points over an index rate, such as the prime rate. When the index rate goes up or down, so does the interest rate that must be paid on the outstanding balance of the term loan. The *prime rate* is the interest rate that banks charge their best—that is, most creditworthy—customers. Theoretically, the prime rate is set separately by every bank, but in practice, all banks follow the lead of the major New York City banks, so there usually is a single prime rate in the United States. The prime rate changes, sometimes quite rapidly, in response to changing inflation expectations and Federal Reserve Board actions. In January 2020, the prime rate stood at 4.75 percent.

Although term loans have many advantages, they have two disadvantages. First, there is a limit to the size of a term loan. Although a term loan can be large, such as when multiple banks combine to make a loan of $100 million or more, most term loans are relatively small, averaging less than $1 million. Also, lenders typically will not extend term loans to the maturity that businesses can attain in a bond financing. Therefore, term loans are inappropriate for use in financing assets with very long lives, such as clinic buildings or long-term care facilities.

Bonds

bond
Long-term debt issued by a business or government unit and generally sold in $1,000 or $5,000 increments to a large number of individual investors.

Like a term loan, a **bond** is a long-term contract under which a borrower agrees to make payments of interest and principal, on specific dates, to the buyer (holder) of the bond (the lender). Individual bonds have denominations of $1,000 or $5,000, but they typically are sold as part of a *bond issue* that contains a large number of individual bonds. Although bonds are similar in many ways to term loans, a bond issue generally is registered with the SEC, advertised, offered to the public through investment bankers, and sold to many different investors. Indeed, thousands of individual and institutional investors may participate when a company, such as Tenet Healthcare (www.tenethealth.com), sells a bond issue, whereas there is typically only one lender in the case of a term loan.

Bonds are categorized as either government (Treasury), corporate, or municipal. *Government bonds*, also called *Treasury bonds*, are issued by the US Treasury and used by the federal government to raise money. The US Treasury issues debt securities with three different maturity ranges. *Treasury bonds*, or *T-bonds*, have original maturities of more than ten years; *Treasury notes*, or *T-notes*, have maturities of two to ten years; and *Treasury bills*, or *T-bills*, have maturities of one year or less. Note that the names of these securities are fixed at the time they are issued even though their maturities shorten over time. Thus, a 20-year T-bond that was issued 15 years ago now has only five years remaining to maturity, but it is still classified as a bond, not a note. Because Treasury bonds cannot be used by healthcare businesses to raise capital (because they are issued by the federal government, not institutions), we will not discuss them in detail in this text.

Corporate Bonds

Corporate bonds are issued by investor-owned businesses, while *municipal bonds* are issued by governments and government agencies **other than the federal government**. The following sections focus primarily on corporate bonds, but much of the discussion also is relevant to municipal bonds. The unique features of municipal bonds are discussed later in this chapter.

Although corporate bonds generally have maturities of 20 to 30 years, both shorter and longer maturities occasionally are used. For example, in 1995, HCA Healthcare (formerly Hospital Corporation of America; see hcahealth.com) issued $200 million worth of 100-year bonds, following the issuance of 100-year bonds by Disney and Coca-Cola in 1993. Since then, several other corporations have issued such bonds. These ultra-long-term bonds had not been used by any firm since the 1920s. Unlike term loans, bonds usually pay only interest over the life of the bond, with the entire amount of principal returned to lenders at maturity.

Most bonds have a *fixed* interest rate, which locks in the rate set at issue for the entire maturity of the bond and minimizes interest payment uncertainty. However, some bonds have a *floating* or *variable rate* that is tied to some interest rate index, so the interest payments move up and down with the general level of interest rates. Floating-rate bonds are more prevalent when rates are high, when the yield curve (which is discussed in the chapter 11 supplement) has a steep upward slope, or when both of these conditions are present. Floating-rate bonds are discussed in more detail in the municipal bonds section.

Some bonds do not pay any interest at all but are sold at a substantial discount from face (principal) value. Such bonds, called **zero-coupon bonds**, provide the bondholder (lender) with capital appreciation rather than interest income. For example, a zero-coupon bond with a $1,000 face value

corporate bond Debt issued (sold) by for-profit businesses, as opposed to government or tax-exempt (municipal) bonds.

zero-coupon bond A bond that pays no interest. It is bought at a discount from par value, so its return comes solely from price appreciation (selling at a price greater than the purchase price or receiving the face value at maturity).

and ten-year maturity might sell for $385.54 when it is issued. An investor who buys the bond would realize a 10 percent annual rate of return if the bond were held to maturity, even though no interest payments would be received along the way. (For tax purposes, however, the difference between par, or face, value and the purchase price is amortized and treated as interest income.) Other bonds, instead of paying interest in cash, pay coupons that grant the lender additional bonds (or a proportion of an additional bond). These bonds are called *payment-in-kind (PIK)* bonds. PIK bonds usually are issued by companies that are in poor financial condition and do not have the cash to pay interest; they tend to be quite risky.

In rare cases, bonds have *step-up provisions*, which stipulate that the interest rate paid on the bond increases if the bond's rating is downgraded. (A downgrade means that the company's financial condition has deteriorated. Bond ratings are discussed in a later section of this chapter.) A step-up provision is risky for the issuing company because it must pay a higher interest rate at the worst possible time—when its financial condition weakens. Conversely, such a provision reduces the risk to bondholders.

The key takeaway here is that bonds in general, and corporate bonds in particular, come in many different flavors. In an introductory healthcare finance text, we can only scratch the surface.

Mortgage Bonds

mortgage bond
A bond issued by a business that pledges real property (land and buildings) as collateral.

With a **mortgage bond**, the issuer pledges certain real assets as security (collateral) for the bond. To illustrate this concept, consider the following example. Central-Texas Healthcare System recently needed $500 million to purchase land and build a new hospital. *First mortgage bonds* in the amount of $300 million, secured by a mortgage on the property, were issued. If Central-Texas defaulted (failed to make the promised payments) on the bonds, the bondholders could foreclose on the hospital and sell the property to satisfy their claims.

Central-Texas could also issue *second mortgage bonds* secured by the same $500 million hospital. In the event of bankruptcy and liquidation, the holders of these second mortgage bonds would have a claim against the property only after the first mortgage bondholders had been paid in full. Thus, second mortgages are sometimes called *junior mortgages*, or *junior liens*, because they are junior in priority to claims of senior mortgages, or first mortgage bonds.

debenture
An unsecured bond, meaning one that has no assets pledged as security (collateral).

Debentures

A **debenture** is an unsecured bond, and as such, it has no lien against specific property as security for the obligation. For example, Central-Texas Healthcare System has $50 million of debentures outstanding. These bonds are not secured by real property but are backed instead by the revenue-producing power of the corporation. Debenture holders, therefore, are *general creditors* whose claims, in the event of bankruptcy, are protected by property not otherwise pledged. In practice, the use of debentures depends on the nature of the firm's assets and its general credit strength. If a firm's credit position is exceptionally strong, it can issue debentures because it simply does not need to pledge specific assets as security. Debentures are also issued by firms with only a small amount of assets suitable as collateral. Finally, firms that have used up their capacity to borrow in the lower-cost mortgage market may be forced to use higher-cost debentures.

Municipal Bonds

Municipal bonds, also called **muni bonds**, are long-term debt obligations issued by states and their political subdivisions, such as counties, cities, port authorities, and toll road or bridge authorities. Short-term municipal securities are used primarily to meet temporary cash needs, while municipal bonds typically are used to finance capital projects (land, buildings, and equipment).

municipal (muni) bond
A tax-exempt bond issued by a government entity, such as a state, city, or healthcare financing authority.

    There are several types of municipal bonds. For example, *general obligation bonds* are secured by the full faith and credit of the issuing municipality (i.e., they are backed by the full taxing authority of the issuer). Conversely, *special tax bonds* are secured by a specified tax, such as a tax on utility services. *Revenue bonds* are bonds that are not backed by taxing power but by the revenues derived from projects such as roads or bridges, airports, and water and sewage systems. Revenue bonds are of particular interest to not-for-profit healthcare providers because they are legally entitled to issue such securities through government-sponsored healthcare financing authorities.

    Not-for-profit healthcare corporations issue large amounts of municipal debt. Such providers issued $20.7 billion of municipal bonds in 2018. As mentioned earlier, floating-rate bonds are riskier to the issuer because future interest costs are uncertain. Conversely, floating-rate bonds are less risky to buyers because rising rates will trigger an increase in the amount of each interest payment. However, virtually all municipal debt has call provisions that permit issuers to replace the floating-rate debt with fixed-rate debt if interest rates rise substantially. The ability to redeem the debt if interest rates soar places a cap on the risk to the borrower as well as on the potential gains to floating-rate bondholders. (Call provisions are discussed in more detail in the next major section of this chapter.)

    Municipal bonds generally are sold in *serial* form—that is, a portion of the issue comes due periodically, anywhere from six months to 30 years or more after issue. Thus, a single issue actually consists of a series of sub-issues of different maturities. In effect, the bond issue is amortized, with a portion of the issue retired every year. The purpose of structuring a bond issue in this way is to match the overall maturity of the issue to the revenue stream of the assets being financed. For example, a new hospital that has a predicted useful life of about 30 years might be financed with a 30-year serial issue. Over time, some of the revenues associated with the new hospital will be used to meet the *debt service requirements* (i.e., the interest and principal payments). At the end of 30 years, the entire issue will be paid off, and the issuer can plan for a replacement facility or a major renovation that would be funded, at least in part, by another debt issue.

Whereas the vast majority of federal government and corporate bonds are held by institutions, close to half of all municipal bonds outstanding are held by individual investors. The primary attraction of most municipal bonds is their exemption from federal and state (in the state of issue) taxes. To illustrate, the interest rate on an A-rated, long-term (20-year) corporate bond in late 2018 was about 4.77 percent,[2] while the rate on a similar risk healthcare muni bond was about 2.9 percent. To an individual investor in the 30 percent federal-plus-state tax bracket, the corporate bond's after-tax yield is $4.77\% \times (1 - 0.30) = 4.77\% \times 0.7 = 3.34\%$, while the muni bond's after-tax yield is the same as its before-tax yield, 2.9 percent. This yield differential on otherwise similar securities illustrates why investors in high tax brackets are so enthusiastic about municipal bonds.

Key Equation: After-Tax Yield on Taxable Bonds
For investors, the yield (return) on a taxable bond is reduced by the payment of income taxes. Suppose a taxable bond offers an 8 percent interest rate (yield). To an investor paying 30 percent in taxes, the after-tax yield is only 5.6 percent:

$$AT = BT \times (1 - T)$$
$$= 8.0\% \times (1 - 0.30)$$
$$= 8.0\% \times 0.70 = 5.6\%.$$

Here, AT is the after-tax yield, BT is the before-tax yield, and T is the tax rate (in decimal form).

Most healthcare municipal bonds are issued by large hospitals in amounts of $100 million or more because the administrative costs associated with stand-alone issues make them cost prohibitive for small hospitals needing only small amounts of debt financing. To provide the benefits associated with tax-exempt financing to small hospitals, many state hospital associations have established municipal *bond pools.* These pools raise funds by issuing municipal bonds that are then loaned to not-for-profit hospitals that are too small to "tap" the muni market directly. To avoid abuses of tax-sheltered debt, federal law requires that at least 95 percent of the bond pool be lent to individual hospitals within three years.

In contrast to corporate bonds, municipal bonds are not required to be registered with the SEC. However, prior to bringing municipal debt to market, issuers must prepare an *official statement* that contains relevant financial information about the issuer and the nature of the bond issue. In addition, issuers are required to (1) provide annual financial statements that update the information contained in the official statement and (2) release information on material events that can affect bond values as such events occur. This information is not sent directly to investors but rather goes to data banks that can be accessed by investment bankers, mutual fund managers, and institutional investors. In theory, because the information is made available to investment bankers who handle public trades, any individual who wants to buy or sell a municipal bond also has access to information that affects the bond's value.

Private Versus Public Placement

Most bonds, including Treasury, corporate, and municipal, are sold primarily through investment bankers to the public at large. For an illustration of the use of municipal bonds by a healthcare provider, consider the $56 million in municipal bonds issued in March 2018 by the Bay Area Health Facilities Authority. The authority is a public body created under Florida's Health Facilities Authorities Law for the sole purpose of issuing health facilities municipal revenue bonds for qualifying healthcare providers. For this particular bond issue, the provider is Cape Coral Medical Center, a not-for-profit hospital, and the primary purpose of the issue is to raise funds to build and equip a new children's wing. The bonds are secured solely by the revenues of Cape Coral, so the municipal conduit agency—the Bay Area Health Facilities Authority—has no responsibility whatsoever for the interest or principal payments on the issue. Smaller bond issues, typically $10 million or less, often are sold directly to a single buyer or a small group of buyers. Issues placed directly with lenders, or **private placements**, have the same advantages as term loans, which were discussed in a previous section.

Although the interest rate on private placements is generally higher than the interest rate on public issues, the administrative costs of placing an issue, such as legal, accounting, printing, and selling fees, are less for private placements than for public issues. Moreover, because there is direct negotiation between the borrower and lenders, the opportunity is greater to structure bond terms that are more favorable to the borrower than the terms routinely contained in public debt issues.

private placement
The sale of newly issued securities to a single investor or small group of investors.

1. Describe the primary features of the following long-term debt securities:
   a. Term loan
   b. Bond
   c. First mortgage bond
   d. Junior mortgage
   e. Debenture
   f. Municipal bond
2. What are the key differences between a private placement and a public issue?
3. What is the purpose of a bond pool?

Debt Contracts

indenture
A legal document that spells out the rights and obligations of both bondholders and the issuing corporation; in other words, the loan agreement for a bond.

promissory note
A document that specifies the terms and conditions of a loan; also called *loan agreement* or, in the case of bonds, *indenture*.

restrictive covenant
A provision in a bond indenture or loan agreement that protects the interests of lenders by restricting the actions of management.

Debt contracts, which spell out the rights of the borrower and lender(s), have different names depending on the type of debt. The contract between the issuer and bondholders is called an **indenture**. Indentures tend to be long—some run several hundred pages in length. For other types of debt, a similar but much shorter document called a *loan agreement* or **promissory note** is used. Health services managers are most concerned about the overall cost of debt, including administrative costs, as well as any provisions that may restrict the business's future actions. In this section, some relevant debt contract features are discussed.

Restrictive Covenants

Many debt contracts include provisions, called **restrictive covenants**, that are designed to protect creditors from managerial actions that would be detrimental to their best interests. For example, the indenture for Sea Coast Hospital's 2019 municipal bond issue contained several restrictive covenants, including the covenant that the issuer must maintain a minimum current ratio of 2.0. (The current ratio is defined as current assets divided by current liabilities, so a current ratio of 2.0 indicates that current assets are twice as large as current liabilities.) Because the current ratio measures a business's *liquidity*—the ability to meet cash obligations as they come due—a minimum current ratio provides some assurance to bondholders that the interest and principal payments coming due can be covered. If Sea Coast violates any of its restrictive covenants—say, by allowing its current ratio to drop below 2.0—it is said to be in *technical default*. ("Regular" default occurs when an interest or principal payment is not made on time, which is called a *missed payment*.)

Trustees

When debt is supplied by a single (or just a few) creditor(s), there is a one-to-one relationship between the lender and the borrower. However, bond issues can have thousands of lenders, so a single voice is needed to represent bondholders. This function is performed by a **trustee**, usually an institution such as a bank, which represents the bondholders and ensures that the terms of the indenture are being carried out. The trustee is responsible for monitoring the issuer and for taking appropriate action if a covenant violation occurs. What constitutes appropriate action varies with the circumstances. A trustee has the power to *foreclose* on an issue in default, in which case the full amount of principal and unpaid interest is due and payable immediately. However, insisting on immediate payment may result in bankruptcy and possibly large losses on the bonds. In such a case, the trustee may decide that the bondholders would be better served by giving the issuer a chance to work out its financial problems rather than force the business into bankruptcy.

trustee
An individual or institution, typically a commercial bank, that represents the interests of bondholders.

Call Provisions

A **call provision** gives the issuer the right to call a bond for *redemption* prior to maturity; that is, the issuer can pay off the bond in its entirety and *redeem*, or *retire*, the issue. If it is used, the call provision generally states that the firm must pay an amount greater than the initial amount borrowed to redeem the bonds. The additional sum required is defined as a *call premium*.

call provision
A provision in a bond indenture (contract) that gives the issuing company the right to redeem (call) the bonds prior to maturity.

Many callable bonds offer a period of call protection, which protects investors from a call just a short time after the bonds are issued. For example, the 20-year callable bonds issued by Vanguard Healthcare in 2019 are not callable until 2029, which is ten years after the original issue date. This type of call provision is known as a *deferred call*.

The call privilege is valuable to the issuer but potentially detrimental to bondholders, especially if the bond is issued during a period when interest rates are cyclically high. In general, bonds are called when interest rates have fallen: The issuer replaces the old, high-interest issue with a new, lower-interest issue and hence reduces annual interest expense. When this occurs, investors are forced to reinvest the principal returned in new securities at the current (lower) rate. The added risk to lenders of a call provision (discussed later in this chapter) causes the interest rate on a new issue of callable bonds to exceed that on a similar new issue of noncallable bonds.

1. Describe the following debt contract features:
   a. Bond indenture
   b. Restrictive covenant
   c. Trustee
   d. Call provision
2. What is the difference between technical default and "regular" default?
3. What impact does a call provision have on an issue's interest rate?

Credit Ratings

Since the early 1900s, bonds and other types of debt have been assigned quality ratings that reflect their probability of going into default. The three primary rating agencies are Fitch Ratings, Moody's Investors Service, and Standard & Poor's (S&P). All three agencies rate both corporate and munici-pal bonds. Standard & Poor's rating designations are shown in exhibit 11.1, but all three have similar rating designations. Bonds with a BBB or higher rating are called **investment grade**, while BB and lower bonds, called **junk bonds**, are more speculative in nature because they have a higher probability of default than higher-rated bonds.

investment-grade bond
A bond with a BBB or higher rating.

junk bond
A bond with a BB or lower rating.

Rating Criteria
Although the rating assignments are subjective, they are based on both qualitative characteristics, such as quality of management, and quantitative

EXHIBIT 11.1
Standard & Poor's Credit Ratings

Credit Risk	Rating Category
Prime	AAA
Excellent	AA
Upper medium	A
Lower medium	BBB
Speculative	BB
Very speculative	B
	CCC
	CC
Default	D

Note: S&P uses plus and minus modifiers for bond ratings below AAA. Thus, A+ designates the strongest A-rated bond and A– the weakest.

factors, such as a business's financial strength. Analysts at the rating agencies have consistently stated that no precise formula is used to set a firm's rating—many factors are taken into account, but not in a mathematically precise manner. Statistical studies have supported this contention. Researchers who have tried to predict bond ratings on the basis of quantitative data have had only limited success, which indicates that the agencies do indeed use a good deal of judgment to establish bond ratings.

Importance of Ratings

Credit ratings are important to borrowers and lenders. For example, a bond's rating is an indicator of its default risk, so the rating has a direct, measurable influence on the interest rate required by lenders and hence on the firm's cost of debt capital. Second, most corporate (i.e., taxable) bonds are purchased by institutional investors rather than by individuals. Many of these institutions are restricted to investment-grade securities. Also, most individual investors who buy municipal bonds are unwilling to take high risks in their bond purchases. Thus, if an issuer's bonds fall below BBB, new bonds will be harder to sell because the number of potential purchasers is reduced. As a result of their higher risk and more restricted market, low-grade bonds typically carry much higher interest rates than high-grade bonds. For example, in 2019, long-term AAA-rated corporate bonds had an interest rate that was 0.44 percentage points above similar maturity T-bond rates, AA bonds were 0.5 points higher, A bonds were 0.6 points higher, and CCC bonds were 8.04 points higher. Clearly, the interest rate penalty for having a low bond rating is significant.

For Your Consideration
Criticisms of Credit Rating Agencies

Large rating agencies, such as Standard & Poor's, have come under increasing criticism for a multitude of reasons. Here are just a few.

First, the rating agencies have been criticized for being too cozy with the companies they rate. Their close relationships with management, which include frequent meetings and advice on actions that companies should take to maintain their current ratings, foster a familial atmosphere that interferes with independent, unbiased rating judgments. Furthermore, the rating agencies are paid by the companies they rate, rather than by the investors they are meant to protect—a clear conflict of interest.

Second, because the rating business is reputation based (why pay attention to a rating that is not recognized by others?), barriers to market entry are high, and the rating agencies are oligopolists. (An oligopoly is a market that is dominated by just a few sellers.) This means that the rating agencies are somewhat immune to forces that apply to competitive markets and, to an extent, can set their own rules.

Finally, in many instances, the debt markets indicate a company's deteriorating credit quality (through lower bond prices) many months before a rating downgrade occurs. This fact has led many observers to suggest that, rather than rely on ratings, investors and regulators should use credit spreads to make judgments about credit risk. (Credit spreads reflect the difference in yields between interest rates on "safe" debt, such as Treasury securities, and rates on risky debt, such as B-rated bonds.)

What do you think about the validity of credit ratings? Do the criticisms of rating agencies have merit? Can the current credit rating system be improved? If so, how?

Changes in Ratings

A change in a firm's bond rating will have a significant effect on its ability to borrow long-term capital and on the cost of that capital. Rating agencies periodically review outstanding bonds, and occasionally they upgrade or downgrade a bond as a result of the issuer's changed circumstances. Also, an announcement that a company plans to sell a new debt issue, or to merge with another company and pay for the acquisition by exchanging bonds for the stock of the acquired company, will trigger an agency review and possibly lead to a rating change. If a firm's situation has deteriorated somewhat but its bonds have not been reviewed and downgraded, it may choose to use a term loan or short-term debt rather than finance through a public bond issue. This may postpone a rating agency review until the situation has improved.

SELF-TEST QUESTIONS

1. What are the three major rating agencies?
2. What are some criteria that the rating agencies use when assigning ratings?
3. How do bond ratings affect the cost of debt to the issuing firm?

Interest Rate Components

As discussed previously, investors require compensation for time value, inflation, and risk. The relationship is formalized for stock investments by the capital asset pricing model, discussed in chapter 10. For debt investments, the rate of return (i.e., the interest rate) required by investors consists of several components. By understanding the components, it is possible to gain insights into why interest rates change over time, differ among borrowers, and even differ on separate issues by the same borrower.

Real Risk-Free Rate

real risk-free rate (RRF)
The rate of interest on a riskless investment in the absence of inflation.

The base on which all interest rates are built is the **real risk-free rate (RRF)**. This is the rate that investors would demand on a debt security that is *totally riskless* when there is *no inflation*. Thus, the RRF compensates investors for the time value of money, but it considers no other factors. Although the RRF is difficult to measure, it is thought to fall somewhere in the range of 2 to 4 percent. In the real world, inflation is rarely zero, and most debt securities

have some risk; thus, the actual interest rate on a given debt security will typically be higher than the real risk-free rate.

Inflation Premium

Inflation has a major impact on required interest rates because it erodes the
purchasing power of the dollar and lowers the value of investment returns.
Creditors, who are the suppliers of debt capital, are well aware of the impact
of inflation. Thus, they build an **inflation premium (IP)** into the interest
rate that is equal to the expected inflation rate over the life of the security.

For example, suppose that the real risk-free rate is 3 percent ($RRF = 3\%$)
and inflation is expected to be 2 percent ($IP = 2\%$) during the next year. The
rate of interest on a one-year riskless debt security would be 3% + 2% = 5%.

The rate of inflation built into interest rates is the rate of inflation
expected in the future, not the rate experienced in the past. The latest reported
figures may show an annual inflation rate of 3 percent, but that is for a past
period. If investors expect a 2 percent inflation rate in the future, 2 percent
will be built into the current rate of interest. Also, the inflation rate reflected
in any interest rate is the average rate of inflation expected *over the life of the
security*. The inflation rate built into a one-year bond is the expected inflation
rate for the next year, but the inflation rate built into a 30-year bond is the
average rate of inflation expected over the next 30 years. The combination
of the RRF and the IP is called the **risk-free rate (RF)**, which incorporates
inflation expectations but does not incorporate any risk factors. In this
example, $RF = 5\%$.

Default Risk Premium

The risk that a borrower will default (i.e., not make the promised payments)
has a significant impact on the interest rate set on a debt security. This risk,
along with the possible consequences of default, is captured by a **default risk
premium (DRP)**. Treasury securities have no default risk; thus, they carry
the lowest interest rates on taxable securities in the United States. For corporate and municipal bonds, the higher the bond's rating, the lower its default
risk. All else being equal, the lower the default risk, the lower the DRP and
interest rate.

Liquidity Premium

A **liquid asset** is one that can be sold quickly at a predictable fair market price
and thus can be converted to a known amount of cash on short notice. Active
markets, which provide liquidity, exist for Treasury securities and for the
stocks and bonds of larger corporations. Securities issued by small companies,

**inflation premium
(IP)**
The premium that
debt investors add
to the real risk-free
(base) interest rate
to compensate for
inflation.

risk-free rate (RF)
The rate of interest
on a riskless
investment when
inflation effects
are considered.

**default risk
premium (DRP)**
The premium
that creditors
demand (add to
the base interest
rate) for bearing
default risk. The
greater the default
risk, the higher
the default risk
premium.

liquid asset
An asset that
can be quickly
converted to cash
at its fair market
value.

including healthcare providers that issue municipal bonds, are *illiquid*—once bought, they can be resold by the owner, but not quickly and not at a predictable price. Furthermore, illiquid securities are normally difficult to sell and have relatively high *transaction costs*. (Transaction costs include commissions, fees, and other expenses associated with selling securities.)

liquidity premium (LP)
The premium that debt investors add to the base interest rate to compensate for lack of liquidity.

If a security is illiquid, investors will add a **liquidity premium (LP)** when they set their required interest rate. It is difficult to measure liquidity premiums with precision, but a differential of at least 2 percentage points is thought to exist between the least liquid and the most liquid securities of similar default risk and maturity.

Price Risk Premium

As demonstrated later in the section on bond valuation, the market value (price) of a long-term bond declines sharply when interest rates rise. Because interest rates can and do rise, all long-term bonds, including Treasury bonds, have an element of risk called **price risk**. For example, assume an individual bought a 30-year Treasury bond for $1,000 when the long-term interest rate on Treasury securities was 7 percent. If, ten years later, T-bond rates had risen to 14 percent, the value of the bond would have fallen to under $600. That would represent a sizable loss on the investment, which demonstrates that long-term bonds—even US Treasury bonds—are not riskless.

price risk
The risk that rising interest rates will lower the values of outstanding debt.

As a general rule, the price risk of bonds of any organization, whether it is the US government, Brookdale Senior Living, or Cape Coral Community Hospital, grows as the maturity of the bond lengthens. Therefore, a **price risk premium (PRP)**, which is tied directly to the term to maturity, must be included in the interest rate. The effect of price risk premiums is to raise interest rates on long-term bonds relative to rates on short-term bonds. This premium, like the other risk premiums, is difficult to measure, but it seems to vary over time; it rises when interest rates are more volatile and uncertain and falls when they are more stable. In recent years, the price risk premium on 30-year T-bonds appears to have been generally in the range of 0.5 to 2 percentage points.

price risk premium (PRP)
The premium that debt investors add to the base rate to compensate for bearing price risk.

Call Risk Premium

Bonds that are callable can be redeemed by the issuer prior to maturity, and hence buyers have uncertain holding periods. This uncertainty makes callable bonds riskier for investors than those that are noncallable. To compensate for bearing call risk, investors charge a **call risk premium (CRP)** on callable bonds. The amount of the premium depends on such factors as the interest rate on the bond, current interest rate levels, and time to first call (the call deferral period). Historically, call risk premiums have been in the range of 30

call risk premium (CRP)
The premium that debt investors add to the base rate to compensate for bearing call risk.

to 50 basis points (a basis point is 1/100th of 1 percent, or 0.01 percent, so 30 basis points is equal to $30 \times 0.0001 = 0.3\%$).

Combining the Components

When all the interest rate components are taken into account, the interest rate required on any debt security can be expressed as follows:

$$\text{Interest rate} = RRF + IP + DRP + LP + PRP + CRP.$$

First consider one-year Treasury bills. Assume that RRF is 2 percent and inflation is expected to average 3 percent in the coming year. Because T-bills have no default, liquidity, or call risk and almost no price risk, the interest rate on a one-year T-bill would be 5 percent:

$$\text{Interest rate}_{\text{T-bill}} = RRF + IP + DRP + LP + PRP + CRP$$
$$= 2\% + 3\% + 0 + 0 + 0 + 0 = 5\%.$$

As discussed previously, the combination of RRF and IP is the risk-free rate, so $RF = 5\%$. In general, the rate of interest on short-term Treasury securities (T-bills) is used as a proxy for the *short-term* risk-free rate.

Consider another illustration, the callable 30-year corporate bonds issued by HealthWest Corporation. Assume that these bonds have an inflation premium of 4 percent; default risk, liquidity, and price risk premiums of 1 percent each; and a call risk premium of 40 basis points. Under these assumptions, these bonds would have an interest rate of 9.4 percent:

$$\text{Interest rate}_{\text{30-year bonds}} = RRF + IP + DRP + LP + PRP + CRP$$
$$= 2\% + 4\% + 1\% + 1\% + 1\% + 0.4\% = 9.4\%.$$

> ## *Key Equation: Required Rate of Return on a Debt Security*
> The required rate of return (interest rate) on a debt security consists of a base rate plus premiums to compensate investors for inflation and risk:
>
> $$\text{Interest rate} = RRF + IP + DRP + LP + PRP + CRP.$$
>
> Here, RRF is the real risk-free (base) rate, IP is the inflation premium, DRP is the default risk premium, LP is the liquidity premium, PRP is the price risk premium, and CRP is the call risk premium.

When interest rates are viewed as the sum of a base rate plus premiums for inflation and risk, it is easy to visualize the underlying economic forces that cause interest rates to vary among different issues and over time.

SELF-TEST QUESTIONS

1. Write out an equation for the required interest rate on a debt security.
2. What is the difference between the real risk-free rate (RRF) and the risk-free rate (RF)?
3. Do the interest rates on Treasury securities include a default risk premium? A liquidity premium? A price risk premium? Explain your answer.
4. Why are callable bonds riskier for investors than similar bonds without a call provision?
5. What is price risk? What type of debt securities would have the largest price risk premium?

Debt Valuation

Now that we have covered the basics of long-term debt financing, the next step is to understand how investors value debt securities. Debt (and other security) valuation concepts are important to health services managers for many reasons. Perhaps most important, capital is the lifeblood of any business. In fact, one of the most common reasons for business failure is insufficient capital. Managers must understand how investors make decisions about security investments. This knowledge is useful for managers of all businesses, who must understand how lenders value debt securities, and especially for managers of investor-owned firms, who must worry about stock price maximization.

In addition, for health services managers to make financially sound decisions regarding real-asset (capital) investments, such as land, buildings, and equipment, it is necessary to estimate the business's cost of capital. Security valuation is a necessary skill in this process, which is covered in detail in chapter 13.

General Valuation Model

Because the financial values of investment opportunities (both real assets and securities) stem from streams of expected cash flows, most investments are valued by the same four-step process:

1. **Estimate the expected cash flow stream.** Estimating the cash flow stream involves forecasting the expected cash flow in each period during the life of the asset. For some assets, such as Treasury securities, the estimation process is quite easy because the interest and principal repayment stream is specified by contract. For other assets, such as the stock of a biotechnology start-up company that is not yet paying dividends or a healthcare provider's new service line, the estimation process can be difficult.

2. **Assess the riskiness of the stream.** The next step is to assess the riskiness of the estimated cash flow stream. The cash flows of most assets are not known with certainty, but they are best represented by probability distributions. The more uncertain these distributions, the greater the riskiness of the cash flow stream. Again, in some situations, it will be fairly easy to assess the riskiness of the estimated cash flow stream; in other situations, it may be quite difficult.

3. **Set the required rate of return.** The required rate of return on the cash flow stream is established on the basis of the stream's riskiness and the returns available on alternative investments of similar risk. In essence, the *opportunity cost* principle discussed in chapter 9 is applied here. By investing in one asset, the funds are no longer available for alternative investments. This opportunity cost sets the required rate of return on the asset being valued.

4. **Discount and sum the expected cash flows.** Each expected cash flow is discounted at the asset's required rate of return, and the present values are summed to find the value of the asset.

The following time line formalizes the valuation process:

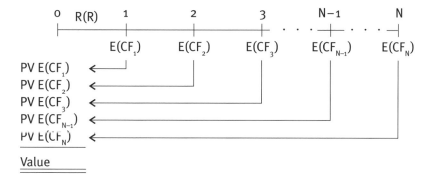

Here, $E(CF_t)$ is the expected cash flow in each period t, $R(R)$ is the required rate of return (i.e., the opportunity cost rate) on the asset, and N is the number of periods for which cash flows are expected. The periods can be months, quarters, semiannual periods, or years, depending on the frequency of the cash flows expected from the asset.

The general valuation model can be applied to both *financial assets (securities)*, such as stocks and bonds, and *real (physical) assets*, such as buildings, equipment, and even whole businesses. Each asset type requires a somewhat different application of the general valuation model, but the basic approach remains the same. In this chapter, the general valuation model is applied to debt securities (bonds). In the chapters that follow, the model is applied to stocks and to real assets.

Definitions

To begin, here are some features of bonds that will come into play:

par value
The stated (face) value of a bond; generally, the principal amount that must be repaid to the issuer.

maturity date
The date on which the principal amount of a loan must be repaid.

coupon (interest) rate
The stated annual rate of interest on a bond, which is equal to the coupon payment divided by the par value.

coupon payment
The dollar amount of annual interest on a bond.

- **Par value.** The *par value*, also called *par*, is the stated (face) value of the bond. It is often set at $1,000 or $5,000. The par value generally represents the amount of money the business borrows (per bond) and promises to repay at some future date.

- **Maturity date.** Bonds generally have a specified maturity date on which the par value will be repaid. For example, Big Sky Healthcare, a large, integrated group practice, issued $50 million worth of $1,000 par value bonds on January 1, 2020. The bonds will mature on December 31, 2029, so they had a 15-year maturity at the time they were issued. The effective maturity of a bond declines each year after issue. Thus, at the beginning of 2021, Big Sky's bonds will have a 14-year maturity, and so on.

- **Coupon rate.** A bond requires the issuer to pay a specific amount of interest each year or, more typically, each six months. The rate of interest is called the *coupon interest rate*, or just the *coupon rate*. The rate may be variable, in which case it is tied to some index, such as 2 percentage points above the prime rate. More commonly, the rate will be fixed over the life (maturity) of the bond. For example, Big Sky's bonds have a 10 percent coupon rate, so each $1,000 par value bond pays $0.10 \times \$1,000 = \$100$ in interest each year. The dollar amount of annual interest, in this case $100, is called the **coupon payment**.

- **New issues versus outstanding bonds.** A bond's value is determined by its coupon payment—the higher the coupon payment, all else held constant, the higher its value. At the time a bond is issued, its coupon rate is generally set at a level that will cause the bond to sell at its par value. In other words, the coupon rate is set at the rate that investors require to buy the bond (i.e., the *going rate*). A bond that has just been issued is called a *new issue*. After the bond has been on the market for about a month, it is classified as an *outstanding bond*, or a *seasoned issue*. New issues sell close to par, but because a bond's coupon payment is generally fixed, changing economic conditions (and interest rates) will cause a seasoned bond to sell for more or less than its par value.

- **Debt service requirement.** Firms that issue bonds are concerned with their total *debt service requirement*, which includes both interest expense and repayment of principal. For Big Sky, the debt service requirement (payment) is $0.10 \times \$50$ million = $5 million per year until maturity. In 2034, the firm's debt service requirement will be $5 million in interest plus $50 million in principal repayment. Thus, the total debt service requirement on the issue is $(15 \times \$5) + \$50 = \$125$ million. In Big Sky's case, only interest is paid until maturity, so the entire principal amount must be repaid at that time. As discussed earlier, many municipal bonds are serial issues structured so

that the debt service requirements are relatively constant over time. In this situation, the issuer pays back a portion of the principal during each year.

Healthcare in Practice

Origins of the Term *Coupon Payment*

The term *coupon payment* dates back to the time when all bonds were *bearer bonds* and physical possession of the bond certificate provided proof of ownership. Coupons, one for each scheduled interest payment over the life of the bond, were printed on the certificate. Here is an example of a coupon from the 1922 Mecca Temple (New York) construction bonds:

To collect an interest payment, bondholders would remove, or "clip," the appropriate coupon and send it to the issuer or take it to a bank, where it would be exchanged for the dollar payment. Today, all bonds are registered bonds, and the issuer (through an agent) automatically sends interest payments to the registered owner.

The Basic Bond Valuation Model

Bonds typically call for the payment of a specific amount of interest for a specific number of years and for the repayment of par on the bond's maturity date. A bond represents an annuity plus a lump sum, and its value is calculated as the present value of this cash flow stream. Here are the cash flows from Big Sky's bonds on a time line:

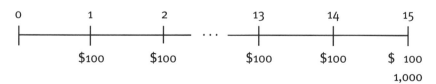

If the bonds had just been issued, and the coupon rate was set at the current interest rate for bonds of this risk, then the required rate of return on the bonds, $R(R_d)$, would be 10 percent. (The subscript d stands for debt.) Because the value of a bond is simply the present value of the bond's cash flows, discounted to time 0 at a 10 percent discount rate, the value of the bond at issue was $1,000:

Present value of a 15-year, $100 payment annuity at 10 percent = $ 760.61
Present value of a $1,000 lump sum discounted 15 years = ___239.39
Value of bond = $1,000.00

There are two approaches to using a spreadsheet to value bonds:

	A	B	C	D
1				
2	10.0%	Rate	Interest rate	
3				
4	$ 100	Value 1	Year 1 coupon	
5	$ 100	Value 1	Year 2 coupon	
6	$ 100	Value 1	Year 3 coupon	
7	$ 100	Value 1	Year 4 coupon	
8	$ 100	Value 1	Year 5 coupon	
9	$ 100	Value 1	Year 6 coupon	
10	$ 100	Value 1	Year 7 coupon	
11	$ 100	Value 1	Year 8 coupon	
12	$ 100	Value 1	Year 9 coupon	
13	$ 100	Value 1	Year 10 coupon	
14	$ 100	Value 1	Year 11 coupon	
15	$ 100	Value 1	Year 12 coupon	
16	$ 100	Value 1	Year 13 coupon	
17	$ 100	Value 1	Year 14 coupon	
18	$ 1,100	Value 1	Year 15 coupon + Principal	
19				
20	$ 1,000.00	=NPV(A2,A4:A18) (entered into Cell A20)		

First, we listed all of the bond's cash flows and used the NPV (net present value) function to value the bond. Note that cell A18 contains $1,100 as the entry, which reflects the $100 interest payment in year 15 plus the $1,000 return of principal:

	A	B	C	D
1				
2	15	Nper	Number of periods	
3	$ 100.00	Pmt	Payment (coupon amount)	
4	$ 1,000.00	Fv	Future value (principal)	
5	10%	Rate	Interest rate	
6				
7				
8	$ 1,000.00	=-PV(A5,A2,A3,A4) (entered into Cell A8)		
9				
10				

Second, we used the PV (present value) function to value the bond. Note that when bonds are being valued, the function requires four arguments (i.e., entries): interest rate, number of payments, payment (coupon amount), and future value. In chapter 9, when we used this function to find the present values of annuities, no future value was entered.

The first approach has the advantage that we can easily visualize the bond's cash flows. The second approach has the advantage of being more compact and requiring fewer entries. To save space, we use the second approach for the remainder of this chapter.

If $R(R_d)$ remained constant at 10 percent over time, what would be the value of the bond one year after it was issued? Now, the term to maturity is only 14 years—that is, $N = 14$. As seen below, the bond's value remains at $1,000:

	A		B	C	D
1					
2	14		Nper	Number of periods	
3	$	100.00	Pmt	Payment (coupon amount)	
4	$	1,000.00	Fv	Future value (principal)	
5	10%		Rate	Interest rate	
6					
7					
8	$	1,000.00	=−PV(A5,A2,A3,A4) (entered into Cell A8)		
9					
10					

As long as the required rate of return remains at 10 percent, the bond's value remains at par, or $1,000.

Suppose that interest rates in the economy fell after the bonds were issued, and as a result, $R(R_d)$ decreased from 10 percent to 5 percent. The coupon rate and par value are fixed by contract, so they remain unaffected by changes in interest rates, but now the discount rate is 5 percent rather than 10 percent. At the end of the first year, with 14 years remaining, the value of the bond would be $1,494.93:

	A		B	C	D
1					
2	14		Nper	Number of periods	
3	$	100.00	Pmt	Payment (coupon amount)	
4	$	1,000.00	Fv	Future value (principal)	
5	5%		Rate	Interest rate	
6					
7					
8	$	1,494.93	=−PV(A5,A2,A3,A4) (entered into Cell A8)		
9					
10					

The arithmetic of the bond value increase should be clear (lower discount rates lead to higher present values), but what is the underlying economic logic? The fact that interest rates have fallen to 5 percent means that if an individual had $1,000 to invest, he or she could buy new bonds like Big Sky's (every day, some 10 to 20 companies sell new bonds), except that these new bonds would only pay $50 in interest each year. Naturally, the individual would favor an annual payment of $100 over one of $50 and hence would be willing to pay more than $1,000 for Big Sky's bonds. All investors would recognize this; as a result, Big Sky's bonds would be bid up in price to $1,494.93, at which point they would provide the same rate of return as new bonds of similar risk—5 percent.

Assuming that interest rates stayed constant at 5 percent over the next 14 years, what would happen to the value of a Big Sky bond? It would fall gradually from $1,494.93 at present to $1,000 at maturity, when the company would redeem each bond for $1,000. This point can be illustrated by calculating the value of the bond one year later, when it has only 13 years remaining to maturity:

	A	B	C	D
1				
2	13	Nper	Number of periods	
3	$ 100.00	Pmt	Payment (coupon amount)	
4	$ 1,000.00	Fv	Future value (principal)	
5	5%	Rate	Interest rate	
6				
7				
8	$ 1,469.68	=–PV(A5,A2,A3,A4) (entered into Cell A8)		
9				
10				

interest (current) yield
The annual interest return on a bond, defined as the interest payment divided by the beginning-of-year price.

The value of the bond with 13 years to maturity is $1,469.68.

If an individual purchased the bond at a price of $1,494.93 and then sold it one year later with interest rates still at 5 percent, a capital loss of $25.25 would be incurred. The rate of return on the bond over the year consists of an **interest (current) yield** plus a **capital gains yield**:

capital gains yield
The percentage capital gain (loss) over some period, defined as the price appreciation (loss) divided by the beginning-of-period price.

Current yield	=	$100 ÷ $1,494.93	=	0.0669	= 6.69%
Capital gains yield	=	–$25.25 ÷ $1,494.93	=	–0.0169	= –1.60%
Total rate of return, or yield	=	$74.75 ÷ $1,494.93	=	0.0500	= 5.00%

Had interest rates risen from 10 to 15 percent during the first year after issue, rather than falling as they did, the value of Big Sky's bonds would have declined to $713.78 at the end of the first year. If interest rates held constant at 15 percent, the bond would have a value of $720.84 at the end of the second year, so the total yield to investors would be as follows:

Current yield	=	$100 ÷ $713.78	=	0.1401	= 14.01%
Capital gains yield	=	$7.06 ÷ $713.78	=	−0.0099	= 0.99%
Total rate of return, or yield	=	$107.06 ÷ $713.78	=	0.1500	= 15.00%

Exhibit 11.2 graphs the values of Big Sky's bonds over time, assuming that interest rates remain constant at 10 percent, fall to 5 percent and remain at that level, and then rise to 15 percent and remain constant at that level. The exhibit illustrates the following important points:

- Whenever the required rate of return on a bond equals its coupon rate, the bond sells at its par value.
- When interest rates and required rates of return fall after a bond is issued, the bond's value rises above its par value and the bond sells at a *premium.*
- When interest rates and required rates of return rise after a bond is issued, the bond's value falls below its par value and the bond sells at a *discount.*
- Bond prices on outstanding issues and interest rates are inversely related. Increasing rates lead to falling prices, and decreasing rates lead to increasing prices.
- The price of a bond will always approach its par value as its maturity date approaches, provided the issuer does not default on the bond.

Note, however, that interest rates do not remain constant over time, so in reality, a bond's price fluctuates both as interest rates in the economy fluctuate and as the bond's term to maturity decreases. In addition, a bond's price will change if there is a change in the creditworthiness of the issuer.

Yield to Maturity on a Bond

Up to this point, a bond's required rate of return and cash flows have been used to determine its value. In reality, investors' required rates of return on securities are not observable, but security prices can be easily determined—at least for securities that are actively traded—by calling a broker or looking at online data sources. Suppose that the Big Sky bond had 14 years remaining to maturity and it was selling at a price of $1,494.93. What rate of return, or **yield to maturity (YTM)**, would be earned if the bond was bought at this

yield to maturity (YTM)
The expected rate of return on a debt security assuming it is held until maturity.

price and held to maturity? To find the answer, 5 percent, use a spreadsheet and the RATE function:

	A	B	C	D
1				
2	14	Nper	Number of periods	
3	$ 1,494.93	Pv	Present value (bond price)	
4	$ (100.00)	Pmt	Payment (coupon amount)	
5	$ (1,000.00)	Fv	Future value (principal)	
6				
7				
8	5.00%	=RATE(A5,A2,A3,A4) (entered into Cell A8)		
9				
10				

The YTM is the *expected rate of return* on a bond, assuming it is held to maturity and no default occurs. It is similar to the total rate of return discussed in the previous section. For a bond that sells at par, the YTM consists entirely of an interest yield, but if the bond sells at a discount or premium, the YTM consists of the current yield plus a positive or negative capital gains yield.

yield to call (YTC)
The expected rate of return on a debt security assuming it is held until it is called.

Bonds that are callable have both a YTM and a **yield to call (YTC)**. The YTC is the expected rate of return on the bond assuming it will be called and assuming the probability of default is zero. The YTC is calculated like the YTM, except that N reflects the number of years until the bond will be called, as opposed to years to maturity, and M reflects the call price rather than the maturity value.

Bond Values with Semiannual Compounding

Virtually all bonds issued in the United States pay interest semiannually, or every six months. To apply the preceding valuation concepts to semiannual bonds, the bond valuation procedures must be modified as follows:

- Divide the annual interest payment (or coupon payment), *INT*, by 2 to determine the dollar amount paid *every six months*.
- Multiply the number of years to maturity, N, by 2 to determine the number of *semiannual interest periods*.
- Divide the annual required rate of return, $R(R_d)$, by 2 to determine the *semiannual required rate of return*.

To illustrate the use of the semiannual bond valuation model, assume that the Big Sky bonds pay $50 every six months rather than $100 annually. Thus, each interest payment is only half as large, but there are twice as many payments. When the going rate of interest is 5 percent annually, the value of Big Sky's bonds with 14 years left to maturity is $1,499.12:

	A	B	C	D
1				
2	28	Nper	Number of periods	
3	$ 50.00	Pmt	Payment (coupon amount)	
4	$ 1,000.00	Fv	Future value (principal)	
5	2.5%	Rate	Interest rate	
6				
7				
8	$ 1,499.12	=−PV(A5,A2,A3,A4) (entered into Cell A8)		
9				
10				

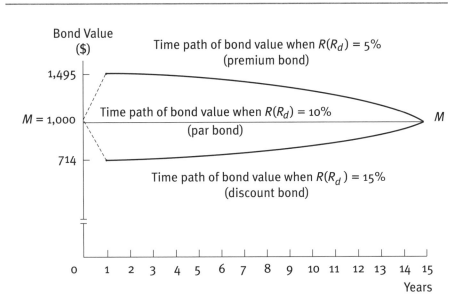

EXHIBIT 11.2
Time Path of the Value of a 15-Year, 10% Coupon, $1,000 Par Value Bond When Interest Rates Are 5%, 10%, and 15%

	Bond Value at a Required Rate of Return of		
Year	5%	10%	15%
0	—	$1,000.00	—
1	$1,494.93	1,000.00	$ 713.78
2	1,469.68	1,000.00	720.84
3	1,443.16	1,000.00	728.97
.	.	.	.
.	.	.	.
.	.	.	.
13	1,092.97	1,000.00	918.71
14	1,047.62	1,000.00	956.52
15	1,000.00	1,000.00	1,000.00

Similarly, if the bond were actually selling for $1,400 with 14 years to maturity, its YTM would be 5.80 percent:

	A	B	C	D
1				
2	28	Nper	Number of periods	
3	$ 1,400.00	Pv	Present value (bond price)	
4	$ (50.00)	Pmt	Payment (coupon amount)	
5	$ (1,000.00)	Fv	Future value (principal)	
6				
7				
8	2.90%	=RATE(A2,A4,A3,A5) (entered into Cell A8)		
9				
10				

The value for I (or rate), 2.90 percent, is the *periodic (semiannual) YTM*, so it is necessary to multiply it by 2 to get the *annual YTM*. It is convention in the bond markets to quote all rates on a stated annual basis, which is fine when bonds—all of which have semiannual coupons—are being compared. However, when the returns on securities with different periodic payments are being compared, all rates of return should be expressed as effective annual rates. The effective annual YTM on the bond is $(1.029)^2 - 1.0 = 1.0588 - 1.0 = 0.0588 = 5.88\%$, compared with the stated rate of 5.80%.

Interest Rate Risk

interest rate risk
The risk to current debtholders that stems from interest rate changes. Interest rate risk has two components: price risk and reinvestment rate risk.

reinvestment rate risk
The risk that falling interest rates will lower the returns on cash flows from bond investments that are reinvested during the life of the bond (or investment horizon).

Interest rates change over time, and such changes create risk for lenders. The overall risk created by changing interest rates is called **interest rate risk**. We will use bonds to illustrate interest rate risk, although such risk applies to all fixed-rate debt securities.

There are two components of interest rate risk. First, as illustrated in our discussion of bond valuation, an increase in interest rates leads to a decline in the values of outstanding bonds. Because interest rates can increase at any time, bondholders face the risk of losses on their holdings. This risk is called *price risk*. Second, many bondholders buy bonds to build funds for future use. These bondholders reinvest the interest (and perhaps principal) cash flows as they are received. If interest rates fall, bondholders will earn a lower rate on the reinvested cash flows, which will have a negative impact on the future value of their holdings. This risk is called **reinvestment rate risk**.

An investor's exposure to price risk depends on the maturity of the bonds. To illustrate, exhibit 11.3 shows the values of $1,000 par value bonds with 1-year and 14-year maturities at several different market interest rates. Notice how much more sensitive the price of the 14-year bond is to changes in interest rates. In general, the longer the maturity of the bond, the greater its price change in response to a given change in interest rates. Thus, bonds with longer maturities are exposed to more price risk.

Although a 1-year bond exposes the buyer to less price risk than a 14-year bond, it carries more reinvestment rate risk. If the holding period

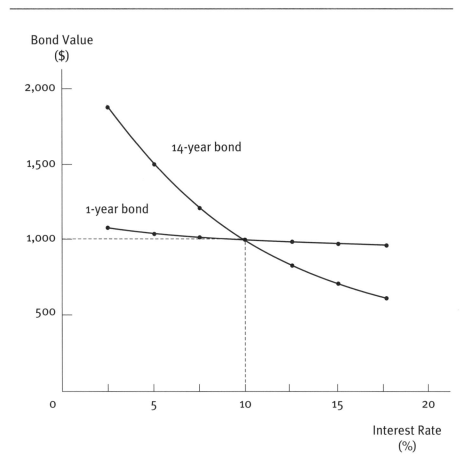

EXHIBIT 11.3
Value of Long-Term and Short-Term 10% Annual Coupon Rate Bonds at Different Market Interest Rates

Current Market Interest Rate	Bond Value	
	1-Year Bond	14-Year Bond
2.5%	$1,073.17	$1,876.82
5.0	1,047.62	1,494.93
7.5	1,023.26	1,212.23
10.0	1,000.00	1,000.00
12.5	977.78	838.45
15.0	956.52	713.78
17.5	936.17	616.25

For Your Consideration

How Safe Are Treasury Bonds?

In the popular press, Treasury bonds (T-bonds) are commonly referred to as being ultra-safe. The conventional wisdom goes something like this: "The US Treasury issues various securities of differing maturities. Like any widely traded security, you can buy them when they are issued and hold them to maturity or buy and sell them in the market at any time. Because Treasury securities are backed by the US government, they are the ultimate safe investment."

But are T-bonds, which have the longest maturities of all Treasury securities, really the ultimate safe investment? That depends on how you define *safe*. Sure, they are safe from default risk, but they carry a great deal of price risk. To illustrate, in the summer of 2019, the interest rate on 30-year T-bonds was roughly 3 percent. If you bought a 30-year bond then at its $1,000 par value and interest rates rose to 6 percent in 2020, your bond, with 29 years left to maturity, would be worth only $590. If interest rates continued to rise, to 8 percent in 2021, the bond, with 28 years left to maturity, would be worth only $446. (In 1981, the rate on 30-year T-bonds was more than 13 percent, so the numbers in this illustration are within the realm of possibility.)

In your view, are Treasury bonds as safe as some people claim? Should they be sold with a "warning label"? Under what conditions do T-bonds make the most sense for investors? When do they make the least sense? In August 2011, Standard & Poor's downgraded US Treasury debt from AAA to AA+. What effect should that action have on the values of bonds outstanding at the time of the downgrade?

is more than one year, the principal and interest will have to be reinvested after one year. If interest rates fall, the return earned during the second year will be less than the return earned during the first year. Reinvestment rate risk is the second dimension of interest rate risk.

Clearly, bond investors face both price risk and reinvestment rate risk as a result of interest rate fluctuations over time. Which type of risk is most meaningful to a particular investor depends on the circumstances, but in general, interest rate risk, including both price and reinvestment rate risk, is reduced by matching the maturity of the bond with the investor's *investment horizon*, or *holding period*.

For example, suppose Hilldale Medical Center received a $50 million contribution that it plans to use in five years to establish a proton beam therapy complex. By investing the contribution in five-year bonds, the hospital would minimize its interest rate risk because it would be matching its investment horizon. Price risk would be minimized because the bond will mature in five years, and investors will receive par value regardless of the level of interest rates at that time. Reinvestment rate risk is also minimized because only the interest on the bond would have to be reinvested during the life of the bond, which is a less risky situation than if both principal and interest had to be reinvested. Note, however, that reinvestment rate risk could be eliminated if Hilldale purchased five-year *zero-coupon bonds*, which pay no interest but sell at a discount when issued.

1. What is the general valuation model?
2. How are bonds valued?
3. What is meant by a bond's yield to maturity (YTM)? Its yield to call (YTC)?
4. Differentiate between price risk and reinvestment rate risk.

Key Concepts

This chapter provides an overview of long-term debt financing, including how interest rates are determined, the characteristics of the major types of debt securities, and how such securities are valued. The key concepts of this chapter are as follows:

- Any business must have assets to operate; to acquire assets, the business must raise *capital*. Capital comes in two basic forms: *debt* capital and *equity* (or *fund*) capital.

- Capital is allocated through the price system; a price is charged to "rent" money. Lenders charge *interest* on funds they lend, while equity investors receive *dividends* and *capital gains* in return for letting the firm use their money.

- Four fundamental factors affect the cost of money: *investment opportunities*, *time preferences for consumption*, *risk*, and *inflation*.

- *Term loans* and *bonds* are long-term debt contracts under which a borrower agrees to make a series of interest and principal payments on specific dates to the lender. A term loan is generally sold to one (or a few) lenders, while a bond is typically offered to the public and sold to many different investors.

- In general, debt is categorized as *Treasury*, which is debt issued by the federal government; *corporate*, which is debt issued by taxable businesses; and *municipal*, which is debt issued by nonfederal government entities, including debt issued on behalf of not-for-profit healthcare providers. Many types of corporate and municipal bonds exist, including *mortgage bonds*, *debentures*, and *subordinated debentures*. Prevailing interest rates, the bond's

(continued)

(continued from previous page)

riskiness, and tax consequences determine the return required on each type of bond.

- *Revenue bonds* are municipal bonds in which the revenues derived from such projects as roads or bridges, airports, water and sewage systems, and not-for-profit healthcare facilities are pledged as security for the bonds.

- A bond *indenture* (or a term loan *agreement*) is a legal document that spells out the rights of both lenders and borrowers.

- A *trustee* is assigned to make sure that the terms of a bond indenture are carried out.

- Bond indentures typically include *restrictive covenants*, which are provisions designed to protect bondholders against detrimental managerial actions.

- A *call provision* gives the issuer the right to redeem the bonds prior to maturity under specified terms, usually at a price greater than the maturity value (the difference is a *call premium*). A firm will call a bond issue and refund it if interest rates fall sufficiently after the bond has been issued.

- Bonds are assigned *ratings* that reflect the probability of their going into default. The higher a bond's rating, and the greater the probability of recovering bondholder capital if default should occur, the lower its interest rate.

- The *interest rate* required on a debt security is composed of the real risk-free rate (RRF) plus premiums that reflect inflation (IP), default risk (DRP), liquidity (LP), price risk (PRP), and call risk (CRP):

$$\text{Interest rate} = RRF + IP + DRP + LP + PRP + CRP.$$

- Bonds call for the payment of a specific amount of *interest* for a specific number of years and for the *repayment of par* on the bond's maturity date. Like most assets, a bond's value is simply the present value of the expected cash flow stream.

- The annual rate of return on a bond consists of an *interest*, or *current*, *yield* plus a *capital gains yield*. Assuming constant interest rates, a bond selling at a *discount* will have a positive capital gains yield, while a bond selling at a *premium* will have a negative capital gains yield.

(continued)

- A bond's *yield to maturity (YTM)* is the rate of return earned on a bond if it is held to maturity and no default occurs. The YTM for a bond that sells at par consists entirely of an interest yield, but if the bond sells at a discount or premium, the YTM consists of the current yield plus a positive or negative capital gains yield.
- Bondholders face *price risk* because bond values change when interest rates change. An investor's exposure to price risk depends on the maturity of the bonds.
- Bondholders face *reinvestment rate risk* when the investment horizon exceeds the maturity of the bond issue. Taken together, price risk and reinvestment rate risk comprise *interest rate risk*, which stems from the fact that interest rates rise and fall over time.

(continued from previous page)

Long-term debt is a major source of capital for health services organizations. Thus, it is necessary for health services managers to be familiar with the basics of debt financing and how it is valued. Furthermore, learning how to value long-term debt provides an excellent introduction to the entire concept of asset valuation. The topics covered in this chapter are useful throughout the remainder of the book.

Questions

11.1. The four fundamental factors that affect the supply of and demand for investment capital—which affect interest rates—are investment opportunities, time preferences for consumption, risk, and inflation. Explain how each factor affects the cost of money.

11.2. The interest rate required by investors on a debt security can be expressed by the following equation:

Interest rate = $RRF + IP + DRP + LP + PRP + CRP$.

Define each term in the equation and explain how it affects the interest rate.

11.3. Briefly describe the following types of debt:
a. Term loan
b. Bond
c. Mortgage bond

        d. Senior debt; junior debt

        e. Debenture

        f. Municipal bond

11.4. Briefly explain the following debt features:

        a. Indenture

        b. Restrictive covenant

        c. Trustee

        d. Call provision

11.5. a. (1) What are the three primary bond rating agencies?

           (2) What do bond ratings measure?

           (3) How do investors interpret bond ratings?

           (4) What is the difference between an A-rated bond and a B-rated bond?

        b. (1) Why are bond ratings important to investors?

           (2) Why are ratings important to businesses that issue bonds?

11.6. a. What is interest rate risk?

        b. What is price risk?

        c. What is reinvestment rate risk?

11.7. Is this statement true or false? "The values of outstanding bonds change whenever the going rate of interest changes. In general, short-term interest rates are more volatile than long-term rates, so short-term bond prices are more sensitive to interest rate changes than are long-term bond prices." Explain your answer.

Problems

11.1. Assume Venture Healthcare sold bonds that had a ten-year maturity, a 12 percent coupon rate with annual payments, and a $1,000 par value.

        a. Suppose that two years after the bonds were issued, the required interest rate fell to 7 percent. What would be the bonds' value?

        b. Suppose that two years after the bonds were issued, the required interest rate rose to 13 percent. What would be the bonds' value?

        c. What would be the value of the bonds three years after issue in each scenario above, assuming that interest rates stayed steady at either 7 percent or 13 percent?

11.2. Twin Oaks Health Center has a bond issue outstanding with a coupon rate of 7 percent and four years remaining until maturity.

The par value of the bond is $1,000, and the bond pays interest annually.

a. Determine the current value of the bond if present market conditions justify a 14 percent required rate of return.

b. Now, suppose Twin Oaks's four-year bond had semiannual coupon payments. What would be its current value? (Assume a 7 percent semiannual required rate of return. However, the actual rate would be slightly less than 7 percent because a semiannual coupon bond is slightly less risky than an annual coupon bond.)

c. Assume that Twin Oaks's bond had a semiannual coupon but 20 years remaining to maturity. What would be the current value under these conditions? (Again, assume a 7 percent semiannual required rate of return, although the actual rate would probably be greater than 7 percent because of increased price risk.)

11.3. Tideview Home Health Care, Inc., has a bond issue outstanding with eight years remaining to maturity, a coupon rate of 10 percent with interest paid annually, and a par value of $1,000. The current market price of the bond is $1,251.22.

a. What is the bond's yield to maturity?

b. Now, assume that the bond has semiannual coupon payments. What is its yield to maturity in this situation?

11.4. Homecare Inc. has three bond issues outstanding. All three bonds pay $100 in annual interest plus $1,000 at maturity. Bond S has a maturity of five years, bond M has a 15-year maturity, and bond L matures in 30 years.

a. What is the value of each of these bonds when the required interest rate is 5 percent, 10 percent, and 15 percent?

b. Why is the price of bond L more sensitive to interest rate changes than the price of bond S?

11.5. Turndale Health System has bonds outstanding that have four years remaining to maturity, a coupon interest rate of 9 percent paid annually, and a $1,000 par value.

a. What is the yield to maturity on the issue if the current market price is $829?

b. If the current market price is $1,104?

c. Would you be willing to buy one of these bonds for $829 if you required a 12 percent rate of return on the issue? Explain your answer.

11.6. Six years ago, Bradford Community Hospital issued 20-year municipal bonds with a 7 percent annual coupon rate. The bonds were called today for a $70 call premium—that is, bondholders received $1,070 for each bond. What is the realized rate of return for those investors who bought the bonds for $1,000 when they were issued?

11.7. Regal Health Plans issued a 12 percent annual coupon bond with a $1,000 par value a few years ago. The bond now has ten years remaining to maturity and sells for $1,100. The bond has a call provision that allows Regal to call the bond in four years at a call price of $1,060.

  a. What is the bond's yield to maturity?

  b. What is the bond's yield to call?

11.8. Jane Smith, MD, has had a great year in her pediatrics practice, and she has cash that she wants to invest. Her financial adviser suggests she buy a seven-year, $1,500 par value bond with an annual coupon rate of 10 percent and three years remaining to maturity. Dr. Smith decides to explore her options. She discovers that new, similarly risky bonds have an average annual rate of return of 12 percent. Bank certificates of deposit are returning 5 percent annually on average while a mutual fund investing in high-risk growth stocks has an average annual rate of return of 20 percent. If Dr. Smith follows her financial adviser's advice, what is the maximum amount she should pay for the bond? Explain your answer.

11.9. Orange District Hospital issued a 30-year, 10 percent annual coupon bond (par value $1,000) two years ago. The bond now has 28 years remaining to maturity and sells for $1,400. The bond has a call provision that allows the hospital to call the bond in ten years at a call price of $1,100. If an investor expects a call and requires a 6.5 percent rate of return, will the investor be likely to purchase the bond? Explain your answer.

Selected Cases

Two cases in *Gapenski's Cases in Healthcare Finance*, sixth edition, are applicable to this chapter: Case 13: Pacific Healthcare (A); and Case 14: Senior Care Enterprises.

Notes

1. Authors' calculation per Optum data, www.optum.com.
2. Obtained from the Federal Reserve Bank of St. Louis, "20-Year High Quality Market (HQM) Corporate Bond Spot Rate," https://fred.stlouisfed.org/series/HQMCB20YR.

Resources

Arduino, K. 2018. "Healthcare Capital Markets Outlook: Short-Term Opportunities Versus Long-Term Uncertainty." *Healthcare Financial Management* 72 (5): 36–43.

———. 2017a. "Amid Change, Focus on Nimbleness and Affordability." *Healthcare Financial Management* 71 (2): 58–59.

———. 2017b. "Time to Revisit Private Placement Debt." *Healthcare Financial Management* 71 (10): 92–93.

Bruton, P. W. 2018. "The Rise, Fall, and Possible Return of Variable-Rate Demand Bonds." *Healthcare Financial Management* 72 (5): 50–54.

Healthcare Financial Management Association. 2018. "Optimizing Capital Structure Decisions Under the New Tax Law." *Healthcare Financial Management* 72 (8): A1–4.

Jordahl, E. A. 2017. "Terminating Swap Positions." Healthcare Financial Management Association. Published December 1. www.hfma.org/Content.aspx?id=57108.

Lalangas, E., D. Kroll, and A. Carlson. 2018. "The Tax Cuts and Jobs Act Takeaways for Healthcare Finance Leaders." *Healthcare Financial Management* 72 (4): 28–31.

Sahrbeck, J. B. 2015. "Timing Tax-Exempt Bond Refunds." *Healthcare Financial Management* 69 (9): 112.

For current (updated daily) interest rate information, see the Federal Reserve System's website at www.federalreserve.gov/releases/h15. This site includes data on commercial paper, corporate bonds, and other rates in addition to the rates on Treasury securities.

For information on bond ratings, see Standard & Poor's: www.standardand poors.com.

CREDIT ENHANCEMENT, TERM STRUCTURE OF INTEREST RATES, AND ECONOMIC FACTORS THAT INFLUENCE INTEREST RATE LEVELS

11

Credit Enhancement

Credit enhancement involves the use of strategies designed to improve a bond issue's rating. One of the most common forms of credit enhancement is *bond insurance*. Here is how it works: Regardless of the inherent credit rating of the issuer, the bond insurer guarantees that bondholders will receive the promised interest and principal payments. Thus, bond insurance protects investors against default by the issuer. Because the insurer gives its guarantee that payments will be made, an insured bond carries the credit rating of the insurance company rather than that of the bond issuer.

Bond insurance gives the issuer access to a lower interest rate, but not without a cost. Bond insurers typically charge an up-front fee, stated as a percentage of the total debt service over the life of the bond. The lower the issuer's inherent credit rating and the worse the outlook for the sector, the higher the cost of bond insurance. Upon careful analysis, the insurance costs on many issues appear to fully negate the value inherent in lower interest payments. Still, such "economically neutral" deals often appeal to issuers because insurance protects investors, and the reputation of the issuer, against future uncertainty. A provider with a solid rating today—say, A+—could easily fall on hard times 20 or so years down the road. Credit enhancement allows the issuer's creditworthiness to decline without having to explain the reasons to the investment community.

Historically, about half of all municipal healthcare bond issues carried insurance. However, many bond insurers were caught up in the 2008 financial crisis of derivative contracts, subprime mortgages, and collateralized mortgage obligations. Every AAA-rated bond insurer was downgraded, and many were forced out of business. In 2019, there was only one hospital bond insurer writing coverage on new issues (Assured Guaranty Corporation, with a rating of AA–).

Instead of commercial bond insurance, many hospitals have turned to federal hospital mortgage insurance provided by the Federal Housing Administration (FHA), a part of the US Department of Housing and Urban Development. This insurance is referred to as FHA 242. Since its inception in 1968, the FHA 242 program has insured more than $20 billion in hospital loans used for facilities construction. Hospitals with more than 50 percent of patient days attributable to acute care are eligible for FHA insurance on both taxable and tax-exempt debt with fixed interest rates having maturities of up to 25 years after construction completion. FHA 242 debt is the equivalent of at least an AA rating, which is higher than most hospitals' inherent rating.

SELF-TEST QUESTIONS

1. What does the term *credit enhancement* mean?
2. Why would healthcare issuers seek bond insurance?
3. What is the FHA 242 program?

The Term Structure of Interest Rates

At certain times, short-term interest rates are lower than long-term rates; at other times, short-term rates are higher than long-term rates; and at yet other times, short-term and long-term rates are roughly equal. The relationship between long- and short-term rates, which is called the *term structure* of interest rates, is important to health services managers who must decide whether to borrow by issuing long- or short-term debt and to investors who must decide whether to buy long- or short-term debt. It is important to understand how interest rates on long- and short-term debt are related to one another.

To examine the current term structure, look up the interest rates on debt of various maturities by a single issuer (usually the US Treasury) in a source such as the *Wall Street Journal*. For example, the tabular section of exhibit S11.1 presents interest rates for Treasury securities of different maturities on two dates. The set of data for a given date, when plotted on a graph, is called a *yield curve*. As shown in the exhibit, the yield curve changes both in position and in shape over time. Had the yield curve been drawn during late July 2006, it would have been essentially horizontal because long-term and short-term bonds at that time had about the same rate of interest.

On average, long-term rates have been higher than short-term rates, so the yield curve usually slopes upward. An upward-sloping curve is expected if the inflation premium is relatively constant across all maturities because the price risk premium applied to long-term issues will push long-term rates above short-term rates. Because an upward-sloping yield curve is most prevalent, this shape is also called a normal yield curve. Conversely, a yield curve that slopes

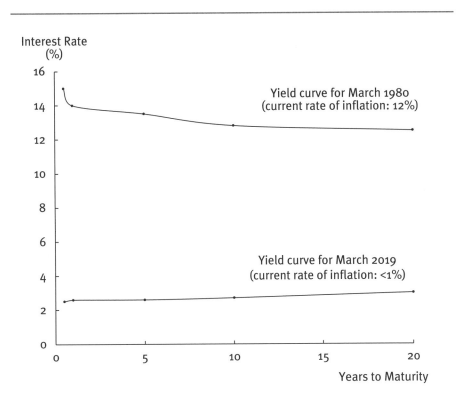

EXHIBIT S11.1
US Treasury
Debt Interest
Rates on Two
Dates

Term to Maturity	March 1980	March 2019
6 months	15.0%	2.5%
1 year	14.0	2.6
5 years	13.5	2.6
10 years	12.8	2.7
20 years	12.5	3.0

downward is called an inverted, or abnormal, yield curve. Thus, the yield curve for March 1980 is inverted, but the one for March 2019 is normal.

Exhibit S11.1 shows yield curves for US Treasury securities, but the curves could have been constructed for similarly rated corporate or municipal (i.e., tax-exempt) debt, if the data were available. In each case, the yield curve would be approximately the same shape but would differ in vertical position. For example, had the yield curve been constructed for Kindred Healthcare (www.kindredhealthcare.com), a for-profit nursing home operator, it would fall above the Treasury curve because interest rates on corporate debt include default risk premiums, whereas Treasury rates do not. Conversely, the curve for Baptist Medical Center (www.baptistjax.com), a not-for-profit hospital, would probably fall below the Treasury curve because the tax-exemption benefit, which lowers the interest rate on tax-exempt securities, generally out-weighs the default risk premium. In every case, however, the riskier the issuer (i.e., the lower the debt is rated), the higher the yield curve plots on the graph.

Health services managers use yield curve information to make deci-sions regarding debt maturities. To illustrate, assume that it is December 2018 and that the yield curve for March 2019 in exhibit S11.1 applies to Baptist Medical Center. Now, assume that the hospital plans to issue $10 million of debt to finance a new outpatient clinic with a 30-year life. If it borrowed in 2019 on a short-term basis—say for one year—Baptist's interest cost for that year would be 2.6 percent, or $260,000. If it used long-term (20-year) financing, its cost would be 3.0 percent, or $300,000. Therefore, at first glance, it would seem that Baptist should use short-term debt.

However, if the hospital used short-term debt, it would have to renew the loan every year at the then-current short-term rate. Although unlikely, it is possible that interest rates could soar to 1980 levels. If this happened, at some point in the future, the hospital might be paying 14 percent, or $1.4 million per year. Conversely, if Baptist used long-term financing in 2019, its interest costs would remain constant at $300,000 per year, so an increase in interest rates in the economy would not hurt the hospital.

Financing decisions would be easy if managers could accurately forecast interest rates. Unfortunately, predicting future interest rates with consistent accuracy is somewhere between difficult and impossible—people who make a living by selling interest rate forecasts say it is difficult, but many others say it is impossible. Sound financial policy, therefore, calls for a mix of long- and short-term debt, as well as equity, so that the business can survive in all but the most severe, and unlikely, interest rate environments. Furthermore, the optimal financing policy depends in an important way on the maturities of the firm's assets: In general, to reduce risk, managers try to match the maturities of the financing with the maturities of the assets being financed. This issue is addressed again in chapter 16, when current asset financing policies are discussed.

SELF-TEST QUESTIONS

1. What is a yield curve, and what information is needed to create this curve?
2. What is the difference between a normal yield curve and an abnormal one?
3. If short-term rates are lower than long-term rates, why may a business still choose to finance with long-term debt?
4. Explain the following statement: "A firm's financing policy depends in large part on the nature of its assets."

Economic Factors That Influence Interest Rate Levels

The general level of interest rates, as opposed to the rate set on a particular debt issue, and the shape of the yield curve are influenced by economic factors. The three most important factors are (1) Federal Reserve policy, (2) federal budgetary policy, and (3) the overall level of economic activity.

Federal Reserve Policy

The money supply has a significant impact on the level of economic activity and the inflation rate, which affect the level of interest rates. In the United States, the money supply and short-term interest rates are controlled by the *Federal Reserve Board* (the *Fed*). If the Fed wants to stimulate the economy, it increases the growth of the money supply and lowers the short-term interest rate that banks charge one another to borrow funds. Alternatively, if the Fed believes that the economy is overheated and inflation will be a problem in the future, it tightens (reduces) the money supply and raises short-term rates. During periods when the Fed is actively intervening in the credit markets, interest rates are affected and the yield curve may be temporarily distorted— that is, short-term rates may temporarily be "too high" or "too low." Typically, the impact of Fed actions on short-term interest rates is much greater than on long-term rates.

Federal Budgetary Policy

If the federal government spends more than it receives in tax revenues, it runs a deficit. Typically the shortfall is covered by government borrowing (issuing Treasury securities), which increases the demand for debt capital and raises the general level of interest rates. The relative impact on short-term and long-term rates depends on how the deficit is financed. Reliance on short-term debt would raise short-term rates, while reliance on long-term debt would increase long-term rates. Over the past several decades, the federal government has, except for a few years, had an annual deficit, which has pushed the national debt to more than $22 trillion. Clearly, federal borrowing has exerted upward pressure on the overall level of interest rates. Because the government uses both short- and long-term borrowing to finance its deficits, the impact on the yield curve is uncertain.

Level of Economic Activity

Business conditions have a significant effect on interest rates. Consumer demand slows during recessions and low-growth periods, which means that fewer goods and services are sold, especially durable goods (houses, automobiles, and the like). At the same time, companies hire fewer employees and spend less on new capital assets (land, buildings, and equipment). The net result is downward pressure on inflation and on the demand for borrowed funds, resulting in downward pressure on interest rates. At the same time, the Fed is trying to stimulate the economy by increasing the money supply and lowering short-term rates. In general, these conditions tend to have a greater impact on short-term rates than on long-term rates because (1) the Fed operates in the short end of the credit markets and (2) long-term inflation expectations are not as volatile as short-term expectations. The story is reversed when the economy is booming.

SELF-TEST QUESTIONS

1. Describe three economic factors that influence the general level of interest rates.
2. Do these factors have a greater influence on short-term rates or long-term rates? Explain.

EQUITY FINANCING AND SECURITIES MARKETS

Learning Objectives

After studying this chapter, readers will be able to

- Describe the key features associated with equity financing of for-profit businesses.
- Discuss the rights and privileges of common stockholders.
- Explain the need for and the ways that not-for-profit businesses obtain equity financing.
- Conduct simple valuation analyses of common stock.
- Explain the concepts of market equilibrium and efficiency.
- Discuss the risk/return trade-off.

Introduction

Long-term debt financing was discussed in chapter 11, including how interest rates are set in the economy; the features of long-term debt securities; and how debt securities, particularly bonds, are valued. The second major source of capital to healthcare businesses is *equity financing*. In investor-owned, or for-profit, businesses, equity financing is obtained externally from owners purchasing equity stakes in the business and internally by retaining earnings within the business. The equivalent financing in not-for-profit corporations, which is sometimes called **fund capital**, is raised externally through contributions and grants and internally, as in for-profit businesses, by retaining earnings. From a financial perspective, equity and fund financing serve the same basic purpose, so the generic term *equity* is used to refer to all nondebt capital, regardless of a business's ownership.

In this chapter, we cover the same general issues that were presented in chapter 11, but we focus on equity financing. In addition, information is provided on market equilibrium and efficiency. The chapter 12 supplement contains material related to capital financing: the market for common stock, securities market regulation, and the investment banking process.

fund capital
Equity capital in a not-for-profit corporation, typically obtained from contributions and grants and by retaining earnings; on the balance sheet, often called *net assets*.

Equity in For-Profit Businesses

In for-profit businesses, equity financing is supplied by the owners of the business, either directly through the purchase of an equity interest in the business or indirectly through earnings retention. Because most large for-profit businesses are organized as corporations, the discussion here focuses on corporate stockholders as opposed to proprietors or partners, although many of the concepts apply to all owners.

Common stockholders are the owners of for-profit corporations, and as such, they have certain rights and privileges. The most important of these rights and privileges are discussed in the following sections. Some for-profit businesses use *preferred stock*, which is a form of equity financing that combines features of both debt and common stock. However, very few healthcare businesses use preferred stock financing, so this type of equity is not covered here.

Claim on Residual Earnings

The reason that most people buy *common stock* is to earn a return. In reality, they are buying the right to a proportionate share of the *residual earnings* of the corporation. A business's net income, which is the residual earnings after all expenses have been paid, belongs to the firm's stockholders. Some portion of net income may be paid out in *dividends,* in which case stockholders receive cash payments by virtue of their ownership interest in the business. Traditionally, dividend-paying corporations have paid dividends quarterly. However, some corporations are now paying dividends annually. The advantage of annual dividends is the reduction in administrative costs associated with paying dividends. There are other ways for investor-owned businesses to return funds to owners—for example, through stock repurchases.

The portion of net income that is retained within the business (i.e., not paid out as dividends) ultimately will be invested in new assets, which presumably will increase the firm's earnings, and hence dividends, over time. An increasing dividend stream means that the stock will be more valuable in the future than it is today because dividends will be higher—for example, in five years—than they are now. Thus, stockholders typically expect to be able to sell their stock at some time in the future at a higher price than they paid for it, thereby realizing a *capital gain*.

To illustrate the payment of dividends, consider exhibit 12.1, which lists the annual per share dividend payment and earnings, as well as the average annual stock price, for Big Sky Healthcare from 2009 through 2019. Over the ten growth periods, Big Sky's dividend grew by 275 percent, or at an average annual rate of 14.1 percent. At the same time, the firm's stock price grew by 247 percent, producing an average annual rate of return of 13.2 percent.

Year	Annual per Share Dividend ($)	Annual per Share Earnings ($)	Average Annual Stock Price ($)
2009	$0.20	$0.48	$ 7.70
2010	0.23	0.55	10.95
2011	0.23	0.52	11.00
2012	0.23	0.58	10.40
2013	0.48	0.85	15.30
2014	0.52	1.10	18.70
2015	0.58	1.25	20.60
2016	0.58	0.45	19.50
2017	0.65	1.35	23.20
2018	0.70	1.50	24.40
2019	0.75	1.55	26.70

EXHIBIT 12.1
Big Sky
Healthcare:
Selected
Financial Data,
2009–2019

Although Big Sky's dividend growth *averaged* 14.1 percent annually over the period, it was not a *constant* 14.1 percent each year. Firms often hold the dividend constant for several years to allow earnings to climb to a point that a higher dividend payment clearly is warranted. For example, Big Sky kept its dividend at $0.23 a share from 2010 through 2012, while earnings per share were flat at about $0.55.

In general, managers are reluctant to reduce dividends because investors interpret lower dividends as a signal that management forecasts poor earnings ahead. Thus, when Big Sky saw its earnings per share temporarily tumble from $1.25 in 2015 to $0.45 in 2016, it maintained its $0.58 per share dividend. Big Sky was able to pay a cash dividend that exceeded earnings in 2016 because the firm's cash flow, which generally exceeds net income, easily supported the dividend. When earnings picked up again in 2017, Big Sky increased its dividend to $0.65.

If a firm is experiencing temporary financial difficulties, it might borrow the funds necessary to pay the dividend expected by stockholders rather than lower or omit the payment. The conventional wisdom among corporate managers is that "like diamonds, dividends are forever." The reason is that a dividend cut—or worse yet, an omission—sends a signal that often triggers a sell-off, which, in turn, substantially lowers the firm's stock price and places management in a precarious position. Thus, dividends typically are cut only under extreme circumstances and after all other reasonable options have been exhausted.

Over the entire period, Big Sky proved to be a good investment for stockholders. For example, assume that the stock was purchased for $7.70 in 2009, a $0.20 dividend was paid on the stock, and then the stock was sold one year later for $10.95. For simplicity, assume that the dividend payment, rather than occurring quarterly, was paid at the end of the one-year holding period. Thus, $7.70 was paid for the stock, and one year later $10.95 + $0.20 = $11.15 was received, for a rate of return of 44.8 percent. However, investors who bought Big Sky's stock in 2011 or 2015 and then sold it one year later would have had a capital loss rather than a capital gain on the sale, even though they would have received quarterly dividends over each one-year holding period. As we discussed earlier, holding the stock for the entire ten-year period would have resulted in dividend income plus a 13.2 percent annual capital gain. (This simple example illustrates that, in general, holding stocks for longer periods is less risky than holding stocks for shorter periods.) We discuss stock valuation in more detail later in this chapter.

Control of the Firm

Common stockholders have the right to elect a firm's board of directors, which, in turn, elects the officers who will manage the business. In small firms, the major stockholders often assume all of the management leadership positions. In large, publicly owned firms, managers typically own some stock, but their personal holdings are insufficient to allow them to exercise voting control. Thus, stockholders can remove the management of most publicly owned firms if they decide that a management team is ineffective.

State and federal laws stipulate how stockholder control is exercised. First, corporations must hold an election of directors periodically, usually once a year, with the vote taken at the annual meeting. In many corporations, one-third of the directors are elected each year for a three-year term. Each share of stock has one vote; thus, the owner of 1,000 shares has 1,000 votes. Stockholders can appear at the annual meeting and vote in person, but typically they transfer their right to vote to a second party by means of a *proxy*. Management always solicits stockholders' proxies and usually gets them. However, if common stockholders are dissatisfied with current management, an outside group may solicit the proxies in an effort to overthrow management and take control of the business. Such a bid for control is known as a **proxy fight**.

A *hostile takeover* occurs when control of the company changes hands without approval by the managers of the firm being bought. Managers who do not have majority control are concerned about hostile takeovers. One of the most common tactics to thwart a hostile takeover is to place a **poison pill** provision in the corporate charter. A poison pill typically permits stockholders of the firm that is taken over to buy shares of the firm that instituted the

proxy fight
An attempt to take control of a corporation by soliciting the votes (proxies) of current shareholders.

poison pill
A provision in a company's charter that makes it an unattractive hostile takeover target.

takeover at a greatly reduced price. Obviously, shareholders of the acquiring firm do not want an outside group to get bargain-priced stock, so such provisions effectively stop hostile takeovers. Although poison pill provisions of this type might appear to be illegal, they have withstood all court challenges. The ultimate effect of poison pills is to force acquiring firms to get the approval of the managers of the firm they are seeking to control prior to the takeover. Although the stated reason for poison pills is to protect shareholders against a hostile takeover at a price that is too low, many people believe that they are designed to protect managers more than stockholders.

The Preemptive Right

Common stockholders sometimes have the right to purchase any new shares sold by the firm; this is called the **preemptive right**. The purpose of the preemptive right is twofold. First, it protects the present stockholders' position of control. If it were not for this safeguard, the management of a corporation facing criticism from stockholders could secure its position by issuing and then purchasing a large number of additional shares. Management would thereby gain control of the corporation and frustrate current stockholders.

preemptive right The right that gives current shareholders the opportunity to purchase any newly issued shares (in proportion to their current holdings) before they are offered to the general public.

The second, and more important, purpose of the preemptive right is that it protects stockholders against dilution of value should new shares be issued at less than the current market price. For example, suppose HealthOne HMO has 1,000 shares of common stock outstanding, each with a price of $100, for a total market value of $100,000. If an additional 1,000 shares were sold to friends and relatives of management at $50 a share, or for $50,000, this would presumably raise the total market value of HealthOne's stock to $150,000. When the new market value is divided by the new number of shares outstanding, the price per share is $75. HealthOne's old stockholders thus lose $25 per share, and the new stockholders have an instant profit of $25 per share.

As this simplistic example demonstrates, selling common stock at a price below the current market price dilutes value and transfers wealth from the present stockholders to those who purchase the new shares. The preemptive right, which gives current stockholders the first opportunity to buy any new shares, protects them against such dilution of value.

SELF-TEST QUESTIONS

1. How do common stock investors usually receive returns?
2. How do common stockholders exercise their right of control?
3. What is the preemptive right, and what is its purpose?

Types of Common Stock

Although most for-profit corporations issue only one type of common stock, in some instances, several types of stock are used to meet the special needs of the company. Generally, when special classifications of stock are used, one type is designated *class A*, another *class B*, and so on. For this reason, such stock is called **classified stock**.

classified stock
The term used to distinguish between stock classes when a business uses more than one type of common stock.

Small, new companies that seek to obtain funds from outside sources frequently use classified stock. For example, when Genetic Research, Inc. (www.gen-res.com), went public, its class A stock was sold to the public and paid a dividend, but it carried no voting rights for five years. Its class B stock was retained by the organizers of the company and carried full voting rights for five years, but dividends could not be paid on the class B stock until the company had established its earning power by building up retained earnings to a designated level. The firm's use of classified stock allowed the public to take a position in a conservatively financed growth company without sacrificing income, while the founders retained absolute control during the crucial early stages of the firm's development. At the same time, outside investors were protected against excessive withdrawals of funds by the original owners. As is often the case in such situations, the class B stock was also called *founders' shares*.

Class A, class B, and so on have no standard meanings. Most firms have no classified shares, but a firm that does could designate its class B shares as founders' shares and its class A shares as those sold to the public. Other firms could use the A and B designations for entirely different purposes.

1. What is meant by *classified stock*?
2. Give one reason for using classified stock.

Procedures for Selling New Common Stock

For-profit corporations can sell new common stock in a variety of ways. In this section, we describe the most common methods.

Rights Offerings

As discussed previously, common stockholders often have the *preemptive right* to purchase any additional shares sold by the firm. If the preemptive right is contained in a particular firm's charter, the company must offer any newly issued common stock to existing stockholders. If the charter does not prescribe a preemptive right, the firm can choose to sell to its existing stockholders or to the public at large. If it sells its newly issued shares to existing stockholders, the stock sale is called a **rights offering**. Each stockholder is issued an *option* to buy a certain number of the new shares at a price below the current market price. The precise terms of the option are listed on a certificate called a *stock purchase right*, or simply a *right*. Stockholders who do not wish to purchase any additional shares in the company can sell their rights to another person who does want to buy the stock.

Public Offerings

If the preemptive right exists in a company's charter, it must sell new stock through a rights offering. If the preemptive right does not exist, the company may choose to offer the new shares to the general public through a **public offering**. Procedures for public offerings are discussed in detail in the chapter 12 supplement.

Private Placements

In a *private placement*, securities are sold to one or a few investors, generally institutional investors. Private placements are most common with bonds, but they also occur with stock. The primary advantages of private placements are lower administrative costs and greater speed, because the shares do not have to go through the Securities and Exchange Commission (SEC) (www.sec.gov) registration process.

The primary disadvantage of private placements is that the securities, because they are unregistered, must be sold to an "accredited" investor—usually an insurance company, a mutual fund, or a pension fund. Furthermore, in the event that the original purchaser wants to sell privately placed securities, they must be resold to other accredited investors. Currently, the SEC allows any institution with a portfolio of $100 million or more to buy and sell private placement securities. Because thousands of institutions have assets that exceed this limit, there is a large market for the resale of private placements, and they are becoming more popular with issuers.

Employee Stock Purchase Plans

Many companies have plans that allow employees to purchase stock of the employing firm on favorable terms. Such plans are generically referred to as *employee stock purchase plans*. Under executive incentive *stock option plans*, key managers are given options to purchase stock at a fixed price. These managers generally have a direct, material influence on the company's fortunes, so if they perform well, the stock price will go up and the options will become valuable.

Also, many companies have *stock purchase plans* for lower-level employees. For example, Texas Health Plans, Inc., a regional investor-owned

rights offering
The mechanism by which new common stock is offered to existing shareholders; each stockholder receives an option (right) to buy a specific number of new shares at a given price.

public offering
The sale of newly issued securities to the general public through an investment banker.

health insurer, permits employees who are not participants in its stock option plan to allocate up to 10 percent of their salary to its stock purchase plan. The funds are then used to buy newly issued shares at 85 percent of the market price on the purchase date. The company's contribution—the 15 percent discount—is not *vested* in an employee until five years after the purchase date. Thus, the employee cannot realize the benefit of the company's contribution without working an additional five years. This type of plan is designed both to improve employee performance and to reduce employee turnover.

Dividend Reinvestment Plans

dividend reinvestment plan (DRIP)
A plan under which the dividends paid to a stockholder are automatically reinvested in the company's common stock.

Many large companies have **dividend reinvestment plans (DRIPs)**, whereby stockholders can automatically reinvest their dividends in the stock of the corporation. There are two basic types of DRIPs: plans that involve only old stock that is already outstanding and plans that involve newly issued stock. In either case, the stockholder must pay income taxes on the dollar amount of the dividends, even though stock, rather than cash, is received.

Under both types of DRIP, stockholders must choose between continuing to receive cash dividends and using the cash dividends to buy more stock in the corporation. Under the *old stock* type of plan, a bank, acting as a trustee, takes the total funds available for reinvestment from each quarterly dividend, purchases the corporation's stock on the open market, and allocates the shares purchased to the participating stockholders on a pro rata basis. The brokerage costs of buying the shares are low because of volume purchases, so these plans benefit small stockholders who do not need cash for current consumption.

The *new stock* type of DRIP provides for dividends to be invested in newly issued stock; hence, these plans raise new capital for the firm. No fees are charged to participating stockholders, and some companies offer the new stock at a discount of 3 to 5 percent below the prevailing market price. The companies absorb these costs as a trade-off against the issuance costs that would be incurred if the stock were sold through investment bankers rather than through the DRIP.

Direct Purchase Plans

Some companies have *direct purchase plans*, which allow stockholders to purchase additional stock directly from the company. Many of these plans grew out of DRIPs, which were expanded to allow participants to purchase shares in excess of the dividend amount. In direct purchase plans, investors usually pay little or no brokerage fees, and many plans offer convenient features such as fractional share purchases, automatic purchases by bank debit, and quarterly statements. Although employee purchase plans, DRIPS, and direct purchase plans are excellent ways for employees and individual investors to purchase stock, they typically do not raise large sums of new capital for firms. Other methods must be used when a business has greater equity needs.

SELF-TEST QUESTIONS

1. What is a rights offering?
2. What is a private placement, and what are its primary advantages over a public offering?
3. Briefly, what are employee stock purchase plans?
4. What is a dividend reinvestment plan?
5. What is a direct purchase plan?

Equity in Not-for-Profit Corporations

Investor-owned corporations have two sources of equity financing: retained earnings and new stock sales. Not-for-profit businesses can and do retain earnings, but they do not have access to the equity markets—that is, they cannot sell common stock to raise equity capital. Although rare, some types of not-for-profit healthcare corporations can sell shares to raise capital. However, such "stock" does not pay dividends and cannot be sold at a profit. This form of not-for-profit corporation is used mostly to finance not-for-profit clinics, whereby the physicians who will practice in the clinic contribute the start-up capital. When physicians leave the clinic, their initial capital investment is returned. Not-for-profit corporations can, however, raise equity capital through *government grants* and *charitable contributions.*

Federal, state, and local governments are concerned about the provision of healthcare services to the general population. Therefore, these public entities often make grants to not-for-profit providers to help offset the costs of services rendered to patients who cannot pay for those services. Sometimes these grants are nonspecific, but often they are meant to provide specific services, such as neonatal intensive care to needy infants.

As for charitable contributions, individuals, pure charities, and many businesses are motivated to contribute to not-for-profit health services organizations for a variety of reasons, including concern for the well-being of others, the recognition that often accompanies large contributions, and tax deductions. Because only contributions to not-for-profit entities are tax deductible, this source of funding is, for all practical purposes, not available to investor-owned health services organizations. Although charitable contributions are not a substitute for profit retention, charitable contributions can be a significant source of fund capital. A study conducted in 2018 noted that in 2012, 52 percent of not-for-profit hospitals received $826,080 on average in charitable contributions.[1]

Most not-for-profit hospitals received their initial, start-up equity capital from religious, educational, or government entities, and today, some hospitals continue to receive funding from these sources. However, since the 1970s, these sources have provided a much smaller proportion of hospital funding, forcing not-for-profit hospitals to rely more on profits and outside contributions. In addition, state and local governments, which are facing significant financial pressures, are finding it more difficult to fund grants to healthcare providers.

Finally, legislative bodies and tax authorities increasingly are forcing not-for-profit hospitals to "earn" their favorable tax treatment by providing a certain amount of charity care. Even more severe, some cities have pressured not-for-profit hospitals to make "voluntary" payments to the city to make up for lost property tax revenue. These trends reduce the ability of not-for-profit health services organizations to raise equity capital by grants and contributions; the result is increased reliance on making money the old-fashioned way—by earning it.

On the surface, investor-owned corporations may appear to have a significant advantage in raising equity capital. In theory, new common stock can be issued at any time and in any reasonable amount. Conversely, charitable contributions are much less certain. The planning, solicitation, and collection periods can take years, and pledges are not always collected. Therefore, charitable contributions that are expected may not materialize. Also, the proceeds of new stock sales may be used for any purpose, but charitable contributions often are *restricted*, in which case they can be used only for a designated purpose.

For Your Consideration
The Green Bay Packers

What do the Green Bay Packers have in common with the Mayo Clinic? It turns out that they are both not-for-profit organizations, but there is a surprising difference: The Packers have stockholders.

The Green Bay Packers, Inc., became a publicly owned, not-for-profit corporation in 1923, when the original articles of incorporation were filed with Wisconsin's secretary of state. The corporation is governed by a board of directors and a seven-member executive committee. In 2019, 5,009,562 shares were owned by 361,169 stockholders—but these shares are not like most stock. They pay no dividends and cannot be sold on the open market; they can only be sold back to the corporation at the same price at which they were purchased. Furthermore, any profits earned by the corporation must be donated to charity.

One of the more remarkable business stories in American sports, the team has been kept financially viable over the years by its shareholders. Fans have come to the team's financial rescue on several occasions, including the sale of $24 million in stock in 1998 for stadium improvements. To protect against someone taking control of the team, the articles of incorporation prohibit any person from owning more than 200,000 shares.

Did you know that some types of not-for-profit corporations can issue stock, although it is rarely done? In what situations might such a model be used in healthcare? What restrictions would have to be placed on the stock and the stockholders?

In reality, however, managers of investor-owned corporations do not have complete freedom to raise capital by selling new common stock. First, the issuance expenses associated with a new common stock issue are not trivial. Second, if market conditions are poor and the stock is selling at a low price, a new stock issue can dilute the value of existing shares and harm current stockholders. Finally, new stock issues may be viewed by investors as a signal that the firm's stock is overvalued, and new issues often drive the stock price lower.

For all these reasons, managers of investor-owned corporations generally would rather not issue new common stock. The key point here is that while for-profit health services organizations have greater access to equity capital than not-for-profit organizations, the differential access to equity capital may not be as great an advantage as it initially appears to be. The greatest advantage is for young, growing businesses that need a great deal of new capital. More mature companies have much less flexibility in raising new equity capital.

SELF-TEST QUESTIONS

1. What are the sources of equity (i.e., fund capital) available to not-for-profit firms?
2. Are not-for-profit corporations at a disadvantage when it comes to raising equity capital? Explain your answer.

Common Stock Valuation

For many reasons, the valuation of common stocks is a difficult and perplexing process. To begin, the type of valuation model used depends on the characteristics of the firm being valued. For stock valuation purposes, there are three distinct types of investor-owned businesses:

1. **Start-up businesses.** A business in its infancy generally pays no dividends because any earnings must be reinvested in the business to fund growth. To make matters worse, start-up firms often take years to make a profit, so there is no track record of positive earnings to use as a basis for a cash flow forecast. Under such conditions, the general valuation (discounted cash flow) model cannot be applied because the value of such a business stems more from opportunities than from the cash flows produced by existing product or service lines. Even if most of the opportunities do not materialize, one or two could turn into

blockbusters and create a highly successful business. With such firms, *option pricing techniques,* which are beyond the scope of this book, can be used, at least in theory, to value the stock. In reality, valuations on these firms are not much more than a shot in the dark, and their stock prices are based mostly on qualitative factors, including emotions. As a result, stock prices of start-up businesses usually are volatile.

2. **Young businesses.** If a firm successfully passes through its initial start-up phase, it often reaches a point at which it has more or less predictable positive earnings but still requires reinvestment of these earnings, so no dividends are paid. In such cases, it is possible to value the entire firm, as well as the stock of the firm, on the basis of the *expected earnings stream.* In such a valuation, the expected earnings stream is discounted, or *capitalized,* to find the current value of the firm. Then, the value of the debt is stripped off to estimate the value of the common stock.

3. **Mature businesses.** Mature firms generally pay relatively predictable dividends, and hence the future dividend stream can be forecast with reasonable confidence. In such cases, the common stock can be valued on the basis of the present value of the *expected dividend stream.* We illustrate this approach in the following sections.

The Dividend Valuation Model

A common stock with a predictable dividend stream can be valued using the general valuation model applied to the expected dividend stream. This approach is called the *dividend valuation model.*

Basic Definitions

The variables used in the illustration include the following:

- $E(D_t)$ = Dividend the stockholder *expects* to receive at the end of year t. D_0 is the most recent dividend, which has already been paid and is known with certainty; $E(D_1)$ is the first dividend expected, and for valuation purposes, it is assumed to be paid *at the end* of one year; $E(D_2)$ is the dividend expected at the end of two years; and so forth. $E(D_1)$ represents the *first* cash flow a new purchaser of the stock will receive. D_0, the dividend that has just been paid, is known with certainty, but all future dividends are expected values, so the estimate of any $E(D_t)$ may differ among investors. (Note that stocks generally pay dividends quarterly, so theoretically, they should be evaluated on a quarterly basis. However, in stock valuation, most analysts work on an annual basis because the data are not precise enough in most situations to warrant the refinement of a quarterly model.)

- P_0 = Actual *market price* of the stock today.
- $E(P_t)$ = Expected price of the stock at the end of each year t. $E(P_0)$ is the *value* of the stock today, as seen by a particular investor based on an estimate of the stock's expected dividend stream and riskiness; $E(P_1)$ is the price expected at the end of one year; and so on. Thus, whereas P_0, the current stock price, is fixed and identical for all investors, $E(P_0)$ differs among investors depending on each investor's assessment of the stock's riskiness and dividend stream. $E(P_0)$, each investor's estimate of the value today, could be above or below P_0, but an investor would buy the stock only if the estimate of $E(P_0)$ were equal to or greater than P_0.
- $E(g_t)$ = Expected growth rate in dividends in each future year t. Investors may use different $E(g_t)$s to evaluate a firm's stock. In reality, $E(g_t)$ is normally different for each year t. However, the valuation process can be simplified by assuming that $E(g_t)$ is constant across time.
- $R(R_e)$ = Required rate of return on the stock, considering both its riskiness and the returns available on other investments. We use the subscript e (for equity) to identify the return as a stock return.
- $E(R_e)$ = Expected rate of return on the stock. $E(R_e)$ could be above or below $R(R_e)$, but an investor would buy the stock only if his or her $E(R_e)$ were equal to or greater than $R(R_e)$. Note that $E(R_e)$ is an *expectation*. A return of $E(R_e)$ = 15% may be expected if Tenet Healthcare stock were purchased today. If conditions in the market or prospects at Tenet take a turn for the worse, however, the realized return may be much lower than expected, perhaps even negative.
- $E(D_1) \div P_0$ = Expected **dividend yield** on a stock during the first year. If a stock is expected to pay a dividend of $1 during the next 12 months, and its current price is $10, then its expected dividend yield is $1 \div $10 = 0.10 = 10\%$.

  dividend yield The annual dividend divided by current stock price.

- $[E(P_1) - P_0] \div P_0$ = Expected *capital gains yield* on the stock during the first year. If the stock sells for $10 today, and it is expected to rise to $10.50 at the end of the year, then the expected capital gain is $E(P_1) - P_0 = $10.50 - $10.00 = 0.50, and the expected capital gains yield is $[E(P_1) - P_0] \div P_0 = $0.50 \div $10 = 0.050 = 5\%$.

Expected Dividends as the Sole Basis for Stock Values

In the discussion of debt valuation in chapter 11, the value of a bond was found by adding the present value of the interest payments over the life of the bond to the present value of the bond's maturity, or par, value. In essence, a bond's value is the present value of the cash flows expected from the bond. Similarly, the value of a stock according to the dividend valuation model is calculated as the present value of a stream of cash flows. What are the cash flows that dividend-paying stocks provide to their holders? First, consider an investor who buys a stock with the intention of holding it in her family forever. In this situation, all the investor and her heirs will receive is a stream of dividends, and the value of the stock today is calculated as the present value of an infinite stream of dividends.

Now consider a more typical case in which an investor expects to hold the stock for a finite period and then sell it. What would be the value of the stock in this case? The value of the stock is again the present value of the expected dividend stream. To understand this, recognize that for any individual investor, expected cash flows consist of expected dividends plus the expected price of the stock when it is sold. However, the sale price received by the current investor will depend on the dividends that some future investor expects to receive. Therefore, for all present and future investors in total, expected cash flows must be based on expected future dividends. To put it another way, unless a business is liquidated or sold to another concern, the cash flows it provides to its stockholders consist only of a stream of dividends; therefore, the value of a share of its stock must be the present value of that expected dividend stream.

Occasionally, stock shares could have additional value, such as the value of a controlling interest when an investor buys 51 percent of a company's outstanding stock or the added value brought about by a takeover bid. However, in most situations, the sole value inherent in stock ownership stems from the dividends that are expected to be paid by the company to its shareholders.

Investors periodically lose sight of the long-run nature of stocks as investments and forget that to sell a stock at a profit, it is necessary to find a buyer who will pay the higher price. Suppose that a stock's value is analyzed on the basis of expected future dividends, and the conclusion is that the stock's market price exceeds a reasonable value. If an investor buys the stock anyway, he would be following the "bigger fool" theory of investment: The investor may be a fool to buy the stock at its excessive price, but he believes that when he is ready to sell, an even bigger fool will be found.

Constant Growth Stock Valuation

If the projected stream of dividends follows a systematic pattern, it is possible to develop a simplified (i.e., easier to evaluate) version of the dividend valuation model. Although only a few firms have dividends that actually grow at a constant rate, constant growth is often assumed because it simplifies the forecasting process. For a constant growth company, the expected dividend growth rate is constant for all years, so $E(g_1) = E(g_2) = E(g_3)$ and so on, which implies that $E(g_t)$ becomes simply $E(g)$. Under this assumption, the dividend in any future year t may be forecast as $E(D_t) = D_0 \times [1 + E(g)]^t$, where D_0 is the last dividend paid, and hence known with certainty, and $E(g)$ is the constant expected rate of growth.

To illustrate, if Minnesota Health Systems, Inc. (MHS), just paid a dividend of $1.82 (i.e., $D_0 = \$1.82$), and if investors expect a 10 percent constant dividend growth rate, the dividend expected in one year will be $E(D_1) = \$1.82 \times 1.10 = \$2.00$; $E(D_2)$ will be $\$1.82 \times (1.10)^2 = \$2.20$; and the dividend expected in five years will be $E(D_5) = D_0 \times [1 + E(g)]^5 = \$1.82 \times (1.10)^5 = \$2.93$.

The Value of a Constant Growth Stock

When $E(g)$ is assumed to be constant, a stock can be valued using a simplified model called the *constant growth model*:

$$E(P_0) = \frac{D_0 \times [1 + E(g)]}{R(R_e) - E(g)} = \frac{E(D_1)}{R(R_e) - E(g)},$$

where $R(R_e)$ is the required rate of return on the stock. If $D_0 = \$1.82$, $E(g) = 10\%$, and $R(R_e) = 16\%$ for MHS, the value of its stock would be $33.33:

$$E(P_0) = \frac{\$1.82 \times 1.10}{0.16 - 0.10} = \frac{\$2.00}{0.06} = \$33.33.$$

	A		B	C	D
1					
2	$	1.82	D_0	Last dividend payment	
3		10.0%	E(g)	Expected growth rate	
4		16.0%	R(R_e)	Required rate of return	
5					
6					
7					
8	$	33.37	=A2*(1+A3)/(A4–A3) (entered into Cell A8)		
9					
10					

For the constant growth model to be valid, the required rate of return on the stock must be greater than its constant dividend growth rate—that is, $R(R_e)$ must be greater than $E(g)$. If the constant growth model is used when $R(R_e)$ is not greater than $E(g)$, the results will be meaningless. However, this problem does not affect the model's usefulness because no company could grow over the long run at a rate that exceeds the required rate of return on its stock. Although the constant growth model is applied here to stock valuation, it can be used in any situation in which cash flows are growing at a constant rate.

How does an investor determine the required rate of return on a particular stock, $R(R_e)$? One way is to use the security market line (SML) of the capital asset pricing model, as discussed in chapter 10. Assume that MHS's market beta (β), as reported by a financial advisory service, is 1.6. Assume also that the risk-free interest rate (the rate on long-term Treasury bonds) is 5 percent, and the required rate of return on the market is 12 percent. According to the SML, the required rate of return on MHS's stock is approximately 16 percent:

$$R(R_{MHS}) = RF + [R(R_M) - RF] \times \beta$$
$$= 5\% + (12\% - 5\%) \times 1.6$$
$$= 5\% + (7\% \times 1.6)$$
$$= 5\% + 11.2\%$$
$$= 16.2\% \approx 16\%.$$

Key Equation: Constant Growth Stock Valuation

If a stock exhibits a constant dividend growth rate, it can be valued by this equation:

$$E(P_0) = \frac{D_0 \times [1 + E(g)]}{R(R_e) - E(g)} = \frac{E(D_1)}{R(R_e) - E(g)}.$$

Here, $E(P_0)$ is the stock's value (expected price), D_0 is the last dividend paid, $E(D_1)$ is the next expected dividend, $E(g)$ is the expected constant dividend growth rate, and $R(R_e)$ is the required rate of return on the stock. To illustrate, assume the next expected dividend is $0.50, the constant dividend growth rate is 4.0 percent, and the required rate of return on the stock is 10 percent. With these estimates, the stock's value is $8.33:

$$E(P_0) = \frac{\$0.50}{0.10 - 0.04} = \frac{\$0.50}{0.06} = \$8.33.$$

Remember, in the SML, RF is the risk-free rate; $R(R_M)$ is the required rate of return on the market, or the required rate of return on a $\beta = 1.0$ stock; and β is MHS's market beta.

	A	B	C	D
1				
2	1.6	β	Beta coeficient	
3	5.0%	RF	Risk-free rate	
4	12.0%	R(R$_M$)	Required return on market	
5				
6				
7				
8	16.2%	=A3+(A4−A3)*A2 (entered into Cell A8)		
9				
10				

Growth in dividends occurs primarily as a result of growth in earnings per share (EPS). Earnings growth, in turn, results from a number of factors, including the general inflation rate in the economy and the amount of earnings the company retains and reinvests. Regarding inflation, if output in units is stable, and if both sales prices and input costs increase at the inflation rate, EPS also will grow at the inflation rate. EPS will also grow as a result of the reinvestment, or plowback, of earnings. If the firm's earnings are not all paid out as dividends (i.e., if a fraction of earnings is retained), the dollars of investment behind each share will rise over time, which should lead to growth in productive assets and growth in earnings and dividends.

In the constant growth model, the most critical input is $E(g)$—the expected constant growth rate in dividends. Investors can make their own $E(g)$ estimates on the basis of historical dividend growth, but $E(g)$ estimates are also available from brokerage and investment advisory firms.

Expected Rate of Return on a Constant Growth Stock

The constant growth model can be rearranged to solve for $E(R_e)$, the *expected rate of return*. In its normal form, the required rate of return, $R(R_e)$, is an input into the model, but when it is rearranged, the expected rate of return, $E(Re)$, is found. This transformation requires that the required rate of return equal the expected rate of return, or $R(R_e) = E(R_e)$. This equality holds if the stock is in equilibrium, a condition that will be discussed later in this chapter. After solving the constant growth model for $E(R_e)$, this expression is obtained:

$$E(R_e) = \frac{D_0 \times [1 + E(g)]}{P_0} + E(g) = \frac{E(D_1)}{P_0} + E(g).$$

If an investor buys MHS's stock today for $P_0 = \$33.33$ and expects the stock to pay a dividend $E(D_1) = \$2.00$ one year from now, and if dividends grow at a constant rate $E(g) = 10\%$ in the future, the expected rate of return on that stock is 16 percent:

$$E(R_{MHS}) = \frac{\$2.00}{\$33.33} + 10.0\% = 6.0\% + 10.0\% = 16.0\%.$$

In this form, $E(R_e)$, the expected total return on the stock, consists of an expected dividend yield, $E(D_1) \div P_0 = 6\%$, plus an expected growth rate or capital gains yield, $E(g) = 10\%$.

	A		B	C	D
1					
2	$	33.33	P$_0$	Stock price	
3	$	2.00	E(D$_1$)	Next expected dividend	
4		10.0%	E(g)	Expected growth rate	
5					
6					
7					
8		16.0%	=A3/A2+A4 (entered into Cell A8)		
9					
10					

Suppose this analysis had been conducted on January 1, 2020: P_0 = \$33.33 is MHS's January 1, 2020, stock price and $E(D_1)$ = \$2.00 is the dividend expected at the end of 2020. What is the value of $E(P_1)$, the company's expected stock price, at the end of 2020 (the beginning of 2021)? The constant growth model would again be applied, but this time the 2021 dividend, $E(D_2) = E(D_1) \times [1 + E(g)] = \$2.00 \times 1.10 = \$2.20$, would be used:

$$E(P_1) = \frac{E(D_2)}{R(R_e) - E(g)} = \frac{\$2.20}{0.06} = \$36.67.$$

Notice that $E(P_1)$ = \$36.67 is 10 percent greater than P_0 = \$33.33: \$33.33 × 1.10 = \$36.67. Thus, a capital gain of \$36.67 − \$33.33 = \$3.34 would be expected during 2020, which results in a capital gains yield of 10 percent:

$$\text{Capital gains yield} = \frac{\text{Capital gain}}{\text{Beginning price}} = \frac{\$3.34}{\$33.33} = 0.100 = 10.0\%.$$

Key Equation: Expected Rate of Return on a Constant Growth Stock
If a stock exhibits a constant dividend growth rate, its expected rate of
return can be estimated as follows:

$$E(R_e) = \frac{D_0 \times [1 + E(g)]}{P_0} + E(g) = \frac{E(D_1)}{P_0} + E(g).$$

Here, $E(R_e)$ is the expected rate of return, D_0 is the last dividend paid,
$E(g)$ is the expected constant dividend growth rate, P_0 is today's price,
and $E(D_1)$ is the next expected dividend.

To illustrate, assume the next expected dividend is \$0.50, the
constant dividend growth rate is 4.0 percent, and the current stock
price is \$8.33. With these estimates, the expected rate of return is 10.0
percent:

$$E(R_e) = \frac{\$0.50}{\$8.33} + 0.04 = 0.06 + 0.04 = 0.10 = 10.0\%.$$

If the analysis were extended, in each future year, the expected capital
gains yield would always equal $E(g)$ because the stock price would grow at
the 10 percent constant dividend growth rate. The expected dividend yield
in 2021 (year 2) could be found as follows:

$$\text{Dividend yield} = \frac{E(D_2)}{E(P_1)} = \frac{\$2.20}{\$36.67} = 0.060 = 6\%.$$

The dividend yield for 2022 (year 3) could also be calculated, and again it
would be 6 percent. Thus, for a constant growth stock, the following conditions must hold:

- The dividend is expected to grow forever (or at least for a long time) at
  a constant rate, $E(g)$.
- The stock price is expected to grow at this same rate.
- The expected dividend yield is a constant.
- The expected capital gains yield is also a constant, and it is equal to $E(g)$.
- The expected total rate of return in any year t, which of necessity is
  a constant, is equal to the expected dividend yield plus the expected
  capital gains yield (growth rate).

The term *expected* should be clarified—it means expected in a statistical sense. Thus, if MHS's dividend growth rate is expected to remain constant at 10 percent, that means the growth rate in each year can be represented by a probability distribution with an expected value of 10 percent—not that the growth rate is expected to be exactly 10 percent in each future year. In this sense, the constant growth assumption is reasonable for many large, mature companies.

Nonconstant Growth Stock Valuation

What happens when a company does not meet the constant growth assumption? For example, what if MHS's dividend were expected to grow at 30 percent for three years and then settle down to a constant growth rate of 10 percent? Under these nonconstant growth conditions, the value of MHS stock would be $53.86, which is significantly higher than the $33.33 value of the stock assuming 10 percent constant growth. Dividend growth of 30 percent for three years followed by 10 percent constant growth creates a more valuable expected dividend stream than straight constant growth at 10 percent. In this situation, the constant growth model does not apply, so it is necessary to apply a nonconstant growth model to value the stock. Although nonconstant stock valuation models are not complicated, they are beyond the scope of an introductory book on healthcare finance.

SELF-TEST QUESTIONS

1. What are three approaches to valuing common stocks, and when does each apply?
2. Does the holding period matter when using the dividend valuation model?
3. Write out and explain the valuation model for a constant growth stock.
4. What are the assumptions of the constant growth model?
5. Show the constant growth model in the form of its expected rate of return.
6. What are the key features of constant growth regarding dividend yield and capital gains yield?

Security Market Equilibrium

Investors will want to buy a security if its expected rate of return exceeds its required rate of return—or, put another way, when its value exceeds its current price. Conversely, investors will want to sell a security when its required rate of return exceeds its expected rate of return—that is, when its current price exceeds its value. When more investors want to buy a security than to sell it, its price is bid up. When more investors want to sell a security than to buy it, its price falls. In *equilibrium*, two conditions must hold:

1. The expected rate of return on a security must equal its required rate of return.
2. The market price of a security must equal its value.

If these conditions do not hold, trading will occur until they do. Of course, security prices are not constant. A security's price can swing wildly as new information becomes available to the market that changes investors' expectations concerning the security's cash flow stream or risk or when the general level of returns (i.e., interest rates) changes. However, evidence suggests that securities prices, especially prices of securities that are actively traded, such as those issued by the US Treasury or by large firms, adjust rapidly to disequilibrium situations. Thus, most people believe that the bonds of the US Treasury and the bonds and stocks of major corporations are generally in equilibrium. The key to the rapid movement of securities prices toward equilibrium is informational efficiency, which is discussed in the next section.

SELF-TEST QUESTIONS

1. What is meant by *security market equilibrium*?
2. What securities are most likely to be in equilibrium?

Informational Efficiency

A securities market—say, the market for long-term US Treasury bonds—is *informationally efficient* if (1) all information relevant to the values of the securities traded can be obtained easily and at low cost and (2) the market contains many buyers and sellers who act *rationally* on this information. If these conditions hold, current market prices will have embedded in them all information of possible relevance; hence, future price movements will be based solely on *new* information as it becomes known.

The **efficient markets hypothesis (EMH)**, which has three forms, formalizes the theory of informational efficiency:

1. The *weak form* of the EMH holds that all information contained in *past price movements* is fully reflected in current market prices.

efficient markets hypothesis (EMH) The theory that stocks are always in equilibrium and it is impossible for investors to consistently earn excess returns (beat the market).

Therefore, information about recent trends in a security's price is of no value in choosing which securities will outperform other securities.

2. The *semistrong form* of the EMH holds that current market prices reflect all *publicly available information*. Spending hours analyzing economic data and financial reports makes no sense because whatever information is found, good or bad, has already been absorbed by the market and embedded in current prices.

3. The *strong form* of the EMH holds that current market prices reflect *all relevant information,* whether publicly available or privately held. If this form holds, then even investors with "inside information," such as corporate officers, would find it impossible to earn abnormal returns— returns in excess of what is justified by the riskiness of the investment.

The EMH, in any of its three forms, is merely a hypothesis, so it is not necessarily true. However, hundreds of empirical tests have been conducted to try to prove or disprove the EMH, and the results are surprisingly consistent. Most tests support the weak and semistrong forms of the EMH for well-developed markets, such as the US markets for large firms' stocks and bond issues and for Treasury securities. Supporters of these forms of the EMH note that there are some 100,000 or so full-time, highly trained professional analysts and traders operating in these markets. Furthermore, many of these analysts and traders work for businesses such as Citigroup, Fidelity Investments, Merrill Lynch, and Prudential that have billions of dollars available to take advantage of undervalued securities. Finally, as a result of disclosure requirements and electronic information networks, new information about heavily followed securities is almost instantaneously available. Security prices in these markets adjust almost immediately as new developments occur, and prices reflect all publicly available information.

Virtually no one, however, believes that the strong form of the EMH holds. Studies of legal purchases and sales by individuals with inside information indicate that insiders can make abnormal profits by trading on that information. It is even more apparent that insiders can make abnormal profits if they trade illegally on specific information that has not been disclosed to the public, such as a takeover bid or a research and development breakthrough.

The EMH has important implications both for securities investment decisions and for business financing decisions. Because security prices appear to generally reflect all public information, most actively followed and traded securities are in equilibrium and fairly valued. Being in equilibrium does not mean that new information cannot cause a security's price to soar or to plummet, but it does mean that most securities are neither undervalued nor overvalued. Therefore, over the long run, an investor with no inside information can expect to earn only a return on a security that compensates for the amount of risk assumed. In the short run—for example, a year—an investor can expect to earn only a return that is the same as the average for securities of equal risk. In other words, investors should not expect to "beat the market" after adjusting for risk. Also, because the EMH applies to most bond markets, bond prices and interest rates reflect all current public information. Consistently forecasting future interest rates accurately is impossible because interest rates change in response to new information.

For managers, the EMH indicates that managerial decisions generally should not be based on perceptions about the market's ability to properly price the firm's securities or on perceptions about the direction of future interest rates. In other words, managers should not attempt to time security issues to catch stock prices while they are high or interest rates while they are low. However, in some situations, managers may have information about their own firms that is unknown to the public. This condition, called *asymmetric information*, can affect managerial decisions. For example, suppose a drug manufacturer has made a breakthrough in cancer research but wants to maintain as much secrecy as possible about the new drug. During final development and testing, the firm might want to delay any new securities offerings because securities could probably be sold under more favorable terms once the announcement is made. Managers can, and should, act on inside information for the benefit of their firms, but inside information cannot legally be used for personal profit.

Are markets really efficient? If markets were not efficient, better managers of stock and bond mutual funds and pension plans would be able to consistently outperform the broad averages over long periods of time. In fact, few managers can consistently earn returns that beat the broad averages, and during most years, the vast majority of actively managed mutual funds underperform the market. In any given year, some mutual fund managers will outperform the market and others will underperform the market—this is certain. But for an investor to beat the market by investing in mutual funds, he must identify the successful managers beforehand, which seems difficult, if not impossible, to do.

In spite of the evidence, many theorists, and even more Wall Street experts, believe that pockets of inefficiency do exist. In some cases, entire markets may be inefficient. For example, the markets for securities issued by small firms may be inefficient because there are neither enough analysts ferreting out information on these companies nor sufficient numbers of investors trading these securities. Many people also believe that individual securities traded in efficient markets are occasionally priced inefficiently, or that investor emotions can drive prices too high during good times (such as the "dot-com bubble" of the late 1990s) or too low during bad times (such as the 2007–2009 recession). Indeed, if investors are driven more by greed and emotion than by rational assessments of security values, markets may not really be as efficient as claimed by supporters of the EMH.

Benjamin Graham, a well-respected stock market pundit, described the EMH as a theory that "could have great practical importance if it coincided with reality."[2] Graham proposed that the price of every stock consists of two components: investment value and a speculative element. Investment value measures the worth of all the cash flows a company will generate in the future, while the speculative element is driven by sentiment and emotions, such as hope, greed, fear, and regret. The market is highly efficient at identifying investment value. However, the speculative element is prone to large and rapid swings that can swamp investment value.

Whether the market is truly efficient, partially efficient, or totally inefficient seems to have little bearing on how easy it is to beat. We know this because so-called investment experts would have much better results than they do, as evidenced by the fact that only 3 percent of actively managed mutual funds deliver results that exceed those merely due to chance.[3]

In closing our discussion of market efficiency, we can discuss what it means to "beat the market." First, consider the short run—say, one year. You may hold a portfolio of stocks that realizes a 20 percent return in a given year. Is that a good return? Yes. Over the past 80 or so years, a diversified investment in stocks averaged an annual return of roughly 10 percent. However, the 20 percent return in any given year does not mean that you beat the market in that year. To actually beat the market, you must realize a return that is higher than the average return on similar portfolios of stocks (portfolios that have the same risk as yours). If the

---

For Your Consideration
Behavioral Finance

Behavioral finance is a field of study that proposes psychology-based theories to explain stock market anomalies. Proponents argue that investors are not nearly as rational as traditional finance theory makes them out to be. Of course, the idea that psychology drives stock market movements flies in the face of the EMH. In fact, *behaviorists,* as they are called, contend that, rather than being unusual, irrational behavior is commonplace. Here is one of the experiments they cite to support that view.

Suppose you are given a choice of a sure **$50** or a coin flip in which you could win either **$100** or nothing. Most people, being risk averse, would pocket the sure **$50**. Now, suppose you are confronted with this choice: a sure loss of **$50** or a coin flip in which you could lose either **$100** or nothing. Now, most people would choose the coin toss, although the value inherent in flipping the coin is equivalent in both scenarios. The idea here is that people tend to view the possibility of recouping a loss as more important than the possibility of greater gain.

The priority of avoiding losses also affects investor behavior. It is common for investors to watch a particular stock plummet in value but refuse to sell because it would "lock in" the

(continued)

average return (benchmark) on a similar-risk portfolio for that year was 25 percent, some portfolios did better than average and others did worse, including yours. If market efficiency holds, those that did better in one year will not be able to consistently beat the relevant benchmark year after year.

What about the long run? Over the long run—say, 20 or more years—beating the market means a return in excess of what is commensurate with the risk undertaken. For a portfolio of average-risk stocks, this means an average annual return of greater than 10 percent (based on historical performance).

(continued from previous page)

loss coupled with the belief that the price will eventually bounce back to the value it had once achieved.

Although behavioral finance offers no investment miracles, perhaps it can help investors train themselves to watch their own behavior and, in turn, avoid mistakes that would be detrimental to their personal wealth.

What are your views on behavioral finance? Is there anything to it? Does it make more sense than market efficiency? Do you believe that knowledge of behavioral finance can help you beat the market?

We really do not know whether it is possible to beat the market by skill or whether it is just a matter of luck. Nevertheless, it is wise for both investors and managers to consider the implications of market efficiency when making investment and financing decisions. Investors who believe that they can beat the market should at least recognize that there is a lot of evidence that tells us that most people who try will ultimately fail.

SELF-TEST QUESTIONS

1. What two conditions must hold for markets to be efficient?
2. Briefly, what is the efficient markets hypothesis (EMH)?
3. What are the implications of the EMH for investors and managers?
4. What is meant by the phrase *beat the market*?

The Risk/Return Trade-Off

Most financial decisions involve choosing between alternative courses of action. For example, should a hospital invest its excess funds in Treasury bonds that yield 4 percent or in Tenet Healthcare (www.tenethealth.com) bonds that yield 7 percent? Should a group practice buy a replacement piece of equipment now or wait until next year? Should a joint venture outpatient diagnostic center purchase a small, limited-use MRI system or a large, more expensive multipurpose system?

Generally, alternative courses of action have different expected rates of return, and it may be tempting to automatically accept the choice with the higher expected return. However, this approach to financial decision-making would be incorrect. In *efficient markets*, alternatives that offer higher returns also entail higher risk. The correct question to ask when making financial decisions is not which alternative has the higher expected rate of return, but which alternative has the higher return *after adjusting for risk*. In other words, which alternative has the higher return over and above the return commensurate with that alternative's riskiness?

To illustrate the *risk/return trade-off*, suppose Tenet Healthcare stock has an expected rate of return of 11 percent, while its bonds yield 7 percent. Does this mean that investors should flock to buy the firm's stock and ignore the bonds? No. The higher expected rate of return on the stock merely reflects the fact that the stock is riskier than the bonds. Investors who are not willing to assume much risk will buy Tenet's bonds, while those who are less risk averse will buy the stock. From the perspective of Tenet's managers, financing with stock is less risky than with debt, so the firm is willing to "pay" the higher cost of equity to limit the firm's risk exposure.

Despite the hypothesized efficiency of major securities markets, the markets for products and services (i.e., the markets for real assets such as diagnostic equipment) are usually not efficient; returns are not necessarily related to risk. Hospitals, group practices, and other healthcare businesses can make real-asset investments and achieve returns in excess of those required to compensate for the riskiness of the investment. Furthermore, the market for *innovation* (i.e., the market for ideas) is not efficient, which means it is possible for people like Mark Zuckerberg, one of the founders of Facebook, to become multibillionaires at a relatively young age. However, when excess returns are found in the product, service, or idea markets, new entrants quickly join the innovators, and competition over time usually forces rates of return down to efficient market levels. As a result, later entrants can only expect returns that are commensurate with the risks involved.

SELF-TEST QUESTIONS

1. Explain the risk/return trade-off.
2. In what markets does this trade-off hold?

Key Concepts

This chapter contains a wealth of material on equity financing, including valuation and market efficiency. The key concepts of this chapter are as follows:

- The most important *common stockholder* rights are the *claim on residual earnings, control of the firm,* and the *preemptive right.*
- New common stock may be sold by for-profit corporations in six ways: on a pro rata basis to existing stockholders through a *rights offering;* through investment bankers to the general public in a *public offering;* to a single buyer, or small number of buyers, in a *private placement;* to employees through an *employee stock purchase plan;* to shareholders through a *dividend reinvestment plan;* and to individual investors by *direct purchase.*
- A *closely held corporation* is one that is owned by a few individuals, who typically are the firm's managers.
- A *publicly owned corporation* is one that is owned by a large number of individuals, most of whom are not actively involved in its management.
- Not-for-profit firms do not have access to the equity markets. However, *charitable contributions,* which are tax deductible to the donor, and *government grants* constitute unique equity sources for not-for-profit firms.
- The *value* of a share of stock of a dividend-paying company is found by *discounting* the stream of *expected dividends* by the stock's required rate of return.
- The value of a stock whose dividends are expected to grow at a constant rate for many years is found by applying the *constant growth model:*

$$E(P_0) = \frac{D_0 \times [1 + E(g)]}{R(R_e) - E(g)} = \frac{E(D_1)}{R(R_e) - E(g)}.$$

(continued)

(continued from previous page)

- The *expected rate of return* on a stock consists of an *expected dividend* yield plus an *expected capital gains* yield. For a constant growth stock, both the expected dividend yield and the expected capital gains yield are constant over time, and the expected rate of return can be found by this equation:

$$E(R_e) = \frac{D_0 \times [1 + E(g)]}{P_0} + E(g) = \frac{E(D_1)}{P_0} + E(g).$$

- The *efficient markets hypothesis (EMH)* holds that (1) stocks are always in equilibrium and fairly valued and (2) it is impossible for an investor to consistently beat the market. Thus, managers should not try to forecast future interest rates or time security issues.
- In efficient markets, alternatives that offer higher returns must also have higher risk; this is called the *risk/return trade-off.* The implication is that investments must be evaluated on the basis of both risk and return.

The coverage of long-term financing continues in chapter 13 with a discussion of how managers choose between debt and equity financing. Chapter 13 also covers the cost of capital, an important concept that provides the benchmark required rate of return used in capital investment analyses.

Questions

12.1. a. What is the preemptive right?
       b. Why is it important to shareholders?
12.2. Why might an investor-owned firm choose to issue different classes of common stock?
12.3. Describe the primary means by which investor-owned firms raise new equity capital.
12.4. What are the similarities and differences between equity capital in investor-owned firms and fund capital in not-for-profit firms?
12.5. What is the general approach for valuing a share of stock of a dividend-paying company?

12.6. Two investors are evaluating the stock of Beverly Enterprises for possible purchase. They agree on the stock's risk and on expectations about future dividends. However, one investor plans to hold the stock for five years, while the other plans to hold the stock for 20 years. Which of the two investors would be willing to pay more for the stock? Explain your answer.

12.7. Evaluate the following statement: One of the assumptions of the constant growth model is that the required rate of return must be greater than the expected dividend growth rate. Because of this assumption, the constant growth model is of limited use in the real world.

12.8. a What is the efficient markets hypothesis (EMH)?
       b. What are its implications for investors and managers?

12.9. a. What is meant by risk/return trade-off?
       b. Does this trade-off hold in all markets?

Problems

12.1. An investor is considering buying the stock of two home health companies that are similar in all respects except the proportion of earnings paid out as dividends. Both companies are expected to earn $6 per share in the coming year, but company D (for dividends) is expected to pay out the entire amount as dividends, while company G (for growth) is expected to pay out only one-third of its earnings, or $2 per share. The companies are equally risky, and their required rate of return is 15 percent. D's constant growth rate is zero and G's is 8.33 percent. What are the intrinsic values of stocks D and G?

12.2. Medical Corporation of America (MCA) has a current stock price of $36, and its last dividend (D_0) was $2.40. In view of MCA's strong financial position, its required rate of return is 12 percent. If MCA's dividends are expected to grow at a constant rate in the future, what is the firm's expected stock price in five years?

12.3. A broker offers to sell shares of Bay Area Healthcare, which just paid a dividend of $2 per share. The dividend is expected to grow at a constant rate of 5 percent per year. The stock's required rate of return is 12 percent.
       a. What is the expected dollar dividend over the next three years?
       b. What is the current value of the stock and the expected stock price at the end of each of the next three years?

c. What is the expected dividend yield and capital gains yield for each of the next three years?

d. What is the expected total return for each of the next three years?

e. How does the expected total return compare with the required rate of return on the stock? Does this make sense? Explain your answer.

12.4. Assume the risk-free rate is 6 percent and the market risk premium is 6 percent. The stock of Clinicians Care Alliance (PCA) has a beta of 1.5. The last dividend paid by PCA (D_0) was $2 per share.

a. What would PCA's stock value be if the dividend were expected to grow at a constant:
  - −5 percent?
  - 0 percent?
  - 5 percent?
  - 10 percent?

b. What would be the stock value if the growth rate were 10 percent but PCA's beta fell to:
  - 1.0?
  - 0.5?

12.5. Better Life Nursing Home, Inc., has maintained a dividend payment of $4 per share for many years. The same dollar dividend is expected to be paid in future years. If investors require a 12 percent rate of return on investments of similar risk, determine the value of the company's stock.

12.6. Jane's sister-in-law, a stockbroker at Invest, Inc., is trying to get Jane to buy the stock of HealthWest, a regional HMO. The stock has a current market price of $25, its last dividend ($D_0$) was $2.00, and the company's earnings and dividends are expected to increase at a constant growth rate of 10 percent. The required return on this stock is 20 percent. From a strict valuation standpoint, should Jane buy the stock?

12.7. Lucas Clinic's last dividend (D_0) was $1.50. Its current equilibrium stock price is $15.75, and its expected growth rate is a constant 5 percent. If the stockholders' required rate of return is 15 percent, what is the expected dividend yield and expected capital gains yield for the coming year?

12.8. St. John Medical, a surgical equipment manufacturer, has been hit hard by increased competition. Analysts predict that earnings and dividends will decline at a rate of 5 percent annually into the foreseeable future. If the firm's last dividend (D_0) was $2.00 and the investors' required rate of return is 15 percent, what will be the company's stock price in three years?

12.9. California Clinics, an investor-owned chain of ambulatory care clinics, just paid a dividend of $2 per share. The firm's dividend is expected to grow at a constant rate of 5 percent per year, and investors require a 15 percent rate of return on the stock.

    a. What is the stock's value?

    b. Suppose the riskiness of the stock decreases, which causes the required rate of return to fall to 13 percent. Under these conditions, what is the stock's value?

    c. Return to the original 15 percent required rate of return. Assume that the dividend growth rate estimate is increased to a constant 7 percent per year. What is the stock's value?

12.10. Humana Inc.'s last dividend (D_0) was $1.12, and its earnings and dividends are expected to increase at a constant growth rate of 12 percent. Humana's (www.humana.com) market beta is 1.16. If the current risk-free rate is 5 percent and the required rate of return on the market portfolio is 12 percent, what is the company's current expected stock price?

12.11. You are considering investing in the stock of Encompass Health (formerly HealthSouth). You do some market research and learn that the company's last dividend was $0.84 and the company's market beta is 1.35. You estimate that earnings and dividends will increase at a constant growth rate of 8 percent. If the current risk-free rate is 5 percent and the required rate of return on the market portfolio is 12 percent, what is the maximum amount you would be willing to pay for the company's stock?

Selected Case

One case in *Gapenski's Cases in Healthcare Finance*, sixth edition, is applicable to this chapter: Case 15: Pacific Healthcare (B).

Notes

1. Herring, B., D. Gaskin, H. Zare, and G. Anderson. 2018. "Comparing the Value of Nonprofit Hospitals' Tax Exemption to Their Community Benefits." *Inquiry* 55: 46958017751970. https://doi.org/10.1177/0046958017751970.

2. Graham, B. 2020. "Mr. Market." Accessed January 24. http://cs
   investing.org/wp-content/uploads/2012/07/mr-market-by-ben
   -graham_final.pdf.

3. Fama, E. F., and K. R. French. 2009. "Luck Versus Skill in the Cross
   Section of Mutual Fund Returns." *Social Science Research Network.*
   Revised February 8, 2010. http://papers.ssrn.com/sol3/papers.cfm
   ?abstract_id=1356021.

Resources

Anderson, D. G., M. Potter, and D. E. Morris. 2018. "Improving Performance and
    Enhancing Innovation with Venture Investing." *Healthcare Financial Man-
    agement* 72 (3): 44–53.

Arduino, K. 2018. "Healthcare Capital Markets Outlook: Short-Term Opportunities
    Versus Long-Term Uncertainty." *Healthcare Financial Management* 72 (5):
    36–43.

Bannow, T. 2018. "High Prices Test Private Equity's Ability to Close Healthcare
    Deals." *Modern Healthcare* 48 (29): 8.

Braun, J. C., and J. M. Holloway. 2009. "An Empirical Analysis of Health Care IPOs
    and SEOs." *Journal of Health Care Finance* 35 (4): 42–63.

Cleverley, W. O., and J. O. Cleverley. 2005. "Philanthropy: The Last Frontier for
    Capital Funding." *Journal of Healthcare Management* 50 (5): 290–93.

Dillingham, W. J. 2018. "Recent Trends in Healthcare Philanthropy and Founda-
    tions." *Healthcare Financial Management* 72 (3): 54–59.

Healthcare Financial Management Association. 2018. "Optimizing Capital Structure
    Decisions Under the New Tax Law." *Healthcare Financial Management* 72
    (8): A1–4.

———. 2003. *How Are Hospitals Financing the Future? Access to Capital in Health
    Care Today.* Westchester, IL: Healthcare Financial Management Association.

Jarvis, W. F. 2011. "Endowment Income for the Post-Reform Era." *Healthcare
    Financial Management* 65 (5): 132–33.

Lalangas, E., D. Kroll, and A. Carlson. 2018. "The Tax Cuts and Jobs Act Takeaways
    for Healthcare Finance Leaders." *Healthcare Financial Management* 72 (4):
    28–31.

Livingston, S. 2018. "Surge in Private Equity Deals Causes Some Alarm." *Modern
    Healthcare* 48 (25): 8.

Taddey, A. J. 2014. "Strategic Capital Planning as a Key Management Tool." *Health-
    care Financial Management* 68 (9): 142–44.

Zweig, J. 2010. "Inefficient Markets Are Still Hard to Beat." *Wall Street Journal.*
    Published January 9.

12

THE MARKET FOR COMMON STOCK, SECURITIES MARKETS REGULATION, AND THE INVESTMENT BANKING PROCESS

The Market for Common Stock

The stocks of most small, publicly owned corporations are not listed on an exchange and hence are called *unlisted*. Such stocks trade in the *over-the-counter (OTC) market*, which consists of a network of dealers connected by computer. The roughly 10,000 companies that are traded in the OTC market usually are very risky and typically do not meet the standards required to be accepted on an exchange.

Most large, publicly owned corporations are listed on one of the *stock exchanges*—either the NASDAQ (formerly the National Association of Securities Dealers Automated Quotations) or the New York Stock Exchange (NYSE). For example, AgeX Therapeutics, Inc. (www.agexinc.com), which develops therapeutics for age-related degenerative diseases, was listed on the NYSE in 2014. More than 3,300 stocks are listed on the NASDAQ, while roughly 2,800 are listed on the NYSE, but because of the larger size of its listed firms, the NYSE historically has dominated the NASDAQ in terms of the market value of stocks listed.

Many people believe that listing is beneficial to both the firm and its stockholders. Listed firms receive a certain amount of free advertising and publicity, and their listed status may elevate their prestige and reputation, which could have positive implications for stock price. These factors, as well as the enhanced safeguards against illegal trading practices offered by exchanges, provide good reasons for businesses to list their stock on one of the exchanges when it meets listing requirements.

Institutional investors, such as pension funds, insurance firms, and mutual funds, own about 60 percent of all common stocks. However, the institutions buy and sell relatively actively, so they account for about 75 percent of all transactions. Thus, the institutions have the greatest influence on the prices of individual stocks.

Stock market transactions can be classified into three categories:

1. **The new issue market.** A small firm typically is owned by its management and a handful of private investors. At some point, if the firm is to grow further, its stock must be sold to the general public, which is referred to as *going public*. The market for stock that is in the process of going public is often called the *new issue market*, and the issue is called an *initial public offering (IPO)*. For example, in 2018, Vapotherm, Inc. (www.vapotherm.com), a medical technology company that develops, manufactures, and markets noninvasive ventilatory support devices, raised close to $536 million in an IPO by selling 4 million shares at $14 per share.

2. **The primary market.** Also in 2018, Acadia Pharmaceuticals Inc. (www.acadia-pharm.com), a biopharmaceutical company focused on discovering and developing innovative medicines that address unmet needs, sold more than 10.8 million shares of new common stock at a price of $18.51 per share for an aggregate offering of almost $200 million, before underwriting discounts, commissions, and estimated expenses. Because the shares sold were newly created, the issue was defined as a *primary market* offering, but because the business was already publicly held, the offering was not an IPO. Corporations prefer to obtain equity by retaining earnings because of the issuance costs and market pressure associated with the sale of new common stock. Still, if a firm requires more equity funds than can be generated from retained earnings, a stock sale may be necessary.

3. **The secondary market.** If the owner of 100 shares of Tenet Healthcare (www.tenethealth.com) sells the stock, the trade is said to have occurred in the secondary market. Thus, the market for outstanding, or used, shares is defined as the *secondary market*. More than 1.5 million shares of Tenet were bought and sold daily on the NYSE in 2018, but the firm did not receive a dime from these transactions.

SELF-TEST QUESTIONS

1. What is an initial public offering (IPO)?
2. What is meant when a stock is *listed*? What about when a stock is *unlisted*?
3. What are the differences between shares that Tenet Healthcare sells in the primary market and its shares being sold in the secondary market?

Securities Market Regulation

Sales of securities are regulated by the *Securities and Exchange Commission (SEC)* (www.sec.gov) and, to a lesser extent, by the Federal Reserve Board (www.federalreserve.gov) and each state. Here are the primary elements of SEC regulation:

- The SEC has jurisdiction over all *interstate* offerings of new securities to the public in amounts of $1.5 million or more.
- Newly issued securities must be registered with the SEC at least 20 days before they are offered to the public. The *registration statement* provides the SEC with financial, legal, and technical information about the company, and the *prospectus* summarizes this information for investors. SEC lawyers and accountants analyze the registration statement and the prospectus; if the information is inadequate or misleading, the SEC will delay or stop the public offering.
- After the registration becomes effective, new securities may be offered, but any sales solicitation must be accompanied by the prospectus. Preliminary, or *red herring*, prospectuses may be distributed to potential buyers during the 20-day waiting period, but no sales may occur during this time. The red herring prospectus contains all the key information that will appear in the final prospectus, except the price, which is generally set after the market closes the day before the new securities are actually offered to the public. (The term *red herring* has several definitions. Its use here stems from the fact that red herring are used as bait for larger fish. Thus, the prospectus is meant to entice investors into buying the security.)
- If the registration statement or prospectus contains misrepresentations or omissions of material facts, any purchaser who suffers a loss may sue for damages. Severe penalties may be imposed on the issuer or its officers, directors, accountants, engineers, appraisers, underwriters, and all others who participated in the preparation of the registration statement or prospectus.
- The SEC also regulates all national stock exchanges. Companies whose securities are listed on an exchange must file annual reports with both the SEC and the exchange.
- The SEC has control over corporate insiders. Officers, directors, and major stockholders must file monthly reports of changes in their holdings of the corporation's stock.

- The SEC has the power to prohibit manipulation by such devices as *pools* (i.e., large amounts of money used to buy or sell stocks to artificially affect prices) or *wash sales* (i.e., sales between members of the same group to record artificial transaction prices).
- The SEC has control over the form of the proxy and the way the company uses it to solicit votes.

Control over the use of credit to buy securities (primarily common stock) is exercised by the Federal Reserve Board through *margin requirements*, which specify the maximum percentage of the purchase price that can be financed by brokerage borrowings. The current margin requirement is 50 percent, so a stock investor can borrow up to half of the cost of a stock purchase from his or her broker. If the price of a stock bought on margin falls, the margin money (50 percent of the original value) becomes more than half of the current value, and the investor is forced to put up additional personal funds. Such a demand for more personal money is known as a *margin call*. The amount of additional funds required depends on the *maintenance margin*, which is set by the broker supplying the loan. When a large proportion of trades are on margin and the stock market begins a retreat, the volume of margin calls can be substantial. Because most investors who buy on margin do not have a large reserve of personal funds, they are forced to sell some stock to meet margin calls, which, in turn, can accelerate a market decline.

States also exercise control over the issuance of new securities within their boundaries. Such control is usually supervised by a corporation commissioner or someone with a similar title. State laws that relate to security sales are called *blue sky laws* because they were put into effect to keep unscrupulous promoters from selling securities that offered the "blue sky" (something wonderful) but actually had no assets or earnings to back up the promises.

The securities industry itself realizes the importance of stable markets, sound brokerage firms, and the absence of price manipulation. Therefore, the Financial Industry Regulatory Authority (FINRA) (www.finra.org) was established in 2007 by the consolidation of existing regulatory agencies as the primary independent regulator for all securities firms doing business in the United States. FINRA's mission is to protect investors by ensuring that the securities industry operates fairly and honestly. It oversees the work of 3,726 brokerage firms and approximately 630,132 registered securities representatives as well the OTC market and stock exchanges. FINRA has approximately 3,600 employees in its two primary offices in Washington, DC, and New York City and 16 regional offices around the country.

In general, government regulation of securities trading, as well as industry self-regulation, is designed to ensure that investors receive information that is as accurate as possible, that no one artificially manipulates the market price of a given security, and that corporate insiders do not take advantage of their position to profit in their companies' securities at the expense of others. Neither the SEC nor state regulators nor the industry itself can prevent investors from making foolish decisions, but they can and do help investors obtain the best information possible, which is the first step in making sound investment decisions.

SELF-TEST QUESTIONS

1. What is the purpose of securities market regulation?
2. What agencies and groups are involved in such regulation?
3. What is a prospectus?
4. What is a margin requirement?
5. What are "blue sky" laws?

Chapter 12 Supplement

The Investment Banking Process

Investment banks are the companies, such as Citigroup, JPMorgan Chase & Co., and Merrill Lynch, that help businesses sell securities to the public. When new securities will be sold to the public, the first step is to select an *investment banker*. This can be a difficult decision for a firm that is going public. However, an older firm that has already "been to market" will have an established relationship with an investment banker. Changing bankers is easy, though, if the firm is dissatisfied with past performance.

The procedures followed in issuing new securities are collectively known as the *investment banking process*. Generally, the following key decisions regarding the issuance of new securities are made jointly by the issuing company's managers and the investment bankers that will handle the deal:

- **Dollars to be raised.** How much new capital is needed?
- **Type of securities used.** Should common stock, bonds, another security, or a combination of securities be used? Furthermore, if common stock is to be issued, should it be done as a rights offering, by a direct sale to the general public, or by a private placement?
- **Contractual basis of issue.** If an investment banker is used, will the banker work on a best efforts basis or will the banker underwrite the issue? In a best efforts sale, the banker guarantees neither the price nor the sale of the securities, only that it will put forth its best efforts to sell the issue. On an *underwritten issue*, the company does get a guarantee because the banker agrees to buy the entire issue and then

resell the securities to its customers. Bankers bear significant risk in underwritten offerings because the banker must bear the loss if the price of the security falls between the time the security is purchased from the issuer and the time of resale to the public.

- **Banker's compensation and other expenses.** The investment banker's compensation (if a banker is used) must be negotiated. Also, the firm must estimate the other *issuance expenses* (often called *flotation costs*) it will incur in connection with the issue—lawyers' fees, accountants' costs, printing and engraving, and so on. In an underwritten issue, the banker will buy the issue from the company at a discount below the price at which the securities are to be offered to the public, with this spread being set to cover the banker's costs and to provide a profit. In a best efforts sale, fees to the investment banker are normally set as some percentage of the dollar volume sold. Issuance costs as a percentage of the proceeds are higher for stocks than for bonds, and they are higher for small than for large issues. The relationship between size of issue and issuance cost primarily is a result of the existence of fixed costs—certain costs must be incurred regardless of the size of the issue, so the percentage cost is quite high for small issues. To illustrate, issuance costs for a $5 million bond issue are about 5 percent, while the costs drop to about 1 percent for issues more than $50 million. For a stock issue, the costs are about 12 percent and 4 percent, respectively.

- **Setting the offering price.** Usually, the *offering price* is based on the existing market price of the stock or the yield to maturity on outstanding bonds. On initial public offerings, however, pricing decisions are much more difficult because there is no existing market price for guidance. The investment banker will have an easier job if the issue is priced relatively low, but the issuer of the securities naturally wants as high a price as possible. Conflict of interest on price therefore arises between the investment banker and the issuer. If the issuer is financially sophisticated and makes comparisons with similar security issues, the investment banker will be forced to price the new security close to its true value.

After the company and its investment banker have decided how much money to raise, the types of securities to issue, and the basis for pricing the issue, they will prepare and file a registration statement and a prospectus (if needed). The final price of the stock or the interest rate on a bond issue is set at the close of business the day the issue clears the SEC, and the securities are offered to the public the following day.

Investors are required to pay for securities within ten days, and the investment banker must pay the issuing firm within four days of the official commencement of the offering. Typically, the banker sells the securities within a day or two after the offering begins. However, on occasion, the banker miscalculates, sets the offering price too high, and thus is unable to move the issue. At other times, the market declines during the offering period, forcing the banker to reduce the price of the stock or bonds. In either instance, on an underwritten offering, the firm receives the agreed-upon dollar amount, so the banker must absorb any losses incurred.

Because they are exposed to large potential losses, investment bankers typically do not handle the purchase and distribution of issues single-handedly unless the issue is a small one. If the sum of money involved is large, investment bankers form *underwriting syndicates* in an effort to minimize the risk that each banker carries. The banking house that sets up the deal is called the *lead*, or *managing*, *underwriter*.

In addition to the underwriting syndicate, on larger offerings even more investment bankers are included in a *selling group*, which handles the distribution of securities to individual investors. The selling group includes all members of the underwriting syndicate, plus additional dealers who take relatively small percentages of the total issue from members of the underwriting syndicate. Thus, the underwriters act as *wholesalers*, while members of the selling group act as *retailers*. The number of investment banks in a selling group depends partly on the size of the issue but also on the number and types of buyers. For example, the selling group that handled a recent $92 million municipal bond issue for Adventist Health System/Sunbelt (now Advent Health, www.adventhealth.com) consisted of three members, while the one that sold $1 billion in B-rated junk bonds for National Medical Enterprises (now Tenet Healthcare) consisted of eight members.

SELF-TEST
QUESTIONS

1. What types of decisions must the issuer and its investment banker make?

2. What is the difference between an underwritten and a best efforts issue?

3. Are there any conflicts that might arise between the issuer and the investment banker when setting the offering price on a securities issue?

CAPITAL STRUCTURE AND THE COST OF CAPITAL

Learning Objectives

After studying this chapter, readers will be able to

- Explain the effects of debt financing on a business's risk and return.
- Discuss the factors that influence the choice between debt and equity financing.
- Describe the general process for estimating a business's corporate cost of capital.
- Estimate the component costs as well as the overall (corporate) cost of capital for any healthcare business.
- Explain the economic interpretation of the corporate cost of capital and how it is used to make capital investment decisions.

Introduction

In chapters 11 and 12, we noted that businesses use two types of capital: debt and equity. In this chapter, we discuss two key issues related to financing. The first issue is the choice between debt and equity financing. Because debt and equity have different characteristics, managers must choose the blend that creates the optimal risk and return structure for the organization.

The second key issue is the overall cost of a business's financing. Because the suppliers of debt and equity capital establish required rates of return on that capital, it is not costless to the business. Managers must understand capital costs and be able to estimate the overall cost of financing to their businesses. With such an estimate, managers are better able to assess the financial consequences of capital investment opportunities such as the acquisition of land, buildings, and equipment.

Capital Structure Basics

capital structure
The structure of a business's financing mix as shown on the balance sheet, often expressed as the percentage of debt financing; for example, 35 percent debt.

The mix of debt and equity financing used by a business is called its **capital structure**, which typically is measured by the structure of the liabilities and equity section of the business's balance sheet. One of the most perplexing questions facing health services managers is how much debt financing, as opposed to equity (or fund) financing, organizations should use. This decision involves several related questions: Is there an optimal mix of debt and equity? In other words, is there an **optimal capital structure**? If optimal capital structures do exist, do hospitals have different optimal structures than home health agencies or ambulatory surgery centers? If so, what factors lead to these differences? How do managers identify the optimal capital structures for their businesses? These questions, although difficult to answer, are important to the financial well-being of any business.

SELF-TEST QUESTIONS

1. What is a business's capital structure?
2. What are some questions relevant to the capital structure decision?

optimal capital structure
The mix of debt and equity financing that management believes is most appropriate for the business; generally based on both quantitative and qualitative factors.

Impact of Debt Financing on Accounting Risk and Return

To fully understand the consequences of capital structure decisions, it is essential to understand the effects of debt financing on a business's risk and return as reflected in its balance sheet and income statement.[1] Consider the situation facing Great Health, Inc., a for-profit (investor-owned) company that is just being formed. Its founders have identified two financing alternatives for the business: all equity (all common stock) and 50 percent debt.

Exhibit 13.1 contains the business's projected financial statements under the two financing alternatives. To begin, consider the balance sheets shown in the top portion of the exhibit. Great Health requires $100,000 in current assets and $100,000 in fixed assets to begin operations. (We keep the values small for ease of illustration.) The asset requirements for any business depend on the nature and size of the business rather than on how the business will be financed, so the asset section of the balance sheet is unaffected by the financing mix. However, the type of financing does affect the liabilities and equity section. Under the all-equity alternative, Great Health's owners will put up the entire $200,000 needed to purchase the required assets. If 50 percent debt financing is used, the owners will contribute only $100,000, and the remaining $100,000 will be obtained from creditors—say, a bank loan with a 10 percent interest rate.

	All Equity	50% Debt
Balance Sheets:		
Current assets	$100,000	$100,000
Fixed assets	100,000	100,000
Total assets	$200,000	$200,000
Bank loan (10% cost)	$ 0	$100,000
Common stock	$200,000	$100,000
Total liabilities and equity	$200,000	$200,000
Income Statements:		
Revenues	$150,000	$150,000
Operating costs	100,000	$100,000
Operating income	50,000	50,000
Interest expense	$ 0	$ 10,000
Taxable income	$ 50,000	$ 40,000
Taxes (30%)	$ 15,000	$ 12,000
Net income	$ 35,000	$ 28,000
Return on investment	17.5%	28%
Total dollar return to investors	$ 35,000	$ 38,000

EXHIBIT 13.1
Great Health, Inc.: Projected Financial Statements Under Two Financing Alternatives

What is the impact of the two financing alternatives on Great Health's projected first year's income statement? Revenues are projected to be $150,000 and operating costs are forecast at $100,000, so the firm's operating income is expected to be $50,000. Because a business's capital structure does not affect revenues or operating costs, the operating income projection is the same under both financing alternatives.

However, interest expense must be paid if debt financing is used. Thus, the 50 percent debt alternative results in a 0.10 × $100,000 = $10,000 annual interest charge, while no interest expense occurs if the firm is all-equity financed. The result is taxable income of $50,000 under the all-equity alternative and a lower taxable income of $40,000 under the 50 percent debt alternative. Because the business anticipates being taxed at a 30 percent federal-plus-state rate, the expected tax liability is 0.30 × $50,000 = $15,000 under the all-equity alternative and 0.30 × $40,000 = $12,000 under the 50 percent debt alternative. Finally, when taxes are deducted from the income stream, the business expects to earn $35,000 in net income if it is all-equity financed and $28,000 in net income if 50 percent debt financing is used.

At first glance, the use of 50 percent debt financing appears to be the *inferior* financing alternative. After all, if 50 percent debt financing is used, the business's projected net income will fall by $35,000 – $28,000 = $7,000. But the conclusion that 50 percent debt financing is a bad choice requires closer examination. What is most important to the owners of Great Health is not the business's net income but the return expected on their equity investment.

return on equity (ROE)
Net income divided by the book value of equity; measures the dollars of earnings per dollar of equity investment.

The best measure of return to the owners of a business is the rate of **return on equity (ROE)**, which is defined as net income divided by the book value of equity. Under all-equity financing, the projected ROE is $35,000 ÷ $200,000 = 0.175 = 17.5%, but under 50 percent debt financing, the projected ROE increases to $28,000 ÷ $100,000 = 28%. The key to the increased ROE is that although net income decreases when debt financing is used, so does the amount of equity needed, and the equity requirement decreases proportionally more than net income.

The bottom line of this analysis is that debt financing can increase the owners' expected rate of return. Because the use of debt financing increases, or leverages up, the return to equity holders, such financing is often called **financial leverage**. The use of financial leverage is merely the use of debt financing.

financial leverage
The use of fixed cost financing; typically debt financing for healthcare providers.

To view the impact of financial leverage from a different perspective, take another look at the income statements in exhibit 13.1. The total dollar return to all investors (i.e., the owners and the bank), is $35,000 in net income when the company is all-equity financed but $28,000 in net income + $10,000 of interest = $38,000 when 50 percent debt financing is used. Thus, the use of debt financing increases the projected total dollar return to investors by $38,000 – $35,000 = $3,000. Where did the extra $3,000 come from? The answer is, from the taxman. Taxes are $15,000 if the business is all-equity financed but only $12,000 if 50 percent debt financing is used, and $3,000 less in taxes means $3,000 more for investors. Because the use of debt financing reduces taxes, more of a firm's operating income is available for distribution to investors, including the owners and creditors.

At this point, Great Health's financing decision seems like a no-brainer. Given only these two financing alternatives, 50 percent debt financing should be used because it promises the owners a higher rate of return. Unfortunately, there is a catch: The use of financial leverage not only increases the owners' projected return but also increases their risk.

To demonstrate the risk-increasing characteristics of debt financing, consider exhibit 13.2, which recognizes that Great Health, like all businesses, is risky. The first year's revenues and operating costs, listed in exhibit 13.1, are *not* known with certainty but are expected values taken from probability

	All Equity			50% Debt			EXHIBIT 13.2
Probability	0.25	0.50	0.25	0.25	0.50	0.25	Great Health, Inc.: Partial
Operating income	$0	$50,000	$100,000	$ 0	50,000	100,000	Income
Interest expense	0	0	0	10,000	10,000	10,000	Statements in
Taxable income	$0	$50,000	$100,000	($10,000)	$40,000	$90,000	an Uncertain
Taxes (30%)	0	15,000	30,000	(3,000)	12,000	27,000	World
Net income	$0	$35,000	$ 70,000	($ 7,000)	$28,000	$63,000	
ROE	0	17.5%	35%	–7%	28%	63%	
Expected ROE		17.5%			28%		
Standard deviation of ROE		12.4%			24.7%		

distributions. Great Health's founders believe that operating income could be as low as zero or as high as $100,000 in the business's first year of operation. Furthermore, there is a 25 percent chance of the worst and the best cases occurring and a 50 percent chance that the exhibit 13.1 forecast, with an operating income of $50,000, will be realized.

The assumptions regarding uncertainty in the future profitability of the business lead to three different ROEs for each financing alternative. The expected ROEs are the same as when uncertainty was ignored (i.e., 17.5 percent if the firm is all-equity financed and 28 percent when 50 percent debt financing is used). For example, the expected ROE under all-equity financing is (0.25 × 0%) + (0.50 × 17.5%) + (0.25 × 35%) = 17.5%. However, the uncertainty in operating income produces uncertainty (risk) in the owners' return. If the owners' risk is measured by the standard deviation of ROE (stand-alone risk), the return is twice as risky in the 50 percent debt financing alternative: 24.7 percent standard deviation of ROE versus 12.4 percent standard deviation in the zero-debt alternative.

The increase in risk is apparent without even calculating the standard deviations. If all-equity financing is used, the worst return that can occur is an ROE of zero. However, with 50 percent debt financing, an ROE of –7 percent can occur. In fact, with no operating income to pay the $10,000 interest to the bank in the worst-case scenario, the owners would either have to put up additional equity capital to pay the interest due (assuming insufficient depreciation cash flow) or declare the business bankrupt. Clearly, the use of 50 percent debt financing increases the riskiness of the owners' investment.

This simple example illustrates two key points about the use of debt financing:

1. A business's use of debt financing increases the expected rate of return on equity to the owners. There is, however, a necessary condition for leveraging to work: For the use of debt financing to increase owners' rate of return, the inherent return on the business (i.e., the return before any financing costs) must be greater than the interest rate on the debt. The inherent return on the business in the Great Health illustration is 25 percent [$50 in operating income divided by $200 in assets], and debt financing costs only 10 percent, so the use of debt financing increases ROE.

2. At the same time that the return increases, the use of debt financing also increases owners' risk. In the Great Health example, 50 percent debt financing doubled the owners' risk as measured by standard deviation of ROE.

When risk is considered, the ultimate decision on which financing alternative should be chosen is not so clear-cut. The zero-debt alternative has a lower expected ROE but also lower risk. The 50 percent debt alternative offers a higher expected ROE but carries with it more risk. Thus, the decision is a classic risk/return trade-off: Higher returns can be obtained only by assuming greater risk. What Great Health's founders need to know is whether the higher return is *enough* to compensate them for the higher risk assumed. To complicate the decision even more, an almost unlimited number of debt-level choices are available, not just the 50/50 mix used in the illustration. This example illustrates that health services managers face a difficult decision in identifying a business's optimal capital structure.

SELF-TEST QUESTIONS

1. What is the impact of debt financing on owners' rate of return?
2. What is the impact of debt financing on owners' risk?
3. What is the basis for choosing the optimal level of debt financing?

Capital Structure Theory

At the end of the previous section, Great Health's founders were left in a quandary because debt financing brings with it both higher returns and higher risk. *Capital structure theory*, which was developed for investor-owned businesses, attempts to resolve this dilemma. If the relationship between the use of debt financing and equity value (stock price) were known, the optimal capital structure could be identified.

There are many competing theories of capital structure, but one theory—the **trade-off model**—is most widely accepted. In general, this theory tells managers that an optimal capital structure does exist for every business. Furthermore, the optimal structure balances the tax advantages of debt financing against the increased risk that arises when debt financing is used. The trade-off theory is summarized in exhibit 13.3. Here, the proportion of debt in a firm's capital structure is plotted on the *x* axis, while the *y* axis plots the individual costs of debt and equity and the combined cost of the two financing sources. The focus in the graph is not on the absolute level of debt financing but rather on the *proportion of debt financing used:* Larger firms have higher dollar values of debt than do smaller firms. Furthermore, growing firms increase the amounts of both debt and equity on their balance sheets on a regular basis. In exhibit 13.3, we assume that the business's assets are held constant; what changes, and hence what is shown on the *x* axis, is the proportion of debt: 0 percent (no debt), 10 percent, 20 percent, and so on, up to 100 percent (i.e., all debt).

trade-off model
A capital structure model that hypothesizes that a business's optimal capital structure balances the costs and benefits associated with debt financing.

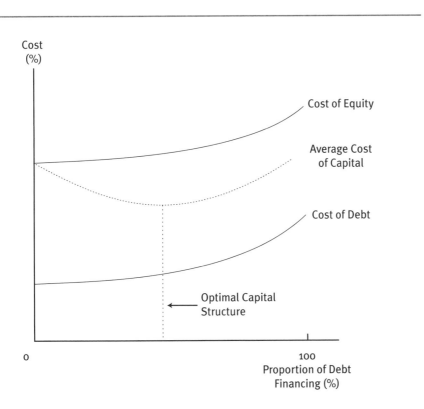

EXHIBIT 13.3
Trade-Off Theory of Capital Structure

To begin our interpretation of the graph, consider the relationship between the cost of debt and the proportion of debt financing. As a business uses a greater proportion of debt financing, the risk to creditors increases because the greater the debt service requirement, the higher the probability that default will occur. In essence, the greater the proportion of debt financing, the riskier the lender's position becomes. Because the lender wants more compensation to assume more risk, the cost of debt (the interest rate) increases as the proportion of debt increases. However, the cost of debt increases slowly at low and moderate proportions of debt because the incremental risk to lenders is relatively small when additional debt is taken on; however, it increases more rapidly as more debt is used. Thus, in exhibit 13.3, the cost-of-debt line first rises slowly, and as more debt is used, it rises at a faster rate.

As discussed in the Great Health illustration, the use of debt financing also increases the risk to equity holders. Furthermore, the greater the proportion of debt in a business's financing mix, the greater this risk becomes. The cost of equity (the return required by equity investors) also increases with the proportion of debt financing, as does the cost of debt. The primary difference between the cost-of-debt and cost-of-equity curves is not their shape but where they are located on the graph. The cost of equity is higher than the cost of debt because owners face more risk than do creditors. (Equity holders have a residual claim on the earnings of the firm, while creditors' claims are fixed by contract.) Furthermore, the effective (true) cost of debt relative to equity is further decreased because interest payments are tax deductible to the business while returns paid to equity holders are not. Thus, as shown in exhibit 13.3, the cost of equity is appreciably greater than the cost of debt at any proportion of debt.

In practice, firms tend to use some, but not all, debt financing; they use a blend of the two major sources of financing. Under these conditions, what is most relevant to the business is not just the cost of debt or just the cost of equity but rather the weighted average (blended) cost of the two components. The weighted average cost is shown on the graph as a dotted line labeled "average cost of capital." At zero debt (the y axis), the firm is all-equity financed, so its average cost of all capital is simply its cost of equity. When a business first starts using debt financing, it adds a lower cost component to its capital structure, and hence the average cost of financing decreases.

However, as the proportion of debt financing increases, both the cost of equity and the cost of debt increase, and at an increasing rate. At some point, the increasing component costs outweigh the fact that more of the lower-cost debt component is being used, and the average cost of capital bottoms out. Beyond this point, the average cost of capital begins to increase. The point at which a business's overall (average) cost of capital is minimized defines the firm's *optimal capital structure*. At this proportion of debt financing, overall financing costs are minimized. Capital, like labor, is an input to the firm, and the firm's financial condition is maximized at any given output when its input costs are minimized.

Once the optimal capital structure, or perhaps an *optimal range*, has been identified for a business, its managers will finance asset acquisitions in a way that keeps the firm at its optimal structure. Thus, the optimal capital structure becomes the target for future financing. For this reason, a firm's optimal capital structure is also called its **target capital structure**.

Although theory indicates that an optimal capital structure exists, it turns out that it is not easy in practice to identify this structure for any given business. However, there is some good news associated with exhibit 13.3. Empirical studies confirm that the average cost-of-capital curve, similar to the one plotted in the exhibit, has a relatively shallow shape. Thus, variations in debt usage from the optimal structure do not have a significant impact on capital costs, and hence it is not essential that managers identify exactly a business's optimal structure. Furthermore, even if a precise optimal structure could be identified, modest movements away from this structure, which commonly occur in practice, will not materially affect financial performance.

> **target capital structure**
> The capital structure (mix of debt and equity) that a business strives to achieve and maintain over time; generally the same as (or very close to) the optimal capital structure.

SELF-TEST QUESTIONS

1. What is the relationship between a business's use of debt financing and its cost of debt? Its cost of equity? Its overall cost of capital?
2. How is the optimal capital structure defined?
3. Why is the optimal capital structure often called the *target capital structure*?
4. Is it critical that the precise structure be identified and followed?

Identifying the Optimal Capital Structure in Practice

Unfortunately, capital structure theory, as illustrated by the graph in exhibit 13.3, cannot provide managers with the optimal capital structure for a given business. This is because the component costs, particularly the cost of equity, cannot be estimated with any confidence for different capital structures. Thus, health services managers must apply judgment in choosing a capital structure. The qualitative analysis involves several factors, and in one situation, a particular factor may have great importance, while the same factor may be relatively unimportant in another situation. The following are some of the more important qualitative issues that managers must consider in setting a business's target capital structure.

Amount of Business Risk

business risk
The risk inherent in the operations of a business, assuming it uses zero-debt financing.

A certain amount of risk, called **business risk**, is inherent in business operations even when no debt financing is used. This risk is associated with the ability of managers to forecast future profitability. The more difficult the forecasting process, the greater the inherent risk of the business. To illustrate, refer to exhibit 13.2. Great Health's business risk can be measured by the standard deviation of ROE, *assuming the firm uses no debt financing*. Thus, the business risk of Great Health is 12.4 percent. If zero-debt financing is used, return on equity is equal to return on assets, so business risk is measured by the inherent uncertainty in the return on a business's assets.

When debt financing is used, equity holders bear additional risk. In a capital structure context, the risk added when debt financing is used is called *financial risk*. For Great Health, the standard deviation of ROE when no debt financing is used is 12.4 percent. Thus, at zero debt, the total risk (all business risk) is 12.4 percent. But when 50 percent debt financing is used, the total risk is 24.7 percent, which consists of 12.4 percent business risk and 12.3 percent financial risk. The difference between the standard deviations of ROE with and without debt financing measures the amount of financial risk. Using a mix of half debt and half equity doubles the risk to the owners of a business, as measured by the standard deviation of ROE.

In general, managers will place some limit on the amount of total risk, which includes business and financial risk, undertaken by a business. Thus, the greater the inherent business risk, the less "room" there is for the use of financial leverage and the lower the optimal proportion of debt financing will be.

Lender and Rating Agency Attitudes

Regardless of a manager's own analysis of the proper capital structure for a business, there is no question that lenders' and rating agencies' attitudes are frequently important determinants of financial structure. In the majority of situations, corporate managers discuss the business's financial structure with lenders and rating agencies and give much weight to their advice. Often, managers want to maintain some target debt rating—say, single A. Furthermore, rating agencies publish guidelines that link firms' capital structures within an industry to specific bond ratings, so guidance is readily available.

If a particular business's management is so confident of the future that it seeks to use debt financing beyond the norms of its industry, lenders may be unwilling to accept such debt levels, or they may do so only at a high price. In effect, lenders and rating agencies set an absolute limit on the proportion of debt financing that can be used by any business, as well as some bounds on the amount of debt that can be raised at reasonable interest rates.

Reserve Borrowing Capacity

Firms generally maintain a **reserve borrowing capacity** that preserves the ability to issue debt when conditions dictate. In essence, managers want to maintain *financial flexibility*, which is defined in a capital structure context as the ability to access, at any time, alternative forms of capital under reasonable terms. For example, suppose Merck (www.merck.com) had just successfully completed a research and development program for a new drug, and its internal projections forecast much higher earnings in the future. However, the new earnings are not yet anticipated by investors, and hence they are not reflected in the price of its stock. If Merck needed additional capital, its managers would not want to issue stock; they would prefer to finance with debt until the higher earnings materialized and were reflected in the stock price. Then they could sell an issue of common stock, retire the debt, and return the firm to its target capital structure. To maintain this reserve borrowing capacity, businesses often use less debt than other factors may indicate should be used. It is the desire to maintain a reserve borrowing capacity that leads managers to set a target capital structure that uses less debt financing than theoretically optimal.

> **reserve borrowing capacity**
> The practice of businesses to use less than the theoretical optimal amount of debt to ensure easy access to new debt at reasonable interest rates regardless of circumstances.

Industry Averages

Presumably, managers act rationally, so the capital structures of other firms in the industry, particularly industry leaders, should provide insights into the optimal structure. In general, there is no reason to believe that the managers of one firm are better than the managers of another firm. If one firm has a capital structure that is significantly different from that of other firms in its industry, the managers of that firm should identify the unique circumstances that contribute to the anomaly. If unique circumstances cannot be identified, then it is doubtful that the firm has identified the correct target structure.

Asset Structure

Firms whose assets are suitable as security (collateral) for loans pay lower interest rates on debt financing than do other firms and hence tend to use more debt. Thus, hospitals tend to use more debt than do companies involved in biotechnology research.

Summary

In closing this major section, note that managers consider all of the factors listed here, to a greater or lesser degree, when setting a business's optimal capital structure. The amount of debt identified as the target capital structure defines the business's **debt capacity**; businesses with a large debt capacity

> **debt capacity**
> The amount of debt considered optimal for the business (the target capital structure).

use a higher proportion of debt financing, while businesses with a low debt capacity use a lower proportion.

1. Is the capital structure decision mostly objective or mostly subjective?
2. What is the difference between business risk and financial risk?
3. What are some of the factors that managers must consider when setting the target capital structure?
4. What is meant by a business's debt capacity?

Not-for-Profit Businesses

Our discussion of capital structure thus far has focused on investor-owned businesses. What about not-for-profit corporations? The same general concepts apply—namely, some debt financing is good, but too much is bad. However, not-for-profit firms have a unique problem: They cannot go to the capital markets to raise equity capital. If an investor-owned firm has more capital investment opportunities than it can finance with retained earnings and debt financing, it can always raise the needed funds with a new stock issue. It may be costly, but it can be done. Additionally, it is quite easy for investor-owned firms to adjust their capital structures. If they are financially underleveraged (using too little debt), they can simply issue more debt and use the proceeds to repurchase stock. On the other hand, if they are financially overleveraged (using too much debt), they can issue additional equity and use the proceeds to refund debt.

Not-for-profit businesses do not have access to the equity markets; their sources of equity capital consist of government grants, private contributions, and excess revenues (retained earnings). Managers of not-for-profit corporations do not have the same degree of flexibility in capital investment or capital structure decisions as do their proprietary counterparts. Thus, it is sometimes necessary for not-for-profit businesses to delay new projects, even profitable ones, because of funding insufficiencies or to use more than the optimal amount of debt to finance needed services.

Although such actions may be required in certain situations, not-for-profit managers must recognize that these strategies are suboptimal. Project delays mean that needed services are not being provided on a timely basis. Using more debt than is optimal pushes the firm beyond the point of the greatest net benefit of debt financing, increasing capital costs above the minimum.

The ability of not-for-profit businesses to garner government grants, attract private contributions, and generate earnings plays an important role in establishing their competitive positions. A business that has an adequate amount of equity (fund) capital can operate at its optimal capital structure and thus minimize capital costs. To illustrate this point, consider two not-for-profit hospitals that are similar in all respects, except that one has more equity capital and can operate at its optimal structure, while the other has insufficient equity capital and must use more debt financing than is optimal. In effect, the hospital with insufficient equity must operate with an inefficient capital structure. The former has a significant competitive advantage because it can either offer more services at the same cost by using additional, suboptimal debt financing or offer matching services at lower costs.

Sufficient equity capital provides not-for-profit businesses with the flexibility to offer all of the necessary services and still operate at the lowest capital cost structure. Like companies that have low operating cost structures, not-for-profit businesses that have low capital cost structures—that is, they operate at their optimal capital structures—have an advantage over their competitors that have higher capital cost structures.

Healthcare in Practice

Debt Use in the Healthcare Sector

Capital structure theory identifies several factors that are important to the capital structure decision. Two of the most important factors are the amount of business risk and the asset structure of the organization. Firms with greater business risk tend to use less debt financing, and firms with a large amount of brick-and-mortar assets, which can be used as loan collateral, tend to use more debt financing.

Now consider three important healthcare sectors: hospitals, medical equipment manufacturers, and biotechnology companies. On average, which of these sectors do you believe uses the most debt financing and which uses the least? Which sector sits in the middle?

Now, how did you reach your conclusions? Does it make any difference if the hospitals are for-profit or not-for-profit? After you have your answers, go to https://finance.yahoo.com/sector/healthcare to see whether you were right. Choose some key firms and go to their statistics page to check their debt/equity ratios.

SELF-TEST QUESTIONS

1. What unique problems do managers of not-for-profit businesses face regarding capital structure decisions?
2. Why is capital structure important to the managers of not-for-profit businesses?

Using the Target Capital Structure

How does a business's target capital structure influence its managerial decisions? First and foremost, as described in the remainder of this chapter, businesses use the target capital structure to define the weights used in the corporate cost-of-capital estimate. In addition, the target capital structure is used to guide financing decisions. If a business is underleveraged (using too little debt) compared with its target, new financing should focus on debt. Conversely, if the business is overleveraged (using too much debt), new financing should focus on equity.

However, other factors influence the financing decision besides the target capital structure. One important factor is the relative cost and availability of debt versus equity financing. Because of the influence of other factors on financing decisions, it is not unusual for a business's actual capital structure to stray, sometimes rather far, from the target structure. For this reason, it is better to think of the target capital structure as a range of values than as a single (point) value. For example, Goldcoast Healthcare has estimated its optimal structure to be 40 percent debt financing, which implies 60 percent equity financing. But Goldcoast's managers have set the business's target capital structure as a range—35 to 45 percent debt.

1. How does a business's target capital structure influence its financing decisions?
2. Why is it best to specify the target capital structure as a range rather than as a single value?

Cost-of-Capital Basics

Up to this point in the chapter, we have focused on the choice between debt and equity financing. Once that decision is made, a business will raise capital over time in such a way as to maintain (or move toward) its target structure. Of course, other considerations also come into play when raising new capital, but over the long run, a business will attempt to keep its capital structure close to the target.

corporate cost of capital (CCC)
The weighted average of a business's capital (financing) costs; also, the discount rate that reflects the overall (average) risk of the entire business.

Now, we turn our attention to estimating the cost of financing at the target structure. The ultimate goal of the cost-of-capital estimation process is to estimate a business's **corporate cost of capital (CCC)**, which represents the blended, or average, cost of a business's financing mix. This cost, in turn, is used as the baseline required rate of return, or *hurdle rate*, when evaluating a business's capital investment opportunities. For example, assume that Bayside Memorial Hospital has a CCC of 10 percent. If a new investment in magnetic resonance imaging (MRI) equipment, which has been judged to have average risk, is expected to return at least 10 percent, it is financially attractive to the hospital. If the MRI is expected to return less than 10 percent, accepting it will have an adverse effect on the hospital's financial soundness. In effect, the CCC sets the **opportunity cost rate** for new capital investment.

> **opportunity cost rate**
> The rate of return expected on alternative investments similar in risk to the investment being evaluated; also called *hurdle rate*.

The CCC is a weighted average of the *component financing* (i.e., debt and equity) *costs*. After the component costs have been estimated, they are combined to form the CCC. Thus, the first step in the cost-of-capital estimation process is to estimate both the cost of debt and the cost of equity. However, before we discuss the mechanics of cost estimation, some other issues regarding the corporate cost-of-capital estimation process must be considered.

Capital Components

The first task in estimating a business's CCC is to determine which sources of capital on the liabilities and equity side of the balance sheet should be included in the estimate. In general, the CCC focuses on the cost of *permanent capital* (long-term capital) because these sources are used to finance capital asset acquisitions (land, buildings, and equipment). Thus, for most businesses, the relevant capital components are *equity* and *long-term debt*. Typically, short-term debt is used only for temporary financing of current assets to support seasonal or cyclical fluctuations in volume, so it is not included in the cost-of-capital estimate. However, if a business does use short-term debt as part of its permanent financing mix, such debt should be included. As discussed in chapter 16, the use of short-term debt to finance permanent assets is very risky and is not common under normal conditions.

Tax Effects

In developing component costs, the issue of taxes arises for investor-owned companies. Should the component costs be estimated on a before-tax or after-tax basis? As discussed in the previous section on capital structure, debt financing creates a tax benefit for the business because interest expense is tax deductible, while equity financing has no impact on taxes. This tax benefit can be handled in several ways when working with capital costs, but the most common way is to include it in the cost-of-capital estimate. Thus, the tax benefit associated with debt financing will be recognized in the component cost-of-debt estimate, resulting in an after-tax cost of debt. For not-for-profit corporations, the benefit that arises from the issuance of tax-exempt debt will be incorporated directly into the cost estimate because investors require a lower-than-market interest rate on tax-exempt (municipal) debt.

Historical Versus Marginal Costs

Two sets of capital costs can be estimated: *historical*, or *embedded*, *costs*, which reflect the cost of funds raised in the past, and *new*, or *marginal*, *costs*, which measure the cost of funds to be raised in the future. Historical costs are important for many purposes. For example, payers that reimburse on a cost basis are concerned with embedded costs. However, the primary purpose of estimating a business's CCC is to use it in making capital investment decisions, which involve future asset acquisitions and future financing. Thus, for our purposes here, the relevant costs are the marginal costs of new funds to be raised during some future planning period—say, a year—and not the cost of funds raised in the past.

SELF-TEST QUESTIONS

1. What is the basic concept of the CCC?
2. What financing sources are typically included in a firm's cost-of-capital estimate?
3. Should the component costs be estimated on a before-tax or after-tax basis?
4. Should the component costs reflect historical or marginal costs?

Cost of Debt Capital

Although the overall cost-of-capital estimation process is the same, some of the details of component cost estimation differ depending on ownership type. We begin our discussion by focusing on large, publicly traded for-profit businesses. Along the way, we point out some of the differences in cost estimation between investor-owned and not-for-profit businesses. Later in the chapter, we discuss some unique features of cost-of-capital estimation in small businesses.

It is unlikely that a business's managers will know at the start of a planning period the exact types and amounts of debt that will be issued in the future; the type of debt used will depend on the specific assets to be financed and on market conditions as they develop over time. However, a firm's managers do know what types of debt the firm typically issues. For example, Bayside Memorial Hospital, a not-for-profit hospital, typically uses bank debt to raise short-term funds to finance seasonal or cyclical working capital needs and 30-year tax-exempt (municipal) bonds to raise long-term debt capital. Because Bayside does not use short-term debt to finance permanent assets, its managers include only long-term debt in their corporate cost-of-capital estimate, and they assume that this debt will consist solely of 30-year tax-exempt bonds.

Suppose that Bayside's managers are estimating the hospital's corporate cost of capital for the coming year. How should they estimate the hospital's *cost of debt*? Bayside's managers would begin by discussing current and prospective interest rates with the hospital's investment bankers, the institutions that help companies obtain financing. Assume that the municipal bond analyst at Suncoast Securities, Inc., Bayside's investment banker, states that a new 30-year tax-exempt healthcare issue would require semiannual interest payments of $30.50 ($61 annually) for each $1,000 par value bond issued. Thus, municipal bond investors currently require a $61 ÷ $1,000 = 0.061 = 6.1% return on Bayside's 30-year bonds.

The true cost of the issue to Bayside would be somewhat higher than 6.1 percent because the hospital must incur administrative expenses, or *flotation costs*, to sell the bonds. However, such expenses are typically small on bond issues, so their impact on the cost-of-debt estimate is inconsequential, especially when the uncertainty inherent in the entire cost-of-capital estimation process is considered. Therefore, it is common practice to ignore flotation costs when estimating debt costs. Bayside follows this practice, so its managers would estimate the hospital's cost of debt as 6.1 percent:

$$\text{Tax-exempt cost of debt} = R(R_d) = 6.1\%.$$

A taxable healthcare provider would use the technique just described to estimate its before-tax cost of debt. However, the tax benefits of interest payments must then be incorporated into the estimate. To illustrate, consider Ann Arbor Health Care, Inc., an investor-owned company. The company's investment bankers indicate that a new 30-year taxable bond issue would require a yield of 10 percent. Because the firm's federal-plus-state tax rate is 30 percent, its after-tax cost of debt estimate is 7 percent:

$$\text{After-tax cost of debt} = R(R_d) \times (1 - T)$$
$$= 0.10 \times (1 - 0.30)$$
$$= 0.10 \times 0.7 = 7\%.$$

The cost of debt to an investor-owned (taxable) firm is an after-tax cost because the effective cost is reduced by the $(1 - T)$ term. By reducing Ann Arbor's component cost of debt from 10 percent to 7 percent, the cost-of-debt estimate has incorporated the benefit associated with interest payment tax deductibility.

Key Equation: Taxable Component Cost of Debt

For a for-profit business, the effective cost of debt is calculated as follows:

$$\text{Effective cost of debt} = R(R_d) \times (1 - T).$$

Here, $R(R_d)$ is the before-tax cost of debt (required interest rate), and T is the tax rate. For example, if a for-profit business's before-tax cost of debt is 8 percent and its tax rate is 30 percent, its effective (after-tax) cost of debt is 5.6 percent:

$$\text{Effective cost of debt} = 8\% \times (1 - 0.30)$$
$$= 8\% \times 0.70 = 5.6\%.$$

The formula for the taxable component cost of debt also works for not-for-profit businesses. In this situation, the cost of debt (interest rate) already reflects the tax-exempt feature of municipal debt and the tax rate is zero. In general, the effective cost of debt is roughly comparable for investor-owned and not-for-profit businesses of similar risk. Investor-owned firms have the benefit of tax deductibility of interest payments, while not-for-profit firms have the benefit of being able to issue lower-interest-rate, tax-exempt debt.

SELF-TEST QUESTIONS

1. What are some methods used to estimate a firm's cost of debt?
2. What is the impact of flotation costs on the cost of debt? Are these costs generally material?
3. For investor-owned firms, how is the before-tax cost of debt converted to an after-tax cost?
4. Not-for-profit businesses can issue tax-exempt debt and pay a lower interest rate on debt financing than for-profit businesses can. Does this mean that debt financing generally is less costly for not-for-profit businesses?

Cost of Equity Capital

Investor-owned businesses raise equity capital by selling new common stock and by retaining earnings for use by the firm rather than paying them out as dividends to shareholders. Not-for-profit businesses raise equity capital through contributions and grants, as well as by generating an excess of revenues over expenses, none of which can be paid out as dividends. In this section, we describe how to estimate the cost of equity capital both to investor-owned and not-for-profit businesses.

Cost of Equity to Investor-Owned Businesses

The cost of debt is based on the return (interest rate) that investors require on debt securities. The *cost of equity* to investor-owned businesses can be defined similarly: It is the rate of return that investors require on a firm's common stock. At first glance, equity raised through *retained earnings* may appear to be a costless source of capital to investor-owned businesses. The reason that a cost of capital must be assigned to all forms of equity financing involves the *opportunity cost principle*. An investor-owned firm's net income belongs to its common stockholders. Employees are compensated by wages, suppliers are compensated by cash payments for supplies, bondholders are compensated by interest payments, governments are compensated by tax payments, and so on. The residual earnings of a business—its net income—belong to the stockholders and "pay the rent" on owner-supplied capital.

Management can either pay out earnings in the form of dividends or retain earnings for reinvestment in the business. If the business retains part of the earnings, an opportunity cost is incurred; stockholders could have received these earnings as dividends and then invested this money in stocks, bonds, real estate, commodity futures, and so on. Thus, a business should earn on its retained earnings at least as much as its stockholders could earn on *alternative investments of similar risk*. If the firm cannot earn as much as stockholders can earn on similar risk investments, the firm's net income should be paid out as dividends rather than retained for reinvestment within the business. What rate of return can stockholders expect to earn on other investments of equivalent risk? The answer is $R(R_e)$—the required rate of return on equity. Investors can earn this return either by buying more shares of the firm in question or by buying the stock of similar firms.

Large, investor-owned businesses use three primary methods in the estimation process: the capital asset pricing model (CAPM), the discounted cash flow (DCF) model, and the debt cost plus risk premium model. These methods are not mutually exclusive, because no single approach dominates the estimation process. In practice, all approaches should be used to estimate the cost of equity, and then the final value should be chosen on the basis of management's confidence in the estimates at hand.

Capital Asset Pricing Model Approach

The *capital asset pricing model*, which we introduced in chapter 10, is a widely accepted financial model that specifies the equilibrium risk/return relationship on common stocks. Basically, the model assumes that investors consider only one factor when setting required rates of return—the volatility of returns on the stock compared with the volatility of returns on a well-diversified stock portfolio called the *market portfolio*, or just the *market*. The measure of risk in the CAPM is the stock's *market beta coefficient*.

Within the CAPM, the actual equation that relates risk to return is the *security market line (SML)*:

$$R(R_e) = RF + [R(R_M) - RF] \times \beta = RF + (RP_M \times \beta).$$

Managers can estimate the required rate of return on the firm's equity, $R(R_e)$, given estimates of the risk-free rate, RF; the beta of the stock, β; and the required rate of return on the market, $R(R_M)$. This estimate, in turn, can be used as an estimate of the firm's cost of equity.

The starting point for the CAPM cost-of-equity estimate is the risk-free rate (RF). Unfortunately, there is no security in the United States that is truly riskless. Treasury securities are essentially free of default risk, but long-term T-bonds will suffer capital losses if interest rates rise, and a portfolio invested in short-term T-bills will provide a volatile earnings stream because the rate paid on T-bills varies over time. Because we cannot, in practice, find a truly riskless rate on which to base the CAPM, what rate should we use? Most analysts use the rate on Treasury bonds.

There are many reasons for favoring a T-bond rate, including the fact that T-bill rates are volatile because they are directly affected by actions taken by the Federal Reserve Board. Perhaps the most persuasive argument is that common stocks are generally viewed as long-term securities, and although a particular stockholder may not have a long investment horizon, the majority of stockholders do invest on a long-term basis. Therefore, it is reasonable to think that stock returns embody long-term inflation expectations similar to those embodied in bonds rather than the short-term inflation expectations embodied in T-bills. On this account, the cost of equity should be more highly correlated with T-bond rates than with T-bill rates. T-bond rates can be found in local newspapers, in the *Wall Street Journal*, and on numerous websites. Generally, the yield on ten-year T-bonds is used as the proxy for the risk-free rate.

The required rate of return on the market, and its derivative, the market risk premium, $RP_M = R(R_M) - RF$, can be estimated on the basis of either historical returns or expected returns. The most widely used set of historical market returns is provided by Morningstar. It examines market data over long periods (from 1926 to present) to determine the average annual rates of return and standard deviations of various classes of securities.[2] In general, most users of the CAPM believe the historical market risk premium falls in the range of 4 to 6 percentage points.

The last parameter needed for a CAPM cost-of-equity estimate is the stock's beta coefficient. Unfortunately, beta measures how risky a stock was *in the past*, whereas investors are interested in *future* risk. A given company might have appeared safe in the past, but things may have changed and its future risk may be judged to be higher than its past risk, or vice versa. In general, is future risk sufficiently similar to past risk to warrant the use of historical betas in a CAPM framework? For individual firms, historical betas are often not stable, so past risk is often *not* a good predictor of future risk.

Furthermore, betas can be calculated over different time periods, and different measures for the market return can be used, so different financial advisory services report different betas for the same company. The choice is a matter of judgment and data availability, for there is no right beta. With luck, the betas derived from different sources will, for a given company, be close together. If they are not, confidence in the CAPM cost-of-equity estimate will be diminished.

To illustrate the CAPM approach, consider Ann Arbor Health Care, which has a beta coefficient, β, of 1.50. Furthermore, assume that the current yield on T-bonds, RF, is 6 percent and that the best estimate for the current market risk premium, RP_M, is 5 percentage points. In other words, the current required rate of return on the market, $R(R_M)$, is 11 percent. All the required input parameters have been estimated, and the SML equation can be solved as follows:

$$
\begin{aligned}
R(R_e) &= RF + [R(R_M) - RF] \times \beta_{AAHC} \\
&= 6\% + (11.0\% - 6\%) \times 1.50 \\
&= 6\% + (5.0\% \times 1.50) \\
&= 6\% + 7.5\% = 13.5\%.
\end{aligned}
$$

According to the CAPM, Ann Arbor's required rate of return on equity is 13.5 percent.

Key Equation: Security Market Line of the Capital Asset Pricing Model
Introduced in chapter 10, the SML provides the relationship between a stock's required rate of return and its portfolio (market) risk as measured by its beta coefficient:

$$R(R_e) = RF + [R(R_M) - RF] \times \beta.$$

Here, $R(R_e)$ is the required rate of return on equity, RF is the risk-free rate, $R(R_M)$ is the required rate of return on the market portfolio, and β is the beta coefficient.

What does the 13.5 percent estimate for $R(R_e)$ imply? In essence, equity investors believe that Ann Arbor's stock, with a beta of 1.50, is more risky than the average stock with a beta of 1.00. With a risk-free rate of 6 percent and a market risk premium of 5 percentage points, an average firm, with $\beta = 1.00$, has a required rate of return on equity of 6% + (5% × 1.00) = 6% + 5% = 11%. Thus, according to the CAPM, equity investors require 250 basis points (2.50 percentage points) more return for investing in Ann Arbor Health Care, with $\beta = 1.50$, than for an average stock, with $\beta = 1.00$.

There is a great deal of uncertainty in the CAPM estimate of the cost of equity. Some of this uncertainty stems from the fact that there is no assurance that the CAPM is correct—that is, that the CAPM accurately describes the risk/return choices of stock investors. In addition, a great deal of uncertainty exists in the input parameter estimates, especially the required rate of return on the market and the beta coefficient. Because of these uncertainties, it is highly unlikely that Ann Arbor's true, but unobservable, cost of equity is 13.5 percent. Instead of picking single values for each parameter, it may be better to develop high and low estimates and then combine all of the high and low estimates to develop a range, rather than a point estimate, for $R(R_e)$.

Discounted Cash Flow Approach

The second approach to estimating the cost of equity is the *discounted cash flow approach*, which uses the dividend valuation model as its basis. As we discussed in chapter 12, if a company has an established track record of paying dividends and if the dividend is expected to grow each year at a constant rate, $E(g)$, the *constant growth model* can be used to estimate the expected rate of return on the stock, $E(R_e)$:

$$E(R_e) = \frac{D_0 \times [1 + E(g)]}{P_0} + E(g) = \frac{E(D_1)}{P_0} + E(g).$$

Because stock prices typically are in equilibrium, the expected rate of return, $E(R_e)$, is also the required rate of return, $R(R_e)$.

As in the CAPM approach, there are three input parameters in the DCF model. Current stock price, P_0, is readily available for firms that are actively traded. Ann Arbor Health Care's stock is traded in the over-the-counter market, so its stock price can be determined easily. At the time of the analysis, Ann Arbor's stock price was $40.

Next year's dividend payment, $E(D_1)$, is also relatively easy to estimate. Ann Arbor's managers can obtain this estimate from the firm's five-year financial plan. For an outsider, dividend data on larger publicly traded firms are available from brokerage houses and investment advisory firms. Ann

Arbor Health Care is followed by several analysts at major brokerage houses, and their consensus estimate for next year's dividend payment is $2.50, so for purposes of this analysis, $E(D_1) = \$2.50$. If next year's dividend estimate is not available, the current dividend, D_0, along with the expected growth rate can be used to make the estimate.

Key Equation: Constant Growth Dividend Valuation Model

If a company's dividends are expected to grow at a constant rate forever, a simple model, introduced in chapter 12, can be used to value its stock:

$$E(R_e) = \frac{D_0 \times [1 + E(g)]}{P_0} + E(g) = \frac{E(D_1)}{P_0} + E(g).$$

Here, $E(R_e)$ is the expected rate of return on equity, which in equilibrium equals $R(R_e)$, the required rate of return on equity; D_0 is the last dividend paid; $E(g)$ is the expected constant dividend growth rate; P_0 is the current stock price; and $E(D_1)$ is the next expected dividend.

The dividend growth rate is the most difficult of the DCF model parameters to estimate. Although historical earnings and dividend data can be analyzed directly to estimate growth rates, most finance professionals rely on expert analysts for growth rate estimates. Analysts forecast and publish growth rate estimates for most of the larger publicly owned companies. For example, *Value Line* provides such forecasts on about 1,700 companies, and all of the larger brokerage houses provide similar forecasts. Assume that analysts who follow Ann Arbor Health Care's stock expect, on average, a dividend growth rate of 7 to 8 percent.

To illustrate the DCF approach, consider the data developed thus far for Ann Arbor Health Care. The company's current stock price, P_0, is $40, and its next expected annual dividend, $E(D_1)$, is $2.50. Furthermore, with an $E(g)$ estimate of 7 to 8 percent, the midpoint, 7.5 percent, will be used as our final estimate. Thus, the DCF estimate for Ann Arbor Health Care's cost of equity is 13.8%:

$$R(R_e) = \frac{E(D_1)}{P_0} + E(g)$$

$$= \frac{\$2.50}{\$40} + 7.5\% = 6.3\% + 7.5\% = 13.8\%.$$

Debt Cost Plus Risk Premium Approach

The *debt cost plus risk premium* approach relies on the fact that stock investments are riskier than debt investments; hence, the cost of equity for any business can be thought of as the before-tax cost of debt to that business plus a risk premium:

$$R(R_e) = R(R_d) + \text{Risk premium.}$$

The cost of debt is relatively easy to estimate, so the key input to this model is the risk premium.

Note that the risk premium used here is not the same as the market risk premium used in the CAPM. The market risk premium is the amount that investors require above the *risk-free rate* to invest in an average-risk common stock. Here, we need the risk premium above the firm's own *before-tax cost of debt*. How might this new risk premium be estimated? Using the data from above, we know that the cost of equity for an average-risk ($\beta = 1.00$) stock is 11 percent. Furthermore, assume that the cost of debt for an average firm, which has roughly an A rating, is 7 percent. Thus, for an average firm, the risk premium of the cost of equity over the cost of debt is 11% – 7% = 4 percentage points.

Empirical work suggests that the risk premium used in the debt cost plus risk premium model ranges from 3 to 5 percentage points. When interest rates are high in the economy, this risk premium tends to be at the lower end of the range, while lower interest rates often lead to higher risk premiums. Perhaps the greatest weakness of this approach is that there is no assurance that the risk premium for the average firm is the same as the risk premium for the firm in question—in this case, Ann Arbor Health Care. Thus, the risk premium method does not have the theoretical precision that the other models do. On the other hand, the input values required by the debt cost plus risk premium model are fewer and easier to estimate than in the other models.

> *Key Equation: Debt Cost Plus Risk Premium Approach*
>
> A business's cost of equity can be estimated by adding a risk premium to the business's before-tax cost of debt:
>
> $$R(R_e) = R(R_d) + \text{Risk premium.}$$
>
> Here, $R(Re)$ is the cost of equity, $R(R_d)$ is the before-tax cost of debt, and the risk premium is the amount of return required above the cost of debt to induce investors to buy the business's stock.

With a before-tax cost-of-debt estimate of 10 percent and a current risk premium estimate of 4 percentage points, the debt cost plus risk premium estimate for Ann Arbor's cost of equity is 14 percent:

$$R(R_e) = R(R_d) + \text{Risk premium} = 10\% + 4\% = 14\%.$$

Comparison of the Capital Asset Pricing Model, Discounted Cash Flow, and Debt Cost Plus Risk Premium Methods

We have presented three methods for estimating the cost of equity. The CAPM estimate for Ann Arbor was 13.5 percent, the DCF estimate was 13.8 percent, and the debt cost plus risk premium estimate was 14 percent. At this point, judgment is required. Most analysts would conclude that the three results are sufficiently consistent to warrant the use of a cost-of-equity estimate of 13.5 to 14 percent. We choose 13.9 percent as our final estimate because of our concern over the input values used in the CAPM estimate. In general, analysts must judge the relative merits of each estimate and then choose a final estimate that seems most reasonable under the circumstances. This choice typically is made on the basis of the analyst's confidence in the input parameters of each approach.

Cost of Equity to Not-for-Profit Businesses

Not-for-profit businesses raise equity (fund) capital in two basic ways: (1) by receiving contributions and grants and (2) by earning an excess of revenues over expenses (retained earnings). In this section, we first discuss some views regarding the cost of fund capital, and then we illustrate how this cost can be estimated.

Our primary purpose in this chapter is to develop a corporate cost-of-capital estimate that can be used in making capital investment decisions. Thus, the estimated cost represents the cost of using capital to purchase fixed (capital) assets, rather than for alternative uses. What is the cost of using equity capital for real-asset investments within not-for-profit businesses? There are several positions that can be taken on this question.[3]

1. **Fund capital has a zero cost.** The rationale here is that (1) contributors do not expect a monetary return on their contributions, and (2) the firm's stakeholders, especially the patients and insurers who pay more for services than is warranted by the firm's tangible costs, do not require an explicit return on the capital retained by the firm. With no explicit return required by the suppliers of equity capital, the cost of that capital is zero.

2. **Fund capital has a cost equal to the return forgone on short-term securities investments.** When a not-for-profit firm receives

contributions or retains earnings, it can always invest these funds in short-term securities (highly liquid, safe securities) rather than purchase real assets (property and equipment). Thus, fund capital has a relatively low opportunity cost that should be acknowledged; this cost is roughly equal to the return available on a portfolio of short-term, low-risk securities such as T-bills.

3. **Fund capital has a cost equal to the expected growth rate of the business's assets.**[4] Assume that a hospital must increase its total assets by 8 percent per year to keep pace with an increasing patient load. To purchase the required assets without increasing its proportion of debt financing, the hospital must grow its equity capital at an 8 percent rate. In this way, the hospital can finance asset growth by growing both debt and equity at the same 8 percent rate, allowing it to hold the proportion of debt constant. If the hospital earned zero return on its existing fund capital, it would be unable to add new assets without increasing its debt ratio or relying on grants and contributions to provide the needed equity. Even if no volume growth is expected, a not-for-profit business must earn a return on its fund capital just to replace its existing asset base as assets wear out or become obsolete. New equity capital is required because new assets generally will cost more than the ones being replaced, so depreciation cash flow in itself will not be sufficient to replace older assets as needed. The bottom line here is that not-for-profit businesses must earn a return on equity merely to support dollar growth in assets; the greater the growth rate, including that caused by inflation and technology improvements, the greater the return that must be earned.

4. **Fund capital has a cost equal to that required to maintain the business's creditworthiness.** One of the factors that rating agencies consider when assigning debt ratings is the profitability of the business: All else being equal, the higher the profitability of the business, the better the credit rating. In general, managers of not-for-profit healthcare businesses have some target debt rating that they seek to achieve (or maintain). Furthermore, rating agencies publish profitability measures, including return on equity, that they consider to be appropriate for each debt rating. Thus, to maintain the business's desired rating, managers must achieve the return on equity recommended by the rating agencies, which, in turn, sets the business's cost-of-equity target.

5. **Fund capital has a cost equal to the cost of equity to similar for-profit businesses.** The rationale here rests on the opportunity cost

concept as discussed in the second argument, but the opportunity cost is now defined as the return available from investing fund capital in *alternative investments of similar risk*. To illustrate, suppose Bayside, a not-for-profit corporation, receives $500,000 in unrestricted contributions in 2019 and also retains $4.5 million in earnings, so it has $5 million of new fund capital available for investment. The $5 million could be (1) used to purchase assets related to its core business, such as an outpatient clinic; (2) temporarily invested in securities with the intent of purchasing healthcare assets sometime in the future; (3) used to retire debt; (4) used to pay management bonuses; (5) placed in a non-interest-bearing account at the bank; and so on. If Bayside uses this capital to invest in real assets, it will be deprived of the opportunity to use the capital for other purposes, so an opportunity cost must be assigned that reflects the riskiness associated with an equity investment in hospital assets. What return is available on securities with similar risk to hospital assets? The answer is the return expected from investing in the stock of an investor-owned hospital business, such as Ann Arbor Health Care. Instead of using fund capital to purchase real healthcare assets, Bayside could always use the funds to buy the stock of a for-profit hospital corporation and delay the purchase of a real asset until sometime in the future.

With these five positions in mind, which one should prevail in practice? Unfortunately, the answer is not clear-cut. However, at a minimum, a not-for-profit business should require a return on its equity investments in real assets that is as large as its projected asset growth rate. In that way, the business is setting the minimum rate of return that will, if it is achieved, ensure the financial stability of the organization. Thus, the expected growth rate sets the minimum required rate of return, and hence the minimum cost of equity, for not-for-profit businesses. However, if the rating agency's target return on equity is greater than the growth rate target, the rating agency's target should be used as the required return on equity to maintain the business's creditworthiness.

However, to recover all opportunity costs fully, including the opportunity cost of employing equity capital in healthcare assets, the real-asset investments must offer an expected financial return equal to the return expected on similar-risk securities investments. Thus, the true economic opportunity cost of equity to a not-for-profit healthcare provider is the rate that could be earned on stock investments in similar investor-owned firms.

For Your Consideration

Choosing a Cost of Equity When Estimates Vary Widely

Suppose you are estimating the cost of capital for a large, publicly traded, for-profit hospital chain. First, you estimated the cost of debt to be 7.2 percent. Then, you applied the three methods of estimating the hospital's cost of equity, with the following results:

CAPM	13.6%
DCF	6.8%
Debt cost plus risk premium	11.2%

Your next task is to choose a single value for the cost of equity.

How do you estimate a single value from these widely different estimates? Should you merely average the three estimates, or should other factors be considered? Does the fact that the DCF estimate is less than the cost of debt influence your decision? What is your best single (point) estimate for the hospital's cost of equity?

Using this cost of equity, a not-for-profit business requires that all costs, including full opportunity costs, be considered in the cost-of-capital estimate. Note that full opportunity costs do not have to be recovered on every new capital investment undertaken. Not-for-profit businesses do invest in projects that are beneficial in ways other than financial, so the cost-of-capital estimate does not set an absolute limit on new investment. We do believe, however, that healthcare managers should be aware of the true financial opportunity costs inherent in capital investments, and the only way this can be accomplished is to use the cost of equity to similar for-profit businesses as the cost of fund capital.

Although the "full opportunity cost" approach appears to be the most correct theoretically, many would argue that the unique mission of not-for-profit businesses precludes securities investments as realistic alternatives to healthcare plant and equipment investments because securities investments do not contribute directly to the mission of providing healthcare services. If that is the case, the cost of fund capital should be the greater of the expected growth rate and the creditworthiness-maintaining rate.

SELF-TEST QUESTIONS

1. What are the three primary methods of estimating a for-profit firm's cost of equity?
2. What is the best proxy for the risk-free rate in the CAPM method? Why?
3. How would you choose between widely different cost-of-equity estimates?
4. What is the cost of fund capital to not-for-profit healthcare businesses?

Corporate Cost of Capital

The final step in the cost-of-capital estimation process is to combine the debt and equity cost estimates to form the **CCC.** As discussed earlier in this chapter, each firm has a target capital structure—that is, the particular mix of debt and equity that minimizes its average cost of capital. Furthermore, when a firm raises new capital, it tries to finance it in a way that will keep the actual capital structure close to its target over time.

Here is the general formula for the corporate cost of capital (CCC) for all firms, regardless of ownership:

$$CCC = [w_d \times R(R_d) \times (1 - T)] + [w_e \times R(R_e)],$$

where w_d and w_e are the target weights for debt and equity, respectively. The cost of the debt component, $R(R_d)$, will be an average if the firm uses several types of debt for its permanent financing. Alternatively, the equation could be expanded to include multiple debt terms. Investor-owned firms would use their marginal tax rate for T, while T would be zero for not-for-profit businesses.

> **Key Equation: Corporate Cost of Capital (CCC)**
> A business's corporate cost of capital is estimated using this equation:
>
> $$CCC = [w_d \times R(R_d) \times (1 - T)] + [w_e \times R(R_e)].$$
>
> Here, CCC is the corporate cost of capital, w_d is the weight of debt financing in the target capital structure, $R(R_d)$ is the cost of debt, T is the tax rate, w_e is the weight of equity, and $R(R_e)$ is the cost of equity.

The CCC represents the cost of each *new* dollar of capital raised rather than the average cost of all the dollars raised in the past. Because the primary interest is in obtaining a cost of capital for use in capital investment analysis, a *marginal cost* is required. Furthermore, the CCC formula implies that each new dollar of capital will consist of both debt and equity that is raised, at least conceptually, in proportion to the firm's target capital structure.

The Corporate Cost of Capital for Investor-Owned Firms
To illustrate the CCC calculation for investor-owned firms, consider Ann Arbor Health Care, which has a target capital structure of 60 percent debt

and 40 percent equity. As previously estimated, the company's before-tax cost of debt, $R(R_d)$, is 10 percent; its tax rate, T, is 30 percent; and its cost of equity, $R(R_e)$, is 13.8 percent. Using these data, we estimate Ann Arbor's CCC to be 9.7 percent:

$$CCC = [w_d \times R(R_d) \times (1 - T)] + [w_e \times R(R_e)]$$
$$= [0.60 \times 10\% \times (1 - 0.30)] + (0.40 \times 13.8\%)$$
$$= 9.7\%.$$

Conceptually, every dollar of new capital that Ann Arbor obtains consists of 60 cents of debt with an after-tax cost of 7 percent and 40 cents of equity with a cost of 13.8 percent. The average cost of each new dollar is 9.7 percent. In any one year, Ann Arbor may raise all its required new capital by issuing debt, by retaining earnings, or by selling new common stock. But over the long run, Ann Arbor plans to use 60 percent debt financing and 40 percent equity financing, and these weights must be used in the CCC estimate regardless of the actual financing plans for the near term.

The Corporate Cost of Capital for Not-for-Profit Firms

The CCC for not-for-profit businesses is estimated in the same way as for investor-owned firms. To illustrate, the CCC for Bayside, assuming a target capital structure of 50 percent debt and 50 percent equity, and using the estimates for the component costs that were developed earlier, is 10 percent:

$$CCC = [w_d \times R(R_d) \times (1 - T)] + [w_e \times R(R_e)]$$
$$= [0.50 \times 6.1\% \times (1 - 0)] + (0.50 \times 13.8\%)$$
$$= 10.0\%.$$

Note that we have assigned the full opportunity cost of equity capital to Bayside, which is the cost of equity to similar for-profit businesses (13.9 percent).

Businesses, regardless of ownership, cannot raise unlimited amounts of new capital in any given year at a constant cost. Eventually, as more new capital is raised, investors will require higher returns on debt and equity capital, even if the capital is raised in accordance with the firm's target structure. Thus, the CCC, as estimated here for Ann Arbor and Bayside, is only valid when the amount required for capital investment falls within the firm's normal range. If capital is required in amounts that far exceed those normally raised, the CCC must be subjectively adjusted upward to reflect the higher costs involved.

1. What is the general formula for the CCC?
2. What weights should be used in the formula? Why?
3. What is the primary difference between the CCC for investor-owned and not-for-profit firms?
4. Is the CCC affected by short-term financing plans? Explain your answer.
5. Is the CCC constant regardless of the amount of new capital required? Explain your answer.

Cost-of-Capital Estimation for Small Businesses

The guidance given thus far in this chapter has focused on the cost-of-capital estimation process for large healthcare businesses. What if the business is small, such as a solo practice, a small group practice, or a small freestanding hospital? The estimation process is the same as described, but the manner in which the component costs are estimated must be handled differently.

Estimating the Cost of Debt

Small businesses typically obtain most of their debt financing from commercial banks, so a business's commercial loan officer will be able to provide some insights into the cost of future debt financing. Alternatively, managers of small businesses can look to marketplace activity for guidance; that is, the interest rate currently being set on the debt issues of similar-risk firms can be used as an estimate of the cost of debt. Here, similar risk can be judged by subjective analysis (same field, similar size, similar use of debt, and so on). In many cases, the prime rate gives small businesses a benchmark for bank loan rates. If the business has borrowed from commercial banks in the past, its managers will know the historical premium charged above the prime rate for the business's bank debt. An awareness of the current interest rate environment generally permits managers to make a reasonable estimate for their own business's cost of debt, even when the business is small.

Estimating the Cost of Equity

Although estimating the cost of debt for a small business is relatively easy, the cost-of-equity estimate is more problematic because such businesses do not have publicly traded stock. Here are some points to note.

Debt Cost Plus Risk Premium Approach

Perhaps the easiest way to estimate the cost of equity for a small business is to use the debt cost plus risk premium approach. Because the cost of debt is relatively easy to estimate, it is equally easy to add some risk premium—say, 4 percentage points—to the business's before-tax cost of debt to obtain its cost-of-equity estimate. However, this estimate can only be considered a starting point estimate because the risk premiums applicable to small businesses may be much larger than those estimated for large firms.

pure play approach
A method for estimating the base cost of equity for a small business whereby the cost of equity of a similar large, publicly traded business is used as a proxy value.

Pure Play Approach

As an alternative to the debt cost plus risk premium approach, a proxy publicly traded firm in the same line of business can be identified and its beta used to estimate the equity risk of the small business. This technique is called the **pure play approach**. To illustrate, suppose the beta for a publicly traded practice management firm is 0.88. *If the riskiness inherent in practice management is the same as the risk involved in the ownership of a small group practice*, a beta of 0.88 can be used to proxy the ownership risk. Then, the CAPM approach can be used to estimate the small business's cost of equity.

To use the pure play approach for a small business, the assumption must be made that the risk to the owners of the publicly traded proxy firm is the same as the risk to the owners of the small business. However, there are several important differences between the ownership of stock in a large corporation and the ownership of a small group practice. First, the geographic and business line diversification of a large business typically makes ownership less risky than a similar position in a small, localized, single-line business. Second, most stockholders of large businesses hold that stock as part of a well-diversified investment portfolio. In a small group practice, employment earnings are highly correlated with investment returns on the practice. Third, stock owned in an investment portfolio is highly liquid; the owner can sell it quickly at a fair market price with a single

---

For Your Consideration
Why Not Apply the Actual Financing Costs?

Assume that a group practice is evaluating a new clinic proposal having a total cost of $10 million. The entire cost will be financed with an 8 percent long-term bank loan. With a 30 percent tax rate, the effective (after-tax) cost of the financing is $8\% \times (1 - T) = 8\% \times (1 - 0.30) = 8\% \times 0.70 = 5.6\%$, while the business's CCC is 10 percent. Proponents of the project argue that the correct discount rate should be the effective cost of debt financing (5.6 percent) because that represents the cost of the financing that actually will be used for the project.

However, the practice's financial manager insists that the correct discount rate is 10 percent (if the project has average risk). The argument rests on two points: (1) The practice could not obtain a $10 million bank loan if there were no equity in the business. Thus, the opportunity cost rate has to include an implied equity contribution. (2) If the practice used 5.6 percent on this project, it would have to use 13 percent (the estimated cost of equity) on projects that were actually financed with equity financing. This

(continued)

phone call. Conversely, an ownership position in a small group practice is difficult to sell.

All of these factors suggest that the ownership risk of a small owner-managed business is greater than for stockholders of large companies, so the cost of equity is higher than that calculated using the CAPM and a proxy company.

Build-Up Method

When estimating the cost of equity for small businesses, it is common to use an approach called the **build-up method**. Here, the cost of equity of a similar large business is used as the base, or starting point. Then, adjustments, or premiums, are added to account for the differences between large and small businesses.

Size premium. Although returns data on businesses as small as a group practice are not readily available, studies using historical returns data indicate that the cost of equity for the smallest stocks listed on the New York Stock Exchange—those in the bottom decile of market value—is about 4 percentage points higher than the cost of equity for large businesses—those in the S&P 500. This premium, added to compensate for the additional risk inherent in the ownership of small, as opposed to large, businesses, is called the *size premium*. It can be argued that the size premium is even larger than 4 percentage points for firms so small that their equity is not publicly traded. The bottom line here is that when the cost of equity of a small business is estimated on the basis of equity costs to similar large businesses, an additional premium must be added to account for the size differential.

Liquidity premium. Because an ownership position in a small business is less liquid than the stock of a large corporation, a liquidity premium is commonly added when estimating the cost of equity for a small business. This premium is generally thought to be about 2 percentage points. Note, however, that if an investor has a control position (more than 50 percent ownership), some of the risk associated with small business ownership is reduced.

Unique-risk premium. Some small businesses have unique risk. For example, the success of a start-up business might depend on new, unproven technology. Or the success of a small business might depend on the intellectual capital or managerial prowess of one person. In such situations, it is not uncommon to add a premium of 5 percentage points or more to account for the unique risk.

(continued from previous page)

would create an unusual capital budgeting system in which projects with a 10 percent internal rate of return would be financially acceptable in the years when debt financing is used but unacceptable in the years when equity financing is used.

What do you think? Should the actual financing be used to set the hurdle rate on new projects, or should all projects (of average risk) be evaluated using the CCC regardless of the actual financing mix?

---

build-up method
A method for estimating the cost of equity for a small business that starts with a base rate and then adds premiums to account for size, liquidity, and unique risk characteristics.

To illustrate the build-up method, consider a small medical practice. The cost of equity to a large practice management company is found as follows:

$$R(R_e) = RF + [R(R_M) - RF] \times \beta$$
$$= 6\% + (11\% - 6\%) \times 0.88$$
$$= 6\% + (5\% \times 0.88) = 10.4\%.$$

Here, we use a pure play beta of 0.88 along with the market data used in previous examples to obtain a base cost of equity of 10.4 percent.

Now, using the build-up method, and assuming a size premium of 4 percentage points and a liquidity premium of 2 percentage points, we obtain the following cost-of-equity estimate:

$$\text{Cost of equity} = 10.4\% + 4\% + 2\% = 16.4\%.$$

If any unique risk is identified for this practice, the cost-of-equity estimate could be even higher.

Although the estimation process clearly is more difficult for small businesses, it may be even more important for small businesses to recognize their CCC than it is for large businesses. The reason is that owners of small businesses often have their livelihoods as well as their equity investments tied to the business. Using the techniques described in this section, even a small business owner can take a stab at estimating the business's CCC.

SELF-TEST QUESTIONS

1. What are the problems faced by small businesses when estimating the CCC?
2. What is the size premium? Liquidity premium? Unique-risk premium?
3. Describe the build-up method for estimating a small business's cost of equity.

An Economic Interpretation of the Corporate Cost of Capital

Thus far, the focus of the cost-of-capital discussion has been on the mechanics of the estimation process. In closing, it is worthwhile to step back from the mathematics of the process and examine the economic interpretation of the CCC.

The component cost estimates that make up a firm's CCC—the costs of debt and equity—are based on the returns that investors require to supply capital to the business. In turn, investors' required rates of return are based on the opportunity costs borne by investing in the debt and equity of the firm in question, rather than in alternative investments of similar risk. These opportunity costs to investors, when incorporated into the firm's CCC, establish the *opportunity cost* to the business. In other words, the CCC is the return that the business could earn by investing in alternative investments that have the same risk as its own real assets. From a purely financial perspective, if a business (especially one that is investor owned) cannot earn its CCC on new capital investments, no new investments should be made and no new capital should be raised. If existing investments are not earning the CCC, they should be terminated, the assets liquidated, and the proceeds returned to investors for reinvestment elsewhere.

However, the CCC is not the appropriate minimum rate of return for all new real-asset investments. The required rates of return set by investors on the business's debt and equity are based on perceptions regarding the riskiness of their investments, which in turn are based on two factors: (1) the inherent riskiness of the business (i.e., business risk) and (2) the amount of debt financing used (i.e., financial risk). Thus, the firm's inherent business risk and capital structure are embedded in its CCC estimate.

Because firms have different business risk and use different proportions of debt financing, they have different CCCs. Differences in capital costs are most pronounced for firms in different fields. Still, even firms in the same field can have different business risk, and capital structure differences among such firms can compound CCC differences.

The primary purpose of estimating a business's CCC is to help make capital budgeting decisions; that is, the cost of capital will be used as the benchmark capital budgeting **hurdle rate**, or minimum return necessary for a project to be financially attractive. The business can always earn its cost of capital by investing in selected stocks and bonds that in the aggregate have the same risk as the firm's assets, so it should not invest in real assets unless it can earn at least as much. However, remember that the CCC reflects opportunity costs based on the aggregate risk of the business (i.e., the riskiness of the firm's average project). Thus, the CCC can be applied without modification only to those projects under consideration that have average risk, where *average* is defined as that amount applicable to the firm's currently held assets in the aggregate. If a project under consideration has risk that differs significantly from that of the firm's average asset, the CCC must be adjusted to account for the differential risk when the project is being evaluated.

To illustrate the concept, Bayside's CCC, 10 percent, is probably appropriate for use in evaluating a new outpatient clinic that has risk similar to the

hurdle rate
The minimum required rate of return on an investment; also called *opportunity cost rate* or *discount rate.*

hospital's average project, which involves the provision of healthcare services. Clearly, it would not be appropriate to apply Bayside's 10 percent CCC without adjustment to a new project that involves establishing a managed care subsidiary; this project does not have the same risk as the hospital's average asset.

As discussed in chapter 10, investors require higher returns for riskier investments. Thus, a high-risk project must have a higher **project cost of capital** than a low-risk project does. Exhibit 13.4 illustrates the relationship between project risk, the CCC, and project costs of capital. The exhibit illustrates that Bayside's 10 percent CCC is the appropriate hurdle rate *only* for an *average-risk* project (project A), where *average* means a project that has the same risk as the aggregate business. Project L, which has less risk than Bayside's average project, has a project cost of capital of 8 percent, which is less than the CCC capital. Project H, with more risk than the average project, has a higher project cost of capital of 12 percent.

The key point here is that the CCC is simply a benchmark that will be used as the basis for estimating project costs of capital. It is not a one-size-fits-all rate that can be used whenever an opportunity cost is needed in a financial analysis. This point will be revisited in chapter 15 when capital investment risk considerations are addressed.

project cost of capital
The discount rate (hurdle rate or opportunity cost rate) that reflects the unique risk of a project.

EXHIBIT 13.4
Bayside Memorial Hospital: Corporate and Project Costs of Capital

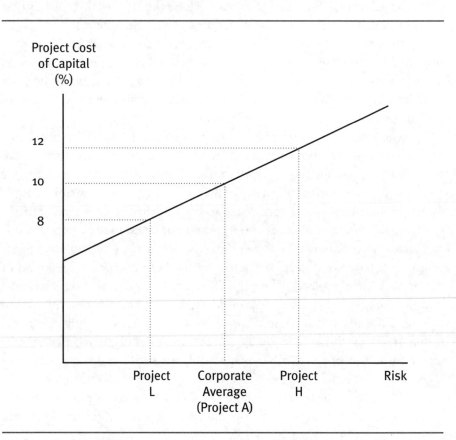

Finally, note that large healthcare systems often have subsidiaries that operate in diverse lines of business, for example, inpatient care, outpatient care, long-term care, and insurance. When this situation exists, for capital investment purposes it is best to estimate **divisional costs of capital** in addition to the CCC. Whereas the overall cost of capital reflects the aggregate risk of the business, the divisional costs of capital reflect the unique risks (and perhaps unique capital structure) of each division (business line). (In chapter 15, we explore the concept of divisional costs of capital in more detail.)

divisional cost of capital
The discount rate (hurdle rate or opportunity cost rate) that reflects the unique risk of a division within a corporation.

SELF-TEST QUESTIONS

1. Explain the economic interpretation of the CCC.
2. Is the CCC the appropriate opportunity cost for all projects that a business evaluates?
3. Draw a graph similar to the one shown in exhibit 13.4 and explain its implications.
4. Should large businesses estimate divisional costs of capital? Explain your answer.

Key Concepts

This chapter discusses optimal capital structure and the corporate cost of capital—two important concepts in healthcare finance. The key concepts of this chapter are as follows:

- The choice between debt and equity financing involves a risk/ return trade-off. The use of debt financing can *leverage up* the return to owners or, in not-for-profit firms, the return on fund capital. However, the use of debt financing also *increases the risk* to owners or, in not-for-profit businesses, to the community stakeholders.
- The *optimal*, or *target*, *capital structure* is the structure that minimizes the average cost of capital to the business. The target amount of debt financing is also called the business's *debt capacity*.
- Finance theory is of limited help in setting a firm's target structure. Thus, in making the capital structure decision,

(continued)

(continued from previous page)

health services managers must consider a wide range of factors, including the following: business risk, lender and rating agency attitudes, reserve borrowing capacity, industry averages, and asset structure.

- Managers of not-for-profit businesses must grapple with the same capital structure decisions as the managers of investor-owned firms. However, not-for-profit firms do not have the same flexibility in making financing decisions because they cannot issue common stock.

- In estimating a firm's corporate cost of capital (CCC), the *component cost of debt* is the *after-tax* cost of new debt. For taxable firms, it is found by multiplying the before-tax cost of new debt by $(1 - T)$, where T is the firm's marginal tax rate, so the effective cost of debt is $R(R_d) \times (1 - T)$. For not-for-profit firms, the debt is often tax exempt, but no other tax effects apply, so the component cost of debt is merely the tax-exempt $R(R_d)$.

- The *cost of equity* to investor-owned firms is the return that its stockholders could obtain by investing in the stocks of similar-risk companies. For large, publicly traded companies, it usually is estimated by using three methods: the *capital asset pricing model (CAPM)* approach, the *discounted cash flow (DCF)* approach, and the *debt cost plus risk premium* approach.

- For not-for-profit firms, the *cost of equity (fund capital)* can be estimated in several ways. First, the full opportunity cost approach uses the *cost of equity* of similar investor-owned firms. Alternatively, the cost of equity can be estimated by the *expected growth rate* of the business or the return-on-equity target set by *rating agencies* to maintain a desired bond rating.

- Each firm has a *target capital structure*, and the target weights are used to estimate the firm's *corporate cost of capital (CCC):*

$$CCC = [w_d \times R(R_d) \times (1 - T)] + [w_e \times R(R_e)].$$

- The CCC for small businesses is estimated using the same techniques that are used for large businesses. However, the estimation of the component costs, particularly the cost of equity, becomes more difficult.

(continued)

(continued from previous page)

- The *build-up method* is used to estimate the cost of equity for a small business. This method uses the *pure play method* (cost of equity of a similar large business) or the debt cost plus risk premium method to establish a starting point, and then adds (1) a *size premium*, (2) a *liquidity premium*, and (3) any *unique-risk premium*.
- When making *capital investment decisions*, a business will use the CCC as the *hurdle rate* for average-risk projects. A firm with divisions that operate in diverse lines of business should use divisional costs of capital for the same purpose.

The concepts developed in this chapter play a vital role in making capital investment decisions and are revisited in chapters 14 and 15.

Questions

13.1. Critique this statement: "The use of debt financing lowers the net income of the firm, so debt financing should be used only as a last resort."

13.2. What is meant by a firm's *debt capacity*?

13.3. Discuss some factors that health services managers must consider when setting a firm's target capital structure. Consider both investor-owned and not-for-profit firms in your answer.

13.4. Is the corporate cost-of-capital estimate based on historical or marginal costs? Why?

13.5. What capital components are typically included when estimating a firm's CCC?

13.6. How may a firm's cost of debt be estimated?

13.7. a. Why is there a cost to retained earnings in investor-owned businesses?

b. What are the three methods commonly used to estimate the cost of equity?

c. Is the risk premium in the CAPM the same as the risk premium in the debt cost plus risk premium model?

d. How would you estimate the cost of equity (fund capital) for a not-for-profit business?

e. How would you estimate the cost of equity for a small investor-owned business?

13.8. What is the economic interpretation of the CCC?

13.9. Is the CCC the same for all firms? Explain your answer.

13.10. For any given firm, can the CCC be used as the hurdle rate for all projects under consideration? Explain your answer.

Problems

13.1. Seattle Health Plans currently uses zero-debt financing. Its operating income (earnings before interest and taxes, or EBIT) is $1 million, and it pays taxes at a 30 percent rate. It has $5 million in assets and, because it is all-equity financed, $5 million in equity. Suppose the firm is considering replacing half of its equity financing with debt financing bearing an interest rate of 8 percent.

a. What impact would the new capital structure have on the firm's net income, total dollar return to investors, and return on equity (ROE)?

b. Redo the analysis, but now assume that the debt financing would cost 15 percent.

c. Return to the initial 8 percent interest rate. Now, assume that EBIT could be as low as $500,000 (with a probability of 20 percent) or as high as $1.5 million (with a probability of 20 percent). There remains a 60 percent chance that EBIT would be $1 million. Redo the analysis for each level of EBIT, and find the expected values for the firm's net income, total dollar return to investors, and ROE. What lesson about capital structure and risk does this illustration provide?

d. Repeat the analysis required for Part a, but now assume that Seattle Health Plans is a not-for-profit corporation and pays no taxes. Compare the results with those obtained in part a.

13.2. Calculate the after-tax cost of debt for the Wallace Clinic, a for-profit healthcare provider, assuming that the coupon rate set on its debt is 11 percent and its tax rate is

a. 0 percent.

b. 20 percent.

c. 30 percent.

13.3. St. Vincent's Health Care has a target capital structure of 35 percent debt and 65 percent equity. Its cost-of-equity (fund capital) estimate is 13.5 percent and its cost-of-tax-exempt-debt estimate is 7 percent. What is the hospital's CCC?

13.4. Richmond Clinic has obtained the following estimates for its costs of debt and equity at different capital structures:

Percent Debt	After-Tax Cost of Debt	Cost of Equity 0%
0%	—	16%
20	6.6%	17
40	7.8	19
60	10.2	22
80	14.0	27

What is the firm's optimal capital structure? (Hint: Calculate its corporate cost of capital at each structure. Also, note that data on component costs at alternative capital structures are not reliable in real-world situations.)

13.5. Medical Group is a large for-profit group practice. Its dividends are expected to grow at a constant rate of 7 percent per year into the foreseeable future. The firm's last dividend (D_0) was $2, and its current stock price is $23. The firm's beta coefficient is 1.6; the rate of return on 20-year T-bonds currently is 5 percent; and the expected rate of return on the market, as reported by a large financial services firm, is 8 percent. The firm's target capital structure calls for 50 percent debt financing, the interest rate required on the business's new debt is 10 percent, and its tax rate is 30 percent.

a. What is Medical Group's cost-of-equity estimate according to the DCF method?

b. What is the cost-of-equity estimate according to the CAPM?

c. On the basis of your answers to parts a and b, what would be your final estimate for the firm's cost of equity?

d. What is your estimate for the firm's CCC?

13.6. Morningview Nursing Home, a not-for-profit corporation, is estimating its CCC. Its tax-exempt debt currently requires an interest rate of 6.2 percent, and its target capital structure calls for 60 percent debt financing and 40 percent equity (fund capital) financing. The estimated costs of equity for selected investor-owned healthcare companies are as follows:

GlaxoSmithKline	15.0%
Long-Term Care Group Inc.	16.4
Encompass Health	17.4
Humana	18.8

a. What is the best estimate for Morningview's cost of equity?

b. What is the firm's CCC?

13.7. Golden State Home Health, Inc., is a large, California-based for-profit home health agency. Its dividends are expected to grow at a constant rate of 5 percent per year into the foreseeable future. The firm's last dividend (D_0) was $1, and its current stock price is $10. The firm's beta coefficient is 1.2; the rate of return on 20-year T-bonds currently is 4 percent; and the expected rate of return on the market, as reported by a large financial services firm, is 8 percent. Golden State's target capital structure calls for 60 percent debt financing, the interest rate required on its new debt is 9 percent, and the firm's tax rate is 30 percent.

a. What is the firm's cost-of-equity estimate according to the DCF method?

b. What is the cost-of-equity estimate according to the CAPM?

c. On the basis of your answers to parts a and b, what would be your final estimate for the firm's cost of equity?

d. What is your estimate for the firm's CCC?

13.8. A local entrepreneur is looking for investors in a new company that will develop mobile apps for behavioral health. The company requires $15 million in start-up funds. It can be capitalized with 100 percent equity financing or with 30 percent debt and 70 percent equity. EBIT is $3 million, and the company will pay taxes at a rate of 30 percent. Debt financing would bear an interest rate of 7 percent.

a. What would be the firm's net income, total dollar return to investors, and ROE with 100 percent equity financing?

b. What would be the firm's net income, total dollar return to investors, and ROE with 30 percent debt financing and 70 percent equity financing?

c. What factors should the investors consider when deciding on the appropriate capital structure?

13.9. A relatively small medical group practice is trying to estimate its CCC. The practice is 100 percent equity financed. The rate of return on 20-year Treasury bonds is currently 4 percent, and the expected rate of return on the market is 8 percent. A large practice management firm has a beta coefficient of 0.9. Market research indicates that the cost of equity for very small firms is approximately 4 percentage points higher than the cost of equity for large firms. Moreover, the investors in the small group practice face liquidity risk and thus determine that a liquidity premium of 2 percentage points is appropriate.

a. What is the best estimate of the firm's CCC?

   b. How would your estimate of the CCC change if the success of the medical group practice was highly dependent on the reputation of a single physician in the group?

Selected Cases

Two cases in *Gapenski's Cases in Healthcare Finance*, sixth edition, are applicable to this chapter: Case 17: Southeastern Homecare; and Case 18: RN Temps, Inc.

Notes

1. The use of preferred stock has roughly the same effect on a business's risk and return, and hence its capital structure decision, as debt financing. However, most businesses in the health services sector do not use preferred stock.

2. For a complete discussion of historical risk premiums, including a discussion of arithmetic and geometric averages, see Morningstar, Inc. 2013. *Ibbotson SBBI 2013 Classic Yearbook: Market Results for Stocks, Bonds, Bills, and Inflation 1926–2012.* Chicago: Morningstar Inc.

3. For one of the classic works on this topic, see Conrad, D. A. 1984. "Returns on Equity to Not-for-Profit Hospitals: Theory and Implementation." *Health Services Research* 19 (1): 41–63. Also, see the follow-up articles by M. V. Pauly, D. A. Conrad, and J. B. Silvers and R. T. Kauer in the April 1986 issue of *Health Services Research.*

4. For an excellent discussion of this issue, see Cleverley, W. O. 1982. "Return on Equity in the Hospital Industry: Requirement or Windfall?" *Inquiry* 19 (2): 150–59.

Resources

Arduino, K. 2018. "Healthcare Capital Markets Outlook: Short-Term Opportunities Versus Long-Term Uncertainty." *Healthcare Financial Management* 72 (5): 36–43.

Cleverley, W. O., and J. O. Cleverley. 2005. "The Link Between a Formal Debt Policy and Replacement Reserves." *Journal of Healthcare Management* 50 (3): 148–50.

Gordon, D. C. 2010. "Squeezing the Funding You Need from Today's Capital Sources." *Healthcare Financial Management* 64 (4): 46–55.

Healthcare Financial Management Association. 2018. "Optimizing Capital Structure Decisions Under the New Tax Law." *Healthcare Financial Management* 72 (8): A1–A4.

Jordahl, E. A. 2017. "Terminating Swap Positions." Healthcare Financial Management Association. Published December 1. www.hfma.org/Content.aspx?id =57108.

Jordahl, E. A., R. Freel, and D. Ratliff. 2016. "Four Current Market Concepts for Advance Refunding." *Healthcare Financial Management* 70 (12): 70–71.

Jordahl, E. A., M. Robbins, and M. Sedlmeier. 2016. "Meeting New Equipment Needs and Reducing Capital Costs." *Healthcare Financial Management* 70 (7): 60–62.

Smith, D. G., J. R. C. Wheeler, H. L. Rivenson, and K. L. Reiter. 2000. "Sources of Project Financing in Health Care Systems." *Journal of Health Care Finance* 26 (4): 53–58.

Trussel, J. 2012. "A Comparison of the Capital Structures of Nonprofit and Proprietary Health Care Organizations." *Journal of Health Care Finance* 39 (1): 1–11.

Wedig, G. J., M. Hassan, and M. A. Morrisey. 1996. "Tax-Exempt Debt and the Capital Structure of Nonprofit Organizations: An Application to Hospitals." *Journal of Finance* 51 (4): 1247–83.

Wheeler, J. R. C., D. G. Smith, H. L. Rivenson, and K. L. Reiter. 2000. "Capital Structure Strategy in Health Care Systems." *Journal of Health Care Finance* 26 (4): 42–52.

CAPITAL INVESTMENT DECISIONS

In part V, we focused on capital acquisition (long-term financing), including capital structure decisions and cost-of-capital estimation—in other words, how businesses raise the funds to buy needed land, buildings, and equipment and how they estimate the cost of those funds. In part VI, we turn our attention to the capital investment decision, focusing on how those funds can be deployed (spent) in the most financially efficient manner.

Our discussion of capital investment decisions spans two chapters. The most critical part of the decision process involves cash flow estimation, because the financial attractiveness of proposed projects stems solely from the cash flows they are expected to produce. Chapter 14 covers the basic concepts of capital investment analysis, including how to estimate a project's cash flows and how to measure its expected financial impact. In addition to cash flow estimation, risk is an important consideration in capital budgeting. Chapter 15 explains how to assess the risk of a project and incorporate that assessment into the capital investment decision process.

THE BASICS OF CAPITAL BUDGETING

Learning Objectives

After studying this chapter, readers will be able to

- Explain how managers use project classifications and post-audits in the capital budgeting process.
- Discuss the role of financial analysis in health services capital budgeting decisions.
- Explain the key issues involved in cash flow estimation.
- Describe the usefulness and methods applied in breakeven and profitability analyses.
- Conduct basic capital budgeting analyses.

Introduction

This chapter focuses on long-term (fixed) asset acquisition decisions, which involve the expenditure of capital funds. Such decisions commonly are called **capital budgeting decisions** because the listing of all capital investments (projects) to be undertaken in the future is known as the *capital budget*. Capital budgeting decisions are among the most critical decisions that health services managers must make. First and most important, the results of capital budgeting decisions generally affect the business for an extended period. If a business invests too heavily in facilities and equipment (fixed assets), it will have too much capacity and its costs will be too high. On the other hand, a business that invests too little in fixed assets may face two problems: technological obsolescence and inadequate capacity. A healthcare provider without the latest technology will lose patients to its more up-to-date competitors and deprive its patients of the best healthcare diagnostics and treatments available.

Effective capital budgeting procedures provide several benefits to businesses. A business that forecasts its needs for capital assets can plan those purchases carefully and thus negotiate the highest-quality assets at the best prices. In addition, asset expansion typically involves substantial expenditures, and because large amounts of funds are not usually at hand, they must be raised externally. Good capital budgeting practices permit a business to identify its

capital budgeting decisions
The process of selecting a business's capital (long-term asset) investments; the list of investments chosen constitutes a business's *capital budget*.

financing needs and sources well in advance, which ensures both the lowest possible financing costs and the availability of funds as they are needed.

Project Classifications

Although the careful analysis of capital investment proposals has many benefits, such efforts can be costly. For certain projects, a detailed analysis may be warranted; for others, simpler procedures should be used. Accordingly, healthcare businesses generally classify projects into categories and then analyze those in each category differently. For example, Ridgeland Community Hospital uses the following classifications:

- **Category 1: Mandatory replacement.** Category 1 consists of expenditures required to replace worn-out or damaged equipment necessary to the operations of the hospital. Because these expenditures are mandatory, they are usually made with only limited analyses and decision processes.
- **Category 2: Discretionary replacement.** This category includes expenditures made to replace serviceable but obsolete equipment. The purpose of these projects generally is to lower costs or to provide more clinically effective services. Because category 2 projects are not mandatory, a more detailed decision process is generally required to support the expenditure than that needed for category 1 projects.
- **Category 3: Expansion of existing services or markets.** Expenditures to increase capacity or expand within markets currently being served by the hospital are included here. These decisions are more complex, so even more detailed analysis is required, and the final decision is made at a higher level within the organization.
- **Category 4: Expansion into new services or markets.** These are projects necessary to provide new services or to expand into geographic areas not currently being served. Such projects involve strategic decisions that could change the fundamental nature of the hospital, and they normally require the expenditure of large sums of money over long periods of time. Invariably, a particularly detailed analysis is required, and the board of trustees generally makes the final decision as part of the hospital's strategic plan.
- **Category 5: Safety or environmental projects.** This category consists of expenditures necessary to comply with government orders, labor agreements, accreditation requirements, and so on. Unless the expenditures are large, category 5 expenditures are treated like category 1 expenditures.

- **Category 6: Other.** This category is a catchall for projects that do not fit neatly into another category. The primary determinant of how category 6 projects are evaluated is the amount of funds required.

In general, relatively simple analyses and only a few supporting documents are required for replacement decisions and safety or environmental projects, especially those that are mandatory. A more detailed analysis is required for expansion and other projects.

Within each category, projects are classified by size: Larger projects require increasingly detailed analyses and approval at a higher level within the hospital. For example, department heads can authorize spending up to $25,000 on discretionary replacement projects, while the full board of directors must approve expansion projects that cost more than $5 million.

SELF-TEST QUESTIONS

1. What is the primary advantage of classifying capital projects?
2. What are some typical classifications?
3. What role does project size (cost) play in the classifications?

The Role of Financial Analysis in Healthcare Capital Budgeting

For investor-owned businesses, in which maximizing owner wealth is the primary goal, the role of financial analysis in capital investment decisions is clear. Projects that contribute to owner wealth should be undertaken, while those that do not should be ignored. But what about not-for-profit businesses, which do not have wealth maximization as a goal? In such businesses, an appropriate goal is providing high-quality, cost-effective service to the communities served. (A strong argument could be made that this should also be the goal of investor-owned businesses in the health services sector.) In this situation, capital budgeting decisions must consider many factors besides a project's financial implications. For example, the needs of the medical staff and the good of the community also must be taken into account. In many instances, noneconomic factors will outweigh financial considerations.

Nevertheless, good decision-making and the future viability of healthcare businesses require that the financial impact of capital investments be fully recognized. If a healthcare provider takes on a series of highly unprofitable projects that meet nonfinancial goals, and such projects are not offset by profitable ones, the firm's financial condition will deteriorate. If this situation persists over time, the provider will eventually lose its financial viability and could even be forced into bankruptcy and closure. Of course, not-for-profit businesses can offset some project losses with contributions and grants. However, long-run financial sustainability is best ensured by striving for operating profitability rather than depending on less reliable sources of funds.

Because bankrupt firms cannot meet a community's needs, even managers of not-for-profit businesses must consider a project's potential impact on the firm's financial condition. Managers may make a conscious decision to accept a project with a poor financial prognosis because of its nonfinancial virtues, but it is important that managers know the financial impact up front, rather than be surprised when the project drains the firm's financial resources. Financial analysis provides managers with relevant information about a project's financial impact and helps managers make better decisions, including those decisions based primarily on nonfinancial considerations.

SELF-TEST QUESTIONS

1. What is the role of financial analysis in capital budgeting decision-making within for-profit firms?
2. Why is project financial analysis important in not-for-profit businesses?

Overview of Capital Budgeting Financial Analysis

The financial analysis of capital investment proposals typically involves four steps:

1. Estimate the project's expected cash flows, which consist of the following:
   a. The capital outlay, or cost
   b. The operating cash flows
   c. The terminal (ending) cash flow
   Cash flow estimation is discussed in the next section.
2. Assess the riskiness of the estimated cash flows. Risk assessment is discussed in chapter 15.
3. Given the riskiness of the project, estimate the project's cost of capital (opportunity cost or discount rate). As discussed in chapter 13, the corporate cost of capital reflects the aggregate risk of the business's assets—that is, the riskiness inherent in the average project. If the project being evaluated does not have average risk, the corporate

cost of capital must be adjusted to reflect the risk differential. Risk incorporation is also discussed in chapter 15.

4. Assess the financial impact of the project. Several measures can be used for this purpose; we discuss four in this chapter.

SELF-TEST QUESTION

> 1. Explain the four steps in capital budgeting financial analysis.

Cash Flow Estimation

The most critical, as well as most difficult, step in evaluating capital investment proposals is *cash flow estimation*. This step involves estimating the investment outlays, the annual net operating flows expected when the project goes into operation, and the cash flows associated with project termination. Many variables are involved in cash flow estimation, and many individuals and departments participate in the process. Making accurate projections of the costs and revenues associated with a large, complex project is difficult, so forecast errors can be quite large. Thus, it is essential that risk analyses be performed on prospective projects.

Neither the difficulty nor the importance of cash flow estimation can be overstated. However, if the concepts discussed in the next sections are observed, errors that often arise can be minimized.

Incremental Cash Flows

The relevant cash flows to consider when evaluating a new capital investment are the project's **incremental cash flows**, which are defined as the business's cash flows in each period if the project is undertaken minus the cash flows if the project is not undertaken:

$$\text{Incremental } CF_t = CF_{t(\text{Business with project})} - CF_{t(\text{Business without project})}.$$

incremental cash flow
A cash flow that arises solely from a project that is being evaluated and hence should be included in the project analysis.

In this equation, the subscript t specifies a time period—often years. CF_0 is the incremental cash flow during year 0, which is generally assumed to be the beginning of the project; CF_1 is the incremental cash flow during the first year; CF_2 is the incremental cash flow during year 2; and so on. In practice, the early incremental cash flows, particularly in year 0, are usually cash outflows—the costs associated with getting the project up and running. As the project begins to generate revenues, the incremental cash flows normally turn positive.

In practice, it typically is not feasible to forecast the cash flows of a business with and without a new project. Thus, the actual estimation process focuses on the cash flows unique to the project being evaluated. However, if a doubt ever arises as to whether a particular cash flow is relevant to the analysis, it is often useful to fall back on the basic definition given here.

Cash Flow Versus Accounting Income

Accounting income statements prepared in accordance with generally accepted accounting principles (GAAP) are, in some respects, a mix of apples and oranges. For example, accountants deduct labor costs (which are cash outflows) from revenues (which may not be entirely cash). (For healthcare providers, most of the collections are from third-party payers, and payment may not be received until several months after the service is provided.) At the same time, the income statement does not recognize capital outlays (which are cash flows), but it does deduct depreciation expense (which is not a cash flow). In capital investment decisions, it is critical that decisions be based on the actual dollars flowing into and out of the business, because a business's true profitability—and hence its ability to provide healthcare services—depends on its cash flows and not on income as reported in accordance with GAAP. Note, however, that accounting items can influence cash flows because items such as depreciation can affect tax or reimbursement cash flows.

Cash Flow Timing

Financial analysts must be careful to account for the timing of cash flows. Accounting income statements are for periods, such as years or quarters, so they do not reflect exactly when revenues and expenses occur during the period. In theory, capital budgeting cash flows should be analyzed exactly as they occur. Of course, there must be a compromise between accuracy and practicality. A time line with daily cash flows would, in theory, provide the most accuracy, but daily cash flow estimates are difficult to perform, unwieldy to use, and probably no more accurate than annual cash flows. Thus, in most cases, analysts simply assume that all cash flows occur at the end of each year. However, for projects with regular, easy-to-forecast cash flows, it may be more appropriate to assume that cash flows occur every six months or even quarterly or monthly.

Project Life

One of the first decisions that must be made in forecasting a project's cash flows is the life of the project. Is it necessary to forecast cash flows for 20 years, or is five years sufficient? Many projects, such as a new hospital or ambulatory care clinic, have long productive lives. In theory, a cash flow forecast should extend for the full life of a project, yet most managers would have little confidence in any cash flow forecasts beyond the near term. Thus, most organizations set an arbitrary limit on the project life assumed in capital budgeting analyses—often five or ten years. If the forecast life is less than the arbitrary limit, the forecast life is used to develop the cash flows. If the forecast life exceeds the limit, project life is truncated and the operating cash flows beyond the limit are ignored in the analysis.

Although cash flow truncation is a practical solution to a difficult problem, it creates another problem: The value inherent in the cash flows beyond the truncation point is lost to the project. This problem can be addressed either objectively or subjectively. The standard procedure at some organizations is to estimate the project's **terminal value**, which is the esti-mated value of the cash flows beyond the truncation point. Sometimes, the terminal value is estimated as the *liquidation value* of the project at that point in time. If the terminal value is too difficult to estimate, the fact that some portion of the project's cash flow value is being ignored should, at a minimum, be recognized by decision makers. The saving grace is that cash flows forecast well into the future typically contribute a small amount to a project's initial profitability estimate. For example, a $100,000 terminal value projected ten years in the future contributes only about $38,500 to the project's value when the project cost of capital (discount rate) is 10 percent.

Some projects have short lives, and hence the analysis can extend over the project's entire life. In such situations, the assets associated with the project may still have some value remaining when the project is terminated. The cash flow expected to be realized from selling the project's assets at ter-mination is called the **salvage value**. Even if a project is terminated for "old age," any cash flow that arises by virtue of scrap value must be included in the project's cash flow estimates. For investor-owned businesses, such asset sales typically will trigger tax consequences, which are discussed in the cash flow estimation example presented in the next major section.

terminal value
An estimate of the value of the cash flows beyond the truncation point when a project's cash flows are arbitrarily truncated.

salvage value
The expected market value of an asset (project) at the end of its useful life.

Sunk Costs

A **sunk cost** refers to an outlay that has already occurred or has been irrevocably committed, so it is an outlay that is unaffected by the current decision to accept or reject a project. To illustrate, suppose that in 2020, Ridgeland Community Hospital is evaluating the purchase of a lithotripter system. To help in the decision, the hospital hired and paid $10,000 to a consultant in 2019 to conduct a marketing study. This cash flow is not relevant to the capital investment decision; Ridgeland cannot recover it regardless of whether the lithotripter is purchased. Cash flows that are not relevant to the analysis are called **nonincremental cash flows**. Sometimes a project appears to be unprofitable when *all* of its associated costs, including sunk costs, are considered. However, on an *incremental* basis, the project may be profitable and should be undertaken. Thus, the correct treatment of sunk costs may be critical to the decision.

Opportunity Costs

All relevant *opportunity costs* must be included in a capital investment analysis. To illustrate, one opportunity cost involves the use of the funds required to finance the project. If a business uses its capital to invest in project A, it cannot use the capital to invest in project B or for any other purpose. The opportunity cost associated with capital use is accounted for in the project cost of capital, which represents the return that the business could earn by investing in alternative investments of similar risk. The mathematics of the discounting process forces the opportunity cost of capital to be considered in the analysis.

There are other types of opportunity costs that arise in capital budgeting analyses. For example, assume that Ridgeland's lithotripter would be installed in a freestanding facility and that the hospital currently owns the land on which the facility would be constructed. In fact, the hospital purchased the land ten years ago at a cost of $50,000, but the current market value of the property is $130,000, after deducting legal and real estate fees. When evaluating the lithotripter, the value of the land cannot be disregarded merely because no cash outlay is necessary. An opportunity cost is inherent in the use of the property because using the property for the lithotripter facility deprives Ridgeland of its use for other purposes. The property might be used for a walk-in clinic, an ambulatory surgery center, or a parking garage rather than sell it. But the best measure of its value to Ridgeland, and hence the opportunity cost inherent in its use, is the cash flow that could be realized by selling it.

By considering the property's current market value, Ridgeland is letting market forces assign the value for the land's best alternative use. Thus, the lithotripter project should have a $130,000 opportunity cost charged against it. The opportunity cost is the property's $130,000 net market value, irrespective of whether the property was acquired for $50,000 or $200,000.

Effects on Existing Business Lines

Capital budgeting analyses must consider the effects of the project under consideration on the firm's existing business lines. Such effects can be either positive or negative; when negative, it is often called *cannibalization*. To illustrate, assume that some of the patients who are expected to use Ridgeland's new lithotripter would have been treated surgically at the hospital; so these surgical revenues will be lost if the lithotripter facility goes into operation. Thus, the incremental cash flows to Ridgeland are the flows attributable to the lithotripter, *less* those lost from forgone surgery services.

On the other hand, new patients who use the lithotripter may use ancillary services provided by the hospital. In this situation, the incremental net cash flows generated by the lithotripter patients' utilization of other services should be credited to the lithotripter project. If possible, both positive and negative effects on other projects should be quantified, but at a minimum they should be noted so that these effects are subjectively considered when the final decision regarding the project is made.

Shipping, Installation, and Related Costs

When a business acquires new equipment, it often incurs substantial costs for shipping and installation or for other related activities. These charges must be added to the invoice price of the equipment to determine the overall cost of the project. Also, the full cost of the equipment, including shipping and installation charges, typically is used as the basis for calculating depreciation charges. Thus, if Ridgeland purchases intensive care monitoring equipment that costs $800,000, but another $200,000 is required for shipping and installation, the full cost of the equipment would be $1 million, and this amount would be the starting point (cost basis) for both tax calculations (when applicable) and all depreciation calculations.

Changes in Current Accounts

Normally, expansion projects require additional inventories, and expanded patient volumes also lead to additional accounts receivable. The increase in these current assets must be financed, just as an increase in fixed assets must be financed. (Increases on the asset side of the balance sheet must be offset by matching increases on the liabilities and equity side.) However, accounts payable and accruals will probably also increase as a result of the expansion, and these current liability funds will reduce the net cash needed to finance the increase in inventories and receivables.

The impact of such changes in current accounts must be recognized in a capital budgeting analysis. If the increase in current assets exceeds the increase in current liabilities, this amount is as much a cash cost to the project as the dollar cost of the asset. Such projects must be charged an additional amount above the dollar cost of the new fixed asset to reflect the net financing needed for current asset accounts. Alternatively, if the increase in current liabilities assets exceeds the increase in current assets, the project generates a positive cash flow. In this situation, the increase in liabilities exceeds the project's current asset requirements, and this cash flow partially offsets the cost of the asset's acquisition.

As the project approaches termination, inventories will be sold off and not replaced, and receivables will be converted to cash without new receivables being created. In effect, the business will recover its change in current accounts when the project is terminated. This will result in a cash flow that is equal but *opposite* in sign to the cash flow that arises at the beginning of a project.

For healthcare providers, for which inventories often represent a very small part of the investment in new projects, the change in current accounts often can be ignored without materially affecting the results of the analysis. However, when a project requires a large positive change in current accounts (current assets increase by a much greater amount than current liabilities), failure to consider the net change will result in an overstatement of the project's profitability.

Inflation Effects

Inflation effects can have a considerable influence on a project's profitability, so inflation must be considered in any sound capital budgeting analysis. As discussed in chapter 13, a firm's corporate cost of capital is a weighted average of its costs of debt and equity. These costs are estimated on the basis of investors' required rates of return, for which investors incorporate an inflation premium. For example, a debt investor might require a 5 percent return on a ten-year bond in the absence of inflation. However, if inflation is expected to average 4 percent over the coming ten years, the investor would require a 9 percent return. Thus, both equity and debt investors add an inflation premium to their required rates of return to help protect them against the loss of purchasing power that stems from inflation.

Because inflation effects are already embedded in the corporate cost of capital, and because this cost will be used as the starting point to discount the cash flows in the profitability measures, inflation effects must also be built into the project's estimated cash flows. If cash flow estimates do not include inflation effects, but a discount rate is used that includes inflation effects, the profitability of the project will be understated.

The most effective way to deal with inflation is to apply inflation effects to each cash flow component using the best available information about how each component will be affected. Because it is impossible to estimate future inflation rates with much precision, errors will probably be made. Often, inflation is assumed to be *neutral* (i.e., it is assumed to affect all revenue and cost components, except depreciation, equally). However, at certain times, it is common for costs to be rising faster than revenues or vice versa. Thus, in general, it is better to apply different inflation rates to each cash flow component. For example, net revenues might be expected to increase at a 3 percent rate, while labor costs might be expected to increase at a 5 percent rate. Inflation adds to the uncertainty and risk of a project under consideration as well as to the complexity of the capital budgeting analysis. Fortunately, computers and spreadsheet programs can easily handle the mechanics of inflation analysis.

Strategic Value

Sometimes a project will have value in addition to that inherent in its cash flows. **Strategic value** is the value that stems from future investment opportunities that can be undertaken only if the project currently under consideration is accepted.

strategic value
The value of future investment opportunities that can be undertaken only if the project currently under consideration is accepted.

To illustrate this concept, consider a hospital management company that is analyzing a management contract for a hospital in Hungary, which is its first move into Eastern Europe. On a stand-alone basis, this project might be unprofitable, but the project might provide entry into the Eastern European market, which could open the door to a range of highly profitable new projects. Or consider Ridgeland Community Hospital's decision to start a kidney transplant program. The financial analysis of this project showed the program to be unprofitable, but Ridgeland's managers considered kidney transplants to be the first step in an aggressive transplant program that not only would be profitable but also would enhance the hospital's reputation for technological and clinical excellence, thereby contributing to the hospital's overall profitability.

In theory, the best way to deal with strategic value is to forecast the cash flows from the follow-on projects, estimate their probabilities of occurrence, and then add the expected cash flows from the follow-on projects to the cash flows of the project under consideration. In practice, this is usually impossible to do because either the follow-on cash flows are too nebulous to forecast or the potential follow-on projects are too numerous to quantify. At a minimum, decision makers must recognize that some projects have strategic value, and this value should be qualitatively considered when making capital budgeting decisions.

1. Briefly discuss the following concepts associated with cash flow estimation:
   a. Incremental cash flow
   b. Cash flow versus accounting income
   c. Cash flow timing
   d. Project life
   e. Terminal value
   f. Salvage value
   g. Sunk costs
   h. Opportunity costs
   i. Effects on current business lines
   j. Shipping and installation costs
   k. Changes in current accounts
   l. Inflation effects
   m. Strategic value

2. Evaluate the following statement: "Ignoring inflation effects and strategic value can result in *overstating* a project's financial attractiveness."

Cash Flow Estimation Example

Up to this point, we have discussed several critical aspects of cash flow estimation. In this section, we illustrate some of the concepts already covered and introduce several others that are important to good cash flow estimation.

For Your Consideration
Cash Flow Estimation Bias

As you know, cash flow estimation is the most critical and most difficult part of the capital budgeting process. Cash flows often must be forecast many years into the future, and estimation errors (some of which may be large) are bound to occur.[1] However, as long as cash flow estimates are unbiased and the errors are random, they will tend to offset one another if many projects are being considered. Thus, in the aggregate, realized profitability will be close to that expected.

(continued)

The Basic Data

Consider the situation facing Ridgeland in its evaluation of a new magnetic resonance imaging (MRI) system. The system costs $1.5 million, and the not-for-profit hospital would have to spend another $1 million for site preparation and installation. Because the system would be installed in the hospital, the space to be used has a low, or zero, market value to outsiders, so no opportunity cost has been assigned to account for the value of the site.

The MRI system is estimated to have weekly utilization (i.e., volume) of 40 scans, and each scan, on average, would cost the hospital $15 in supplies. The system is expected to be in operation 50 weeks a year, with the remaining two weeks devoted to maintenance. The estimated average charge per scan is $500, but 25 percent of this amount, on average, is expected to be lost to charity care patients, contractual allowances, and bad debt losses. Thus, the average reimbursement per scan is $500 × 0.75 = $375. Ridgeland's managers developed the project's forecast revenues by conducting the revenue analysis contained in exhibit 14.1.

The MRI system would require one technician, resulting in an incremental increase in annual labor costs of $50,000, including fringe benefits. Cash overhead costs would increase by $10,000 annually if the MRI is activated. The equipment would require maintenance, which would be furnished by the manufacturer for an annual fee of $150,000, payable at the end of each year of operation. For book purposes, the MRI will be depreciated by the straight-line method over a five-year life.

The MRI system is expected to operate for five years, at which time the hospital's master plan calls for a new imaging facility. The hospital plans to sell the MRI at that time for an estimated $750,000 salvage value, net of

(continued from previous page)

Unfortunately, there is evidence that some managers tend to overstate revenues and understate costs, which results in an upward bias in estimated profitability.[2] If this occurs, more projects will be accepted than would be the case if no bias existed. There are several reasons for cash flow estimation bias. Perhaps managers have an incentive to maximize department size rather than profitability. Or managers may become emotionally attached to their project proposals and are unable to make objective estimates.

Do you think that cash flow estimation bias exists in healthcare providers? If so, why might that be the case? What are some steps that senior management could take to eliminate, or at least reduce, the bias?

EXHIBIT 14.1
Ridgeland Community Hospital: MRI System Revenue Analysis

Payer	Number of Scans per Week	Charge per Scan	Total Charges	Basis of Payment	Net Payment per Scan	Net Revenue
Medicare	10	$500	$ 5,000	Fixed fee	$370	$ 3,700
Medicaid	5	500	2,500	Fixed fee	350	1,750
Private insurance	9	500	4,500	Full charge	500	4,500
Blue Cross	5	500	2,500	Percent of charge	420	2,100
Managed care	7	500	3,500	Percent of charge	390	2,730
Self-pay	4	500	2,000	Full charge	55	220
Total	40		$20,000			$15,000
Average			$ 500			$ 375

EXHIBIT 14.2
Ridgeland Community Hospital: MRI Project Cash Flow Analysis

	0	1	2	3	4	5
			Cash Revenues and Costs			
1. System cost	($1,500,000)					
2. Related expenses	(1,000,000)					
3. Net revenues		$750,000	$787,500	$826,875	$868,219	$ 911,629
4. Labor costs		50,000	52,500	55,125	57,881	60,775
5. Maintenance costs		150,000	157,500	165,375	173,644	182,326
6. Supplies		30,000	31,500	33,075	34,729	36,465
7. Incremental overhead		10,000	10,500	11,025	11,576	12,155
8. Depreciation		350,000	350,000	350,000	350,000	350,000
9. Operating income		$160,000	$185,500	$ 212,275	$240,389	$ 269,908
10. Taxes		0	0	0	0	0
11. Net operating income		$160,000	$185,500	$ 212,275	$240,389	$ 269,908
12. Depreciation		350,000	350,000	350,000	350,000	350,000
13. Net salvage value						750,000
14. Net cash flow	($2,500,000)	$510,000	$535,500	$562,275	$590,389	$1,369,908

Note: Totals are rounded.

removal costs. The inflation rate is estimated to average 5 percent over the period, and this rate is expected to affect all revenues and costs except depreciation. Ridgeland's managers initially assume that projects under evaluation have average risk, and thus the hospital's 10 percent corporate cost of capital is the appropriate project cost of capital (opportunity cost discount rate). In chapter 15, we demonstrate that a risk assessment of the project may indicate that a different cost of capital is appropriate.

Although the MRI project is expected to take away some patients from the hospital's other imaging systems, new MRI patients are expected to generate revenues for some of the hospital's other departments. On net, the two effects are expected to balance out—that is, the cash flow loss from other imaging systems is expected to be offset by the cash flow gain from other services used by new MRI patients.

Cash Flow Analysis (Not-for-Profit Businesses)

The first step in the financial analysis is to estimate the MRI site's net cash flows. This analysis is presented in exhibit 14.2, which shows the key points of the analysis by line number.

- **Line 1.** Line 1 contains the estimated cost of the MRI system. In general, capital budgeting analyses assume that the first cash flow, normally an outflow, occurs at the end of year 0. Expenses, or cash outflows, are shown in parentheses.
- **Line 2.** The related site construction expense, $1,000,000, is also assumed to occur at year 0.
- **Line 3.** Annual net revenues = Weekly volume × Weeks of operation per year × Net revenue per scan = 40 × 50 × $375 = $750,000 in the first year. The 5 percent inflation rate is applied to all charges and costs that would likely be affected by inflation, so the amount shown on line 3 increases by 5 percent over time. Although most of the operating revenues and costs would occur more or less evenly over the year, it is difficult to forecast exactly when the flows would occur. Furthermore, there is significant potential for large errors in cash flow estimation. For these reasons, operating cash flows are often assumed to occur at the end of each year. Also, we assume that the MRI system could be put into operation quickly. If this were not the case, the first year's operating flows would be reduced. In some situations, it might take several years from the first investment cash flow to the point when the project is operational and begins to generate revenues.
- **Line 4.** Labor costs are forecast to be $50,000 during the first year, and they are assumed to increase over time at the 5 percent inflation rate.

- **Line 5.** Maintenance fees must be paid to the manufacturer at the end of each year of operation. These fees are assumed to increase at the 5 percent inflation rate.
- **Line 6.** Each scan uses $15 of supplies, so supply costs in the first-year total 40 × 50 × $15 = $30,000, which are expected to increase each year by the inflation rate.
- **Line 7.** If the project is accepted, overhead cash costs will increase by $10,000 in the first year. Note that the $10,000 expenditure is a *cash cost* that is related directly to the acceptance of the MRI project. Existing overhead costs that are arbitrarily allocated to the MRI project are *not* incremental cash flows and thus should not be included in the analysis. Overhead costs are also assumed to increase over time at the inflation rate.
- **Line 8.** Book depreciation in each year is calculated by the straight-line method, assuming a five-year depreciable life. The depreciable basis is equal to the capitalized cost of the project, which includes the cost of the asset and related construction, less the estimated salvage value. Thus, the depreciable basis is ($1,500,000 + $1,000,000) − $750,000 = $1,750,000, and the straight-line depreciation in each year of the project's five-year depreciable life is $1,750,000 ÷ 5 = $350,000. Note that depreciation is based solely on acquisition costs, so it is unaffected by inflation. Also, note that the exhibit 14.2 cash flows are presented in a generic format that can be used by both investor-owned and not-for-profit hospitals. Depreciation expense is not a cash flow but an accounting convention that amortizes the cost of a fixed asset over its revenue-producing life. Because Ridgeland is tax exempt, depreciation will not affect taxes, and because depreciation is added back to the cash flows on line 12, *depreciation could be totally omitted from the cash flow analysis.*
- **Line 9.** Operating income in each year is calculated as net revenues less all operating expenses.
- **Line 10.** Ridgeland is a not-for-profit hospital and does not pay taxes; thus, this line contains zeros.
- **Line 11.** Ridgeland pays no taxes, so the project's net operating income equals its operating income.
- **Line 12.** Because depreciation, a noncash expense, was included on line 8, it must be added back to the project's net operating income in each year to obtain each year's net cash flow.
- **Line 13.** The project is expected to be terminated after five years, at which time the MRI system would be sold for an estimated $750,000. This salvage value cash flow is shown as an inflow at the end of year 5.

- **Line 14.** The project's net cash flows consist of a $2,500,000 investment at year 0 followed by five years of cash inflows.

   The cash flows shown in exhibit 14.2 do not include interest expense on any debt financing that might be required to fund the project. On average, Ridgeland will finance new projects in accordance with its target capital structure, which consists of 50 percent debt financing and 50 percent equity (fund) financing. The costs associated with this financing mix, including both interest costs and the opportunity cost of equity capital, are incorporated into the firm's 10 percent corporate cost of capital. Because the cost of debt financing is included in the discount rate that will be applied to the cash flows, recognition of interest expense in the cash flows would be double counting.

Cash Flow Analysis (For-Profit Businesses)

The cash flow analysis presented in exhibit 14.2 can be easily modified to reflect tax implications if the analyzing organization is a for-profit business. To illustrate, assume that the MRI project is being evaluated by Ann Arbor Health Care Inc., an investor-owned hospital chain. Assume also that all of the project data presented earlier apply to Ann Arbor, except that the MRI falls into the *Modified Accelerated Cost Recovery System (MACRS)* five-year class for tax depreciation and the firm has a 30 percent tax rate.

   Exhibit 14.3 contains Ann Arbor's cash flow analysis. Note the following differences from the not-for-profit analysis performed in exhibit 14.2:

- **Line 8.** Depreciation expense must be modified to reflect *tax depreciation* rather than *book depreciation*. Tax depreciation is calculated using the MACRS as specified in current tax laws. Each year's tax depreciation is found by multiplying the asset's depreciable basis, *without reduction by the estimated salvage value*, by the appropriate depreciation factor. In this illustration, the depreciable basis is $2,500,000, and the MRI system falls into the MACRS five-year class, so the MACRS factors specified by the tax code are 0.20, 0.32, 0.19, 0.12, 0.11, and 0.06, in years 1 to 6, respectively. Thus, the tax depreciation in year 1 is 0.20 × $2,500,000 = $500,000, in year 2 the depreciation is 0.32 × $2,500,000 = $800,000, and so on. (Tax laws are complex and change often. Therefore, this book does not include a complete discussion of MACRS. For more information, see either the Internal Revenue Service [IRS] publication pertaining to depreciation or any of the many tax guidebooks available at bookstores or online.)
- **Line 10.** Taxable firms must reduce the operating income on line 9 by the amount of taxes. Taxes, which appear on line 10, are computed by multiplying the line 9 pretax operating income by the firm's marginal

EXHIBIT 14.3
Ann Arbor Health Care Inc.: MRI Project Cash Flow Analysis

	0	1	2	3	4	5
				Cash Revenues and Costs		
1. System cost	($1,500,000)					
2. Related expenses	(1,000,000)					
3. Net revenues		$750,000	$787,500	$826,875	$868,219	$ 911,629
4. Labor costs		50,000	52,500	55,125	57,881	60,775
5. Maintenance costs		150,000	157,500	165,375	173,644	182,326
6. Supplies		30,000	31,500	33,075	34,729	36,465
7. Incremental overhead		10,000	10,500	11,025	11,576	12,155
8. Depreciation		500,000	800,000	475,000	300,000	275,000
9. Operating income		$ 10,000	($264,500)	$ 87,275	$290,389	$ 344,908
10. Taxes		3,000	(79,350)	26,183	87,117	103,472
11. Net operating income		$ 7,000	$ 185,150	$ 61,093	$203,272	$ 241,436
12. Depreciation		500,000	800,000	475,000	300,000	275,000
13. Net salvage value						$ 570,000
14. Net cash flow	($2,500,000)	$507,000	$614,850	$536,093	$503,272	$1,086,436

Note: Totals are rounded.

tax rate. For example, the project's taxes for year 1 are 0.30 × $10,000 = $3,000. The taxes shown for year 2 are a negative $79,350. In this year, the project is expected to lose $264,500, and hence Ann Arbor's taxable income, assuming that its existing projects are sufficiently profitable, will be reduced by this amount if the project is undertaken.

This reduction in Ann Arbor's overall taxable income would lower the firm's tax bill by T × Reduction in taxable income = 0.30 × $264,500 = $79,350.[3]

- **Line 12.** The MACRS depreciation amount, because it is a noncash expense, is added back in line 12.

- **Line 13.** Investor-owned firms will normally incur a tax liability on the sale of a capital asset at the end of the project's life. According to the IRS, the value of the MRI system at the end of year 5 is the *tax book value*, which is the depreciation that remains on the tax books. For the MRI, five years' worth of depreciation would be taken, so only one year of depreciation remains. The MACRS factor for year 6 is 0.06, so by the end of year 5, Ann Arbor has expensed 0.94 of the MRI's depreciable basis and the remaining tax book value is 0.06 × $2,500,000 = $150,000. Thus, according to the IRS, the value of the MRI system is $150,000. When Ann Arbor sells the system for its estimated salvage value of $750,000, it realizes a "profit" of $750,000 − $150,000 = $600,000, and it must repay the IRS an amount equal to 0.3 × $600,000 = $180,000. The $180,000 tax bill recognizes that Ann Arbor took too much depreciation on the MRI system, so it represents a *recapture* of the excess tax benefit taken over the five-year life of the system. The $180,000 in taxes reduces the cash flow received from the sale of the MRI equipment, so the salvage value net of taxes is $750,000 − $180,000 = $570,000.

As can be seen by comparing line 14 in exhibits 14.2 and 14.3, all else being equal, the taxes paid by investor-owned firms tend to reduce a project's net operating cash flows and net salvage value, reducing the project's financial attractiveness.

Replacement Analysis

We used Ridgeland's MRI project to illustrate how the cash flows from an *expansion project* are analyzed. All businesses, including Ridgeland, also make *replacement decisions*, in which a new asset is considered to replace an existing asset that could, if not replaced, continue in operation. The cash flow analysis for a replacement decision is somewhat more complex than for an expansion decision because the cash flows from the existing asset must be considered.

Again, the key to cash flow estimation is to focus on the *incremental cash flows*. If the new asset is acquired, the existing asset can be sold, so the current market value of the existing asset is a cash inflow in the analysis. The incremental flows are the cash flows expected from the replacement asset less the flows that the existing asset would produce if not replaced. By applying the incremental cash flow concept, we can estimate the correct cash flows for replacement decisions.

SELF-TEST QUESTIONS

1. Briefly describe how a project cash flow analysis is constructed.
2. Is it necessary to include depreciation expense in a cash flow analysis by a not-for-profit provider? Explain your answer.
3. What are the key differences in cash flow analyses performed by investor-owned and not-for-profit businesses?
4. How do expansion and replacement cash flow analyses differ?

payback period
The number of years it takes for a business to recover its investment in a project without considering the time value of money.

Breakeven Analysis

Breakeven analysis was introduced in chapter 5 in conjunction with breakeven volume in an accounting profit analysis. Now, the breakeven concept is applied in a project analysis setting. In project analyses, many different types of breakeven can be determined. Rather than discuss all possible types of breakeven, here we focus on one type—time breakeven.

Payback is defined as the expected number of years required to recover the investment in a project, so *payback*, or **payback period**, measures time breakeven. To illustrate, consider the net cash flows for the MRI project contained on line 14 in exhibit 14.2. The best way to determine the MRI's payback is to construct the project's *cumulative cash flows* as shown in exhibit 14.4. The cumulative cash flow at any point in time is simply the sum of all the cash flows (with proper sign indicating an inflow or outflow) that have

Healthcare in Practice
Discounted Payback

The *discounted payback* is a breakeven measure similar to the conventional payback, except that the cash flows in each year are discounted to year 0 by the project's cost of capital (but kept at their original positions on the time line) prior to calculating the cumulative cash flows and payback. Thus, the discounted payback solves the conventional payback's problem of not considering the project's cost of capital in the payback calculation.

The table below contains the calculation for Ridgeland's MRI project. Note that each entry in the middle column is the matching annual cash

(continued)

occurred up to that point. Thus, in exhibit 14.4, the cumulative cash flow at year 0 is −$2,500,000; at year 1, it is −$2,500,000 + $510,000 = −$1,990,000; in year 2, it is −$2,500,000 + $510,000 + $535,500 = −$1,990,000 + $535,500 = −$1,454,500; and so on.

As shown in the rightmost column of exhibit 14.4, the $2,500,000 investment in the MRI project will be recovered at the end of year 5 if the cash flow forecasts are correct. Furthermore, if the cash flows are assumed to come in evenly during the year, breakeven will occur $301,836 ÷ $1,369,908 = 0.22 years into year 5, so the MRI project's payback is 4.22 years.

Initially, payback was used by managers as the primary financial evaluation tool in project analyses. For example, a business might accept all projects with paybacks of five years or less. However, payback has two serious deficiencies when it is used as a project selection criterion. First, payback ignores all cash flows that occur after the payback period. To illustrate, Ridgeland might be evaluating a competing project that has the same cash flows as the MRI

(continued from previous page)

flow discounted at the 10 percent cost of capital for the number of years it occurs in the future. For example, the discounted year 2 cash flow is $535,500 ÷ (1.10)^2 = $442,562.

Year	Annual Cash Flows	Discounted Cash Flows	Cumulative Cash Flows
0	($2,500,000)	($2,500,000)	($2,500,000)
1	510,000	463,636	(2,036,304)
2	535,500	442,562	(1,593,802)
3	562,275	422,446	(1,171,356)
4	590,389	403,244	(768,112)
5	1,369,908	850,605	82,493

Now, with the counted instead of raw cash flows, the payback is 4 + (768,112 ÷ 850,605) = 4.90 years. Because time value is recognized in the discounted payback, it takes longer than the conventional payback (4.22 years) to recover the initial investment.

What do you think? Is the discounted payback a better measure of time breakeven than the conventional payback? Does it solve all the conventional payback's problems?

project in years 0 through 5. However, the alternative project might have a cash inflow of $2 million in year 6. Both projects would have the same payback, 4.22 years, and hence be ranked the same, even though the alternative project clearly is better from a financial perspective. Second, payback ignores the opportunity costs associated with the capital employed. For these reasons, payback generally is no longer used as the primary evaluation tool.

In spite of its shortcomings, payback is useful in capital investment analysis. The shorter the payback, the more quickly the funds invested in a project will become available for other purposes and the more *liquid* the project. Also, cash flows expected in the distant future are generally regarded as being riskier than near-term cash flows, so shorter payback projects generally are less *risky* than those with longer paybacks. Therefore, payback is often used as a rough measure of a project's liquidity and risk.

EXHIBIT 14.4
Ridgeland
Community
Hospital: MRI
System Annual
and Cumulative
Cash Flows

Year	Annual Cash Flows	Cumulative Cash Flows
0	($2,500,000)	($2,500,000)
1	510,000	(1,990,000)
2	535,500	(1,454,500)
3	562,275	(892,225)
4	590,389	(301,836)
5	1,369,908	1,068,072

**SELF-TEST
QUESTIONS**

1. What is payback?
2. What are the benefits of payback?
3. What are its deficiencies when used as the primary evaluation tool?

Return on Investment (Profitability) Analysis

**return on
investment (ROI)**
The estimated
financial return on
an investment. In
capital budgeting
analysis, ROI can
be measured
either in dollars or
percentage (rate
of) return.

Up to this point, the chapter has focused on cash flow estimation and break-even analysis. Perhaps the most important element in a project's financial analysis is its expected profitability, which generally is expressed by **return on investment (ROI)**, measured either in dollars or in percentage (rate of) return. In the next sections, we discuss one dollar measure and two rate-of-return ROI measures.

Net Present Value

Net present value (NPV), first discussed in chapter 9, is a profitability (or dollar ROI) measure that uses discounted cash flow (DCF) techniques, so it is often referred to as a *DCF profitability measure*. To apply the NPV method:

- Find the present (time 0) value of each net cash flow, including both inflows and outflows, when discounted at the project's cost of capital.
- Sum the present values. This sum is defined as the project's net present value.
- If the NPV is positive, the project is expected to be profitable, and the higher the NPV, the more profitable the project. If the NPV is zero, the project breaks even in an economic sense. If the NPV is negative, the project is expected to be unprofitable.

With a project cost of capital of 10 percent, the NPV of Ridgeland's MRI project is calculated as follows:

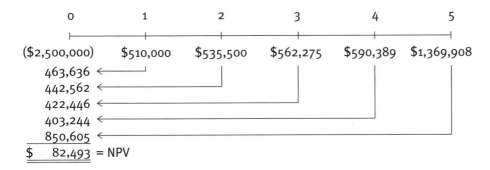

Spreadsheets have NPV functions that easily perform the mathematics if given the cash flows and cost of capital.[4] Here is the spreadsheet solution:

	A	B	C	D
1				
2	10.0%		Project cost of capital	
3	$ (2,500,000)		Cash flow 0	
4	510,000		Cash flow 1	
5	535,500		Cash flow 2	
6	562,275		Cash flow 3	
7	590,389		Cash flow 4	
8	1,369,908		Cash flow 5	
9				
10	$ 82,493	=NPV(A2,A4:A8)+A3 (entered into Cell A10)		

Here, we have merely entered the net cash flows into the spreadsheet. In a typical project analysis, the spreadsheet would be used for the cash flow analysis, with the last row of the analysis containing the net cash flows. The project's NPV is calculated in cell A10 using the NPV function. The first entry in the function (A2) is the discount rate (project cost of capital), while the second entry (A4:A8) designates the range of cash inflows from years 1 through 5. Because the NPV function calculates NPV one period before the first cash flow entered in the range, it is necessary to start the range with year 1 rather than year 0. Finally, to complete the calculation in cell A10, A3 (the initial outlay) is added to the NPV function. The end result, $82,493, is displayed in cell A10.

The rationale behind the NPV method is straightforward. An NPV of zero signifies that the project's cash inflows are just sufficient to (1) return the capital invested in the project and (2) provide the required rate of return on that capital (the opportunity cost of capital). If a project has a positive NPV, it is generating excess cash flows, and these excess cash flows are available to management to reinvest in the business and, for investor-owned firms, to pay bonuses (if the firm is a proprietorship or partnership) or dividends. If a project has a negative NPV, its cash inflows are insufficient to compensate the firm for the capital invested or perhaps even insufficient to recover the initial investment, so the project is unprofitable and acceptance would cause the financial condition of the firm to deteriorate. For investor-owned firms, NPV is a direct measure of the contribution of the project to owners' wealth, so NPV is considered by many academics and practitioners to be the best measure of project profitability.

The NPV of the MRI project is $82,493, so on a present value basis, the project is expected to generate a cash flow excess of more than $80,000. Thus, the project is economically profitable, and its acceptance would have a positive impact on Ridgeland's financial condition.

Internal Rate of Return
Whereas NPV measures a project's dollar profitability, internal rate of return (IRR), which is another DCF profitability measure, measures a project's percentage profitability (i.e., its expected rate of return).

Mathematically, IRR is defined as the discount rate that equates the present value of the project's expected cash inflows to the present value of the project's expected cash outflows, so the IRR is simply the discount rate that forces the NPV of the project to equal *zero*. Spreadsheets have IRR functions that rapidly calculate IRRs. Simply input the project's cash flows, and the computer computes the IRR.

For Ridgeland's MRI project, the IRR is that rate that causes the sum of the present values of the cash inflows to equal the $2,500,000 cost of the project:

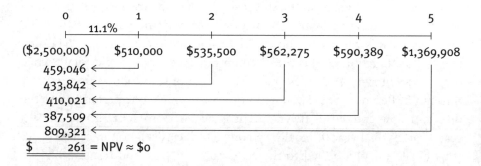

When all of the MRI project's cash flows are discounted at 11.1 percent, the NPV of the project is approximately zero. Thus, the MRI project's IRR is 11.1 percent. Put another way, the project is expected to generate an 11.1 percent rate of return on its $2,500,000 investment. Note that the IRR is like a bond's yield to maturity: It is the rate of return expected on the investment assuming that all the cash flows anticipated actually occur.

Here is the spreadsheet solution:

	A	B	C	D
1				
2	10.0%		Project cost of capital	
3	$ (2,500,000)		Cash flow 0	
4	510,000		Cash flow 1	
5	535,500		Cash flow 2	
6	562,275		Cash flow 3	
7	590,389		Cash flow 4	
8	1,369,908		Cash flow 5	
9				
10	11.1%	= IRR (A3:A8) (entered into Cell A10)		

Note that we have placed the IRR function in cell A10; the entry in the IRR function (A3:A8) specifies the range of cash flows to be used in the calculation. The answer, 11.1%, is displayed in cell A10.

If the IRR exceeds the project cost of capital, a surplus is projected to remain after recovering the invested capital and paying for its use, and this surplus accrues to the firm's stockholders (in Ridgeland's case, to its stakeholders). If the IRR is less than the project cost of capital, however, taking on the project imposes an expected financial cost on the firm's stockholders or stakeholders. The MRI project's 11.1 percent IRR exceeds its 10 percent project cost of capital. Thus, as measured by IRR, the MRI project is profitable and its acceptance would enhance Ridgeland's financial condition.

Comparison of the NPV and IRR Methods

Consider a project with a zero NPV. In this situation, the project's IRR must equal its cost of capital. The project has zero expected profitability, and acceptance would neither enhance nor diminish the firm's financial condition. To have a positive NPV, the project's IRR must be greater than its cost of capital, and a negative NPV signifies a project with an IRR less than its cost of capital. Thus, projects deemed profitable by the NPV method will also be deemed profitable by the IRR method.

In the MRI example, the project would have a positive NPV for all costs of capital less than 11.1 percent. If the cost of capital were greater than 11.1 percent, the project would have a negative NPV. In effect, the NPV and IRR are perfect substitutes for each other in measuring whether or not a project is profitable. Note, however, that when mutually exclusive projects are being analyzed (i.e., two or more projects are being analyzed but only one can be chosen), NPV and IRR rankings can conflict—that is, project A could have the higher NPV, but project B could have the higher IRR. In such situations, the NPV method is generally considered to be the best measure of profitability.

Modified Internal Rate of Return

In general, academics prefer the NPV profitability measure. This preference stems from two factors: (1) NPV measures profitability in dollars, which is a direct measure of the contribution of the project to the value of the business, and (2) both the NPV and the IRR, because they are DCF techniques, require an assumption about the rate at which project cash flows can be reinvested, and the NPV method has the better assumption.

To further explain the second point, consider the MRI project's year 2 net cash flow of $535,500. In effect, the discounting process inherent in the NPV and IRR methods automatically assigns a reinvestment rate to this cash flow; that is, both the NPV and IRR methods assume that Ridgeland has the opportunity to reinvest the $535,500 year 2 cash flow in other projects, and each method automatically assigns a reinvestment (earnings) rate to this flow for years 3, 4, and 5. The NPV method assumes reinvestment at the project cost of capital, 10 percent, while the IRR method assumes reinvestment at the IRR rate, 11.1 percent.

Which is the better assumption—reinvestment at the cost of capital or reinvestment at the IRR rate? In Ridgeland's MRI project, it does not make much difference. However, in some projects, the difference in NPV and IRR measures is significantly affected by the reinvestment rate assumption. Here's the logic behind favoring the cost of capital as the better assumption: Theoretically, a business will take on all projects that exceed the cost of capital. Thus, at the margin, the returns from capital reinvested within the firm are more likely to be at or close to the cost of capital than at the project's IRR, especially for projects with exceptionally high or low IRRs. Furthermore, a business can obtain outside capital at a cost roughly equal to the cost of capital, so cash flows generated by a project could be replaced by capital having this cost. In general, reinvestment at the cost of capital is a better assumption than reinvestment at the IRR rate, and hence NPV is a theoretically better measure of profitability than IRR.[5]

Even though academics strongly favor the NPV method, practicing managers prefer the IRR method because it is more intuitive for most people to analyze investments in terms of percentage (rates of) return than dollars of NPV. Thus, an alternative rate-of-return measure has been developed that eliminates the primary problem with IRR. This method is the **modified IRR (MIRR)**, and it is calculated as follows:

modified internal rate of return (MIRR)
A project return-on-investment measure similar to internal rate of return but using the assumption of reinvestment at the cost of capital.

- Discount all the project's net cash *outflows* back to year 0 at the project cost of capital.
- Compound all the project's net cash *inflows* forward to the last (terminal) year of the project, at the project cost of capital. This value is called the *inflow terminal value.*

- The discount rate that forces the present value of the inflow terminal value to equal the present value of costs is the MIRR.

Applying these steps to Ridgeland's MRI project produces a MIRR of about 10.7 percent:

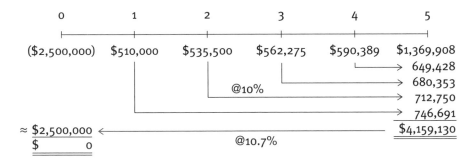

Here is the spreadsheet solution for the MIRR:

	A	B	C	D
1				
2	10.0%		Project cost of capital	
3	$ (2,500,000)		Cash flow 0	
4	510,000		Cash flow 1	
5	535,500		Cash flow 2	
6	562,275		Cash flow 3	
7	590,389		Cash flow 4	
8	1,369,908		Cash flow 5	
9				
10	10.7%	= MIRR (A3:A8,A2,A2)		

The MIRR function is placed in cell A10. The first entry in the function (A3:A8) is the range of cash flows, while the next two entries (A2,A2) are the project cost of capital. (The MIRR function allows the reinvestment rate to differ from the project cost of capital: The first of the two entries is the project cost of capital, and the second is the reinvestment rate. For our purposes, the two rates are the same.) The resulting MIRR, 10.7%, is displayed in cell A10.

The MIRR method, by compounding the cash inflows forward at 10 percent, forces the reinvestment rate to equal 10 percent, which is the project cost of capital. Note that the MIRR for the MRI project is less than the project's IRR because the cash inflows are reinvested at only 10 percent rather than at the project's 11.1 percent IRR. In general, the MIRR is less than the IRR when the IRR is greater than the cost of capital, but it is greater than the IRR when the IRR is less than the cost of capital. In effect, the IRR overstates the profitability of profitable projects and understates the profitability of unprofitable projects. By forcing the correct reinvestment rate, the MIRR method provides decision makers with a theoretically better measure of a project's expected rate of return than does the IRR.

The MIRR has other advantages over the IRR besides the proper reinvestment rate. Primarily, it avoids potential problems when a project has *non-normal* cash flows. A project with normal cash flows has one or more outflows followed by one or more inflows, while one with non-normal cash flows has outflows occurring after one or more inflows have occurred. In the non-normal situation, it is possible for a project to have two IRRs or even to have no IRR. These unusual results occur because of the mathematics of the IRR calculation. The MIRR overcomes these problems, so it is the only rate-of-return measure that can be applied to some projects.[6]

1. Briefly describe how to calculate net present value (NPV), internal rate of return (IRR), and modified IRR (MIRR).
2. What is the rationale behind each method?
3. Why is MIRR a better rate-of-return measure than IRR?
4. Do the three methods lead to the same conclusions regarding project profitability? Explain your answer.

Some Final Thoughts on Breakeven and Profitability Analyses

Although we have discussed one breakeven and three profitability measures, there are many other measures that are commonly used in project financial analyses. Because each measure contributes slightly different information about the financial consequences of a project, managers should not focus on a single measure. A thorough financial analysis of a new project includes numerous financial measures, and capital budgeting decisions are enhanced if all information inherent in all measures is considered in the process.

However, just as it would be foolish to ignore any of the quantitative measures, it would be foolish to base capital budgeting decisions solely on these measures. The uncertainties in the cash flow estimates for many projects are such that the resulting quantitative measures can be viewed only as rough estimates. Furthermore, organizational missions and strategic factors are important elements in capital budgeting decision-making. Thus, qualitative factors should play an important role in the decision process. (We discuss one approach, project scoring, in a later section.)

Finally, managers should be cautious of potential projects that have high expected profitability. In a highly competitive environment, there would be no highly profitable projects available because the marketplace would have already identified these opportunities and taken advantage of them. Thus, high-profitability projects must have some underlying rationale, such as market dominance or innovation, that justifies the profitability. Even then, under most circumstances, the project's high profitability will be eroded over time by competition.

SELF-TEST QUESTIONS

1. Evaluate the following statement: "The difficulty in calculating numerous breakeven and profitability measures restricts the amount of information available in capital budgeting analyses."
2. Should capital budgeting analyses look at only one breakeven or profitability measure? Explain your answer.
3. Why should projects with high expected profitability be viewed with some skepticism?

Capital Budgeting in Not-for-Profit Businesses

Although the capital budgeting techniques discussed so far are appropriate for use by all businesses when assessing the financial impact of a proposed project, a not-for-profit business has the additional consideration of meeting its charitable mission. In this section, we discuss two models that extend the capital budgeting decision to include a charitable mission.

Net Present Social Value Model

The financial analysis techniques discussed so far have focused exclusively on the cash flow implications of a proposed project. Some healthcare businesses, particularly not-for-profit providers, have the goal of producing social services along with commercial services. For such firms, the proper analysis of proposed projects must systematically consider the *social value* of a project along with its purely financial, or cash flow, value.

When social value is considered, the *total net present value (TNPV)* of a project can be expressed as follows:[7]

$$TNPV = NPV + NPSV.$$

net present social value (NPSV)
The present value of a project's social value; added to the financial net present value (NPV) to obtain a project's total value.

Here, *NPV* represents the conventional NPV of the project's cash flow stream and *NPSV* is the **net present social value** of the project. The *NPSV* term, which represents managers' assessment of the social value of a project, clearly differentiates capital budgeting in not-for-profit firms from that in investor-owned firms. In evaluating each project, a project is acceptable if its TNPV is greater than or equal to zero. This means that the sum of the project's financial and social values is at least zero, so when both facets of value are considered, the project has positive, or at least nonnegative, worth. Probably not all projects will have social value, but if a project does, it is considered formally in this decision model. However, no project should be accepted if its NPSV is negative, even if its TNPV is positive.

Furthermore, to ensure the financial viability of the firm, the sum of the conventional NPVs of all projects initiated in a planning period must equal or exceed zero. If this restriction were not imposed, social value could displace financial value over time, and a business could not continue to provide social value without financial integrity. Note, however, that not-for-profit providers may be able to use contributions and grants to offset some, or even all, of any aggregate negative NPV created by the acceptance of projects with positive social value but negative financial value.

> **Key Equation: Net Present Social Value Model**
> The net present social value (NPSV) model incorporates both financial and social value into a single model:
>
> $$TNPV = NPV + NPSV.$$
>
> Here, *TNPV* is total net present value, *NPV* is the net present value of the project's financial worth, and *NPSV* is the present value of the project's social worth. Although NPSV is difficult to estimate, this model formalizes the concept that not-for-profit providers should consider both social and financial value when making capital budgeting decisions.

NPSV is the sum of the present (year 0) values of each year's social value. In essence, the suppliers of fund capital to a not-for-profit firm never receive a cash return on their investment. Instead, they receive a return on their investment in the form of social dividends. These dividends take the form of services that have social value to the community, such as charity care, medical research and education, and myriad other services that, for one reason or another, do not pay their own way. Services provided to patients at a price equal to or greater than the full cost of production do not create social value. Similarly, if government entities purchase care directly for beneficiaries of a program or support research, the resulting social value is created by the funding organization as opposed to the service provider.

In estimating a project's NPSV, first it is necessary to estimate in dollar terms the social value of the services provided in each year. When a project provides services to individuals who are willing and able to pay for those services, the value of those services is captured by the amount that the individuals actually pay. Thus, the value of the services provided to those who cannot pay, or to those who cannot pay the full amount, can be estimated by the average net price paid by those individuals who are able to pay. Next, a discount rate must be applied to the social value cash flows. In general, providers should require a return on their social value stream that approximates the return available on the equity investment in for-profit firms that offer the same services.

This approach to valuing social services has intuitive appeal, but certain implementation problems merit further discussion:

Healthcare in Practice
Accounting Rate of Return

The accounting rate of return (ARR) uses accounting information to measure the profitability of an investment. Although there are alternative ways of performing the calculation, the generic formula is as follows:

Accounting rate of return =
Average net profit ÷ Average investment.

Here, both profit and investment are measured in accounting terms and averaged over the life of the project. For example, a five-year project that cost $100,000 and has a zero salvage value would have an average investment of $100,000 ÷ 5 = $20,000. If the aggregate profit over the five years were forecast to be $25,000, the average annual net profit would be $5,000. Thus, the project's ARR would be $5,000 ÷ $20,000 = 25%.

Proponents of the ARR cite the following advantages: (1) It is simple to use and understand; (2) it can be readily calculated from accounting data, unlike NPV and IRR; (3) it incorporates the entire stream of income as opposed to looking at only a single year.

What is your opinion of the ARR? Does it have any weaknesses compared with NPV and IRR? Should healthcare organizations use ARR to make capital budgeting decisions?

- Price is a fair measure of value only if the payer has the capacity to judge the true value of the service provided. Many observers of the health services sector would argue that information asymmetries between providers and purchasers inhibit the ability of purchasers to judge true value.
- The fact that most payments for healthcare services are made by third-party payers may result in price distortions. For example, insurers may be willing to pay more for services than an individual would pay in the absence of insurance; alternatively, the market power of some insurers,

such as Medicare, may result in a price that is less than individuals would be willing to pay.

- A great deal of controversy exists over the true value of treatment in many situations. Suppose that some people are entitled to whatever healthcare is available, regardless of cost, and are not required to pay for the care personally. Even though society as a whole must cover the cost, people may demand a level of care that is of questionable value. For example, should large sums be spent to keep a comatose 92-year-old alive for a few more days? If the true value to society of such an expenditure is zero, assigning a high social value just because that is its cost makes little sense.

Although the NPSV model formalizes the capital budgeting decision process applicable to not-for-profit healthcare firms, few organizations actually attempt to quantify NPSV. However, not-for-profit providers should, at a minimum, subjectively consider the social value inherent in projects under consideration.

Project Scoring

project scoring
An approach to project assessment that considers both financial and nonfinancial factors.

Managers of not-for-profit businesses, as well as managers of most investor-owned firms, recognize that nonfinancial factors should be considered in any capital budgeting analysis. The NPSV model examines only one other factor, and it is difficult to implement in practice. Thus, many businesses use a quasi-subjective **project scoring** approach to capital budgeting decisions that attempts to capture both financial and nonfinancial factors. Exhibit 14.5, which is used by Ridgeland, illustrates one such approach.

Ridgeland ranks projects on three dimensions: stakeholder, operational, and financial. Within each dimension, multiple factors are examined and assigned scores that range from 2 points for very favorable impact to –1 point for negative impact. The scores within each dimension are added to obtain scores for each of the three dimensions, and then the dimension scores are summed to obtain a total score for the project. The total score gives Ridgeland's managers a feel for the relative values of projects under consideration when all factors, including financial, are taken into account.

Ridgeland's managers recognize that the scoring system is completely arbitrary, so a project with a score of 10, for example, is not necessarily twice as good as a project that scores 5. Nevertheless, Ridgeland's project scoring approach forces its managers to address multiple issues when making capital budgeting decisions, and it does provide a relative ranking of projects under consideration. Although Ridgeland's approach should not be used at other organizations without modification for organizational- and sector-unique

EXHIBIT 14.5
Ridgeland
Community
Hospital:
Project Scoring
Matrix

	Relative Score			
Criteria	2	1	0	−1
Stakeholder Factors				
Physicians	Strongly support	Support	Neutral	Opposed
Employees	Greatly helps morale	Helps morale	No effect	Hurts morale
Visitors	Greatly enhances visit	Enhances visit	No effect	Hurts image
Social value	High	Moderate	None	Negative
Operational Factors				
Outcomes	Greatly improves	Improves	No effect	Hurts outcomes
Length of stay	Documented decrease	Anecdotal decrease	No effect	Increases
Technology	Breakthrough	Improves current	Adds to current	Lowers
Productivity	Large decrease in FTEs	Decrease in FTEs	No change in FTEs	Adds FTEs
Financial Factors				
Life cycle	Innovation	Growth	Stabilization	Decline
Payback	Less than 2 years	2–4 years	4–6 years	Over 6 years
IRR	Over 20%	15–20%	10–15%	Less than 10%
Correlation	Negative	Uncorrelated	Somewhat positive	Highly positive

Stakeholder factor score   _____

Operational factor score   _____

Financial factor score   _____

   Total score   _____

circumstances, it does provide insights into how a matrix might be developed that is unique to a business.

1. Describe the net present social value (NPSV) model of capital budgeting.
2. Describe the construction and use of a project scoring matrix.

The Post-audit

Capital budgeting is not a static process. If there is a long lag between a project's acceptance and its implementation, any new information concerning either capital costs or the project's cash flows should be analyzed before the start-up occurs. Furthermore, the performance of each project should be

post-audit
The feedback
process in which
the performance of
projects previously
accepted is
reviewed and
actions are taken
if performance
is below
expectations.

monitored throughout the project's life. The process of formally monitoring project performance over time is called the **post-audit**. It involves comparing actual results with those projected, explaining why differences occur, and analyzing potential changes to the project's operations, including replacement or termination.

The post-audit has several purposes:

- **Improve forecasts.** When managers systematically compare projections to actual outcomes, estimates tend to improve. Conscious or unconscious biases can be identified and, one hopes, eliminated; new forecasting methods are sought as the need for them becomes apparent; and managers tend to do everything better, including forecasting, if they know that their actions are being monitored.
- **Develop historical risk data.** Post-audits permit managers to develop historical data on new project analyses regarding risk and expected rates of return. These data can be used to make judgments about the relative risk of future projects.
- **Improve operations.** Managers run businesses, and they can perform at higher or lower levels of efficiency. When a forecast is made, for example, by the surgery department, the department director and medical staff are, in a sense, putting their reputations on the line. If costs are above predicted levels and volume is below expectations, the managers involved will strive, within ethical bounds, to improve the situation and to bring results into line with forecasts. As one hospital CEO put it, "You academics worry only about making good decisions. In the health services sector, we also have to worry about making decisions good."
- **Reduce losses.** Post-audits monitor the performance of projects over time, so the first indication that termination or replacement should be considered often arises when the post-audit indicates that a project is performing poorly.

SELF-TEST QUESTIONS

1. What is a post-audit?
2. Why are post-audits important to the efficiency of a business?

Using Capital Budgeting Techniques in Other Contexts

The techniques developed in this chapter can help health services managers make a number of decisions in addition to project selection. One example is the use of NPV and IRR to evaluate corporate merger opportunities.

Healthcare companies often acquire other companies to increase capacity or expand into other service areas, among other reasons. A key element of any merger analysis is the valuation of the target company. Although the cash flows in such an analysis may be structured differently than in project analysis, the same evaluation tools are applied.

Managers also use capital budgeting techniques when deciding whether or not to divest assets or reduce staffing. Like capital budgeting, these actions require an analysis of the impact of the decision on the firm's cash flows. When eliminating personnel, businesses typically spend money up front in severance payments but then receive benefits in the form of lower labor costs in the future. When assets are sold, the pattern of cash flows is reversed—that is, cash inflows occur when the asset is sold, but any future cash inflows associated with the asset are sacrificed. (If future cash flows are negative, the decision, at least from a financial perspective, should be easy.) In both situations, the techniques discussed in this chapter, perhaps with modifications, can be applied to assess the financial consequences of the action.

SELF-TEST QUESTION

1. Can capital budgeting tools be used in different settings? Explain your answer.

Key Concepts

This chapter discusses the basics of capital budgeting. The key concepts of this chapter are as follows:

- *Capital budgeting* is the process of analyzing potential expenditures on fixed assets and deciding whether the firm should undertake those investments.
- A capital budgeting financial analysis consists of four steps: (1) *estimate the expected cash flows*, (2) *assess the riskiness of those flows*, (3) *estimate the appropriate cost-of-capital discount rate*, and (4) *determine the project's profitability and breakeven characteristics*.
- The most critical and most difficult step in analyzing a project is estimating the *incremental cash flows* that the project will generate.
- In determining incremental cash flows, *opportunity costs* (i.e., the cash flows forgone by using an asset) must be considered, but

(continued)

(continued from previous page)

sunk costs (i.e., cash outlays that cannot be recouped) are not included. Furthermore, any impact of the project on the firm's *other projects* must be included in the analysis.

- *Tax laws* generally affect investor-owned firms in three ways: (1) Taxes reduce a project's operating cash flows; (2) tax laws prescribe the depreciation expense that can be taken in any year; and (3) taxes affect a project's salvage value cash flow.

- Capital projects often require changes in *current accounts* in addition to the investment in fixed assets. Such changes represent a cash flow that, if material, must be included in the analysis. The net change in current accounts is recovered when the project is terminated.

- A project may have some *strategic value* that is not accounted for in the estimated cash flows. At a minimum, strategic value should be noted and considered qualitatively in the analysis.

- The *effects of inflation* must be considered in project analyses. The best procedure is to build inflation effects directly into the component cash flow estimates.

- Time breakeven, which is measured by the *payback period*, provides managers with insights concerning a project's liquidity and risk.

- Project profitability is assessed by *return on investment (ROI)* measures. The two most commonly used ROI measures are net present value and internal rate of return.

- *Net present value (NPV)*, which is simply the sum of the present values of all the project's net cash flows when discounted at the project's cost of capital, measures a project's expected dollar profitability. An NPV greater than zero indicates that the project is expected to be profitable after all costs, including the opportunity cost of capital, have been considered. Furthermore, the higher the NPV, the more profitable the project.

- *Internal rate of return (IRR)*, which is the discount rate that forces a project's NPV to equal zero, measures a project's expected rate of return. If a project's IRR is greater than its cost of capital, the project is expected to be profitable, and the higher the IRR, the more profitable the project.

- The NPV and IRR profitability measures provide identical indications of profitability; that is, a project that is judged to be profitable by its NPV will also be judged profitable by its IRR.

(continued)

(continued from previous page)

However, when mutually exclusive projects are being evaluated, NPV might rank a different project higher than IRR. This difference can occur because the two measures have different *reinvestment rate assumptions*—IRR assumes that cash flows can be reinvested at the project's IRR, while NPV assumes that cash flows can be reinvested at the project's cost of capital.

- The *modified internal rate of return (MIRR)*, which forces a project's cash flows to be reinvested at the project's cost of capital, is a better measure of a project's percentage rate of return than the IRR.
- The *net present social value (NPSV) model* formalizes the capital budgeting decision process for not-for-profit firms.
- Firms often use *project scoring* subjectively to incorporate a large number of factors, including financial and nonfinancial, into the capital budgeting decision process.
- The *post-audit* is a key element in capital budgeting. By comparing actual results with predicted results, managers can improve both operations and the cash flow estimation process.
- Capital budgeting techniques are used in a wide variety of settings in addition to project evaluation.

The discussion of capital investment decisions continues in chapter 15, which focuses on risk assessment and incorporation.

Questions

14.1. a. What is capital budgeting? Why are capital budgeting decisions so important to businesses?
   b. What is the purpose of placing capital projects into categories such as mandatory replacement or expansion of existing products, services, or markets?
   c. Should financial analysis play the dominant role in capital budgeting decisions? Explain your answer.
   d. What are the four steps of capital budgeting analysis?

14.2. Briefly define the following cash flow estimation concepts.
   a. Incremental cash flow
   b. Cash flow versus accounting income
   c. Sunk cost

    d. Opportunity cost

    e. Changes in current accounts

    f. Strategic value

    g. Inflation effects

14.3. Describe the following project breakeven and profitability measures. Be sure to include each measure's economic interpretation.

    a. Payback

    b. Net present value (NPV)

    c. Internal rate of return (IRR)

    d. Modified internal rate of return (MIRR)

14.4. Critique this statement: "NPV is a better measure of project profitability than IRR because NPV leads to better capital investment decisions."

14.5. a. Describe the net present social value (NPSV) model.

    b. What is a project scoring matrix?

14.6. What is a post-audit? Why is the post-audit critical to good investment decision-making?

14.7. From a purely financial perspective, are there situations in which a business would be better off choosing a project with a shorter payback over one that has a larger NPV?

Problems

14.1. Winview Clinic is evaluating a project that costs $52,125 and has expected net cash inflows of $12,000 per year for eight years. The first inflow occurs one year after the cost outflow, and the project has a cost of capital of 12 percent.

    a. What is the project's payback?

    b. What is the project's NPV? Its IRR? Its MIRR?

    c. Is the project financially acceptable? Explain your answer.

14.2. Better Health, Inc., is evaluating two investment projects, each of which requires an up-front expenditure of $1.5 million. The projects are expected to produce the following net cash inflows:

Year	Project A	Project B
1	$ 500,000	$2,000,000
2	1,000,000	1,000,000
3	2,000,000	600,000

   a. What is each project's IRR?

   b. What is each project's NPV if the cost of capital is 10 percent? 5 percent? 15 percent?

14.3. Capitol Healthplans, Inc., is evaluating two different methods for providing home health services to its members. Both methods involve contracting out for services, and the health outcomes and revenues are not affected by the method chosen. Therefore, the incremental cash flows for the decision are all outflows. Here are the projected flows:

Year	Method A	Method B
0	($300,000)	($120,000)
1	(66,000)	(96,000)
2	(66,000)	(96,000)
3	(66,000)	(96,000)
4	(66,000)	(96,000)
5	(66,000)	(96,000)

   a. What is each alternative's IRR?

   b. If the cost of capital for both methods is 9 percent, which method should be chosen? Why?

14.4. Great Lakes Clinic has been asked to provide exclusive healthcare services for next year's World Exposition. Although flattered by the request, the clinic's managers want to conduct a financial analysis of the project. There will be an up-front cost of $160,000 to get the clinic in operation. Then, a net cash inflow of $1 million is expected from operations in each of the two years of the exposition. However, the clinic has to pay the organizers of the exposition a fee for the marketing value of the opportunity. This fee, which must be paid at the end of the second year, is $2 million.

   a. What are the cash flows associated with the project?

   b. What is the project's IRR?

   c. Assuming a project cost of capital of 10 percent, what is the project's NPV?

   d. What is the project's MIRR?

14.5. Assume that you are the chief financial officer at Porter Memorial Hospital. The CEO has asked you to analyze two proposed capital investments—project X and project Y. Each project requires a net investment outlay of $10,000, and the cost of capital for each project is 12 percent. The projects' expected net cash flows are as follows:

Year	Project X	Project Y
0	($10,000)	($10,000)
1	6,500	3,000
2	3,000	3,000
3	3,000	3,000
4	1,000	3,000

   a. Calculate each project's payback period, net present value (NPV), and internal rate of return (IRR).

   b. Which project (or projects) is financially acceptable? Explain your answer.

14.6. The director of capital budgeting for Big Sky Health Systems, Inc., has estimated the following cash flows in thousands of dollars for a proposed new service:

Year	Expected Net Cash Flow
0	($100)
1	70
2	50
3	20

The project's cost of capital is 10 percent.

   a. What is the project's payback period?

   b. What is the project's NPV?

   c. What is the project's IRR? Its MIRR?

14.7. Michigan Health Center, a for-profit hospital, is evaluating the purchase of new diagnostic equipment. The equipment, which costs $600,000, has an expected life of five years and an estimated pretax salvage value of $200,000 at that time. The equipment is expected to be used 15 times a day for 250 days a year for each year of the project's life. On average, each procedure is expected to generate $80 in collections, which is net of bad debt losses and contractual allowances, in its first year of use. Thus, net revenues for year 1 are estimated at 15 × 250 × $80 = $300,000.

     Labor and maintenance costs are expected to be $100,000 during the first year of operation, while utilities will cost another $10,000 and cash overhead will increase by $5,000 in year 1. The cost for expendable supplies is expected to average $5 per procedure during the first year. All costs and revenues, except depreciation, are expected to increase at a 5 percent inflation rate after the first year.

The equipment falls into the MACRS five-year class for tax depreciation and is subject to the following depreciation allowances:

Year	Allowance
1	0.20
2	0.32
3	0.19
4	0.12
5	0.11
6	0.06
	1.00

The hospital's tax rate is 30 percent, and its corporate cost of capital is 10 percent.

a. Estimate the project's net cash flows over its five-year estimated life. (Hint: Use the following format as a guide.)

	Year					
	0	1	2	3	4	5
Equipment cost						
Net revenues						
Less: Labor/maintenance costs						
Utilities costs						
Supplies						
Incremental overhead						
Depreciation						
Operating income						
Taxes						
Net operating income						
Plus: Depreciation						
Plus: Equipment salvage value						
Net cash flow						

b. What are the project's NPV and IRR? (Assume for now that the project has average risk.)

14.8. You have been asked by the president and CEO of Kidd Pharmaceuticals to evaluate the proposed acquisition of a new labeling machine for one of the firm's production lines. The machine's price is $50,000, and it would cost another $10,000 for transportation and installation. The machine falls into the MACRS three-year class, and hence the tax depreciation allowances are

0.33, 0.45, and 0.15 in years 1, 2, and 3, respectively. The machine would be sold after three years because the production line is being closed at that time. The best estimate of the machine's salvage value after three years of use is $20,000. The machine would have no effect on the firm's sales or revenues, but it is expected to save Kidd $20,000 per year in before-tax operating costs. The firm's tax rate is 30 percent and its corporate cost of capital is 10 percent.

a. What is the project's net investment outlay at year 0?

b. What are the project's operating cash flows in years 1, 2, and 3?

c. What are the terminal cash flows at the end of year 3?

d. If the project has average risk, is it expected to be profitable?

14.9. The staff of Jefferson Memorial Hospital has estimated the following net cash flows for a satellite food services operation that it may open in its outpatient clinic:

Year	Expected Net Cash Flow
0	($100,000)
1	30,000
2	30,000
3	30,000
4	30,000
5	30,000
5 (salvage value)	20,000

The year 0 cash flow is the investment cost of the new food service, while the final amount is the terminal cash flow. (The clinic is expected to move to a new building in five years.) All other flows represent net operating cash flows. Jefferson's corporate cost of capital is 10 percent.

a. What is the project's IRR? Its MIRR?

b. Assuming the project has average risk, what is its NPV?

c. Now, assume that the operating cash flows in years 1 through 5 could be as low as $20,000 or as high as $40,000. Furthermore, the salvage value cash flow at the end of year 5 could be as low as $0 or as high as $30,000. What are the worst-case and best-case IRRs? The worst-case and best-case NPVs?

14.10. BetterCare Insurance Company is considering the development of a case management program for its insured diabetics. BetterCare has estimated that the case management program will cost $200,000 in development and start-up costs. Once the program is operational, BetterCare estimates that the program will reduce utilization, and therefore claims payments, for its diabetic population. Net cash flows, calculated as claims-related savings less program operational costs, are estimated to be as follows:

Years 1–5 ($25,000) per year cash outflow as the program is ramping up
Years 6–10 $75,000 per year cash inflow as the program starts generating better outcomes

   a. Assuming BetterCare's corporate cost of capital is 15%, on purely financial grounds, should BetterCare invest in the program?

   b. Now, assume the program is able to generate positive outcomes sooner. If the expected case flows were as follows, would your answer change?

Years 1–2 ($25,000) per year cash outflow as the program is ramping up
Years 3–10 $75,000 per year cash inflow as the program starts generating better outcomes

14.11. Assume that you are the chief financial officer at General Hospital. The CEO has asked you to analyze two proposed capital investments—project X and project Y. Each project requires a net investment outlay of $75,000, and the cost of capital for each project is 10 percent. The projects' expected net cash flows are as follows:

Year	Project X	Project Y
0	($75,000)	($75,000)
1	20,000	50,000
2	20,000	15,000
3	20,000	15,000
4	30,000	10,000

   a. Calculate each project's net present value (NPV) and internal rate of return (IRR).

   b. Which project (or projects) is financially acceptable? If you reach different conclusions regarding the financial acceptability of project X and project Y, explain why, given that both projects return total cash flows of $90,000 over the four years.

Selected Case

One case in *Gapenski's Cases in Healthcare Finance*, sixth edition, is applicable to this chapter: Case 14: Jones Memorial Hospital.

Notes

1. For a discussion of the cash flow estimation practices of some large firms, as well as some estimates of the inaccuracies involved, see Pohlman, R. A., E. S. Santiago, and F. L. Markel. 1988. "Cash Flow Estimation Practices of Large Firms." *Financial Management* 17 (2): 71–79.
2. For more on cash flow estimation bias, see Pruitt, S. W., and L. J. Gitman. 1987. "Capital Budgeting Forecast Biases: Evidence from the *Fortune* 500." *Financial Management* 16 (1): 46–51.
3. If Ann Arbor did not have taxable income to offset in year 2 and had no taxable income to offset in previous years, the loss would have to be carried forward and hence the tax benefit would not be immediately realized. In this situation, the tax shield value of the loss would be reduced because it would be pushed into the future rather than recognized immediately. Note that IRS regulations pertaining to the carryback of losses change often to reflect changing economic conditions. At this time, businesses can elect to carry back losses three, four, or five years.
4. The NPV is the same as the cumulative DCF shown for year 5 in the discounted payback table. In essence, NPV can be thought of as the total cumulative DCF of the project.
5. One could argue that not-for-profit businesses do not have unlimited access to capital, and thus such firms cannot replace project cash flows with external capital. Furthermore, not-for-profit businesses usually do not have sufficient capital to accept all projects that have positive NPVs, so the return on a not-for-profit firm's marginal project may not equal the firm's cost of capital. Nevertheless, for not-for-profit businesses, the average aggregate return on projects will usually be close to the firm's cost of capital, so the cost of capital is still a better reinvestment rate than the project's IRR, especially when projects with exceptionally high or low IRRs are being evaluated.
6. For a more complete discussion of projects with non-normal cash flows, see Brigham, E. F., and M. C. Ehrhardt. 2013. "Cash Flow Estimation and Risk Analysis." In *Financial Management: Theory and*

Practice, 14th ed., chap. 11. Mason, OH: South-Western Cengage Learning.

7. This section is drawn primarily from an article by Wheeler, J. R. C., and J. P. Clement. 1990. "Capital Expenditure Decisions and the Role of the Not-for-Profit Hospital: An Application of the Social Goods Model." *Medical Care Review* 47 (4): 467–86.

Resources

Casolari, C., and S. Womack. 2010. "Prioritizing Capital Projects When Cash Is Scarce." *Healthcare Financial Management* 64 (3): 114, 116.

The TeachMeFinance website has several tutorial-type discussions that cover aspects of financial management. For a capital budgeting tutorial, see
Clarke, R. L., and R. Wolfert. 2003. "Capital Allocation: Three Cases of Financing for the Future." *Healthcare Financial Management* 57 (10): 58–62.

For additional resources relevant to this chapter, see
Arduino, K. 2018. "The Increasing Importance of Strategic Capital Planning." *Healthcare Financial Management* 72 (2): 76–77.
Devine, K., T. J. Kloppenborg, and P. O'Clock. 2010. "Project Measurement and Success: A Balanced Scorecard Approach." *Journal of Health Care Finance* 36 (4): 38–50.
Evanoo, J., and D. Cameron. 2010. "The Case to Replace: Developing a Sound Capital Equipment Strategy." *Healthcare Financial Management* 64 (2): 84–90.
Grauman, D. M., G. Neff, and M. M. Johnson. 2011. "Capital Planning for Clinical Integration." *Healthcare Financial Management* 65 (4): 57–66.
Guimond, J. P. 2016. "Have You Looked at Your Capital Process Lately?" *Healthcare Financial Management* 70 (5): 64–69.
Healthcare Financial Management Association. 2004. "Inside the Real World of Capital Allocation." *Healthcare Financial Management* 58 (12): 81–86.
Hegwer, L. R. 2016. "Capital Planning for a New Era." *Healthcare Financial Management* 70 (5): 60–63.
Henley, R. J., and M. A. Zimmerman. 2005. "10 Proven Strategies for Reducing Equipment Costs." *Healthcare Financial Management* 59 (5): 78–81.
Jasuta, L. 2016. "Rolling Capital/Managing Investments in a Value-Based Care World." *Healthcare Financial Management* 70 (6): 82–89.
Laskaris, J., and K. Regan. 2013. "The New Break-Even Analysis." *Healthcare Financial Management* 67 (12): 88–95.

McCue, M. J. 2011a. "Association of Market, Organizational and Financial Factors with the Number, and Types of Capital Expenditures." *Health Care Management Review* 36 (1): 67–77.

———. 2011b. "Capital Expenditure Trends in California Hospitals: 2002–2007." *Hospital Topics* 89 (1): 9–15.

Parrott, B. 2018. "Why Age Is Not Enough: A Better Approach to Equipment Replacement." *Healthcare Financial Management* 72 (5): 44–49.

Poplan, B. 2011. "Making Informed Capital Investment Decisions for Clinical Technology." *Healthcare Financial Management* 65 (2): 64–68.

Reiter, K. L., D. G. Smith, R. C. Wheeler, and H. L. Rivenson. 2000. "Capital Investment Strategies in Health Care Systems." *Journal of Health Care Finance* 26 (4): 31–41.

Reiter, K. L., and P. H. Song. 2013. "Hospital Capital Budgeting in an Era of Transformation." *Journal of Health Care Finance* 39 (3): 14–22.

———. 2011. "The Role of Financial Market Performance in Hospital Capital Investment." *Journal of Health Care Finance* 37 (3): 38–51.

Reiter, K. L., J. R. C. Wheeler, and D. G. Smith. 2008. "Liquidity Constraints on Hospital Investment When Credit Markets Are Tight." *Journal of Health Care Finance* 35 (1): 24–33.

Stewart, L. J. 2012. "Analysis of Capital Spending and Capital Financing Among Large U.S. Nonprofit Health Systems." *Journal of Health Care Finance* 38 (3): 1–15.

PROJECT RISK ANALYSIS

Introduction

Chapter 14 covered the basics of capital budgeting, including cash flow estimation, breakeven analysis, and return on investment (ROI) (profitability) measures. This chapter extends the discussion of capital budgeting to include risk analysis, which is composed of three elements: defining the type of risk relevant to the project, measuring the project's risk, and incorporating the risk assessment into the capital budgeting decision process. Although risk analysis is a key element in all financial decisions, the importance of capital investment decisions to a healthcare business's success or failure makes risk analysis vital in such decisions.

The higher the risk associated with an investment, the higher its required rate of return. This principle is just as valid for healthcare businesses that make capital expenditure decisions as it is for individuals who make personal investment decisions. Thus, the ultimate goal in project risk analysis is to ensure that the cost of capital used as the discount rate in a project's ROI analysis properly reflects the riskiness of that project. The corporate cost of capital, which is covered in detail in chapter 13, reflects the cost of capital to the organization based on its aggregate risk—that is, based on the riskiness of the firm's average project.

In project risk analysis, a project's risk is assessed relative to the firm's average project: Does the project under consideration have average risk, below-average risk, or above-average risk? The corporate cost of capital is then adjusted to reflect any differential risk, resulting in a *project cost of capital*. In general, above-average-risk projects are assigned a project cost of capital that is higher than the corporate cost of capital, average-risk projects are evaluated at the corporate cost of capital, and below-average-risk projects are assigned a discount rate that is less than the corporate cost of capital. (Note that when capital budgeting is conducted at the divisional level, the adjustment process is handled in a similar manner, but the starting value is the divisional cost of capital.)

Types of Project Risk

Three types of financial risk can be defined in a capital budgeting context:

1. **Stand-alone risk**, which assumes the project is held in isolation and ignores portfolio effects within the business and among its owners (equity investors).
2. **Corporate risk**, which views the risk of a project within the context of the business's portfolio of projects.
3. **Market risk**, which views the project from the perspective of the business's owners, who are assumed to hold a well-diversified portfolio of stocks.

The type of risk that is most relevant to a particular capital budgeting decision depends on the business's type of ownership and the number of projects it holds.

Stand-Alone Risk

coefficient of variation
A statistical measure of an investment's stand-alone risk calculated by dividing the standard deviation of returns by the expected return. The result is the amount of stand-alone risk per unit of return.

Stand-alone risk is present in a project whenever there is a chance of a return that is less than the expected return. In effect, **a project is risky whenever its cash flows are not known with certainty**, because uncertain cash flows mean uncertain profitability. Furthermore, the greater the probability of a return far below the expected return, the greater the risk. Stand-alone risk can be measured by the *standard deviation*, or **coefficient of variation**, of the project's profitability (ROI), which is often measured by net present value (NPV), internal rate of return (IRR), or modified internal rate of return (MIRR). Because standard deviation and coefficient of variation measure the dispersion of a distribution around its expected value, the larger these values, the greater the probability that the project's ROI will be far below that expected.

Conceptually, stand-alone risk is relevant in only one situation: when a not-for-profit business is evaluating its first project. In this situation, the project will be operated in isolation, so no portfolio diversification is present—the business does not have a collection of different projects, nor does it have owners who hold diversified portfolios of investments.

Corporate Risk

In reality, businesses usually offer many different products or services, and thus they can be thought of as having a large number (perhaps hundreds) of individual projects. For example, MinuteMan Healthcare, a New England not-for-profit managed care company, offers healthcare services to a large number of diverse employee groups in numerous service areas, and each group can be considered a separate project. In this situation, the stand-alone risk of a project under consideration by MinuteMan is not relevant because the project will not be held in isolation. The relevant risk of a new project to MinuteMan is its contribution to the business's overall risk (the impact of the project on the variability of the overall profitability of the business). This type of risk, which is relevant when the project is part of a not-for-profit business's portfolio of projects, is called *corporate risk*.

A project's corporate risk depends on the context (i.e., the firm's other projects), so a project may have high corporate risk to one business but low corporate risk to another, particularly when the two businesses operate in widely different industries.

Market Risk

Market risk is generally viewed as the relevant risk for projects being evaluated by large, investor-owned businesses. In such businesses, the owners hold large, diversified portfolios of securities investments (stocks and bonds of many firms), which can be thought of as large, diversified portfolios of individual projects. Because the goal of owner wealth maximization implies that a project's returns, as well as its risk, should be defined and measured from the owners' perspective, the riskiness of an individual project to a well-diversified owner is its contribution to the riskiness of a well-diversified stock portfolio.

SELF-TEST QUESTIONS

1. What are the three types of project risk?
2. How is each type of project risk measured, both in absolute and relative terms?

Relationships Among Stand-Alone, Corporate, and Market Risk

After discussing the three types of project risk and the situations in which each is relevant, it is tempting to conclude that stand-alone risk is almost never important because not-for-profit businesses should focus on a project's corporate risk and investor-owned firms should focus on a project's market risk. Unfortunately, the situation is not that simple.

First, it is almost impossible in practice to quantify a project's corporate or market risk. However, as demonstrated in the next section, it is possible to get a rough idea of the relative stand-alone risk of a project. Thus, managers can make statements such as "project A has above-average risk," "project B has below-average risk," or "project C has average risk," all in the stand-alone sense. After a project's stand-alone risk has been assessed, the primary factor in converting stand-alone risk to corporate or market risk is correlation. If a project's returns are expected to be highly positively correlated with the firm's returns, high stand-alone risk translates to high corporate risk. Similarly, if the business's returns are expected to be highly correlated with the stock market's returns, high corporate risk translates to high market risk. The same relationships hold when the project is judged to have average or low stand-alone risk.

Most projects will be in a business's primary line of business. Because all projects in the same line of business are generally affected by the same economic factors, such projects' returns are usually highly correlated. When this situation exists, a project's stand-alone risk is a good proxy for its corporate risk. Furthermore, most projects' returns are also positively correlated with the returns on other assets in the economy—most assets have high returns when the economy is strong and low returns when the economy is weak. When this situation holds, a project's stand-alone risk is a good proxy for its market risk.

Thus, for most projects, the stand-alone risk assessment also gives good insights into a project's corporate and market risk. The only exception is when a project's returns are expected to be independent of or negatively correlated with the business's average project. In these situations, considerable judgment is required because the stand-alone risk assessment will overstate the project's corporate risk. Similarly, if a project's returns are expected to be independent of or negatively correlated with the market's returns, the project's stand-alone risk overstates its market risk.

1. What type of project risk generally is the most measurable?
2. How are the types of project risk related?

Risk Analysis Illustration

To illustrate project risk analysis, consider Ridgeland Community Hospital's evaluation of a new magnetic resonance imaging (MRI) system that was presented in chapter 14. Exhibit 15.1 contains the project's cash flow analysis. If all of the project's component cash flows were known with certainty, its projected profitability would be known with certainty, and hence the project would have no risk. However, in virtually all project analyses, future cash flows and hence profitability are uncertain—and in many cases highly uncertain—so risk is present.

The starting point for analyzing a project's risk involves estimating the uncertainty inherent in the project's cash flows. Most of the individual cash flows in exhibit 15.1 are subject to uncertainty. For example, volume was projected at 40 scans per week. However, actual utilization will almost certainly be higher or lower than the 40-scan forecast. In effect, the volume estimate is really an expected value taken from some probability distribution of potential utilization, as are many of the other values listed in exhibit 15.1. Graphs of the distributions of the variables could be relatively tight (peaked with small tails), reflecting small standard deviations and low risk, or they could be relatively flat (rounded with large tails), denoting a great deal of uncertainty about the variable in question and hence a high degree of risk. In other words, high confidence in the forecast variables typically translates to low risk, while low confidence signifies high risk.

The nature of the component cash flow distributions and their correlations with one another determine the nature of the project's profitability distribution and thus the project's risk. In the following sections, three quantitative techniques for assessing a project's risk are discussed: sensitivity analysis, scenario analysis, and Monte Carlo simulation.[1] In a later section, we present a qualitative approach to risk assessment. Remember that our focus here is on the stand-alone risk of the project. After the stand-alone risk is assessed, we will use judgment to translate that assessment into corporate and market risk (if relevant).

EXHIBIT 15.1
Ridgeland Community Hospital: MRI Project Cash Flow Analysis

	0	1	2	3	4	5
			Cash Revenues and Costs			
1. System cost	($1,500,000)					
2. Related expenses	(1,000,000)					
3. Net revenues		$750,000	$787,500	$826,875	$868,219	$ 911,629
4. Labor costs		50,000	52,500	55,125	57,881	60,775
5. Maintenance costs		150,000	157,500	165,375	173,644	182,326
6. Supplies		30,000	31,500	33,075	34,729	36,465
7. Incremental overhead		10,000	10,500	11,025	11,576	12,155
8. Depreciation		350,000	350,000	350,000	350,000	350,000
9. Operating income		$160,000	$185,500	$ 212,275	$240,389	$ 269,908
10. Taxes		0	0	0	0	0
11. Net operating income		$160,000	$185,500	$ 212,275	$240,389	$ 269,908
12. Depreciation		350,000	350,000	350,000	350,000	350,000
13. Net salvage value						750,000
14. Net cash flow	($2,500,000)	$510,000	$535,500	$562,275	$590,389	$1,369,908

Profitability Measures:
Net present value (NPV) = $82,493
Internal rate of return (IRR) = 11.1%
Modified internal rate of return (MIRR) = 10.7%

1. What condition creates project risk?
2. What makes one project riskier than another?
3. What type of risk is being assessed initially?

Sensitivity Analysis

Historically, **sensitivity analysis** has been classified as a risk assessment tool. In reality, it is not very useful in assessing a project's risk. However, it does have significant value in project analysis, so we discuss it in some detail here.

sensitivity analysis
A project analysis technique that assesses how changes in a single input variable, such as utilization, affect profitability.

Many of the variables that determine a project's cash flows are subject to some type of probability distribution that is not known with certainty. If the realized value of such a variable is different from its expected value, the project's profitability will differ from its expected value. Sensitivity analysis shows exactly how much a project's profitability—net present value (NPV), internal rate of return (IRR), or modified internal rate of return (MIRR)—will change in response to a given change in a single input variable, with other input variables held constant.

Sensitivity analysis begins with a *base case* developed using *expected values* (in the statistical sense) for all uncertain variables. To illustrate, assume that Ridgeland's managers believe that all of the MRI project's component cash flows are known with relative certainty except for weekly volume and salvage value. The expected values for these variables (volume = 40, salvage value = $750,000) were used in exhibit 15.1 to obtain the base case NPV of $82,493. Sensitivity analysis is designed to provide managers the answers to such questions as these: What if volume is more or less than the expected level? What if salvage value is more or less than expected? (Typically, more than two variables are examined in a sensitivity analysis; here, we use only two to keep the illustration manageable.)

Change from Base Case Level	Net Present Value (NPV)	
	Volume	Salvage Value
−30%	($814,053)	($ 57,215)
−20	(515,193)	(10,646)
−10	216,350	35,923
0	82,493	82,493
10	381,335	129,062
20	680,178	175,631
30	979,020	222,200

EXHIBIT 15.2
MRI Project Sensitivity Analysis

In a sensitivity analysis, each uncertain variable is changed by a fixed percentage above and below its expected value, while all other variables are held constant at their expected values. Thus, all input variables except one are held at their base case values. The resulting NPVs (or IRRs or MIRRs) are recorded and plotted. Exhibit 15.2 contains the NPV sensitivity analysis for the MRI project, assuming that there are only two uncertain variables: volume and salvage value.

Note that the NPV is a constant $82,493 when there is no change in any of the variables because a 0 percent change re-creates the base case. Managers can examine the values in exhibit 15.2 to get a feel for which input variable has the greatest impact on the MRI project's NPV—the larger the NPV change for a given percentage input change, the greater the impact. Considering only these two variables, we see that the MRI project's NPV is affected by changes in volume more than by changes in salvage value. This result should be somewhat intuitive because salvage value is a single cash flow in the analysis, whereas volume influences the cash flow in each year that the MRI is in operation.

Often, the results of sensitivity analyses are shown in graphical form. For example, the exhibit 15.2 sensitivity analysis is graphed in exhibit 15.3.

EXHIBIT 15.3
Sensitivity
Analysis Graphs

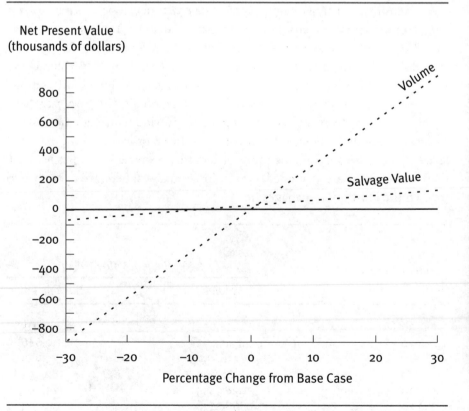

Here, the slopes of the lines show how sensitive the MRI project's NPV is to changes in each of the two uncertain input variables—the steeper the slope, the more sensitive the NPV is to a change in the variable. The sensitivity lines intersect at the base case values—0 percent change from base case level and $82,493. Spreadsheet models are ideally suited for performing sensitivity analyses because such models both automatically recalculate NPV when an input value is changed and facilitate graphing.[2]

Exhibit 15.3 vividly illustrates that the MRI project's NPV is very sensitive to changes in volume but only mildly sensitive to changes in salvage value. When a sensitivity plot has a negative slope, it indicates that *increases* in the value of that input variable *decrease* the project's NPV. If two projects were being compared, the one with the steeper sensitivity lines would be regarded as riskier because a relatively small error in estimating a variable— for example, volume—would produce a large error in the project's projected NPV. If information were available on the sensitivity of NPV to input changes for Ridgeland's average project, similar judgments regarding the riskiness of the MRI project could be made relative to the firm's average project.

Although sensitivity analysis is classified as a risk assessment tool, it has severe limitations in this role. For example, suppose that Ridgeland Community Hospital had a contract with a health maintenance organization (HMO) that guaranteed a minimum MRI usage at a fixed reimbursement rate. In that situation, the project would not be very risky, despite the sensitivity analysis showing the NPV to be highly sensitive to changes in volume. In general, a project's *stand-alone* risk, which is what a sensitivity analysis measures, depends on both the sensitivity of its profitability to changes in key input variables and the ranges of likely values of these variables. Because sensitivity analysis considers only the first factor, its results can be misleading. Furthermore, sensitivity analysis does not consider any interactions among the uncertain input variables; it considers each variable independently.

In spite of the shortcomings of sensitivity analysis as a risk assessment tool, it does provide managers with valuable information. First, it provides profitability breakeven information for the project's uncertain variables. For example, exhibits 15.2 and 15.3 show that a decrease of just a few percent in expected volume makes the project unprofitable, whereas the project remains profitable even if salvage value falls by more than 10 percent. Although somewhat rough, this breakeven information is clearly valuable to Ridgeland's managers.

Second, and perhaps more important, sensitivity analysis helps managers identify which input variables are *most critical* to the project's profitability and hence to the project's financial success. In this example, volume is clearly the most critical input variable of the two being examined, so Ridgeland's managers should ensure that the volume estimate is the best possible. A small overestimate in volume can make the project seem very attractive financially when evaluated, yet the actual results could easily be disappointing. The concept here is that Ridgeland's managers have a limited amount of time to spend on analyzing the MRI project, and sensitivity analysis enables them to focus on what's most important.

In addition, sensitivity analysis can be useful after a project has been initiated. For example, assume that Ridgeland's MRI project is accepted and the first post-audit indicates that the project is not meeting its financial expectations. Ridgeland's managers must take actions to try to improve the project's financial results. But what actions should they take? Sensitivity analysis identifies the variables that have the greatest impact on profitability. Thus, managers can try to influence those variables that have the greatest potential for improving financial performance, such as volume, rather than those variables that have little impact on profitability.

1. Briefly describe sensitivity analysis.
2. What type of risk does it attempt to measure?
3. Is sensitivity analysis a good risk assessment tool? If not, what is its value in the capital budgeting process?

Scenario Analysis

Scenario analysis is a stand-alone risk analysis technique that considers the impact of changes in key variables on NPV, the likely range of the variable values, and the interactions among variables. To conduct a scenario analysis, managers pick a "bad" set of circumstances (e.g., low volume, low salvage value), an average or "most likely" set, and a "good" set. The resulting input values are then used to create a probability distribution of NPV.

To illustrate scenario analysis, assume that Ridgeland's managers regard a drop in weekly volume below 30 scans as unlikely and a volume above 50 as also improbable. On the other hand, salvage value could be as low as $500,000 or as high as $1 million. The most likely (and expected) values are 40 scans per week for volume and $750,000 for salvage value. Thus, a volume of 30 and a $500,000 salvage value define the lower bound, or worst-case scenario, while a volume of 50 and a salvage value of $1 million define the upper bound, or best-case scenario.

Ridgeland can now use the *worst, most likely,* and *best case* values for the input variables to obtain the NPV that corresponds to each scenario.

Ridgeland's managers used a spreadsheet model to conduct the analysis; exhibit 15.4 summarizes the results. The most likely (base) case results in a positive NPV; the worst case produces a negative NPV; and the best case results in a large, positive NPV. These results can now be used to determine the expected NPV and standard deviation of NPV. To do so, an estimate is needed of the probabilities of occurrence of the three scenarios. Suppose that Ridgeland's managers estimate that there is a 20 percent chance of the worst case occurring, a 60 percent chance of the most likely case occurring, and a 20 percent chance of the best case occurring. Of course, it is difficult to estimate scenario probabilities with any confidence.

Exhibit 15.4 contains a discrete distribution of returns, so the expected NPV can be found as follows:

$$\text{Expected NPV} = [0.20 \times (-\$819{,}844)] + (0.60 \times \$82{,}493)$$
$$+ (0.20 \times \$984{,}829) = \$82{,}493.$$

The expected NPV in the scenario analysis is the same as the base case NPV, \$82,493. The results are consistent because, when coupled with scenario probabilities, the values of the uncertain variables used in the scenario analysis—30, 40, and 50 scans for volume and \$500,000, \$750,000, and \$1,000,000 for salvage value—produce the same expected values used in the exhibit 15.1 base case analysis. If inconsistencies exist between the base case NPV and the expected NPV in the scenario analysis, the two analyses have inconsistent input value assumptions.

Using the distribution of NPVs, we can calculate the standard deviation (denoted by σ):

$$\sigma_{NPV} = [0.20 \times (-\$819{,}844 - \$82{,}493)^2 + 0.60 \times (\$82{,}493 - \$82{,}493)^2$$
$$+ 0.20 \times (\$989{,}829 - \$82{,}493)^2]^{1/2}$$
$$= \$570{,}688.$$

Scenario	Probability of Outcome	Volume	Salvage Value	NPV
Worst case	0.20	30	$ 500,000	($819,844)
Most likely case	0.60	40	750,000	82,493
Best case	0.20	50	1,000,000	984,829
Expected value		40	$ 750,000	$ 82,493
Standard deviation				$570,688
Coefficient of variation				6.9

EXHIBIT 15.4
MRI Project
Scenario
Analysis

The standard deviation of NPV measures the MRI project's stand-alone risk. Ridgeland's managers can compare the standard deviation of NPV of this project with the uncertainty inherent in Ridgeland's aggregate cash flows, or average project. Often, the coefficient of variation (CV) is used to measure the stand-alone risk of a project: $CV = \sigma_{NPV} \div E(NPV) = \$570,688 \div \$82,493 =$ for the MRI project. CV measures the risk per unit of return and is a better measure of comparative risk than standard deviation, especially when projects have widely differing NPVs. If Ridgeland's average project has a CV of 4.0, the MRI project would be judged to be riskier than the firm's average project, so it would be classified as having above-average risk. (We use NPV as the ROI measure in this scenario analysis, but we could have focused on either IRR or MIRR.)

Scenario analysis can also be interpreted in a less mathematical way. The worst-case NPV, a loss of about \$800,000 for the MRI project, represents an estimate of the worst possible financial consequences of the project. If Ridgeland can absorb such a loss in value without much impact on its financial condition, the project does not represent a significant financial danger to the hospital. Conversely, if such a loss would mean financial ruin for the hospital, its managers might be unwilling to undertake the project, regardless of its profitability under the most likely and best-case scenarios. Note that the risk of the project is *not* changing in these two situations. The difference is in the ability of the organization to *bear* the risk inherent in the project.

Although scenario analysis provides useful information about a project's stand-alone risk, it is limited in two ways. First, it considers only a few states of the economy, so it provides information on only a few potential profitability outcomes for the project. In reality, an almost infinite number of possibilities exist. Although the illustrative scenario analysis contained only three scenarios, it could be expanded to include more states of the economy—say, five or seven. However, there is a practical limit to how many scenarios can be included in a scenario analysis.

Second, scenario analysis, at least as it is normally conducted, implies a definite relationship among the uncertain variables—that is, the analysis assumes that the worst value for volume (30 scans per week) will occur at the same time as the worst value for salvage value (\$500,000) because the worst-case scenario is defined by combining the worst possible value of each uncertain variable. Although this relationship (all worst values occurring together) may hold in some situations, it may not hold in others. For example, if volume is low, the MRI may have less wear and tear and will be worth more after five years of use. The worst value for volume, then, should be coupled with the best salvage value. Conversely, poor volume may be symptomatic of poor medical effectiveness of the MRI, leading to limited demand for used equipment and a low salvage value. Scenario analysis tends to create extreme profitability values for the worst and best cases because it automatically combines all worst and best input values, even if those values have only a remote chance of occurring together. The problem can be mitigated, but not eliminated, by assigning relatively low probabilities to the best-case and worst-case scenarios or by using more than three scenarios. The next section describes a stand-alone risk assessment method, Monte Carlo simulation, that addresses both the limited number of states and extreme profitability problems.

A **word of warning** regarding the relationship between profitability and risk analyses is in order here. When conducting a scenario analysis, it is natural to consider both the resulting profitability (NPV in the illustration) and risk. However, it is possible for inconsistencies in the input variable assumptions to cause the expected NPV from the scenario analysis to differ from the base case NPV. A scenario analysis is conducted for the **sole purpose of assessing a project's stand-alone risk.** A scenario analysis is *not* conducted to estimate a project's profitability. Thus, once the risk determination has been made (for example, in a later section Ridgeland judges the MRI project to have above-average risk), the scenario analysis plays no further role in the project evaluation. As you will see, the project risk determination feeds back into the base case analysis to make the final judgment regarding the project's financial worth.

---

1. Briefly describe scenario analysis.
2. What type of risk does it attempt to measure?
3. What are its strengths and weaknesses?

SELF-TEST QUESTIONS

Monte Carlo Simulation

Monte Carlo simulation, so named because it developed from the mathematics of casino gambling, describes uncertainty in terms of *continuous probability distributions,* which have an infinite number of outcomes rather than just a few *discrete* values. Monte Carlo simulation provides a more realistic view of a project's risk than scenario analysis and can be installed as an add-on to a spreadsheet program. Because most financial analysis today is done with spreadsheets, Monte Carlo simulation is accessible to virtually all health services organizations, large and small.

The first step in a Monte Carlo simulation is to create a model that calculates the project's net cash flows and profitability measures, as was done for Ridgeland's MRI project. The relatively certain variables are estimated as

Monte Carlo simulation
A computerized risk analysis technique that uses continuous distributions to represent the uncertain input variables.

single, or point, values in the model, while continuous probability distributions are used to specify the uncertain cash flow variables. After the model has been created, the simulation software automatically executes the following steps:

1. The Monte Carlo program chooses a single random value for each uncertain variable on the basis of its specified probability distribution.
2. The values selected for each uncertain variable, along with the point values for the relatively certain variables, are combined in the model to estimate the net cash flow for each year.
3. Using the net cash flow data, the model calculates the project's profitability—for example, as measured by NPV. A single completion of these three steps constitutes one iteration, or run, in Monte Carlo simulation.
4. The Monte Carlo software repeats the above steps many times (e.g., 5,000). Because each run is based on different input values, each run produces a different NPV.

The result of the simulation is an NPV probability distribution based on a large number of individual scenarios, which encompasses almost all of the likely financial outcomes. Monte Carlo software usually displays the results of the simulation in both tabular and graphical forms and automatically calculates summary statistical data such as expected value and standard deviation.[3]

For an illustration of Monte Carlo simulation, again consider Ridgeland Community Hospital's MRI project. As in the scenario analysis, the illustration has been simplified by specifying the distributions for only two key variables: weekly volume and salvage value. Weekly volume is not expected to vary by more than ±10 scans from its expected value of 40 scans. Because this situation is symmetrical, the normal (bell-shaped) distribution can be used to represent the uncertainty inherent in volume. In a normal distribution, the expected value plus or minus three standard deviations will encompass almost the entire distribution. Thus, a normal distribution with an expected value of 40 scans and a standard deviation of $10 \div 3 = 3.33$ scans is a reasonable description of the uncertainty inherent in weekly volume.

A triangular distribution is chosen for salvage value because it specifically fixes the upper and lower bounds, whereas the tails of a normal distribution are, in theory, limitless. The triangular distribution is also used extensively when the input distribution is nonsymmetrical because it can easily accommodate skewness. Salvage value uncertainty was specified by a triangular distribution with a lower limit of $500,000, a most likely value of $750,000, and an upper limit of $1 million.

The basic MRI model containing these two continuous distributions was used, plus a Monte Carlo add-on to the spreadsheet program, to conduct

Expected NPV	$ 82,498
Minimum NPV	($951,760)
Maximum NPV	$ 970,191
Probability of a positive NPV	62.8%
Standard deviation	$256,212
Skewness	0.002

EXHIBIT 15.5
Simulation
Results
Summary

a simulation with 5,000 iterations. The output is summarized in exhibit 15.5, and the resulting probability distribution of NPV is plotted in exhibit 15.6. The mean, or expected, NPV, $82,498, is about the same as the base case NPV and expected NPV indicated in the scenario analysis, $82,493. In theory, all three results should be the same because the expected values for all input variables are the same in the three analyses. However, there is some randomness in the Monte Carlo simulation, which leads to an expected NPV that is slightly different from the others. The more iterations that are run, the more likely the Monte Carlo NPV will be the same as the base case NPV, assuming the assumptions are consistent.

The standard deviation of NPV is lower in the simulation analysis because the NPV distribution in the simulation contains values within the entire range of possible outcomes, while the NPV distribution in the scenario analysis contains only the most likely value and best-case and worst-case extremes.

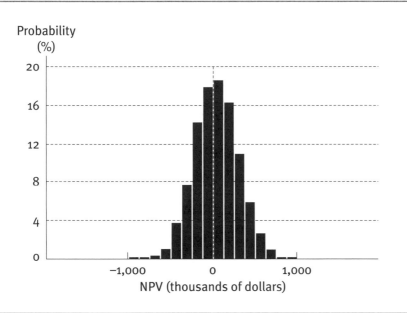

EXHIBIT 15.6
NPV Probability
Distribution

In this illustration, one value for volume uncertainty is specified for all five years; that is, the value chosen by the Monte Carlo software for volume in year 1—for example, 40 scans—is used as the volume input for the remaining four years in that iteration of the simulation analysis. As an alternative, the normal distribution for year 1 could be applied to each year separately, which would allow the volume forecasts to vary from year to year. Then, the Monte Carlo software might choose 35 as the value for year 1, 43 as the year 2 input, 32 for year 3, and so on. This approach, however, may not do a good job of describing real-world behavior—high usage in the first year presumably means strong acceptance of the MRI system and high usage in the remaining years. Similarly, low usage in the first year probably portends low usage in future years.

The volume and salvage value variables were treated as independent in the simulation—that is, the value chosen by the Monte Carlo software from the salvage value distribution was not related to the value chosen from the volume distribution. Thus, in any run, a low volume can be coupled with a high salvage value and vice versa. If Ridgeland's managers believe that high utilization at the hospital indicates a strong national demand for MRI systems, they can specify a positive correlation between these variables. A positive correlation would tend to increase the riskiness of the project because a low-volume pick in one iteration cannot be offset by a high-salvage-value pick. Conversely, if the salvage value is more a function of the technological advances that occur over the next five years than local utilization, it may be best to specify the variables as independent, as is done in this example.

As in scenario analysis, the project's simulation results must be compared with a similar analysis of the firm's average project. If Ridgeland's average project were considered to have less stand-alone risk when a Monte Carlo simulation was conducted, the MRI project would be judged to have above-average stand-alone risk.

For Your Consideration
How Many Scenarios in a Scenario Analysis?

In the scenario analysis of Ridgeland's MRI project, we used three scenarios. However, three is not a magic bullet—the more scenarios that are used, the more information that is obtained from the analysis. Furthermore, more scenarios lessen the problem associated with extreme values because the best and worst scenarios can be assigned low probabilities (which are probably realistic) without causing the risk inherent in the project to be understated.

While more scenarios add realism and provide more information for decision makers, a greater number of scenarios increases forecasting difficulty and makes the analysis more time consuming. Furthermore, the greater the number of scenarios, the more difficulty in interpreting the results. Thus, the entire process is easier if three scenarios are used rather than, say, nine.

What do you think? Are three scenarios sufficient, or should more be used? How many scenarios are too many? Is it better to have an odd number of scenarios than an even number? Is there an optimal number of scenarios?

Monte Carlo simulation has two primary advantages over scenario analysis: (1) All possible input variable values are considered, and (2) correlations among the uncertain inputs can be incorporated into the analysis. However, there is a downside to these two advantages: Although it is mechanically easy to input the probability distributions for the uncertain variables as well as their correlations into a Monte Carlo simulation, it is much more difficult to determine what those distributions and correlations are. The problem is that the more information a risk analysis technique requires, the harder it is to develop the data with any confidence; hence, managers can be left with an elegant result of questionable value.

SELF-TEST QUESTIONS

1. Briefly, what is Monte Carlo simulation?
2. What type of risk does it attempt to measure?
3. What are its strengths and weaknesses?

Qualitative Risk Assessment

In some situations, it may be difficult to conduct a quantitative risk assessment—the numbers are just too difficult to predict. In these situations, rather than ignore differential risk, some healthcare businesses use a more subjective approach. More and more healthcare organizations are using qualitative risk assessment techniques to confirm quantitative assessment results or as the sole basis for the risk assessment. For example, one large healthcare clinic uses five questions to qualitatively assess project risk:

- Does the project require additional market share or represent a new service initiative?
- Is the project outside the scope of current management expertise?
- Does the project require difficult-to-recruit technical specialists?
- Will the project put us in competition with a strong competitor?
- Does the project require the use of new, unproven technology?

To assess project risk, each yes answer is assigned one point, while each no answer receives zero points. If the total point count for the project is zero, it is judged to have low risk; one or two points indicate moderate risk, and three or more points indicate high risk. Although such a subjective approach initially appears to have little theoretical foundation, a closer examination reveals that each question in the above list is tied to cash flow uncertainty. Thus, the greater the number of yes answers, the greater the cash flow uncertainty and hence the greater the stand-alone risk of the project.

The value of using the qualitative risk assessment approach in conjunction with a quantitative risk assessment is that it forces managers to think about project risk in alternative frameworks. If the quantitative and qualitative assessments do not agree, it is clear that the project's risk assessment requires more consideration.

1. Describe qualitative risk assessment.
2. Why does it work?
3. Assume a quantitative risk assessment has been conducted on a project. Is a qualitative risk assessment necessary?

Incorporating Risk into the Decision Process

Thus far, the MRI illustration has demonstrated that it is difficult to quantify a project's riskiness. It may be possible to reach the general conclusion that one project is more or less risky than another or to compare the riskiness of a project with the aggregate risk of the firm, but it is difficult to develop a precise measure of project risk. This lack of precision in measuring project risk adds to the difficulties involved in incorporating differential risk into the capital budgeting decision.

There are two methods for incorporating project risk into the capital budgeting decision process: (1) the certainty equivalent method, which adjusts a project's expected cash flows to reflect project risk, and (2) the risk-adjusted discount rate method, which deals with differential risk by changing the cost of capital. Although the risk-adjusted discount rate method is used by most businesses, there are some theoretical advantages to using the certainty equivalent method. Furthermore, it raises some interesting issues related to the risk-adjustment process.

The Certainty Equivalent Method

The *certainty equivalent (CE) method* follows directly from the concept of *utility theory*, which is used by economists to explain how individuals make choices among risky alternatives.[4] Under the CE approach, managers must first evaluate a cash flow's risk and then specify, with certainty, how much money would be required to be indifferent between the riskless (certain) sum and the risky cash flow's expected value. To illustrate, suppose that you are offered two choices:

1. **Flip a coin.** If it's heads, you win $1 million; if it's tails, you get nothing. The expected value of the gamble is $(0.5 \times \$1,000,000) + (0.5 \times \$0) = \$500,000$, but the actual outcome will be either zero or $1 million, so the gamble is quite risky.
2. **Do not flip the coin.** Simply pocket $400,000 in cash.

If you are indifferent to the two alternatives, $400,000 is the CE amount for this particularly risky expected $500,000 cash flow. The riskless $400,000 provides the same satisfaction (utility) as the risky $500,000 expected return. In general, investors are risk averse, so the CE amount for this gamble will be something less than the $500,000 expected value. But each person has their own CE value—the greater the degree of risk aversion, the lower the CE amount.

The CE concept can be applied to capital budgeting decisions, at least in theory, in this way:

1. Convert each net cash flow of a project to its CE value. Here, the riskiness of *each net cash flow* is assessed, and a CE cash flow is chosen on the basis of that risk. The greater the risk, the greater the difference between the net cash flow's expected value and its lower CE value. (If a net cash outflow is being adjusted, the CE value is higher than the expected value. The unique risk adjustments required on cash outflows are discussed in a later section.)
2. Once each cash flow is expressed as a CE, discount the project's CE cash flow stream by the *risk-free rate* (adjusted for taxes if necessary) to obtain the project's "differential risk-adjusted" NPV.[5] Here, the term *differential risk-adjusted* implies that the unique risk of the project, compared with the overall risk of the business, has been incorporated into the decision process. The risk-free rate is used as the discount rate because CE cash flows are analogous to risk-free cash flows.
3. A positive differential risk-adjusted NPV indicates that the project is profitable even after adjusting for differential project risk.

The CE method is simple and neat. Furthermore, it can easily handle differential risk among the *individual* net cash flows. For example, the final year's CE cash flow might be adjusted downward an additional amount to account for salvage value risk if that risk is considered to be greater than the risk inherent in the operating cash flows.

Unfortunately, there is no practical way to estimate a risky cash flow's CE value. There is no benchmark available to help make the estimate, so each individual would have her own estimate, and these could vary significantly. Also, the risk assessment techniques—for example, scenario analysis—focus on profitability and hence measure the stand-alone risk of a project in its entirety. This process provides no information about the riskiness of individual cash flows, so there is no basis for adjusting each cash flow for its own unique risk.

The Risk-Adjusted Discount Rate Method

risk-adjusted discount rate (RADR)
A discount rate that accounts for the specific riskiness of the investment being analyzed.

In the **risk-adjusted discount rate (RADR)** method, expected cash flows are used in the valuation process, and the risk adjustment is made to the discount rate (opportunity cost of capital). All average-risk projects are discounted at the firm's corporate cost of capital, which represents the opportunity cost of capital for average-risk projects; high-risk projects are assigned a higher cost of capital; and low-risk projects are discounted at a lower cost of capital.

One advantage of the RADR method is that the process has a starting benchmark—the firm's corporate cost of capital. This discount rate reflects the riskiness of the business in the aggregate, or the riskiness of the business's average project. Another advantage is that project risk assessment techniques identify a project's aggregate risk—the combined risk of all of the cash flows—and the RADR applies a single adjustment to the cost of capital rather than attempting to adjust individual cash flows. However, the disadvantage is that there typically is no theoretical basis for setting the size of the RADR adjustment, so the amount of adjustment remains a matter of judgment.

The RADR method has one additional disadvantage. It combines the factors that account for time value (the risk-free rate) and the adjustment for risk (the risk premium): Project cost of capital = Differential risk-adjusted discount rate = Risk-free rate + Risk premium. The CE approach, on the other hand, keeps the risk adjustment and time value separate: Time value is accounted for in the discount rate, and risk is accounted for in the cash flows. By lumping together risk and time value, the RADR method compounds the risk premium over time—just as interest compounds over time, so does the risk premium. This compounding of the risk premium means that the RADR method automatically assigns more risk to cash flows that occur in the distant future, and the further into the future, the greater the implied risk. Because the CE method assigns risk to each cash flow individually, it does not impose any assumptions regarding the relationship between risk and time.

Key Equation: Risk-Adjusted Discount Rate Theoretical Model
The RADR model is one method used to incorporate risk in the capital budgeting decision process. It is based on the following concept:

Project cost of capital = Risk-free rate + Risk premium.

The idea here is that the risk-free rate accounts for the time value of money, while the risk premium accounts for the unique (below-average, average, or above-average) risk of the project.

The RADR method, with a constant discount rate applied to all cash flows of a project, implies that risk increases with time. This imposes a greater burden on long-term projects, so short-term projects will tend to look better financially than long-term projects. For most projects, the assumption of increasing risk over time is probably reasonable because cash flows are more difficult to forecast the further one moves into the future. However, managers should be aware that the RADR approach automatically penalizes distant cash flows, and an explicit penalty based solely on cash flow timing is not warranted unless some specific additional source of risk can be identified.

SELF-TEST QUESTIONS

1. What are the differences between the CE and RADR methods for risk incorporation?
2. What assumptions about time and risk are inherent in the RADR method?

Making the Final Decision

In most project risk analyses, it is impossible to assess the project's corporate or market risk quantitatively, so managers are left with only an assessment of the project's stand-alone risk. Because Ridgeland Community Hospital is a not-for-profit organization, corporate risk is the most relevant risk in capital budgeting decisions. What is the MRI project's corporate risk? The MRI project, like most projects being evaluated by Ridgeland, is in the same line of business—the provision of patient services—as the firm's other projects. Under these circumstances, it is likely that the returns on the MRI project would be highly correlated with Ridgeland's aggregate returns (overall profitability). Thus, Ridgeland's managers concluded that the stand-alone risk assessment is a good proxy for the project's corporate risk, and the MRI project was categorized as high-risk.

The business's corporate cost of capital provides the basis for estimating a project's differential risk-adjusted discount rate—average-risk projects are discounted at the corporate cost of capital, high-risk projects are discounted at a higher cost of capital, and low-risk projects are discounted at a rate below the corporate cost of capital. Unfortunately, there is no good way of specifying exactly how much higher or lower these discount rates should be. Given the present state of the art, risk adjustments are necessarily judgmental and somewhat arbitrary.

Ridgeland's standard procedure is to add 4 percentage points to its 10 percent corporate cost of capital when evaluating high-risk projects, and to subtract 2 percentage points when evaluating low-risk projects. Thus, to estimate the high-risk MRI project's differential risk-adjusted NPV, the project's expected (base case) cash flows shown in exhibit 15.1 are discounted at 10% + 4% = 14%. This rate is called the *project cost of capital*, as opposed to the corporate cost of capital, because it reflects the risk characteristics of a specific project rather than the aggregate risk characteristics of the business (or average project). The resultant NPV is –$200,017, so the project becomes unprofitable when the analysis is adjusted to reflect its high risk. Ridgeland's managers may still decide to go ahead with the MRI project for other reasons, but at least they know that its expected profitability is not sufficient to make up for its risk.

Key Equation: Risk-Adjusted Discount Rate Implementation Model
The RADR method is implemented as follows:

Project cost of capital = Corporate cost of capital + Risk adjustment.

Here, the corporate cost of capital is used as the base rate (starting point), and a risk adjustment is applied if the project has non-average risk. For above-average-risk projects, the risk premium is added to the base rate, while the risk premium is subtracted for those projects judged to have below-average risk.

To illustrate, assume a project having above-average risk is being evaluated. The corporate cost of capital is 10 percent, and the standard adjustment amount is 3 percentage points. With these assumptions, the project cost of capital is 13 percent:

Project cost of capital = Corporate cost of capital + Risk adjustment
= 10% + 3% = 13%.

1. How do most firms incorporate differential risk into the capital budgeting decision process?
2. Is the risk adjustment objective or subjective?
3. What is a project cost of capital?

Adjusting Cash Outflows for Risk

Although most projects are evaluated on the basis of profitability, some projects are evaluated solely on the basis of cost. Such evaluations are done when it is impossible to allocate revenues to a particular project, or when two competing projects will produce the same revenue stream. For example, suppose that Greenbriar Oncology Associates must choose between two ways of disposing of its medical waste. There is no question about the need for the project, and neither method will affect the medical practice's revenue stream. In this case, the decision will be based on the present value of expected future costs—that is, the method with the lower present value of costs will be chosen.

Exhibit 15.7 contains the forecast annual costs associated with each method. The in-house system would require a large expenditure at year 0 to upgrade the practice's current disposal system, but the yearly operating costs would be relatively low. Conversely, if Greenbriar contracted for disposal services with an outside vendor, it would have to pay only $25,000 up front to initiate the contract. However, the annual contract fee would be $200,000 a year.

If both methods were judged to have average risk, Greenbriar's corporate cost of capital, 10 percent, would be applied to the cash flows to

Year	In-House System	Outside Contract
0	($500,000)	($ 25,000)
1	(75,000)	(200,000)
2	(75,000)	(200,000)
3	(75,000)	(200,000)
4	(75,000)	(200,000)
5	(75,000)	(200,000)
Present value of costs at a discount rate of:		
10%	($784,309)	($783,157)
14%	—	($ 711,616)
6%	—	($867,473)

EXHIBIT 15.7
Greenbriar Oncology Associates: Waste Disposal Analysis

obtain the present value (PV) of costs for each method. Because the PVs of costs for the two waste disposal systems ($784,309 for the in-house system and $783,157 for the contract method) are roughly equal at the 10 percent discount rate, on the basis of financial considerations alone, Greenbriar's managers are indifferent as to which method should be chosen.

However, Greenbriar's managers actually believe that the contract method is much riskier than the in-house method. The cost of modifying the current system is known almost to the dollar, and operating costs can be predicted fairly well. Furthermore, with the in-house system, operating costs are under the control of Greenbriar's management. Conversely, if Greenbriar relies on the contractor for waste disposal, the practice is more or less stuck with continuing the contract because it will lose in-house capability. Because the contractor was only willing to guarantee the price for one year, the bid may have been lowballed and large price increases will occur in future years. The two methods have about the same PV of costs when both are considered to have average risk, so which method should be chosen if the contract method is judged to have high risk? Clearly, if the costs are the same under a common discount rate, the lower-risk in-house project should be chosen.

Now, try to incorporate this intuitive differential risk conclusion into the quantitative analysis. Conventional wisdom is to increase the corporate cost of capital for high-risk projects, so the contract cash flows would be discounted using a project cost of capital of 14 percent, which is the rate that Greenbriar applies to high-risk projects. But at a 14 percent discount rate, the contract method has a PV of costs of only $711,616, which is about $70,000 lower than for the in-house method. If the discount rate were increased to 20 percent on the contract method, it would appear to be $161,000 cheaper than the in-house method. Thus, the riskier the contract method is judged to be, the better it looks.

Something is obviously wrong here. To penalize a *cash outflow* for higher-than-average risk, it must have a *higher* present value, not a *lower* one. Therefore, a cash outflow that has above-average risk must be evaluated with a lower-than-average cost of capital. Recognizing this, Greenbriar's managers applied a 10% – 4% = 6% discount rate to the high-risk contract method's cash flows. This produces a PV of costs for the contract method of $867,473, which is about $83,000 more than the PV of costs for the average-risk in-house method.

The appropriate risk adjustment for cash outflows is also applicable to other situations. For example, the city of Detroit offered Ann Arbor Health Care Inc. the opportunity to use a city-owned building in one of the city's blighted areas for a walk-in clinic. The city offered to pay to refurbish the building, and all profits made by the clinic would accrue to Ann Arbor. However, after ten years, Ann Arbor would have to buy the building from the city at the then-current market value. The market value estimate that Ann Arbor used in its analysis was $2 million, but the realized cost could be much greater, or much less, depending on the economic condition of the neighborhood at that time. The project's other cash flows were of average risk, but this single outflow had higher risk, so Ann Arbor lowered the discount rate that it applied to this one cash flow. This action created a higher present value for the $2 million cost (outflow) and hence lowered the project's NPV.

The bottom line here is that the risk adjustment for cash outflows is the opposite of the adjustment for cash inflows. When cash outflows are being evaluated, higher risk leads to a lower discount rate.[6]

SELF-TEST QUESTIONS

1. Why are some projects evaluated on the basis of present value of costs?
2. Is there any difference between the risk adjustments applied to cash inflows and cash outflows? Explain your answer.
3. Can differential risk adjustments be made to single cash flows, or must the same adjustment be made to all of a project's cash flows?

Divisional Costs of Capital

In theory, project costs of capital should reflect both a project's differential risk and its differential *debt capacity*. The logic here is that if a project's optimal financing mix is significantly different from the business in the aggregate, the weights used in estimating the corporate cost of capital do not reflect the weights appropriate to the project. Because of the difficulties encountered in estimating a project's debt capacity (its optimal capital structure), such adjustments are rarely made in practice.

Even though it is not common to make capital structure adjustments for individual projects, firms often make both capital structure and risk adjustments when developing divisional costs of capital. To illustrate, a for-profit healthcare system might have one division that invests primarily in real estate for medical uses and another division that runs an HMO. Clearly, each division has its own unique business risk and optimal capital structure. The low-risk, high-debt-capacity real estate division could have a cost of capital of 10 percent, while the high-risk, low-debt-capacity HMO division could have a cost of capital of 14 percent. The health system itself, which consists of 50 percent real estate assets and 50 percent HMO assets, would have a corporate cost of capital of 12 percent.

If all capital budgeting decisions within the system were made on the basis of the overall system's 12 percent cost of capital, the process would be biased in favor of the higher-risk HMO division. The cost of capital would be too low for the HMO division and too high for the real estate division. Over time, this cost-of-capital bias would result in too many HMO projects being accepted and too few real estate projects, which would skew the business line mix toward HMO assets and increase the overall risk of the system. The solution to the cost-of-capital bias problem is to use *divisional costs of capital*, rather than the overall corporate cost of capital, in the capital budgeting decision process.

Unlike individual project costs of capital, divisional costs of capital often can be estimated with some confidence because it is usually possible to identify publicly traded firms that are predominantly in the same line of business as the subsidiary. For example, the cost of capital for the HMO division could be estimated

---

For Your Consideration

Uncertainty in Initial Cash Outflows

In many capital budgeting situations, the initial cost of a project, especially when it occurs only at time 0, is assumed to be known with certainty. The idea here is that in most cases bids have already been received from vendors, so the initial cost can be predicted with relative precision. However, in some circumstances, there can be substantial uncertainty in initial costs. For example, there can be a great deal of uncertainty in the cost of a building that will not be constructed for several years. Or there can be uncertainty in the cost of a major construction project that will take several years to complete.

When there is uncertainty in initial cost, how should that risk be incorporated into the analysis? If the entire cost, or even the major portion, occurs at time 0, the discount rate is not applied to the cash flow, so the risk-adjusted discount rate method will not get the job done.

What do you think? Can the CE method be used? Assume that time 0 costs on a project could be $100,000 or $150,000 with equal probability, so the expected initial cost is $125,000. What is your estimate of the CE cash flow? (Hint: Remember that risk adjustments to cash outflows are the opposite of those applied to inflows.)

by looking at the debt and equity costs and capital structures of the major for-profit HMOs such as Humana and UnitedHealth Group. With such market data at hand, it is relatively easy to develop divisional costs of capital. As a final check, the weighted average of the divisional costs of capital should equal the firm's corporate cost of capital.

1. In theory, should project cost-of-capital estimates include capital structure effects?
2. Should all divisions of a firm use the firm's corporate cost of capital as the benchmark rate in making capital budgeting decisions?
3. How might a business go about estimating its divisional costs of capital?

An Overview of the Capital Budgeting Decision Process

The discussion of capital budgeting thus far has focused on how managers evaluate individual projects. For capital planning purposes, health services managers also need to forecast the total number of projects that will be undertaken and the dollar amount of capital needed to fund the projects. The list of projects to be undertaken, along with the cost of each project and the total cost, is called the *capital budget*.

While every healthcare provider estimates its capital budget in its own unique way, some procedures are common to all firms. The procedures followed by Seattle Health System are used to illustrate the process:

1. The chief financial officer (CFO) estimates the system's corporate cost of capital. As discussed in chapter 13, this estimate depends on market conditions, the business risk of the system's assets in the aggregate, and the system's optimal capital structure.
2. The CFO then scales the corporate cost of capital up or down to reflect the unique risk and capital structure features of each division. Assume that the system has three divisions: LRD (low-risk division), ARD (average-risk division), and HRD (high-risk division).
3. Managers in each of the divisions evaluate the risk of the proposed projects to their divisions, categorizing each project as LRP (low-risk project), ARP (average-risk project), or HRP (high-risk project). These project risk classifications are based on the riskiness of each project relative to the other projects in the division, not to the system in the aggregate.

Exhibit 15.8 summarizes Seattle Health System's overall capital budgeting process. It uses the same adjustment amounts as does Ridgeland: 4 percentage points for high risk and 2 percentage points for low risk. Thus, the corporate cost of capital is adjusted upward to 14 percent in the high-risk division and downward to 8 percent in the low-risk division. The same adjustment—4 percentage points upward for high-risk projects and 2 percentage points downward for low-risk projects—is applied to differential risk projects in each division. The end result is a range of project costs of capital within the system that runs from 18 percent for high-risk projects in the high-risk division to 6 percent for low-risk projects in the low-risk division.

This process creates a capital budget that incorporates each project's debt capacity (at least at the divisional level) and risk. However, managers also must consider other possible risk factors that may not have been included in the quantitative analysis. For example, could a project under consideration significantly increase the system's liability exposure? Conversely, does the project have any strategic or social value or other attributes that could affect its profitability? Such additional factors must be considered, at least subjectively, before a final decision can be made. Typically, if the project involves new products or services and is large (in capital requirements) relative to

EXHIBIT 15.8
Seattle Health System: Project Cost of Capital Chart

Corporate cost of capital = 10%	HRD cost of capital = 14%	High-risk project	18%
		Average-risk project	14%
		Low-risk project	12%
	ARD cost of capital = 10%	High-risk project	14%
		Average-risk project	10%
		Low-risk project	8%
	LRD cost of capital = 8%	High-risk project	12%
		Average-risk project	8%
		Low-risk project	6%

the size of the firm's average project, the additional subjective factors will be important to the final decision; one large mistake can bankrupt a firm, so "bet the company" decisions are not made lightly. On the other hand, a decision on a small replacement project would be made mostly on the basis of numerical analysis.

Ultimately, capital budgeting decisions require an analysis of a mix of objective and subjective factors such as risk, debt capacity, profitability, medical staff needs, and social value. The process is not precise, and often there is a temptation to ignore one or more important factors because they are nebulous and difficult to measure. Despite the imprecision and subjectivity, a project's risk, as well as its other attributes, should be assessed and incorporated into the capital budgeting decision process.

---

1. Describe a typical capital budgeting decision process.
2. Are decisions made solely on the basis of quantitative factors? Explain your answer.

Capital Rationing

Standard capital budgeting procedures assume that for-profit businesses can raise virtually unlimited amounts of capital to meet capital budgeting needs. Presumably, as long as the business is investing the funds in profitable (positive NPV) projects, it should be able to raise the debt and equity needed to fund all worthwhile projects. In addition, standard capital budgeting procedures assume that a business will raise the capital needed to finance its optimal capital budget roughly in accordance with its target capital structure.

This picture of a firm's capital financing and capital investment process is probably appropriate for most investor-owned firms. However, not-for-profit businesses do not have unlimited access to capital. Their equity capital is limited to retentions, contributions, and grants, and their debt capital is limited to the amount supported by the equity capital base. Thus, not-for-profit businesses, and even investor-owned firms on occasion, face periods in which the capital needed for investment in new projects exceeds the amount of capital available. This situation is called **capital rationing**.

If capital rationing exists, and the business has more acceptable projects than capital, then, *from a financial perspective,* the firm should accept that set of capital projects that maximizes aggregate NPV and still meets the

capital rationing
The situation that occurs when a business has more attractive investment opportunities than it has capital to invest.

capital constraint. This approach can be called "getting the most bang for the buck" because it picks projects that have the most positive impact on the firm's financial condition.

profitability index (PI)
A project return-on-investment measure defined as the present value of cash inflows divided by the present value of outflows. It measures the number of dollars of inflow per dollar of outflow (on a present value basis), or the "bang for the buck."

An ROI measure not yet discussed, **the profitability index (PI)** is useful under capital rationing. The PI is defined as the present value (PV) of cash inflows divided by the PV of cash outflows. Thus, for Ridgeland's MRI project discussed earlier in the chapter, PI = $2,582,493 ÷ $2,500,000 = 1.03. The PI measures a project's dollars of profitability per dollar of investment, all on a PV basis. In other words, it measures the bang for the buck. The MRI project promises three cents of profit for every dollar invested, which indicates it is not very profitable. (The PI of 1.03 is before adjusting for risk. After adjusting for risk, the project's PI is less than 1.00, indicating that the project is unprofitable.) In a capital rationing situation, the optimal capital budget is determined first by listing all profitable projects in descending order of PI. Then, projects are selected from the top of the list downward until the available capital is used up.

Of course, in healthcare businesses, priority may be assigned to some low or even negative PI projects, which is fine as long as these projects are offset by the selection of profitable projects that prevent the low-profitability priority projects from eroding the business's financial condition.

1. What is capital rationing?
2. From a financial perspective, how are projects chosen when capital rationing exists?
3. What is the profitability index, and why is it useful under capital rationing?

Key Concepts

This chapter, which continues the discussion of capital budgeting started in chapter 14, focuses on risk assessment and incorporation. The key concepts of this chapter are as follows:

- Three separate and distinct types of *project risk* can be identified and defined: (1) stand-alone risk, (2) corporate risk, and (3) market risk.
- A project's *stand-alone risk* is the relevant risk if the project is the sole project of a not-for-profit firm. It is a function of the

(continued)

(continued from previous page)

project's profit uncertainty and is generally measured by the *standard deviation* of net present value (NPV). Stand-alone risk is often used as a proxy for corporate and market risk because (1) corporate and market risk are often impossible to measure and (2) the three types of risk are usually highly correlated.

- *Corporate risk* reflects the contribution of a project to the overall riskiness of the business. Corporate risk ignores stockholder diversification, so it is the relevant risk for most not-for-profit businesses.

- *Market risk* reflects the contribution of a project to the overall riskiness of owners' well-diversified portfolios. In theory, market risk is the relevant risk for investor-owned firms, but many people argue that corporate risk is also relevant to owners, and it is certainly relevant to a firm's other stakeholders.

- Three quantitative techniques are commonly used to *assess* a project's stand-alone risk: (1) sensitivity analysis, (2) scenario analysis, and (3) Monte Carlo simulation.

- *Sensitivity analysis* shows how much a project's profitability—for example, as measured by NPV—changes in response to a given change in an input variable such as volume, with other things held constant.

- *Scenario analysis* defines a project's best, most likely, and worst cases and then uses these data to measure its stand-alone risk.

- Whereas scenario analysis focuses on only a few possible outcomes, *Monte Carlo simulation* uses continuous distributions to reflect the uncertainty inherent in a project's component cash flows. The result is a probability distribution of NPV, or internal rate of return (IRR), that provides a great deal of information about the project's riskiness.

- In many situations, it is impractical to conduct a quantitative project risk assessment. In such situations, many healthcare businesses use a *qualitative approach* to risk assessment.

- There are two methods for incorporating project risk into the capital budgeting decision process: (1) the *certainty equivalent (CE) method*, in which a project's expected cash flows are adjusted to reflect project risk, and (2) the *risk-adjusted discount rate (RADR) method*, in which differential risk is dealt with by changing the cost of capital.

(continued)

(continued from previous page)

- Projects are generally classified as above-average, average, or below-average risk on the basis of their stand-alone risk assessment. Above-average-risk projects are evaluated at a *project cost of capital* that is greater than the firm's corporate cost of capital. Average-risk projects are evaluated at the firm's corporate cost of capital, while below-average-risk projects are evaluated at a rate less than the corporate cost of capital.
- When evaluating *risky cash outflows,* the risk adjustment process is reversed—that is, lower rates are used to discount more risky cash flows.
- *Capital rationing* occurs when a business does not have access to sufficient capital to fund all profitable projects, so the best financial outcome results from accepting the set of projects that has the highest aggregate NPV. In such situations, the profitability index (PI) is a useful profitability (ROI) measure.
- Ultimately, capital budgeting decisions require an analysis of a mix of objective and subjective factors such as risk, debt capacity, profitability, medical staff needs, and service to the community. The process is not precise, but good managers do their best to ensure that none of the relevant factors is ignored.

This chapter concludes our discussion of capital investment decisions. Chapter 16 examines the revenue cycle and current accounts management.

Questions

15.1. a. Why is risk analysis so important to the capital budgeting process?
   b. Describe the three types of project risk. Under what situation is each of the types most relevant to the capital budgeting decision?
   c. Which type of risk is easiest to measure in practice?
   d. Are the three types of project risk usually highly correlated? Explain your answer.
   e. Why is the correlation among project risk measures important?

15.2. a. Briefly describe sensitivity analysis.
   b. What are its strengths and weaknesses?

15.3. a. Briefly describe scenario analysis.

     b. What are its strengths and weaknesses?

15.4. a. Briefly describe Monte Carlo simulation.

     b. What are its strengths and weaknesses?

15.5. a. How is project risk incorporated into a capital budgeting analysis?

     b. Suppose that two mutually exclusive projects are being evaluated on the basis of cash costs. How would risk adjustments be applied in this situation?

15.6. What is the difference between the corporate cost of capital and a project cost of capital?

15.7. What is meant by the term *capital rationing*? From a purely financial standpoint, what is the optimal capital budget under capital rationing?

15.8. Santa Roberta Clinic has estimated its corporate cost of capital to be 11 percent. What are reasonable values for the project costs of capital for low-risk, average-risk, and high-risk projects?

15.9. Describe the qualitative approach to risk assessment. Why does this approach, which does not rely on numerical data, work?

Problems

15.1. The managers of Merton Medical Clinic are analyzing a proposed project. The project's most likely NPV is $120,000, but as evidenced by the following NPV distribution, there is considerable risk involved:

Probability	NPV
0.05	($700,000)
0.20	(250,000)
0.50	120,000
0.20	200,000
0.05	300,000

    a. What are the project's expected NPV and standard deviation of NPV?

    b. Should the base case analysis use the most likely NPV or the expected NPV? Explain your answer.

15.2. Heywood Diagnostic Enterprises is evaluating a project with the following net cash flows and probabilities (Prob.):

Year	Prob. = 0.2	Prob. = 0.6	Prob. = 0.2
0	($100,000)	($100,000)	($100,000)
1	20,000	30,000	40,000
2	20,000	30,000	40,000
3	20,000	30,000	40,000
4	20,000	30,000	40,000
5	30,000	40,000	50,000

The year 5 values include salvage value. Heywood's corporate cost of capital is 10 percent.

a. What is the project's expected (i.e., base case) NPV assuming average risk? (Hint: The base case net cash flows are the expected cash flows in each year.)

b. What are the project's most likely, worst-case, and best-case NPVs?

c. What is the project's expected NPV on the basis of the scenario analysis?

d. What is the project's standard deviation of NPV?

e. Assume that Heywood's managers judge the project to have lower-than-average risk. Furthermore, the company's policy is to adjust the corporate cost of capital up or down by 3 percentage points to account for differential risk. Is the project financially attractive?

15.3. Consider the project contained in problem 14.7 in chapter 14.

a. Perform a sensitivity analysis to see how NPV is affected by changes in the number of procedures per day, average collection amount, and salvage value.

b. Conduct a scenario analysis. Suppose that the hospital's staff concluded that the three most uncertain variables were number of procedures per day, average collection amount, and the equipment's salvage value. Furthermore, the following data were developed:

Scenario	Probability	Number of Procedures	Average Collection	Equipment Salvage Value
Worst	0.25	10	$ 60	$100,000
Most likely	0.50	15	80	200,000
Best	0.25	20	100	300,000

c. Finally, assume that California Health Clinic's average project has a coefficient of variation of NPV in the range of 1.0–2.0. (Hint: The coefficient of variation is defined as the standard deviation of NPV divided by the expected NPV.) The hospital adjusts for risk by adding or subtracting 3 percentage points to its 10 percent corporate cost of capital. After adjusting for differential risk, is the project still profitable?

d. What type of risk was measured and accounted for in parts b and c? Should this be of concern to the hospital's managers?

15.4. The managers of United Medtronics are evaluating the following four projects for the coming budget period. The firm's corporate cost of capital is 14 percent.

Project	Cost	IRR
A	$15,000	17%
B	15,000	11
C	12,000	15
D	20,000	13

a. What is the firm's optimal capital budget?

b. Now, suppose Medtronics's managers want to consider differential risk in the capital budgeting process. Project A has average risk, project B has below-average risk, project C has above-average risk, and project D has average risk. What is the firm's optimal capital budget when differential risk is considered? (Hint: The firm's managers *lower* the IRR of high-risk projects by 3 percentage points and *raise* the IRR of low-risk projects by the same amount.)

15.5. Arc Managed Care Company is evaluating two different computer systems for handling provider claims. There are no incremental revenues attached to the projects, so the decision will be made on the basis of the present value of costs. Arc's corporate cost of capital is 10 percent. Here are the net cash flow estimates in thousands of dollars:

Year	System X	System Y
0	($500)	($1,000)
1	(500)	(300)
2	(500)	(300)
3	(500)	(300)

    a. Assume initially that both systems have average risk. Which one should be chosen?

    b. Assume that system X is judged to have high risk. Arc accounts for differential risk by adjusting its corporate cost of capital up or down by 2 percentage points. Which system should be chosen?

15.6. University Health Center has three divisions: Real Estate, with an 8 percent cost of capital; Health Services, with a 10 percent cost of capital; and Managed Care, with a 12 percent cost of capital. The center's risk adjustment procedures call for adding 3 percentage points to adjust for high risk and subtracting 2 percentage points for low risk. Construct a diagram such as the one in exhibit 15.8 that illustrates the range of project costs of capital for the center.

15.7. Refer to the table developed in problem 15.5 for University Health Center. Assume the Managed Care Division is evaluating a project with the net cash flows and probabilities shown in the table below. Assume the Managed Care Division has judged the project to have lower-than-average risk. Is the project financially attractive?

Year	Prob. = 0.3	Prob. = 0.4	Prob. = 0.3
0	($100,000)	($100,000)	($100,000)
1	20,000	30,000	40,000
2	20,000	30,000	40,000
3	20,000	30,000	40,000
4	20,000	30,000	40,000

15.8. Pediatric Partners is evaluating a project with the following net cash flows and probabilities:

Year	Prob. = 0.25	Prob. = 0.5	Prob. = 0.25
0	($75,000)	($75,000)	($75,000)
1	15,000	20,000	30,000
2	15,000	20,000	30,000
3	15,000	20,000	30,000
4	15,000	20,000	30,000
5	20,000	30,000	40,000

The year 5 values include salvage value. Pediatric Partners' corporate cost of capital is 12 percent.

a. What is the project's expected (i.e., base case) NPV assuming average risk? (Hint: The base case net cash flows are the expected cash flows in each year.)

b. What are the project's most likely, worst-case, and best-case NPVs?

c. What is the project's expected NPV on the basis of the scenario analysis?

d. What is the project's standard deviation of NPV?

e. Assume that Pediatric Partners' managers judge the project to have higher-than-average risk. Furthermore, the practice's policy is to adjust the corporate cost of capital up or down by 2 percentage points to account for differential risk. Is the project financially attractive?

Selected Cases

Three cases in *Gapenski's Cases in Healthcare Finance*, sixth edition, are applicable to this chapter: Case 20: Coral Bay Hospital; Case 21: National Rehabilitation Centers; and Case 22: Northwest Suburban Health System.

Notes

1. Another risk analysis method, *decision tree analysis*, is particularly useful when a project is structured with a series of decision points, or stages, that allow cancellation prior to full implementation. For more information on decision tree analysis, see chapter 12 in Pink, G. H., and P. H. Song. 2020. *Gapenski's Understanding Healthcare Financial Management*. Chicago: Health Administration Press.

2. Spreadsheet programs have data table functions that automatically perform sensitivity analyses. After the table is roughed in, the spreadsheet automatically calculates and records a project's NPV, or some other value, in the appropriate cells.

3. *Skewness* measures the degree of symmetry of a distribution. A skewness of zero indicates a symmetric distribution, positive skewness indicates a distribution that is skewed to the right (its right tail is longer than its left), and negative skewness indicates a distribution that is skewed to the left (its left tail is longer than its right). The absolute value of the number indicates the degree of skewness—the larger the number, the more skewed the distribution.

4. Economists use utility theory to explain how individuals make choices among risky alternatives.

5. The risk-free rate does not incorporate the tax advantage of debt financing, so such benefits to taxable firms should be incorporated directly into the cash flows when the CE method is used. Alternatively, the discount rate can be determined using the corporate cost-of-capital formula, but with the risk-free rate in place of the costs of debt and equity. The discount rate calculated in this way is the risk-free rate with the tax advantage included, so it can be applied to the CE cash flows without tax adjustments.

6. What happens when the cash flows being discounted include both inflows and outflows so that the proper risk adjustment is not obvious? The solution is to try an adjustment and see what happens. For example, if the corporate cost of capital is 10 percent and the mixed cash flow project is judged to have high risk, discount the cash flows at 14 percent. If the NPV of the project increases, the adjustment clearly is wrong because an adjustment for high risk should penalize the project. Thus, the correct adjustment is to decrease the cost of capital—say, to 6 percent.

Resources

Casolari, C., and S. Womack. 2010. "Prioritizing Capital Projects When Cash Is Scarce." *Healthcare Financial Management* 64 (3): 114–16.

Holmes, R. L., R. E. Schroeder, and L. F. Harrington. 2000. "Objective Risk Adjustment Improves Calculated ROI for Capital Projects." *Healthcare Financial Management* 54 (12): 49–52.

Vianueva, D. 2011. "Healthcare Capital Projects: How to Avoid Common Problems." *Healthcare Financial Management* 65 (4): 86–90.

Williams, D. R., and P. H. Hammes. 2007a. "Real Option Logic for Healthcare Entrepreneurial Growth and Survival." *Healthcare Financial Management* 61 (5): 76–79.

———. 2007b. "Real Options Reasoning in Healthcare: An Integrative Approach and Synopsis." *Journal of Healthcare Management* 52 (3): 170–87.

VII

OTHER TOPICS

Up to this point, our discussion of financial management has focused primarily on long-term, or strategic, management decisions. In part VII, we move first to more immediate, short-term decision-making. Then, in the final chapter, we focus on financial condition analysis, which will act as a capstone to many of the topics covered throughout the book.

Chapter 16 focuses on managing short-term accounts—such as cash, receivables, short-term debt, and payables. In addition to discussing individual accounts, this chapter covers the revenue cycle, which ties together health services operations, billing, and collections. An understanding of these topics is critical to sound financial management at all health services organizations. In chapter 17, we discuss how to assess the financial condition of a business. If managers are to plan for the future, they must know the current financial status of the business.

REVENUE CYCLE AND CURRENT ACCOUNTS MANAGEMENT

Learning Objectives

After studying this chapter, readers will be able to

- Discuss in general terms how businesses manage cash and marketable securities.
- Describe the construction and use of cash budgets.
- Explain the key elements of the revenue cycle and the issues involved in its management.
- Explain the basics of receivables management and why it is so important to the revenue cycle.
- Describe the basic framework for supply chain management.
- Explain the alternatives available for short-term financing, including the use of security to obtain loans.

Introduction

In our discussion of financial management leading up to this chapter, the general focus has been on long-term, strategic decisions. Another important element of healthcare finance involves the management of short-term (current) accounts, such as cash, receivables, inventories, and payables. In corporate finance, the management of current accounts is called *working capital management*.

This chapter begins with an overview of current accounts management, followed by a brief discussion of the management of each current asset account plus revenue cycle management. These topics tie together health services operations, billing, and collections. The chapter closes with a discussion of the types of short-term financing used by healthcare providers.

An Overview of Current Accounts Management

Current accounts management involves all current assets and most current liabilities. The primary goal of current accounts management is to support the operations of the business at the lowest possible cost. Clearly, a business must have the level of current assets necessary to meet its operational requirements. However, it is imprudent to hold too high a level because of the costs of carrying those assets.

To illustrate the requirement for short-term financing and to review the current asset and current liability accounts, consider the situation facing Sun Coast Clinics, Inc., a for-profit operator of four walk-in clinics in South Florida. Exhibit 16.1 contains the firm's December 2020 and April 2021 balance sheets. The provision of ambulatory care services in this part of Florida is a seasonal business. The peak season for Sun Coast is December through April, when the population of the area soars because of winter tourism and the arrival of "snow birds" (i.e., retired individuals who typically live in the North during the summer and fall months but move to residences in Florida for the winter).

In December of each year, Sun Coast is finishing its slow season and preparing for its busy season. Thus, the clinic's accounts receivable are relatively low, but its cash and inventories are relatively high. (In this example, the cash account also contains cash equivalents, which are highly liquid securities with maturities of three months or less.) By the end of April, Sun Coast has completed its busy season, so its accounts receivable are relatively high, but its cash and inventories are relatively low in preparation for the slow summer season. On the current liabilities side, Sun Coast's accounts payable and accruals are relatively high at the end of April, just after the busy season.

Consider what happens to Sun Coast's total current assets and total current liabilities over the December-to-April period. Current assets increase from $200,000 to $240,000, driven by the increase in accounts receivable. The clinic has been providing services and incurring costs for labor and supplies; however, patient or third-party payments for those services have not yet been collected. Thus, the clinic must increase its capital by $40,000—an increase on the assets

Healthcare in Practice
Working Capital

The term *working capital* originated in the United States in the 1700s, when Yankee peddlers were the main source of goods for many farmers in remote areas of the Northeast. These merchants loaded up their wagons with goods and set off on a regular route to peddle their wares. According to the economic definitions of capital (assets) versus labor, the peddler's horse and wagon constituted the business's fixed capital (fixed assets), while the merchandise was called *working capital* because it was what was sold, or turned over, to produce a profit. Over the years, use of the term has evolved so that today, the term *gross working capital* is defined as current assets, while *net working capital* is defined as current assets minus current liabilities.

	December 2020	April 2021
Cash	$ 30	$ 20
Accounts receivable	155	210
Inventories	15	10
Total current assets	$200	$240
Net fixed assets	500	500
Total assets	$700	$740
Accounts payable	$ 30	$ 40
Accruals	15	25
Notes payable	105	125
Total current liabilities	$150	$190
Long-term debt	150	140
Common equity	400	410
Total liabilities and equity	$700	$740

EXHIBIT 16.1
Sun Coast
Clinics, Inc.:
End-of-Month
Balance Sheets
(in thousands)

side of the balance sheet must be financed by an increase on the liabilities and equity side. The higher volume of purchases and labor expenditures associated with increased services is partially financed by a $20,000 spontaneous increase in accounts payable and accruals, from $30,000 + $15,000 = $45,000 in December to $40,000 + $25,000 = $65,000 in April. In other words, while the clinic is waiting to collect its receivables, it is also waiting to pay some of its bills. However, the net result is an additional $40,000 – $20,000 = $20,000 current asset financing requirement in April, which Sun Coast obtained from the bank as a short-term loan (notes payable). Therefore, at the end of April, Sun Coast showed notes payable of $125,000, up from $105,000 in December. Unlike accounts payable and accrued expenses, bank loans come with an explicit cost—namely, the interest the bank charges for use of the funds. This is called a *carrying cost*. As this example shows, increases in short-term assets are not free.

These fluctuations for Sun Coast result from seasonal factors. Similar fluctuations in current asset requirements, and hence in financing needs, can occur because of business cycles; typically, current asset requirements and financing needs contract during recessions and expand during boom times.

SELF-TEST QUESTIONS

1. What is the goal of current accounts management?
2. Describe how seasonal volume fluctuations influence current asset levels and financing requirements.

Cash Management

Businesses need *cash*, which includes both actual cash on hand and cash held in commercial checking accounts, to pay for labor and materials, buy fixed assets, pay taxes, service debt, and so on. However, cash is a *nonearning asset*—it provides no return. Thus, similar to the overall goal of current accounts management, the goal of cash management is to minimize the amount of cash the business must hold to conduct its normal activities while having sufficient cash on hand to support operations. Maintaining sufficient cash ensures that a business is *liquid*, which means that it can meet its cash obligations as they come due. Conversely, a business that is illiquid cannot easily generate the cash needed to meet its obligations, and its operations suffer.

A key element in a business's cash management process is the cash budget, which we discuss in the next major section of this chapter. In essence, the cash budget tells managers how effective they are in applying the cash management techniques discussed in the following subsections.

Managing Float

float
The difference between the balance shown on a business's (or individual's) checkbook and the balance shown on the bank's books.

A well-run business has more money in its checking account than the balance shown in its checkbook. *Net float*, or just **float**, is the difference between the balance shown in the bank's records and the balance in the business's checkbook. Alternatively, float can be calculated as the sum of the business's two component floats: disbursement and collections.

To illustrate net float and its components, assume that Gainesville Primary Care writes checks in the amount of $5,000 each day. As the checks are written, the amounts are deducted from the checkbook balance. It takes six days for these checks to be mailed, delivered, deposited, and cleared and for the amounts to be deducted from the clinic's bank account. As a result, the clinic's checkbook will show a balance that is $6 \times \$5,000 = \$30,000$ less than the balance on the bank's records. Considering only disbursements, the clinic's actual balance at the bank is $30,000 greater than the amount shown on its checkbook, so it has a positive $30,000 *disbursement float*.

Now assume the clinic receives checks in the amount of $5,000 daily, but it loses four days while they are being deposited and cleared. This difference will result in $4 \times \$5,000 = \$20,000$ of

---

For Your Consideration

Credit Cards—The Ultimate Float for Individuals

Businesses, especially those with large amounts of checks written and received, can take advantage of the float inherent in checking accounts. But for most individuals, the volume of checking activity makes float management impractical. However, there is a good source of float available to individuals: credit cards.

When you charge a purchase on a credit card (but not a debit card), you are given a grace period to pay it off. So as long as you pay the

(continued)

collections float. Because of the delay in depositing and clearing checks, the clinic's balance at the bank is $20,000 less than that on its checkbook, which represents a negative collections float of $20,000.

The clinic's net float, which is the sum of the positive $30,000 disbursement float and negative $20,000 collections float, is $10,000. On average, the clinic's balance at the bank is $10,000 larger than the balance on its checkbook. Some businesses are so good at managing float that they carry a negative checkbook balance but have a positive balance at the bank. For example, one medical equipment manufacturer stated that its bank records show an average cash balance of about $200,000, while its own checkbook balance is *minus* $200,000—it has $400,000 of net float.

A firm's net float is a function of its ability to speed up collections on checks received and to slow down collections on checks written. Efficient businesses go to great lengths to speed up the processing of incoming checks, thus putting the funds to work faster, and they try to delay their own payments as long as possible (without engaging in unethical or illegal practices).

A 2018 Federal Reserve Payments Study found that the number of checks written decreased by 3.6 percent from 2015 to 2016 and by 4.8 percent from 2016 to 2017.[1] However, many people still pay their healthcare expenses by check, particularly the elderly and poor, who tend to be high users of the healthcare system. Therefore, checks will likely be used for the foreseeable future, and well-run businesses continue to recognize the value inherent in float.

Acceleration of Receipts

Managers have searched for ways to collect receivables faster since the day that credit transactions began. Although cash collection is the responsibility of a firm's managers, the speed with which checks are cleared depends on the banking system. Several techniques are now used to speed collections and to get funds where they are needed, but the three most popular are lockbox services, concentration banking, and electronic claims processing. This section covers lockbox services and concentration banking. The discussion of electronic claims processing appears later in this chapter.

(continued from previous page)

full amount within the grace period, you are not charged interest. In essence, you buy now and pay later without any interest charges. Because you receive the food or merchandise or service now and pay for it, say, 40 days later, the bank that issues the credit card is extending you an interest-free loan. Smart people use credit cards for the convenience and for the value of the float. However, credit cards are only a good deal when you have the financial means to pay them off in full by the payment date.

What do you think about credit cards? In what situations are they a benefit to individuals? How can credit cards be abused? Do you own a credit card? Do you use it wisely?

lockbox
A post office box used by a business to receive checks at a location other than the corporate headquarters.

Lockboxes are one of the oldest cash management tools, and virtually all banks that offer cash management services offer lockbox services. In a lockbox system, incoming checks are sent to post office boxes rather than to corporate headquarters. For example, Health SouthWest, a regional HMO headquartered in Oklahoma City, has its Texas members send their payments to a box in Dallas, its New Mexico members send their checks to Albuquerque, and so on, rather than have all checks sent to Oklahoma City. A local bank collects the contents of each post office box (which is called "the lockbox") and deposits the checks into the company's local account. The bank then provides the HMO with daily records of the receipts collected, usually via an electronic data transmission system in a format that permits online updating of the firm's receivables accounts.

A lockbox system reduces the time required for a business to receive incoming checks, deposit them, and get them cleared through the banking system, so the funds are available for use more quickly. This time reduction occurs because mail time and check collection time are both reduced if the lockbox is located in the same geographic area as the customer. Lockbox services can increase the availability of funds by one to four days over the regular system for firms with customers over a large geographic area.

Although lockbox systems are efficient in speeding up collections, the firm's cash is spread among many banks. The primary purpose of *concentration banking* is to mobilize funds from decentralized receiving locations, whether they are lockboxes or decentralized company locations, into one or more central cash pools. In a typical concentration system, the firm's collection banks record the deposits received each day. Based on the firm's disbursement needs, the funds are then transferred from these collection points to a concentration bank. Concentration accounts allow firms to take maximum advantage of economies of scale in cash management and investment. Health SouthWest uses an Oklahoma City bank as its concentration bank. The HMO cash manager uses this pool for short-term investing or reallocation among its other banks.

Automated Clearing House (ACH)
An electronic communication network for transmitting data from one financial institution to another.

Electronic systems make concentration banking easy. The **Automated Clearing House (ACH)** is a communication network that sends data from one financial institution to another. Instead of using paper checks, the ACH creates electronic files that place all transactions for a particular bank in a single file and then send it to that bank. In addition to the ACH, *Fedwire* is used to move large sums between banks. Between the two systems, trillions of dollars are efficiently moved among banks on a daily basis.

Disbursement Control

Accelerated collections represent one side of using float, while controlling fund outflows is the other. Efficient cash management can only result if both inflows and outflows are managed effectively.

No single action controls disbursements more effectively than *payables centralization*. This permits the firm's managers to evaluate the payments coming due for the entire business and to meet those needs in an organized and controlled manner. Centralized disbursement also permits more efficient monitoring of payables and float balances. However, centralized disbursement does have a downside—centralized offices may have difficulty making all payments promptly, which can create ill will with suppliers and disqualify the business from receiving prompt-payment discounts.

Zero-balance accounts (ZBAs) are special disbursement accounts that have a zero-dollar balance on which checks are written. Typically, a firm establishes several ZBAs in the concentration bank and funds them from a *master account*. As checks are presented to a ZBA for payment, funds are automatically transferred from the master account, which is an interest-earning account. If the master account has a negative balance, it is replenished by borrowing from the bank against a line of credit or by selling some securities from the firm's marketable securities portfolio. ZBAs simplify the control of disbursements and cash balances and hence reduce the amount of idle (i.e., non-interest-bearing) cash.

Whereas ZBAs are typically established at concentration banks, *controlled disbursement accounts* can be set up at any bank. In fact, controlled disbursement accounts were initially used only in relatively remote banks, so this technique was originally called *remote disbursement*. The basic technique is simple: Controlled disbursement accounts are not funded until the day's checks are presented against the account. The key to controlled disbursement is the ability of the bank that has the account to report the total amount of checks received for clearance each morning. This early notification gives a firm's managers sufficient time to wire funds to the controlled disbursement account to cover the checks presented for payment.

> **zero-balance account (ZBA)**
> A bank account having a zero balance that is established by a business to handle disbursements of a particular type. Funds are transferred to ZBAs from a master account as needed to cover the checks written.

Matching the Costs and Benefits of Cash Management

Although the techniques discussed earlier can reduce cash balance requirements, implementing these procedures is not a costless operation. How far should a firm go in making its cash operations more efficient? As a general rule, the firm should incur these expenses only so long as the marginal returns exceed the marginal costs.

The value of careful cash management depends on the opportunity costs of funds invested in cash, which, in turn, depend on the current rate of interest. For example, in the early 1980s, when interest rates were relatively high, businesses devoted a great deal of care to cash management. Today, with interest rates much lower, cash management is less valuable. Clearly, larger businesses, with larger cash balances, can better afford to hire the personnel necessary to maintain tight control over their cash positions.

Because cash management is an element of business operations in which economies of scale are present, banks place considerable emphasis on developing and marketing these services. Thus, banks can generally provide cash management services to smaller companies at lower costs than companies can achieve by operating in-house cash management systems.

1. What is float?
2. How do firms use float to increase cash management efficiency?
3. What are some methods businesses can use to accelerate receipts?
4. What are some methods businesses can use to control disbursements?
5. How should cash management actions be evaluated?

The Cash Budget

In chapter 8, in our discussion of financial planning and budgeting, we focused on the operating budget, which provides managers with numerous insights into the efficiency of an organization's operations. However, the operating budget is based on accrual accounting principles and does not provide managers with much information about a business's cash position. This situation is remedied by the **cash budget**.

cash budget
A schedule that lists a business's expected cash inflows, outflows, and net cash flows for some future period.

To create a cash budget, managers forecast cash collections and fixed asset and inventory requirements, along with the times such payments are expected. This information is combined with cash outlay projections for operating and financial expenses such as wages and benefits, interest payments, tax payments, and so on to produce a report showing the organization's projected cash inflows and outflows over some specified period. Generally, the cash budget consists of individual monthly cash budgets forecast for one year, plus a more detailed daily or weekly cash budget for the coming month. The monthly cash budget is used for liquidity planning purposes, and the daily or weekly budget is used for actual cash control.

Creating a cash budget does not require the application of a complex set of accounting rules. Rather, all the entries in a cash budget represent the actual movement of cash into or out of the organization. To illustrate, exhibit 16.2 contains a monthly cash budget that covers six months of 2021 for Mission County Homecare, a small for-profit home healthcare company. Mission's cash budget, which is broken down to three sections, is typical, although there is a great deal of variation in formats used by different organizations. For ease of illustration, the cash budget is constrained to relatively few lines.

EXHIBIT 16.2
Mission County Homecare: May–October Cash Budget

	March	April	May	June	July	August	September	October
Collections Worksheet:								
1. Billed charges	$50,000	$50,000	$100,000	$150,000	$200,000	$100,000	$100,000	$50,000
2. Collections:								
a. Within 30 days (19.6%)			19,600	29,400	39,200	19,600	19,600	9,800
b. 30–60 days (70%)			35,000	70,000	105,000	140,000	70,000	70,000
c. 60–90 days (10%)			5,000	5,000	10,000	15,000	20,000	10,000
3. Total collections			$ 59,600	104,400	154,200	174,600	109,600	89,800
Supplies Worksheet:								
4. Amount of supplies ordered		$10,000	$ 15,000	$ 20,000	$ 10,000	$ 10,000	$ 5,000	
5. Payments made for supplies			$ 10,000	$ 15,000	20,000	10,000	10,000	$ 5,000
Net Cash Gain (Loss):								
6. Total collections (from line 3)			$ 59,600	$104,400	$154,200	$274,600	$109,600	$ 89,800
7. Total purchases (from line 5)			$ 10,000	$ 15,000	$ 20,000	$ 10,000	$ 10,000	$ 5,000
8. Wages and salaries			60,000	70,000	80,000	60,000	60,000	60,000
9. Rent			2,500	2,500	2,500	2,500	2,500	2,500
10. Other expenses			1,000	1,500	2,000	1,000	1,000	500
11. Taxes				20,000		50,000	20,000	
12. Payment for capital assets								
13. Total payments			$ 73,500	$109,000	$104,500	$123,500	$ 93,500	$ 68,000
14. Net cash gain (loss)			($ 13,900)	($ 4,600)	$ 49,700	$ 51,100	$ 16,100	$ 21,800
Surplus/Deficit Summary:								
15. Cash at beginning with no borrowing			$ 15,000	$ 1,100	($ 3,500)	$ 46,200	$ 97,300	$113,400
16. Cash at end with no borrowing			$ 1,100	($ 3,500)	$ 46,200	$ 97,300	$113,400	$135,200
17. Target cash balance			10,000	10,000	10,000	10,000	10,000	10,000
18. Cumulative surplus (deficit)			($ 8,900)	($ 13,500)	$ 36,200	$ 87,300	$103,400	$125,200

The first section of Mission's cash budget contains the *collections work-sheet*, which translates the billing for services provided into cash revenues. Because of its location in a summer resort area, Mission's patient volume, and hence billings, peak in July. However, like most health services organizations, Mission rarely collects when services are provided. What is relevant from a cash budget perspective is not when services are provided or when billings occur but when cash is collected. Based on previous experience, Mission's managers know that most collections occur 30 to 60 days after billing. In fact, Mission's managers have created a collections worksheet that allows them to forecast, with some precision, the timing of collections. This worksheet was used to convert the billings shown on line 1 of exhibit 16.2 into the collection amounts shown on lines 2 and 3.

To illustrate the relationship between billings and collections, consider the $100,000 of billed charges forecast for May. Of this amount, $19,600 (19.6 percent) is expected to be collected in May (within 30 days), $70,000 (70 percent) is expected to be collected in June (30–60 days after billing), and $10,000 (10 percent) is expected to be collected in July (60–90 days after billing). Thus, of the $100,000 in May billings, $19,600 + $70,000 + $10,000 = $99,600 is expected to be collected, so a small amount ($400 or 0.4 percent) is forecast to be a bad debt loss (an implicit price concession). If this pattern of collections is expected to continue, then the organization can forecast all future cash collections using a similar method. For example, the $104,400 of cash collections expected in June represents the following: (0.196 × $150,000 billed charges in June) + (0.70 × $100,000 billed charges in May) + (0.10 × $50,000 billed charges in April) = $29,400 + $70,000 + $5,000 = $104,400.

The next section of Mission's cash budget is the *supplies worksheet*, which accounts for timing differences between supply order and purchase. Mission's patient volume forecasts, which are used to predict the billing amounts shown on line 1, are also used to forecast the supplies (primarily medical) needed to support patient services. These supplies are ordered and received one month prior to expected usage, as shown on line 4. However, Mission's suppliers do not demand immediate payment. Rather, Mission has, on average, 30 days to pay for supplies after they are received, so the actual payment occurs one month after purchase, as shown on line 5.

The next section combines data from the collections and supplies worksheets with other projected cash outflows to show the *net cash gain (loss)* for each month. Cash from collections is shown on line 6. Lines 7 through 12 list cash payments that are expected to be made during each month, including payments for supplies. Then, all payments are summed, with the total shown on line 13. The difference between expected cash receipts and cash payments, line 6 minus line 13, is the net cash gain or loss during the month, which is shown on line 14. For May, there is a forecast net cash outflow of $13,900 (the parentheses indicate a negative cash flow).

Although line 14 contains the "meat" of the cash budget, lines 15 through 18 (the surplus/deficit summary) extend the basic budget data to show Mission's monthly forecast cumulative cash position. Line 15 shows the forecast cash on hand at the beginning of each month, assuming that no borrowing takes place. Mission is expected to enter the budget period, the beginning of May, with $15,000 of cash on hand. For each succeeding month, line 15 is merely the value shown on line 16 for the previous month. The values on line 16, which are obtained by adding lines 14 and 15, show the cash on hand at the end of each month, assuming no borrowing takes place. For May, Mission expects a cash loss of $13,900 on top of a starting balance of $15,000, for an ending cash balance of $1,100, in the absence of any borrowing. This amount is the cash on hand at the beginning of June, with no borrowing amount, shown on line 15.

To continue, Mission's target cash balance (i.e., the amount that it wants on hand at the beginning of each month), which is shown on line 17, is $10,000. The target cash balance is subtracted from the forecast ending cash with no borrowing amount to determine the firm's monthly deficit (shown in parentheses) or surplus (shown without parentheses). Because Mission expects to have ending cash in May, as shown on line 16, of only $1,100, it will have to obtain $1,100 – $10,000 = –$8,900 to bring the cash account up to the target balance of $10,000. If this amount is borrowed, as opposed to obtained from other sources such as liquidating marketable securities, the total loan outstanding will be $8,900 at the end of May. (The assumption here is that Mission will not have any loans outstanding on May 1.)

The cumulative cash surplus or deficit is shown on line 18; a positive value indicates a cash surplus, while a negative value indicates a deficit. The surplus cash or deficit shown on line 18 is a cumulative amount. Thus, Mission is projected to require $8,900 in May; it has a cash shortfall during June of $4,600, as reported on line 14, so its total deficit projected for the end of June is $8,900 + $4,600 = $13,500, as shown on line 18.

The same procedures are followed in subsequent months. Patient volume and billings are projected to peak in July, accompanied by increased payments for supplies, wages, and other items. However, collections are projected to increase by a greater amount than costs, and Mission expects a $49,700 net cash inflow during July. This amount is sufficient to pay off the cumulative loan (if one is used) of $13,500 and have a $36,200 cash surplus on hand at the end of the month.

Patient volume, and the resulting operating costs, are expected to fall sharply in August, but collections will be the highest of any month because they will reflect the high June and July billings. As a result, Mission would normally be forecasting a healthy $101,100 net cash gain during the month. However, the company expects to make a cash payment of $50,000 to purchase a new computer system during August, so the forecast net cash gain is reduced to $51,100. This net gain adds to the surplus, so August is projected to end with $87,300 in surplus cash. If all goes according to the forecast, later cash surpluses will enable Mission to end this budget period with a surplus of $125,200.

Mission's managers use the cash budget for liquidity planning purposes. For example, the exhibit 16.2 cash budget indicates that Mission will need to obtain $13,500 in total to get through May and June. Thus, if the firm does not have any marketable securities to convert to cash, it will have to arrange some type of financing (loan) to cover this period. Furthermore, the budget indicates a $125,200 cash surplus at the end of October. Mission's managers will have to consider how these funds can best be used. Perhaps the money should be paid out to owners as dividends or bonuses, used for fixed asset acquisitions, or be temporarily invested in marketable securities for later use within the business. This decision will be made on the basis of Mission's overall financial plan.

This brief illustration shows the mechanics and managerial value of the cash budget. However, before concluding the discussion, several additional points need to be made. First, if cash inflows and outflows are not uniform during the month, a monthly cash budget could seriously understate a business's peak financing requirements. The data in exhibit 16.2 show the situation expected on the last day of each month, but on any given day during the month, it could be quite different. For example, if all payments had to be made on the fifth of each month, but collections came in uniformly throughout the month, Mission would need to borrow cash to cover within-month shortages. For example, August's $123,500 cash payments may be made before Mission receives the full $174,600 in collections. In this situation, Mission would have to obtain some amount of cash to cover shortfalls in August, even though the end-of-month cash flow after all collections had been made is positive. In this case, Mission would have to prepare a weekly or daily cash budget to indicate such borrowing needs.

Also, because the cash budget represents a forecast, all the values in exhibit 16.2 are *expected* values. If actual patient volume, collection times, supplies purchases, wage rates, and so on differ from forecast levels, the projected cash deficits and surpluses will be incorrect. Thus, there is a reasonable chance that Mission may need to obtain a larger amount of funds than is indicated on line 18.

Because of the uncertainty of the forecasts, spreadsheets are particularly well suited for constructing and analyzing cash budgets. For example, Mission's managers could change any assumption—say, projected monthly volume or the time third-party payers take to pay—and the cash budget would automatically and instantly be recalculated. This would show Mission's managers exactly how the firm's cash position changes under alternative operating assumptions. Typically, such an analysis is used to determine the size of the credit line needed to cover temporary cash shortages.[2] In Mission's case, such an analysis indicated that a $20,000 credit line is sufficient.

1. Why do organizations need a cash budget?
2. Does the cash budget require an extensive knowledge of accounting principles?
3. In your view, what is the most important line of the cash budget?

Marketable Securities Management

Many businesses hold temporary portfolios of short-term securities called **marketable securities**. On the balance sheet, short-term securities with maturities of three months or less are lumped in with cash and often labeled *cash and cash equivalents*. Short-term securities with maturities between three months and one year are reported separately as *short-term investments*. Although cash and marketable securities management are discussed in separate sections, in practice, they cannot be separated from one another because management of one implies management of the other.

There are two primary reasons for holding marketable securities: (1) They serve as an interest-earning substitute for cash balances, and (2) they are used to hold funds that are being accumulated to meet a specific large, near-term obligation, such as a tax payment or capital expenditure.

In general, the key characteristic sought in marketable securities investments is safety (preservation of principal). Most health services managers are willing to give up some return to ensure that funds are available, in the amounts expected, when needed. Large businesses, with large amounts of surplus cash, often directly own securities such as Treasury bills (short-term debt issued by the federal government).

Conversely, smaller businesses are more likely to invest with a bank or a money market mutual fund because a small firm's volume of investment simply does not warrant hiring specialists to manage a marketable securities portfolio. Small businesses often use a mutual fund and write checks on the fund to bolster the cash account as the need arises.[3] Interest rates on mutual funds are somewhat lower than rates on direct investments of equivalent risk because

marketable securities
Securities that are held in lieu of cash, typically safe, short-term securities such as Treasury bills; called *cash equivalents* or *short-term investments* when listed on the balance sheet.

of management fees. However, for smaller companies, net returns may well be higher on mutual funds because no in-house management expense is required.

The bottom line here is that, regardless of size, businesses' marketable securities portfolios consist almost exclusively of safe, liquid investments that can be sold at any time at a predictable price.

1. Why do firms hold marketable securities?
2. How are these holdings reported on the balance sheet?
3. What are some securities that are commonly held as marketable securities?
4. Why are these securities preferred?

Revenue Cycle Management

One of the hottest topics in healthcare finance today is revenue cycle management. Its importance stems from the fact that most healthcare providers are not paid the entire amount due for services at the same time services are rendered. Thus, providers incur cash costs for facilities, supplies, and labor but do not receive immediate payment to cover those costs. In fact, hospitals and medical practices have to wait an average of 50 days to collect from third-party payers.

revenue cycle
The set of recurring activities and related information processing required to provide patient services and collect for those services.

The **revenue cycle** is defined as the set of recurring business activities and related information processing necessary to bill for and collect the revenues due for services provided. More pragmatically, the revenue cycle at provider organizations should ensure that patients are properly categorized by payment obligation, that correct and timely billing takes place, and that the correct payment is promptly received.

Revenue cycle activities typically are broken down into four phases based on when they occur: (1) those that occur before the service is provided, (2) those that occur simultaneously with the service, (3) those that occur after the service is provided, and (4) those that are continuous. The following are some examples of revenue cycle activities listed by phase.[4]

Before-Service Activities
- **Preservice insurance verification.** The insurance status of the patient is identified immediately after the outpatient visit (or inpatient stay) is scheduled to ensure that the patient actually has the insurance indicated when the appointment was made.

- **Precertification/prior authorization (if necessary).** If the insurance verification indicates that the payer requires *precertification*, it should be done immediately. Without precertification for services that require it, the provider runs the risk of having the claim (bill) denied even though the services were provided.
- **Preservice patient financial counseling.** The patient should be counseled regarding the payer's and patient's payment responsibilities. It is not fair to present a large bill to an unsuspecting patient after the service is rendered.

At-Service Activities

- **Time-of-service insurance verification.** The patient's insurance status should be re-verified with both the patient and the payer at the time of service to ensure that no changes have occurred since the initial verification.
- **Service documentation/claims production.** The services provided should be documented in a way that facilitates correct claims submission. The documentation process should ensure that (1) the provider fully and correctly documents all diagnoses and services provided, (2) the services provided are coded in accordance with the payer's claim system, (3) the code reflects the highest legitimate reimbursement amount, and (4) the claim is formatted in accordance with payer guidelines and contains all required information.

After-Service Activities

- **Claims submission.** The claim should be submitted to the payer as quickly as possible after the service is rendered. However, speed should not take precedence over accuracy because incomplete and inaccurate billing accounts for a large proportion of late payments.
- **Third-party follow-up.** If payment is not received within 30 days, a reminder should be sent.
- **Denials management.** Claims denial by third-party payers is one of the major impediments to timely reimbursement. Typically, most denials are caused by improper precertification or incomplete or erroneous claims submission. Prompt claims resubmission is essential to good revenue cycle management.
- **Payment receipt and posting.** When the reimbursement is received, it must be properly deposited and credited. This activity ends the revenue cycle.

Continuous Activities

- **Monitoring.** Once revenue cycle activities are identified and timing goals are set for each activity, the provider should implement a system of metrics (key indicators) to ensure that these goals are being met.
- **Review and improvement.** The key indicators monitoring the revenue cycle must be continually reviewed and any deficiencies corrected.

The revenue cycle requires constant attention because the external factors that influence it are constantly changing. Also, problems that occur at any point in the revenue cycle tend to have ripple effects—that is, a problem that occurs early in the cycle can create additional problems at later points in the cycle. For example, failure to obtain required precertification can lead to claim denial, which at best means delayed payment and at worst means no payment at all.

The ability of healthcare providers to convert services rendered into cash is critical to their financial performance. Problems in the revenue cycle lead to lost and late payments, both of which degrade provider revenues and financial condition. You can think of the provider as furnishing to the payer an interest-free loan that covers the costs of the services rendered. The faster the loan is repaid, the better for the lender (provider).

Monitoring Revenue Cycle Performance

The ultimate goal of revenue cycle management is to convert services provided into cash reimbursement as quickly as possible. Thus, a provider's patient accounts receivable plays a key role in assessing performance. The total amount of accounts receivable outstanding at any given time is determined by two factors: (1) the volume of services provided and (2) the average length of time between services and collections.

For Your Consideration

Revenue Cycle Management in Medical Practices

As in hospitals, revenue cycle management is an important contributor to profitability in medical practices. Yet many physicians struggle with the idea that they are businesspeople as well as clinicians.

One of the problems frequently encountered in medical practices is the lack of physician engagement in revenue cycle management. To create the most efficient revenue cycle process, it is essential that all physicians, especially the lead physician, be fully committed to the effort. Without a high level of executive sponsorship, small problems can quickly turn into large ones.

When physicians are fully engaged in revenue cycle management, it becomes clear that the process is of utmost importance to the success of the practice and that the entire team needs to be on board. This is particularly true when new processes or technologies are being introduced.

What do you think about the need for physician involvement in revenue cycle management? Can't the office manager and billing and collections staff handle the task? What can be done to encourage physicians to be more supportive of the organization's business practices?

For example, suppose Home Infusion, Inc., a home health care business, begins operations on January 1 and on the first day starts to provide services to patients billed at $1,000 each day. For simplicity, assume that all patients have the same insurance, that it takes Home Infusion two days to submit patients' bills, and that it takes the insurer another 18 days to make the payments. Thus, it takes 20 days from delivery of service to receipt of payment.

At the end of the first day, Home Infusion's accounts receivable will be $1,000; they will rise to $2,000 by the end of the second day; by January 20, they will rise to $20,000. On January 21, another $1,000 will be added to receivables, but, assuming that the insurer pays the full amount for services provided 20 days earlier, payments for services provided on January 1 will reduce receivables by $1,000, so total accounts receivable will remain constant at $20,000. If either patient volume or the collection period changes, the amount in accounts receivable will change.

Monitoring Overall Revenue Cycle Performance

If a service is provided for cash, the payment is received at that time, but if the service is provided on credit, the payment is not actually received until the account is collected. If the account is never collected, the payment is never received. Thus, healthcare managers must closely monitor receivables to ensure that they are being collected in a timely manner and to uncover any deterioration in the *quality* of receivables. Early detection can help managers take corrective action before the situation has a significant negative impact on the organization's financial condition. (Receivables quality is defined as the likelihood that the receivables will be collected in a timely manner and without losses.)

The common approach to monitoring revenue cycle performance, both in the aggregate and by specific activity, is by using metrics. Generically, a *metric* is a single quantitative indicator—usually a ratio—that can be used to measure the performance of some process. The primary purpose of metrics is to monitor performance and aid in the identification of corrective action plans if performance is subpar. In this section, we discuss two metrics that monitor overall revenue cycle performance: average collection period and aging schedule.

Average Collection Period. Suppose that Home Infusion provides an average of ten home health visits a day at an average net charge of $100 per visit, for a total of $1,000 in *average daily billings (ADB)*. Assuming 250 workdays a year, the company's annual billings total $1,000 × 250 = $250,000. Furthermore, assume that all services are paid by two third-party payers: One pays for half of the billings 15 days after the service is provided,

average collection period (ACP)
The average length of time it takes a business to collect its receivables; also called *days sales outstanding (DSO)* or *days in patient accounts receivable.*

and the second pays for the other half of billings in 25 days. Home Infusion's **average collection period (ACP)**, also called *days in patient accounts receivable*, is 20 days.

$$ACP = (0.5 \times 15 \text{ days}) + (0.5 \times 25 \text{ days}) = 20 \text{ days.}$$

Assuming a constant uniform rate of services provided, and hence billings, the accounts receivable balance at any point in time will be equal to $ADB \times ACP$. Home Infusion's receivables balance would be $20,000:

$$\text{Receivables balance} = ADB \times ACP = \$1,000 \times 20 = \$20,000.$$

What is the cost implication of carrying $20,000 in receivables? The $20,000 on the left side of the balance sheet must be financed by an equivalent amount on the right side. Home Infusion uses a bank loan, which has an interest rate of 8 percent, to finance its receivables. Thus, over a year, the firm must pay the bank $0.08 \times \$20,000 = \$1,600$ in interest to carry its receivables balance. The cost associated with carrying other current assets can be thought of in a similar way.

> **Key Equations: Average Collection Period and Receivables Balance**
> The average collection period (ACP) is a weighted average of the time it takes an organization to collect its receivables. Assume payer A takes 20 days to pay and contributes 40 percent of a provider's receivables, while payer B takes 50 days and contributes 60 percent. The ACP, then, is 38 days:
>
> $$ACP = (0.4 \times 20 \text{ days}) + (0.6 \times 50 \text{ days})$$
> $$= 8 + 30 = 38 \text{ days.}$$
>
> With the ACP known, the receivables balance is calculated as follows:
>
> $$\text{Receivables balance} = ADB \times ACP,$$
>
> where ADB is average daily billings. For example, if a provider has $5,000 in average daily billings and an ACP of 38 days, its receivables balance is $190,000:
>
> $$\text{Receivables balance} = ADB \times ACP$$
> $$= \$5,000 \times 38$$
> $$= \$190,000.$$

The ACP, which is a measure of the average length of time it takes patients (or third-party payers) to pay their bills, often is compared with the sector median ACP. For example, if the home health sector median ACP is 22 days, versus Home Infusion's 20-day ACP, its collections department is doing a better-than-average job. Note, however, that even though Home Infusion's payers are, on average, paying faster than the 22-day sector median, its two payers are paying in 15 days and 25 days. Thus, the firm's collections department should take a hard look to see whether the ACP of the 25-day payer can be reduced to the sector median or even to the 15 days of the other payer.

Why is it so important to minimize a business's ACP? To illustrate, assume that Home Infusion's ACP is 25 days, and its receivables balance is $25,000. Assuming an 8 percent cost of financing (carrying) its receivables, the annual carrying cost to Home Infusion is 0.08 × $25,000 = $2,000. But at its actual ACP of 20 days, its carrying cost is only 0.08 × $20,000 = $1,600. Thus, by reducing its ACP by five days, Home Infusion reduced its receivables carrying cost by $400 annually. "No big deal," you say. True, but now consider a 500-bed hospital with $100 million in receivables and a 60-day ACP, which implies average daily billings (ADB) of $100 million ÷ 60 = $1.67 million. A reduction of ACP by five days would reduce the receivables balance to $1.67 million × 55 = $91.85 million, or by about $8 million. Assuming the same 8 percent cost of carrying receivables, the savings amounts to a substantial 0.08 × $8 million = $0.64 million = $640,000. In addition, the hospital would receive a one-time cash flow of $8 million as the receivables balance is reduced. It should be apparent that immediate cash flow as well as large savings can be obtained by reducing a business's ACP and hence its receivables balance.

Aging Schedules. An **aging schedule** breaks down a firm's receivables by the age of each account. To illustrate, exhibit 16.3 contains the December 31, 2020, aging schedules of two home health companies: Home Infusion and Home Care. Both firms offer the same services and show the same total receivables balance. However, Home Infusion's aging schedule indicates that it is collecting its receivables faster than Home Care is. Only 50 percent of Home Infusion's receivables are more than ten days old, but 55 percent of Home Care's receivables are more than ten days old. More important, Home Care has receivables that are more than 30 days old and even some that are more than 40 days old. Based on a sector median ACP of 22 days, Home Care's managers should be concerned about the efficiency of the firm's collections efforts and the ability of the late payers to make the payments due.

Aging schedules cannot be constructed from the type of summary data reported in a firm's financial statements; they must be developed from the

aging schedule
A table that expresses a business's accounts receivable by how long each account has been outstanding.

EXHIBIT 16.3
Aging
Schedules for
Two Firms

Age of Account (Days)	Home Infusion		Home Care	
	Value of Account	Percentage of Total Value	Value of Account	Percentage of Total Value
0–10	$10,000	50%	$ 9,000	45%
11–20	7,500	38	5,000	25
21–30	2,500	12	3,000	15
31–40	0	0	2,000	10
Over 40	0	0	1,000	5
Total	$20,000	100%	$20,000	100%

firm's accounts receivable ledger. However, well-run businesses have computerized accounts receivable records. Thus, it is easy to determine the age of each invoice, sort electronically by age categories, and generate an aging schedule. In addition, some providers show account aging on patient billing statements.

Monitoring Specific Revenue Cycle Activities

Of course, overall revenue cycle performance is a function of how well the specific revenue cycle activities are performed. The following are five metrics, of many, that are commonly used to measure the performance of specific revenue cycle activities:

1. **Cost to collect.** This metric is used to measure the overall cost-effectiveness of an organization's revenue cycle management. It is defined as Total revenue cycle costs ÷ Total amount collected. The idea here is that it makes no sense to spend $1.50 to collect $1.

2. **Point-of-service collection rate.** This metric is defined as Point-of-service collections ÷ Total patient collections. Its purpose is to measure the percentage of the monies owed by patients that is collected when the service is rendered. Clearly, the more money that is collected at the time of service, the better. Collection when the patient is at the facility saves the cost of billing and ensures that the payment is made.

3. **Initial denial rate.** This metric, which is a broad measure of billing efficiency, is defined as Number of initial claims denied ÷ Number of claims submitted. Here, the higher the metric value, the greater the cost of collecting payments due from insurers. Claims denials increase revenue cycle costs in three ways. First, denials require additional work, and hence cost, at the billing organization. Second,

denials delay the receipt of payment, which increases the cost of carrying the receivables balance. Third, if the denial is permanent, the claim is never paid and the cost of service is borne by the provider.

4. **Registration quality score.** This metric measures the effectiveness of the patient registration process. It is defined as Number of correct patient demographic and insurance data elements at registration ÷ Total number of data elements. A high score indicates good up-front patient data collection and prevents downstream revenue cycle defects.

5. **Charge lag days.** This metric measures the time it takes from the day a service is provided to the day a bill is sent to the payer (patient or insurer). It is defined as Total days between service and billing ÷ Number of bills. Note this definition gives the average lag days over some time period. The metric could also be calculated by payer (patient, Medicaid, or others). Clearly, on average, the faster that bills are generated and sent, the quicker the collection.

Before we end our discussion of specific metrics, it is useful to consider what makes a good metric. First and foremost, metrics are supposed to measure process performance. So good metric design starts with defining what the fundamental purpose is for the process being assessed. Only after having defined the process purpose can a discussion begin about measuring performance. In the case of the revenue cycle, the fundamental purpose can be defined as identifying the correct amount "owed" to the organization for services rendered and converting that amount into cash.

Second, recognize that metrics are used to provide the organizational focus to ensure that resources are aimed at the correct activities. To further this concept, selected metrics, coupled with associated goals, are used to define incentive pay plans to motivate staff to achieve the desired results. With these goals in mind, here are several characteristics of good metrics:

- Metrics must directly measure the degree of "success" of the process purpose.
- Metrics must be measurable and quantitative.
- Metrics must be objective and precise.
- Metrics must be measurable over time.
- Metrics should be easily defined and understood by all affected managers and staff.

While the performance monitoring objective of metrics is apparent to most individuals, the human component evades many. Metrics play a

EXHIBIT 16.4
Hospital
Sector's
Receivables Mix

Payer	Percentage of Total Accounts Receivable
Medicare	30.9%
Managed care	22.5
Self-pay	13.2
Medicaid	13.1
Commercial insurers	11.6
Other	8.7
	100.0%

Data from Aspen Publishers, *Hospital Accounts Receivable Analysis*, 2015.

major role not only in motivating staff to work better but also in communicating organizational goals and objectives. In high-performing organizations, managers and staff have a sense of purpose related to their daily activities, and metrics play a fundamental role in communicating how this purpose is achieved.

Unique Problems Faced by Healthcare Providers

Although the general principles of revenue cycle management discussed up to this point are applicable to all businesses, healthcare providers face some unique problems. The most obvious problem is the billing complexity created by the third-party payer system. For example, rather than having to deal with a single billing system that applies to all customers, providers have to deal with the rules and regulations of many different government and private insurers that use different payment methodologies. Thus, providers have to maintain large staffs of specialists who report to a *patient accounts manager*.

EXHIBIT 16.5
Hospital
Sector's
Aggregate
Aging Schedule

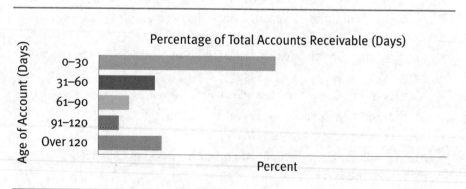

Data from Aspen Publishers, *Hospital Accounts Receivable Analysis*, 2015.

For an illustration of the problem, consider exhibit 16.4, which contains the receivables mix for the hospital sector. Many of the categories listed in the exhibit include multiple payers, so the actual number of payers can easily run into the hundreds.

Exhibit 16.5 provides information on how long it takes hospitals to collect receivables. Because of the large number of payers and the complexities involved in billing and follow-up actions, hospitals clearly have a great deal of difficulty collecting bills in a timely manner. On average, it takes about 50 days to collect a receivable. However, this number has decreased in recent years as hospital managers have become increasingly aware of the costs associated with carrying receivables and as automated systems have made the collections process more efficient. Despite the positive trend, about 33 percent of receivables still were more than 60 days old. In addition, the American Hospital Association estimated the cost of uncompensated care (hospital care provided for which no payment was received from the patient or insurer) in 2017 to be about $38.4 billion, or 4.2 percent of total expenses.[5]

To help providers collect from managed care plans in a timely fashion, many states have enacted laws that mandate "prompt" payment. For example, New York State requires that all undisputed claims by providers be paid by plans within 45 days of receipt. If prompt payment is not made, fines are assessed.[6]

The Revenue Cycle and Value-Based Payment

Value-based reimbursement models are shifting some of the financial accountability that used to be borne by payers onto healthcare providers. Thus, there is an increasing need to monitor not only revenue cycle processes but also quality measures that contribute to the overall payments that providers receive. Much of the data needed to make improvements in care quality and patient outcomes, identify high-risk patients to better manage population health, and accurately classify patients for risk stratification and adjustment reside in providers' clinical data systems. Many providers are investing in advanced data analytics tools that allow them to monitor quality and outcomes data in real time so that they can make adjustments to better manage the revenue cycle and maximize their collections.

In addition, the proliferation of high-deductible health plans is making claims management more complex. Revenue cycle activities such as patient financial counseling, communication and price transparency, and efficient billing and collection practices are becoming critical as patients assume a greater role in managing their care.

1. What is the revenue cycle?
2. What four phases make up the revenue cycle?
3. Why is proper management of the revenue cycle critical to the financial performance of healthcare providers?
4. Explain how a firm's receivables balance is built up over time and why there are costs associated with carrying receivables.
5. Briefly discuss two metrics used to monitor overall revenue cycle performance.
6. What are some of the unique problems healthcare providers face in managing receivables?
7. What are some implications for the revenue cycle of value-based payment?

Supply Chain Management

supply chain management
The management of the procurement, storage, and utilization of supplies; also called *inventory management*.

The overall management of inventory, including purchasing, transportation, storage, and use or disposal, is called **supply chain management** or *inventory management*. Inventories are an essential part of virtually all business operations. As is the case with accounts receivable, inventory levels depend heavily on volume. However, whereas receivables build up after services have been provided, inventories must be acquired **ahead** of time. This is a critical difference, and the necessity of forecasting patient volume before establishing target inventory levels makes inventory management a difficult task. Also, because errors in inventory levels can lead either to catastrophic consequences for patients or excessive carrying cost, supply chain management in health services organizations is as important as it is difficult.

Proper supply chain management requires close coordination among the marketing, purchasing, patient services, and finance departments. The patient services department is generally the first to spot changes in demand. These changes must be worked into the company's purchasing and operating schedules, and the financial manager must arrange any financing that will be needed to support inventory buildups. Improper communication among departments, poor volume forecasts, or both can lead to disaster.

The key to cost-effective supply chain management is information technology. *Inventory control systems* start with an inventory count in memory, and, as withdrawals are made, the system records them and revises the inventory balance. When the order point is reached, the system automatically places an order, and when the order is received, the system increases the recorded balance. A good supply chain management system must be dynamic. A large provider may stock thousands of different items of inventory. Increased or decreased use of these items may have no correlation with an increase or decrease in aggregate utilization of services. As the usage rate for an item begins to rise or fall, the supply chain manager must adjust its balance to avoid running short or ending up with obsolete items. If the change in the usage rate appears to be permanent, the *base inventory* level should be recomputed, the *safety stock* should be reconsidered, and the computer model used in the control process should be reprogrammed.

Today, many health services providers use the **just-in-time (JIT) approach** to supply chain management. JIT is a management strategy aimed at minimizing costs by having inventory items arrive on-site shortly before they are needed. This simple concept reduces the costs associated with carrying large inventories at any given point in time.

To illustrate the use of JIT systems among providers, consider Bayside Memorial Hospital, which consumes large quantities of medical supplies each year. A few years ago, the hospital maintained a 25,000-square-foot warehouse to hold its medical supplies. However, as cost pressures mounted, the hospital closed its warehouse and sold the inventory to a major hospital supplier. Now the supplier is a full-time partner of Bayside in ordering and delivering the products of some 400 hospital supply companies.

Bayside's supply chain streamlining process began with daily deliveries to the hospital's loading dock but soon expanded to a JIT system called *stockless inventory*. Now the supplier fills orders in exact, sometimes small, quantities and delivers them directly to departments inside the hospital, including the operating rooms and nursing floors. Bayside's managers estimate that the stockless system has saved the hospital about $1.5 million a year since it was instituted, including $350,000 from staff reductions and $1,150,000 from inventory and facilities reductions. In addition, the hospital has converted space that was previously used as storerooms to patient care and other cash-generating uses. The distributors that offer stockless inventory systems typically add 3 to 5 percent service fees, but many large hospitals with high supplies costs can still realize savings on total inventory costs.

However, the stockless inventory concept has its own set of problems. The major concern is that a *stock-out*, which occurs when a needed inventory item is not available, will cause a serious problem. In addition, some hospital managers are concerned that such systems create too much dependence on a single supplier, and that the cost savings will disappear as prices increase.

just-in-time (JIT) approach
A supply chain management technique that requires suppliers to deliver inventory items in relatively small quantities as they are needed, which reduces the amount of inventory stock held; there are several variations of JIT systems.

For Your Consideration

The GS1 System of Standards

Founded in 1977, GS1 is an international not-for-profit organization dedicated to the improvement of supply chain efficiency. GS1's primary activity is the development of the GS1 System, a series of standards composed of four key elements: bar codes, which are used to automatically identify items; eCom, which creates standardized business inventory messaging data; Global Data Synchronization, which allows multiple businesses to have consistent inventory data; and EPCglobal, which establishes a system that uses radio frequency chips to track items across the entire supply chain.

In the US healthcare sector, many companies—from manufacturers to distributors to end users such as hospitals—are actively supporting the adoption of GS1 standards. The goals of the companies involved include enhanced patient safety, improved supply chain management, enhanced drug control, and better connectivity to electronic health records.

What do you think of the GS1 standards concept? How can bar codes and radio frequency chips enhance patient safety? Do you think that the adoption of GS1 standards will increase or decrease supply chain costs?

As stockless inventory systems become more prevalent in hospitals, more and more hospitals are relying on outside contractors that assume both inventory management and supplier roles. In effect, hospitals are beginning to outsource supply chain management. For example, some hospitals are experimenting with an inventory management program known as *point-of-service distribution*, which is one generation ahead of stockless systems. Under point-of-service programs, the supplier delivers supplies, intravenous solutions, medical forms, and so on to the supply rooms. The supplier owns the products in the supply rooms until the hospital uses them, at which time the hospital pays for the items.

In addition to reducing inventories, outside supply chain managers are often better at ferreting out waste than are their in-house counterparts. For example, an inventory management company found that one hospital was spending $600 on products used in open heart surgery, while another was spending only $420. Because there was no meaningful difference in the procedure or outcomes, the higher-cost hospital was able to change the medical devices used in the surgery and pocket the difference.

In an even more advanced form of supply chain management, some hospitals negotiate with suppliers to furnish materials on the basis of how much medical care is delivered, rather than the type and number of products used. In such agreements, providers pay suppliers a set fee for each unit of patient service provided—for example, $125 for each case-mix-adjusted patient day. Under this type of system, a hospital ties its supplies expenditures to its revenues, which, at least for now, are for the most part tied to the number of units of patient service. The end of the evolution of inventory management techniques for healthcare providers is expected to be some form of capitated payment; providers will pay suppliers a previously agreed-upon fee regardless of actual future patient volume and regardless of the amount of supplies actually consumed.

1. Why is good supply chain management important to a firm's success?
2. Describe some recent trends in supply chain management by healthcare providers.

Current Liability Management

At this point in the chapter, we conclude our discussion of current assets management and turn our attention to current liabilities management. We begin with accruals and trade credit, after which we cover short-term debt financing.

Accruals

Firms generally pay employees on a weekly, biweekly, or monthly basis, so the balance sheet will typically show some accrued wages. Similarly, the firm's estimated income taxes (if applicable); the Social Security and income taxes withheld from employee payrolls; and any required sales, workers' compensation, and unemployment taxes are generally paid on a weekly, monthly, or quarterly basis. Thus, as discussed in chapter 4, the balance sheet accruals account typically includes both taxes and wages.

Accruals increase automatically, or spontaneously, as a firm's operations expand. Furthermore, this type of short-term debt is free in the sense that no explicit interest is paid on funds raised through accruals. However, a firm cannot ordinarily control the amount of accruals on its balance sheet because the timing of wage payments is set by economic forces and sector custom, and tax payment dates are established by law. Because accruals represent free financing, businesses should use all of the accrual financing they can obtain, but managers have little control over the levels of such accounts.

Accounts Payable (Trade Credit)

Firms often make purchases from other firms on credit. Such debt is recorded on the balance sheet as an *account payable*. Accounts payable, or *trade credit*, is the largest single category of short-term debt for many businesses. Because very small companies typically do not qualify for financing from other sources, they rely especially heavily on trade credit.

Trade credit is another spontaneous source of financing in the sense that it arises from ordinary business transactions. For example, suppose that a hospital purchases an average of $2,000 a day of supplies on terms of net 30 days—meaning that it must pay for goods 30 days after the invoice date.

On average, the hospital will owe 30 × $2,000 = $60,000 to its suppliers, assuming that the hospital's managers act rationally and do not pay before the credit is due. If the hospital's volume, and consequently its purchases, were to double, its accounts payable would also double to $120,000. Simply by growing, the hospital would have spontaneously generated an additional $60,000 of financing. Similarly, if the terms under which it bought supplies were extended from 30 to 40 days, the hospital's accounts payable would expand from $60,000 to $80,000. Thus, both greater volume and a longer credit period generate additional financing for a business.

credit policy
Generically, a business's rules and regulations regarding granting credit and collecting from buyers that take credit; for healthcare providers, the business's policy regarding self-pay and indigent patients.

Firms that sell on credit have a **credit policy** that includes certain *terms of credit*. For example, Lake Michigan Medical Supply Company sells on terms of 2/10, net 30—meaning that a 2 percent discount is given if payment is made within ten days of the invoice date, with the full invoice amount being due and payable within 30 days if the discount is not taken. Suppose that East Chicago Health System buys an average of $12 million of medical and surgical supplies from Lake Michigan each year, less a 2 percent discount, for net purchases of $11,760,000 ÷ 360 = $32,666.67 per day. For the sake of simplicity, suppose that Lake Michigan is East Chicago Health System's only supplier. If East Chicago Health System takes the discount, paying at the end of the tenth day, its payables will average 10 × $32,666.67 = $326,667, so East Chicago Health System will, on average, be receiving $326,667 of credit from its only supplier, Lake Michigan Medical Supply Company.

Suppose now that the system's managers decide not to take the discount. What effect will this decision have on the system's financial condition? First, East Chicago Health System will begin paying invoices after 30 days, so its accounts payable will increase to 30 × $32,666.67 = $980,000. Lake Michigan will now be supplying East Chicago Health System with $980,000 – $326,667 = $653,333 of additional trade credit. The health system could use this additional credit to pay off bank loans, expand inventories, increase fixed assets, build up its cash account, or even increase its own accounts receivable.

Note that we used $32,666.67 for average daily sales, which is based on the discounted price of the surgical supplies, regardless of whether East Chicago Health System takes the discount. In general, businesses treat the discounted price of supplies as the "true" cost when reporting expenses on the income statement. If the business does not take the discount, the cost difference is reported separately on the income statement as an expense called "discounts lost." Thus, we used the discounted price to reflect the cost of the supplies in both instances.

East Chicago Health System's additional credit from Lake Michigan has a cost: It is forgoing a 2 percent discount on its $12 million of purchases, so its costs will rise by $240,000 per year. Dividing this $240,000 cost by the amount of additional credit provides the implicit approximate percentage cost of the added trade credit:

$$\text{Approximate \% cost} = \frac{\$240,000}{\$653,333} = 36.7\%.$$

Assuming that East Chicago Health System can borrow from its bank or from other sources at an interest rate less than 36.7 percent, it should not expand its payables by forgoing discounts.

The following equation can be used to calculate the approximate percentage cost, on an annual basis, of forgoing discounts:

$$\text{Approximate \% cost} = \frac{\text{Discount percent}}{100 - \text{Discount percent}}$$
$$\times \frac{360}{\text{Days credit received} - \text{Discount period}}.$$

The numerator of the first term, Discount percent, is the cost per dollar of credit, while the denominator in this term, 100 – Discount percent, represents the funds made available by not taking the discount. Thus, the first term is the *periodic* cost rate of the trade credit—in this example, East Chicago Health System must spend $2 to gain $98 of credit, for a periodic rate of 2 ÷ 98 = 0.0204 = 2.04%. The second term shows how many times each year this cost is incurred—in this example, 360 ÷ (30 – 10) = 360 ÷ 20 = 18 times. Putting the two terms together, the approximate cost of forgoing the discount when the terms are 2/10, net 30 is computed as follows:

$$\text{Approximate \% cost} = \frac{2}{98} \times \frac{360}{20} = 0.0204 \times 18$$
$$= 0.367 = 36.7\%.$$

The cost of trade credit can be reduced by paying late—that is, by paying beyond the date that the credit terms allow. This strategy is called *stretching*. If East Chicago Health System could get away with paying Lake Michigan in 60 days rather than in the specified 30, the effective credit period would become 60 – 10 = 50 days, and the approximate cost would drop from 36.7 percent to (2 ÷ 98) × (360 ÷ 50) = 14.7%. During a recession, businesses may be able to get away with late payments to suppliers, but they will also suffer a variety of problems associated with stretching accounts payable and being branded as a slow payer.

On the basis of the preceding discussion, it is clear that trade credit usually consists of two distinct components:

free trade credit
The amount of credit received from a supplier that has no explicit cost attached; in other words, credit received during the discount period.

1. **Free trade credit** is credit received during the discount period. For East Chicago Health System, the free trade credit amounts to ten days' net purchases, or $326,667.

2. **Costly trade credit** is credit in excess of the free credit. The cost of this credit is implied because it is obtained only if the discount is forgone. For East Chicago Health System, the amount of costly trade credit is $653,333.

costly trade credit
The credit taken by a company from a vendor in excess of the free trade credit.

From a finance perspective, managers should view trade credit in this way. First, the actual price of supplies is the discounted price—that is, the price that would be paid on a cash purchase. Any credit that can be taken without an increase in price is free credit that should be taken. Second, if the discounted price is the actual price, the added amount that must be paid if the discount is not taken is, in reality, *a finance charge* for additional credit. A business should take the additional credit only if the finance charge is less than the cost of alternative credit sources.

> **Key Equation: Approximate Cost of Trade Credit**
> The approximate cost of the costly portion of trade credit can be calculated as follows:
>
> $$\text{Approximate \% cost} = \frac{\text{Discount percent}}{100 - \text{Discount percent}}$$
> $$\times \frac{360}{\text{Days credit received} - \text{Discount period}}.$$

To illustrate, assume a vendor offers terms of 3/10, net 60, which means that a 3 percent discount is offered if the bill is paid in ten days, but the full amount is due in 60 days if the discount is not taken. In this case, the approximate cost of not taking the discount is 22.3 percent:

$$\text{Approximate \% cost} = \frac{3}{(100-3)} \times \frac{360}{(60-10)} = \frac{3}{97} \times \frac{360}{50}$$
$$= 0.0309 \times 7.2$$
$$= 0.223 = 22.3\%.$$

In the example, East Chicago Health System should take the $326,667 of free credit offered by Lake Michigan Medical Supply Company. Free credit is good credit. However, the cost rate of the additional $653,333 of costly trade credit is approximately 37 percent. The system has access to bank loans at a lower interest rate, so it does not take the additional credit. Under the terms of trade found in most industries, the costly component involves a relatively high percentage cost, so stronger firms avoid using it.

Short-Term Debt Financing

Short-term debt, which is a current liability account, has three primary advantages over long-term debt (discussed in chapter 11). First, a short-term loan can be obtained much faster than long-term credit. Lenders will insist on a more thorough financial examination before extending long-term credit, and the loan agreement (or bond indenture) will have to be spelled out in considerable detail because a lot can happen during the life of a 20-year loan (or bond). Thus, businesses that require funds in a hurry look to the short-term credit markets.

Second, if the need for funds is temporary (seasonal or cyclical), a firm may not want to commit to long-term debt for the following reasons:

1. Issuance costs—sometimes called *flotation costs*—are generally higher for long-term debt than for short-term debt. Issuance costs are the administrative costs associated with obtaining financing. For debt financing, these costs include legal and accounting fees, printing costs, loan application fees, and credit assessment fees.
2. Although long-term debt can be repaid early, provided that the loan agreement includes a prepayment provision, prepayment penalties can be expensive. Accordingly, if a firm thinks its need for funds may diminish in the near future, it should choose short-term debt for the greater flexibility it provides.
3. Long-term loan agreements typically contain restrictive covenants that constrain the firm's future actions. Short-term credit agreements are generally much less onerous in this regard.
4. The interest rate on short-term debt generally is lower than the rate on long-term debt. Thus, when coupled with lower issuance costs, short-term debt can have a significant total cost advantage over long-term debt.

In spite of these advantages, short-term debt has one serious disadvantage: It subjects the firm to more risk than long-term financing. First, if a firm borrows on a long-term basis, its interest costs will be relatively stable over time, but if it uses short-term debt, its interest expense can fluctuate widely. For example, the short-term rate that banks charge large corporations (the prime rate) more than tripled over a two-year period in the early 1980s, rising from 6.25 to 21 percent. Many firms that had borrowed heavily on a short-term basis simply could not meet their rising interest costs, and as a result, bankruptcies hit record levels during that period.

Second, the principal amount on short-term debt comes due on a regular basis. If the business's financial condition deteriorates, it may be unable to repay this debt when it matures. Furthermore, the business may be in such a weak financial position that the lender will not extend the loan. Such a scenario can result in severe problems for the borrower, which could force the business into bankruptcy.

Commercial banks, whose short-term loans generally appear on firms' balance sheets as *notes payable*, are an important source of short-term financing for many health services businesses. The banks' influence is actually greater than it appears from the dollar amounts they lend because banks provide *nonspontaneous* funds. As a business's financing needs increase, it requests its bank provide the additional funds. If the request is denied, the firm may be forced to abandon attractive growth opportunities.

Although banks make longer-term loans, the bulk of their lending is on a short-term basis (about two-thirds of all bank loans mature in a year or less). Bank loans to businesses are frequently written as 90-day notes, so the loan must be repaid or renewed at the end of 90 days. When a bank loan is approved, the agreement is executed by signing a *promissory note*, which is similar to a bond indenture or loan agreement but much less detailed. When the note is signed, the bank credits the borrower's checking account with the amount of the loan, while both cash and notes payable increase on the borrower's balance sheet.

Compensating Balances

compensating balance
A minimum checking account balance that a business must maintain to compensate the bank for other services or loans.

Banks sometimes require borrowers to maintain a checking account balance equal to 10 to 20 percent of the face amount of a short-term loan. This requirement is called a **compensating balance**, and such balances raise the effective interest rate on the loan. For example, suppose that Pine Garden Nursing Home needs an $80,000 bank loan to pay off maturing obligations. If the loan requires a 20 percent compensating balance, the nursing home must borrow $100,000 to obtain a usable $80,000, assuming that the business does not have an "extra" $20,000 around to use as a compensating balance. If the stated interest rate is 8 percent, the effective cost rate is 10 percent: $0.08 \times \$100,000 = \$8,000$ in interest expense divided by $80,000 of usable funds equals 10 percent.

Lines of Credit

One common type of short-term loan is the **line of credit**, sometimes called a *revolving credit agreement* or just *revolver*. The contract on such loans specifies the maximum credit the bank will extend to the borrower over some specified period of time. For example, on December 31, a bank loan officer might indicate to Pine Garden's manager that the bank will provide up to $80,000 during the forthcoming year. If, on January 10, Pine Garden borrows $15,000 against the line, this would be called *taking down* $15,000 of the credit line. This takedown would be credited to the nursing home's checking account at the bank, and before repayment of the $15,000, Pine Garden could borrow additional amounts up to a total of $80,000 outstanding at any one time.

> **line of credit**
> A loan arrangement in which a bank agrees to lend some maximum amount to a business over some designated period.

Lines of credit generally are extended for one year or less, and borrowers typically have to pay an up-front commitment fee of 0.5 to 1 percent of the total amount of the line. Interest is paid only on the amount of the credit line that is actually used. As a general rule, the rate of interest on credit lines is pegged to the prime rate, so the cost of the loan can vary over time if interest rates change. Pine Garden's rate was set at prime plus 0.5 percentage points.

Secured Short-Term Debt

Generally, short-term debt used by healthcare providers is unsecured, meaning that no specific assets are pledged as collateral. Given a choice, it is ordinarily better to borrow on an unsecured basis because the administrative costs associated with secured loans are often high. However, weak businesses may find that they can borrow only if they put up some form of security to protect the lender or that they can borrow at a much lower rate by using security. Within the healthcare sector, the most common form of collateral is accounts receivables.

Accounts receivable financing involves either the pledging of receivables or the selling of receivables. The *pledging* of accounts receivable is characterized by the fact that the lender not only has a claim against the dollar amount of the receivables but also has recourse against the pledging firm. This means that if the person or firm that owes the receivable does not pay, the business that borrows against the receivable must take the loss. Therefore, the risk of default on the accounts receivable pledged remains with the borrowing firm. When receivables are pledged, the payer is not ordinarily notified about the pledging, and payments are made on the receivables in the same way as when receivables are not used as loan security.

The second form of receivables financing is *factoring*, or *selling accounts receivable*. In this type of secured financing, the receivables account is purchased by the capital supplier, generally without recourse to the selling business. In a typical factoring transaction, the buyer of the receivables pays the seller about 90 to 95 percent of the face value of the receivables. When receivables are factored, the person or business that owes the receivable is often notified of the transfer and is asked to make payment directly to the company that bought the receivables. Because the factoring firm assumes the risk of default on accounts, it must perform a credit check on the receivables prior to the purchase. Accordingly, *factors*, which are the firms that buy receivables, can provide not only money but also a credit department for the borrower. Incidentally, the same financial institutions that make loans against pledged receivables also serve as factors. Thus, depending on the circumstances and the wishes of the borrower, a financial institution will provide either form of receivables financing.

Because healthcare providers tend to carry relatively large amounts of receivables, such businesses are prime candidates for receivables financing. The sale of these receivables, especially by hospitals that are experiencing liquidity problems, represents one way to reduce carrying cost and stimulate cash flow.

Although receivables financing is one way to reduce current assets and financing costs, critics contend that such programs are too expensive. Because of the costs involved, most receivables financing programs are used by providers that have serious liquidity (cash flow) problems, although programs are being developed that can provide benefits even to well-run businesses that are not facing a liquidity crunch.

SELF-TEST QUESTIONS

1. What are accruals, and what is their role in short-term financing?
2. What is the difference between free and costly trade credit?
3. How might a hospital that expects to have a cash shortage sometime during the coming year make sure that needed funds will be available?
4. What is the current asset most commonly pledged as security for short-term loans?

Key Concepts

This chapter examines current asset management and financing. The key concepts of this chapter are as follows:

- The goal of current asset management and financing is to *support the business's operations* at the lowest possible cost without taking undue risks.

- The *primary goal of cash management* is to reduce the amount of cash held to the minimum necessary to conduct business in a financially efficient manner.

- *Float* is the difference between the balance shown in a business's (or individual's) checkbook and the balance shown on the bank's books.

- *Float management techniques* include *accelerating collections* and *controlling disbursements.*

- *Lockboxes* are used to accelerate collections. A *concentration banking system* consolidates the collections into a centralized pool that can be managed more efficiently than a large number of individual accounts.

- Three techniques for controlling disbursements are *payables centralization, zero-balance accounts,* and *controlled disbursement accounts.*

- Businesses can reduce their cash balances by holding *marketable securities.* Marketable securities serve both as a *substitute for cash* and as a *temporary investment* for funds that will be needed in the near future. Safety is the primary consideration when selecting marketable securities.

- The implementation of a sophisticated cash management system is costly, and all cash management actions must be evaluated to ensure that the benefits exceed the costs.

- A *cash budget*, which is the primary cash management tool, forecasts the cash inflows and outflows of an organization with the goal of identifying expected surpluses and shortfalls.

(continued)

(continued from previous page)

- In general, *monthly* cash budgets are used for planning purposes, while *weekly* or *daily* budgets are used for cash management purposes.

- The *revenue cycle* includes all activities associated with billings and collections for services provided.

- The revenue cycle can be broken down into four activity categories, depending on when they occur: (1) *before-service* activities, (2) *at-service* activities, (3) *after-service* activities, and (4) *continuous* activities.

- When a business sells goods to a customer on credit, an *account receivable* is created.

- Businesses use *aging schedules* and *average collection period (ACP)* data to monitor overall revenue cycle performance.

- In addition, *metrics* are used to monitor the performance of individual revenue cycle activities.

- Proper *supply chain (inventory) management* requires close coordination among the marketing, purchasing, patient services, and finance departments. Because the cost of holding inventory can be high and stock-outs can be disastrous, inventory management is important.

- *Just-in-time (JIT)* systems are used to minimize inventory costs and, simultaneously, to improve operations.

- The advantages of short-term debt are the *speed* with which short-term loans can be arranged, increased *flexibility*, and the fact that short-term *interest rates* are generally *lower* than long-term rates. The principal disadvantages of short-term credit are that borrowers must bear *extra risk* because lenders can demand payment on short notice and that the cost of the loan will increase if interest rates rise.

- *Accruals*, which are recurring short-term liabilities, represent free spontaneous credit.

- *Accounts payable*, or *trade credit*, arises spontaneously as a result of purchases on credit. Businesses should use all the *free trade credit* they can obtain, but they should use *costly trade credit* only if it is less expensive than alternative sources of short-term debt.

- *Bank loans* are an important source of short-term credit. When a bank loan is approved, a *promissory note* is signed.

(continued)

(continued from previous page)

- Banks sometimes require borrowers to maintain *compensating balances*, which are deposit requirements set between 10 and 20 percent of the loan amount. Compensating balances raise the effective rate of interest on bank loans.
- *Lines of credit*, or *revolving credit agreements*, are formal understandings between the bank and the borrower in which the bank agrees to extend some maximum amount of credit to the borrower over some specified period.
- Sometimes a borrower will find that it is necessary to borrow on a *secured basis*, in which case the borrower uses assets, primarily accounts receivable in the healthcare sector, as collateral for the loan.

This chapter focuses on the revenue cycle and current accounts management rather than the long-term concepts covered in earlier chapters. In the final chapter in the text, chapter 17, we cover financial performance analysis.

Questions

16.1. a. What is the goal of cash management?

  b. Briefly describe float and the following associated cash management techniques:
   - Receipt acceleration
   - Disbursement control

16.2. a. What is a cash budget, and how is it used?

  b. Should depreciation expense appear on a cash budget? Explain your answer.

16.3. a. Give two reasons why businesses hold marketable securities.

  b. Which types of securities are most suitable for holding as marketable securities?

  c. Suppose Southwest Regional Medical Center has just raised $6 million in new capital that it plans to use to build three freestanding clinics, one each year over the next three years. (For the sake of simplicity, assume that equal payments have to be made at the end of each of the next three years.) What securities should be bought for the firm's marketable securities portfolio, assuming that the firm has no other excess cash? (Hint: Consider both the type and maturity of the securities.)

   d. Now, consider the situation faced by the Huntsville Physical
      Therapy Group. It has accumulated $20,000 in cash above its
      target cash balance, and it has no immediate needs for this excess
      cash. However, the firm may at any time need some or all of the
      $20,000 to meet unforeseen cash needs. What securities should
      be bought for the firm's marketable securities portfolio?

16.4. a. What is meant by the term *revenue cycle*?
       b. What are the three sets of activities that make up the revenue
          cycle?
       c. What is the overall goal of revenue cycle management?

16.5. a. Define the term *average collection period (ACP)*.
       b. How is ACP used to monitor overall revenue cycle
          performance?
       c. What is an aging schedule?
       d. How is an aging schedule used to monitor overall revenue cycle
          performance?

16.6. a. What is a metric?
       b. What role do metrics play in revenue cycle management?

16.7. a. What is a just-in-time (JIT) inventory system?
       b. What are the advantages and disadvantages of JIT systems?
       c. Can JIT inventory systems be used by healthcare providers?
          Explain your answer.

16.8. Describe the three major sources of short-term financing.

16.9. a. What is the difference between free trade credit and costly trade
          credit?
       b. Should businesses use all the free trade credit that they can get?
          Explain your answer.
       c. Should businesses use all the costly trade credit they can get?
          Explain your answer.

16.10. Explain briefly how healthcare providers typically obtain secured
       short-term financing.

Problems

16.1. On a typical day, Park Place Clinic writes $1,000 in checks. It
       generally takes four days for those checks to clear. Each day the
       clinic typically receives $1,000 in checks that take three days to
       clear. What is the clinic's average net float?

16.2. Drugs 'R Us operates a mail-order pharmaceutical business on the
       West Coast. The firm receives an average of $325,000 in payments

per day. On average, it takes four days for the firm to receive payment, from the time customers mail their checks to the time the firm receives and processes them. A lockbox system that consists of ten local depository banks and a concentration bank in San Francisco would require Drugs 'R Us to pay a fixed fee of $6,500 per month. Under this system, customers' checks would be received at the lockbox locations one day after they are mailed, and the daily total would be wired from each local bank to the concentration bank at a cost of $9.75 per wire (this additional fee would be paid by Drugs 'R Us). Assume that Drugs 'R Us could earn 10 percent on marketable securities and that there are 260 working days and hence 260 transfers from each lockbox location per year.

a. What is the total annual cost of operating the lockbox system?

b. What is the dollar benefit of the lockbox system to Drugs 'R Us?

c. On purely financial grounds, should the firm initiate the lockbox system?

16.3. Suppose one of the suppliers to Seattle Health System offers terms of 3/20, net 60.

a. When does the system have to pay its bills from this supplier (assuming it abides by the credit terms)?

b. What is the approximate cost of the costly trade credit offered by this supplier? (Assume 360 days per year.)

16.4. Langley Clinics, Inc., buys $400,000 in medical supplies each year (at gross prices) from its major supplier, Consolidated Supplies, which offers Langley terms of 2.5/10, net 45. Currently, Langley is paying the supplier the full amount due on day 45, but it is considering taking the discount, paying on day 10, and replacing the costly trade credit with a bank loan that has a 10 percent annual cost.

a. What is the amount of free trade credit that Langley obtains from Consolidated Supplies? (Assume 360 days per year throughout this problem.)

b. What is the amount of costly trade credit?

c. What is the approximate annual cost of the costly trade credit?

d. Should Langley replace its trade credit with the bank loan? Explain your answer.

e. If the bank loan is used, how much of the trade credit should be replaced?

16.5. Milwaukee Surgical Supplies, Inc., has gross sales for the year of $1,200,000. The collections department estimates that 30 percent of the customers pay on the tenth day, 40 percent pay on the thirtieth day, and the remaining 30 percent pay, on average, 40 days after the purchase. (Assume 360 days per year.)

    a. What is the firm's average collection period?

    b. What is the firm's current receivables balance?

    c. What would be the firm's new receivables balance if Milwaukee Surgical toughened up on its collection policy, with the result that all customers previously paying on day 40 now paid on the thirtieth day?

    d. Suppose that the firm's cost of carrying receivables was 8 percent annually. How much would the toughened credit policy save the firm in annual receivables carrying cost? (Assume that the entire amount of receivables had to be financed.)

16.6. Fargo Memorial Hospital has annual net patient service revenues of $14,400,000. It has two major third-party payers, plus some of its patients are self-payers. The hospital's patient accounts manager estimates that 10 percent of the hospital's paying patients (its self-payers) pay on day 30, 60 percent pay on day 60 (payer A), and 30 percent pay on day 90 (payer B).

    a. What is Fargo's average collection period? (Assume 360 days per year throughout this problem.)

    b. What is the firm's current receivables balance?

    c. What would be the firm's new receivables balance if a newly proposed electronic claims system resulted in collecting from third-party payers in 45 and 75 days, instead of in 60 and 90 days?

    d. Suppose the firm's annual interest rate on short-term debt was 10 percent. If the electronic claims system costs $30,000 a year to lease and operate, should it be adopted? (Assume that the entire receivables balance has to be financed.)

16.7. Healthcare Associates (HA) is in the process of preparing a cash budget for December. HA had the following results for the past three months:

	Net patient service revenue	Amount of the month's revenue still uncollected (i.e., in accounts receivable) at the end of November
September	$150,000	$ 0
October	120,000	12,000
November	180,000	54,000

HA has no uncollectible accounts. In December, HA is expecting $200,000 in net patient service revenue. If HA expects the same pattern of cash collection as in previous months, what should be budgeted for *total cash collections* in December in HA's cash budget?

16.8. North Carolina Pediatric Partners has forecast billed charges for the first six months of the year as shown in the following table. Based on historical collection patterns, North Carolina Pediatric Partners expects to collect charges as follows: 5 percent within 30 days, 85 percent within 60 days, and 5 percent within 90 days. The remaining 5 percent is expected to be uncollectible. What should be budgeted for cash collections in each of the months January through June?

Month	Billed Charges	Cash Collections
January	$ 99,000	?
February	99,000	?
March	99,000	?
April	105,000	?
May	105,000	?
June	105,000	?

Selected Cases

Four cases in *Gapenski's Cases in Healthcare Finance*, sixth edition, are applicable to this chapter: Case 26: Mountain Village Clinic; Case 27: Foster Pharmaceuticals; Case 28: Clarinda Community Hospital; and Case 29: Milwaukee Regional Health System.

Notes

1. Board of Governors of the Federal Reserve System. 2018. The Federal Reserve Payments Study—2018 Annual Supplement. Accessed February 14, 2020. www.federalreserve.gov/paymentsystems/2018 -December-The-Federal-Reserve-Payments-Study.htm.

2. A *credit line* is an agreement between a borrower and a financial institution that obligates the institution to furnish credit over some

period—typically a year—up to the agreed amount. The borrower may use some, all, or none of the credit line. Usually, borrowers must pay an up-front fee—called a *commitment fee*—for the credit guarantee.

3. Money market mutual funds cannot be used as a replacement for commercial checking accounts because the number of checks that can be written against such funds normally is limited to just a few per month.

4. There is no universally accepted description of revenue cycle activities. Different professional organizations tend to include somewhat different sets of activities. Still, the basic premise remains the same: Revenue cycle management encompasses the information systems, policies, and methodologies used to review patients' and insurers' financial obligations, document services provided, translate the services into appropriate billing amounts, issue invoices, and collect the correct payments—all in a timely manner.

5. American Hospital Association. 2019. Uncompensated Care Fact Sheet. Published January. www.aha.org/system/files/2019-01 /uncompensated-care-fact-sheet-jan-2019.pdf.

6. New York State. Department of Financial Services. 2002. "Re: Prompt Pay." Published July 24. www.dfs.ny.gov/insurance/ogco2002 /rg207242.htm.

Resources

Baker, K. B. 2016. "Aligning Systems for Improved Revenue Cycle Performance." *Healthcare Financial Management* 70 (9): 44–51.

Boggs, S. L. 2010. "Physician Practice and Hospital Revenue Cycle Drivers: What's the Difference?" *Healthcare Financial Management* 64 (9): 40–46.

Brody, P. 2007. "The Time Is Right for Supply Chain Synchronization." *Healthcare Financial Management* 6 (1): 94–98.

Burns, W., and A. Harmon. 2016. "Reducing Administrative Write-Offs Through Improved Denial Management." *Healthcare Financial Management* 70 (7): 30–33.

DeLuca, M., and C. Smith. 2010. "Building a World-Class A/P Function." *Healthcare Financial Management* 64 (3): 100–106.

D'Eramo, M., and L. Umbreit. 2005. "Thinking Inside the (Lock)Box: Using Banking Technology to Improve the Revenue Cycle." *Healthcare Financial Management* 59 (8): 90–93.

Doody, D. 2010. "Alternative Strategies: A Better Alternative." *Healthcare Financial Management* 64 (5): 42–45.

———. 2007. "Measuring Up: Investment Policies and Practices in Not-for-Profit Health Care." *Healthcare Financial Management* 61 (1): 124–28.

Freeman, T., and S. Stephen. 2011. "What Makes a Physician Revenue Cycle Tick." *Healthcare Financial Management* 65 (9): 63–67.

French, C. J., and T. H. Dodd. 2010. "Are Alternative Investments the Right Approach for Your Organization?" *Healthcare Financial Management* 64 (4): 72–77.

Glaser, J. 2011. "Strengthening Revenue Cycle Capabilities in an Era of Reform." *Healthcare Financial Management* 65 (5): 48–52.

Hammer, D. C. 2005. "Performance Is Reality: How Is Your Revenue Cycle Holding Up?" *Healthcare Financial Management* 59 (7): 49–56.

Healthcare Financial Management Association. 2018. "Transforming Accounts Payable: Opportunities, Challenges, and Next Steps." Published July 31. www.hfma.org/Content.aspx?id=61336.

———. 2016a. "Leveraging Data Analytics to Improve the Revenue Cycle." Published August 1. www.hfma.org/RevCycleAnalytics.

———. 2016b. "Transforming the Disbursement Cycle: Four Steps for Selecting a Diversified Payment Strategy." Published June 1. https://api.hfma.org/Content.aspx?id=49444.

———. 2013a. "10 Key Revenue Cycle Technology Considerations for the Future." *Healthcare Financial Management* 67 (9): 51–58.

———. 2013b. "10 Revenue Cycle Improvement Ideas from HFMA's MAP Award Winners." *Healthcare Financial Management* 67 (10): 70–78.

———. 2012. "Supply Chain Benchmarking Presents Opportunity for Added Cost Savings." *Healthcare Financial Management* 66 (11): 164–65.

———. 2011. "Research Shows Path to Revenue Cycle Gains Through Effective Benchmarking." *Healthcare Financial Management* 65 (9): 49–54.

———. 2004. "Linking Supply Costs and Revenue: The Time Has Come." *Healthcare Financial Management* 58 (5): 97–98.

Jarvis, W. F. 2013. "Rethinking Asset Allocation: The Case for Portfolio Diversification." *Healthcare Financial Management* 67 (5): 140–42.

Jordahl, E. A., and D. Ratliff. 2017. "Refocus Treasury Functions for Continued High Volatility." *Healthcare Financial Management* 71 (7): 54–56.

Kapel, A. S., J. McCormack, I. R. Merkatz, and J. Oliva. 2004. "Increasing Up-Front Collections." *Healthcare Financial Management* 58 (3): 82–88.

Kowalski, J. C. 2009. "Needed: A Strategic Approach to Supply Chain Management." *Healthcare Financial Management* 63 (6): 90–98.

Leach, R., M. Daymont, J. Roby, L. Metro, and S. Walter. 2012. "A Multidisciplinary Approach to Denials Prevention." *Healthcare Financial Management* 66 (3): 108–12.

Mason, D. 2011. "Increasing Up-Front Payments with a Preservice Financial Checklist." *Healthcare Financial Management* 65 (9): 104–8.

Melling, J. 2017. "Preparing for Value-Based Payment: Fundamental Change That Encompasses the Revenue Cycle." *Healthcare Financial Management* 71 (5): 60–66.

Rauscher, S., and J. R. C. Wheeler. 2010. "Hospital Revenue Cycle Management and Payer Mix: Do Medicare and Medicaid Undermine Hospitals' Ability to Generate and Collect Patient Care Revenue?" *Journal of Health Care Finance* 37 (2): 81–95.

Reiter, K. L., H. L. Rivenson, D. G. Smith, and J. R. C. Wheeler. 2011. "Cash Holdings of Not-for-Profit Hospitals." *Journal of Health Care Finance* 38 (2): 24–38.

Rivenson, H. L., and D. G. Smith. 2013. "Finance Theory and Hospital Cash Balances." *Journal of Health Care Finance* 39 (3): 23–31.

Rivenson, H. L., J. R. C. Wheeler, D. G. Smith, and K. L. Reiter. 2000. "Cash Management in Health Care Systems." *Journal of Health Care Finance* 26 (4): 56–69.

Saharia, D. 2016. "Revenue Cycle Leakage: 5 Red Flags Indicating Major Inefficiencies." *Healthcare Financial Management* 70 (9): 60–64.

Singh, S. R., and J. R. C. Wheeler. 2012. "Hospital Financial Management: What Is the Link Between Revenue Cycle Management, Profitability, and Not-for-Profit Hospitals' Ability to Grow Equity?" *Journal of Healthcare Management* 57 (5): 325–41.

Van Londen, J., and P. Zimmerman. 2012. "Cutting Costs in Your Own Backyard: Opportunities in Financial Services." *Healthcare Financial Management* 66 (3): 93–97.

Work, M. 2010. "Automating the OR Supply Chain at Memorial Hermann Healthcare System." *Healthcare Financial Management* 64 (10): 100–104.

FINANCIAL CONDITION ANALYSIS

Learning Objectives

After studying this chapter, readers will be able to

- Explain the purposes of financial statement and operating indicator analyses.
- Describe the primary techniques used in financial statement and operating indicator analyses.
- Conduct basic financial statement and operating indicator analyses to assess the financial condition of a business.
- Describe the problems associated with financial statement and operating indicator analyses.
- Describe how key performance indicators (KPIs) and dashboards can be used to monitor the financial condition of a business.

Introduction

One of the most important characteristics of a healthcare organization is its *financial condition*: Does the business have the financial capacity to perform its mission? Many judgments about financial condition are made on the basis of **financial statement analysis**, which focuses on the data contained in a business's financial statements. Financial statement analysis is applied to historical data, which reflect the results of past managerial decisions, and to forecast data, which constitute the road map for the business's future. Thus, managers use financial statement analysis both to assess current condition and to plan for the future.

Although financial statement analysis provides a great deal of important information regarding financial condition, it does not provide much insight into the operational *causes* of that condition. Thus, financial statement analysis is often supplemented by **operating indicator analysis**, which uses operating data not usually found in an organization's financial statements—such as occupancy, patient mix, length of stay, and productivity measures—to identify factors that contributed to the assessed financial condition. Operating

financial statement analysis
The process of using data contained in financial statements to make judgments about a business's financial condition.

operating indicator analysis
The process of using operating indicators to help explain a business's financial condition.

indicator analysis allows managers to identify and implement strategies that will ensure a sound financial condition in the future.

Financial condition analysis involves a number of techniques that extract information contained in a business's financial statements and elsewhere and combine it in a form that helps stakeholders make judgments about the organization's financial condition and operations. Often, the result is a list of organizational strengths and weaknesses. This chapter discusses several analytical techniques used in financial condition analyses, some related topics, and the problems inherent in such analyses. Along the way, you will discover that financial condition analysis generates a great deal of data. A difficulty in assessing financial condition is separating the important from the unimportant and presenting the results in a simple, easy-to-understand, and easy-to-monitor format. Thus, we close the chapter with some ideas about data presentation. In addition to the chapter content, the chapter 17 supplement discusses four topics: market value ratios, common size analysis, percentage change analysis, and economic value added (EVA).

Financial Statement Analysis

As you learned in chapters 3 and 4, generally accepted accounting principles require businesses to prepare four *financial statements:* (1) the *income statement,* (2) the *statement of changes in equity,* (3) the *balance sheet,* and (4) the *statement of cash flows.* Together, these statements give an accounting picture of an organization's operations and financial position. Because financial statement data are well organized and easily understood, such statements provide a logical starting point for analyzing an organization's financial condition.

In much of this chapter, Riverside Memorial Hospital, a 450-bed not-for-profit facility, is used to illustrate financial condition analysis. Although a hospital is being used to illustrate the techniques, they can be applied to any health services setting. Simplified versions of Riverside's three primary financial statements are contained in exhibits 17.1, 17.2, and 17.3. Riverside's income statements and balance sheets (exhibits 17.2 and 17.3) will be examined in later sections when we discuss ratio analysis and other tools that are used to interpret the data. For now, our focus is on the statement of cash flows, which can be interpreted without the aid of additional data or tools.

The statement of cash flows (exhibit 17.1) can be thought of as an income statement that has been converted from accrual accounting to cash accounting. In essence, the statement of cash flows reports where a business gets its cash and what it does with that cash.

EXHIBIT 17.1
Riverside
Memorial
Hospital:
Statement of
Cash Flows,
Year Ended
December
31, 2020 (in
thousands)

Cash flows from operating activities:

Operating income	$6,474
Adjustments:	
Depreciation	4,130
Increase in accounts receivable	(1,102)
Increase in inventories	(195)
Decrease in accounts payable	(438)
Increase in accrued expenses	229
Net cash flow from operations	$9,098
Cash flows from investing activities:	
Investment in property and equipment	($4,293)
Investment in short-term securities	(2,000)
Net cash flow from investing	($6,293)
Cash flows from financing activities:	
Nonoperating income	$2,098
Repayment of long-term debt	(2,150)
Repayment of notes payable	(3,262)
Lease principal repayment	(323)
Net cash flow from financing	($3,637)
Net increase (decrease) in cash and equivalents	($ 832)
Beginning cash and equivalents	3,095
Ending cash and equivalents	$2,263

The statement is organized into three main sections: (1) cash flows from operating activities, (2) cash flows from investing activities, and (3) cash flows from financing activities. In addition, there is a short section that reconciles the net cash flow reported on the statement with the change in cash reported on the balance sheet. In the statement, cash coming into the hospital (inflows) is shown as a positive number, while cash being spent (outflows) is shown as a negative number (shown in parentheses).

The first section of the statement shows cash generated by and used in operations during 2020. For Riverside, operations provided $9,098,000 in net cash flow. The income statement reported $6,474,000 in operating income and $4,130,000 in depreciation, for $10,604,000 in operating cash flow. But as part of its operations, Riverside invested $1,297,000 in current assets (receivables and inventories) and reduced its spontaneous liabilities (payables and accruals) by $209,000. The end result, *net cash flow from operations*, is $10,604,000 – $1,297,000 – $209,000 = $9,098,000.

The next section of the statement of cash flows focuses on investments in fixed assets and securities. Riverside spent $4,293,000 on capital expenditures in 2020 and invested $2,000,000 in short-term securities, for a net cash outflow from investing of $6,293,000.

Is the $4,293,000 invested in fixed assets a large or small amount? The first section of the statement of cash flows reports depreciation expense of $4,130,000 for 2020, so the hospital spent only slightly more than its depreciation expense on new fixed assets. Thus, it is replacing fixed assets at approximately the same rate that existing fixed assets are losing value.

Riverside's financing activities, shown in the third section, highlight the fact that the hospital received $2,098,000 in nonoperating income (unrestricted contributions and investment income) and used $2,150,000 + $3,262,000 + $323,000 = $5,735,000 in cash to pay off previously incurred long-term debt, short-term debt, and lease obligations. The net effect of the hospital's financing activities was a *net cash outflow from financing* of $3,637,000. When the three major sections are totaled, Riverside had a $9,098,000 − $6,293,000 − $3,637,000 = $832,000 *net decrease in cash* (i.e., net cash outflow) during 2020. The bottom of exhibit 17.1 reconciles the 2020 net cash flow with the ending cash balance shown on the balance sheet. Riverside began 2020 with $3,095,000; experienced a cash outflow of $832,000 during the year; and ended the year with $3,095,000 − $832,000 = $2,263,000 in its cash and equivalents account, as verified by the value reported on the balance sheet (exhibit 17.3).

Riverside's statement of cash flows shows nothing unusual or alarming. It does show that the hospital's operations were inherently profitable, at least in 2020. Had the statement showed an operating cash loss, Riverside's managers would have had something to worry about; if the losses continued, such a drain could threaten the financial viability of the hospital. The statement of cash flows also provides easily interpretable information about Riverside's financing and fixed asset investing activities for the year. For example, Riverside's cash flow from operations was used primarily to purchase replacement fixed assets, invest in short-term securities, and pay off notes payable and long-term debt. Such uses of operating cash flow do not raise red flags regarding the hospital's financial actions.

Managers and investors must pay close attention to the statement of cash flows. Financial condition is driven by cash flows, and the statement gives a good picture of the annual cash flows generated by the organization.[1] An examination of exhibit 17.1 (or better yet, a series of such exhibits going back the last five years and projected five years into the future) would give Riverside's managers and creditors an idea of whether the hospital's operations are self-sustaining—that is, whether the business is generating the cash flows necessary to pay its bills, including those associated with the capital employed. Although the statement of cash flows is filled with valuable information, the bottom line tells little about the business's financial condition, because operating losses can be covered by financing transactions such as borrowing or selling new common stock (if investor owned), at least in the short run.

SELF-TEST QUESTIONS

1. What type of financial performance information is provided in the statement of cash flows?
2. What is the difference between net income and cash flow, and which is more meaningful to a business's financial condition?
3. Does the fact that a business's cash position has improved provide much insight into the year's financial results?

Financial Ratio Analysis

The next step in most financial condition analyses is to examine the business's other financial statements. We analyzed Riverside's statement of cash flows first because this statement is formatted in a way that facilitates interpretation without further data manipulation. Now we examine the income statement and balance sheet. Although these statements contain a wealth of financial information, it is difficult to make meaningful judgments about financial condition by merely examining the statements' raw data. To illustrate, one medical group practice may have $5,248,760 in long-term debt and interest charges of $419,900, while another may have $52,647,980 in debt and interest charges of $3,948,600. The true burden of these debts, and each practice's ability to pay the interest and principal due on them, cannot be easily assessed without additional data analyses, such as those provided by ratio analysis.

Financial ratio analysis combines data from the balance sheet and income statement to create single numbers whose financial significance is easily interpreted (i.e., numbers that measure aspects of financial condition). In the case of the debt and interest payments just described, ratios could be constructed that relate each practice's debt to its assets and the interest it pays to the income it has available for payment.

Generally, ratios are grouped into categories to make them easier to interpret. We use the data presented in exhibits 17.2 and 17.3 to calculate an illustrative sampling of financial ratios for 2020 for Riverside Memorial

financial ratio analysis
The process of creating and analyzing ratios from financial statement data to assess a business's financial condition.

EXHIBIT 17.2
Riverside
Memorial
Hospital:
Statement of
Operations
(Income
Statements),
Years Ended
December 31,
2020 and 2019
(in thousands)

	2020	2019
Revenues:		
Net patient service revenue	$103,174	$ 91,929
Premium revenue	5,232	4,622
Other revenue	3,644	6,014
Total operating revenues	$112,050	$102,565
Expenses:		
Nursing services	$ 58,285	$ 56,752
Dietary services	5,424	4,718
General services	13,198	11,655
Administrative services	11,427	11,585
Employee health and welfare	10,250	10,705
Malpractice insurance	1,320	1,204
Depreciation	4,130	4,025
Interest expense	1,542	1,521
Total expenses	$105,576	$102,165
Operating income	$ 6,474	$ 400
Nonoperating income	2,098	1,995
Net income	$ 8,572	$ 2,395

Hospital. To aid interpretation, the ratios are compared with hospital peer group average ratios.

To assess their relative performance, many healthcare organizations compare their financial ratios with average or median values of ratios for similar organizations. For example, Optum annually publishes the *Almanac of Financial and Operating Indicators*, which provides five-year trend information on more than 70 financial ratios for hospitals. The ratios are reported for peer groups because meaningful comparisons require "apples-to-apples" comparisons. Financial performance and condition can vary substantially among hospitals of different size, geographic location, teaching status, ownership, payment method, and other characteristics. For example, small rural hospitals tend to be less profitable, treat a higher percentage of Medicare and Medicaid patients, and have less cash than urban hospitals. If a small rural hospital wants to assess its financial performance, comparing its financial ratios with those of other small rural hospitals would be meaningful—comparison with an academic medical center would not be realistic or helpful. Therefore, the comparative data in this chapter are termed "peer group averages" to denote average values of ratios for hospitals similar to Riverside Memorial Hospital. The stated peer group averages are for illustrative use only and do not reflect actual performance for any hospital group. In accordance with standard practice, we call the comparative data *averages*, but in reality, they are *median* values. Median values are better for comparisons because they are not biased by extremely high or low values in the data set.

Profitability Ratios

Profitability is the net result of a large number of managerial policies and decisions, so **profitability ratios** provide one measure of a business's aggregate financial performance.

profitability ratios
A group of ratios that measure different dimensions of a business's profitability.

Total Margin

The *total margin*, often called the *total profit margin* or just *profit margin*, is net income divided by all revenues, including both operating revenues and nonoperating income:

$$\text{Total margin} = \frac{\text{Net income}}{\text{Total revenues}} = \frac{\$8,572}{\$114,148} = 0.075 = 7.5\%.$$

Industry average = 5.0%.

Total revenues are defined as net operating revenues plus nonoperating income, so Total revenues = $112,050 + $2,098 = $114,148. Riverside's total margin of 7.5 percent shows that the hospital makes 7.5 cents on each dollar of revenue. The total margin measures the ability of the organization to generate revenues from all sources and to control expenses. All else being equal, the higher the total margin, the lower the expenses relative to revenues. Riverside's total margin is well above the peer group average of 5.0 percent, indicating good expense control. How good? The sector data source also reports quartiles; for total margin, the upper quartile was 8.4 percent, meaning that 25 percent of hospitals had total margins higher than 8.4 percent. Although Riverside's total margin was better than average, it was not as good as the top 25 percent of hospitals.

Riverside's relatively high total margin could mean that the hospital's charges are relatively high, its costs are relatively low, its nonoperating revenue is relatively high, or some combination of these factors. A thorough operating indicator analysis would help pinpoint the cause, or causes, of Riverside's high total margin.

Operating Margin

Another useful margin ratio is the *operating margin*, defined as operating income divided by patient-related (operating) revenues:

$$\text{Operating margin} = \frac{\text{Operating income}}{\text{Net operating revenues}} = \frac{\$6,474}{\$112,050} = 0.058 = 5.8\%.$$

Industry average = 3.5%.

The advantage of operating margin is that it focuses on core business activities and hence removes the influence of financial (investment) gains and losses, which are unrelated to operations and often are transitory. Riverside's total margin was 7.5 percent, while its operating margin was only 5.8 percent, compared with the peer group average of 3.5 percent. Removing nonoperating income (primarily unrestricted contributions and investment returns) lowers profitability, but Riverside's core operations are more profitable than the peer group average, which is good news. Note, though, that the format of many healthcare organizations' financial

EXHIBIT 17.3
Riverside
Memorial
Hospital:
Balance Sheets,
December 31,
2020 and 2019
(in thousands)

	2020	2019
Assets:		
Cash and equivalents	$ 2,263	$ 3,095
Short-term investments	4,000	2,000
Net patient accounts receivable	21,840	20,738
Inventories	3,177	2,982
Total current assets	$ 31,280	$ 28,815
Gross property and equipment	$ 145,158	$ 140,865
Accumulated depreciation	25,160	21,030
Net property and equipment	$ 119,998	$ 119,835
Total assets	$ 151,278	$ 148,650
Liabilities:		
Accounts payable	$ 4,707	$ 5,145
Accrued expenses	5,650	5,421
Notes payable	2,975	6,237
Total current liabilities	$ 13,332	$ 16,803
Long-term debt	$ 28,750	$ 30,900
Finance lease obligations	1,832	2,155
Total long-term liabilities	$ 30,582	$ 33,055
Net assets (equity)	$ 107,364	$ 98,792
Total liabilities and net assets	$ 151,278	$ 148,650

statements makes this ratio difficult to determine without additional information. Furthermore, the definition of operating margin varies depending on data availability.

Return on Assets

The ratio of net income to total assets measures the *return on total assets*, often called simply *return on assets (ROA)*:

$$\text{Return on assets} = \frac{\text{Net income}}{\text{Total assets}} = \frac{\$8,572}{\$151,278} = 0.057 = 5.7\%.$$

Peer group average = 4.8%.

Riverside's 5.7 percent ROA—which means that each dollar of assets generated 5.7 cents in profit—is well above the 4.8 percent peer group average. ROA tells managers how productively, in a *financial sense*, a business is using its assets. The higher the ROA, the greater the net income for each dollar invested in assets and hence the more productive the assets. ROA measures both a business's ability to control expenses, as expressed by the total margin, and its ability to use its assets to generate revenue.

Return on Equity

The ratio of net income to total equity (net assets) measures the *return on equity (ROE)*:

$$\text{Return on equity} = \frac{\text{Net income}}{\text{Total equity}} = \frac{\$8,572}{\$107,364} = 0.080 = 8.0\%.$$

Peer group average = 8.4%.

Riverside's 8.0 percent ROE is slightly below the 8.4 percent peer group average. The hospital was able to generate 8.0 cents of income for each dollar of equity investment, while the average hospital produced 8.4 cents. ROE is especially meaningful for investor-owned businesses because owners use ROE to determine how well the business's managers are using owner-supplied capital. For not-for-profit businesses such as Riverside, boards of trustees and managers use ROE to determine how well, in *financial terms*, its community-supplied capital is being used.

Riverside's 2020 margin measures and ROA were above the peer group average, yet the hospital's ROE was below the average. As we explain later in the section on Du Pont analysis, this seeming inconsistency is a result of the hospital's low use of debt financing.

Liquidity Ratios

One of the first concerns of most managers, and the major concern of a firm's creditors, is the business's *liquidity*. Will the business be able to meet its cash obligations as they come due? **Liquidity ratios** are designed to answer that question. Riverside has debts totaling more than $13 million (i.e., its current liabilities) that must be paid off within the coming year. Will the hospital be able to make these payments? A full liquidity analysis requires the use of a *cash budget*, which we discussed in chapter 16. However, by relating the amount of cash and other current assets to current obligations, ratio analysis provides a quick, easy-to-use, rough measure of liquidity.

liquidity ratios
Ratios that measure the ability of a business to meet its cash obligations as they come due.

Current Ratio

The *current ratio* is calculated by dividing current assets by current liabilities:

$$\text{Current ratio} = \frac{\text{Current assets}}{\text{Current liabilities}} = \frac{\$31,280}{\$13,332} = 2.3, \text{ or } 2.3 \text{ times.}$$

Peer group average = 2.0.

The current ratio tells managers that the immediate liquidation of Riverside's current assets at book value would provide $2.30 of cash for every $1 of current liabilities. If a business is beginning to have financial difficulty, it will begin paying its accounts payable more slowly, building up short-term bank loans (notes payable), and so on. If these current liabilities rise faster than current assets, the current ratio will fall, which could spell trouble. Because the current ratio is an indicator of the extent to which short-term claim obligations are covered by assets that are expected to be converted to cash in the near term, it is a commonly used measure of liquidity.

Riverside's current ratio is slightly above the peer group average. Because current assets should be converted to cash in the near future, it is highly probable that these assets could be liquidated at close to their stated values. With a current ratio of 2.3, the hospital could liquidate current assets at only 43 percent of book value and still pay off current creditors in full. (To determine the minimum proportion of current assets that must be converted to cash to meet current obligations, divide the number 1 by the current ratio. For Riverside, 1 ÷ 2.3 = 0.43, or 43 percent. This proportion is confirmed by noting that 0.43 × $31,280,000 = $13,332,000, the amount of current liabilities.)

Days Cash on Hand

The current ratio measures liquidity on the basis of balance sheet accounts (in economic parlance, *stocks*) as opposed to income statement items (*flows*). However, the true measure of a business's liquidity is whether it can meet its payments as they come due, so liquidity is more related to cash inflows and outflows than it is to assets and liabilities. The *days-cash-on-hand ratio* is a better measure of liquidity than the current ratio.

$$\text{Days cash on hand} = \frac{\text{Cash and equivalents + Short-term investments}}{(\text{Expenses} - \text{Depreciation}) / 365}$$

$$= \frac{\$2,263 + \$4,000}{(\$105,576 - \$4,130) / 365} = \frac{\$6,263}{\$277.93} = 22.5 \text{ days.}$$

Peer group average = 30.6 days.

The denominator of the equation *estimates* average daily cash expenses by stripping out noncash expenses (depreciation) from reported total expenses and then dividing by 365. The numerator is the amount of cash and securities available to make those cash payments. Because Riverside's days cash on hand is lower than the peer group average, its liquidity position as measured by days cash on hand is worse than that of the average hospital.

For Riverside, the two measures of liquidity, current ratio and days cash on hand, give conflicting results. Perhaps the average hospital has a greater proportion of cash and equivalents and short-term investments in its current assets mix than Riverside. Perhaps Riverside had an extraordinary need for cash in 2019 and 2020. Further analysis would be required to make a supportable judgment concerning Riverside's liquidity position. Remember, though, that the cash budget, which we discussed in chapter 16, is the primary tool used by managers to ensure liquidity.

Debt Management (Capital Structure) Ratios

The extent to which an organization uses debt financing, or *financial leverage*, is an important measure of financial performance for several reasons. First, by raising funds through debt, owners of for-profit businesses can maintain control with a limited investment. For not-for-profit organizations, debt financing allows more services to be provided than if the organization were solely financed with contributions and earnings. Next, creditors look to equity capital to provide a margin of safety; if the owners (or community) have provided only a small proportion of total financing, the risks of the enterprise are borne mainly by its creditors. Finally, if a business earns more on investments financed with borrowed funds than it pays in percentage interest, its ROE is increased.

Debt management ratios fall into two categories:

1. **Capitalization ratios** use balance sheet data to determine the extent to which borrowed funds have been used to finance assets.
2. **Coverage ratios** use income statement data to determine the extent to which fixed financial charges are covered by reported profits.

debt management ratios
A group of ratios that measure the extent of a business's financial leverage (capital structure).

The two sets of ratios are complementary, so most financial statement analyses examine both types.

Capitalization Ratio 1: Total Debt to Total Assets (Debt Ratio)

The ratio of total debt to total assets (total liabilities and equity), called the *debt ratio*, measures the percentage of total capital provided by creditors:

$$\text{Debt ratio} = \frac{\text{Total debt}}{\text{Total assets}} = \frac{\$43,914}{\$151,278} = 0.290, \text{ or } 29.0\%.$$

Peer group average = 42.3%.

For this ratio, debt typically is defined as *all debt*, including current liabilities. In essence, debt is defined here as everything on the capital side of the balance sheet except equity. However, this ratio has many variations, many of which use different definitions of debt.

Creditors prefer low debt ratios because the lower the ratio, the greater the cushion against creditors' losses in the event of bankruptcy and liquidation. Conversely, owners of for-profit firms may seek high leverage either to leverage up returns or because selling new stock would mean giving up some degree of control. In not-for-profit organizations, managers may seek high leverage to offer more services.

Riverside's debt ratio is 29.0 percent, meaning its creditors have supplied less than one-third of the business's total financing. Put another way, each dollar of assets was financed with 29 cents of debt and, consequently, 71 cents of equity. (The *equity ratio* is defined as 1 − Debt ratio, so Riverside's equity ratio is 71 percent.) Because the average debt ratio for the peer group is more than 40 percent, Riverside uses significantly less debt than the average hospital. The low debt ratio indicates that the hospital would find it relatively easy to borrow additional funds, presumably at favorable rates.

Note that the *debt-to-equity ratio*, defined as Total debt ÷ Total equity, is a close relative of the debt ratio. These ratios are transformations of one another and provide the same information but with a different twist. Both the debt ratio and debt-to-equity ratio increase as a business uses a greater proportion of debt financing, but the debt ratio rises linearly and approaches a limit of 100 percent, while the debt-to-equity ratio rises at a faster rate and approaches infinity. Lenders, in particular, prefer to use the debt-to-equity ratio rather than the debt ratio because it tells them how much capital creditors have provided to the organization *per dollar of equity capital*. The higher this ratio, the riskier the creditors' position. Other analysts tend to prefer the debt ratio because it makes it easier to visualize the liabilities and equity mix on the balance sheet.

Capitalization Ratio 2: Debt-to-Capitalization Ratio

The *debt-to-capitalization ratio*, which is long-term debt divided by *long-term capital* (long-term debt plus equity), focuses on the proportion of debt used in a business's permanent (long-term) capital structure. This ratio is also called the *long-term-debt-to-capitalization ratio* or just *capitalization ratio*. (Note that we include finance lease obligations in our definition of long-term debt because such obligations are similar to long-term debt.)

$$\text{Debt-to-capitalization ratio} = \frac{\text{Long-term debt}}{\text{Long-term debt} + \text{Equity}}$$

$$= \frac{\$30,582}{\$30,582 + \$107,364} = 0.222, \text{ or } 22.2\%.$$

Peer group average = 34.6%.

Many analysts believe that the debt-to-capitalization ratio best reflects the capital structure of a business. This belief is based on the fact that most businesses use as much spontaneous free credit (current liabilities less short-term bank loans) as they can get. Furthermore, short-term interest-bearing debt typically is used only to fund *temporary* current asset needs. Thus, the "true" capital structure of a business—the one that reflects its target structure—is best reflected by a ratio that focuses on permanent (long-term) financing.

Riverside's debt-to-capitalization ratio is 22.2 percent, compared with the peer group average of 34.6 percent. This low use of debt financing in Riverside's permanent capital mix confirms the conclusion made earlier that the hospital has unused debt capacity.

Coverage Ratio 1: Times Interest Earned Ratio

The *times interest earned (TIE) ratio* is determined by dividing earnings before interest and taxes (EBIT) by interest charges. EBIT is used in the numerator because it represents the amount of accounting income that is available to pay interest expense. For a not-for-profit organization, which does not pay taxes, EBIT = Net income + Interest expense, whereas for a for-profit business, EBIT = Net income + Interest expense + Taxes. Riverside's TIE ratio is 6.6:

$$\text{TIE ratio} = \frac{\text{EBIT}}{\text{Interest expense}} = \frac{\$8,572 + \$1,542}{\$1,542} = \frac{\$10,114}{\$1,542} = 6.6.$$

Peer group average = 4.0.

The TIE ratio measures the number of dollars of accounting income (as opposed to cash flow) available to pay each dollar of interest expense. In essence, it is an indicator of the extent to which income can decline before it is less than annual interest costs. Failure to pay interest can bring legal action by the firm's creditors, possibly resulting in bankruptcy.

Riverside's interest is covered 6.6 times, so it has $6.60 of accounting income to pay each dollar of interest expense. Because the peer group average TIE ratio is four times, the hospital is covering its interest charges by a relatively high margin of safety. Thus, the TIE ratio reinforces the previous conclusions based on the debt and debt-to-capitalization ratios—namely, that the hospital could easily expand its use of debt financing.

Coverage ratios are often better measures of a firm's debt utilization than capitalization ratios because coverage ratios discriminate between low-interest-rate debt and high-interest-rate debt. For example, a medical group practice might have $10 million of 4 percent debt on its balance sheet, while another might have $10 million of 8 percent debt. If both practices have the same income and assets, both will have the same debt ratio. However, the group that pays 4 percent interest will have lower interest charges and hence will be in better financial condition than the group that pays 8 percent. This difference in financial condition is captured by the TIE ratio.

Coverage Ratio 2: Cash Flow Coverage Ratio

Although the TIE ratio is easy to calculate, it has three major deficiencies. First, leasing is a common form of financing, and the TIE ratio ignores lease payments, which, like debt payments, are contractual obligations. Second, many debt contracts require that principal payments be made over the life of the loan, rather than only at maturity. Thus, most organizations must meet fixed financial charges associated with debt financing besides interest payments. Finally, the TIE ratio ignores the fact that accounting income, whether measured by EBIT or net income, does not reflect the actual cash flow available to meet a business's fixed payments.

These deficiencies are corrected in the *cash flow coverage (CFC) ratio*, which shows the amount by which cash flow covers fixed financial requirements. Here is Riverside's 2020 CFC ratio assuming the hospital had $1,368,000 of lease payments and $2,000,000 of required debt principal repayments:

$$\text{CFC ratio} = \frac{\text{EBIT} + \text{Lease payments} + \text{Depreciation expense}}{\text{Interest expense} + \text{Lease payments} + \text{Debt principal} / (1-T)}$$

$$= \frac{\$10,114 + \$1,368 + \$4,130}{\$1,542 + \$1,368 + \$2,000 / (1-0)} = \frac{\$15,612}{\$4,910} = 3.2.$$

Peer group average = 2.3.

Like its TIE ratio, Riverside's CFC ratio exceeds the peer group average, indicating that Riverside is better at covering total fixed payments with cash flow than is the average hospital. This fact should be reassuring both to creditors and to management as it reinforces the view that Riverside has untapped debt capacity.

You may be wondering why the term $(1 - T)$ is applied to the debt principal. Investor-owned firms must make principal repayments with *after-tax dollars*, and hence they must earn more pretax dollars to both pay taxes and make the principal repayment. The *grossed-up* amount, which results from dividing the principal amount by $(1 - T)$, gives the amount of pretax dollars needed to cover the required principal repayments. Thus, the calculation, which contains pretax dollars in the numerator, now has pretax dollars in the denominator and hence is consistent in format.

Asset Management (Activity) Ratios

The next group of ratios, the **asset management ratios**, is designed to measure how effectively a business's assets are being utilized. These ratios help answer whether the amount of each type of asset reported on the balance sheet seems reasonable, too high, or too low in view of current (or projected) operating levels. Riverside and other hospitals must borrow or raise equity capital to acquire assets. If they have too many assets for the volume of services provided, their capital costs will be too high and their profits will be depressed. Conversely, if the level of assets is too low, volume may be lost or vital services not offered.

asset management ratios
Financial statement analysis ratios that measure how effectively a firm is managing its assets.

Fixed Asset Turnover Ratio

The *fixed asset turnover ratio*, also called the *fixed-asset utilization ratio*, measures the utilization of property and equipment. It is the ratio of total (all) revenues to net fixed assets (property and equipment):

$$\text{Fixed asset turnover} = \frac{\text{Total revenues}}{\text{Net fixed assets}} = \frac{\$114,148}{\$119,998} = 0.95.$$

Peer group average = 2.2.

Note that total revenues include both operating and nonoperating revenues: $112,050 + $2,098 = $114,148. Also, net fixed assets are listed on the balance sheet as net property and equipment.

Riverside's ratio of 0.95 indicates that each dollar of fixed assets generated 95 cents in total revenue. This value compares poorly with the peer group average of 2.2 times, indicating that Riverside is not using its fixed assets as productively as is the average hospital. (The lower-quartile value for the sector is 1.8; thus, Riverside falls in the bottom 25 percent of all hospitals in its fixed asset utilization.)

Before condemning Riverside's management for poor performance, it should be pointed out that a major problem arises from the use of the fixed asset turnover ratio for comparative purposes. Recall that most asset values listed on the balance sheet reflect historical costs rather than current market values. Inflation and depreciation have caused the values of many assets that were purchased in the past to be understated. Therefore, if an old hospital that acquired much of its plant and equipment years ago is compared with a new hospital with the same physical capacity, the old hospital, because it has a much lower book value of fixed assets, would report a much higher turnover ratio. This difference in fixed asset turnover is more reflective of the inability of financial statements to deal with inflation than of any inefficiency on the part of the new hospital's managers.

Total Asset Turnover Ratio

The *total asset turnover ratio* measures the turnover, or utilization, of all of a business's assets. It is calculated by dividing total (all) revenues by total assets:

$$\text{Total asset turnover} = \frac{\text{Total revenues}}{\text{Total assets}} = \frac{\$114{,}148}{\$151{,}278} = 0.75.$$

Peer group average = 0.97.

Again, note that total revenues include both operating and nonoperating revenues.

Each dollar of total assets generated 75 cents in total revenues. Riverside's total asset turnover ratio is below the peer group average, but not as far below as its fixed asset turnover ratio. Thus, relative to the peer group, the hospital is using its current assets better than its fixed assets. Such judgments can be confirmed by examining Riverside's current asset turnover. In 2020, Riverside's current asset turnover ratio (Total revenues ÷ Total current assets) is 3.6, compared with the peer group average of 3.4, so the hospital is slightly above average in its utilization of current assets.

Days in Patient Accounts Receivable

Days in patient accounts receivable is used to measure effectiveness in managing receivables. This measure of financial performance, which is sometimes classified as a liquidity ratio rather than an asset management ratio, has many names, including *average collection period (ACP)* and *days sales outstanding (DSO)*. It is computed by dividing net patient accounts receivable by average daily patient revenue to find the number of days that it takes an organization, on average, to collect its receivables. In theory, the denominator of this ratio should focus on revenues other than immediate cash payments, but this information generally is unavailable, so net patient services revenue is used.

Also, note that premium and other revenue is not included in the calculation because such revenue typically is collected before or at the time services are provided, and hence it does not affect receivables.

$$\text{Days in patient accounts receivable} = \frac{\text{Net patient accounts receivable}}{\text{Net patient service revenue} / 365}$$

$$= \frac{\$21,840}{\$103,174 / 365} = \frac{\$21,840}{\$282.67} = 77.3 \text{ days.}$$

Peer group average = 64.0 days.

Riverside is not doing as well as the average hospital in collecting its receivables. It is important that businesses collect their receivables as soon as possible. Clearly, Riverside's managers should strive to increase the hospital's performance in this key area.

Average Age of Plant

The *average age of plant* gives a rough measure of the average age in years of a business's fixed assets (net property and equipment):

$$\text{Average age of plant} = \frac{\text{Accumulated depreciation}}{\text{Depreciation expense}} = \frac{\$25,160}{\$4,130} = 6.1 \text{ years.}$$

Peer group average = 9.1 years.

Riverside's physical assets are newer than those of the average hospital. Thus, the hospital is offering more up-to-date facilities than average, and it will probably have fewer capital expenditures in the near future. On the other hand, Riverside's net fixed-asset valuation is relatively high, which, as pointed out earlier, biases the hospital's fixed-asset and total asset turnover ratios downward. This fact raises serious questions about the interpretation of the turnover ratios calculated previously.

Comparative and Trend Analyses

When conducting financial ratio analysis, the value of a particular ratio, in the absence of other information, reveals almost nothing about a business's financial

For Your Consideration

How Many Ratios Are Enough?

In our discussion of financial ratio analysis, we discussed 14 ratios that are commonly used to interpret financial statement data. Although that may seem like a lot of ratios, our discussion just scratched the surface.

Without too much additional work, you could probably compile a list of 50 financial ratios. Yet studies have shown that about 90 percent of the information contained in financial statements can be uncovered using about ten carefully selected ratios.

How many ratios do you think are enough? Does it matter how the ratios are selected? Is there a cost to using more ratios than necessary? What is the disadvantage of generating too much data?

comparative analysis
The comparison of key financial and operational measures of one business with those of comparable businesses or sector averages; also called *benchmarking.*

trend analysis
A ratio analysis technique that examines the value of a ratio over time to see whether it is improving or deteriorating.

condition. For example, if a nursing home management company has a current ratio of 2.5, it is virtually impossible to say whether that is good or bad. Additional data are needed to interpret the results of this ratio analysis. In the discussion of Riverside's financial ratios, the focus was on **comparative analysis**—that is, the hospital's ratios were compared with the average ratios for the peer group. Another useful ratio analysis tool is **trend analysis**, which analyzes the trend of a single ratio over time. Trend analysis gives clues about whether a business's financial situation is improving, holding constant, or deteriorating.

It is easy to combine comparative and trend analyses in a single graph, such as the one shown in exhibit 17.4. Here, Riverside's ROE (the solid line) and peer group average ROE data (the dashed lines) are plotted for the past five years. The graph shows that the hospital's ROE was declining faster than the sector average from 2016 through 2019, but that it rose above the sector average in 2020. Other ratios can be analyzed in a similar manner.

EXHIBIT 17.4
Riverside Memorial Hospital: ROE Analysis, 2016–2020

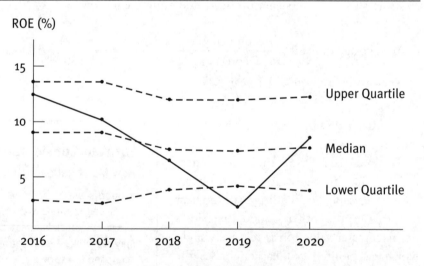

Return on Equity (ROE)				
			Sector	
Year	Riverside	Lower Quartile	Median	Upper Quartile
2016	12.5%	2.6%	8.6%	13.3%
2017	10.0	2.5	8.6	13.3
2018	6.7	2.8	7.2	12.0
2019	2.4	4.1	7.2	12.1
2020	8.0	3.8	7.4	12.3

1. What is the purpose of ratio analysis?
2. What are two ratios that measure profitability?
3. What are two ratios that measure liquidity?
4. What are two ratios that measure debt management?
5. What are two ratios that measure asset management?
6. How can comparative and trend analyses be used to interpret a ratio?

Tying the Financial Ratios Together: Du Pont Analysis

Financial ratio analysis provides a great deal of information about a business's financial condition, but it does not provide an overview or tie any of the ratios together. **Du Pont analysis**, so named because managers at the Du Pont Company developed it, provides an overview of a business's financial condition and helps managers and investors understand the relationships among several ratios. The analysis decomposes ROE, one of the most important measures of a business's profitability, into the product of three other ratios, each of which has an important economic interpretation. The result is the *Du Pont equation:*

Du Pont analysis
A financial statement analysis tool that decomposes return on equity into three components: profit margin, total asset turnover, and equity multiplier.

$$ROE = \text{Total margin} \times \text{Total asset turnover} \times \text{Equity multiplier}$$

$$\frac{\text{Net income}}{\text{Total equity}} = \frac{\text{Net income}}{\text{Total revenues}} \times \frac{\text{Total revenues}}{\text{Total assets}} \times \frac{\text{Total assets}}{\text{Total equity}}.$$

Riverside's 2020 data are used to illustrate the Du Pont equation:

$$\frac{\$8,572}{\$107,364} = \frac{\$8,572}{\$114,148} \times \frac{\$114,148}{\$151,278} \times \frac{\$151,278}{\$107,364}$$

$$8.0\% = 7.5\% \times 0.75 \times 1.4$$

$$= 5.6\% \times 1.4.$$

In the Du Pont equation, the product of the first two terms on the right side is return on assets (ROA), so the equation can also be written as *ROE = ROA* × Equity multiplier. Riverside's 2020 total margin was 7.5 percent, so the hospital made 7.5 cents profit on each dollar of total revenue. Furthermore, assets were turned over (or created revenues) 0.75 times during the year, so the hospital earned a return of 7.5% × 0.75 = 5.6% on its assets. Aside from a rounding error, this value for ROA is roughly the same as was calculated previously in our ratio analysis discussion.

If the hospital used only equity financing, its 5.6 percent ROA would equal its ROE. However, creditors supplied 29 percent of Riverside's capital, while equity holders (the community) supplied the rest. Because the 5.6 percent ROA belongs exclusively to the suppliers of equity capital, which makes up only 71 percent of total capital, Riverside's ROE is higher than its 5.6 percent ROA. Specifically, ROA must be multiplied by the *equity multiplier*, which shows the amount of assets working for each dollar of equity capital, to obtain the ROE of 8.0 percent. This 8.0 percent ROE could be calculated directly: *ROE* = Net income ÷ Total equity = $8,572 ÷ $107,364 = 8.0%. However, the Du Pont equation shows how total margin, which measures *expense control*; total asset turnover, which measures *asset utilization*; and financial leverage, which measures *debt utilization*, interact to determine ROE.

Key Equation: Du Pont Analysis

The Du Pont equation decomposes a business's return on equity (ROE) into the product of three other ratios:

$$ROE = \text{Total margin} \times \text{Total asset turnover} \times \text{Equity multiplier}.$$

The value of this equation stems from the fact that the total margin measures expense control, the total asset turnover measures asset utilization, and the equity multiplier measures debt utilization. Du Pont analysis is particularly useful when the equation can be compared with both benchmark equations and previous years' results.

Riverside's managers use the Du Pont equation to suggest how to improve the hospital's financial condition. To influence the profit margin, Riverside must increase revenues and/or reduce costs. Thus, the hospital's marketing staff can study the effects of raising charges, or lowering them to increase volume; moving into new services or markets with higher margins; entering into new contracts with managed care plans; and so on. Furthermore, management accountants can study the expense items and, while working with department heads and clinical staff, can seek ways to reduce costs. More specific ideas regarding actions needed to improve financial condition will be gleaned from an operating indicator analysis, which is discussed in a later section of this chapter.

Regarding total asset turnover, Riverside's analysts, while working with both clinical and marketing staffs, can investigate ways of reducing investments in different types of assets or increasing the productivity of existing assets. Finally, the hospital's financial staff can analyze the effects of alternative financing strategies on the equity multiplier (i.e., debt utilization), seeking to hold down interest expenses and the risks of debt while still using debt to leverage up ROE.

The Du Pont equation provides a useful comparison between a business's performance as measured by ROE and the performance of an average hospital. For example, here is the comparative analysis for 2020:

Riverside: ROE = 7.5%   ×   0.75 × 1.4
                         =   5.6%   × 1.4 = 8.0%.
Peer group average: ROE = 5.0%   ×   0.97 × 1.7
                         =   4.8%   × 1.7 = 8.4%.

The Du Pont analysis tells managers and creditors that Riverside has a significantly higher profit margin, and thus better control over expenses, than the average hospital. However, the average hospital has better total asset turnover, so Riverside is getting below-average utilization from its assets. In spite of the average hospital's advantage in asset utilization, Riverside's superior expense control outweighs its utilization disadvantage because its ROA of 5.6 percent is higher than the peer group average ROA of 4.8 percent. Finally, the average hospital has offset Riverside's advantage in ROA by using more financial leverage, although Riverside's lower use of debt financing decreases its risk. The result is that Riverside gets somewhat less return on its equity capital than does the average hospital.

One potential problem with Du Pont and ratio analyses applied to not-for-profit organizations, especially hospitals, is that a large portion of their net income may come from nonoperating sources. If nonoperating revenues are highly variable and unpredictable, ROE and the ratios as previously defined may be a poor measure of the hospital's inherent profitability. All applicable ratios, as well as the Du Pont analysis, could be recast to focus on operations by using operating revenue and operating income in lieu of total (all) revenues and net income.

SELF-TEST QUESTIONS

1. Explain how the Du Pont equation combines several ratios to obtain an overview of a business's financial condition.
2. Why might a focus on operating revenue and operating income be preferable to a focus on total revenue and net income?

Other Analytical Techniques

common size analysis
A technique to analyze a business's financial statements that expresses income statement items and balance sheet accounts as percentages rather than in dollars.

percentage change analysis
A technique to analyze a business's financial statements that expresses the year-to-year changes in income statement items and balance sheet accounts as percentages.

Besides ratio and Du Pont analyses, two additional financial statement analysis techniques are commonly used in financial condition analysis. In **common size analysis**, all income statement items are divided by total revenues and all balance sheet items are divided by total assets. Thus, a common size income statement shows each item as a percentage of total revenues, and a common size balance sheet shows each account as a percentage of total assets. The advantage of common size statements is that they facilitate comparisons of income statements and balance sheets over time and across companies because they remove the influence of the scale (size) of the business.

Another frequently used technique when analyzing financial statements is **percentage change analysis**. Here, the percentage changes in the balance sheet accounts and income statement items from year to year are calculated and compared. In this format, it is easy to see which accounts and items are growing faster or slower than others and thus to identify which are under control and which are out of control.

The conclusions reached in common size and percentage change analyses generally parallel those derived from ratio analysis. Occasionally, however, a serious deficiency is highlighted only by one of the three analytical techniques, while the other two techniques fail to bring the deficiency to light. Thus, a thorough financial statement analysis usually consists of a Du Pont analysis to provide an overview and then includes several different techniques such as ratio, common size, and percentage change analyses. For illustrations of common size and percentage change analyses, see the supplement to this chapter.

SELF-TEST QUESTIONS

1. What advantage do common size statements have over regular statements when conducting a financial statement analysis?
2. What is percentage change analysis, and why is it useful?
3. Which analytical techniques should be used in a complete financial statement analysis?

operating indicator
A ratio that focuses on operating data rather than financial data.

Operating Indicator Analysis

Operating indicator analysis goes one step beyond financial statement analysis by examining operating variables to *explain* a business's financial condition. Like the financial ratios, **operating indicators** are typically grouped into major categories to make interpretation easier. For hospitals, the following are the most commonly used categories:

- Profit indicators
- Price indicators
- Volume (utilization) indicators
- Length-of-stay indicators
- Intensity-of-service indicators
- Efficiency indicators
- Unit cost indicators

   Because of the large number of operating indicators used in a typical analysis, the indicators cannot be discussed in detail here. However, to give you an appreciation for this type of analysis, we discuss seven commonly used hospital operating indicators—one from each category. Note that most of the data needed to calculate operating indicators are not contained in the financial statements. More complete data are required for this type of analysis.

Profit per Discharge
Profit per discharge, a profit indicator, provides a measure of the amount of profit on inpatient services earned per discharge. Note that this measure is "raw," in the sense that it is not adjusted for case mix, which we discuss later, or local wage conditions. Often, operating indicators are calculated in both raw and adjusted forms. In 2020, Riverside's managerial accounting system reported $87,740,000 of inpatient service revenue, $84,865,000 of inpatient costs, and 18,281 patient discharges. Thus, Riverside's profit per discharge was $157:

$$\text{Profit per discharge} = \frac{\text{Inpatient profit}}{\text{Total discharges}} = \frac{\$87,740,000 - \$84,865,000}{18,281}$$

$$= \frac{\$2,875,000}{18,281} = \$157.$$

Peer group average = $73.

   Compared with the peer group average, Riverside's inpatient services are more than twice as profitable. It is not uncommon in today's tight reimbursement environment for hospitals to lose money (as measured by accounting profit) on inpatient services. In fact, with a peer group average profit per discharge of only $73, half of the hospitals are making less than $73, which indicates that a significant percentage of hospitals are losing money on inpatient services. Most, however, make up the losses with profits from other services or from nonoperating income.

Net Price per Discharge

Net price per discharge, which is one of many price indicators, measures the average inpatient revenue collected on each discharge. Based on the data presented in the discussion of the profit-per-discharge indicator, Riverside's net price per discharge for 2020 was $4,800:

$$\text{Net price per discharge} = \frac{\text{Net inpatient revenue}}{\text{Total discharges}} = \frac{\$87,740,000}{18,281} = \$4,800.$$

Peer group average = $5,056.

Riverside collects less per discharge than the average hospital; however, we have already seen that Riverside makes a profit of $157 on each discharge, so its inpatient services cost structure must be proportionally even lower than the peer group average. Riverside's ability to make a profit on each discharge could be attributed to a lower-than-average case mix, which measures the average intensity of services provided, or to an aggressive cost management program.

Occupancy Rate (Percentage)

Occupancy rate, one of many volume indicators, measures the utilization of a hospital's licensed beds and hence fixed assets. Because overhead costs are incurred on all assets whether used or not, higher occupancy spreads fixed costs over more patients and hence increases per patient profitability. Based on 95,061 inpatient days in 2020, Riverside's occupancy rate was 57.9 percent:

$$\text{Occupancy rate} = \frac{\text{Inpatient days}}{(\text{Number of licensed beds} \times 365)} = \frac{95,061}{450 \times 365} = 57.9\%.$$

Peer group average = 45.4%.

Riverside has a higher occupancy rate than the average hospital and hence is using its inpatient fixed assets more productively. Note that this conclusion contradicts the financial statement analysis interpretation of the hospital's 2020 fixed asset turnover ratio. While that ratio is affected by inflation, accounting convention, and the amount of assets devoted to other functions, the occupancy rate is not. Hence, it is a superior measure of pure asset utilization, at least with respect to inpatient utilization. On this basis, Riverside's managers appear to be doing a good job, relative to the sector, of using the hospital's inpatient fixed assets. This measure can also be applied to staffed beds. In Riverside's case, the two measures of capacity are the same, but some hospitals have fewer staffed beds than licensed beds.

Average Length of Stay

Average length of stay (ALOS), or just *length of stay (LOS)*, is the number of days an average inpatient is hospitalized with each admission. ALOS and an alternative version adjusted for case mix are the sole LOS indicators. Riverside's 2020 LOS was 5.2 days:

$$LOS = \frac{\text{Inpatient days}}{\text{Total discharges}} = \frac{95,061}{18,281} = 5.2 \text{ days}.$$

Peer group average = 4.7 days.

On average, Riverside keeps its patients in the hospital slightly longer than the average hospital. In general, that longer stay is considered to have a negative impact on inpatient profitability because most hospitals have a reimbursement mix heavily weighted toward prospective (episodic) payment. With payment fixed per discharge, lower LOS typically leads to lower costs and hence higher profitability (unless premature discharges result in readmissions and related penalties).

All Patient Case-Mix Index

The *all patient case-mix index* is one of several intensity-of-service indicators. The concept of measuring case mix was first applied to Medicare patients; hence, many hospitals calculate both a Medicare case-mix index and an all-patient case-mix index. Case mix is based on diagnosis; diagnoses requiring more complex treatments are assigned a higher value. The idea is to be able to differentiate (on average) between hospitals that provide relatively simple, and hence low-cost, services from those that provide highly complex and costly services. Case-mix values assigned to diagnoses are periodically recalibrated, with the intent of forcing the average hospital to have a case-mix index of 1.0. In general, case mix is related to size because large hospitals typically offer a more complex set of services than small hospitals do. Furthermore, case-mix values tend to be high at teaching hospitals (greater than 1.5) because the most complex cases often are transferred to such hospitals.

Riverside's all-patient case-mix index was 1.12 for 2020, which is slightly below the peer group average of 1.15. Thus, the patients that Riverside admits to the hospital require about the same intensity of services that patients at the average hospital require, which tells us that inpatient revenues and costs are not influenced by having a patient mix that is either relatively simple to treat or relatively complex.

Inpatient FTEs per Occupied Bed

The number of *inpatient full-time equivalents (FTEs) per occupied bed* is a measure of workforce productivity and hence an indicator of efficiency. The lower the number, the more productive the workforce. When the focus is on inpatient productivity, inpatient FTEs are used. The measure can also be adapted to outpatient productivity. Needless to say, there are many situations in a hospital setting in which it is difficult to allocate FTEs to the type of service provided. With an inpatient workforce of 1,251 FTEs, Riverside's inpatient FTEs per occupied bed was 4.8 in 2020:

$$\text{Inpatient FTEs per occupied bed} = \frac{\text{Inpatient FTEs}}{\text{Average daily census}}$$

$$= \frac{1,251}{0.579 \times 450} = \frac{1,251}{260.55} = 4.8.$$

Peer group average = 5.6.

The average daily census—the number of patients hospitalized on an average day—was calculated by multiplying Riverside's occupancy rate (57.9 percent = 0.579) by the number of licensed beds (450). With higher-than-average labor productivity coupled with better fixed asset utilization, it is no surprise that Riverside's inpatient services are more profitable than those of the average hospital.

Salary per FTE

Salary per FTE, a unit cost indicator, provides a simple measure of the relative cost of the largest resource item used in the hospital sector—labor. With total salaries of $83,038,613 in 2020 and 2,681 total FTEs, Riverside's salary per FTE in 2020 was $30,973:

$$\text{Salary per FTE} = \frac{\text{Total salaries}}{\text{Total FTEs}} = \frac{\$83,038,613}{2,681} = \$30,973.$$

Peer group average = $32,987.

Now, we can see that Riverside's above-average profitability is enhanced by both worker productivity and control over wages and benefits.

In a full operating indicator analysis, many more indicators would be examined in an attempt to identify the operating strengths and weaknesses that underlie a business's financial condition. Although operating indicator analysis has been illustrated using the hospital sector, the concepts can be applied to any healthcare business, although the indicators would differ. Also, operating indicators are interpreted in the same way as financial ratios (i.e., by performing comparative and trend analyses).

1. What is the difference between financial statement analysis and operating indicator analysis?
2. Why is operating indicator analysis important?
3. Describe several metrics commonly used in operating indicator analysis.

Limitations of Financial Ratio and Operating Indicator Analyses

While financial ratio and operating indicator analyses can provide a great deal of useful information regarding a business's operations and financial condition, such analyses have limitations that necessitate care and judgment. This section highlights some of the problem areas. To begin, many large healthcare businesses operate a number of services in different lines of business, and in such cases, it is difficult to develop meaningful comparative data. This problem tends to make financial statement and operating indicator analyses somewhat more useful for providers with a single service line than for large, multiservice companies.

Next, generalizing about whether a particular ratio or indicator is good or bad is often difficult. For example, a high current ratio may show a strong liquidity position, which is good, or an excessive amount of current assets, which is bad. Similarly, a high asset turnover ratio may denote either a business that uses its assets efficiently or one that is undercapitalized and cannot afford to acquire enough assets. In addition, firms often have some ratios and indicators that look good and others that look bad, which make a firm's overall financial position, strong or weak,

For Your Consideration
Inflation Accounting

Inflation accounting (also called *replacement cost accounting* or *current cost accounting*) describes a range of accounting systems designed to correct problems arising from historical cost accounting under inflation. It was widely used in the nineteenth and early twentieth centuries, but it was mostly replaced by historical cost accounting in the 1930s after asset values were devastated by the Great Depression.

Historical cost accounting leads to two basic problems. First, many of the historical numbers appearing on financial statements are not economically relevant because prices have changed since they were incurred. Second, the numbers on financial statements represent dollars expended at different points of time. Thus, adding cash of $10,000 held on December 31, 2020, with a $10,000 cost of land acquired in 1965 makes little sense because inflation has caused the two amounts to represent

(continued)

(continued from previous page)

significantly different levels of purchasing power. Under inflation accounting, the $10,000 cash would be added to the current market value of the land, say, $50,000, which equalizes the purchasing power of the two amounts.

During the past 50 years, accounting standards have encouraged companies to supplement historical cost-based financial statements with price level (inflation)–adjusted statements, but few companies have done so. Additionally, in the 1970s, the Financial Accounting Standards Board reviewed a draft proposal that would mandate price level–adjusted statements. However, because of stringent opposition from companies, the proposal was never adopted.

What do you think? Would it be easy to estimate the current values of balance sheet assets? What are the advantages and disadvantages of inflation accounting? Should generally accepted accounting principles be revised to require inflation accounting?

difficult to determine. For this reason, significant judgment is required when analyzing financial and operating performance.

Another problem is that different accounting practices can distort financial statement ratio comparisons. For example, firms can use different accounting conventions to value cost of goods sold and ending inventories. During inflationary periods, these differences can lead to ratio distortions.

Finally, inflation effects can distort balance sheets and income statements. Numerous reporting methods have been proposed to adjust accounting statements for inflation, but no consensus has been reached on how to do this or on the practical usefulness of the resulting data. Nevertheless, accounting standards encourage, but do not require, businesses to disclose supplementary data to reflect the effects of general inflation. Inflation effects tend to make ratio comparisons over time for a given business, and across businesses at any point in time, less reliable than would be the case in the absence of inflation.

SELF-TEST QUESTIONS

1. Briefly describe some of the problems encountered when performing financial statement analysis and operating indicator analysis.
2. Explain how inflation effects created problems in the Riverside illustration.

Benchmarking

Most techniques for evaluating financial condition require comparisons to make meaningful judgments. In the previous examination of selected financial ratios and operating indicators, Riverside's ratios were compared with peer group average ratios. However, like most businesses, Riverside's managers go one step further—they compare their ratios not only with peer group averages but also with sector leaders and primary competitors. The technique of comparing ratios against selected standards is called **benchmarking**, while the comparative ratios are called *benchmarks*. Riverside's managers benchmark against peer group averages; against National/GFB Healthcare and Pennant Hospital, which are two leading for-profit hospital businesses; and against Woodbridge Memorial Hospital and St. Anthony's, which are its primary local competitors.

benchmarking
The comparison of performance metrics, such as financial ratios, of one business against those of similar businesses and sector averages; also called *comparative analysis*.

To illustrate the concept of benchmarking, consider how Riverside's analysts present total margin data to the firm's board of trustees:

	2020		2019
National/GFB	9.8%	National/GFB	9.6%
Sector top quartile	*8.4*	*Sector top quartile*	*8.0*
St. Anthony's	8.0	St. Anthony's	7.9
Riverside	**7.5**	Pennant Hospital	5.0
Sector median	*5.0*	*Sector median*	*4.7*
Pennant Hospital	4.8	**Riverside**	**2.3**
Sector lower quartile	*1.8*	*Sector lower quartile*	*2.1*
Woodbridge Memorial	0.5	Woodbridge Memorial	(1.3)

Benchmarking permits Riverside's managers to easily see where the firm stands relative to its competition in any given year and over time. As the data show, Riverside was roughly in the middle of the pack in 2020 with respect to its primary competitors and two large investor-owned hospital chains, although its performance was better than the average hospital. Its 2019 performance was significantly worse, so it improved substantially from 2019 to 2020. Although benchmarking is illustrated with one ratio, other ratios can be analyzed similarly. For presentation purposes, bar charts (which are color coded for ease of recognition and interpretation) are often used in benchmarking analyses.

All comparative analyses require comparative data. Such data are available from a number of sources, including commercial suppliers, federal and state government agencies, and sector trade groups. Each data supplier uses a somewhat different set of ratios designed to meet its own needs. Thus, the comparative data source selected dictates the ratios that will be used in the analysis. Also, there are minor and sometimes major differences in ratio definitions between data sources—for example, one source may use a 365-day year, while another uses a 360-day year. Or one source might use operating values, as opposed to total values, when constructing ratios. It is very important to know the specific definitions used in the comparative data because definitional differences between the ratios being calculated and the comparative ratios can lead to erroneous interpretations and conclusions. Thus, the first task in any ratio analysis is to identify the comparative data set and the ratios to be used. The second task is to make sure the ratio definitions used in the analysis match those from the comparative data set.

> 1. What is benchmarking?
> 2. Why is it important to be familiar with the comparative data set?

Key Performance Indicators and Dashboards

Financial statement data are usually created on an annual and quarterly basis, whereas operating indicator data are generated much more often, even daily. Financial condition analyses produced from this information may include hundreds of *metrics* (ratios and other measures). Although annual and quarterly financial condition analyses are always performed, managers need to monitor financial condition on a more regular basis so that problem areas can be identified and corrective action taken in a timely manner. However, performing financial condition analyses, say, on a weekly basis, would overload managers, and as a result, important findings could be missed.

key performance indicator (KPI)
A financial statement ratio or operating indicator that is considered by management to be critical to mission success.

To help solve the data overload and timeliness problems, many healthcare businesses use **key performance indicators (KPIs)** and dashboards. KPIs are a *limited number* of financial and operating indicator metrics that measure performance critical to the success of an organization. In essence, they assess the current state of the business, measure progress toward organizational goals, and facilitate prompt managerial action to correct deficiencies.

The KPIs chosen by any business depend on the line of business and its mission, goals, and objectives. In addition, KPIs usually differ by timing. For example, a hospital might have a daily KPI of number of net admissions (admissions minus discharges), while the corresponding quarterly and annual KPI might be occupancy rate. Clearly, the number of KPIs used must be kept to a minimum to allow managers to focus on the most important aspects of financial and operating performance.

dashboard
A format for presenting a business's key performance indicators that resembles the dashboard of an automobile.

Dashboards are a common way to present an organization's KPIs. The term stems from an automobile's dashboard, which presents key information (e.g., speed, engine temperature, oil pressure) about the car's performance. Often, the KPIs are shown as gauges, which allow managers to quickly interpret the indicators. The basic idea is to allow managers to monitor the business's most important financial and operating metrics on a regular basis (daily for some metrics) in a form that is easy to read and interpret.

1. What is a key performance indicator (KPI)? A dashboard?
2. How are KPIs and dashboards used in financial condition analysis?

Key Concepts

The primary purpose of this chapter is to present the techniques used by managers and investors to assess an organization's financial condition. The main focus is on financial condition as reflected in a business's financial statements, although operating data are also introduced to explain a business's current financial status. The key concepts of this chapter are as follows:

- *Financial statement analysis*, which is designed to identify a firm's financial condition, focuses on the firm's financial statements. *Operating indicator analysis*, which uses data typically found outside of the financial statements, provides insights into why a firm is in a given financial condition.

- *Financial ratio analysis*, which focuses on financial statement data, is designed to reveal the relative financial strengths and weaknesses of a company compared with other companies in the same sector, and to show whether the business's financial condition has been improving or deteriorating over time.

- The *Du Pont equation* indicates how the total margin, the total asset turnover ratio, and the use of debt interact to determine the rate of return on equity. It provides a good overview of a business's financial condition.

- *Liquidity ratios* indicate the business's ability to meet its short-term obligations.

- *Asset management ratios* measure how effectively managers are using the business's assets.

- *Debt management ratios* reveal the extent to which the firm is financed with debt and the extent to which operating cash flows cover debt service and other fixed-charge requirements.

- *Profitability ratios* show the combined effects of liquidity, asset management, and debt management on operating results.

(continued)

(continued from previous page)

- Ratios are analyzed using *comparative analysis*, in which a firm's ratios are compared with peer group averages or those of another firm, and *trend analysis*, in which a firm's ratios are examined over time.
- In a *common size analysis*, a business's income statement and balance sheet are expressed in percentages. This facilitates comparisons between firms of different sizes and for a single firm over time.
- In *percentage change analysis*, the differences in income statement items and balance sheet accounts from one year to the next are expressed in percentages. In this way, it is easy to identify those items and accounts that are growing appreciably faster or slower than average.
- *Benchmarking* is the process of comparing the performance of a particular company with that of a group of benchmark companies, often sector leaders and primary competitors.
- Financial condition analysis is hampered by some serious problems, including *development of comparative data*, *interpretation of results*, and *inflation effects*.
- *Key performance indicators (KPIs)* are a limited number of *metrics* that focus on those measures that are most important to an organization's mission success. Often, KPIs are presented in a format that resembles a *dashboard*.

Financial condition analysis has its limitations, but if used with care and judgment, it can provide managers with a sound picture of an organization's financial condition as well as identify those operating factors that contributed to that condition.

Questions

17.1. a. What is the primary difference between financial statement analysis and operating indicator analysis?

   b. Why are both types of analyses useful to health services managers and investors?

17.2. Should financial statement and operating indicator analyses be conducted only on historical data? Explain your answer.

17.3. One asset management ratio, the inventory turnover ratio, is defined as sales (i.e., revenues) divided by inventories. Why would this ratio be important for a medical device manufacturer or a hospital management company?

17.4. a. Assume that Pennant and the Wood Group, two operators of nursing homes, have fiscal years that end at different times—say, one in June and one in December. Would this fact cause any problems when comparing ratios between the two companies?

b. Assume that two companies that operate walk-in clinics both had the same December year-end, but one was based in Aspen, Colorado, a winter resort, while the other operated in Cape Cod, Massachusetts, a summer resort. Would their locations lead to problems in a comparative analysis?

17.5. a. How does inflation distort ratio analysis comparisons, both for one company over time and when different companies are compared?

b. Are only balance sheet accounts or both balance sheet accounts and income statement items affected by inflation?

17.6. a. What is the difference between trend analysis and comparative analysis?

b. Which is more important?

17.7. Assume that a large managed care company has a low return on equity (ROE). How could Du Pont analysis be used to identify possible actions to help boost ROE?

17.8. Regardless of the specific line of business, should all healthcare businesses use the same set of ratios when conducting a financial statement analysis? Explain your answer.

17.9. What are key performance indicators (KPIs)? What is a dashboard?

Problems

17.1. a. Modern Medical Devices has a current ratio of 0.5. Which of the following actions would improve (i.e., increase) this ratio?
  • Use cash to pay off current liabilities.
  • Collect some of the current accounts receivable.
  • Use cash to pay off some long-term debt.
  • Purchase additional inventory on credit (i.e., accounts payable).
  • Sell some of the existing inventory at cost.

b. Assume that the company has a current ratio of 1.2. Now which of the above actions would improve this ratio?

17.2. Southern Physicians, a medical group practice, is just being formed. It will need $2 million of total assets to generate $3 million in revenues. Furthermore, the group expects to have a profit margin of 5 percent. The group is considering two financing alternatives. First, it can use all-equity financing by requiring each physician to contribute his or her pro rata share. Alternatively, the practice can finance up to 50 percent of its assets with a bank loan. Assuming that the debt alternative has no impact on the expected profit margin, what is the difference between the expected ROE if the group finances with 50 percent debt versus the expected ROE if it finances entirely with equity capital?

17.3. Riverside Memorial's primary financial statements are presented in exhibits 17.1, 17.2, and 17.3.

    a. Calculate Riverside's financial ratios for 2019. Assume that Riverside had $1,000,000 in lease payments and $1,400,000 in debt principal repayments in 2019. (Hint: Use the book discussion to identify the applicable ratios.)

    b. Interpret the ratios. Use both trend and comparative analyses. For the comparative analysis, assume that the peer group average data presented in the book are valid for both 2019 and 2020.

17.4. Consider the following financial statements for BestCare HMO, a not-for-profit managed care plan:

BestCare HMO
Statement of Operations and Change in Net Assets
Year Ended June 30, 2020
(in thousands)

Revenue:	
Healthcare premiums	$26,682
Fees and other revenue	1,689
Interest and other income	242
Total revenues	$28,613
Expenses:	
Healthcare costs	$15,154
General and administrative expenses	7,893
Selling expenses	3,963
Interest expense	385
Total expenses	$27,395
Net income	$ 1,218
Net assets, beginning of year	$ 900
Net assets, end of year	$ 2,118

BestCare HMO
Balance Sheet
June 30, 2020
(in thousands)

Assets:	
Cash and cash equivalents	$2,737
Net premiums receivable	821
Other current assets	387
Total current assets	$3,945
Net property and equipment	$5,924
Total assets	$9,869
Liabilities and Net Assets:	
Healthcare costs payable	$2,145
Accrued expenses	929
Unearned premiums	141
Current portion of long-term debt	241
Total current liabilities	$3,456
Long-term debt	$4,295
Total liabilities	$7,751
Net assets (equity)	$2,118
Total liabilities and net assets	$9,869

a. Perform a Du Pont analysis on BestCare. Assume that the peer group average ratios are as follows:

Total margin	3.8%
Total asset turnover	2.1
Equity multiplier	3.2
Return on equity (ROE)	25.5%

b. Calculate and interpret the following ratios for BestCare:

	Peer Group Average
Return on assets (ROA)	8.0%
Current ratio	1.3
Days cash on hand	41 days
Average collection period	7 days
Debt ratio	69%
Debt-to-equity ratio	2.2
Times interest earned (TIE) ratio	2.8
Fixed asset turnover ratio	5.2

17.5. Consider the following financial statements for Green Valley Nursing Home, Inc., a for-profit, long-term care facility:

Green Valley Nursing Home, Inc.
Statement of Income and Retained Earnings
Year Ended December 31, 2020

Revenue:	
Resident services revenue	$3,163,258
Other revenue	106,146
Total revenues	$3,269,404
Expenses:	
Salaries and benefits	$1,515,438
Medical supplies and drugs	966,781
Insurance and other	406,357
Depreciation	85,000
Interest	206,780
Total expenses	$3,180,356
Operating income	$89,048
Income tax expense	31,167
Net income	$ 57,881
Retained earnings, beginning of year	$ 199,961
Retained earnings, end of year	$ 257,842

Green Valley Nursing Home, Inc.
Balance Sheet
December 31, 2020

Assets	
Current Assets:	
Cash and cash equivalents	$ 105,737
Marketable securities	200,000
Net accounts receivable	215,600
Supplies	87,655
Total current assets	$ 608,992
Property and equipment	$2,250,000
Less accumulated depreciation	356,000
Net property and equipment	$1,894,000
Total assets	$2,502,992

Liabilities and Shareholders' Equity

Current Liabilities:

Accounts payable	$72,250
Accrued expenses	192,900
Notes payable	100,000
Current portion of long-term debt	80,000
Total current liabilities	$ 445,150
Long-term debt	$1,700,000
Total liabilities	$2,145,150

Shareholders' Equity:

Common stock, $10 par value	$ 100,000
Retained earnings	257,842
Total shareholders' equity	$ 357,842
Total liabilities and shareholders' equity	$2,502,992

a. Perform a Du Pont analysis on Green Valley. Assume that the peer group average ratios are as follows:

Total margin	3.5%
Total asset turnover	1.5
Equity multiplier	2.5
Return on equity (ROE)	13.1%

b. Calculate and interpret the following ratios:

	Peer Group Average
Return on assets (ROA)	5.2%
Current ratio	2.0
Days cash on hand	22 days
Average collection period	19 days
Debt ratio	71%
Debt-to-equity ratio	2.5
Times interest earned (TIE) ratio	2.6
Fixed asset turnover ratio	1.4

c. Assume that there are 10,000 shares of Green Valley's stock outstanding and that some recently sold for $45 per share.
   • What is the firm's price/earnings ratio?
   • What is its market/book ratio?

(Hint: These ratios are discussed in the supplement to this chapter.)

17.6. Examine the peer group average ratios given in problems 17.4 and 17.5. Explain why the ratios are different between the managed care and nursing home industries.

17.7. Recent financial statements for the Heart Hospital are provided below:

The Heart Hospital
Balance Sheet
September 30, 2020
(in thousands)

Current assets:	
Cash	$14,202
Accounts receivable, net	5,918
Medical supplies inventory	1,211
Prepaid expenses and other current assets	1,429
Total current assets	$22,760
Property, plant, and equipment, net	$33,769
Other assets	901
Total assets	$57,430
Current liabilities:	
Accounts payable	$ 1,910
Accrued compensation and benefits	2,543
Other accrued liabilities	1,843
Current portion of long-term debt	2,064
Total current liabilities	$ 8,360
Long-term debt	21,640
Total liabilities	$30,000
Owners' equity	$27,430
Total liabilities and owners' equity	$57,430

The Heart Hospital
Statement of Operations
Year Ended September 30, 2020
(in thousands)

Net patient service revenue	$64,505
Operating expenses:	
Personnel expense	$21,707
Medical supplies expense	15,047

(continued)

Other operating expenses	9,721
Depreciation expense	2,625
Total operating expenses	$49,100
Income from operations	$15,405
Other income (expenses):	
Interest expense	($ 1,322)
Interest and other income, net	159
Total other income (expenses), net	($ 1,163)
Net income	$14,242

a. Perform a Du Pont analysis on the Heart Hospital. Assume that the peer group average ratios are as follows:

Total margin	15.0%
Total asset turnover	1.5
Equity multiplier	1.67
Return on equity (ROE)	37.6%

b. Calculate and interpret the following ratios for the Heart Hospital:

	Peer Group Average
Return on assets (ROA)	22.5%
Current ratio	2.0
Days cash on hand	85 days
Average collection period	20 days
Debt ratio	40%
Debt-to-equity ratio	0.67
Times interest earned (TIE) ratio	5.0
Fixed asset turnover ratio	1.4

17.8. Refer to the financial statements for the Heart Hospital in problem 17.7. Prepare a common size balance sheet (where each account is expressed as a percentage of total assets) and a common size income statement (where each account is expressed as a percentage of total revenues). What do the common size balance sheet and income statement reveal about the Heart Hospital?

(Hint: Common size analysis is illustrated in the supplement to this chapter.)

Selected Cases

Two cases in *Gapenski's Cases in Healthcare Finance*, sixth edition, are applicable to this chapter: Case 23: Commonwealth Health Plans; and Case 24: River Community Hospital (A).

Note

1. Takeover specialists in investment banking firms always focus on an organization's cash flows. To them, cash flows are the primary determinant of a business's value.

Resources

Boblitz, M. C. 2006. "Looking Out the Window: Market Intelligence for a View of the Real World." *Healthcare Financial Management* 60 (7): 47–53.

Brown, B. 2016. "Using Business Intelligence to Bring Financial Challenges into Focus." *Healthcare Financial Management* 70 (8): 54–63.

Burkhardt, J. H., and J. R. Wheeler. 2013. "Examining Financial Performance Indicators for Acute Care Hospitals." *Journal of Health Care Finance* 39 (3): 1–13.

Cleverley, W. O. 2014. "Time to Replace Adjusted Discharges." *Healthcare Financial Management* 68 (5): 84–89.

Cleverley, W. O., and J. O. Cleverley. 2005. "Scorecards and Dashboards: Using Financial Metrics to Improve Performance." *Healthcare Financial Management* 59 (7): 64–69.

Conner, B. 2017a. "The New Revenue Recognition Standard: Where Organizations Stand." *Healthcare Financial Management* 71 (10): 30–33.

———. 2017b. "Whatever Happened to Charity Care in Financial Statements?" *Healthcare Financial Management* 71 (1): 30–32.

Coyne, J. S., and S. G. Singh. 2008. "The Early Indicators of Financial Failure: A Study of Bankrupt and Solvent Health Systems." *Journal of Healthcare Management* 53 (5): 333–46.

Grant, J. L. 2007. "A Primer on EVA for Health Care Providers." *Journal of Health Care Finance* 33 (3): 22–39.

Kaufman, K. 2008. "Managing Risk in a Challenging Financial Environment." *Healthcare Financial Management* 62 (8): 45–50.

Kirby, S., and B. Robertson. 2009. "Start Small and Build Toward Business Intelligence." *Healthcare Financial Management* 63 (1): 96–103.

Kirk, M. A., G. M. Holmes, and G. H. Pink. 2012. "Achieving Benchmark Financial Performance in CAHs: Lessons from High Performers." *Healthcare Financial Management* 66 (4): 116–22.

Love, D., L. Revere, and K. Black. 2008. "A Current Look at the Key Performance Measures Considered Critical by Health Care Leaders." *Journal of Health Care Finance* 34 (3): 19–34.

Parkinson, J., P. Tsasis, and M. Porporato. 2007. "A Critical Review of Financial Measures Are Reported in the Ontario Hospital Balanced Scorecard." *Journal of Health Care Finance* 34 (2): 48–57.

Pieper, S. K. 2005. "Reading the Right Signals: How to Strategically Manage with Scorecards." *Healthcare Executive* 20 (3): 9–14.

Pink, G. H., I. McKillop, E. G. Schraa, C. Preyra, C. Montgomery, and G. R. Baker. 2001. "Creating a Balanced Scorecard for a Hospital System." *Journal of Health Care Finance* 27 (3): 1–20.

Price, C. A., A. E. Cameron, and D. Price. 2005. "Distress Detectors: Measures for Predicting Financial Distress in Hospitals." *Healthcare Financial Management* 59 (8): 74–80.

Robertson, B., and C. Wieland. 2007. "Intelligent and Actionable Dashboards." *Healthcare Financial Management* 61 (9): 141–43.

Rohloff, R. 2017. "Creating a Better Healthcare Analysis Paradigm." *Healthcare Financial Management* 71 (11): 106–7.

Schuhmann, T. M. 2008. "Hospital Financial Performance: Trends to Watch." *Healthcare Financial Management* 62 (7): 59–66.

Selivanoff, P. 2017. "Taking Control of Pay-for-Performance Contracts." *Healthcare Financial Management* 71 (8): 58–65.

Shapiro, M. D. 2007. "Economic Value Added: Can It Apply to an S Corporation Medical Practice?" *Healthcare Financial Management* 61 (8): 78–82.

Shoemaker, W. 2011. "Benchmarking Boon: Tapping Publicly Available Data to Improve Performance." *Healthcare Financial Management* 65 (6): 88–94.

Vélez-González, H., R. Pradhan, and R. Weech-Maldonado. 2011. "The Role of Non-financial Performance Measures in Predicting Hospital Financial Performance: The Case of For-Profit System Hospitals." *Journal of Health Care Finance* 38 (2): 12–23.

Watkins, A. L. 2003. "A Balanced Perspective: Using Nonfinancial Measures to Assess Financial Performance." *Healthcare Financial Management* 57 (11): 76–80.

Wyatt, J. 2004. "Scoreboards, Dashboards, and KPIs: Keys to Integrated Performance Measurement." *Healthcare Financial Management* 58 (2): 76–80.

17

MARKET VALUE RATIOS, COMMON SIZE ANALYSIS, PERCENTAGE CHANGE ANALYSIS, AND ECONOMIC VALUE ADDED

Market Value Ratios

In addition to the financial ratios discussed in chapter 17, another group of financial ratios focuses on stockholder metrics. For investor-owned firms with publicly traded stock, ratios that relate the firm's stock price to its earnings and book value per share can be developed. Such market value ratios give managers an indication of what investors think of the firm's past performance and future prospects as indicated by stock price. If the firm's liquidity, asset management, debt management, and profitability ratios are all good, its stock price (and hence market value ratios) will likely be high.

Price/Earnings Ratio

The *price/earnings (P/E) ratio* shows how much investors are willing to pay per dollar of reported profits. Suppose the stock of General Home Care, an investor-owned home health care company, sells for $28.50, while the firm had 2020 earnings per share (EPS) of $2.20. Then, its P/E ratio would be 13.0:

$$\text{P/E ratio} = \frac{\text{Price per share}}{\text{Earnings per share}} = \frac{\$28.50}{\$2.20} = 13.0.$$

Peer group average = 15.2.

P/E ratios are higher for firms with high growth prospects, all else held constant, but they are lower for riskier firms. General's P/E ratio is slightly below the average of its peer investor-owned home health care companies, which suggests that the company is regarded as being riskier than most, as having poorer growth prospects, or both.

Market/Book Ratio

The ratio of a stock's market price to its book value of equity gives another indication of how investors regard the company. Companies with relatively high rates of return on equity generally sell at higher multiples of book value than those with low returns. General Home Care reported $80 million in total equity on its 2020 balance sheet, and the firm had 5 million shares outstanding, so its *book value per share* is $80 ÷ 5 = $16.00. Dividing the price per share by the book value per share gives a *market/book (M/B)* ratio of 1.8:

$$\text{M/B ratio} = \frac{\text{Price per share}}{\text{Book value per share}} = \frac{\$28.50}{\$16.00} = 1.8.$$

Peer group average = 2.1.

Investors are willing to pay slightly less for each dollar of General's book value than for that of an average home health care company in General's peer group.

SELF-TEST QUESTION

1. What are two ratios that measure market value for publicly traded investor-owned businesses?

Common Size Analysis

Analytical techniques other than ratio analysis can be used to interpret financial statements. In *common size analysis,* all income statement items are divided by total revenues, and all balance sheet items are divided by total assets. Thus, a common size income statement shows each item as a percentage of revenues, and a common size balance sheet shows each account as a percentage of total assets. The significant advantage of common size statements is that they facilitate comparisons of income statements and balance sheets over time and across firms because they compensate for scale (size) differentials.

Exhibit S17.1 contains Riverside's common size income statement for 2020, along with the common size statement for the hospital sector. An analysis of the common size statements shows few significant differences between Riverside and the sector. Perhaps the most important difference is that Riverside's operating income is well above average while its nonoperating income is well below average. Although having a higher income from core operations is good, Riverside's managers should examine its contributions

	Riverside	Peer Group Average
Revenues:		
Net patient service revenue	90.4%	87.4%
Premium revenue	4.6	7.2
Other revenue	3.2	2.4
Total operating revenues	98.2%	97.0%
Expenses:		
Nursing services	51.1%	50.7%
Dietary services	4.8	4.7
General services	11.6	11.5
Administrative services	10.0	10.2
Employee health and welfare	9.0	9.2
Malpractice insurance	1.2	1.0
Depreciation	3.6	3.0
Interest expense	1.4	1.9
Total expenses	92.5%	92.2%
Operating income	5.7%	4.8%
Nonoperating income	1.8	3.0
Net income	7.5%	5.0%

EXHIBIT S17.1
Riverside Memorial Hospital: Common Size Income Statement for 2020

Note: This table contains inconsistencies because values are rounded to the nearest tenth of a percent.

and endowments to see whether better management could result in higher nonoperating income. Additionally, a lower percentage of Riverside's revenue comes from capitated contracts and other patient-related sources than is true of the average hospital.

Exhibit S17.2 contains Riverside's common size balance sheet for 2020, along with peer group average data. Three striking differences are revealed: (1) Riverside's current assets are significantly lower than the peer group average, (2) its net property and equipment are significantly higher, and (3) it uses far less debt financing than the average hospital.

SELF-TEST QUESTIONS

1. How are common size statements created?
2. What advantage do common size statements have over regular statements when conducting a financial statement analysis?

EXHIBIT S17.2
Riverside
Memorial
Hospital:
Common Size
Balance Sheet
for 2020

	Riverside	Peer Group Average
Assets:		
Cash and cash equivalents	1.5%	3.7%
Short-term investments	2.6	2.0
Accounts receivable	14.4	17.2
Inventories	2.1	2.5
Total current assets	20.6%	25.4%
Gross property and equipment	96.0%	90.1%
Accumulated depreciation	16.6	15.5
Net property and equipment	79.4%	74.6%
Total assets	100.0%	100.0%
Liabilities:		
Accounts payable	3.1%	3.9%
Accrued expenses	3.7	4.1
Notes payable	2.0	3.2
Total current liabilities	8.8%	13.3%
Long-term debt	19.0%	36.5%
Finance lease obligations	1.2	0.9
Total long-term liabilities	20.2%	37.4%
Net assets (equity)	71.0%	49.3%
Total liabilities and net assets	100.0%	100.0%

Note: This table contains inconsistencies because values are rounded to the nearest tenth of a percent.

Percentage Change Analysis

Another technique frequently used when analyzing financial statements is *percentage change analysis*. In this analysis, the percentage changes in the individual items on the income statement and accounts on the balance sheet over some period are calculated and compared. In this format, it is easy to see which items are growing faster or slower than others, and hence which of them are under control and which are out of control.

To illustrate percentage change analysis, consider Riverside's income statements shown in exhibit S17.3, where the 2019 and 2020 items have been converted into percentage changes. Note that Riverside's net patient service revenue grew at a 12.2 percent rate, while at the same time, nursing

	2020	2019	Percentage Change
Revenues:			
Net patient service revenue	$103,147	$ 91,929	12.2%
Premium revenue	5,232	4,622	13.2
Other revenue	3,644	6,014	−39.4
Total operating revenues	$112,050	102,565	9.2%
Expenses:			
Nursing services	$ 58,285	$ 56,752	2.7%
Dietary services	5,424	4,718	15.0
General services	13,198	11,655	13.2
Administrative services	11,427	11,585	−1.4
Employee health and welfare	10,250	10,705	−4.2
Malpractice insurance	1,320	1,204	9.6
Depreciation	4,130	4,025	2.6
Interest expense	1,542	1,521	1.4
Total expenses	$105,576	$102,165	3.3%
Operating income	$ 6,474	$ 400	1,518.5%
Nonoperating income	2,098	1,995	5.2
Net income	$ 8,572	$ 2,395	258.0%

EXHIBIT S17.3
Riverside Memorial Hospital: Statements of Operations (Income Statements), Years Ended December 31, 2020 and 2019 (in thousands) with Percentage Changes

services expenses grew by only 2.7 percent. Conversely, dietary services expenses grew at 15.0 percent. This information tells Riverside's managers that revenues associated with patients grew faster than nursing expenses (which is a positive trend for the hospital), but dietary services expenses grew faster than revenues (which is a negative trend). Other items on the income statement would be analyzed in a similar manner. Also, percentage change analysis could be applied to balance sheet accounts in the same way as our income statement illustration.

The conclusions reached in a percentage change analysis, as well as in a common size analysis, generally parallel those derived from ratio analysis. However, occasionally, a serious deficiency is highlighted only by one of the three analytical techniques, while the other two techniques fail to reveal the deficiency. Thus, a thorough financial statement analysis includes a Du Pont analysis to provide an overview and also includes ratio, common size, and percentage change analyses.

Economic Value Added

Up to this point, we have focused on using different techniques to evaluate the financial condition of a business. In many situations, it is useful to have a single measure that provides information on both financial condition and managerial performance. That measure is *economic value added (EVA)*, which focuses on managerial effectiveness in a given year. The basic formula for EVA is as follows:

$$EVA = NOPAT - (\text{Total capital} \times \text{Corporate cost of capital}),$$

where *NOPAT* is net operating profit after taxes.

In the EVA equation, NOPAT can be thought of as revenues minus all operating costs, including taxes (if applicable) but excluding interest expense. It is actually calculated as follows:

$$EBIT \times (1 - T),$$

where *EBIT* is earnings before interest and taxes.

Total capital is the sum of the book values of investor-supplied (interest-bearing) debt and equity, while the corporate cost of capital is the business's cost of financing. In essence, EVA measures the dollar profit above the economic dollar cost of creating that profit. Because the calculation of EVA does not require market value data, it can be applied to both for-profit and not-for-profit businesses.

To illustrate the EVA concept, consider Riverside Memorial Hospital's EVA performance in 2020. The hospital had $8,572,000 of net income and $1,542,000 in interest expense, for NOPAT of $10,114,000. Its investor-supplied capital was $2,975,000 in notes payable, $30,582,000 in long-term debt and finance lease obligations, and $107,364,000 in equity, for total capital of $140,921,000. Assuming a 7 percent corporate cost of capital, Riverside's 2020 EVA was $249,530:

$$EVA = \$10,114,000 - (\$140,921,000 \times 0.07)$$
$$= \$10,114,000 - \$9,864,470$$
$$= \$249,530.$$

Riverside's EVA of $249,530 tells its managers that the hospital generated a positive economic income in 2020. In essence, it needed $140,921,000 in investor-supplied capital to generate $10,114,000 in operating profit. The $140,921,000 in capital required to support operations had an overall cost of 7 percent, so the dollar cost to obtain the capital was $9,864,470. Because operations earned more in "profit" than it cost to generate that profit, the hospital had positive economic income (EVA).

EVA is an estimate of a business's true economic profit for the year, and it differs substantially from accounting profitability measures such as net income. EVA represents the residual income that remains after *all costs*, including the opportunity cost of the employed equity capital, have been recognized. Conversely, accounting profit is formulated without imposing a charge for equity capital. EVA depends on both operating efficiency and balance sheet management: Without operating efficiency, profits will be low; without efficient balance sheet management, there will be too many assets, and hence too much capital, which results in higher-than-necessary dollar capital costs.

For investor-owned businesses, there is a direct link between EVA and the value of the business—the higher the EVA, the greater the value to owners. For not-for-profit firms, equity capital is a scarce resource that must be managed well to ensure the financial viability of the organization, and hence its ability to continue to perform its stated mission. EVA lets managers know how well they are doing in managing this scarce resource because the higher the EVA in any year, the better the job managers are doing in using the organization's contributions and earnings to create value for the community. Of course, EVA measures only economic value; any social value created by the equity capital is ignored and, therefore, must be subjectively considered. EVA can be applied to divisions as well as to entire businesses, and the charge for capital should reflect the risk and capital structure of the business unit, whether it is the aggregate business or an operating division.

In practice, the calculation of EVA is much more complex than presented here because many accounting issues must be addressed properly when estimating a firm's NOPAT. Nevertheless, the brief discussion here illustrates that a business's true economic profitability depends on both income statement profitability and effective use of balance sheet assets. Specifically, EVA is improved by (1) increasing revenues and decreasing costs, and hence increasing NOPAT; (2) decreasing the amount of assets used to create NOPAT; and (3) decreasing the business's capital costs. Of course, all of this is easier said than done, and there are potential negative consequences associated with these actions. Still, the EVA model provides a good (but perhaps overly simple) road map to financial excellence.

SELF-TEST QUESTIONS

1. What is economic value added (EVA), and how is it measured?
2. Why is EVA a better measure of financial performance than accounting measures such as earnings per share and return on equity?
3. What does EVA tell managers about how to achieve good financial performance?

GLOSSARY

accountable care organization (ACO): A network of healthcare providers joined together for the purpose of increasing patient service quality and reducing costs.

accounting: The field of finance that involves the measuring and recording of events, in dollar terms, that reflect an organization's operational and financial status. *See* financial management.

accounting breakeven: The volume required to produce revenues sufficient to cover all accounting costs; in other words, zero profitability. *See* economic breakeven.

accounting entity: The entity (business) for which a set of financial statements applies.

accounting period: The period (amount of time) covered by a set of financial statements—often a year, but sometimes a quarter or another time period.

accrual accounting: The recording of economic events in the periods in which the events occur, even if the associated cash receipts or payments happen in a different period.

accrued expenses: A business liability that stems from the fact that some obligations, such as wages and taxes, are not paid immediately after the obligations are created.

activity-based costing (ABC): A bottom-up approach to costing that identifies the activities required to provide a particular service, estimates the costs of those activities, and then aggregates those costs.

adverse selection: The problem faced by insurance companies because individuals who are more likely to have claims are also more likely to purchase insurance.

aging schedule: A table that expresses a business's accounts receivable by how long each account has been outstanding.

allocation rate: The numerical value used to allocate overhead costs; for example, $10 of facilities costs per square foot of occupied space.

American Institute of Certified Public Accountants (AICPA): The professional association of public (financial) accountants.

amortized (installment) loan: A loan that is repaid in equal periodic amounts that include both principal and interest payments.

annual report: A report issued annually by an organization to its stakeholders that contains descriptive information and financial statements for the prior year.

annuity: A series of payments of a fixed amount for a specified number of equal periods.

annuity due: An annuity with payments occurring at the beginning of each period. *See* ordinary (regular) annuity.

asset: An item that either possesses or creates economic value for an organization.

asset management ratios: Financial statement analysis ratios that measure how effectively a firm is managing its assets.

Automated Clearing House (ACH): An electronic communication network for transmitting data from one financial institution to another.

average collection period (ACP): The average length of time it takes a business to collect its receivables; also called *days sales outstanding (DSO)* or *days in patient accounts receivable.*

balance sheet: A financial statement that lists a business's assets, liabilities, and equity (fund capital).

benchmarking: The comparison of performance metrics, such as financial ratios, of one business against those of similar businesses and industry averages; also called *comparative analysis.*

beta coefficient (β): A measure of the risk of one investment relative to the risk of a collection (portfolio) of investments.

bond: Long-term debt issued by a business or government unit and generally sold in $1,000 or $5,000 increments to a large number of individual investors.

book value: The value of a business's assets, liabilities, and equity as reported on the balance sheet; in other words, the value in accordance with generally accepted accounting principles (GAAP).

breakeven analysis: A type of analysis that estimates the amount of some variable—such as volume, price, or variable cost rate—that is needed to break even. *See* accounting breakeven; economic breakeven.

budget: A detailed plan, in dollar terms, of how a business and its subunits will acquire and utilize resources during a specified period of time.

budgeting: The process of preparing and using a budget, which is a detailed plan (in dollar terms) that specifies how resources will be obtained and used during some future period.

build-up method: A method for estimating the cost of equity for a small business that starts with a base rate and then adds premiums to account for size, liquidity, and unique risk characteristics.

bundled (global) payment: The fee-for-service payment of a single amount for the complete set of services required to treat a single episode.

business risk: The risk inherent in the operations of a business, assuming it uses zero-debt financing.

call provision: A provision in a bond indenture (contract) that gives the issuing company the right to redeem (call) the bonds prior to maturity.

call risk premium (CRP): The premium that debt investors add to the base rate to compensate for bearing call risk.

capital: The funds raised by a business that will be invested in assets, such as land, buildings, and equipment that support the organizational mission.

capital asset pricing model (CAPM): An equilibrium model that specifies the relationship between a stock's value and its market risk, as measured by beta (β).

capital budgeting: The process of analyzing and choosing new long-term assets such as land, buildings, and equipment.

capital budgeting decisions: The process of selecting a business's capital (long-term asset) investments; the list of investments chosen constitutes a business's *capital budget*.

capital gain (loss): The profit (loss) from the sale of certain investments at more (less) than their purchase price.

capital gains yield: The percentage capital gain (loss) over some period, defined as the price appreciation (loss) divided by the beginning-of-period price.

capital rationing: The situation that occurs when a business has more attractive capital investment opportunities than it has capital to invest.

capital structure: The structure of a business's financing mix as shown on the balance sheet, often expressed as the percentage of debt financing; for example, 35 percent debt.

capitation: A reimbursement methodology that is based on the number of covered lives (or enrollees) as opposed to the amount of services provided.

cash accounting: The recording of economic events when a cash exchange takes place.

cash budget: A schedule that lists a business's expected cash inflows, outflows, and net cash flows for some future period.

chargemaster: A list of all items and services provided by a health services organization containing their gross (list) prices.

chart of accounts: A document that assigns a unique numerical identifier to every account of an organization.

classified stock: The term used to distinguish between stock classes when a business uses more than one type of common stock.

coefficient of variation: A statistical measure of an investment's stand-alone risk calculated by dividing the standard deviation of returns by the expected return. The result is the amount of stand-alone risk per unit of return. *See* standard deviation.

common size analysis: A technique to analyze a business's financial statements that expresses income statement items and balance sheet accounts as percentages rather than in dollars.

comparative analysis: The comparison of key financial and operational measures of one business with those of comparable businesses or sector averages; also called *benchmarking*.

compensating balance: A minimum checking account balance that a business must maintain to compensate the bank for other services or loans.

compounding: The process of finding the future value of a lump sum, an annuity, or a series of unequal cash flows.

contribution margin: The difference between per unit revenue and per unit cost (variable cost rate); in other words, the dollar amount that each unit of volume contributes to covering fixed costs and, once fixed costs are covered, to profit.

conventional budgeting: An approach to budgeting that uses the previous budget as the starting point for creating the new budget. *See* zero-based budgeting.

corporate bond: Debt issued (sold) by for-profit businesses, as opposed to government or tax-exempt (municipal) bonds.

corporate cost of capital (CCC): The weighted average of a business's capital (financing) costs; also, the discount rate that reflects the overall (average) risk of the entire business.

corporation: A legal business entity that is separate and distinct from its owners (or community) and managers.

correlation: The movement relationship between two variables.

correlation coefficient: A standardized measure of correlation that ranges from -1 (variables move perfectly opposite of one another) to $+1$ (variables move in perfect synchronization); denoted by r.

cost: A resource use associated with providing or supporting a specific service.

cost allocation: The process by which overhead costs are assigned (allocated) to individual departments within an organization.

cost center: A business unit that does not generate revenues, hence only its costs can be measured. *See* profit center.

cost driver: The basis on which a cost pool is allocated; for example, square footage for facilities costs.

cost pool: A group of overhead costs to be allocated; for example, facilities costs or marketing costs.

cost-based reimbursement: A fee-for-service reimbursement method based on the costs incurred in providing services.

costly trade credit: The credit taken by a company from a vendor in excess of the free trade credit. *See* free trade credit.

cost-to-charge ratio (CCR): A ratio used to estimate the overhead costs of individual services; defined as the ratio of indirect (overhead) costs to charges (or alternatively, to service revenues).

coupon (interest) rate: The stated annual rate of interest on a bond, which is equal to the coupon payment divided by the par value.

coupon payment: The dollar amount of annual interest on a bond.

credit policy: Generically, a business's rules and regulations regarding granting credit and collecting from buyers that take credit; for healthcare providers, the business's policy regarding self-pay and indigent patients.

credit terms: The statement of terms that extends credit to a buyer.

cross-subsidization (price shifting): A pricing approach in which some payers are charged more than full costs to make up for other payers that are paying less than full costs.

current asset: An asset that is expected to be converted into cash within one accounting period (often a year). *See* fixed assets.

Current Procedural Terminology (CPT) codes: Codes applied to medical, surgical, and diagnostic procedures.

dashboard: A format for presenting a business's key performance indicators that resembles the dashboard of an automobile. *See* key performance indicator.

debenture: An unsecured bond, meaning one that has no assets pledged as security (collateral).

debt capacity: The amount of debt considered optimal for the business (the target capital structure).

debt management ratios: A group of ratios that measure the extent of a business's financial leverage (capital structure).

debt ratio: A debt utilization ratio that measures the proportion of debt (versus equity) financing; typically defined as total debt (liabilities) divided by total assets.

default: When a borrower fails to make a promised debt payment; technical default occurs when the borrower fails to meet one of the restrictions in the loan agreement but is still making the required payments.

default risk premium (DRP): The premium that creditors demand (add to the base interest rate) for bearing default risk. The greater the default risk, the higher the default risk premium.

depreciation: A noncash charge against earnings on the income statement that reflects the "wear and tear" on a business's fixed assets (property and equipment).

depreciation shield: The dollar amount of taxes that will not have to be paid because of the business's depreciation expense.

direct cost: A cost that is tied exclusively to a subunit of an organization, such as the salaries of a department's employees. When a subunit is eliminated, its direct costs disappear. *See* indirect (overhead) cost.

direct method: A cost allocation method in which all overhead costs are allocated directly from the overhead departments to the patient services departments with no recognition that overhead services are provided to other support departments. *See* reciprocal method; step-down method.

discounting: The process of finding the current (present) value of a lump sum, an annuity, or a series of unequal cash flows.

diversifiable risk: The portion of the risk of an investment that can be eliminated by holding the investment as part of a diversified portfolio. *See* market risk.

dividend reinvestment plan (DRIP): A plan under which the dividends paid to a stockholder are automatically reinvested in the company's common stock.

dividend yield: The annual dividend divided by current stock price.

divisional cost of capital: The discount rate (hurdle rate or opportunity cost rate) that reflects the unique risk of a division within a corporation.

double entry system: The system used to make accounting journal entries; called *double entry* because each transaction has to be entered in at least two different accounts.

Du Pont analysis: A financial statement analysis tool that decomposes return on equity into three components: profit margin, total asset turnover, and equity multiplier.

economic breakeven: The volume required to produce revenues sufficient to cover all accounting costs and to provide a specified profit level. *See* accounting breakeven.

effective annual rate (EAR): The interest rate that, under annual compounding, produces the same future value as was produced by more frequent compounding.

efficient markets hypothesis (EMH): The theory that stocks are always in equilibrium and it is impossible for investors to consistently earn excess returns (beat the market).

equity: Assets minus liabilities; in other words, the "book value" of the ownership position of a business.

expected rate of return: The return expected, in a statistical sense, on an investment when the purchase is made.

expense budget: A budget that focuses on the costs of providing goods or services.

expenses: The costs of doing business; the dollar value of resources used to provide goods or services.

fee-for-service: A reimbursement methodology that provides payment each time a service is provided. *See* capitation.

financial accounting: The field of accounting that focuses on the measurement and communication of the economic events and status of an entire organization. *See* managerial (management) accounting.

Financial Accounting Standards Board (FASB): A private organization whose mission is to establish and improve the standards of financial accounting and reporting for private businesses.

financial asset: A security, such as a stock or bond, that represents a claim on a business's cash flows. Financial assets are purchased with the expectation of receiving future payments.

financial leverage: The use of fixed cost financing; typically debt financing for healthcare providers.

financial management: The field of finance that provides the theory, concepts, and tools used by healthcare managers to make financial decisions. *See* accounting.

financial plan: The portion of the operating plan that focuses on the finance function.

financial ratio analysis: The process of creating and analyzing ratios from financial statement data to assess a business's financial condition.

financial risk: In an investment context, the risk that the return on an investment will be less than expected. The greater the chance of earning a return far below that expected, the greater the risk. In a capital structure context, it is the risk added to a business (more precisely, to the business's owners) when debt financing is used. The greater the proportion of debt financing, the greater the financial risk.

financial statement analysis: The process of using data contained in financial statements to make judgments about a business's financial condition.

financial statements: Statements prepared by accountants that convey the financial status of an organization. The four primary statements are the income statement, balance sheet, statement of changes in equity, and statement of cash flows.

fiscal year: The year covered by an organization's financial statements; it usually, but not necessarily, coincides with the calendar year.

fixed assets: A business's long-term assets, such as land, buildings, and equipment; usually labeled *net property and equipment* on the balance sheet. *See* current asset.

fixed cost: A cost that is not related to the volume of services delivered; for example, facilities costs. Total fixed costs do not change if volume remains within the relevant range. *See* variable cost.

flexible budget: A budget based on the static budget assumptions but adjusted to reflect realized volume. *See* static budget.

float: The difference between the balance shown on a business's (or individual's) checkbook and the balance shown on the bank's books.

Form 990: A form filed by not-for-profit organizations with the Internal Revenue Service that reports on governance and charitable activities.

four Cs: A mnemonic for the basic finance activities: costs, cash, capital, and control.

free trade credit: The amount of credit received from a supplier that has no explicit cost attached; in other words, credit received during the discount period. *See* costly trade credit.

full cost pricing: The process of setting prices to cover all costs plus a profit component. *See* marginal cost pricing.

fund accounting: A system for recording financial statement data that categorizes accounts whose use has been limited.

fund capital: Equity capital in a not-for-profit corporation, typically obtained from contributions and grants and by retaining earnings; on the balance sheet, often called *net assets*.

general ledger: The master listing of an organization's primary accounts, which record the transactions that are used to create a business's financial statements.

generally accepted accounting principles (GAAP): The set of guidelines that has evolved to foster the consistent preparation and presentation of financial statements.

Healthcare Common Procedure Coding System (HCPCS): A medical coding system that expands the CPT codes to include nonphysician services and durable medical equipment. *See* Current Procedural Terminology (CPT) codes.

health insurance exchange (HIE): An online marketplace created primarily by the states or the federal government that insurers use to post plan details and consumers use to purchase health insurance.

historical cost: In accounting, the purchase price of an asset.

hurdle rate: The minimum required rate of return on an investment; also called *opportunity cost rate* or *discount rate*.

income statement: A financial statement, prepared in accordance with generally accepted accounting principles (GAAP), that summarizes a business's revenues, expenses, and profitability.

incremental cash flow: A cash flow that arises solely from a project that is being evaluated and hence should be included in the project analysis. *See* nonincremental cash flow.

indenture: A legal document that spells out the rights and obligations of both bondholders and the issuing corporation; in other words, the loan agreement for a bond.

indirect (overhead) cost: A cost that is tied to shared resources rather than to an individual subunit of an organization; for example, facilities costs. *See* direct cost.

inflation premium (IP): The premium that debt investors add to the real risk-free (base) interest rate to compensate for inflation.

inpatient prospective payment system (IPPS): The method, based on diagnosis, that Medicare uses to reimburse providers for inpatient services.

interest (current) yield: The annual interest return on a bond, defined as the interest payment divided by the beginning-of-year price.

interest rate risk: The risk to current debtholders that stems from interest rate changes. Interest rate risk has two components: price risk and reinvestment rate risk.

internal rate of return (IRR): A return-on-investment (ROI) metric that measures expected rate of (percentage) return.

International Classification of Diseases (ICD) codes: Numerical codes for designating diseases plus a variety of signs, symptoms, and external causes of injury.

investment-grade bond: A bond with a BBB or higher rating. *See* junk bond.

investor-owned (for-profit) corporation: A corporation that is owned by shareholders who furnish capital and expect to earn a return on their investment.

junk bond: A bond with a BB or lower rating. *See* investment-grade bond.

just-in-time (JIT) approach: A supply chain management technique that requires suppliers to deliver inventory items in relatively small quantities as they are needed, which reduces the amount of inventory stock held; there are several variations of JIT systems.

key performance indicator (KPI): A financial statement ratio or operating indicator that is considered by management to be critical to mission success.

liability: A fixed financial obligation of an organization.

limited liability partnership (LLP): A partnership form of organization that limits the professional (malpractice) liability of its partners.

line of credit: A loan arrangement in which a bank agrees to lend some maximum amount to a business over some designated period.

liquid asset: An asset that can be quickly converted to cash at its fair market value.

liquidity premium (LP): The premium that debt investors add to the base interest rate to compensate for lack of liquidity.

liquidity ratios: Ratios that measure the ability of a business to meet its cash obligations as they come due.

lockbox: A post office box used by a business to receive checks at a location other than the corporate headquarters.

managed care plan: A combined effort by an insurer and a group of providers that aims both to increase quality of care and to decrease costs.

managerial (management) accounting: The field of accounting that focuses on all levels of an organization and is used internally for managerial decision-making. *See* financial accounting.

marginal cost: The cost of one additional unit of volume; for example, one more inpatient day or patient visit.

marginal cost pricing: The process of setting prices to cover only marginal costs. *See* full cost pricing.

market portfolio: A portfolio that contains all publicly traded stocks; often proxied by some market index, such as the S&P 500.

market risk: The risk of an individual investment when it is held as part of a diversified portfolio as opposed to held in isolation. *See* diversifiable risk.

marketable securities: Securities that are held in lieu of cash, typically safe, short-term securities such as Treasury bills; called *cash equivalents* or *short-term investments* when listed on the balance sheet.

maturity date: The date on which the principal amount of a loan must be repaid.

Medicaid: A federal and state government health insurance program that provides benefits to low-income individuals.

medical coding: The process of transforming medical diagnoses and procedures into universally recognized numerical codes.

medical home: A team-based model of care led by a personal physician who provides continuous and coordinated care throughout a patient's lifetime with a goal of maximizing health outcomes; also called *patient-centered medical home.*

Medicare: A federal government health insurance program that primarily provides benefits to individuals aged 65 or older.

modified internal rate of return (MIRR): A project return-on-investment measure similar to internal rate of return but using the assumption of reinvestment at the cost of capital.

Monte Carlo simulation: A computerized risk analysis technique that uses continuous distributions to represent the uncertain input variables.

moral hazard: The problem faced by insurance companies because individuals are more likely to use unneeded health services when they are not paying the full cost of those services.

mortgage bond: A bond issued by a business that pledges real property (land and buildings) as collateral.

municipal (muni) bond: A tax-exempt bond issued by a government entity such as a state, city, or healthcare financing authority.

net assets: The dollar value, according to GAAP, of a business's assets after subtracting the business's liabilities. In not-for-profit businesses, the term often is used on the balance sheet in place of *equity*.

net income: The total earnings of a business, including both operating and nonoperating income.

net patient accounts receivable (receivables): The amount of money billed for services provided but not yet collected.

net present social value (NPSV): The present value of a project's social value; added to the financial net present value (NPV) to obtain a project's total value.

net present value (NPV): A project return-on-investment (ROI) metric that measures the time value–adjusted expected dollar return. *See* internal rate of return (IRR); modified internal rate of return (MIRR).

net working capital: A liquidity measure equal to current assets minus current liabilities.

nominal (stated) interest rate: The interest rate stated in a debt contract; it does not reflect the effect of any compounding that occurs more frequently than annually. *See* periodic interest rate.

nonincremental cash flow: A cash flow that does not stem solely from a project that is being evaluated; nonincremental cash flows are not included in a project analysis. *See* incremental cash flow.

nonoperating income: The earnings of a business that are unrelated to core activities; for a healthcare provider, the most common sources are contributions and investment income. *See* operating income.

operating budget: A single budget that combines both the revenue and expense budgets.

operating income: The earnings of a business directly related to core activities; for a healthcare provider, earnings are related to patient services. *See* nonoperating income.

operating indicator: A ratio that focuses on operating data rather than financial data.

operating indicator analysis: The process of using operating indicators to help explain a business's financial condition.

operating margin: Operating income divided by net operating revenues; it measures the amount of operating profit per dollar of operating revenues and focuses on the core activities of a business. *See* total (profit) margin.

operating plan: An organizational road map for the future, often spanning five years, but with most detail for the first year. Operating plans must be based on and consistent with the guidance provided in the organization's strategic plan.

opportunity cost: The cost associated with alternative uses of the same funds. For example, if money is used for one investment, it is no longer available for other uses, creating an opportunity cost.

opportunity cost rate: The rate of return expected on alternative investments similar in risk to the investment being evaluated; also called *hurdle rate*.

optimal capital structure: The mix of debt and equity financing that management believes is most appropriate for the business; generally based on both quantitative and qualitative factors. *See* target capital structure.

ordinary (regular) annuity: An annuity with payments occurring at the end of each period.

partnership: A nonincorporated business entity that is created by two or more individuals.

par value: The stated (face) value of a bond; generally, the principal amount that must be repaid to the issuer.

patient service revenue: Revenue that stems solely from the provision of patient services; in some situations, it may only reflect revenue from fee-for-service patients.

payback period: The number of years it takes for a business to recover its investment in a project without considering the time value of money.

payment (PMT): In time value analysis, the dollar amount of an annuity cash flow.

per diem payment: A fee-for-service reimbursement method that pays a set amount for each inpatient day.

percentage change analysis: A technique to analyze a business's financial statements that expresses the year-to-year changes in income statement items and balance sheet accounts as percentages.

periodic interest rate: In time value of money analysis, the interest rate per period; for example, 2 percent quarterly interest, which equals an 8 percent stated (annual) rate. *See* nominal (stated) interest rate.

perpetuity: An annuity that lasts forever (has no maturity date).

poison pill: A provision in a company's charter that makes it an unattractive hostile takeover target.

population health management: The concept that the health of all individuals is improved when the health of the entire population is improved.

portfolio: A number of individual investments held collectively.

portfolio risk: The riskiness of an individual investment when it is held as part of a diversified portfolio (collection of investments) as opposed to held in isolation.

post-audit: The feedback process in which the performance of projects previously accepted is reviewed and actions are taken if performance is below expectations.

preemptive right: The right that gives current shareholders the opportunity to purchase any newly issued shares (in proportion to their current holdings) before they are offered to the general public.

premium revenue: Patient service revenue that stems from capitated patients as opposed to fee-for-service patients.

present value (PV): The beginning amount (current worth) of an investment of a lump sum, an annuity, or a series of unequal cash flows.

price risk: The risk that rising interest rates will lower the values of outstanding debt. *See* interest rate risk; reinvestment rate risk.

price risk premium (PRP): The premium that debt investors add to the base rate to compensate for bearing price risk.

price setter: A business that has the power to set the market prices for its goods or services.

price taker: A business that has no power to influence the prices set by the marketplace (or by government payers).

private placement: The sale of newly issued securities to a single investor or small group of investors.

probability distribution: All possible outcomes of a random event along with their probabilities of occurrence; for example, the probability distribution of rates of return on a proposed investment.

profit analysis: A technique applied to an organization's cost and revenue structure that analyzes the effect of volume changes on costs and profits; also called *CVP (cost-volume-profit) analysis.*

profit and loss (P&L) statement: A statement that summarizes the revenues, expenses, and profitability of either the entire organization or a subunit of it; can be formatted in different ways for different purposes and does not conform to generally accepted accounting principles (GAAP).

profit center: A business unit (in our examples, typically a department) that generates revenues as well as costs, hence its profitability can be measured. *See* cost center.

profitability index (PI): A project return-on-investment measure defined as the present value of cash inflows divided by the present value of outflows. It measures the number of dollars of inflow per dollar of outflow (on a present value basis), or the "bang for the buck."

profitability ratios: A group of ratios that measure different dimensions of a business's profitability.

project cost of capital: The discount rate (hurdle rate or opportunity cost rate) that reflects the unique risk of a project.

project scoring: An approach to project assessment that considers both financial and nonfinancial factors.

promissory note: A document that specifies the terms and conditions of a loan; also called *loan agreement* or, in the case of bonds, *indenture*.

proprietorship: A simple form of business owned by a single individual; also called *sole proprietorship*.

prospective payment: A fee-for-service reimbursement method in which the payment amount is established beforehand by the third-party payer and, in theory, is not directly related to costs or charges.

provider: An organization that provides healthcare services (treats patients).

proxy fight: An attempt to take control of a corporation by soliciting the votes (proxies) of current shareholders.

public offering: The sale of newly issued securities to the general public through an investment banker.

pure play approach: A method for estimating the base cost of equity for a small business whereby the cost of equity of a similar large, publicly traded business is used as a proxy value.

real asset: A physical asset, such as a medical practice or a piece of diagnostic equipment, that has the potential to generate future cash inflows.

real risk-free rate (RRF): The rate of interest on a riskless investment in the absence of inflation.

realized rate of return: The return achieved on an investment when it is terminated.

reciprocal method: A cost allocation method that recognizes all of the overhead services provided by one support department to another. *See* direct method; step-down method.

reinvestment rate risk: The risk that falling interest rates will lower the returns on cash flows from bond investments that are reinvested during the life of the bond (or investment horizon). *See* interest rate risk; price risk.

relative value unit (RVU): A measure of the amount of resources consumed to provide a particular service. When applied to physicians, a measure of the amount of work, practice expenses, and liability costs associated with a particular service.

relative value unit (RVU) method: A method for estimating the overhead costs of individual services based on the intensity of the service provided, as measured by RVUs.

relevant range: The range of volume expected over some planning period. Alternatively, the range over which fixed costs remain constant—if volume falls outside the relevant range, the fixed cost estimate may be invalid.

reserve borrowing capacity: The practice of businesses to use less than the theoretical optimal amount of debt to ensure easy access to new debt at reasonable interest rates regardless of circumstances.

restrictive covenant: A provision in a bond indenture or loan agreement that protects the interests of lenders by restricting the actions of management.

return on equity (ROE): Net income divided by the book value of equity; measures the dollars of earnings per dollar of equity investment.

return on investment (ROI): The estimated financial return on an investment. In capital budgeting analysis, ROI can be measured either in dollars or percentage (rate of) return.

revenue budget: A budget that focuses on the revenues of an organization or its subunits.

revenue cycle: The set of recurring activities and related information processing required to provide patient services and collect for those services.

revenue recognition principle: The concept that revenues must be recognized in the accounting period in which they are realizable and earned.

revenues: Inflows of assets resulting from the exchange of goods or services with customers.

rights offering: The mechanism by which new common stock is offered to existing shareholders; each stockholder receives an option (right) to buy a specific number of new shares at a given price.

risk aversion: The tendency of individuals and businesses to dislike risk. The implication of risk aversion is that riskier investments must offer higher expected rates of return to be acceptable.

risk-adjusted discount rate (RADR): A discount rate that accounts for the specific riskiness of the investment being analyzed.

risk-free rate (RF): The rate of interest on a riskless investment when inflation effects are considered.

salvage value: The expected market value of an asset (project) at the end of its useful life.

scenario analysis: A project risk analysis technique that examines alternative outcomes, generally three, as opposed to only the most likely outcome.

Schedule H: An attachment to Form 990 filed by not-for-profit hospitals that gives additional information on charitable activities.

Securities and Exchange Commission (SEC): The federal government agency that regulates the sale of securities and the operations of securities exchanges.

This agency also has overall responsibility for the format and content of financial statements.

security market line (SML): The portion of the capital asset pricing model (CAPM) that specifies the relationship between market risk and required rate of return.

sensitivity analysis: A project analysis technique that assesses how changes in a single input variable, such as utilization, affect profitability.

social determinants of health: Social, economic, and environmental conditions in the places where people are born, live, grow, learn, work, and play that affect health.

stakeholder: A party that has an interest, often financial, in a business. Stakeholders can be affected by the business's actions, objectives, or policies.

stand-alone risk: The riskiness of an investment that is held in isolation as opposed to held as part of a portfolio (collection of investments).

standard deviation (σ): A statistical measure of the variability (dispersion) of a probability distribution about the mean (expected value). *See* coefficient of variation.

statement of cash flows: A financial statement that focuses on the cash flows that come into and go out of a business.

statement of changes in equity: A financial statement that reports how much of a business's income statement earnings flows to the balance sheet equity account.

static budget: A budget that is prepared at the beginning of a planning period.

statistics budget: A budget that contains the patient volume and resource need assumptions used in all other budgets.

step-down method: A cost allocation method that recognizes some of the overhead services provided by one support department to another. *See* direct method; reciprocal method.

strategic plan: A document that defines the business's long-term direction along with the resources needed to get there.

strategic value: The value of future investment opportunities that can be undertaken only if the project currently under consideration is accepted.

sunk cost: A cost that has already occurred or is irrevocably committed; sunk costs are nonincremental to project analyses and hence should not be included.

supply chain management: The management of the procurement, storage, and utilization of supplies; also called *inventory management*.

target capital structure: The capital structure (mix of debt and equity) that a business strives to achieve and maintain over time; generally the same as (or very close to) the optimal capital structure.

target costing: For price takers, the process of reducing costs (if necessary) to the point at which a profit is earned on the market-determined price.

tax-exempt (not-for-profit) corporation: A corporation that has a charitable purpose, is tax exempt, and has no owners; also called *nonprofit corporation*.

term loan: Long-term debt financing obtained directly from a financial institution, often a commercial bank.

terminal value: An estimate of the value of the cash flows beyond the truncation point when a project's cash flows are arbitrarily truncated.

third-party payer: A generic term for any outside party, typically an insurance company or a government program, that pays for part or all of a patient's healthcare services.

time line: A graphical representation of time and cash flows; may be an actual line or cells on a spreadsheet.

time value analysis: The use of time value of money techniques to value future cash flows; sometimes called *discounted cash flow analysis*.

time-driven activity-based costing (TDABC): An approach to costing that focuses on the entire cost of a patient's cycle of care rather than the cost of individual services.

total (profit) margin: Net income divided by total revenues; it measures the amount of total profit per dollar of total revenues. *See* operating margin.

trade credit: The credit offered to businesses by suppliers (vendors) when credit terms are offered.

trade-off model: A capital structure model that hypothesizes that a business's optimal capital structure balances the costs and benefits associated with debt financing.

traditional costing: The top-down approach to costing that first identifies costs at the department level and then (potentially) assigns those costs to individual services. *See* activity-based costing (ABC).

trend analysis: A ratio analysis technique that examines the value of a ratio over time to see whether it is improving or deteriorating.

trustee: An individual or institution, typically a commercial bank, that represents the interests of bondholders.

underlying cost structure: The relationship between an organization's fixed costs, variable costs, and total costs; also called *cost structure*.

value-based purchasing (VBP): An approach to provider reimbursement that rewards quality and efficiency of care rather than quantity of care.

variable cost: A cost that is directly related to the volume of services delivered and changes in total with changes in volume; for example, the cost of clinical supplies. *See* fixed cost.

variable cost rate: The variable cost of one unit of output (volume).

variance: The difference between what actually happened and what was expected to happen.

variance analysis: A technique used in budgeting in which realized values are compared with budgeted values to help control operations.

yield to call (YTC): The expected rate of return on a debt security assuming it is held until it is called.

yield to maturity (YTM): The expected rate of return on a debt security assuming it is held until maturity.

zero-balance account (ZBA): A bank account having a zero balance that is established by a business to handle disbursements of a particular type. Funds are transferred to ZBAs from a master account as needed to cover the checks written.

zero-based budgeting: An approach to budgeting that starts with a "clean slate" and requires complete justification of all budget items. *See* conventional budgeting.

zero-coupon bond: A bond that pays no interest. It is bought at a discount from par value, so its return comes solely from price appreciation (selling at a price greater than the purchase price or receiving the face value at maturity).

INDEX

Note: Italicized page locators refer to exhibits.

ABOUT THE AUTHORS

Kristin L. Reiter, PhD, is professor and associate chair in the Department of Health Policy and Management in the Gillings School of Global Public Health, and a research fellow in the Cecil G. Sheps Center for Health Services Research, both at the University of North Carolina at Chapel Hill.

She received a bachelor's degree in accounting from Northern Illinois University. She received a master's in applied economics and a doctorate in health services organization and policy, with a concentration in corporate finance, from the University of Michigan. Prior to joining academia, she worked in public accounting, serving not-for-profits and clients in the insurance industry.

Dr. Reiter teaches undergraduate- and graduate-level courses in healthcare accounting and financial management and is involved in research projects examining rural health policy, hospital financial performance, and the business case for quality. In the past 15 years, she has served on audit, finance, and advisory committees of several healthcare professional associations. She is the author or coauthor of more than 50 peer-reviewed articles, and she has presented to academic and professional audiences in the United States, France, and Canada.

Paula H. Song, PhD, is associate professor and residential master's program director in the Department of Health Policy and Management in the Gillings School of Global Public Health, and a research fellow in the Cecil G. Sheps Center for Health Services Research, both at the University of North Carolina at Chapel Hill. Dr. Song's research and teaching interests span healthcare financial management, investment strategies in not-for-profit hospitals, payment reform, and business case evaluation for health initiatives. Dr. Song received a doctorate in health services organization and policy and a master's degree in health services administration and applied economics from the University of Michigan.

Remembering Louis C. Gapenski, PhD

This tribute is reprinted with permission from the *Journal of Healthcare Finance:*

In the field of health care finance, one need not look far to see the impact of Louis "Lou" C. Gapenski, PhD. When he passed away on April 20, 2016, we all lost a gifted scholar, writer, teacher, mentor, and friend. After retiring from the Marine Corps as a Lieutenant Colonel in 1979, Lou earned both an MBA and a PhD in Finance and Economics from the University of Florida. He spent his academic career as a faculty member in the College of Public Health and Health Professions' Department of Health Services Research, Management, and Policy at the University of Florida. If Lou had not decided to embark on this second career, the field of health care finance would not be the same.

By traditional academic metrics, Lou was a successful scholar: many peer-reviewed articles, other publications and book reviews, and presentations at academic and professional conferences. His scholarship offered some of the earliest applications of standard corporate finance theory to healthcare issues, examining topics such as capital structure decisions and financial risk, capital investment methods and return on investment measures, determinants of hospital profitability, and the importance of non-patient revenues to hospitals. A cited reference analysis of his work in healthcare and management using the Web of Science showed the breadth of his influence. His findings have been cited in both peer-reviewed and professional gray literature involving over 200 different authors or co-authors, many of whose names are well known in the field of health care finance today. These authors represented almost 100 different colleges and universities and close to 20 provider, consulting, or government organizations in 19 different countries.

However, Lou was best known for his compendium of best-selling textbooks on corporate finance and healthcare financial management. His collaboration with Eugene Brigham produced a textbook factory: Lou was a coauthor of five editions of *Financial Management: Theory and Practice* (translated into Bulgarian, Chinese, French, Indonesian, Italian, Portuguese, and Spanish), six editions of *Intermediate Financial Management*, and five editions of *Cases in Financial Management*. In the early 1990s, Lou turned his attention to the nascent discipline of healthcare financial management, being among the first to argue that the theory and application of corporate finance was both relevant and necessary to the training of healthcare managers. Over the next twenty-five years, Lou authored seven editions of *Understanding Healthcare Financial Management*, five editions of *Cases in Healthcare Finance*, six editions of *Healthcare Finance: An Introduction to*

Accounting and Financial Management, and two editions of *Fundamentals of Healthcare Finance*. By any standard, this was an extraordinary level of textbook productivity and was a constant source of amazement and curiosity among his colleagues. Lou was once asked "How do you manage to write so many textbooks?" to which he replied "When I get up in the morning, I tell myself that Chapter 1 has to be finished by the end of the day, and then I sit down and do it." We always suspected that his career in the Marines was excellent preparation for the self-discipline required to write textbooks.

Lou's textbooks and casebook in health care finance were novel and innovative in that they offered the rigorous finance training commonly found in business schools, but using language and context that would speak to those whose passion was health care. In all of Lou's work, his commitment to teaching and learning was evident. In planning for new textbooks or new editions of existing books, Lou would reach out to colleagues, students and individuals working in the field, seeking input on how to improve his books and the associated ancillary learning materials. He was eager to receive feedback, and he worked tirelessly to implement the recommendations of those around him. His creativity was apparent in the new features offered in each edition, and the stories and examples he included to engage students and draw them into the subject matter. When Lou originally approached us about becoming co-authors, we had no idea how much we would learn from him about writing textbooks—assessment of learning needs, clear exposition of complex concepts and calculations, development of ancillary learning materials, as well as the business of publishing itself. Better than anyone we knew, Lou understood how to write a good textbook.

Lou has received abundant praise from students for his uncanny ability to clearly explain the most complex or theoretical concepts, and appreciation for his use of humor and stories to create interest and motivate discussion. His talent for teaching carried over into the classroom, where he implemented innovative case-based teaching methods and was recognized for excellence through nineteen teaching awards. He was also regularly asked to teach courses in other programs both in the US and globally, and to conduct seminars at provider organizations including the Mayo Clinic. His work has touched thousands of students and professionals, and his books are undoubtedly on the reference shelves of healthcare leaders everywhere.

While his professional contributions are evident, Lou will also be remembered for his outstanding character. In spreading the sad news of his passing with colleagues throughout the country, it was not uncommon to hear comments such as, "Lou was one of a kind" or "There will never be another like Lou." He was witty, generous, and extraordinarily kind. Lou was a selfless mentor to those around him—quick to provide opportunities, and reluctant to take any of the credit. He was also genuinely interested in getting to know the people with whom he worked. He took the time to develop meaningful and lasting relationships, and he gratefully acknowledged the contributions of all of his partners, colleagues, and collaborators. Along with his wife Jane, Lou generously sponsored lunches, student events, conferences, scholarships and an endowed professorship. Jane was often seen with Lou at healthcare finance–related events, and they were true partners, both with an enduring commitment his life's work.

With the passing of Lou Gapenski, the field of health care finance has lost a great leader and a champion. However, his memory and his legacy will live on in his scholarship, his textbooks, the students he trained, the leaders he inspired, and the colleagues whose lives he impacted for the better. This issue of the *Journal of Healthcare Finance* is dedicated to Lou's memory, and his influence can be seen throughout the work in the pages that follow.

Kristin L. Reiter, PhD, Professor
Paula H. Song, PhD, Associate Professor
Department of Health Policy and Management
Gillings School of Global Public Health
University of North Carolina at Chapel Hill
1104H McGavran-Greenberg Hall, Campus Box 7411
Chapel Hill, North Carolina 27599-7411